THE OXFORD HISTORY
OF ENGLAND

Edited by SIR GEORGE CLARK

THE OXFORD HISTORY OF ENGLAND

Edited by SIR GEORGE CLARK

These volumes have been published.

ENGLAND
1870—1914

By

R. C. K. ENSOR

OXFORD
AT THE CLARENDON PRESS

Oxford University Press, Amen House, London E.C.4

GLASGOW NEW YORK TORONTO MELBOURNE WELLINGTON
BOMBAY CALCUTTA MADRAS KARACHI KUALA LUMPUR
CAPE TOWN IBADAN NAIROBI ACCRA

FIRST PUBLISHED FEBRUARY 1936
REPRINTED MARCH 1936, 1941, 1944, 1946, 1949, 1952, 1960

PRINTED IN GREAT BRITAIN
AT THE UNIVERSITY PRESS, OXFORD
BY VIVIAN RIDLER
PRINTER TO THE UNIVERSITY

PREFACE

THE date at which this volume ends, the outbreak of the European War, is the latest for which there is enough documentary evidence to write English history scientifically. Only a short while ago the zero point must have been placed much farther back; but the wealth added to our evidences in the last ten years is exceptional. It includes, to take only a few instances, Messrs. Gooch and Temperley's *British Documents*, two volumes of Lord Salisbury's *Life*, three of Chamberlain's, all of Asquith's, Redmond's, and Lord Carnarvon's. Any one who has gratefully used these many volumes must be penetrated by the thought of his helplessness without them. There remain certain gaps—a volume yet to come in each of the three cases first-mentioned, and above all the long-expected *Life* of Balfour. But what we have now, vastly outweighs what we still await.

In histories of recent periods it has been common and perhaps usual that names of persons still living should be distinguished from those of the dead by such prefixes as 'Mr.'. The practice is surely a bad one; it creates an entirely unreal line of division, and hampers both writer and readers in their attempt to view the past *sub specie aeternitatis*. Therefore I have here wholly abstained from it. I hope that my decision will in no quarter be interpreted as discourtesy. To living people who have helped to make history, it should scarcely be a ground of complaint that they are treated as historical figures.

Save one, my most outstanding debts are to the Editor of the series, to which this volume belongs, and to two other friends—Dr. J. L. Hammond and Mr. Joseph Owen (late of the Board of Education)—who cheerfully embraced the onerous task of reading the fifteen chapters in manuscript, and made most valuable suggestions on them. I particularly owe it to Dr. Hammond that my attention was directed to the unprinted Gladstone Papers bearing on the problem of Gladstone's conversion to Home Rule. But for my access to these I must also render thanks to the Gladstone Trustees and to their Secretary, Mr. A. Tilney Bassett, who placed freely at my disposal his unique knowledge of the Papers, their order, contents, and handwritings.

No one could write a volume of this kind without seeking information upon a host of particular points from individuals qualified to give it, or from the officials of various important bodies. My debts to such informants are exceedingly numerous; but believing that they will be content with the private expression of my sincere gratitude, I do not propose to display their names here like a row of scalps. By way of historical warrant, however, I ought to mention that the interesting pieces of information from Sir George Leveson-Gower and from Mr. Lloyd George, given in the footnotes on p. 183 and p. 390 respectively, are printed here with their authorization in each case. I should like specially also to thank Mr. J. A. Spender for giving me some information under circumstances, which I need not particularize, but which rendered his action peculiarly generous.

My greatest debt, however, is to my wife; and the fact that that is a common experience among authors, shall not dissuade me from saying so.

R. C. K. E.

TABLE OF CONTENTS

V. MENTAL AND SOCIAL ASPECTS, 1870–86

VI. LORD SALISBURY'S PRIME

IX. ECONOMICS AND INSTITUTIONS, 1886–1900

X. MENTAL AND SOCIAL ASPECTS, 1886–1900

XI. THE UNIONIST DECLINE

XII. EDWARDIAN LIBERALISM

XIII. HEADING FOR CATASTROPHE

XV. MENTAL AND SOCIAL ASPECTS, 1901–14

LIST OF MAPS
(at end)

INTRODUCTION

WHEN the guns of the Franco-Prussian war first thundered in earnest on 4 August 1870 a new epoch began, although Europe at the time did not know it. At midnight of the same day just forty-four years later the sands of Great Britain's ultimatum to Germany ran out; and with them the epoch ended. It is the task of the present volume to trace the history of England during these forty-four years.

Why did the war of 1870 inaugurate a period in a sense in which no other since Waterloo had done? Why was it in a different class from the wars of 1854, of 1859, or of 1866, all of which had engaged Great Powers and two of which helped to unify great nations? For three principal reasons. First because it transferred from France to Germany the political ascendancy over Europe, which the former, with only passing interruptions, had exercised for well beyond two centuries. Secondly, because the singular completeness of the victor's success (he not only won all his objects in six months, but covered the whole of his military expenses by the war indemnity) gave the world a new conception of war's possibilities as an instrument of policy under modern highly-organized conditions. Thirdly, because the defeat of France's professional army by the conscript reservists of Prussia was the triumph of a particular system. It led speedily to the adoption of nation-wide military conscription by all considerable continental states. Europe's long vigil under arms—'powerless from terror of her own vast power'—was the logical outcome, and the catastrophe of 1914 its quasi-inevitable climax.

But the period is also a very distinct one for the internal history of our island; and here (if again we try counting) it may be viewed in at least five different lights. To begin with, it witnessed the conversion of English government into a democracy. Disraeli's Act of 1867 had opened the first breach in the narrow franchise of 1832. But it took a little time to make itself felt, and needed for its completion the Ballot Act of 1872 and the rural franchise extension of 1884. Equally necessary was it that other organs of democracy should be developed besides the central parliament. Such were supplied by the system of elective municipal government; which had its franchise democratized before Disraeli's Act, but was extended in different forms to the rural areas and the metropolis by the County Councils Act of 1888, the Local Government Act of 1894, and the London Government Act of 1899. In the same order of things came the emergence of the trade unions. These bodies had existed long before 1870, but their memberships were comparatively small and their activities semi-illegal. Partly owing to the Trade Union Acts of 1871, 1876, and 1906, partly as a natural result of the interplay between industrialism and popular education, and partly through the brains and character of individual leaders, they gradually developed the great powers whose range first became fully apparent about 1911–12.

Secondly, the same period saw the conversion of the English as a whole into a school-taught and literate people. Mr. Forster's famous act, passed in the summer of 1870, concerns the historian of an earlier period, but all its consequences fall within this one. Mr. Forster made elementary education national (though compulsion was not completed till 1880); Lord Salisbury in 1891 made it free; and the Balfour Act of 1902 combined it with secondary and technical education in something like a single state system administered through the main organs of local government. These acts mark stages; but progress was continual. Already by 1886 out of 2,416,272 voters at the general election in England and Wales only 38,587 were illiterate; though the proportion among voteless adults would no doubt be higher. But in the last decade of our period illiteracy had been razed off our map, taking a considerable proportion of the nation's crime with it; and the fact that parents as well as children had been to school began to create quite new possibilities in spheres like that of public health work.

Thirdly, this is the period in which English agriculture was ruined. It is a common error to suppose that it collapsed with the repeal of the corn laws. On the contrary, it remained the foremost in the world for nearly thirty years longer. It was not till 1872 that the plough reached its maximum extension over English soil. That was the culmination of English wheat-growing under the sheep-and-corn rotations. The slump began soon after; it was acute by 1878. By 1914 the area of arable land in England and Wales had diminished by 3½ million acres or 26 per cent.; the number of persons employed in farming had fallen in almost exactly the same proportion; and the acreage of wheat had shrunk by nearly one half. As, conversely, the population of England and Wales swelled from 22,712,266 at the 1871 census to 36,070,492 at the 1911 census (an increase not far short of 60 per cent. in forty years), it followed that the country's inability to feed itself was sensationally enhanced. To a degree never matched elsewhere in human records on any similar scale, the English became dependent for their daily bread and meat upon sea-borne imports, which could only be purchased by the export of industrial goods or services.

But, fourthly, it was during these same years that English manufacturing industry, for the first time since the advent of the Industrial Revolution, began to find its export trade seriously threatened by foreign competition. The causes and character of this development will be discussed later; we must be content here to note its novelty. In the fifteenth, sixteenth, seventeenth, and eighteenth centuries English exporters had, of course, had rivals abroad. But the objects of foreign trade were then very different. It was rather a luxury than a necessity; a mere fringe on the life of a self-supporting nation. And when after the Industrial Revolution our exports began to be our livelihood, for several generations no foreigners could compete with us on level terms. Trade had its cycles of good and bad; but where we failed to sell it was because our customers abroad lacked purchasing power, not because other nations had supplanted us in their custom. This continued even for a few years after 1870; but then the process of supplanting set in. The United States started producing goods in many lines where hitherto she had bought ours. Country after country in western Europe launched into manufacturing for the world at large. Germany, in particular, multiplied mammoth industrial cities, with soaring birth-rates and mushroom populations, needing export markets to live on no less than we. Foreign trade came thus to wear, as it never had before in history, the aspect of a struggle for existence between rival manufacturing nations; among whom densely populated England ran bigger risks than any other, while no longer enjoying any monopolist lead.

Lastly, this period supplied part of the foundations and most of the superstructure to the British Empire as we now know it. For India alone it was by comparison uneventful. Canada had formed a federal nucleus in 1867, but more than half of her habitable area and six out of her ten provinces were added or constituted from 1870 onwards. Australia was federated in 1900;

the Union of South Africa in 1910; while New Zealand developed from rather a struggling settlement into a prosperous nation during the last two decades of the nineteenth century. The Egyptian campaign of 1885 was the first in which self-governing colonies sent contingents of troops to fight beside those of the mother country. And the Colonial Conference, first called in 1887, was the germ of the Imperial Conference, which has since become so vital for the constitution of a British Commonwealth of Nations. Elsewhere this same period witnessed, especially in the tropics, an enormous amount of 'painting the map red'. Not only was Egypt occupied, the Suez Canal controlled, Upper Burma conquered, and Malaya developed, but (save for the ex-German territories mandated to her after the European war) nearly the whole of Great Britain's immense colonial domains in tropical and sub-tropical Africa were acquired. The phrase, 'the fourth British Empire', which is sometimes applied to these last, may scarcely exaggerate their importance; but she owes them almost entirely to private initiatives. With the exception of Joseph Chamberlain, very few cabinet ministers at the time cared much about their acquisition, or were prepared to spend public money on their development. And though Malaya (thanks to tin and rubber) had progressed rapidly before 1914, this was not true of the African colonies, which in many instances lagged behind those of other powers.

Such are perhaps the main features for England of the period upon whose story we are entering. It is well to start with them clear in our heads, that we may not lack clues in the endless labyrinth of facts and events. But it would be easy to lengthen the list. The student of administration, for instance, will note that side by side with a democratic machinery for ascertaining and expressing the people's will there grew up a bureaucratic machinery for giving it effect. August 31, 1870, the date at which the entry to the Civil Service was thrown open to competitive examination, marks a point of departure. From then onwards may be traced a steady and rapid expansion in the size, number, and efficiency of the government departments, which—followed at short distance by similar expansions on the municipal side—revolutionized the scope and role of government itself. Similarly, to solve the physical problems involved in feeding the over-populated island a whole new and miraculous technology of food transport and preservation—grain elevators, meat and fruit canneries, refrigerating plants, specialized shipping—was developed in this period overseas and here. In the sphere, again, of political controversies nearly the whole of that phase in Anglo-Irish relations which is associated with the phrase 'Home Rule' falls between 1870 and 1914. So, in the sphere of adventurous discovery, do the concluding stages in man's survey of his earth's surface—the unravelling of the last secrets of Africa and the conquest of both the Poles. So again do a host of major scientific discoveries, and many revolutionary inventions in the arts both of peace and war. So, in England, do some very important social developments consequent on legal changes; e.g. the general supersession of direct individual ownership by ownership through limited companies in almost every sphere of industry and trade, and the emancipation, for contractual and property-owning purposes, of married women. So, likewise, does the greater part of the gradual but overwhelming revolution in the English birthrate brought about by the use of contraceptives; and so does a silent but easily distinguished change in the sphere filled by religion.

The country's political history during the forty-four years falls pretty sharply and obviously into three more or less equal sub-periods. The first extends to the defeat and resignation of Gladstone's third cabinet in 1886; the second from thence to the death of Queen Victoria; and the third down to the outbreak of the European war. In the first, the dominant figures are Gladstone, Disraeli, and Parnell; in the second, Salisbury and Joseph Chamberlain; while the third, though it extends four years beyond the death of King Edward, might conveniently be labelled Edwardian. The dividing lines correspond not only to the main changes of current in the country's internal politics, but, within only a few years each way, to those in the orientation of its foreign policy, and also to movements of ideas and periods of cultural development.

The present volume, therefore, has been conformed to this triple division; and the chapters are so grouped as to treat each of the sub-periods in turn under all its main heads. It is believed that this arrangement will be for the convenience of the reader; whose greatest difficulty, when examining a period about which so much is known, must always be not to lose sight of the wood for the trees.

I

GLADSTONE'S PRIME

URING the decade 1870–80 one feature above all others
shaped the surface of British politics—the personal duel,
continuous save for a period following 1874, between two figures
of tremendous stature, Gladstone and Disraeli. Its first few years
fall outside the period of this volume; and what narrowed the
combat to a duel was the death (in October 1865) of Palmerston.
The only quite comparable episode in English history is the
similar rivalry of Pitt and Fox; and the well-known lines, in
which Sir Walter Scott characterized that earlier contest, might
be applied without change to the later. Now as then the champions seemed

> With more than mortal powers endowed;

now as then

> Beneath each banner proud to stand,
> Looked up the noblest of the land;

though in the later case, unlike the earlier, they were not themselves born aristocrats, but the one was a baptized Jew, and the
other (although educated at Eton) came of Scottish merchant-
folk who had made money in the Liverpool slave-trade.

To understand their pre-eminence, one must appreciate the
paramount interest which the English public then took in Parliamentary proceedings. In the seventies of last century there were
no film stars, no football champions, no speed supermen, no male
or female aviators, no tennis heroes or heroines; even cricket
(W. G. Grace started playing in first-class matches in 1864) was
only beginning to be much noticed in the newspapers. The
people's daily fluctuations of excitement, of expectancy, of hero-
worship, which are dissipated now over these and many other
fields, were concentrated then upon the house of commons. The
turf and the pulpit were its only rivals; and neither equalled it,
while the pulpit (by popularizing the taste for oratory) rather
helped its vogue. Parliamentary speeches were reported pro-
minently and at length in all the newspapers; they were read
aloud and discussed in homes and public-houses. Points scored
or lost in debate across the floor of the house of commons were
not merely noted by the members present, but followed with rapt

attention throughout the country. Working men canvassed the form and prospects of parliamentary leaders much as they now do those of dirt-track racers. The dazzle of the brightest lights was unforgettable. As late as 1900 an old village worker in Somerset wished to convey to the present writer his sense of the eminence of a local worthy. 'He held', he said, 'a position in the neighbourhood like that which the late Lord Palmerston used to hold in this country.' Palmerston had then been dead thirty-five years.

Of the mighty protagonists now before us Disraeli celebrated his sixty-sixth birthday in December 1870, and Gladstone his sixty-first in the same month. Both were then at the height of their powers. Disraeli's waned gradually after he was 70, rapidly after 75; and he died at 76. Gladstone, who lived to be 88 and was in office as Prime Minister at 84, nevertheless, like Disraeli, underwent a change about 70. As a consequence, common estimates of him to-day rarely do him full justice. For the phases of his character and record, which to old men now living are a personal memory and which younger men may have overheard on the lips of since-dead relatives, are those from 1880 onwards, when, though still phenomenal, he was altogether past his best. One has to get behind this, and study at first hand the speeches, newspapers, and other contemporary records of the sixties and seventies, to realize his almost incredible magnitude in his prime. Then for a period of years he displayed all-round parliamentary powers, which it is difficult to believe can ever have been quite equalled, and which in one situation after another simply astounded friend and foe alike. It is not the least part of Disraeli's credit that in presence of such a human tornado he never lost his footing or his nerve, but by the cool and dexterous use of his own very different resources—in particular through the strange partnership of a daring imagination with a resilient and inscrutable irony—was able always to maintain a fighting front.

Gladstone had taken office as prime minister for the first time in 1868 at the head of a party formed by a fusion of whigs, Peelites, and radicals, to which the term 'liberal' was first regularly applied in England. Born of Disraeli's (1867) extension of the franchise, this was the greatest reforming Parliament since that born of the original extension in 1832. The sessions of 1869 and 1870 fall outside the present volume; in the first the Irish Church had been disestablished; in the second two other measures of prime importance, the first Irish Land Act and the great English Education Act, had become law. At the same time an Order in Council of 4 June 1870 had thrown open to competitive examination the entry (as from 31 August) to nearly all branches of the civil service except the foreign office. Such had been the first instalments of reform from a government intent on realizing in many further directions the aim which they all embodied, viz. to abolish class privileges and unbar to all the doors of political, economic, and cultural opportunity.

Debates on them still occupied the public mind of the United Kingdom, when in August the thunders of the Franco-Prussian war pealed out, if not from a blue sky, at any rate with a shock very little prepared for. The army estimates in the previous spring had been for less than £13 millions, and provided less than 110,000 regulars *and reservists* to be available for service abroad, including all those needed for our many overseas garrisons. Ten thousand was the largest expeditionary force that the war office could contemplate; and only by paring and scraping could the necessary 9 infantry battalions of 850 men be constituted for it.[1] Thus the spectacle of a war, in whose first stage Prussia and her associates mobilized under arms 475,000 men with adequate reserves behind them, laid suddenly bare the relative impotence of Great Britain to interfere on the Continent.

At two points, nevertheless, her interference was soon needed. The first was Belgium, whose neutrality we had guaranteed together with France, Prussia, Austria, and Russia by the Treaty of London in 1839. This neutrality had been deemed a British and a Prussian, but not a French, interest. As far back as 1852 Napoleon III (then prince president of France) had signed a decree annexing Belgium, but withdrew it before publication. In 1870, between the declaration of war and the start of the fighting, Bismarck published a draft treaty with the same object, three or four years old,[2] and in the handwriting of Napoleon III's ambassador, Benedetti. Gladstone thereupon took prompt action. He invited both France and Prussia to sign short treaties reaffirming the guarantee of 1839, and providing that, if the armies of either country violated the neutrality of Belgium, Great Britain

---

[1] Sir Robert Biddulph, *Lord Cardwell at the War Office* (1904), pp. 64–5.
[2] It probably dated from 1866, but Bismarck made it appear to date from 1867. Cp. Albert Sorel, *Histoire Diplomatique de la Guerre Franco-Allemande* (1875), i. 25–8; G. Rothan, *La Politique Française en 1866* (1875), pp. 382–4.

would co-operate with the other for its defence. Bismarck's assent was the prompter; but by 9 August (when France's military embarrassments were already such as to discourage her provoking wider trouble) that of Napoleon III's government followed. An important British interest was thus successfully safeguarded, and a precedent set for the attitude of the Asquith cabinet in 1914. The latter, however, was not a complete one; since Gladstone's pledge of action was limited to co-operation in and for Belgium, and carried no engagement to participate otherwise in the general operations of the war.

The other challenge came from Russia. Bismarck, when he engaged his country in single combat with France, had to face risks of intervention by Austria, Italy, Russia, and Great Britain. He was not the kind of statesman to 'wait and see' till they materialized; but at once took steps to divide and distract the neutral world. So, among other things, he suggested[1] to Prince Gortchakov, the Russian Chancellor, that he should denounce those clauses of the (1856) Treaty of Paris, which provided for the neutralization of the Black Sea, and forbade Russia to maintain on it military or naval establishments. Gortchakov delayed action till the fall of Metz had made it certain that France could not help Great Britain to enforce the clauses. But at the end of October 1870 he denounced them. The Powers most directly challenged by this were Great Britain and Turkey.

The Turks were furious, but dared not act alone. Nor could Great Britain without continental support, of which none was in fact forthcoming. Lord Granville,[2] who had become Foreign Secretary following the death of Lord Clarendon in the previous July, handled the situation with tact and dignity. In his first dispatch he abstained from arguing whether the object desired by Russia could be conceded or not. But he insisted firmly on the principle that, before a single Power can free itself from any of the stipulations of a treaty, it must obtain the consent of the other signatory Powers. The effect of unilateral denunciation (like Gortchakov's) is, he said, 'to bring the entire authority and effi-

[1] See Bismarck's *Gedanken und Erinnerungen* (1898); tr. by A. J. Butler as *Bismarck the Man and the Statesman*, ii. 113–14.
[2] George, second Earl Granville, b. 1815. Educated at Eton and Christ Church, Oxford; M.P. 1836–46, when he succeeded to the peerage; foreign secretary, 1851; president of the council, 1853; leader of house of lords, 1855; in office under Palmerston, 1859–65; colonial secretary, 1868–70; foreign secretary, 1870–4 and 1880–5; colonial secretary, 1886; d. 1891.

cacy of treaties under the discretionary control of each one of the Powers who may have signed them; the result of which would be the entire destruction of treaties in their essence'. This appeal to the abstract sanctity of treaties had a double wisdom. It placed the British case upon ground which, for what it was worth, could not easily be shaken. And it opened up the road to a bargain, whereby Russia should concede the form of what was in dispute, and Great Britain the substance. After a good deal of negotiation, which served to blazon the new fact that victorious Prussia dominated Europe, a conference of the Powers was opened (17 January 1871) in London, and a compromise resulted on those lines. A Protocol embodying the principle for which Granville contended was unanimously signed. But treading on its heels came an agreement to abrogate the Black Sea clauses. Face was saved, and Turkey consoled, by a small further modification of the 1856 terms.

Gladstone and Granville deserve credit, on the whole, for the way in which this storm was weathered. They simply had not power to do more. And it may be argued, that the Black Sea clauses implied a derogation from 'natural sovereignty', which could never have been more than temporary in the case of a Great Power. Palmerston, their original begetter, had here as elsewhere shown more vigour than realism. Yet the British public took it badly. They registered a deep sense of Russia's perfidy and deep alarm at her renewed menace—feelings which a few years later came to the surface with dangerously explosive force in the crisis of 1878. Now too was born a popular distrust of Gladstone's leadership in foreign affairs, a seed of grumbling that he had let the country down, which later events sprouted and Disraeli's dexterity watered, till it cast a shadow at the polls in 1874. What subconsciously galled the Englishman of that day was the contrast between his country's gigantic lead over her neighbours in trade, production, invention, mechanical powers and material resources of every kind,[1] and her relegation to an unaccustomed back seat in the councils of Europe.

Following its success over Belgium, and still anxious to localize the conflict, the British government had taken the initiative (later in August 1870) of asking various Powers to exchange assurances that they would not depart from neutrality without previous mutual communication. On this basis, without formal treaties,

[1] See Chapter IV.

Italy, Russia, Austria-Hungary, and some lesser Powers agreed.
No further British move was made. Granville stood firm against
mediation, unless both sides wished it; and as a convinced neutral
turned a deaf ear alike to Thiers when he pleaded for intervention, and to the Prussian ambassador's protests against our supplying war-stores to France. Gladstone agreed with him save
on a single subject. When the Prussian annexation of Alsace-
Lorraine was mooted from the latter part of September onwards,
he took deeply to heart, not the protests of the French about the
inviolability of their soil, but the threat to transfer the provinces
without the consent of their inhabitants. He wanted to approach
the other neutral Powers with a proposal to declare the principle
involved. But Granville and the cabinet over-ruled him. On
the practical point they were right. No such move could succeed,
or could even appear neutral, unless all the greater neutrals joined
in it. And Russia was certain to abstain, owing to her Black Sea
intrigue with Bismarck. Yet it is impossible, in the light of the
years which came after, to read what Gladstone wrote privately
at the time[1] without being struck by his insight and foresight.

Public sympathy in England veered a good deal with the course
of the war. At the outset it was mainly pro-Prussian—partly
because France was supposed to be the aggressor; partly because
the English then felt themselves very much a Protestant country,
and Prussia was a Lutheran Power. But certain elements were
pro-French all through—fashionable people who had frequented
the glittering Paris of the Second Empire, and on the radical side
the then influential Positivists.[2] Following Sedan and Metz,
when the Prussians became plain conquerors and the French
picturesque patriots, sympathy for the under-dog rallied nearly
all England to the French side. It found a blameless and memorable expression after the fall of Paris (28 January 1871), when
London alone sent £80,000 worth of provisions to succour the
starving city. The government's neutral attitude had the support
of the queen. She shared all her subjects' sympathies with
Lutheranism, and could not be cold to the triumphs of her own
son-in-law, the Prussian crown prince. But she instinctively disliked the annexation policy, and in September 1870 went so far
as to dispatch a personal telegram to the King of Prussia, ex-

---

[1] *Life*, by Lord Morley (1903), bk. vi, ch. 5.
[2] See, e.g., Frederic Harrison's eloquent articles in the *Fortnightly Review*, then
edited by John Morley.

pressing in general terms her hope that his country, after its glorious victories, would make an early and magnanimous peace. The king replied in equally general terms, and no more came of it.

The details of that stupendous trial of arms concern European, not English, history. Yet we must not disregard their impact on the English mind. For sheer swift drama nothing in the war of 1914–18 quite compares with them. Few episodes, save the outset, of the later Armageddon were so mobile; and none were ever so fully, freely, and immediately reported in the press. The first real shock occurred at Weissenburg; and within a month thereafter ten battles were fought, 300,000 men were killed, wounded, or made prisoners, the Germans had penetrated 150 miles into France, the Emperor was a captive and his family fugitives, and Paris, then the world's largest city after London and by far its most magnificent, was awaiting under an extemporized Republic the inexorable advance of the besieger. Nor were the incidents less sensational than the results. Sedan (1 September 1870), where the Emperor's great army was surrounded and nearly 100,000 men were killed, wounded, or laid down their arms, was the most striking victory of encirclement since Cannae and Trasimene. Later, the surrender of Metz by Bazaine (14 October 1870) with nearly 120,000 men was the largest military capitulation of which history then held record. Later still persisted the tragic 131-days siege of Paris itself, the very heart of the world's luxury, with its long agony of torn hopes and tarnished heroisms, vain sorties, and remorseless hunger; an object-lesson for London almost at its doors. And last of all, after the surrender to the Germans, the appalling episodes of the Paris Commune of 1871 revealed for the first time in modern history—what Thucydides had known, and what in 1917–19 we saw on a much vaster scale—that, when shock and defeat have battered an organized society beyond a certain point, not only its external but its internal walls collapse, and the worst atrocities of war may be eclipsed by those of revolution.

Swift effects were not wanting outside France, beside the stirring forward of Russia, which we have seen. The entry of King Victor Emmanuel's troops into Rome (20 September 1870) and the completion of Italian unity was one. The union of Germany herself (minus Austria) in a new Bismarck-moulded empire (proclaimed 18 January 1871) was another. Time was yet to show how the spirit of 'blood and iron', which had wrought these mighty changes, was to dominate the world in their working out; and how much the liberal spirit, which for so long had been radiated through Europe from England and France, was to be checked and damped through the catastrophic defeat of what still then was the larger of those two nations.

The war was bound to have some repercussion on British armaments. Gladstone strove to keep it small. On 2 August 1870 parliament voted 20,000 additional men for the army and £2 millions on a Vote of Credit. But by 1871 both public and professional opinion were strongly moved. One of the most successful anonymous pamphlets ever issued, *The Battle of Dorking*, appeared from the pen of a clever Engineer officer,[1] and raised for the first time the spectre of a German invasion of England. The navy estimates of 1871 (moved by Goschen,[2] who had succeeded Childers[3] as first lord, when ill health compelled the latter's retirement) showed a rise of only £385,826 to a total still below £10 millions; though H.M.S. *Devastation*, launched in July, marked a distinct step in the world's progress towards mightier ironclads. But the army estimates went up by £2,866,700—a salmon's leap in those days; and they totalled nearly £16 millions, providing for an addition of 19,980 men to the regulars, including 5,000 to the artillery. Nor was that all. The very able man of affairs, Edward Cardwell,[4] who had been secretary for war since 1868, was determined not merely to expand the army, but to reform it.

The needs were indeed great. Even the rude lessons of the Crimea had left essential mischiefs unhealed. At the top the com-

---

[1] Colonel (afterwards General Sir George) Chesney, then head of the new Indian Civil Engineering College at Cooper's Hill.

[2] George Joachim Goschen, b. 1831, son of German merchant in London. Educated at Rugby and Oriel College, Oxford. As liberal was vice-president, Board of Trade, 1865; chancellor, duchy of Lancaster, 1866; president, Poor Law Board, 1868; first lord, Admiralty, 1871–4. As unionist was chancellor of the Exchequer, 1887–92; converted Consols, 1888; first lord, Admiralty, 1895–1900. Viscount in 1901; d. 1907.

[3] Hugh C. E. Childers, b. 1827, son of Yorkshire clergyman. Educated at Trinity College, Cambridge. In Australia, 1850–7; in parliament as liberal from 1860; first lord, Admiralty, 1868–71; chancellor, duchy of Lancaster, 1872–3; secretary for war, 1880–2; chancellor of the exchequer, 1882–5; home secretary, 1886; d. 1896.

[4] Edward Cardwell, b. 1813 in Liverpool. Educated at Winchester and Balliol College, Oxford. Entered parliament as Peelite, 1842; president, Board of Trade, 1852–5; chief secretary, Ireland, 1859–61; chancellor, duchy of Lancaster, 1861–4; colonial secretary, 1864–6; secretary for war, 1868–74. Viscount in 1874; d. 1886.

mander-in-chief, the duke of Cambridge, opposed all change. And reforming officers below him had long been, as the saying is, in a cleft stick. For on the conservative side were the vested interests which maintained the abuses; while on the liberal side men like Gladstone had taken a purely cheese-paring view of the army, caring too little about efficiency, provided they could screw down the estimates.

Cardwell's place among statesmen is that of the greatest British army reformer during the nineteenth century. In him economy and efficiency met. In 1868 he had abolished flogging in the army during peace-time.[1] This step was opposed by most senior officers, who could quote against it the emphatic opinion of Wellington. Yet it was imperative, if the private soldier's career were to become anything better than a sort of penal servitude for the dregs of the population. It enabled Cardwell two years later to abolish 'bounty money' for recruits, and to discharge known bad characters from the army. Further in 1869 he started withdrawing troops from the self-governing colonies. In the two years 1870–1 units totalling 20,000 men were restored to the home establishment, the colonies being encouraged to raise their own local forces instead. Thus was abandoned another Wellingtonian policy—that of hiding the British army during peace in scattered driblets over distant places. Its motive had been to dodge the traditional hostility of the whigs to a standing army. But it was fatal to strategic economy and to anything beyond battalion training.

Still harder ground was broken in the summer of 1870. Parliament passed an Army Enlistment (short service) Act; and the queen was induced to sign reluctantly (28 June) an Order in Council subordinating the commander-in-chief to the secretary of state. How much further reform might have gone but for Sedan and Metz, it is impossible to say. Cardwell had the great advantage of enjoying Gladstone's financial confidence—so much so that some had backed him for chancellor of the exchequer. But before any thorough army changes could fructify, a very strong obstacle must be removed. This was the system of obtaining commissions and promotions in the army by purchase. It had wide and deep roots throughout upper-class society, and, as we shall see, was eventually only overcome by a sort of *coup d'état*. But for the war of 1870–1 there could hardly have been,

[1] It was not abolished for active service also until 1880.

as there was, a public opinion to sustain Gladstone in such an extreme course.

The story may first be briefly outlined. Cardwell's Army Regulation Bill, 1871, was introduced in the commons. It covered a good deal else besides abolishing purchase; but purchase was the sole issue fought over. After fierce obstruction it was passed, and went to the lords. That house by 155 votes to 130 carried a motion which in form shelved the bill, but in effect defeated it. On the second day following, the government announced that purchase was by royal warrant abolished. As the bill had provided generous compensation for the officers and there would be none at all without its passage, the lords had now perforce to pick it down off their shelf and pass it. Conservatives, and also some radicals (e.g. Professor Fawcett), declaimed shrilly against what they deemed an abuse of the Prerogative. But the country, which wanted security, and felt that purchase had blocked the way to it, simply refused to take notice.

Such being the events in their order, let us now examine their bearings. 'Purchase' as a legally recognized institution went back at least to the decision in *Ive* v. *Ash* (1702). At different times attempts had been made to regulate it, and there existed a tariff of prices which might be lawfully paid; but by the usage of the service large competitive additions were made to these. Service opinion was almost universally in favour of the system. It had been extolled by Wellington in a famous Memorandum of 1833; and in 1841 Lord Melbourne's Commission, which comprised the leading soldiers of the day, had praised it as furthering the promotion and retirement of officers, and thereby making for their physical efficiency. In 1850 the aged Wellington, with two other officers who afterwards became Lord Raglan and Lord Panmure, signed another Report to the same effect. Later reports during the following twenty years were mainly confirmatory. Lord Palmerston upheld the system; as the whig party had done for a century and a half.

Yet its vices were self-evident. It obstructed any re-mapping, however advisable, of the regimental units. It prevented the selection and promotion of officers by merit. It enabled rich youths to buy themselves into positions for which they were quite untrained. Radicals could have criticized it as giving privilege to wealth; soldiers, as bestowing security and high rank upon incompetence. If in fact neither criticism had made headway, it was that England had no notion of the art of war. British officers were expected to be gentlemen and sportsmen; but outside the barrack-yard they were, as Wolseley testified later in retrospect, 'entirely wanting in military knowledge'. The lack of it was deemed no drawback, since Marlborough's and Wellington's officers got on without. Only the rise of Prussian military science, exemplified first in 1866 and then in 1870, availed to shake this complacency.

Even so the number of officers opposed to purchase was tiny. There were now a few in or around the war office. They were all under 40—Colonel Wolseley, lately back from Canada with very great credit for putting down the Red River rebellion; Major George Colley, a leading professor at the staff college; Major Robert Biddulph, Cardwell's military secretary; Captain Henry Brackenbury; and Captain Evelyn Baring (afterwards Lord Cromer), engaged in what eventually became the Intelligence Branch. Though they all attained distinguished careers later,[1] they had nearly every senior officer against them, from the duke of Cambridge down; and in the sequel not even Wolseley himself was ever quite forgiven by the service caste.

With them, but particularly with Wolseley and Baring, Cardwell acted in complete sympathy. So did the under-secretary, Lord Northbrook, who was Baring's first cousin. Gladstone himself became whole-hearted in support. The liberals rallied generally to the anti-privilege argument; great play being made with the case of Lord Cardigan,[2] which, though more than a generation old, was only an extreme example of what purchase would still permit. In the house of commons Disraeli, though officially opposing Cardwell's bill as a government measure, warily left most of the criticism to service members. A knot of colonels fought hard, and Sir Roundell Palmer (not then in the government) accused them of 'endeavouring to baffle the majority by mere consumption of time'. This seems to be the

---

[1] But Cromer's was outside the army, which he virtually quitted on account of this episode.

[2] James, 7th earl of Cardigan (1797–1868), had entered the army in 1824, and almost immediately bought his way into the command of the 15th Hussars. In 1833 he had to leave it, owing to the acquittal of an officer whom he had illegally put under arrest; but three years later he bought himself the command of the 11th Hussars. These proceedings cost him many tens of thousands of pounds, but he was a rich peer who could easily afford them. Fortunately for the reformers his name (though he led the Six Hundred at Balaclava) was unpopular in the service.

first example of obstruction, in the modern sense, in the house of commons; and it is worth noticing that it occurred in the very first parliament elected on a wide franchise. The second extended the evil much farther; and the third, as we shall see, carried it to a crisis.

The debate in the lords also had features which pointed forward. For almost the first time since 1832 the peers were brought into naked and downright conflict with the commons by class motives on a class issue. And in this many whigs, headed by Earl (formerly Lord John) Russell, sided with the tories against the liberals. The whig earl Grey and tory earl of Carnarvon made very similar speeches. Their kernel was that the purchase system kept officering as an occupation for gentlemen, and not a trade for professional men. If it became the latter, it might menace our go-easy oligarchic liberties; and they preferred an inefficient army to an authoritarian state.

The royal warrant procedure, by which the lords' resistance was outflanked, was defended by Gladstone as not involving the Prerogative. What the queen did, he said, was to cancel the warrant, under which purchase was legal, and frame a new one, under which it was not; and this she could do, not by exercising the Prerogative, but under statutory powers conferred by an act of George III.[1] Lord Cairns in the house of lords weightily challenged the legality of this; and in the house of commons, while the attorney-general (Sir R. Collier) rested the government's action on the statute, the solicitor-general (Sir J. Coleridge) relied on the Prerogative. The point is now of minor importance, since Professor Fawcett's fear that the precedent would be repeated and grow into a new tyranny of the Crown over parliament, has in any case not been realized.

To Cardwell and his associates the abolition of purchase was a reform desired less for its own sake than as opening the door to others. Partly by his series of acts, and partly by administrative measures, he transformed the army. The main points of change were these.

First he divided the business of the war department into three sections, of which the newly subordinated commander-in-chief, the surveyor-general of the ordnance, and the financial secretary were to be the respective heads, all acting under the responsibility of the secretary of state. He concentrated the three

[1] 49 Geo. III, c. 126.

branches under one roof by moving the office of the commander-in-chief and the army head-quarters staff from the old Horse Guards in Whitehall to the war office, which was then in Pall Mall. Greatly increased powers and responsibilities were conferred upon the commander-in-chief. He was given command of all the land forces of the Crown, regular and auxiliary, both at home and abroad. As part of the process, the right of appointing officers in the militia, which had hitherto belonged to the lords-lieutenant of counties, was taken from them and transferred to the war office. Here was a distinct blow at the territorial oligarchy.

With this went a measure of staff reform. In almost every other army it had become usual to attach to every general officer one staff officer, who was his *alter ego*. In the British army there were two, and the dualism went right up to the top, where the adjutant-general and the quartermaster-general were of co-equal and rival authority. Cardwell abolished this, and the quartermaster-general at the war office became an officer of the adjutant-general's department. But that was as far as he dared go. The full status of 'chief of staff' was only instituted in wars (and not even then in India); and the army had to wait till the twentieth century before a proper permanent general staff was organized on continental lines.

Next, there was the problem of the men. From Waterloo to 1847 men were enlisted for twenty-one years' service with the colours—practically for life. This was the Wellingtonian system. Together with flogging, it had given army service its penal servitude character; but it had also the fatal disadvantage of rendering impossible a reserve. In 1847 the period was lowered to twelve years; but it was still too long. The lesson of the Franco-Prussian war was the absolute necessity of a trustworthy army reserve of well-trained men in the full vigour of their manhood. Every soldier in the line regiments served more than half his time abroad, most commonly in India or the tropics; and after twelve years their physique was seldom good enough. Cardwell therefore introduced short service. Men were enlisted for six years with the colours and six in the reserves.[1] Senior officers shook their heads, but the system worked, and was the basis of our remarkable success in war throughout the Wolseley period.

---

[1] He would have liked to give an option of three with the colours and nine in the reserves, but his advisers would not go so far.

Recruiting greatly improved, and service in the army became popular, so far as it could while Gladstonian economy maintained the pitifully low rates of pay.

Following this (in 1872–4) the infantry was rearmed with the Martini-Henry rifle. This was the first satisfactory breech-loading rifle in the British army, though after the war of 1866 our old muzzle-loading Enfields had been converted into rather inefficient breech-loaders on the Snider system. It is worth recalling that the prince consort, not long before his death, had vainly urged breech-loaders upon Palmerston as far back as October 1861.

Thirdly, there was the problem of regimental reorganization. The old regiments of the line, which were known by numbers and for the most part lacked any territorial basis,[1] had long histories and strong *esprit de corps*. But few of their battalions could muster more than 500 men. They were hard to recruit and still harder to expand; and they could not develop any organic links with the auxiliary forces—militia and volunteers—which were territorial.

Cardwell, therefore, proceeded to territorialize all infantry of the line. He divided Great Britain and Ireland into sixty-nine infantry regimental districts, each containing the depot of the regiment to be associated with its territory. Each of these county regiments was to comprise at least two regular battalions, with one, two, or three battalions of militia, and generally all the volunteer infantry belonging to the district. With fusions here and dovetailings there, the existing line regiments were fitted into the scheme, and carried their histories, their battle-honours, and their fighting traditions to the depots of the new organization. At first, to smooth over the transition, long and cumbrous titles were bestowed on the resulting units. But it was always intended that they should eventually come to be known by their plain county names, and within less than a generation these were well established. In the twentieth century it probably occurs to few people that the Durhams, say, or the Dorsets owe their existence as such to Cardwell, or that the proud battle-honours of Vittoria or Plassey, which appear on their colours, were earned by units who had nothing to do with either county.

The object of attaching at least two battalions to each depot

---

[1] i.e. any basis in a particular recruiting territory—not in 'Territorials', which were a twentieth-century introduction.

was, that one should be always at the depot, while the other was on foreign service. This was Cardwell's famous 'linked battalion' system. Recruits in those days were nearly all the merest boys, and needed several years' home training before they were fit to send abroad. By alternating the foreign service of the battalions every few years, it was possible to ensure that the units abroad consisted always of seasoned material. To this as much as anything may be attributed the notably good fighting record of British troops overseas between 1871 and 1899.

The cavalry regiments, whose officers wielded more social influence than any, Cardwell dared not touch to reorganize; though he increased the total of their establishments from 8,762 men to 10,422. The artillery he localized like the infantry; though it was imperfectly subdivided owing to the continuance of the system of working the Royal Artillery as a single regiment. Cardwell regarded artillery as an arm in which the mechanistic nation should be relatively strong. He increased its total of horsed guns from 180 to 336, and added about 5,000 men. His efforts here, however, were largely sterilized by the conservatism of the ordnance officers; who actually insisted at this time on *going back* to muzzle-loading cannon, and thereby kept us behind the rest of Europe for a good part of twenty years. On the morrow of the Franco-Prussian war this was truly an astonishing folly; the more so, because the worth of breech-loading artillery in war had been first demonstrated by British gunners in the China war of 1860.

This comprehensive programme of army changes, mostly authorized or foreshadowed by his acts of 1870 and 1871, was Cardwell's daily work, in the teeth of incessant opposition, during the following three years. He had the satisfaction of seeing it achieved beyond reversal before he left office with the fall of the Gladstone government in 1874. He was then completely worn out. He took a peerage and retired into private life.

His reforms during the quarter of a century following left a broad mark on British history. Without them not only would prompt and crucial successes, such as the Egyptian campaign of 1882,[1] have been unobtainable, but the power-prestige, which Lord Salisbury had behind him in his diplomacy, would scarcely have existed in the same way. Not their least exceptional feature

[1] As handsomely admitted in Gladstone's letter to him of 15 September 1882 (Biddulph, op. cit., p. 247).

was their economy. Cardwell left the estimates lower than he found them, and yet he had increased the strength of the army in the United Kingdom by 25 battalions, 156 field guns, and abundant stores, while the reserves available for foreign service had been raised from 3,545 to 35,905 men.

In the reorganization as a whole there were two flaws. One was that the duke of Cambridge remained commander-in-chief, and from then till his resignation in 1895 obstructed progress in the central direction of the army as a fighting machine.[1] The other was the omission to construct a proper general staff, the lack of which led to our blunders and break-downs in the South African campaign of 1899. Their combined effects proved eventually very serious, but the second was a corollary of the first, and the first was beyond any war minister's power to alter at that period.

Here we may take our leave of Cardwell. He was an exceedingly able man, who had seemed designated for a more general political career, as Gladstone's lieutenant and perhaps his successor. Instead, he exhausted his prime on this single vast specialized task; rendering to his country a unique service, for which he has not always been too generously remembered. Among his parliamentary associates at the war office two young men may be mentioned; for we shall meet them again hereafter, both there and in wider fields. One was Mr. Henry Campbell-Bannerman, M.P., who in 1871 became financial secretary. The other was the fifth marquis of Lansdowne, who in 1872, when Lord Northbrook went to India as Viceroy, became undersecretary.

The other reform of most scope carried by the Administration before its fall was that of the English Judicature. Its author was Roundell Palmer, first Lord Selborne;[2] who became lord chancellor in 1872, when Lord Hatherley had to retire owing to loss of eyesight. A speech which he made in the house of commons in 1867, when an ex-attorney-general, had led to the ap-

[1] The duke (1819–1904) was the queen's first cousin, and held his post because she wished (as the prince consort had) that the commander-in-chief should be a member of the royal family. For a characterization of him as an obstructive force, see Field-Marshal Sir W. Robertson, *From Private to Field-Marshal* (1921), 17.

[2] B. 1812. Educated at Rugby, Winchester, and Trinity College, Oxford; the greatest chancery advocate of his day; solicitor-general, 1861; attorney-general, 1863–6; lord chancellor, 1872–4, 1880–5; d. 1895. He, Cardwell the war minister, and Lowe the chancellor of the exchequer, had been friends at school together.

pointment of an exceedingly strong royal commission with Lord Cairns, Disraeli's chancellor, as chairman.[1] This body reported in 1869, and in 1871 Lord Hatherley introduced a bill; but (like an earlier one by Cairns) it was, to quote Lord Selborne, 'too much in skeleton form', and came to nothing.

Lord Selborne long afterwards described the bill, which became the Judicature Act 1873, as 'the work of my own hand, without any assistance beyond what I derived from the labours of my predecessors; and it passed', he added, 'substantially in the form in which I proposed it'. It was indeed an admirable piece of drafting. Lord Cairns supported it heartily, and it was piloted through the house of commons by two law officers, Sir John Coleridge and Sir George Jessel (both afterwards eminent judges), who were highly qualified to speak respectively for the common law and the equity side.

The act was a piece of tidying up upon the largest scale in a field littered with the most venerable survivals from the middle ages. Down to 1873 modern England retained two legal systems side by side—the common law administered in one set of courts, and equity, which overrode it, administered in another. The act 'fused' them by providing that they should be administered concurrently in every court by every judge, and that, where their rules conflicted, the rules of equity should prevail. But it did more; it remodelled the courts themselves. At that time there were still three separate common law courts of unlimited jurisdiction—Queen's Bench, Common Pleas, and Exchequer. Each had a chief and puisne judges; each traced jurisdiction back to Edward I; and the only machinery which kept them at one was the court called the Exchequer Chamber, in which appeals from the judges of any of them were heard by judges of the other two. The Court of Chancery, which administered equity, had since 1851 been regularly organized in two 'instances'—the first manned by the lord chancellor, the master of the rolls, and three vice-

---

[1] The other members were: Lord Hatherley, Sir W. Erle (chief justice of the common pleas), Sir James Wilde (afterwards Lord Penzance), Sir R. Phillimore, Mr. G. Ward Hunt, Mr. H. C. E. Childers, Lord Justice James, Mr. Baron (afterwards Lord) Bramwell, Mr. Justice (afterwards Lord) Blackburn, Sir Montague Smith, Sir R. Collier (afterwards Lord Monkswell), Sir John Coleridge (afterwards Lord Coleridge, Lord Chief Justice), Sir R. Palmer (afterwards Lord Selborne, Lord Chancellor), Sir J. Karslake, Mr. (afterwards Mr. Justice) Quain, Mr. H. Rothery, Mr. Ayrton, Mr. W. G. Bateson, Mr. John Hollams, and Mr. F. D. Lowndes. No English lawyer can fail to note the professional weight of these names. Politically they comprised both parties.

chancellors, the second by two lords justices sitting with the lord chancellor as a court of appeal.[1] Further, special branches of the law, on whose history the Roman system had exerted more influence, were dealt with by three special courts—the High Court of Admiralty, the Court of Probate, and the Court for Divorce and Matrimonial Causes. From decisions in all these seven courts appeal in the final instance lay to the house of lords.

By the Act of 1873 all seven were united to form one Supreme Court of Judicature. An eighth, the London Bankruptcy Court, was left outside at the time, but it came in afterwards. At first the old titles were maintained, and what had been separate courts became separate divisions. But a section of the act authorized the Crown to abolish offices and merge divisions; and by 1880 they were reduced (as had always been intended) to the triple scheme which still obtains. In one respect only did Lord Selborne overshoot his mark. He organized his supreme court in two instances—a high court and an appeal court; and in conformity with the practice of continental judicatures he intended decisions of the latter to be final. So his act abolished the appeal jurisdiction of the house of lords. But this alarmed the peers, and led to a political agitation. The conservative leaders became involved; and following their victory at the polls in 1874 an amending act was passed by Lord Cairns in 1876, restoring a final appeal to the house of lords past the appeal court, and constituting the lords' tribunal for that purpose in the form with which we have since been familiar.

Lord Selborne's reform might be taken as a classic example of spectacular change carried through by consent. The construction of the present Central Law Courts, which was then in hand, no doubt helped to commend unity to the judges and the legal profession. Great tact and patience were nevertheless required to realize it. But the method permitted nothing revolutionary; and the scheme left standing many features which were and are anomalous among the judicatures of Europe. For instance, it provided for no decentralization of even the high court's justice, except on the common law side through the ancient and cumbrous device of travelling assizes; and it retained the necessity, amazing to a continental lawyer, that every kind of appeal

[1] There were also ancient chancery courts in Lancashire and Durham: these Lord Selborne left standing, and they still afford the sole provision made for chancery litigation (above county court level) outside London.

should be heard in London only. Whether Lord Selborne could have innovated more, had he wished, may be argued. But the fate of his scheme for a single appeal does not encourage the idea.

Such being the Gladstone government's two outstanding contributions to national progress during the part of its career subsequent to the outbreak of the Franco-Prussian war, let us now trace the diary and brief chronicle of that period. August 1870 is a watershed in the administration's fortunes. Before that date it had been popular as well as strenuous, backed by a majority in the country no less than in the house. But from about then a change set in. The majority at Westminster remained, though nerve-shaken by adverse by-elections; but that in the constituencies continuously trickled away.

The earliest weakening was due to radical and nonconformist disappointment over the compromise policy of Forster's Education Act. Forster's own constituents at Bradford carried a vote of censure on him at his first meeting after the act was passed. Next, as we have seen, came patriotic misgivings about the London Conference's surrender to Russia in the matter of the Black Sea. A little later came further shocks to patriotic feeling in connexion with the *Alabama* claims. This matter, though not finally settled till 1872, arose wholly out of events in the sixties, and for convenience its fuller treatment in this history has been left to the volume covering that period, where details of its various phases will be given. Here it may suffice to say, that in 1871-2 three separate occasions arose, when British pride was severely wounded. The first was in April of the former year, when the United States asked us to admit inadmissible principles; the second in the following December, when she revived before the arbitrators her so-called Indirect Claims; and the third in September 1872, when the arbitrators called on Great Britain to pay 15,000,000 dollars by way of damages. The Gladstone government had on each of these occasions the moral courage to take a wise but unpopular course. Posterity praises its extreme wisdom; but what stood out at the time was its extreme unpopularity.

The year 1871, besides the big agitation against Cardwell, witnessed a teacup storm over the budget. Down to and including 1870, the finance of the Gladstone government was plain sailing. The chancellor of the exchequer, Robert Lowe,[1] had a buoyant revenue and thrifty colleagues. But in 1871 money had to be found for the army increases inspired by the Franco-Prussian war. Lowe proposed to raise a million by a tax on matches. These were still comparatively a new article in Europe, and some foreign governments had already made money out of them, as not a few have since. Lowe's idea, therefore, was perfectly sound; and the Latin pun *Ex luce lucellum*, which was to adorn the revenue stamps on the match-boxes, is still remembered as typical of his wit and scholarship. However, the match manufacturers protested that, if matches were dearer, people would go back to tinder and their trade would be ruined. Foreign analogies show this to have been absurd; but unluckily for Lowe the principal match factory was in London. A pathetic rabble of its humble workers, chiefly very poor women, marched towards the house of commons, and were dispersed by police. The episode so affected the house that Lowe had to withdraw his tax, and get the money by raising income-tax instead. The fiscal results of this reverse were trifling; but the effect on public opinion, with the 'sporting' interest which was then taken in parliament, was quite appreciable for the government's prestige. Lowe, in particular, never recovered his house of commons reputation, which till then had stood singularly high.

Hubbubs were raised shortly afterwards over two appointments which the prime minister made. One was judicial, the other ecclesiastical. They are known as the Collier and the Ewelme cases. In the first a public reproof was administered to the government by Cockburn, the lord chief justice. There can be little doubt now that he was wrong, and that Hatherley, Gladstone, and Roundell Palmer were right. Yet it is not helpful to a government that it should collide with the lord chief justice.

But a much deeper source of unpopularity lay behind—one which produced results not for a day but for generations. In the summer of 1871 Bruce,[2] the home secretary, introduced his first

[1] B. 1811. Educated at Winchester and University College, Oxford. 1842–50 in Australia, where he was active at the bar and in the politics of Sydney. In 1852 and 1855, held minor offices under Aberdeen and Palmerston; in 1866 led the 'Adullamites' against the Whig Reform Bill; 1868–73, chancellor of the exchequer; 1873–4, home secretary; 1880, created Viscount Sherbrooke. An albino, and, though a great reader, could never use his eyes without pain; d. 1892.

[2] Henry Austin Bruce, b. 1815; educated at Swansea Grammar School; barrister; home secretary, 1868–73; created Lord Aberdare, 1873, and was lord president of the council 1873–4; d. 1895.

and most drastic Licensing Bill. It raised a storm of opposition from the publicans and the liquor trade generally; and as the chief temperance organization in politics, the United Kingdom Alliance, refused (because it did not embody their particular panacea, Local Veto) to give it any effective counter-support, it had to be withdrawn. In 1872 he tried again, and passed a weaker and yet still very contentious act. It was in debate upon this in the house of lords, that the eloquent Dr. Magee, then bishop of Peterborough, made his famous avowal that he would like to see 'England free better than England sober'. Its passage led to actual rioting in various towns; but it was enforced.

From midsummer 1871 till the dissolution of 1874 nearly every public-house in the United Kingdom was an active committee-room for the conservative party. The consequences of this upon actual voting, well attested by contemporary evidence,[1] probably outweighed all the other factors in the government's unpopularity. But the current of it ran deeper; for here—little realized, perhaps, at the time—was one of the source-points in the history of parties. Down to then the liquor industry, like other industrial interests, was apt to be liberal. One member (Stansfeld) of this very cabinet was a brewer. The liberal Dickens had glorified drink. The head of the great firm of Bass sat in parliament from 1848 to 1883 as liberal member for Derby. Till then, too, the conservative party lacked an adequate material basis. Whigs and tories alike in the old oligarchic days had rested on the support of great landed families. After 1832, and again after 1867, the widening of the franchise compelled a corresponding widening of parties; and so the liberal and conservative parties were gradually evolved. But the liberals had been far more successful in enrolling permanent interests under their banner. By championing economic liberty and class emancipation, they had won over the business classes generally. After 1860 they had paid increasing attention to the lower sections of the middle class and the upper strata of the wage-earners; and since these were mainly nonconformist, had enrolled nonconformity. By so doing they revived the historic tie between the tory party and the established church. But Anglicanism alone was neither strong

[1] e.g. *Annual Register*. Gladstone's own view of the 'immediately operative causes' which defeated him at the polls may be read in a letter to his brother Robertson of 6 February 1874: 'I have no doubt what is the principal. We have been borne down in a torrent of gin and beer.' (Morley's *Life*, bk. vi, chap. 14.)

enough nor rich enough for a party to live on. Fertile in ideas, Disraeli had missed the truth that in England no party exists by ideas only; and down to 1870 he had failed to place any strong new interest on his side. That was why his bold franchise bid in 1867 led to his own discomfiture.

But from 1871 onward to the end of our period the conservative party made good this lack. Money, workers, and support of every kind flowed to it inexhaustibly from the liquor trade. The more the liberals came to rely on the chapels, the more the public-houses rallied to their opponents. When political 'machines' developed in the eighties, the need for a permanent large income at the head-quarters of each party was vastly increased. But for money derived from brewers and distillers, it is very doubtful if the conservatives could have met it. Party funds being secret, nothing about them can be affirmed certainly; but nobody will dispute that during the forty years before 1914 a very large conservative income came from this source. Nor was money all. Few people are so well placed to influence voters as publicans; and there practically ceased to be any liberal publicans.

These facts, whose objective interest is considerable, have seldom been objectively discussed. They provide no small part of the explanation why conservatism was so much more successful in the forty years after 1871 than in the forty years before that date. But the liberals made them subjects for question-begging abuse. And the conservatives were a little shamefaced, and avoided talking much about them. It is difficult to see how either attitude was justified. Undeniable evils existed in the liquor traffic, but the better leaders among those engaged in it were not concerned to defend them; while it was neither improper for the trade, nor immoral for a party, to oppose political measures which, whatever one thinks of them, were essentially pointed to the goal of prohibition. Conservative shamefacedness, it may be noted, did not extend from speech to action. For example, one of the purest characters in front bench politics, no less a man than A. J. Balfour, sat from 1885 to 1905 for East Manchester. All the time that he did so, the seat was reputed in the gift of certain local breweries; and the chairman of his committee was the leading representative of the liquor trade in the public life of Manchester.

The by-elections began to tell their story from the date of Bruce's 1871 bill. In the summer of that year the sitting liberal member for East Surrey died; at the by-election the seat was lost, the conservatives being 300 votes up, and the liberals 1,300 down, on a poll of under 7,000. Some months later another liberal seat fell vacant at Plymouth; and it too was lost, though the liberal candidate was local and popular, and the conservative a complete stranger. So the swing continued throughout 1872–3. Yet at Westminster the government not only retained large majorities, but thanks mainly to Gladstone's eloquence had regularly the best of it in debates. In 1871 they carried two measures of much social importance, a Trade Union Act[1] and a University Tests Act. The latter made an epoch in the universities of Oxford and Cambridge, since it threw open for the first time all lay posts, in the colleges as well as the universities, to men of all creeds upon equal terms. Thus the church of England lost one of her last obviously anachronistic privileges; and that it should be withdrawn by so ardent a churchman as Mr. Gladstone lent a certain dignity to the proceeding. Gladstone's assent to the principle (earlier championed by Goschen and Sir John Coleridge) was not quickly won. But, once convinced, he forced the measure through against a house of lords opposition; led, it seems strange to record, by the great Lord Salisbury, who had succeeded to his title three years earlier and taken a similar line against Gladstone's disestablishment of the Irish church. In the same year an act was passed, whereby the Poor Law Board, the local government section of the home office, the medical department of the privy council, and some other oddments were thrown together to form the local government board (precursor of the ministry of health); of which Stansfeld,[2] the author of the act, became the first president, retaining his seat in the cabinet. It was no fault of this capable minister that this was not followed by a large constructive reform of local government throughout the country. But Gladstone neither then nor at any other time, as his letters and policies plainly show, had any adequate sense of the importance of local government.

The following year saw the passage of the Ballot Act 1872. It commended itself as a further step in liberal emancipation. Vot-

---

[1] See Chapter IV.
[2] James Stansfeld, b. 1820. Educated (Dissenter) at University College, London. Brewer, and friend of Mazzini. M.P. 1859–95; minor Ministerial posts, 1863, 1866, 1868, 1869; entered Cabinet as President of the Poor Law Board, 1871. From 1874 to 1886 agitated for repeal of the Contagious Diseases Acts. President of the Local Government Board, 1886; G.C.B. 1895; d. 1898.

ing was for the first time in British experience made secret. The history of this measure (for which there had not been much popular demand, though it had figured in advanced programmes for half a century) illustrates the frequent futility of political prophecy. During the debates both hopes and fears were expressed as to its result in England. Neither were borne out by the sequel; England was not deeply affected. But where the act had revolutionary consequences, which its authors had neither foreseen nor intended, was in Ireland.

A young Irish landowner, then twenty-six years of age and living quietly aloof from politics in the county Wicklow, perceived the possibilities in a flash. Though a protestant, he had imbibed strong anti-English feelings from his American mother; and a certain sympathy with Fenianism had striven in him with a sense of its hopelessness. But 'Now', he said, 'something can be done, if full advantage will be taken of this Ballot Act'. Hitherto the Irish voter, powerless against the intimidation of his social superiors, had returned members to one or other of the two English parliamentary parties. He need do so no longer. 'An independent Irish party, free from the touch of English influence, was the thing wanted, and this party could be elected under the Ballot Act.' The name of the young Irishman was Charles Stewart Parnell; and it is curious to reflect that but for the undesigned gift of this act the whole of his meteoric career, with its profound reactions upon English history for half a century, might never have occurred.[1]

It was from Ireland, as it happened, that the government's first defeat came. At the beginning of 1873 Gladstone grasped a particularly dangerous nettle. He introduced an Irish University Bill. Its difficult aim was to create a university, to which Irish Roman catholics would resort, without going beyond what a protestant parliament would sanction. At first it was well received, and Archbishop Manning, head of the Roman church in England, favoured it; as did Delane of *The Times*. But in fact it fell between two stools. Cardinal Cullen marshalled the Irish hierarchy in opposition, and on the other side it became anathema, not only to the presbyterian general assembly, but to radical educationists headed by Professor Fawcett. Disraeli could not but exploit such an opening, and on the night of March 11–12 the bill was defeated on second reading by 287

[1] Barry O'Brien, *Life of Parnell* (1899), ch. ii.

votes to 284, 43 liberals (including 35 Irish) voting against the government.

On this Gladstone resigned, and suggested that Disraeli should take office with a minority administration. Twelve years later he made an exactly analogous suggestion, when Lord Salisbury was his opponent; and Lord Salisbury acted on it, with bad results to himself. Disraeli, however, was too wily a bird to be caught by chaff; and after a week's crisis the Gladstone cabinet, fearing to risk a dissolution, had to resume its tasks in the same parliament. It attempted nothing more that session beyond passing the great Judicature Act; and soon after the house rose an attempt was made to propitiate public opinion by removing the two most unpopular ministers, Bruce and Lowe,[1] not indeed from the cabinet, but from the posts in which they were obnoxious. Bruce, ennobled as Lord Aberdare, became lord president of the council; Lowe replaced him as home secretary; and Gladstone himself took over his old post at the exchequer. About the same time Coleridge and Jessel both received judgeships, and two notable men, Sir Henry James[2] and Sir William Harcourt,[3] became the new law officers. Lyon Playfair[4] became postmaster-general.

These changes proved short-lived. Early in January 1874 yet another by-election (at Stroud) went against the government; and Gladstone (who ten months earlier had been telling the queen that his work was done, his mandate exhausted, and he himself in need of a long rest) declared on 24 January his intention of dissolving parliament.[5] His oddly chosen platform was

[1] Lowe's removal had been precipitated by the discovery of financial irregularities at the Post Office, for which he, the postmaster-general (Monsell), and the commissioner of public works (Ayrton) had each a ministerial responsibility. Monsell was dismissed; Ayrton, like Lowe, transferred.

[2] B. at Hereford 1828, son of a local doctor. Educated at Cheltenham; very successful barrister; M.P. 1869–95; attorney-general, 1873–4 and 1880–5; declined lord chancellorship and went liberal unionist, 1886; as Lord James of Hereford, was chancellor of the duchy in Salisbury's third cabinet, 1895–1902; d. 1911.

[3] B. 1827, grandson of archbishop of York. Educated at Trinity College, Cambridge; barrister; wrote 'Historicus' letters, 1863; M.P. 1868–1904; professor of international law at Cambridge, 1869; solicitor-general, 1873–4; home secretary, 1880–5; chancellor of the exchequer, 1886 and 1892–5; liberal leader, 1896–8; d. 1904.

[4] B. in India, 1819. Chemist; studied at St. Andrews, Glasgow, London, Giessen; managed print-works at Clithero, 1840–3; professor of chemistry at Edinburgh, 1858–68; M.P. 1868–92; postmaster-general, 1873–4; vice-president of council, 1886; peerage (as Lord Playfair), 1892; d. 1898.

[5] In Lord Askwith's *Life of Lord James of Hereford* (1930) the curious will find given (pp. 65–9) from James's inside knowledge a probably correct explanation of

a proposal to abolish income-tax. A general election followed without delay, and was over by the middle of February. The conservatives secured a majority of 83 in Great Britain; in the whole house of commons, owing to the new emergence of an Irish home rule party, it was harder to compute, but could in no case be reckoned below 48. On 17 February Gladstone resigned. His memorable first administration—by far the most successful of the four which he headed, and under many aspects the greatest during the long reign of Queen Victoria—was at an end.

Two separate topics may close this chapter. The first concerns the situation of the Crown and its wearer.

There can be no doubt that by the beginning of 1871 the queen had grown seriously unpopular. There were many causes. Subconsciously the displacement of a monarchy by a republic in Paris may have operated as one. But the chief was her persistence in retirement since the death of the prince consort over nine years earlier. There was a widespread feeling that she neglected her national duty, and did not earn the large grants made to her and her family by parliament. Thus when in the spring her fourth daughter, Louise, married the eldest son of a wealthy subject, the duke of Argyll, big popular meetings at Birmingham and Nottingham passed resolutions condemning the grants voted to the young couple.

But in this the year proved a turning-point. An illness of the queen in the early autumn recalled some sympathy to her. Much greater sympathy followed very soon after, when on 8 December it became known that the prince of Wales was dangerously ill with enteric fever. For about a week he hung between death and life, while the whole nation listened at the door of his sick-room. On the tenth anniversary of his father's death he turned the corner; and his eventual recovery evoked a burst of enthusiasm which founded his own popularity and restored his mother's. Although thenceforward the queen's reputation grew rapidly,

Gladstone's final haste to dissolve before parliament reassembled. James as attorney-general had advised (contrary to his predecessor, Coleridge) that by taking on the chancellorship of the exchequer Gladstone had accepted an 'office of profit' under the 6 Anne, c. 7, and unless he secured re-election in his constituency, could not speak or vote in the house without incurring penalties. His Greenwich seat was deemed too unsafe for a by-election; but it might be held at a general election, as in fact it was.

till in the last two decades of her life it became almost a religion, her actual power within the state declined. We have seen how Cardwell and Gladstone in 1870 wrested control over the army from her by making the commander-in-chief subject to the secretary of state instead of to the sovereign direct. During Gladstone's first premiership she was not so hostile to him personally, as she afterwards became under Disraeli's tutoring; though their correspondence shows tendencies to estrangement from August 1871 onwards.[1] The liberal leader on his part always treated her with the utmost consideration, and more than once stretched his own influence to the limit in order to make her wishes prevail in an unsympathetic house of commons.

Our other topic is the Ashanti campaign of 1873-4, a 'little war' of more than average interest. It arose substantially out of our embargo on the slave trade, but proximately from the accession in 1867 to the Ashanti throne of a warrior monarch, Kofi Kari-kari ('King Coffee'), and the conclusion in 1871 of an Anglo-Dutch treaty. Under the latter (in exchange for our disinteresting ourselves in the coast of Sumatra) the Dutch transferred to us their forts on the Gold Coast. These had hitherto been dotted along the seaboard in and out with our own, in a manner which prevented either Power from obtaining much territorial control. The chief of them was Elmina, which we took over on 2 April 1872, and which Kofi had long coveted for a coastal slave-emporium.

The Ashantis were an inland group of very warlike, pure negro, fetish-worshipping tribes federated under a king at Kumasi. Access to them was difficult owing to the dense and fever-haunted tropical forest, in and behind which they lived. They had often harried our adjacent 'friendlies' and attacked our settlements with success. In 1824 a British governor, Sir Charles McCarthy, had been killed by them in battle with nearly all his officers; and his skull was in use at Kumasi as a royal drinking-cup. More recently in the sixties they had twice inflicted on us small but unavenged defeats; but our increased activity against slave-trading menaced the chief source of their king's wealth. Kofi now claimed Elmina; and after a bickering negotiation (complicated by his holding four Europeans in captivity at Kumasi) he invaded the British protected area with three armies early in 1873, easily routed the Fanti 'friendlies', and advanced to within

[1] See P. Guedalla, *The Queen and Mr. Gladstone*, i (1933).

twelve miles of the British head-quarters at Cape Coast Castle. Fighting took place in June within Elmina itself, where a few hundred marines, Hausas, and West Indian troops held the fort and won a battle in the town. Fortunately for us, the invaders suffered much from disease.

The Gladstone government, impelled by Lord Kimberley, the colonial secretary, despite the opposition of Goschen, decided to employ soldiers, drive out the enemy, and teach him a permanent lesson. In September Sir Garnet Wolseley sailed for Cape Coast, with the rank of major-general, to combine the positions of administrator and commander-in-chief. An able staff went with him to prepare plans, roads, and transport; and 2,400 white troops followed, but were delayed till nearly Christmas for climatic reasons. Wolseley's problem was to reach Kumasi and return by the end of February; since early in March the worst rainy season would begin and the rivers be flooded. It was essentially a time-campaign. When he arrived at Cape Coast, he found that of 130 Englishmen then ashore only 22 remained fit for duty; and he knew that 'every extra day the war lasted meant more deaths from fever'.

He started on 6 January 1874, and after a great deal of hard fighting in the gloom of the forest, including two pitched battles, reached Kumasi on 4 February with the loss of 16 officers and men killed and something under 400 wounded. The king had fled, and still withheld agreement to terms; whereupon, according to plan, his great palace was destroyed, his capital burned, and the British force marched safely back. On the way messengers bearing gold came after it from the king; a draft treaty was handed to them; and a month later it was signed. The king renounced his claims over the British and ex-Dutch spheres; promised free trade and an open road to Kumasi; pledged himself to endeavour to stop human sacrifices; and undertook to pay a war indemnity of 50,000 ounces of gold by instalments.

The weak point in these terms was that they left intact the Ashanti military confederacy, which had to be tackled again a generation later. Nevertheless the episode was decisive for the history of British West Africa. The fever-stricken Guinea seaboard had a bad name at home, and many would have been willing to see us pushed off it. Wolseley's success averted that; and so saved in the acorn the brilliant modern development of our Gold Coast colony.

The cost of the operations was £900,000. Militarily they reflected great credit on the commander, who received a grant of
£25,000 from parliament for his services. But the other officers
employed were a picked body; and seven of the survivors afterwards became respectively, Field-Marshal Sir Evelyn Wood,
Field Marshal Lord Methuen, General Sir H. Brackenbury,
General Sir Redvers Buller, General Sir W. Butler, General Sir
J. Frederick Maurice, and Lieutenant-General Sir George Colley. The newspaper correspondents were also remarkable; they
were Winwood Reade[1] and H. M. Stanley. The latter, who had
already in 1871 'found Livingstone', was fated subsequently to
pierce the twilight of many African forests, but of none more for-
bidding than the primeval belt whose glooms formed the screen
before blood-stained Kumasi.

[1] Remembered now for a still-read book, *The Martyrdom of Man*.

II

THE RULE OF DISRAELI

DISRAELI, whom the general election of 1874 placed for the first time in his long career at the head of an assured parliamentary majority, was on many showings a master-mind. He saw far and deep, with uncanny flashes of something like prophecy. His position had been won against immense obstacles by brain and will-power alone. For over twenty-five years he had led the conservative party in the house of commons (the longest continuous leadership of which our politics holds record); with but three brief intervals in office between long spells in opposition. Despite his excellence in debate, his main bent was imaginative and constructive; and one must regret that he never had a chance to employ it freely in tasks of government, until he had crossed the threshold of his seventieth year.

Fourteen months earlier his devoted wife had died. To him this was a peculiarly weakening loss; for, though he had a genius for making men follow him and greatly excelled Gladstone in their personal management, his inner nature only derived joy and sustenance from the society of women. After his wife's death he sought to solace his craving, partly in a romantic attachment to two elderly sisters, the countess of Bradford and the dowager countess of Chesterfield;[1] partly in a fantastic devotion towards the person of Queen Victoria; whom he figured as a second Gloriana and styled, to his intimates, 'the Faery'. But these were make-believes; his loneliness was real. Then gout crept over him with intermittent but deadly crescendos; while old age and widowhood proved poor equipments for supporting an office which twice tired out within five years even the iron vigour of Gladstone. That his long Ministry was not more fruitful may largely be thus explained.

But there were other reasons. He could not skate so boldly in office as he had in opposition over the thin ice between his own reforming ideas and the property interests of those who had made him their champion. He had begun life as a radical, diagnosing England as 'two nations', rich and poor, and proclaiming the

---

[1] He wrote to them almost daily, and the letters (edited by Lord Zetland) are valuable documents regarding his premiership. So are his letters to the queen, printed in Buckle's *Life*.

supreme need to make them one. He still cared sincerely for social reform; but few, if any, of his followers in parliament supported him for its sake. Leading the opposition to Gladstone he had taxed his rival's reforms with menacing 'every institution and every interest, every class and every calling in the country' and planning to 'despoil churches and plunder landlords'.[1] Such slogans are defensive, not progressive; they had made him the rallying-point for the interests which were kicking at change. It was a legitimate position for a conservative leader, but not one where he could take reform for his first motto, even when qualified as 'social' to distinguish it from the liberal brand. He needed others, and he chose two—the monarchy and the empire. Both remained written on the conservative banner for half a century after his death.

The second alone had much influence on political events. Between 1874 and 1914, while the person of the monarch may even have gained importance as a figure-head, it steadily lost power as a factor in government. This resulted from the democratizing of parliament in 1867 and 1884; for a constitutional sovereign, while able to stand up against the ministers of an oligarchic parliament in the name of the unrepresented democracy, becomes powerless against men carrying the credentials of democracy itself. After Disraeli's death the process went on under liberals or conservatives indifferently; no memory of his romanticism could move his party to arrest it. But with imperialism the case was different. Though later some liberals cared more for it than some conservatives (Lord Rosebery more than Lord Salisbury, for instance), Disraeli's initiative made it, on the whole, a conservative preserve. And though time altered much from the Disraelian conception (in which India counted for nearly everything, and the self-governing colonies, despite the emphasis laid on them in his famous Crystal Palace speech,[2] for relatively little), yet he here was a genuine founder, and his idea, apart from the bias of his personal Orientalism, proved longer-sighted than his contemporaries could know. Meanwhile the course of his premiership, as we shall see, shows the dazzle of imperialism soon outshining the sober glow of social reform, and luring Disraeli onward, first to triumphant climax, and then to anti-climax.

He began by forming a distinctly able cabinet. His greatest initial catch was Lord Salisbury; who had severed himself from

[1] Speech at Manchester, 3 April 1872.   [2] 24 June 1872.

the conservative front bench in 1867 in dislike of Disraeli's franchise extension, and increased a rising reputation by formidable skirmishing on the party's right flank, till induced now to rejoin as secretary for India. The temper and mind of this great man were remarkably unlike Disraeli's; and it was not till the later stages of the Eastern crisis that they worked really well together. Both had a strong vein of political realism, and both were great makers of epigrams. But the sombre and negative cast of Salisbury's powerful intelligence had little in common, save a kind of Italian subtlety, with the gay adventure, constructive imagination, and incurable romanticism of the older leader. The brilliant but erratic fourth earl of Carnarvon,[1] who had seceded with Salisbury in 1867, rejoined with him now, taking the colonial office. The fifteenth earl of Derby (son of the earl who was thrice premier and 'Rupert of debate') became foreign secretary; while the progressive Lord Cairns, weighty in cabinet, resumed the post of lord chancellor, and the duke of Richmond became President of the council, and leader of the upper house. In the commons the ablest ministers, after their chief, were Sir Stafford Northcote[2] at the exchequer, Gathorne Hardy[3] at the war office, G. Ward Hunt[4] at the admiralty, Richard Assheton Cross[5] at the home office, and Sir Michael Hicks Beach[6] as chief secretary for Ireland. Of these Sir Stafford Northcote stood for sound finance and sober respectability in general. The next two were

[1] Carnarvon (1831–90) had been Salisbury's contemporary both at Eton and at Christ Church, Oxford. Colonial secretary, 1866–7 and 1874–8; Irish viceroy, 1885–6.

[2] B. 1818. Educated at Eton and Balliol College, Oxford. Succeeded to baronetcy, 1851; M.P. 1855–85; financial secretary, treasury, 1859; president, Board of Trade, 1866; chancellor of the exchequer, 1874–80; leader of conservative party in house of commons, 1876–85; created earl of Iddesleigh and appointed first lord, treasury, 1885; foreign secretary, 1886; d. 1887.

[3] B. 1814. Educated at Shrewsbury and Oriel College, Oxford. M.P. 1856–78; created Viscount Cranbrook, 1878; earl, 1892. Minor offices, 1859 and 1866; home secretary, 1867; secretary for war, 1874; for India, 1878; lord president of the council, 1885–92; d. 1906.

[4] B. 1825. Educated at Eton and Christ Church, Oxford. M.P. from 1857; financial secretary to treasury, 1866–8; chancellor of the exchequer, Feb. 1 to December 1868; first lord, admiralty, 1874; died in office (of gout), 1877.

[5] B. 1823. Educated at Rugby and Trinity College, Cambridge. M.P. 1857–86; viscount, 1886. Home secretary, 1874–80 and 1885–6; secretary for India, 1886–92; lord privy seal, 1895–1900; d. 1914.

[6] B. 1837. Educated at Eton and Christ Church, Oxford. Succeeded to baronetcy, 1854; M.P. 1864–1905; chief secretary, Ireland, 1874–8 and 1886–7; colonial secretary, 1878–80; chancellor of the exchequer, 1885–6 and 1895–1902; created viscount St. Aldwyn, 1905; earl, 1914; d. 1916. Nicknamed *Black Michael*.

both capable departmental heads, and Gathorne Hardy a good deal more—one of the best debaters and most esteemed figures in parliament; a counterpart to Cardwell, whom he felicitously succeeded. Cross was a little-known Lancashire bank-director, put straight into high office to frame social reforms, which he did to admiration; he was popularly deemed a 'find' of Disraeli's, but in fact had been at school and college with Lord Derby. Lastly, Sir Michael Hicks Beach, who was not in the cabinet at first, compelled admission to it in the following year by his outstanding ability; a man who, though he never became prime minister, had certainly more capacity for that or any other high office than many whose luck has carried them to the summit.

This strong team had but a weak one facing it; for the defeat of the liberal government had almost redissolved their party into its original and warring elements. Gladstone himself, on resigning office in February 1874, had privately resigned the liberal leadership as well. At his colleagues' request this was temporarily camouflaged as a holiday; and he wrote a formal letter to Lord Granville (12 March 1874), saying that he needed rest, and could not give more than occasional attendance in the house of commons during the present session. But in January of the following year he publicly retired, and Lord Hartington (afterwards the eighth and greatest duke of Devonshire) succeeded him as the liberal leader. The weary ex-premier seems for the time to have thought the scope for reform exhausted—an idea which infuriated a rising school of young radicals, still weak in parliament, but fast coming increasingly to sway the party outside. John Morley in letters and journalism, Sir Charles Dilke in the house of commons, and Joseph Chamberlain in provincial politics, may be taken as types and leaders of these men. Hartington was chosen to conciliate them; of the whigs he was the one whom they least disliked. Their sharpest veto was against Forster; whom nonconformists had never forgiven for the compromises of the 1870 Education Act.[1]

Under the conditions of the period a government starting in February could hardly get into its stride the same year; and the 1874 session was uneventful. Gladstone had promised to abolish income-tax; Northcote was content to lower it by a penny, and

---

[1] See letter of Chamberlain, printed in J. L. Garvin's *Life*, i (1932), 222. Forster, who had been brought up as a quaker (and was the brother-in-law of Matthew Arnold), really stood far nearer the left than Hartington.

spend the rest of a £5½ millions surplus on abolishing the sugar duties and permitting small increases in both army and navy estimates. Cross carried a Licensing Act, which made some prompt concessions to the liquor interests; though they were disappointed at its not more fully repealing Bruce's.[1] Only one attempt was, in fact, made to reverse Liberal legislation, and that was dropped.[2] The chief debates of the session arose over a Public Worship Bill introduced in the house of lords by the archbishop of Canterbury (Dr. Tait) to curb the catholicizing movement in the established church, which was then termed ritualism. The veteran evangelical, Lord Shaftesbury, having considerably altered this by an amendment which set up a lawyer as ecclesiastical judge, Disraeli, under strong pressure from the queen, virtually adopted it as a government measure; and after a conflict between the houses over a detail had been resolved by the commons giving way, it became law, Lord Penzance being transferred from the probate and divorce division to fill the new judgeship. Two of the prime minister's colleagues, Lord Salisbury and Gathorne Hardy, differed from their chief about this measure.[3] On the liberal benches it drew vigorous support from Sir William Harcourt, then and always a zealous Erastian, but was passionately opposed by Gladstone. During the recess the latter contributed an article on ritualism to the *Contemporary Review*, which ran into fifteen editions; and followed it up with a pamphlet on the Vatican Decrees of 1870, of which 100,000 copies were sold within a month.

Trade, which had boomed in England since the Franco-Prussian war, was less good this year. It was the beginning, though not realized at the time, of what economists have since called the Great Depression of the seventies. There were sporadic strikes of coal-miners and iron-workers against reductions of wages; but the movement, that attracted most notice, was the strike of farm labourers in Suffolk, followed by a general lock-out of agricultural trade-unionists in the eastern counties. It

---

[1] The chief parts of the 1872 act, which the 1874 act repealed, were s. 35 (which gave the police a most sweeping right of entry) and ss. 19–22 with the first schedule (which prohibited adulteration). Right of entry was given in more guarded form. The hours of closing were also modified.

[2] An Endowed Schools Act Amendment Bill.

[3] A speech on it by Salisbury evoked Disraeli's famous reference to him (5 August 1874) as 'not a man who measures his words' but 'a great master of gibes and flouts and jeers'. Salisbury never entirely ceased to live up to this description.

lasted eighteen weeks; cost Joseph Arch's National Agricultural
Labourers' Union (founded two years earlier) nearly £25,000;
and ended in the defeat of the 2,400 men locked out, of whom
440 emigrated, while 400 more moved to other parts of England.
But it roused new agrarian sympathies among the urban radicals,
particularly in Birmingham. Abroad the chief scene of unrest
was Spain; where a year of revolutions began with the fall of
Castelar's republic and ended with the legitimist restoration of
Alfonso XII.[1] Otherwise the principal events on the continent
were two peaceful international conferences: that at Berne,
where on 9 October 1874 was signed the International Postal
Convention (still the basis of postal communication between
countries); and that at Brussels (convened by Tsar Alexander II)
on the Laws of War. The declarations signed at the latter
by all the European Powers (but not ratified) revealed a certain
divergence between British and continental views on this topic;
they were twenty-five years later incorporated for the most part
in the first Hague Convention. As a sequel to the Ashanti war
(recounted in our last chapter) Great Britain declared the abolition of slavery on the Gold Coast; and in the Pacific she annexed
the islands of Fiji.[2]

The 1875 session was far more productive—indeed quite an
annus mirabilis for useful domestic legislation. Ministers worked
from half a dozen sides to redeem Disraeli's promises of social
reform. His home secretary, Cross, sponsored a group of important measures—a Trade Union Act amending the Gladstonian
Act of 1871 in a sense decidedly more favourable to the trade
unions;[3] an Artisans' Dwellings Act, which is one of the milestones
in English legislation on the housing problem; and a Sale of Food
and Drugs Act, which was the first really comprehensive measure
on its subject and remained the principal statute till 1928.[4]

---

[1] Castelar was an eloquent contributor to Morley's *Fortnightly Review*, and with
him, as with Gambetta, both Dilke and Morley had certain contacts.

[2] Lord Carnarvon thus defined the motives for their annexation: 'Looking to the
opinion of New Zealand and Australia and, as far as it can be gathered, of parliament and this country, and looking also to the advantages which these islands possess as an intermediate station between America and Australia, and the risks of
great disorders arising unless some government is constituted' (*Queen Victoria's
Letters*, II. ii (1926), 344).

[3] For details see Chapter IV.

[4] Well planned though this act was, it did not repair all the mischief done by
Cross's own repeal in the previous year of the adulteration provisions in Bruce's
Licensing Act. For it only forbade ingredients which would 'render the article

Even more epoch-making was the great Public Health Act 1875.
Mainly a consolidation statute (incorporating features from over
100 acts, many of them local), it roused no controversy. But few
measures have rendered more social service; and until 1937 it
remained the backbone of our sanitary law, despite the passing
of long acts to supplement or amend it in 1907 and 1925. *Sanitas
sanitatum, omnia sanitas* had been the motto propounded by Disraeli in 1872.[1] These admirable statutes proved not only his
own good faith, but the reality of the neglects with which he had
taunted the official liberals. In contrast with the latter, Chamberlain (now the radical mayor of Birmingham) soon came to be
on excellent terms both with Cross and also with Disraeli's president of the local government board, G. Sclater-Booth.[2] By personal interviews he helped them to improve their measures; and
they in turn, when Chamberlain's bold scheme for slum-clear-
ance and rebuilding in central Birmingham required sanction,
gave him very timely support. It has been said that Disraeli's
franchise extension of 1867 was 'the death-warrant of *laisser-
faire*'.[3] Certainly this first full session, in which its author was
free to legislate, drove a remarkable number of nails into *laisser-
faire's* coffin. In the same summer Northcote's budget established
the New Sinking Fund. Its idea was simple. The interest on the
National Debt was then £27,200,000; the Fund was to be £28
millions; there would be a margin of £800,000 to pay off debt
within the first year, and ever-increasing margins in subsequent
years, as the lessening of debt lessened the sum due for interest.
Here too a gap in Gladstone's statesmanship was filled. The one
flaw was the liability of the Fund to be raided by perplexed chancellors of the exchequer. Unfortunately Northcote himself set
the example only four years later, to pay for the Zulu war.

While the main bills went forward in the commons, the lord
chancellor and the duke of Richmond were busy in the lords.
The duke's Agricultural Holdings Act was the first to compensate
displaced tenants for agricultural improvements. Cairns's Land

injurious to health'. Thus it failed to cover such practices as putting salt in beer
to create thirst; which Bruce's Act had expressly prohibited.
  [1] *Selected Speeches* (1882), ii. 511.
  [2] B. 1826. Educated at Winchester, and Balliol College, Oxford. M.P. from
1857; financial secretary, treasury, 1868; president, local government board, 1874–
80; chairman of grand committee in the house of commons, 1880; 1st Baron Basing,
1887; d. 1894.   [3] J. A. Williamson, *The Evolution of England* (1931), 430;
cp. the thesis of A. V. Dicey's *Relation between Law and Public Opinion in England
during the Nineteenth Century* (1905).

Transfer Act dealt with land registration; repealed Lord West-bury's unsuccessful Act of 1862; and laid down the general lines on which the subject has since been treated in England. But by contrast with Cross's, these measures revealed the limitations of conservative reform. They were over-tentative. For the Agri-cultural Holdings Act the liberals substituted a better one eight years later. But the half-hearted methods of Cairns's land regis-tration unfortunately held their ground. To them it is due that England did not secure within the period of this volume the boon of cheap, simple, and secure land-transfer, as practised almost all over the continent and in the Dominions.

This year, like its predecessor, brought declining trade and witnessed some stirrings of social unrest. Over the South Wales coal-field there was a great strike and lock-out, which lasted from January to May and involved ironworkers as well as miners. It was, too, during the summer, that the author[1] of the 'Plimsoll Mark' made (22 July 1875) a memorable 'scene' in the house of commons in protest against the postponement of a bill to prevent the sacrifice of seamen's lives through the overloading of ill-found and over-insured ships. His outburst could be justified by its motive, and in part by its results. A temporary bill went through in a few days, and its principles were made permanent in the Merchant Shipping Act of the following year. But the example of success through disorder did immediate injury to parliament, and has ever since furnished the favourite precedent for those desirous of injuring it further.

Three months after the close of the reforming session Disraeli —his star still in the ascendant—brought off a famous stroke in quite another field. This was the British government's purchase, for £4 millions, of the Khedive Ismail's shares in the Suez Canal Company. Opened only six years earlier, the canal had changed the sea-route from England to India, and transferred to Egypt most of the strategic importance which before belonged to the Cape of Good Hope. Nothing, however, had as yet been done to give us any control, or even *locus standi*, in relation to this vital new artery of empire. But the spendthrift Ismail owned about seven-sixteenths (not actually a controlling interest, be it noted) of the shares in the French company which had constructed it. Already in December 1870, when Lord Granville was foreign secretary and France in the throes of her war with Prussia, he

[1] Samuel Plimsoll (1824–98), the 'sailors' friend'; M.P. 1868–80.

had not merely offered to sell this interest to Great Britain, but had suggested (apparently with Ferdinand de Lesseps's[1] concurrence) that she should buy up the whole of what was then a non-paying concern. This unique opportunity was rejected by the foreign office—very mistakenly, as one can now see. The public knew nothing about it. But the Khedive's financial straits continued. By the middle of November 1875 he was negotiating with two French groups for the mortgage or sale of his shares, when news that they were in the market came again to the foreign office, brought this time by a patriotic journalist, Frederick Greenwood. Once more the department pooh-poohed the idea. But when it got past the ultra-timid Lord Derby to the bold eye of the prime minister, it was seen in a very different light. It is possible, as Mr. Buckle, his biographer, suggests, that through the Rothschilds he had been partly prepared for it; the terms (criticized by Northcote), on which he obtained the money from their firm, rather hint some obligation towards them.[2] Be that as it may, there is no doubt that the decision to purchase was entirely Disraeli's, and that he carried it in the cabinet against strong opposition.

It was recognized both at home and abroad as an act of national leadership. Even in France, where many resented it, the government put a good face on the transaction, and Lesseps issued a circular in its favour. Bismarck professed himself enthusiastic. Gladstone's only criticism was that the bargain might prove bad business. Here he showed less than his usual financial acumen; for in fact during the fifty years following the purchase the original sum was repaid in dividends and interest about eight times over. The English public welcomed it as securing the route to India. In itself it contributed little to this; and its principal direct fruit was merely to assist in obtaining more reasonable tolls for the merchant shipping which used the canal (then nearly four-fifths British). It did, however, give England a new concern and standing in Egypt, which she began almost at once to develop; and this led on, as will be shown later, to her eventually taking control of the country.

The premier's next enterprise brought together two objects of his special interest—the English monarchy and the Indian em-

---

[1] The French engineer (1805–94) who had formed the Suez Canal Company and constructed the canal.

[2] *Life of Beaconsfield*, v (1920), 439–41.

pire. It was a proposal to add 'Empress of India' to the queen's titles. He wanted to utilize—what a successful visit paid by the prince of Wales to India that very winter brought out—the special glamour of monarchy for the Oriental imagination. He felt the difference which it might make to an Indian, if he could regard his sovereign, not as the queen (or king) of a distant and alien island, but as the empress (or emperor) of his own country. The new title by implication recognized the latter as a separate entity in the world, with a monarch of its own who was proud of it; and nobody who now reflects on the trend of the twentieth century towards a distinct and autonomous India federated under the Crown, can deny here the strangely forward-looking quality of Disraeli's thought. By contrast the criticisms, not merely of the caustic Lowe or the cautious Hartington, but of what probably were then a decided majority among educated Englishmen, seem to-day pedantic. They split hairs over the word 'Empress'; recent memories of Napoleon III and Maximilian of Mexico tarnished it; above all, it was 'un-English'. Disraeli replied that it was not for use in England, but in India; and he recalled that it had been sufficiently favoured by Queen Elizabeth for her to let Spenser employ it in his famous dedication of the *Faerie Queene*. Hostile amendments by Hartington in the commons and Shaftesbury in the lords were both defeated; and the new title became law, to the advantage of the Indian connexion. Queen Victoria was deeply galled by the opposition's attitude. It helped to fix the anti-liberal bias of her later years.

The other legislative achievements of 1876 were not remarkable. Lord Cairns carried the amendment to Lord Selborne's Judicature Act, which we noted in the previous chapter.[1] To do him justice, he did so reluctantly; both in 1874 and in 1875 he had tried to pass amendments, which would not have involved giving a double appeal. But the feelings in his party were too strong for him. Only one reforming measure of this year compares with those of 1875—Lord Sandon's Education Act. Forster in 1870 had not made primary education compulsory, for the reason (among others) that the new schools for it had first to be built. The 1876 act compelled local authorities to appoint attendance committees; declared that it was the duty of parents to send their children to school from the age of 5 to that of 10, and

[1] p. 18, above.

later, failing certain certificates of proficiency or attendance, up
to 14; and ordered boards of guardians to pay the fees for children
of very poor parents. Compulsion, though indirectly and tentatively, was thus introduced, and with it a step towards free
education. Northcote's third budget (for over £77¾ millions as
against under £72 millions in the last budget under Gladstone
three years before) showed a slight deficit; and he had to reimpose
the penny which he took off the income-tax in 1874. Therewith
vanished the last hope that Gladstone's idea of abolishing the
tax might be realized. Northcote signalized his sense of its permanence by extending its exemption-limit from £100 to £150.

The other constructive bills brought in this year (which were
neither few nor unimportant) all failed to become law; being,
in effect, snowed under by the pressure of foreign events, to which
we must now turn our attention. Before doing so, let us note the
transference (August 1876) of Disraeli to the house of lords as
earl of Beaconsfield. The motive was the state of his health. His
private letters show how seriously he suffered from gout. In the
house of commons he had set, nevertheless, an example of regular
attendance early and late; and still to outside observation kept
the flag of his old jaunty courage flying.[1] Probably the foreign
crisis was the last straw; for Lord Derby's weakness threw its
burdens increasingly on the prime minister. His wife had been
created Viscountess Beaconsfield four years before her death,
and the new title united him to her memory. His leadership of
the commons devolved upon Northcote; a respectable adjutant,
but not a brilliant captain.

Turkey had been bolstered up by Great Britain and France
in the Crimean war in the belief that she could be induced to set
her house in order. But for the following twenty years that belief
was falsified. By the early seventies her finances grew desperate.
On the one hand she could not pay or organize properly either
her administration or her troops. On the other, her ever-growing
taxes (exacted by tax-farmers) were a spur to local revolts.

At this time Turkey-in-Europe still included most of the Balkan peninsula. Of the four Christian races who, together with
Albanians and Turks, made up its population, the Greeks (only

---

[1] See letter by Prof. A. E. Housman, *The Times*, 25 November 1932, giving his
personal recollection of Disraeli's demeanour in the house a week before he made
his last speech there.

a minority of them) lived in a small independent kingdom (not then including even Thessaly) at the southern end. Similarly of the Serbs a part (but only a minority) lived in what was then the dependent principality of Serbia, or in the independent rock-fastness called Montenegro. Of the Rumanians (or 'Vlachs') the majority lived in the Rumanian principality. By contrast, the Bulgars, who were the single most numerous race in the territory directly ruled by Turkey, had no home of their own outside it. They were almost unknown to European statesmen. But in 1870 the Sultan, at the instance of Russia, allowed them to have a religious head of their own, the 'Exarch', instead of being ranked, as previously, under the Greek patriarch at Constantinople. This change, which took effect in 1872, rapidly stimulated their sense of nationality.

Turkish misrule of the Christian races, being chronic and in-tolerable, could not remain indefinitely a feature of modern Europe. Three broad alternatives might now be discerned: (1) reform of Turkey itself from within; (2) absorption of Tur-key-in-Europe by Russia and Austria-Hungary, with or with-out a partition of the rest of Turkey, in which Great Britain, France, and Italy might find Asiatic or African 'compensations'; (3) development of the Christian races in four independent nation-states, with or without the Moslem Albanians as a fifth. When Great Britain's pro-Turkish policy was crystallized thirty years earlier, it is fair to say that the third alternative had scarcely dawned; and that, if the second were (as it was) deemed irrecon-cilable with British interests, it only remained, with however little confidence, to embrace the first. By 1875 events both in the Balkans and outside it had made the third far more practic-able. It is to the credit of Gladstone and the discredit of Disraeli, that the one saw, and the other missed, what in course of history was to prove the solution. Yet the obstacles to it were far greater than Gladstone realized, and not least (what nobody, save per-haps the Turks, fully appreciated at the time) the deadly rivalries between the Christian races themselves. If Disraeli narrowed his vision to the first two alternatives, so did Andrássy and Gort-chakov.[1] Russia in the seventies was unquestionably an aggres-

---

[1] Gortchakov, as the subsequent terms at San Stefano showed, valued Balkan nationalism solely by way of cloak for Russian advance. Andrássy did not pretend to value it at all. He accurately perceived in the little Serb principality a seed of danger for a dual monarchy which had Serb-speaking populations in both its halves; and his main purpose was, in Bosnia-Herzegovina, to forestall its growth.

sive Power; following the collapse of Napoleon III's European hegemony and the abrogation of the Black Sea clauses, expansionist Pan-Slavism attained its highest vogue among her official classes. Disraeli, with his special interest in India and in England's new route to it, could not be indifferent to the threat which thus overhung the eastern Mediterranean. He sought to parry it, and at the same time to avoid war; and in this dual purpose (whatever be thought of his policy in longer perspective) he succeeded against odds. Where motive and result were so clear, it seems superfluous to impute also (as Gladstone did[1]) a racial bias. Still it is true that Disraeli, although a baptized and conforming member of the Church of England, preserved valued contacts with the heads of the Jewish community in Europe, and that that community was and continued to be extremely pro-Turkish in outlook.

About midsummer 1875, following a bad harvest in 1874, the warlike Serbs of Herzegovina rose in rebellion against taxes. Volunteers from Serbia helped them, and soon the rising spread all over Bosnia. The Powers made various attempts to localize it, Austria-Hungary taking the lead, because her territory adjoined Bosnia, and her foreign minister, Andrássy, was secretly ambitious to occupy it. In August Austria-Hungary, Germany, and Russia (the governments composing the *Dreikaiserbund*) began conferring at Vienna. But Great Britain was not invited; and Disraeli, whose ambassador at Constantinople, Sir H. Elliott, was excessively pro-Turkish, started feeling his way towards a policy of his own. At the Guildhall, on 9 November 1875, he took occasion to assert that British interests in the Eastern Question were not less important than those of the three Eastern Powers.

On 1 December the Sultan sanctioned a scheme of reforms. It was good on paper, but nobody (save perhaps Elliott) believed in it. On 30 December Andrássy issued on behalf of the Eastern Powers a Note, which Disraeli and Lord Derby, against Elliott's opinion, accepted. The Note expressed the fear that (as actually happened) Bulgaria would rise when the snows melted, and Serbia and Montenegro would be drawn into the struggle. To forestall this it proposed another set of reforms. The Sultan accepted them on paper, but obstructed their going any farther. Nationalist feeling began stirring in Turkey, and on 6 May 1876 a Moslem mob at Salonica murdered (with curious impartiality)

[1] Lord Morley, *Life* (1903), bk. vii, ch. iv, § 2.

the German and the French consuls. Punishment and recompense were eventually conceded; but meanwhile (13 May) came a second circular from the Eastern Powers, the so-called Berlin Memorandum. The pith of it was that Turkey should conclude an armistice with the rebels for two months, and during that period carry out the programme of the Andrássy Note. At this point Disraeli and Lord Derby, following Elliott's advice, launched Great Britain on a course of her own. They rejected the Berlin proposals.

Here was a parting of the ways, which was bound to have far-reaching consequences. What was Disraeli's motive? Primarily fear of Russia. He saw behind the Berlin Memorandum two men, Gortchakov and Bismarck, whom he deeply distrusted, and who had once before caballed to trick England over the Black Sea clauses.[1] Linked with them was Andrássy, whom (rightly enough) he regarded as an intriguer playing a double game.[2] The traditional British policy was to support Turkey, and Elliott at Constantinople incarnated it. But it needs to be noted that Elliott's most famous predecessor took another view. Lord Stratford de Redcliffe, now in his ninetieth year, but still mentally vigorous, thought the Memorandum should have been accepted. So did the Opposition leaders, and so did opinion in France. Disraeli himself wavered. On 24 May he ordered the British fleet to Besika Bay; but on 9–10 June he made in secret a fruitless overture to Russia for a direct Anglo-Russian agreement.[3]

The immediate effect was to raise the temperature of Turkish nationalism. A 'reform' Ministry took office. On 30 May 1876 the Sultan Abdul Aziz was deposed, and a week later he committed suicide with a pair of scissors. His successor, Murad V, only reigned three months; on 31 August he too was deposed; and his early death, given out as suicide, followed in due course. The throne passed to Abdul Hamid II, who was destined to retain it for thirty-three years. Meanwhile at the beginning of July Serbia declared war. Her army was commanded and largely officered by Russians; and on 8 July the Tsar Alexander II and the Emperor Franz Josef met at Reichstadt, accompanied by their principal ministers, to divide the skin of the Turkish lion.

[1] p. 4, above.
[2] Letters to Lady Bradford, 6 September 1875 and 13 November 1875.
[3] R. W. Seton-Watson, *Disraeli, Gladstone, and the Eastern Question* (1935), pp. 40–3. The approach was to Shuvalov, the Russian ambassador in London. Disraeli made another, again without result, in February 1877 (ibid., pp. 159–60).

Terms of division were secretly agreed; but Serbia's ensuing defeats made them for the time quite inapplicable. Indeed after Abdul Hamid's accession there was even a withdrawal of the Berlin Memorandum—hailed by Disraeli as justifying the British abstention.

Already, however, before Serbia's entry, events had begun in another area, which, as they tardily and gradually became known to Europe, swung the moral balance heavily against the Porte. Early in May 1876 risings of comitadjis[1] occurred in Bulgaria. In answer the Turkish government let loose against the Bulgar population the armed irregulars known as Bashi-Bazouks. Through May and June they committed appalling massacres, in which both sexes and all ages suffered. In one of the Bulgar administrative districts the subsequent official British estimate was that 12,000 Christians perished. Torture, rape, flogging, and pillage accompanied the killings. The miscreants were rewarded and their leaders decorated; none were punished.

Disraeli was heavily handicapped in dealing with this matter by the mistakes of Elliott, whose pro-Turkish bias long led him to minimize the facts. Elliott himself had one excuse, since the first damning official report from the spot (that of the British vice-consul at Adrianople) failed to reach him. But its contents became known to the *Daily News*, then the organ of advanced liberalism in London; and they came before the public in its pages on 23 June. Relying on Elliott, Disraeli belittled the story, and treated the atrocities as 'to a large extent inventions'. But they were only too true; and each week brought confirmation, till at the beginning of September an official report by Walter Baring, one of Elliott's subordinates, placed an appalling catalogue of horrors beyond further dispute. Disraeli's letters show his own reaction to have been twofold. First, while unable to condemn the ambassador in public, he was justly furious in private at the false position in which his 'lamentable want of energy and deficiency of information'[2] had placed the government. Secondly, he realized that the impression produced in England by events in Bulgaria had 'completely destroyed sympathy with Turkey', and rendered British intervention against a Russian declaration of war 'practically impossible'.[3] Within

---

[1] i.e. armed guerrillas directed by a revolutionary committee.
[2] Letter to Lord Derby, 7 August 1876.
[3] Letter to Elliott, 29 August 1876.

a few days of his writing these last words appeared Gladstone's pamphlet, *The Bulgarian Horrors and the Question of the East*; and with it began the most famous political campaign ever waged by a popular leader in the annals of English democracy. 'From that time forward,' wrote Gladstone[1] twenty years later, 'till the final consummation in 1879–80, I made the Eastern question the main business of my life.'

The pamphlet sold 40,000 copies within three or four days. It contained the famous demand that the Turks should clear out 'bag and baggage'.[2] Gladstone followed it up with a tremendous open-air speech at Blackheath to his constituents, and a little later went on a round of great meetings. Before launching his pamphlet he had secured qualified assents from Hartington and Granville, the liberal leaders; but it really was his personal fight. He swept popular feeling, especially in the north, and not it only; great noblemen backed him, like the duke of Argyll, great publicists, like Delane of *The Times*; the leading historians— Carlyle, Froude, Freeman, Acton, Stubbs, J. R. Green—were found in singular unanimity on his side; with them were Tennyson, Darwin, Ruskin, Burne-Jones, and the higher intelligentsia generally. Gladstone spoke in the spirit of Milton's sonnet *On the late Massacre in Piedmont*; the strength of his eloquence was a massive appeal to elemental humanity and justice. Its political wisdom, beyond this, lay in his discernment of, and reliance on, the spirit of nationality. The workings of his own mind were certainly biased by some less worthy factors—his ecclesiastical interest in the Greek church was one, the personal influence of Madame Novikov,[3] another. But the spell which bound his audiences to him was what J. R. Green called at the time 'his warm ardour for all that is noble and good';[4] and it stirred some of the profoundest depths in the English nature.

To Disraeli (now Lord Beaconsfield) viewing affairs as a diplomat his rival's irruption seemed wholly ill timed. Were not the Moscow Pan-Slavists pressing Russia to start a war of Balkan conquest under pretext of philanthropy? Was it not the task of British statesmanship to hold her back, without war, by showing

[1] Quoted by Morley, *Life*, bk. vii, ch. iv, § 1.
[2] Not, however, (as often supposed) from all Turkey-in-Europe, but from 'the province they have desolated and profaned', i.e. Bulgaria.
[3] A clever Russian lady, then new to England, who came to be for about two decades perhaps the most notable mouthpiece of Tsarist Russia in English society.
[4] *Letters of J. R. Green* (1901), p. 446.

a firm front? Gladstone sabotaged this; for he divided Britain's front, and sanctified Russia's pretext. Thus the duel between the veteran champions returned to the foreground, and with it quite a new intensity inflamed their partisans. Not that the prime minister any longer shared Elliott's tenderness towards Turkey. At the Guildhall in November he might declare in public for Russia's benefit that, if war were forced on England, she 'would not terminate till right was done'. But at Constantinople he put the strongest pressure on the Porte to concede an armistice to the defeated Serbians. Only under threat of Elliott's withdrawal was this obtained. There followed (12 December 1876 to 20 January 1877) a conference of the Powers in the Turkish capital, to which Lord Salisbury was the British delegate. Travelling via Paris, Berlin, Vienna, and Rome, he consulted those governments on his way, and in the conference itself he established very considerable accord with Ignatiev, the Pan-Slavist Russian ambassador, who showed unexpected moderation. The Powers agreed on a programme of reforms, and if Turkey had accepted them, there would have been peace all round. But Turkey would not. The Young Ottoman leader, Midhat Pasha, was now in power, and had induced Abdul Hamid to grant a constitution. Under cover of this he fought the Powers with the usual weapons of Turkish procrastination; and finally, when the Sultan himself favoured accepting their programme, prevailed on the Turkish grand council to reject it. Two motives stiffened Midhat. He believed that the Russian government (with reason, as the event showed) would shrink from engaging its army; and he was not convinced that, when Salisbury threatened leaving Turkey to her fate, he represented the real intention of the British government. For the latter disastrous illusion Elliott and some of his subordinates were in part to blame. There is no evidence that Lord Beaconsfield was; though some passages in his letters show that he was far from understanding or sympathizing with every step in Salisbury's masterly negotiations.

The breakdown of the Constantinople Conference meant a Russo-Turkish war. It did not come at once; there were more parleys, and even another protocol from the Powers to the Porte. But on 24 April 1877 hostilities began. Russia had bought off Austria-Hungary beforehand by a promise of Bosnia-Herzegovina. Great Britain declared neutrality, subject to her vital interests being respected, among which she particularized the maintenance of free communication with the East through the Suez Canal, the exclusion of Egypt from the sphere of military operations, and the recognition by Russia of the inviolability of Constantinople, with the navigation of the Straits. Gortchakov assented on all points. Those regarding Constantinople and the Straits were old, and harked back; those about Egypt and the Canal were new, and pointed forward.

Fighting continued for nine months—till the armistice of Adrianople (31 January 1878). At the beginning the Russians advanced easily. But soon after midsummer, when their armies were entangled in the Balkans, the Turks turned on them, and under two notable new generals, Osman and Suleiman, won a series of victories. Osman Pasha threw himself into a great entrenched camp at Plevna, where he defied and defeated the Tsar's armies for months. These events roused in England a fierce counterblast to the Gladstonian agitation. The old anti-Russian feeling surged up; and the spectacle of the dreaded aggressive Power hurling its huge semi-barbaric hosts in vain against the gallant resistance of a weaker foe, who had for long been Britain's ally, wiped out for many the memory of the Bulgarian massacres. No one felt this more than Queen Victoria, whose mind often mirrored remarkably that of the 'man in the street'.[1] Fortunately her eagerness for war found no echo in the cabinet; though there was a widening cleft there between Lord Carnarvon and Lord Derby, who desired peace at any price, and those who shared the prime minister's view, that the way to save peace and British interests together was to show ourselves unshrinking. Lord Salisbury bridged it till Derby's indecisions became too much for him.[2]

The war was decided by numbers, ruthlessly spent. By 10 December 1877 Plevna was starved out, and Osman capitulated. All knew it for the beginning of the end. But to advance and support large armies through the snow-bound Balkan mountains in midwinter without railways took time; and the final Turkish defeats occurred a month later. In face of them Queen Victoria,

[1] Reading the very crude expression of her attitude in her letters at this time, one is tempted to wonder whether some earlier hint of it may have been what reached Midhat Pasha and induced him to disbelieve the official warnings that Great Britain would stand aside. But of this no evidence exists.

[2] 'Making a featherbed walk', he wrote on 4 October 1876, 'is nothing to the difficulty of making an irresolute man look two inches into the future' (Lady G. Cecil, *Life*, ii. 89). Gathorne Hardy commented similarly in his diary (*Life* (1910), by his son, ii. 49).

in a letter to her premier of 10 January 1878, even mooted her own abdication, so deeply did her warlike spirit resent the 'low tone' of the country and the cabinet. Turkey was now suing Russia for an armistice; but the Tsar's troops still advanced, and on 20 January they occupied Adrianople. The crisis had come. On 23 January the British cabinet ordered the Mediterranean fleet to steam through the Dardanelles to Constantinople, and asked parliament to vote £6 millions for military purposes. A week later Russia granted Turkey an armistice.

The cabinet decision caused Derby and Carnarvon to resign; though when the order to the fleet was countermanded, Derby was persuaded to stay on. A week after the armistice it was reported that the Russians were in Constantinople. The queen pressed her ministers to declare war; but they were content to send a portion of the fleet to Constantinople 'for the protection of life and property', while parliament passed the £6 millions vote without debate. The Russians answered our naval move by moving forward their army; whose outposts sighted the minarets of Stamboul only to gaze at the same time on the warning silhouettes of the British ironclads. A war fever flared up in England; this was the period of the famous music-hall song which added 'Jingoism' to the English vocabulary.[1] And for some months peace was in danger. It was saved by two things—the exhaustion of Russia, who could scarcely face a new war, and the policy of Beaconsfield, who, as is now fairly clear, had never intended to make one. Certainly he would not for the mere purpose of keeping Russian troops out of the Turkish capital; as on 12 February the Turks were finally let know. On 19 February a sort of truce was arranged, whereby Russia undertook not to occupy Gallipoli, in return for Great Britain's not landing troops in Turkey.

But on 3 March 1878 the belligerents signed the treaty of San Stefano. Its terms were strongly Pan-Slavist, and neither Great Britain nor Austria-Hungary could stomach them. Andrássy proposed its revision by a European conference. Russia would not accept unless the scope of discussion were strictly delimited in advance; Great Britain insisted that the conference must have

---

[1] We don't want to fight;
But by Jingo, if we do,
We've got the men, we've got the ships,
We've got the money too.

a free hand, and the whole treaty go into the melting-pot. On 27 March Lord Beaconsfield persuaded his cabinet to call up the reserves immediately and summon to the Mediterranean a large body of Indian troops.[1] These martial decisions were unanimous, save for Lord Derby; who now finally resigned, and was succeeded at the foreign office by Lord Salisbury. The vacancy thus created at the India office was filled by Gathorne Hardy, who went to the House of Lords as Viscount Cranbrook. Carnarvon's post at the colonial office had fallen to Sir M. Hicks Beach.

The new foreign minister had mastered the facts of the Eastern Question more fully than any other British statesman, and he signalized his advent by issuing to the Powers almost at once a most able Circular Note. Though answered at length by Prince Gortchakov, it really convinced the chancelleries, and brought down Bismarck from the fence in favour of an unlimited conference.[2] The outcome was the famous Congress of Berlin (13 June to 13 July 1878). It was the most imposing gathering of diplomats which Europe had seen since the Congress of Vienna sixty-three years earlier; while the choice of meeting-ground marked the continental primacy to which Germany had been raised by the 1870 war. Great Britain sent three representatives —her prime minister, her foreign secretary, and her able Berlin ambassador, Lord Odo Russell.[3] The success of the congress was largely, though not wholly, assured by secret conventions concluded between the Powers beforehand. Great Britain signed three of them—with Russia (30 May), with Austria-Hungary (6 June), and with Turkey (4 June).[4] Within the lines thus chalked, a subtle and at times risky game was played between the

[1] Eventually only 7,000 came; they reached Malta in May. There was a little-known precedent for bringing them; for in 1801 a contingent of 2,000 Indians had reinforced Sir Ralph Abercromby's army against the French in Egypt.

[2] As originally planned, of ambassadors. Gortchakov took the lead in making it a congress of heads of governments and special plenipotentiaries.

[3] Lord Salisbury took his nephew A. J. Balfour with him as his secretary; so that three successive conservative prime ministers of England were among those present. The list similarly included three chancellors of Germany—Bismarck, Hohenlohe, and the then youthful Bülow. To Lord Odo Russell Beaconsfield afterwards offered a peerage; but the head of his family, the duke of Bedford, refused to endow it, on the ground that no Russell should receive a peerage, even for official services, from any but Whig hands. On Gladstone's return to power he relented; and Lord Odo became the first Lord Ampthill. The incident, typical in all but its date, illustrated how closely the ideas of family and party were linked in the minds of the whig magnates.

[4] All were secret. But shortly after the congress began the Anglo-Russian

two veterans of the tournament, Prince Gortchakov (now 80) and Lord Beaconsfield (in his 74th year). The genius for suave yet formidable bargaining, which the latter had matured during forty-one years of parliamentary experience, was abetted by the active support of Andrássy, the acquiescence of Bismarck, and the distrust towards Russia which, in regard to the most contentious issue, inspired Italy and France. There was a crisis on 22 June when Beaconsfield backed up a sort of ultimatum to Russia by ordering a special train; but Bismarck, assured that he was in earnest, prevailed on the Russians to give way. Andrássy obtained all that he wished, and Beaconsfield all that he contended for; while Turkey herself was allowed scarcely more voice in her fate than Germany at Versailles in 1919.

Beaconsfield's return from Berlin was a veritable triumph. In characteristic phrase he told his shouting fellow countrymen that he brought back 'peace with honour'. It was indeed the climax of his personal career. Starting from nothing, he had made himself first a brilliant adventurer, then a party leader, then a national leader, and now a dominant international figure. For the moment all England was with him; and had he dissolved parliament another seven-year mandate seemed assured. He decided against it. The moment passed. Thenceforward fate smiled on him no more.

What was his achievement worth? The treaty of San Stefano had been thoroughly bad. Russia made war in the name of liberty; she made peace in the spirit of annexation. In Asia this was undisguised; though she had been much helped in her campaign by the Christian Armenians, she merely swallowed slices of their territory without any attempt to free their nation, whether under Turkey's flag or her own. And a condition attached to the war indemnity opened prospects of further mouthfuls. In Europe annexation had mostly to be cloaked; but the cloak was thin. The plan was to restrict as much as possible all the non-Slav races, and among the Slavs to plump for the Bulgars; whose political self-consciousness was least developed, and whose language and liturgy were nearest the Russian. Accordingly the Rumanians, despite their war services to Russia, were despoiled of Rumanian Bessarabia, in order that the Tsar might once more control the lower Danube; their 'compensation' in the

Convention was divulged to the *Globe* newspaper by a copying-clerk employed (at 8*d*. an hour!) in the foreign office. No serious harm resulted.

Dobrudja south of its delta was frankly contemptuous. Turkey on the mainland was left in effective ownership of nothing but Thrace, the Chalcidic peninsula, the (almost isolated) city of Salonica, Thessaly, Epirus, and Albania. Nearly all the rest, including large districts in Macedonia which were predominantly Serb or Greek, was shaped into a Big Bulgaria, whose organization was to be in Russian hands. Territorially this formed a quadrilateral between the Danube, the Black Sea, the Aegean, and the mountains of Albania; with ports on both seas, which as Russian bases could command either. Serbia and tiny Montenegro were both enlarged and declared independent; but both remained very small. Greece got nothing, and saw her irredenta, which was larger than herself, partitioned between Turks and Bulgars. Bosnia-Herzegovina was to fly the Turkish flag, but to undergo an international control as proposed by the Constantinople conference. (It was reserved, of course, as 'compensation' for Austria-Hungary.)

The Berlin Congress did a service by destroying this treaty without the cost of further war. But the particular changes which it made, though less unjust on balance, were quite as selfishly inspired. Nothing was done for Rumania—why should anybody save Russia's ally from Russia?[1] Nothing adequate was done for Greece. Big Bulgaria, the main bone of contention, was trisected. The Macedonian vilayets with their Bulgar, Serb, and Greek populations were returned bodily to Turkey; the northern tract (Bulgar) between the Danube and the Balkan range was made a dependent principality to be organized by Russia; the central tract (equally Bulgar) between the Balkan and Rhodope ranges became a special Turkish province (Eastern Rumelia) under a Christian governor. The motive for dividing the last two was purely strategic; it gave the Turks against Russia the military benefit of the Balkan barrier. All this was Beaconsfield's concern. Austria-Hungary, on her part, secured the right to occupy and administer Bosnia-Herzegovina; pushed Montenegro back again from the Adriatic; and reopened between her and Serbia a corridor for her own *Drang nach Osten*[2]—her historic urge towards Salonica.

[1] Great Britain did propose the restoration of her Bessarabian territory, but such quixotic wisdom received no support.

[2] The correct application of this phrase, which by English writers has often been misapplied.

These dispositions are related by so direct a pedigree to the occasions of the Great War in 1914 that they cannot be passed without comment. Two features were especially bad. One was the transfer of Bosnia-Herzegovina to Austria-Hungary in a form which denied, without extinguishing, the irredentist aspirations of Serbia. But no one could stop Andrássy's achieving this; it was the great victory of his brilliant diplomacy—one of those fatal monuments over which the irony of history inscribes Juvenal's line: *Magnaque numinibus vota exaudita malignis.* On Beaconsfield's side of the treaty, the division of Bulgaria south of the Balkan range from Bulgaria north of it did no great harm nor good in the sequel; it was ended within eight years. But his return of the Macedonian vilayets to Turkey without any stipulation for Christian governors was the second fatal mistake. It ushered in thirty-four years of misrule, comitadji-fighting, and massacre in that large and miserable area; and the best that can be said in its favour is that it did not, like the San Stefano treaty, prejudge unfairly the ultimate claims of the rival Christian nationalities.

In his general aim—to fend off Russia from Constantinople— he succeeded remarkably. Nor is the subsequent history of politics in Sofia any proof that what he feared (and Russia hoped) of the Big Bulgaria was mistaken. Big Bulgaria would necessarily have been much more subservient to the Tsar, because she would have had so many Greeks and Serbs to coerce; what enabled little Bulgaria to be independent was her compact homogeneity. Yet this damming of the Russian current had results not foreseen in 1878. In a profounder sense than Bosnia-Herzegovina or Macedonia it caused the 1914 War. For the deeper source of that conflict was the intersection at Constantinople of two rival imperial 'urges'—that of Russia southward to the Mediterranean and that of Germany eastward along the line Berlin–Bagdad. Had the San Stefano settlement stood, Germany's ambition could scarcely have developed this later direction; and although the pressure of her gigantic force seeking imperial outlets in a pre-empted world might in any case have caused an explosion, it would not have been that explosion. And here we may note a later oracle of Lord Beaconsfield's, in a letter of 4 November 1880,[1] that, 'next to making a tolerable settlement for the Porte', his 'great object was to break up, and permanently prevent, the

[1] Quoted by Sir H. Drummond Wolff, *Rambling Recollections* (1908), ii. 265.

alliance of the three Empires', and that he had completely succeeded. It is indeed true that the first rift between St. Petersburg and Berlin, and the first strong drawing-together of Berlin
and Vienna, may alike be dated from this congress; and in that
sense it originated, under Lord Beaconsfield's manipulation, the
grouping from which the World War resulted.

A word more must be said of the congress's dealings with
Turkey-in-Asia. It sanctioned large strategic annexations by
Russia at the south-east corner of the Black Sea, but suppressed
her trick about the war indemnity. It also sanctioned the transfer
of Cyprus to British occupation and administration, as had been
arranged in the Anglo-Turkish Convention of 4 June. By the
latter Great Britain had contracted a defensive alliance with
Turkey, engaging herself to defend Turkey-in-Asia, while the
Sultan pledged himself to introduce reforms and protect the
Christian inhabitants in consultation with her. Little was to
come from this to Englishmen in future, save the mortification of
responsibility for Armenian massacres which they could not prevent. But in judging Lord Beaconsfield's policy one must remember that it was never carried through. He had in mind a very
considerable penetration of the east of Asiatic Turkey by friendly
British influence, so that something like a British protectorate
would link the Mediterranean with Middle Asia and the Persian
Gulf route to India. For this the island of Cyprus lying opposite
Alexandretta was not ill suited; and Lord Beaconsfield sent
British military consuls to Armenia to be the organizers of Turkey's frontier defence. Had the plan continued, it would perhaps
have saved the Armenians; for the military consuls, being of
value to the Turks, might have been listened to by them. But
when Gladstone returned to power in 1880 he withdrew these
officers, and sent ordinary political consuls instead; and they,
being regarded by the Turks as undesired interlopers, were helpless save to witness and report. As for Cyprus, Great Britain's
occupation of Egypt in 1882 gave her fleet the use of ports which
rendered those of the island superfluous. But previously it possessed no other base in the Mediterranean east of Malta, and lay
during the 1876–8 crisis in an open roadstead off the Turkish
coast at Besika Bay. France was the only Power to take umbrage and demand 'compensation'. She was appeased by Great
Britain's secret consent to the seizure of Tunis; which, with en-
couragement from Bismarck, she carried out in 1881.

The settlement after Waterloo had been followed by a period of 38½ years, during which no war occurred between Great Powers. The similar period after the treaty of Berlin was just over 36 years. The difference is not great enough to disentitle Beaconsfield and Bismarck to some, at least, of the credit which it has become fashionable to bestow on Castlereagh and Metternich.

During the 1877 and 1878 sessions, while the Near East absorbed the ageing premier, the trade decline, which had begun three years earlier, deepened into one of the main 'cyclical' depressions of the nineteenth century. Alone it was bad enough, bringing wage-reductions and industrial conflicts in trade after trade. But with it came an entirely new feature—an intense agricultural depression, which extended to every part of Europe served by railways, and which was due to the novel competition of transatlantic prairie-grown grain with European. The economics of this will be shown in Chapter IV; here we note merely the political side. Almost simultaneously in 1879 the bitter cry of the home farmers in the different European countries shaped itself into a demand upon their respective parliaments for a tariff on cereals. In Berlin and in Paris it was heard; Germany and France both imposed duties and, although at high cost to the rest of the community, saved their farms and farmers. In London it was not heard. At the parting of the ways the British government took the other turning.

The peculiar thing is that this happened, not under a liberal ministry aggressively pledged to free trade, but under a conservative premier, and one who three decades earlier had ousted Peel from the leadership of his party on this very issue. Yet what Peel had done then left English agriculture flourishing; from what Beaconsfield did now it has never recovered. Whether his course was right or wrong, it is hard to approve it from his own standpoint, or to regard the speeches[1] in which he justified it as showing his usual long-sightedness. Fundamentally, however, the difference between England and the continent in this matter was military.[2] Country-dwellers were supposed to make the best soldiers. The continent wished to preserve them for conscripts; but England, not having conscription, did not care what became of them.

[1] Especially that of 29 April 1879, which descends to pure Micawberism.
[2] Prince Bülow (*Imperial Germany*, Eng. version (1914), 215) quotes with approval the saying of Prince Guido Henckel: 'Agriculture must provide our soldiers, and industry must pay for them.'

With economic discontent in the country, and Gladstone thundering against the premier on provincial platforms, the opposition at Westminster began to pull itself together. In 1877 the whig leaders first supported the radical demand for the extension of a popular franchise to the county constituencies. Hartington spoke for it; Gladstone gave it his vote; only Lowe and Goschen remained aloof. A by-election in 1876 had brought Chamberlain to the house as member for a safe seat in Birmingham; and the new method of political organization, which held that city for radicalism, began to spread its tentacles outside. A great step was taken when on 31 May 1877, with Mr. Gladstone's presence and blessing, the National Liberal Federation came to birth. Its first head-quarters were at Birmingham, and Chamberlain was its first president. Ostensibly formed to extend to the liberal party all over the country the benefits of organization on the Birmingham model ('the Caucus', as it was then called), it served also to strengthen radicals against whigs within the ranks which uneasily combined them.

Another cloud which began gathering in these years was that of a militant agitation for Irish Home Rule. The phrase 'Home Rule' had been invented by Isaac Butt,[1] as a more positive and less offensive version of the old demand for 'Repeal' of the union. The movement was launched under his inspiration at a Dublin meeting in 1870; and in 1874 it carried some 59 seats at the general election. In that year and the three following Butt, who was both an able and a winning speaker, put his case before the house of commons in a conciliatory and constitutional manner. He was uniformly ignored and rebuffed. In April 1877, when his party's annual home rule motion was defeated by 417 votes to 67, only one English member (Sir Wilfred Lawson) spoke for it, and only eight gave it their votes. The result was that certain of Butt's followers, who preferred more drastic methods, gained the upper hand; and in 1878 he resigned the Irish leadership, and made way for them.

The chief to displace him was Charles Stewart Parnell, a young man of whom we caught a glimpse in the last chapter. Parnell entered parliament at a by-election in April 1875; and by a coin-

[1] B. 1813; educated at Trinity College, Dublin, where he was professor of political economy 1836–41. At first conservative, and opposed O'Connell; 1852–65, in parliament as 'liberal conservative'; 1865–9, appeared as counsel for all the Fenian prisoners; 1871–9, sat as home ruler. Like Parnell, was a protestant; d. 1879.

cidence took his seat on the very day when the first notable effort in Irish obstruction was made—by a Fenian, Joseph Biggar. Some months later he witnessed and pondered the disorderly success of Plimsoll.[1] But it was not till the session of 1877 that he himself came to the front as an obstructionist; having in the interval quietly strengthened his position with the two leading and rival forces in Nationalist Ireland, the Roman Catholic Church and the Irish Republican Brotherhood; to neither of which did he belong. His tactics offended Butt, but he soon brushed Butt aside. By July of that year he and his band had gained such skill in obstruction, that they twice kept the house of commons up all night—the second time till 2 p.m., a 26 hours' sitting. Such performances have since become commonplaces of parliamentarism in many lands. But then they were almost unheard of, and the sensation was immense. Sir Stafford Northcote, as leader of the house, carried two anti-obstructionist rules; the Irishmen soon got round them; and in 1878 he had a committee appointed to consider the problem. But it proved very baffling on its technical side. Early in 1879 he moved six resolutions to deal with it. Five had to be abandoned; and the sixth, after consuming three nights in debate, was passed with amendments which rendered it nugatory.

These manœuvres partly explain why the Disraelian government, after its fruitful start, became so barren of legislation during its later years. But their full effect on Ireland and on Parnell's fortunes was due to the coincidence of the agricultural slump. Just as the liberals had forgotten Ireland when they passed the Ballot Act, so the conservatives forgot her when they decided not to protect farming. In Great Britain a policy, which sacrificed the rural to the urban populations, did at least favour the large majority. But Ireland, save round Belfast, was a nation of agriculturalists; and, excepting the graziers, ruin fell on them all. The vast majority were tenants holding from landlords at rents which the fall in agricultural prices made it impossible to pay. Embittered by differences of religion and race, the relations of landlord and tenant in Ireland had already for two centuries resembled a smouldering civil war. The Gladstone Act of 1870 had given a certain relief; and in 1875 a considered survey by the Dublin correspondent of *The Times* recorded a widespread assuagement.[2] But within three years the crisis in rural economy

---

[1] p. 37 above.   [2] Quoted in *Annual Register*, (134)–(135).

tore it to shreds, and created the worst situation since the famine. The terrible murder of Lord Leitrim in Donegal (2 April 1878) was the first thunderclap in the storm. Two Fenians, frowned on by their organizations, but much helped by fellow members, resolved to seize its opportunities. One was Michael Davitt,[1] who had been released in December 1877 after serving seven years and seven months in penal servitude for treason-felony. The other was John Devoy of the Clan-na-Gael, the American branch of the Irish Republican Brotherhood. At first the agrarian revolt spread unhelped by the parliamentarians. But on 7 June 1879, a month after Butt's death, Parnell threw his mantle over it. On 21 October the Irish National Land League was formed, with Parnell as president, two Fenians (Biggar and Egan) as treasurers, and two more Fenians (Davitt and Brennan) as secretaries. Thenceforward the concerted deployment of Irish revolutionary forces on two fronts—at Westminster and over the Irish countryside—confronted British statesmanship with an unparalleled challenge.

Grave as were these troubles near home, the cabinet was more engrossed, and the public imagination more struck, by two blood-curdling disasters in distant fields—that of Isandhlwana (22 January 1879) and that of Kabul (3 September 1879). Both were incidental to 'forward' policies; and they helped to swing the see-saw of British public opinion heavily against Disraelian imperialism. What had touched its zenith of popularity in July 1878 approached its nadir fourteen months later.

Let us take the South African story first. Lord Carnarvon, who became colonial secretary in 1874, had during his earlier tenure of the same office sponsored the Act of 1867 which federated Canada. It became now his leading idea to federate South Africa. His predecessor, Lord Kimberley, had favoured the project; and the native peril, which then confronted the four white South African communities, gave it much plausibility. But Carnarvon acted without tact. His first proposals were ill

---

[1] Michael Davitt (1846–1906), born co. Mayo; aged 6 when his father was evicted and emigrated to Lancashire; aged 11 when as child-worker in a cotton-mill he lost his right arm in the machinery. Joined I.R.B. 1865; organizing secretary for England and Scotland, 1868; sentenced to twelve years' penal servitude, 1870; released by efforts of Isaac Butt, December 1877; in America and with Henry George, 1878; launched Irish agrarian revolt, 1879; M.P. 1880–99; conflict with Parnell over land nationalization, 1882; anti-Parnellite, 1892; helped the Boers, 1900–2. Chief representative of Collectivism within the Irish Nationalist movement.

received in South Africa; and when he sent out J. A. Froude on a personal mission to explain them, that distinguished historian's two visits (1874 and 1875) only increased the local distrust of Downing Street. A negotiation (1876) with the Orange Free State, whereby the latter for a lump sum of £90,000 abandoned its claim to the Kimberley diamonds field, was Carnarvon's sole success in this quarter.

But by 1876 the problem of white versus black approached a crisis. Besides many minor factors in it, there were two main ones—Zululand and the Transvaal. Zululand was a Bantu military monarchy, whose king, Keshwayo,[1] maintained a highly drilled army of nearly 40,000 celibate athlete-warriors. It had been traditional for each of them to 'wash his spear', and the history of the conquering kingdom (founded by Keshwayo's grandfather) had been one of incessant wars and aggressions. The white communities most threatened were Natal and the Transvaal, and the condition of the latter gave a standing provocation. Its Republic, now under President Burgers, was chronically lawless and insolvent. When by the Sands River Convention of 1852 it had been given its independence, a condition had been made that there should be no slavery. The only effect was that in the Transvaal the word 'apprentice' was substituted for 'slave'. Kaffir children were kidnapped and trained to work in the fields, had their price, and were unprotected by law. Wagon-loads of them were sold or bartered.[2] Moreover groups of individual farmers were constantly encroaching on native lands round them. The result was frequent fighting.

In 1875 in a war against a Bantu chief named Sekukuni the Boers were seriously defeated. Burgers found himself with no troops and an empty treasury. Accordingly he hired a force of filibusters (under one Schlickmann,[3] a Prussian ex-officer), who received no pay or supplies, but were to reimburse themselves by plunder. They committed hideous barbarities, butchering women and children, and cutting the throats of the wounded. Kaffir feeling was stung to desperation; there were mutterings in the Zulu thundercloud; and on 22 September 1876 Lord Carnarvon wrote to the high commissioner that such a war menaced

---

[1] So spelt by Theal and by African scholars generally. But the form in use in England at the time was Cetewayo.

[2] H. Rider Haggard, *Cetewayo and His White Neighbours* (1882), ch. ii.

[3] He had been an unsuccessful digger at the diamond fields. Most of his filibusters seem to have come from there.

the peace of all South Africa, and he must insist on its being stopped.

Early in 1877 strong steps were taken. There had come to England for a conference Sir Theophilus Shepstone, minister for native affairs in Natal, now a man of 60, having started life as a Kaffir interpreter 42 years earlier. He was utterly fearless, and thoroughly understood natives, especially Zulus; but, as events showed, he misjudged the Boers. Carnarvon sent him to the Transvaal to confer with Burgers and discuss confederation, with discretion to arrange bringing the country under the British flag. Arriving in Pretoria with a few civil servants and twenty-five mounted police, he found that Burgers had only 12s. 6d. in the treasury. No taxes and no salaries were being paid; the jails had been opened because they could not feed the prisoners. Sekukuni and Keshwayo were both threatening, and there seemed every prospect of an appalling wipe-out. If Great Britain would not act, Burgers talked of calling in Germany. But he and his friends were willing to be annexed, on two conditions—that they should themselves receive pensions or offices, and that in public they should be allowed to protest against the change. With the first condition it was easy to comply; but Shepstone made the fatal mistake of also accepting the second.[1] After eleven weeks' discussion he proclaimed the annexation of the country (12 April 1877).

Meanwhile Carnarvon had sent to South Africa a new high commissioner—Sir Bartle Frere. Frere was an Indian civilian, whose record in India before, during, and after the Mutiny had been one of solid as well as brilliant success. He had the makings of an admirable viceroy; and had he been appointed instead of Lord Lytton in 1876, the mistakes of the latter's Afghan policy would very probably have been avoided. Of South Africa he knew nothing. He had only been sixteen days in the country when the news of Shepstone's action at Pretoria reached Cape-town. It came to him as a shock, but he could do nothing. Carnarvon, irregularly and unwisely, had given Shepstone a special authority independent of the high commissioner.

[1] Burgers 'actually assisted in the wording of the proclamation, by which independence was to be destroyed, and submitted in turn for the special commissioner's [i.e. Shepstone's] approval the protest which it would be necessary for him to make'! (G. M. Theal, *History of South Africa from 1873 to 1884* (1919), i. 271.) It is not surprising that, when the displaced Boer Government unanimously passed the protest on 11 April, the British representatives were unimpressed. But they were wrong.

Frere decided to address himself to the various native menaces. He spent the rest of 1877 on some successful operations against the Kaffirs in the Transkei, known as the Gaika and Galeka wars. In 1878 he started negotiating with Keshwayo. The first point was to clear up a boundary dispute between Zululand and the Transvaal. This was referred to an arbitration, whose award went mainly in Keshwayo's favour, and all that was incumbent on Frere was to proclaim it. But he had become deeply impressed with the menace of the Zulu military system. In October and November he and the local commander-in-chief, General Thesiger,[1] wrote home repeatedly asking for additional troops against a Zulu war. The cabinet refused them, and urged peace; but later, growing anxious because the quickest message took two to three weeks,[2] they judged it safest to send some. Frere's answer was to launch at the Zulus (11 December 1878) an ultimatum which he knew they could not accept. Thus he committed his country to a serious war, not only without leave, but contrary to instructions.

The Prime Minister in cabinet was exasperated, and nearly all his colleagues favoured recalling Frere. But the queen defended him, as did Hicks Beach, who had become colonial secretary after Carnarvon's departure; and these two prevailed. The ultimatum expired in a month, and on 12 January 1879 Lord Chelmsford marched into Zululand. Ten days later occurred the Isandhlwana disaster. Lured by a Zulu feint the British general led most of his force some way from his camp. When he returned, he found the camp pillaged and almost every living soul in it slaughtered.[3] Under-rating the Zulus, he had neglected the regular precaution of laagering the wagons.[4] The importance of this was illustrated the same night at the small post of Rorke's Drift, where a force of only 103 men with 35 sick in hos-

---

[1] Son of the first Lord Chelmsford (1794–1878), one-time conservative lord chancellor, and father of the notable Indian viceroy (1868–1933). He succeeded to his father's title in December of this year.

[2] There being then no cable beyond Cape Verde.

[3] Fifty white officers and 776 N.C.O.s and men were killed; nearly all belonging to the 24th Regiment (South Wales Borderers), by men of whose 2nd battalion Rorke's Drift also was garrisoned. Only about 40 Europeans got away, all the white civilians (drivers, &c.) being massacred; and about 800 men of various black contingents perished too. All the slain were disembowelled. The Zulu losses were still heavier.

[4] At least two separate Boers—one no less a person than Paul Kruger—had warned him specially about it.

pital held a laager successfully against a great host of Zulus, and
inflicted such losses as mitigated the moral effect of the day's
victory. But Chelmsford had to execute a perilous retreat, and
it was only a day short of four calendar months before his troops
could reoccupy the battle-field and take up the bodies.

The news of Isandhlwana reached England on 11 February,
and the public received it badly. The cabinet at once sent off
to Chelmsford not only all the cavalry, artillery, and stores for
which he asked, but five battalions of infantry instead of his
three. Beaconsfield had been very ill served both by him and by
Frere; yet in parliament he defended each, and did not recall
either. Months passed, and smaller blunders recurred. Early
in June the Prince Imperial of France (only son of Napoleon III),
who served with the British as a volunteer, lost his life in a trifling
skirmish. Just before this the cabinet had decided to send out
Wolseley as commander-in-chief and high commissioner for
Natal. He arrived on 28 June to find Chelmsford carrying out
dispositions which six days later at the battle of Ulundi destroyed
the Zulu army. In the sequel Keshwayo was captured and deported; while Wolseley broke up Zululand into eight principali-
ties under as many separate chiefs.

So ended an inglorious but costly war, to pay for which Sir
Stafford Northcote suspended the Sinking Fund. Opinion in
England was led by Gladstone to view it as a typical example of
Beaconsfield's forward policy and a wanton aggression against
the Zulus. It certainly was not the first, for Frere had acted
against the premier's wishes. Nor was it altogether the second; for
the Zulu military system was not really compatible with settled
life in South Africa, nor could anything but force end it. The
true inopportuneness of the war lay in its bearing on the annexation of the Transvaal. This had gone through without a blow,
because the Boers were in terror of Keshwayo.[1] Had it been
followed up by giving them a constitution like Cape Colony's
under the British flag, it might have been a success. The first
error was to impose an illiberal Crown Colony government. But
the second was to destroy Keshwayo. The removal of his menace
bore the same relation to the subsequent successful revolt of
the Transvaal, as the expulsion of France from Canada in the
eighteenth century bore to the revolt of the thirteen colonies.
The prime fault was Carnarvon's in 1877, when he divided

[1] Theal (op. cit.) disputes this, but the evidence seems against him.

authority between two men—Shepstone and Frere—who took hold of the problem by opposite handles. Militarily most credit belongs to the Zulus. Ineffective with their few fire-arms, they carried spearmanship to the highest level reached by man. But white troops, it must be remembered, had still no machine-guns.

Let us turn now to the Afghan troubles. We must go back to 1876, when the second Lord Lytton[1] was appointed viceroy of India with instructions to seek to induce Sher Ali, then Amir of Afghanistan, to receive a friendly mission. This conformed with a 'forward' theory of forestalling Russian invasion. He was authorized to promise the Amir to continue his subsidy, and also to assist him materially, in a clear case, against unprovoked aggression. But Sher Ali must admit British agents to his frontier positions. There followed early in 1877 a conference at Peshawar between Sir Lewis Pelly and two Afghan representatives. It broke down on the Amir's refusal of the British condition. Meantime in December 1876 the Treaty of Jacobabad, concluded through Captain Sandeman,[2] had confirmed an agreement of 1854 with the Khan of Kalat, which enabled British troops to be stationed at Quetta, a base for striking at Kandahar.

After the breakdown at Peshawar over a year passed. The home government and the viceroy pulled opposite ways. In Europe war threatened; in India famine pressed. But Sher Ali from 1873 onwards had been making military preparations on a vast scale, for which Russia paid.[3] In July 1878 a Russian Mission under General Stoletov appeared in Kabul. On this Lord Lytton announced that a British Mission would be sent likewise. It was dispatched under Sir Neville Chamberlain; but Sher Ali had it turned back at the frontier. There followed a British ultimatum,[4] which the Amir ignored; and finally three British

[1] Edward Robert Lytton (1831–92), son of Edward Bulwer, first Baron Lytton (1803–73), the well-known novelist and politician. Educated at Harrow and Bonn; 1849–74, filled minor diplomatic appointments; 1874–6, minister at Lisbon; 1876–80, viceroy of India; 1887–91, ambassador at Paris. Created earl, 1880. Published many poems, much read in their day, under pseudonym 'Owen Meredith'.

[2] Robert Groves Sandeman (1835–92), afterwards knighted, a Scotsman from Perth, son of a general in the East India Company's service; author of the famous Sandeman system, in which Baluchistan is governed by local chiefs under the Khan of Kalat with the British government as arbiter between them. Had rare power of dealing with chiefs and headmen, all of whom over a vast area he knew personally.

[3] Lord Roberts, *Forty-One Years in India* (1897), ch. xlviii.

[4] At each of the stages leading up to this Lytton worked for war, while, excepting Cranbrook, all the ablest men in the cabinet (Beaconsfield, Salisbury, Cairns, Cross,

armies invaded Afghanistan. The first moved through the
Khyber Pass and took Jalalabad. The second under General
Roberts[1] operated by the Kurram Pass, and won a brilliant victory at Peiwar Kotal. The third, starting from Quetta, occupied
Pishin and (early in January 1879) Kandahar. These movements
overwhelmed Sher Ali; in February, while making for Russian
Turkestan, he died. His son, Yakub Khan, succeeded, and
began negotiating with the British. On 26 May was signed the
treaty of Gandamak. By it the Afghans ceded military control
over the passes, and accepted British control of foreign policy
with a British minister at Kabul. Sir Louis Cavagnari[2] took up
residence there accordingly; and the Beaconsfield government,
though severely criticized, not only by Gladstone at home, but
by men trained after Lord Lawrence's tradition in the Punjab,
seemed brilliantly to have attained all its Afghan objectives.

The blow fell. On 3 September Afghan soldiers, alleged
to be mutinous, stormed the Legation at Kabul. The Minister
and the whole of his suite and escort were massacred. The news
reached England three days later, and created a profound revulsion against the Beaconsfield policy. It was the shock of Isandhlwana redoubled.

The war began over again. Roberts, in what he himself
thought his hardest and best Indian campaign, marched by the
Kurram Pass to Kabul, defeating the rebels at Charasiab on the
way. The ambiguous Yakub, who early had fled to him, abdi-
cated at the capital. In the south the British force at Kandahar
was reinforced. A pause ensued. It was not the end of the
Afghan trouble, but it was as far as we can take it under the
Beaconsfield government and in the present chapter. To this
point the net effect on home opinion had been to fortify Gladstone's anti-Imperialist agitation.

This last reached a climax in the famous Midlothian campaign

and Northcote) were trying to stop him. Their arguments, with the story of how
Lytton got his way, may be studied in Buckle, *Life of Beaconsfield*, vi. 380–8. It is
an extreme instance of a strong cabinet being over-ridden by the 'man on the spot'.
Salisbury blamed Beaconsfield for weakness (Lord Balfour, *Chapters of Autobiography*, p. 114).

[1] Frederick Sleigh Roberts (1832–1914) had by then served twenty-seven years
in India and reached the rank of major-general. This was his first command as a
general officer on active service.

[2] Among Lord Lytton's mistakes was the choice of a man who to the Afghans
was an object of special suspicion. See the evidence of the head missionary of
Peshawar, quoted in J. Martineau's *Life of Frere* (1895), ii. 156–7.

launched by the veteran on 24 November. From Liverpool to Edinburgh with three speeches on the way; a week of Brobdingnagian oratory in Midlothian itself; a visit to Glasgow; and then back in the same manner. What made it historic was not merely the force and scale of Gladstone's eloquence, but the fact that before him it had never been the etiquette for leading British statesmen to 'stump the country' in that fashion. Queen Victoria was scandalized at the innovation. But though Beaconsfield abstained from following suit, it was, of course, the natural corollary of the franchise-widening which he himself had carried.

There was now a marked reunion of liberal forces. But the conservatives were far from realizing how the tide flowed. A by-election at Liverpool had raised their spirits; and after the famous barrister, Sir Edward Clarke, won another for them at Southwark, the Prime Minister judged it opportune (8 March 1880) to announce a dissolution, making Irish Home Rule his main issue. Gladstone followed with his second Midlothian Campaign; and most of the polls were declared in the first week of April. With economic discontent and the Irish vote both on their side, the liberals swept the board. Their majority in the new house of commons was 137 over the conservatives, the Irish nationalists winning 65 seats as a third party. Both Queen Victoria and Lord Beaconsfield were sincerely surprised; a circumstance which shows how little the workings of a democratic electorate had yet come to be understood.

Without meeting the new parliament the conservative cabinet resigned. To its foes the defeat of the Beaconsfield system was like a victory over forces of darkness. Gladstone wrote to the duke of Argyll that it had 'given joy to the large majority of the civilized world'.[1] Radical Morley wrote to radical Chamberlain 'I only now begin to realize what a horrid and dismal time we have had for the last four years'.[2] But perhaps it was less a system than it seemed. Lord Salisbury, in a private confidence, criticized the record of his late chief.[3] He described him as 'a man who, with all his great qualities, was unable to decide a general principle of action, or to ensure that when decided on it should be carried out by his subordinates', and 'a statesman whose only final political principle was that the Party must on

---

[1] Lord Morley, *Life of Gladstone* (1903), bk. vii, ch. viii.
[2] J. L. Garvin, *Life of Chamberlain*, i (1932), 290.
[3] Lord Balfour, *Chapters of Autobiography* (1930), pp. 113–14.

no account be broken up'. 'Exceedingly short-sighted, though very clear-sighted,' he said, 'he neither could nor would look far ahead.' These have since been common charges against many prime ministers. Yet in his own way Lord Beaconsfield was longer-sighted than Lord Salisbury. The latter in January 1902 concluded an Anglo-Japanese Alliance. But it is doubtful whether, as Lord Beaconsfield did,[1] he foresaw it—and the coming dominance of Japan in the Far East—as early as September 1875.

[1] Lord Zetland, *Letters of Disraeli to Lady Bradford and Lady Chesterfield* (1929), i. 287.

III

THE ASCENDANCY OF PARNELL

DOWN to Lord Beaconsfield's resignation, Lord Hartington had been the liberal leader in the commons and Lord Granville in the lords. The queen invited each to form a ministry; but they declined. That new portent, the Midlothian campaign, had in fact swept their claims away. Gladstone had gone behind parliament to the people, which for the first time virtually chose its own premier. He told Hartington (who put the question to him at the queen's request) that he would accept no subordinate office. At once his accession to the highest became inevitable.

But in selecting his ministers he acted differently, and almost kicked down the radical ladder by which he had climbed. Eight of his eleven colleagues in the cabinet were whigs. One of the three others, Forster, had parted company with radicalism ten years earlier; another, John Bright, was now but the shadow of a great name. The only effective radical admitted was Joseph Chamberlain; and to him was assigned the then humblest cabinet office, the board of trade. Even Dilke, whose following in the party was very large and who worked with Chamberlain in a sort of duumvirate, could obtain nothing better than an under-secretaryship—to Granville at the foreign office. Fawcett[1] became postmaster-general outside the cabinet; while Trevelyan,[2] who had worked very hard in the Disraeli parliament, took a post but little higher than he had filled twelve years earlier as a young man of 30. Lowe, however, the veteran anti-Radical, was made Viscount Sherbrooke and dropped.

From this one-sided start much of Gladstone's failure in his 1880–5 administration may be traced. For never in the modern

---

[1] Henry Fawcett, b. 1833; educated at Trinity Hall, Cambridge; blinded by a shooting accident, 1858. Professor of political economy at Cambridge, 1863–84; M.P. 1865–84; postmaster-general, 1880–4; d. 1884.

[2] George Otto Trevelyan, b. 1838, son of Sir Charles Trevelyan (1807–86), the famous civil servant, and nephew of Macaulay, whose life he wrote. Educated at Harrow and Trinity College, Cambridge. M.P. 1865–86 and 1887–97; lord of the admiralty, 1868–70; later took the lead in pressing for extension of popular franchise to counties; parliamentary secretary to the admiralty, 1880–2; chief secretary for Ireland, 1882–4; chancellor, duchy of Lancaster, 1884–5; secretary for Scotland, 1886 and 1892–5. Succeeded to baronetcy, 1886; notable author; O.M. 1911; d. 1928.

era has a triumphant house of commons majority achieved so little. A fever ran in the veins of that parliament, as in those of no other through the nineteenth century. The reason was not merely the continuing economic unrest outside, nor the new phenomenon of two oppositions—an Irish as well as a conservative. It was that, besides normal and open conflict between majority and minorities, there persisted a hidden one within the majority itself, which palsied the government's counsels and zigzagged its policy. Gladstone had induced extremes to meet in attacking Beaconsfield, but not in the pursuit of any positive programme. His own method of adjustment, which was to be radical in the open and whiggish behind the scenes, allowed neither side to feel secure. Now, too, that he was past 70, mere egotism grew on him; and with it a habit of playing the mystery-man and puzzling his followers by unexpected moves.

Discredit dogged the very first meetings of the house of commons. Charles Bradlaugh,[1] well known as a lecturer and pamphleteer against Christianity, had been returned as a radical for Northampton. He claimed to make affirmation of allegiance instead of taking the parliamentary oath. The proper course for the Speaker, Sir Henry Brand,[2] was to allow him to do so, with a warning that he risked being sued for penalties in the courts. The issue turned wholly on the legal construction of certain statutes; and judges, not members of parliament, were the people to decide it. But Brand fumbled, and referred it to the house, which in turn referred it to a select committee. The committee, by a majority of one, decided against the right to affirm; and thereupon Bradlaugh came forward to swear in the ordinary way. Once again Brand fumbled; and instead of safeguarding the clear right of a duly elected member, allowed a debate to develop, which ended in the passage of an arbitrary amendment debarring Bradlaugh from oath and affirmation alike. By these repeated errors a weak Speaker brought about one of the least creditable episodes in the history of parliament. It had been Sir Henry Drummond Wolff and Lord Randolph Churchill (shortly

---

[1] B. in London 1833. Began life as errand-boy; later, enlisted; bought his discharge, 1853; became solicitor's clerk and (under name 'Iconoclast') secularist lecturer. Tried with Mrs. Annie Besant in 1876 for re-publishing a Neo-Malthusian pamphlet; sentenced to 6 months' imprisonment and £200 fine, but conviction quashed on appeal. M.P. from 1880 to 1891, when he died.

[2] 1814–92. Speaker from 1872 to 1884, when he became the first Viscount Hampden.

with A. J. Balfour and John Gorst to form a clique of four; nick-named 'the Fourth Party', but in fact a 'ginger' group inside the conservative opposition), who first saw the political possibilities lurking in the religious issue. Not only might they rally their own benches against the 'Radical atheist', but a great many non-conformist radicals and the whole Irish party (under Cardinal Manning's direct instigation) could be brought into the same lobby. Gladstone, than whom no more devout Churchman lived, pleaded finely for tolerance. But he could not command a majority. The ins and outs of the persecution are not worth tracing here; suffice it that, though Bradlaugh went thrice to his constituency and secured re-election, and though at all times he was willing to take the ordinary oath, he could not sit in parliament as of assured right till 1886.[1] His personal demeanour remained lofty and, save on one occasion, dignified. But the successive incidents, from his committal to the Clock Tower (1880) and his forcible ejection by ten policemen (1881) down to the egregious judicial decision in the Court of Appeal (1885),[2] greatly damaged the ministry by dividing its majority and exhibiting it in postures of impotence. Northcote also showed pitiably; for it was plain that he abetted the bullying by his young bloods, not because he believed in it, but because he feared the bullies.

The new government inherited two problems of empire—in South Africa and in Afghanistan. Both were on the brink of new troubles. In South Africa the Zulus had been crushed, but the annexed Boers were approaching revolt. Dutch opinion throughout South Africa was unanimous in demanding the restoration of the Transvaal republic, which Gladstone's speeches had led them to expect from him. But the cabinet decided against it, and Frere, despite radical protests at home, was not at once recalled. Still working for a federation of the four white communities (Cape Colony, Natal, the Transvaal, and the Orange Free State), he induced the Sprigg Government to propose in the Cape parliament a scheme for a federating conference. It was rejected on 25 June 1880 by the influence of the delegates (Kruger and Joubert) from the Transvaal independence committee. His

---

[1] The knot was then cut by the new Speaker, Peel, who peremptorily refused to allow any member to interfere between another member and the oath. Thereby he rendered ridiculous, not merely the spineless Brand, but the whole record of the fevered 1880–5 house.

[2] 14 Q.B.D. 667.

recall (1 August) followed; but freedom for the Transvaal did not—neither the disannexation, which Gladstone and Hartington had championed out of office, nor the self-government under the Crown, for which Frere had pressed earnestly and still did. By December the Boers' patience was exhausted. They took up arms, and British authority in their land was quickly reduced to four little garrisons, all beleaguered.

Wolseley had by now gone home, and the British forces left in Natal were commanded by Sir George Colley. He was a good officer, but neither he nor any one else had realized that the Boers, who five years earlier under the wretched Burgers régime had let a Kaffir chief defeat them, were, when properly led, the finest mounted infantry in the world. Advancing to the Transvaal border with 1,500 men, he sustained a reverse at Laing's Nek. A month later he advanced again; and on Majuba Hill his little force of 359 men was decisively defeated, and he himself killed (27 February 1881). Piet Joubert commanded with great skill the attacking Boers.

What was Gladstone to do? Go on fighting for an annexation in which he disbelieved, and risk a rebellion of the Cape Dutch? Or make peace, conceding to force what he had refused to reason, and leaving the Boers arrogant as well as injured? He took the latter course. Perhaps, could he have foreseen 1899–1902, he might have chosen otherwise; though, as we shall see later on, the war of those years had many more immediate causes—the growth of the gold-mines, the grievances of the Uitlanders, the Jameson Raid, and the diplomacy of Lord Milner—besides this, which was its most ultimate root. The Pretoria Convention of 1881 recognized the independence of the Transvaal, subject to British suzerainty, including control of its foreign relations. Three years later the London Convention of 1884 modified the terms in certain respects. Trouble was laid up for the future, because this second instrument, while it preserved the British control over treaties (save with the Orange Free State), did not repeat the word suzerainty. Meanwhile in 1883 Paul Kruger, who had headed the revolt, became (at the age of 58) president of the South African republic; to which office he was continuously re-elected while the republic lasted.

In Afghanistan the Beaconsfield Government had already by March 1880 decided to evacuate the north. Lord Lytton had dropped his partition scheme, but proposed retaining a garrison at Kandahar. His successor as viceroy, the Marquess of Ripon,[1] resolved to give up even that. A nephew of Sher Ali, Abdurrahman, was recognized as Amir, and installed at Kabul within three months. Unfortunately Kandahar was treated separately, and in July another Afghan claimant, Ayub Khan, marched against it. General Burrows set out from Kandahar to check him with about 2,500 men, and on the 27th was heavily defeated at Maiwand.[2] Besieged in Kandahar, the remains of the British southern force was in great danger, till relieved by the action of General Roberts from Kabul. Roberts's spectacular march, transporting a force of 10,000 fighting men and over 8,000 camp followers in 23 days for a distance of 313 miles without a base, invites comparisons (though on a smaller scale) with General Sherman's 'march to the sea' through Georgia in 1864.[3] The complete victory, which crowned it, restored our prestige after Maiwand without undoing our decision to evacuate; and after some ups and downs Abdurrahman acquired the whole country. No British resident was sent to Kabul. But by express agreement with the Amir Great Britain was to control his foreign relations, to guarantee him against external aggression, and to pay him a subsidy. On these terms Abdurrahman consolidated his kingdom until his death in 1901.

Ill health had largely disabled Lord Beaconsfield since his fall from office. He delivered his last notable speech in a debate on the evacuation of Kandahar. This was on 9 March 1881, and on 19 April he died. Through forty-four years he had displayed at Westminster a unique personality. Of Gladstone or Palmerston or Peel it may be said that they differed from other parliamentarians rather in size than in kind. Towering over their rank and file like the heroes in Homer, they yet were of like parts and passions with them. Lord Beaconsfield never was. His party had followed him after 1846 because, when they craved for a lead, he gave them one, and no one else could. They came to

---

[1] George Frederick Samuel Robinson, second earl and first marquis, b. 1827. Educated by private tutors only; a 'Christian Socialist' with F. D. Maurice and Kingsley; M.P. 1852; under-secretaryships, 1859 and 1861; secretary for war, 1863; for India, 1866; lord president of the council, 1868–73; became a Roman catholic, 1874; viceroy of India, 1880–4; first lord of the admiralty, 1886; colonial secretary, 1892–5; lord privy seal, 1905–8; d. 1909.

[2] Figures on Burrows's side were: total engaged, 2,476; killed, 934; missing, 175; 2 guns (R.H.A.) lost.

[3] Afghanistan being almost roadless, Roberts had to march without a single wheeled vehicle. His only artillery were three batteries of mountain-guns on mule-back.

trust him, to idolize, and even to love; but they never understood him. And he, with all his passion for England, remained deeply un-English. Idealist and cynic, prophet and tactician, genius and charlatan in one, men took him for a flaunting melodramatist until they experienced him as a deadly fighter. A radical by origin and instinct, he remade the conservative party; but though he ruled its counsels so long, it was only warily and within limits that he ever shaped them to his ideas. Disputes over his career have turned less on facts than on moral values. More than half a century after his death there is still argument about them.

The succession to his party leadership was divided between Lord Salisbury in the lords and Sir Stafford Northcote in the commons. The historic Gladstone-Disraeli duel was over. Gladstone himself remained another fourteen years in public life— far longer, it must be remembered, than any one at the time could foresee. But new men of genius rose up beside him. The eighties brought five into the foremost rank. The eldest of them, Joseph Chamberlain (born 1836), was the son of a dissenting shopkeeper; and he had made his sufficient fortune by his own exertions, not in any of the few genteel professions, where he might have rubbed shoulders with younger sons of hereditary landowners, but as a manufacturer of screws in plebeian Birmingham.[1] The rest of our quintet, however, who were in a remarkable degree born contemporaries—C. S. Parnell (1846), Lord Rosebery (1847), A. J. Balfour (1848), and Lord Randolph Churchill (1849)—were all scions of the landowning oligarchy which had ruled Great Britain and Ireland for two centuries. And subject to personal differences there was not one of them but illustrated typically the strength and weaknesses of the aristocratic temperament. Few then realized their class's impending eclipse; though the fateful decision about agriculture in 1878-9 had in truth already determined it. Almost one might style this brilliant band the last of the patricians.

The dominating issues in home politics during this government's life were Irish. The story in detail is tangled. But its main phases stand fairly distinct.

---

[1] Only two persons of similar origin had sat on a front bench before him— Bright, whom Gladstone had first coaxed into his cabinet in 1868, and W. H. Smith, whom an irresistible *bonhomie* had carried into Beaconsfield's in 1877.

At the outset in 1880 the queen's speech announced that the coercion statute passed by the conservatives would be let lapse on 1 June. Ministers hoped to govern Ireland by the ordinary law. This policy could only have succeeded if coupled with measures of instant relief; for below the surface fury of Michael Davitt's Land League (with campaign-funds now pouring in from America and Australia) the root of the agrarian trouble was, as General Gordon testified in a memorable letter, sheer misery. That of the evicted tenants brooked no delay. Yet it was not till the Irish party had introduced a bill to give them compensation, that the government, after some manœuvring, adopted the principle in a measure of its own. Its second reading in the commons was carried by 299 to 217, but about 50 liberals abstained and 20 voted against. Consequently (by 282 to 51) the lords threw it out; and the year passed leaving the sufferers without legal redress.[1] By autumn they had grown utterly desperate, and the whole fabric of Irish society was shaken. 'Captain Moonlight' ruled three provinces and much of the fourth. Ricks were burned, cattle maimed, dwelling-houses fired into after dark. Individuals woke to find graves dug before their doors; others were dragged from their beds and assaulted by masked bands. Only life was spared; and even that limit disappeared after the atrocious murder of Lord Mountmorres in County Galway.[2] On 19 September, at Ennis, Parnell urged that any one taking a farm from which a tenant had been evicted should be 'isolated from his kind as if he were a leper of old'. The first person to be thus treated was a certain Captain Boycott, the agent of a large landowner in County Mayo; and his name has added a word to the English language. An expedition to relieve him organized

---

[1] The following table (given in Barry O'Brien's *Parnell*, ch. xi) shows clearly how the deepening agricultural depression led to evictions, and how increases in them led on to increases in outrages.

Year	Persons evicted	Agrarian outrages
1877	2,177	236
1878	4,679	301
1879	6,239	863
1880	10,457	2,590

[2] His body with six revolver bullets in it was found within a mile of his house. A cottager near the spot would not allow it to be brought across his threshold for a surgeon to ascertain whether life was extinct. His coffin had to be escorted by armed police; and the drivers refused to carry it from the hearse. His murderers were never discovered.

from Ulster only served to advertise the success of the method; which soon became a universal weapon. When the government could stand it no more, a prosecution for conspiracy was launched (2 November 1880) against the Land League, with Parnell and 13 others named as defendants. The trial was protracted from 13 December to 25 January. It ended in a disagreement of the jury. For the Parnellites the result was a triumph. Bonfires blazed from the Irish hills.

The second phase was coercion. Lord Cowper, the viceroy, and W. E. Forster, the chief secretary, had both been early converted to it by Dublin Castle. Its opponents in the cabinet were Gladstone, Chamberlain, and Bright; but they had to give way. Forster introduced his Coercion Bill on 24 January, and an orgy of obstruction followed. From 31 January to 2 February the house sat forty-one continuous hours; until Speaker Brand, on his own authority, took the division on the first reading. Next day Gladstone moved a closure resolution, and it was carried after tense scenes, during which most of the Irish members were suspended. Its terms mark a modest stage in the tightening of parliamentary procedure; as amended, it laid down that, if a motion declaring the business urgent were supported by forty members rising in their places, it should be put without debate, and, if carried by not less than three to one in a house of not less than 300, should give the Speaker a free hand to regulate the business for the time being. Even with this aid the bill did not become law till 2 March. Its main feature was a suspension of the *Habeas Corpus* Act; it conferred on the Irish executive an absolute power of arbitrary and preventive arrest.

But it was not in Gladstone's statecraft to pursue coercion alone. He must couple redress with it. On 7 April 1881 he brought in his second great measure of Irish land reform. Its completeness astonished Irish and English members alike. Following the report of a commission presided over by Lord Bessborough, it gave the tenants the 'three F's' (Fixity of tenure, Fair rents, Free sale), for which they had been agitating since Butt's day, and against which Northcote had unwisely committed himself the previous autumn. Its chief flaw was its occasion; as too often in England's dealings with Ireland, the administration conceded to violence and crime what it had denied to reason and justice. This fact governed the tactics of Parnell; who never disarmed for an instant, and even persuaded three-fifths of his followers to abstain from supporting the bill on second reading. He did indeed take care to save it from being weakened in committee; but two days after it was through the commons he deliberately provoked a scene there, got himself expelled, and went on to deter the tenants from dropping their agitation and rushing into the act's new land courts. His course was shrewd in every aspect; it won better eventual terms from the courts; and it preserved for him the support of the Irish-American extremists. But how, then, while coercion lasted, could he be left free? At Leeds on 7 October Gladstone declared that 'the resources of civilization were not exhausted'; and six days later the Irish leader was imprisoned in Kilmainham Jail. He had wanted this for private as well as public reasons; having already formed with the wife of Captain O'Shea, an Irish Liberal M.P., the liaison whose disclosure in 1890 ruined him.[1] He was in custody for nearly six months, till April 1882, under rather lax conditions which permitted him not a little communication with the outer world.

Forster's coercion ran on for that period, lasting thus for about a year in all. It was a total failure. True, a No Rent movement, which the Land League launched in answer to Parnell's arrest, came to nothing because the priests opposed it. True, the League, too, was, in form, suppressed. But if we compare the ten months following Forster's act with the ten preceding it, we find that the number of agrarian outrages, instead of declining, had risen by 60 per cent., while the number of homicides and cases of firing at the person had trebled. So matters moved to the third phase— the so-called Kilmainham Treaty. On 10 April Parnell was permitted leave from prison to visit a married sister, whose son was dying in Paris. At Eltham his own daughter, born in February, was also dying; and he went there both on his way to Paris and on his way back. He thus saw O'Shea, through whom communications were opened up by Chamberlain and Gladstone. Both sides wanted a settlement, and there was but one hard obstacle. Some 100,000 Irish tenants owed large arrears of rent. Till these were paid they could not take advantage of the Land Act, but all remained liable to be evicted. Parnell

---

[1] Mrs. O'Shea was expecting a child, who was Parnell's; and he was anxious to be out of the way during her confinement, lest it should precipitate a public disclosure. Prison achieved this, besides conferring the halo of martyrdom. The child was born on 16 February 1882. See Appendix B.

insisted on a bill to wipe the arrears off with a contribution of money from some public source. Chamberlain had already seen the need for this, and to him is due the main credit for meeting it. A secret informal bargain was struck that the government should bring in a satisfactory Arrears Bill, while Parnell should use his influence to end crime and disorder. Co-operation was to replace coercion. Parnell, Dillon, and O'Kelly, the three Irish members in Kilmainham, were released (2 May 1882), as was Davitt from Dartmoor four days later. Lord Cowper, the viceroy, and Forster, the chief secretary, resigned. Their places were taken by Lord Spencer[1] and Lord Frederick Cavendish. The choice of the latter (a younger brother of Lord Hartington, who had married a niece of Mrs. Gladstone) illustrated the premier's preference for whigs. The natural man to have sent was Chamberlain, whose practical genius had procured the treaty.

It was indeed a fair prospect, but tragedy almost immediately overcast it. On 6 May Lord Spencer arrived in Dublin. After the pageant of his entry Lord Frederick Cavendish was walking in the Phoenix Park with Mr. Burke, the under-secretary, when a band of men surprised the pair within sight and hearing of the Viceregal Lodge, and hacked them to death with long surgical knives. The assassins, who for nearly the rest of 1882 baffled detection, belonged to the 'Invincibles'—a small murder club, of which Dublin Castle, arresting suspects right and left, had remained in ignorance. Their object was to kill Burke; Cavendish only suffered because he was in Burke's company. But it was the death of this newly arrived, innocent, and very amiable chief secretary, which made the act appear one of peculiar horror, even to Fenians. Parnell's iron composure was, for once, shaken.[2]

[1] John Poyntz Spencer, fifth earl (1835–1910), had the unique experience of being Gladstone's colleague in all his four cabinets. In 1868–74, and again in 1882–5, he was Irish viceroy; in 1880–2, and again in 1886, lord president of the council; in 1892–5, first lord of the admiralty. Descended from the great earl of Sunderland and the great duke of Marlborough, he was one of the few whig aristocrats who did not desert Gladstone over home rule in 1886. Educated at Harrow and Trinity College, Cambridge. Thrice M.F.H. of the Pytchley. Sobriquet (from the colour of his beard): 'The Red Earl'.

[2] Dilke wrote: 'Early on Sunday morning the 7th, Parnell came to see me with Justin McCarthy. He was white and apparently terror-stricken. He thought the blow was aimed at him and that, if people kept their heads and the new policy prevailed, he himself would be the next victim of the secret societies' (Gwynn and Tuckwell, *Life of Sir Charles W. Dilke*, i. 441). At Westminster Parnell habitually carried a revolver in his overcoat. (Sir Alfred Pease, *Elections and Recollections*, p. 279; Lord Desborough confirmed this to me of his own knowledge.)

He felt, as he told Davitt, that he had himself been stabbed in the back. With Dillon and Davitt he signed a condemnatory manifesto.

Both on his side and on Gladstone's a real attempt was made to save the Kilmainham alliance. The premier sent as Cavendish's successor Trevelyan, an undoubted radical. But a new and stiffer Crimes Bill was inevitable; and, as inevitably, the Parnellites had to oppose it. An Arrears Act was passed, but in a form not generous enough for most of the tenants to be able to use. Moreover the Invincibles were still unknown, and ghastly murders by their organization and others went on increasingly. On 17 August occurred the most horrible, perhaps, of all Irish agrarian crimes, the massacre at Maamtrasna; where an entire household—father, mother, three sons, and a daughter—were stabbed and battered as they slept and left for dead, only one (a little boy) surviving his wounds.[1] The year established a record of 26 murders and 58 attempted murders; but just before it closed, a feature of the new Coercion Act—power to magistrates to hold secret inquiries and examine witnesses on oath, before anybody was definitely charged—bore its fruit in the arrest of the Invincibles. Two of them turned queen's evidence, the most important, James Carey, being a councillor of the Dublin Corporation; and in the following April they were brought to trial. The story of Phoenix Park was completely exposed; five of those concerned in it were hanged, and three sent to penal servitude for life; while Carey, whom it was sought to smuggle away to Natal, was shot dead by an avenger on shipboard before arriving there. As 1883 went on, Irish affairs grew quieter. Parnell was at the height of his influence, and in December received a presentation of £38,000 collected for him all over the world. But alike for personal and political reasons he wanted a temporary appeasement; and, though his colleagues chafed and murmured, the working of the 1881 Land Act helped

---

[1] The ten men concerned in this butchery were seen by watchers, and all subsequently arrested. Two turned queen's evidence, eight were sentenced to death, but only the three who had entered the victims' cabin were actually hanged. Light is thrown on the psychology of parties by the fact that not merely did the Parnellites plead repeatedly for the prisoners, but in July 1885 Lord Randolph Churchill and even Sir Michael Hicks Beach took sides with them as against Lord Spencer. Lord Carnarvon, however, on going into the matter found it quite impossible to do other than Lord Spencer had done. For the dreadful incident at the execution, which so affected Irish feeling, see the account by Mr. F. J. Higginbottom (*The Vivid Life* (1934), pp. 40–3), one of the few eyewitnesses.

him to obtain it. It lasted more or less till the end of this Parliament, despite a series of dynamite outrages in London, which kept England from forgetting that the Irish movement was revolutionary.

We turn now to the government's chief innovation in foreign policy—the British occupation of Egypt.

Following the purchase of the Suez Canal shares in 1875, British interest in Egypt grew. That same month an expert, Stephen Cave, was sent to report on its finances. In April 1876 the extravagant Khedive Ismail suspended payment of his debts, and in May under pressure from France instituted the *Caisse de la Dette publique*. Four Powers (France, Great Britain, Italy, and Austria-Hungary) were invited to nominate commissioners. Lord Derby, however, shrank from nominating one; and it was not till after an Anglo-French Mission (Goschen[1] and Joubert) had visited Egypt, and a Dual Control (with a Frenchman and an Englishman as controllers-general) had been set up, and the *Caisse* had been broadened into a Commission, that early in 1878 two British representatives, Sir C. Rivers Wilson and Major Evelyn Baring,[2] took up their positions in Cairo. Thus began a Franco-British *Condominium*. At first a number of reforms were made, but Ismail soon reacted recklessly against them; and in June 1878 the Powers induced the Sultan to depose him in favour of his son Tewfik. In all this the initiatives came from France, whose government strongly supported the bondholders of the Egyptian debt. Lords Derby, Beaconsfield, and Salisbury were each in turn reluctant to act; and though Baring, less for the bondholders than for good government and peace, was insistent that they should, he had little backing until, in 1880, he left Egypt. In July of that year, after the change of government in England, Egypt made a sort of composition with her creditors.

Already in 1879 there had been a mutiny of the Egyptian army

[1] See note on p. 8, *ante*.

[2] B. 1841 at Cromer Hall, Norfolk; educated at the Ordnance School, Carshalton, and the R.M.A., Woolwich; entered the Royal Artillery, 1858. In India 1872–6 as secretary to his cousin Lord Northbrook, then viceroy; in Egypt 1878–80 controlling finance; in India 1880–3 as financial member of the viceroy's (Lord Ripon's) council; in Egypt 1883–1907 as British consul-general and virtual ruler of the country. Created Baron Cromer, 1892; viscount, 1899; earl, 1901. First cousin to Sir Edward Grey (foreign secretary, 1905–16); d. 1917.

officers to obtain arrears of pay. It was quelled, and the arrears paid up; but discontent remained. The severe retrenchments, which the new European officials demanded in both military and civil establishments, were contrasted bitterly with the high salaries which they themselves drew; and in this way the unrest became anti-foreign. Early in 1881 Colonel Arabi Pasha appeared as leader of a fresh officer-protest, which compelled Tewfik to dismiss his war minister. Arabi, who was a native Egyptian, not a Turk, roused the feelings of his countrymen, not merely against Europeans, but against the official clique of Turks, Circassians, and other Levantines, who were about the Khedive. On 10 September he struck again; surrounded the Khedive's palace; and in the name of the army demanded the dismissal of all the ministers, the convocation of the notables, the establishment of a constitution, and the increase of the army from 4,000 men to 18,000. The khedive was left helpless; he had to accept; and with that the Franco-British *condominium* was critically shaken. The two Powers were united in guarding against an intrusion by Turkey, but in little else. Gambetta, who became French prime minister in November, tried to promote a policy of joint intervention. Granville received his advances coldly. The Gladstone cabinet was divided between its reluctance to intervene and its unwillingness to see another Power intervene without it. With much reason it felt that a joint Anglo-French occupation would be unworkable, and preferred the idea (which France opposed) of employing a Turkish army as the common instrument. On 8 January 1882, at Gambetta's instance, the two Powers declared to Tewfik in a Joint Note that his maintenance on the throne was considered by them indispensable to the welfare of Egypt. The Note only exasperated the Egyptian nationalists; knowing how France, but a few months before, had forcibly transferred Tunis and its Bey from the Ottoman empire to her own, they suspected her of scheming to do the same here. It also gave umbrage to the four other Great Powers; who in a Memorandum to Turkey declared against individual action by France and Great Britain. But on 26 January the Gambetta ministry resigned, after a defeat in the French Chamber on a home issue; and as an immediate result Arabi Pasha carried out (31 January) at Cairo a sort of *coup d'état*, dismissing the prime minister, imposing a new constitution, and making himself minister of war. No intervention followed. M. de Freycinet, who had succeeded Gambetta, represented the view (which was also Clemenceau's) that France must avoid risks outside Europe, in order to meet those within it.[1] Besides, both in England and France there were liberal sympathies with Arabi as an emancipator of his people. Months of criss-cross negotiation followed, in which all the Powers took some part; and the idea of a mandate to Turkey might have gone through, had not the Sultan himself shuffled. Meanwhile Arabi's supporters grew out of hand. In May British and French fleets were sent to Alexandria as a precaution against disorder. On 11 June nationalist riots broke out in the city under their eyes; the victims included fifty Europeans dead and over sixty wounded, the British consul among them. Order was restored by troops of the Khedive; but Arabi remained dominant. His soldiers began feverishly fortifying Alexandria. Admiral Seymour pointed out that the new batteries threatened the fleets, and on 3 July received authority, if the operation were persisted in, to silence the guns and destroy the earthworks. On 11 July things came to a head; the French Admiral Conrad, under orders from Paris, steamed away with his ships; and the English fleet single-handed silenced the forts after a 10½ hours' bombardment. Nine days later the Gladstone cabinet decided to send an army under Sir Garnet Wolseley. France was invited to join, but the Freycinet cabinet would not go beyond defending the Canal. Even that was too much for the French chamber; which on 29 July overthrew the government.

England therefore went forward alone; and Wolseley, by a victory based on that rarest of military feats, a long and completely successful night-march, destroyed the whole power of Arabi at Tel-el-Kebir (13 September 1882). There never was a tidier operation. The British casualties were under 450. A cavalry dash on Cairo succeeded the rout and obtained the surrender of the remaining enemy forces. The fruit of Cardwell's reforms was seen in the promptitude which had collected 16,400 British troops and shipped them with all needful supplies over a sea-distance about equal to the crossing of the Atlantic. This was unparalleled in our military annals, and it backed our diplomacy with a new prestige which lasted till 1899. Where

[1] As Paul Deschanel puts it (*Gambetta*, p. 321 of the English version): 'The whole period of French history that we are studying is dominated by the German terror. ... The disaster of 1882 in the Mediterranean was the direct outcome of our defeats in 1870 on the Continent.'

France, the second continental Power, had shivered on the brink and abandoned the fruits of a seventy-year effort, Great Britain had jumped in and finished her affair in two months.

Yet the end proved only a beginning. Bright, who was a quaker, had resigned from the cabinet on the bombardment of Alexandria. The rest had felt constrained to intervention on account of the Suez Canal; but they hoped we should withdraw again almost at once. Their spokesmen kept saying so. But gradually it was found impossible. Egypt after the collapses of Ismail and Arabi was a house whose roof and walls had fallen in. For the sake, not only of the bondholders, but of many other interests, Europe was bound to insist on its rebuilding. But because of the Canal we could not afford to let another Power come in and do the work. It is a pity that Gladstone and his colleagues were so slow to face this. Following Tel-el-Kebir the world was quite ready for them to declare either annexation or a protectorate; and had they taken the latter course and straightened out the tangle of khedivial obligations to other Powers, it would have saved us many difficulties and dangers later, not only in Egypt, but on the larger chessboard of diplomacy. However, in September 1883 they made an historic appointment. Major Evelyn Baring had been in India since 1880 as finance member of the viceroy's council. He was recalled, knighted, and sent to Egypt as British agent and consul-general. He held the post for over twenty-three years.

Before he reached Cairo a decision had been taken there whose consequences proved a boomerang for the Gladstone cabinet. Two years earlier a native of Dongola, with a varied record as a slave-trader and an Egyptian official, had proclaimed himself a Mahdi, or Messiah, and raised a revolt in Kordofan. Misgovernment throughout the vast areas known as the Egyptian Sudan had since 1880 been so atrocious, that his movement spread like wildfire. For an insolvent and disorganized Egypt the only sane policy was to give way, retaining at furthest Khartoum and the province of Sennaar. But the khedive's ministers wanted more; and encouraged by trivial successes they sent an army under an English officer, Hicks Pasha, to attack the Mahdi in his own country. The British cabinet ought to have vetoed the step, but preferred the Gladstone-Granville attitude of washing its hands. This, as soon appeared, was a fatal mistake. Hicks Pasha and his Egyptians were cut to pieces by the Mahdists

(5 November 1883), and London was confronted with a much aggravated problem.

It was now wisely decided to evacuate the whole Sudan south of Wady Halfa. But a great difficulty arose about the many and scattered Egyptian garrisons. On the Red Sea side, to which the rising had extended, an Egyptian force under a British officer was holding Suakim, and could easily be succoured (as it soon had to be) by British and Indian sea-borne troops. But what of all the inland garrisons whose centre was Khartoum? After much debate between London and Cairo it was decided to dispatch to the Sudan General Charles Gordon.[1] He left London on 18 January 1884, destined originally for Suakim, but diverted at Cairo to Khartoum. Baring's assent had been reluctant; he feared sending an Englishman, lest a British army might be needed to extricate him; and he feared sending Gordon, lest his fanatical courage should lead him too far. Events proved these qualms only too well founded. The plan's chief sponsors inside the government were Hartington, Granville, Northbrook, and Dilke.

Gordon went to Khartoum as governor-general with secret instructions to evacuate, which he made the serious mistake of divulging at Berber on his way up the Nile. But on his arrival in February he formulated another plan; it was to commission Zobeir Pasha as governor-general of the Sudan to hold Khartoum and the Nile valley against the Mahdi. Zobeir was a former slave-trader; Gordon had fought against him and killed his son; but he respected his strong qualities, and wished to use them. What stood in the way was English public sentiment. The cabinet overcame their own distaste for employing a poacher as gamekeeper; but they felt they could not overcome that of the house of commons.[2] Late in March the plan was finally nega-

[1] Charles George Gordon (1833–85) entered the Royal Engineers, 1852; served before Sebastopol, 1855; took part in British capture of Peking, 1860; served under the Chinese government, 1863–5, and suppressed the Tai-Ping rebellion, winning thirty-three battles; served in the Sudan, 1873–6 and 1877–80, suppressing the slave-trade and establishing order over vast areas. He was perhaps the finest specimen of the heroic Victorian type—a Bible-taught Evangelical, fearless, tireless, incorruptible; following the call of duty through fields of desperate adventure. Greatly interested in social questions, he spent much of his spare time during home appointments on 'ragged schools' and other personal work for poor boys. For an exhaustive refutation of the charge of intemperance, light-heartedly revived against him by the late Mr. Lytton Strachey (*Eminent Victorians* (1918), p. 234), see Dr. B. M. Allen's *Gordon and the Sudan* (1931), at pp. 82–101.

[2] Partly because the prime minister was laid up with a throat affection and could

tived. Thenceforth all was drift. In May Berber fell to the Mahdists, and Gordon in Khartoum was cut off. How was he to be extricated? Already Baring (26 March) and Wolseley (8 April) had separately urged the government to make immediate preparations for a military expedition. But Gladstone's one-track mind was immersed in his Reform Bill, and the cabinet inexcusably delayed decision till August. For this Baring afterwards[1] laid the chief blame on the premier; but Harcourt, Granville, and Northbrook must certainly share it. The ministers who most faced the need were Hartington and Selborne.[2]

Four months too late Wolseley was appointed to command an expedition, for which scarcely any preparation had been made. He reached Cairo early in September, and was not able to start from Wady Halfa until 5 October. For three months a most gallant army marched and fought its way against time up the uncharted Nile, while all England counted its daily steps. The river in the 850 miles of its course between Wady Halfa and Khartoum describes two large curves in the form of an S; to cut across the second of these a picked force under Sir Herbert Stewart traversed 150 miles of the Bayuda desert, winning a desperate victory at Abu Klea. Two days later, when close to the river, its general was mortally wounded—a fatal mishap, for his successor was an officer of far less experience and resolution. On the morning of 21 January the force made contact with Gordon's four steamboats sent down from Khartoum. Had they gone upstream with reinforcements that same afternoon they would have

not speak. But they underrated the asset of Gordon's own immense popularity. Lord Morley comments justly on the whole episode: 'To run all the risks involved in the dispatch of Gordon, and then immediately to refuse the request that he persistently represented as furnishing him his only chance, was an incoherence that the Parliament and people of England have not often surpassed' (*Life of Gladstone*, bk. viii, ch. ix, § 5).

[1] Lord Cromer, *Modern Egypt* (1908), ii. 17.

[2] The Gladstone Papers at the British Museum show that in July 1884 a remarkable series of written pleadings on the subject was circulated to the cabinet. They are: (1) a Cabinet Minute by Harcourt against sending a relief expedition, dated the 24th; (2) a Memorandum by Lord Selborne in favour of sending one, dated the 29th; (3) a rejoinder from Gladstone himself against sending, dated the 30th. Harcourt, arguing with obvious animus, based himself mainly on statements by Gordon's brother, Sir H. Gordon, which were well calculated to irritate the cabinet's more pacific section. Selborne took what on the whole must be pronounced an accurate and even prophetic view of the facts and the issue. Gladstone's rejoinder has nearly every merit except realism. It is most cogent and persuasive writing. But we can see now that he misread the evidence and quite misconceived both what was happening at Khartoum and what was likely to happen.

reached the besieged town on the 25th at latest. But the start
was inexcusably delayed for three days; they did not arrive till
the 28th; and the place had been stormed and Gordon killed on
the 26th. It was only by prodigies of ingenious resource that he
had defended it so long.[1]

No single event in Gladstone's career made him more unpopular. Queen Victoria, sharing (as so often) the feelings of
'the man in the street', sent him an angry telegram *en clair*. Much
now is known that was then obscure; and in the light of it the
verdict appears not unjust. Gordon's own conduct contributed
to the disaster—in particular, his unwillingness to leave outlying
garrisons to their fate. But the prime cause was the cabinet's
inconsequence and neglect of facts. A vote of censure in the
commons was only defeated by fourteen votes. On the military
side, however, though the Nile expedition missed its aim, its
conduct was such as to enhance still further our already very high
prestige.

It was decided to retain Suakim in any case, partly as a check
on slave-trading across the Red Sea. But should Wolseley go on
and reconquer Khartoum, or should we withdraw behind the
Wady Halfa frontier? Events in another quarter suddenly enforced the wisdom of the second course. On 30 March 1885 a
Russian force attacked and defeated an Afghan force at Penjdeh,
the centre of a fertile district on the Afghan-Turcoman frontier,
which Russia wished to earmark in advance of the proceedings
of a Boundary Commission. It was a sharp reminder of the threat
to North-west India, and for some weeks Great Britain and Russia seemed on the verge of war. But on this occasion the diplomacy of Gladstone and Granville showed better than on any
other. They happily balanced firmness with conciliation. The
Sudan commitment was promptly liquidated; and a Vote of
Credit for £11 millions (on 27 April) taught Russia that we were
not to be trifled with. But our proposals were moderate and
mediatory; Lord Dufferin, as viceroy, handled the Amir with
much tact; and early in May the tension relaxed. A mooted
compromise, whereby Russia should have Penjdeh while the important Zufilkar Pass, which she also coveted, should go to
Afghanistan, was fiercely criticized by the conservatives; who
even divided the house against the government. By one of the

[1] For the most mature modern study of this famous tragedy, see Dr. B. M. Allen's
Gordon and the Sudan.

ironies of politics they were in office a few months later, and it was by Lord R. Churchill and Lord Salisbury that this compromise, a good one in all the circumstances, was eventually (10 September) carried through. The episode revealed the wisdom of Gladstone's withdrawal from Afghanistan in 1880, which had enabled Afghan Nationalism to show a united front against Russian aggression.

In reviewing these foreign episodes it is necessary to glance back at the orientations of the Great Powers. Since 1871 Germany under Bismarck had been the leading Power, and Bismarck's chief preoccupation had been fear of France. In 1872 he had formed the *Dreikaiserbund*—an *entente* between the German, Russian, and Austrian Emperors. In 1875 the German general staff had pressed for a preventive war to crush France's revival; the idea was nipped in the bud by Tsar Alexander II, with some support from Queen Victoria; but the *Dreikaiserbund* survived this difference. It did not, however, survive the Congress of Berlin in 1878; when the Balkan rivalries of Russia and Austria-Hungary placed Bismarck in a dilemma, and the adroit pressure of Beaconsfield so sharpened it that the German chancellor was compelled to come on the Austrian side and deeply mortified St. Petersburg. There followed in 1879 an alliance between Germany and Austria-Hungary. Meanwhile with the idea of dividing Great Britain from France Bismarck had made repeated suggestions to us to appropriate Egypt; and to effect a similar division between France and Italy he urged France to take Tunis. The latter project rather suited Great Britain, which preferred not to see both shores of the Mediterranean's waspwaist held by a single Power; and at Berlin in 1878 Beaconsfield and Salisbury had urged it on the French delegate, Waddington. It was carried out in 1881, and our own occupation of Egypt in 1882, and both the cleavages which Bismarck desired resulted. That between England and France over Egypt lasted twenty years, and that between France and Italy over Tunis cannot yet be deemed extinct after more than half a century. From both Germany derived far-reaching gains. Italy was driven almost immediately to join her and Austria-Hungary in what thenceforth became the Triple Alliance (20 May 1882). Great Britain's subjection was more subtle. The Gladstone cabinet had followed events without understanding them. They had never wanted to occupy Egypt; and there is nothing to show that they ever measured up what estrangement from France would involve for the occupants of an Egypt which was allowed to remain legally in pawn and in bondage to the Powers at large. They not only missed the opportunity of altering the country's status after Tel-el-Kebir; but in 1884, when an Egyptian loan was in the offing and Baring pressed them to guarantee it, they refused. The consequence was that the 1885 loan of £9 millions was guaranteed by all the European Powers, and all six of them obtained seats on the commission of the debt. Now the commission's powers were such that Egypt could not in the long run be governed without its consent; and as the French and Russian commissioners habitually opposed us, it meant that we could not get on without keeping the Powers of the Triple Alliance—*in primis* Germany—on our side. When Lord Rosebery became foreign secretary in February 1886, Baring put the position to him in plain words.

'The point', he wrote, 'which I venture to press earnestly on your attention is the necessity of working well with Germany. Berlin and not Cairo is the real centre of gravity of Egyptian affairs. If we drift again into the same position in which we were a year ago—that is to say, into a position in which every Power except Italy is unkindly— no efforts to put matters right locally will avail; if, on the other hand, we are well with Bismarck, we have a chance of gradually solving our difficulties here.'[1]

Such was the hidden bondage into which Gladstone's policy delivered us. That it did not detract even more than was the case from our 'splendid isolation' in the period before 1899, may be ascribed partly to Lord Salisbury's diplomatic gifts, partly to the unique position of our navy, and not a little to the reputation which Cardwell's reforms and Wolseley's genius had won for our army as an overseas striking force.

Gladstone's record in foreign affairs has been the subject of much controversy. Many revere him as the great champion of right in international dealings; many others accuse him of sheer incompetence. There is truth behind both views. The watchword of his party was 'Peace, retrenchment, and reform'; and his own twin passions in politics were for justice and for sound finance.

[1] Letter dated 9 February 1886 (quoted in Lord Zetland's *Lord Cromer* at p. 128). The reference to 'a year ago' is to a period when Bismarck, in his early aspirations after colonies, had found Gladstone unaccommodating and had applied the screw. See also Viscount Grey, *Twenty-Five Years*, i. 7–11, for a striking description of the same situation six years later.

He was a peace-lover, and he disliked on principle any kind of 'forward' policy, partly because it might be unjust, partly because it was likely to increase expenditure. In the harsh Bismarckian age he stood for the humaner liberalism of the mid-nineteenth century; and the value of that attitude can be appreciated to-day, when we see to what Bismarckianism led. But unlike Disraeli, he never really studied or understood the subtler realities of foreign affairs and the relationships of the Powers. Lord Cromer, who had intimate experience, and down to 1884 had been a liberal with radical leanings, pronounced him 'wholly ignorant' in this domain.[1] His supporters blamed him for occupying Egypt in 1882; his adversaries, for abandoning Gordon in 1884. Yet the first course was inevitable, and the second, though distressing, left no permanent mark on the world. His real fault was that when he went into Egypt he went half-heartedly and without forethought; and consequently did so on the wrong terms. Their mischief was only overcome in Egypt itself by Cromer's extraordinary talent; but outside they prevented Great Britain right down to 1914 from ever exerting a free and completely detached influence on the groupings of the other Powers. This was a real factor in the eventual Armageddon.

We resume now the course of home affairs. Down to the beginnings of 1884 the English radicals who returned Gladstone to power four years earlier had got very little for their votes. Ireland so constantly 'blocked the way', that in the first three sessions no large controversial government measure affecting England was attempted. The year 1880 saw the passage of a Burials Act, which laid to rest a long-standing nonconformist grievance; and of the Ground Game Act, which similarly remedied an old complaint of tenant farmers. Chamberlain at the board of trade took up Plimsoll's work for sailors, and cleverly got through a Seamen's Wages Act and a Grain Cargoes Act. In 1881 flogging was finally abolished in both the army and the navy. 1882 brought two acts of far-reaching social importance. One, the Married Women's Property Act (following but greatly extending an act of 1870), granted to married women for the first time in England rights of separate ownership over every kind of property, assimilating them in this respect to the unmarried. The other, the Settled Land Act, broke down the bars on land transfer, which a dozen

[1] Lord Zetland, *Lord Cromer* (1932), p. 121.

generations of conveyancers had contrived for the protection of the great hereditary estates, and enabled settled land to be freely sold or let on long building lease, subject only to the capital sums thus realized being paid over to trustees of the settlement. These acts were not party measures; the lord chancellor, Selborne, carried the first, and his conservative predecessor, Earl Cairns, the second; but both, in fact, illustrated and promoted the passing of the English governing class from a landowning to a commercial basis. In the same year Chamberlain sponsored the first Electric Lighting Act—unhappily on lines which later proved mischievous. In 1883, with better inspiration, he passed two very big commercial measures—the Bankruptcy Act and the Patents Act; and Sir Henry James, the attorney-general, carried the first reasonably effective Corrupt Practices Act to prevent abuses at elections. The greater output this year perhaps came about because the house of commons for the first time tried delegating work to 'Grand' or 'Standing' Committees.

But by now the disappointed radicals could endure being baulked no longer. They had found in Chamberlain a spokesman of shattering force. The speeches which he then delivered electrified England with a demagogic and class-war note never heard before from a minister of the Crown. Here, for instance, is his famous retort (30 March 1883) to an attack by one of the conservative leaders:

'Lord Salisbury constitutes himself the spokesman of a class—of the class to which he himself belongs, who *toil not neither do they spin*; whose fortunes—as in his case—have originated by grants made in times gone by for the services which courtiers rendered kings, and have since grown and increased, while they have slept, by levying an increased share on all that other men have done by toil and labour to add to the general wealth and prosperity of the country.'

Terrible words, unlocking pent forces never hitherto in England made so articulate. By autumn he had forced the cabinet to find time and courage for a first-class controversial measure—franchise reform. Since 1867 there had been different electorates in the borough and in the county constituencies. In the former, householders had a vote as such; in the latter, they had not. Thus the towns were democratic, but the English countryside remained under the territorial oligarchy—an electoral difference which corresponded (save in mining areas) to a difference in the structure of social life. In the seventies an agitation for democratizing the county franchise had been pioneered by Trevelyan, who annually moved a motion about it. In 1877 Hartington, representing the whigs, had, as we saw in our last chapter, accepted the principle. But now, when it came to details, there were some to which he strongly demurred; and it was only after a severe struggle that Chamberlain overcame his resistance in the cabinet. Early in 1884 the bill passed the commons easily, Goschen alone opposing it from the whig angle. But in the lords the conservatives were very hostile; Lord Salisbury was an extremist on the question; and as they durst not kill the bill directly, they held it up with a demand that a Redistribution Bill should be passed first, reckoning that in the storm of local jealousies raised by the latter both bills would founder.[1] Gladstone denied the right of the second chamber to force a dissolution on this issue, and called an autumn session to resubmit the bill. Meanwhile a fierce popular agitation stirred the country; the phrases 'the Peers against the People' and 'Mend them or end them' (coined by Chamberlain and Morley respectively) now first became battle-cries; and the veteran Bright propounded a scheme, not so unlike that enacted twenty-seven years later, whereby the lords were to have a suspensory instead of an absolute veto. But there were many in high places who dreaded extremes—not least the queen and the prime minister; and eventually by a direct negotiation between Gladstone and Salisbury the Franchise Bill and a scheme of redistribution were passed as agreed measures. The United Kingdom electorate was raised from about 3 millions to about 5 millions. Seventy-nine towns of less than 15,000 population ceased to be seats; 36 of less than 50,000 lost one of their two members. The universities and the boroughs between 50,000 and 165,000 alone remained two-member constituencies; the rest of the country, rural and urban, was artificially chopped up into single-member divisions; and the historic *communitates* (counties and boroughs) ceased to be, as such, the basis of the house of commons. The individual for the first time became the unit, and numerical equality ('one vote, one value') the master principle.

Two features of this legislation call for comment. First, it extended the franchise to Ireland on the same terms as England,

---

[1] These tactics were not extemporized; they had been foreseen and recommended by Lord Beaconsfield himself on the morrow of the 1880 election (Earl (A. J.) Balfour, *Chapters of Autobiography* (1930), p. 126).

while maintaining the full number of Irish seats. Secondly, it abolished the plural-member[1] system under which the house of commons had been predominantly elected, substituting single-member constituencies. The first meant that all over Ireland, outside the north-east corner, liberals and tories would be swept away, and Parnell would reign supreme over a parliamentary contingent much larger than a population basis warranted. The second put a stop to the liberal party's convenient device of running whigs and radicals in double harness, one of each per contest. This really spelled the end of the whigs. Neither feature was designed to effect what it actually did. The first (against which Hartington had striven) was pressed by Chamberlain and the radicals on grounds of abstract principle; Parnell, grimly aware of what it would mean in practice, sat very tight, doing what occasions required of him, no more. The second was urged by Hicks Beach on the disinterested ground that, unless two-member counties were divided, their new electorates would be unwieldy.

Whatever stimulus the franchise victory brought to the flagging fortunes of the government was soon dissipated by the news of the tragedy at Khartoum. Thenceforward it was doomed. Apart from the Penjdeh affair and the Sudan evacuation, the only important political episode before its fall was an attempt of Chamberlain, supported by Gladstone, to promote for Ireland a scheme of devolution involving county boards and a national council. At one stage he thought to obtain the assent of Parnell through O'Shea; though that unreliable intermediary only ended by sowing mutual distrust in the two men. Later, Cardinal Manning secured for him the support of the Irish hierarchy. But the scheme, opposed by the viceroy, Lord Spencer, failed to pass the cabinet, all the commoners except Hartington being in its favour and all the peers save Granville against. The cleavage which had paralysed the Administration for so much of its five years was complete. A tender of Chamberlain's resignation was followed by Dilke's, and the government was for some weeks on the verge of breaking up, when it was defeated in the house. Parnell had been approached from another side. Lord

[1] In addition to the prevailing two-member constituencies there had been created in 1867 a certain number with three, in which each elector had only two votes; the object being to give the third seat to the minority, where any large minority existed. But these also were now swept away.

Randolph Churchill, now by far the most active and aggressive force in the conservative party, had publicly angled for his support on terms of discontinuing coercion; and this offer had been confirmed in a secret official undertaking given to Justin McCarthy, Parnell's first lieutenant.[1] Consequently on 8 June 1885, when Hicks Beach moved an amendment to the budget, the Irish vote enabled it to be carried by 264 to 252. As many as 76 liberals did not vote. Gladstone resigned the next day.

The situation was very like that of March 1873, when Disraeli warily refused office and Gladstone had to go on again. But Lord Salisbury was less wary; and after exacting a pledge of tolerance from his opponent pending the general election, he formed a minority government (24 June 1885), which lasted almost exactly seven months. Perhaps the most notable thing about this ministry was the choice of its head. At that date it was inevitable; for the conservative leadership in the house of commons was practically in dispute between Sir Stafford Northcote and Lord Randolph Churchill. The latter, who had risen like a meteor in the lifetime of the parliament, filled the part of a conservative Chamberlain. As the radical leader fought the whigs, so the tory democrat had fought his party's 'old gang'; and as Chamberlain had riveted his power by forming the National Liberal Federation, so Lord Randolph centred his on the National Union of Conservative Associations—a 'caucus' directly copying the liberal one. In 1884 he had brought off against his official leaders a bold and precarious stroke, resigning from the chair of the National Union and being triumphantly re-elected. At present he was just too young, and his already unrivalled popularity too recent, for him to take office as the party leader; but conceivably he might have done so had Gladstone lasted his full term. In that case conservatism would have resumed Disraeli's tradition; for Churchill was a democrat and a social reformer. Salisbury was neither; a very great foreign minister, he represented in home affairs the merely anti-progressive section of his party. At a period when swiftly changing conditions called for legislative action, he stood nearly always on the side of doing nothing. Nor was his new post congenial; 'he complained', said Lord Carnarvon in November 1885, 'of his office of Prime Minister, which he detested, though he liked the

[1] See McCarthy's detailed account in his speech at Hull, 15 December 1887.

Foreign Office'.[1] Yet his elevation in this interim fashion had long results. It made him premier for over 13½ out of the next 17 years.

The cabinet was composed mainly of ex-ministers. Its chief new-comer was Churchill, who became secretary for India. Earl Cairns having died the previous April, a Tory lawyer of far less progressive outlook, Hardinge Giffard, took his place on the woolsack with the title Lord Halsbury. The earl of Carnarvon, who had twice quitted a Disraeli ministry—in 1867 with, and in 1878 without, the approval of Lord Salisbury—went to Ireland as viceroy. For the rest, Northcote became earl of Iddesleigh and lord president of the council, and Hicks Beach became chancellor of the exchequer and leader of the house of commons. Lord Salisbury's promising nephew, A. J. Balfour, entered the cabinet as president of the local government board.

Only two episodes of note occurred during the seven months. One was the annexation of Upper Burma, for which, as Indian secretary, Lord Randolph Churchill was immediately responsible. Lower (or, as it was then called, British) Burma had been conquered in the wars of 1824 and 1852, and was administered from Rangoon by a chief commissioner under the government of India. Upper Burma remained a native kingdom with its capital at Mandalay. The last king, Thibaw (then spelt Theebaw), who reigned from 1878, was barbarous and incompetent. His ministers thought nothing of appointing notorious brigands as provincial governors. Lord Salisbury was against intervention; but the French in Tongking, flushed with conquest, began sending emissaries into Burma. After a temporary check in Tongking they were reconsidering their position, when Thibaw chose the moment to commit the final outrage of confiscating the Bombay-Burma Company's property, in order to transfer its rights to French rivals. Unaware that the French were no longer inclined to accept the transfer, he refused arbitration. In October we sent an ultimatum; in November 10,000 troops from India occupied Mandalay, after suffering barely a dozen casualties. Thibaw was deported; and on 1 January 1886 the whole kingdom was annexed to the Crown. But a sporadic struggle, half warfare and half dacoity, went on for another two years.

The other episode concerned Ireland. The conservatives had

[1] Sir Arthur Hardinge, *The Fourth Earl of Carnarvon* (1925), iii. 198.

come in by Parnell's support, and were anxious to retain it. They redeemed their promise about coercion. The system of 'firm government', which Lord Spencer had carried out for three years with steadily increasing success, came abruptly to an end. The Irish leader had advocated a peasant proprietary; and to please him there was carried the first state-assisted scheme of Irish land purchase—known as Lord Ashbourne's Act. The new viceroy, who had passed the act federating Canada in 1867 and whom we saw trying to federate South Africa in our last chapter, favoured giving Ireland a home rule status similar to that of a Canadian province inside the dominion. In July he held special secret conversations with Justin McCarthy, and on one famous occasion (1 August 1885) with Parnell himself. Ten months later, in debate before the vote on the Home Rule Bill, Parnell revealed this approach; and the conservatives excused it as tentative (which it clearly was) and unauthorized (which it certainly was not). We know now that Lord Carnarvon consulted Lord Salisbury before the interview, and reported fully to him at Hatfield immediately after. As for Parnell, he cared not from whom he got Home Rule, provided he got it. Party for party, he rather preferred the conservatives, because they could control the house of lords. Confident in his coming strength, he declared in August that the Irish in the new parliament would have 'a platform with only one plank, and that one plank National Independence'. With the English press in full cry, both Hartington and Chamberlain rebuked this. But Churchill's and Salisbury's speeches noticeably refrained from doing so, and Gladstone's Hawarden manifesto kept a wide door open.

The month of September brought a diversion in the form of a tremendous series of election speeches delivered by Chamberlain all over the country. This was his famous campaign for the 'unauthorized programme'. His scheme of social and agrarian reform looks moderate enough in the perspective of to-day, but it made the ears of every one who heard it tingle. The queen was horrified, and Lord Iddesleigh called him Jack Cade. The country discerned that, after Gladstone, he was now the strongest personality in English politics. Unhappily for himself Parnell did not see it. He and Chamberlain were blinded towards each other by O'Shea's deception.

Meanwhile, wholly unknown to the public and his principal colleagues, Gladstone was viewing politics from a quite new angle.[1] At least as far back as the beginning of August he had reached the momentous conclusion that home rule must come. Two things had especially helped to convert him—first, the reversal of Lord Spencer's policy by the conservatives, which supplied public proof that Ireland could never be treated consistently and outside party in the house of commons; and secondly, the conversion (which, of course, was an official secret) of some very highly placed men in Dublin Castle, including Sir Robert Hamilton, who four years earlier had succeeded the murdered Burke as its head. But in his seventy-sixth year the veteran ex-Premier was not at all anxious to sponsor a change of this magnitude himself. To convert the liberals would be difficult, and, if he succeeded, would only throw the conservative party, including the house of lords, against the policy. Pondering the precedents of 1829 (Catholic Emancipation), 1846 (repeal of the Corn Laws), and 1867 (democratization of the franchise), he asked himself whether the better method would not be that which they exemplified— reform by a conservative leader receiving liberal support against his own dissentients. And much that he knew or had been told led him to expect such a role from Lord Salisbury.[2] Accordingly, while convinced of the need in his own mind, he was very anxious to do nothing which might queer the conservative government's pitch. He felt that he must keep his lips sealed; for Lord Salisbury could not easily commend to his followers anything that already bore a liberal hall-mark. He felt also a profound distaste for anything like 'bidding' between the parties for the Irish vote. That Parnell had contacts with Lord Carnarvon he knew from the best source—Parnell himself.

But to the Irish leader 'bidding' appeared naturally in a different light. His duty was to secure in advance of the general election the best terms that he could for his cause. He had a valuable asset to trade with—the Irish vote in the English boroughs; it had been well drilled, and he could throw it which way he chose. His regular intermediary in negotiating with Gladstone was Mrs. O'Shea; and on 30 October, a few weeks after Lord Salisbury had made a remarkably pro-Irish speech

[1] Cp. Lord Morley's *Life* (bk. ix, ch. 1); Lord Gladstone, *After Thirty Years* (1928), p. 282; Barry O'Brien, *Life of Parnell*, ch. 18; J. L. Garvin, *Life of Joseph Chamberlain*, ii (1933), bk. vi. But see Appendix A, *infra*, for some lights thrown on the matter by unpublished documents in the Gladstone Papers.

[2] Cp., e.g., G. W. E. Russell, *Malcolm MacColl: Memoirs and Correspondence* (1914), p. 122. But again see Appendix A.

at Newport, he forwarded through her a 'scheme' of so much home rule as he would like Gladstone to adopt. The dose was moderate—more so than Gladstone's own bill of the following year. But the liberal statesman returned no answer until after the general election, and his public utterances were of Delphic ambiguity. Nothing was left for Parnell to do but to make the best bargain that he could with the tories. Nobody now knows just what his understanding was, for it must have been contingent upon something which did not happen, viz. a conservative, or at least a conservative-Parnellite, majority. But on 21 November, two days before the first pollings, he cast the die. A manifesto was issued ordering the Irish in Great Britain to vote conservative.

The electoral result was soon seen. Partly through the Irish vote and partly because they had not forgotten Gordon, London, Liverpool, Manchester, and the towns generally, turned against Gladstone. But in the counties the new electors, kindled by the 'unauthorized programme', repaid the party which had enfranchised them. On balance the majority of liberals over conservatives in the new house totalled 86. Parnell, however, had swept catholic Ireland, and his swollen following reached exactly the same figure.[1] Thus the situation for which he had been working during five years was realized with fantastic precision. He became visibly the arbiter in parliament; though, while he could keep either English party out of office, only the liberals were strong enough for him to put them in.

On 19 December, after all but a few of the results were known, Mrs. O'Shea on Parnell's behalf wrote to Gladstone again, asking for an answer about his 'scheme'. Gladstone replied at once, and correspondence was resumed, yet still upon the basis that the tory-Parnellite alliance continued, and that Gladstone wanted it to continue. As late as Christmas Eve he declared in a letter to her (i.e. in effect, to Parnell): 'My wish and hope still are, that Ministers should propose some adequate and honourable plan for settling the question of Irish government, and that the Nationalists should continue in amicable relations with them for that purpose.' A few days earlier, meeting Balfour at the duke of Westminster's house, he had told him (and through him

---

[1] In 1880 the Irish home rulers elected had nominally numbered 60. But many of these were really liberals, and Parnell's fighting nucleus comprised only about 35. In 1885 the whole 86 were solid.

Lord Salisbury) that, if the conservatives took this course, they could count on his support. But even as he spoke the prospect was doomed. The fatal blow had been dealt by Gladstone's son and secretary, Herbert. From good but mistaken motives, and under circumstances that need not concern us, the young man on 15 December disclosed to certain editors the secret of his father's conversion. Statements based on his indiscretion appeared in two papers on the 17th and in all the press on the 18th. It was impossible for Gladstone to deny them save in terms which could easily be seen through; and after Christmas speculation about his attitude drowned every other topic in politics. Events moved almost at once towards a rupture of the alliance between Parnell and the tories, and the substitution of one between him and Gladstone. Carnarvon gave up the viceroyalty, and the chief secretary, Sir W. Hart Dyke, also resigned. Gladstone was left to break, as best he could, the effect of his conversion on his colleagues and his party generally; while the conservatives reformed to fight on new and favourable ground as the defenders of the Union against moonlighters and cattle-maimers.

Things could scarcely have turned out worse for home rule. On the surface both English parties showed badly. Lord Salisbury looked as if he dropped Parnell because the election results deprived him of usefulness; while Gladstone incurred the charge of corruptly capitulating to the Irish chief for the sake of regaining office. Neither tale was true, but the latter was by far the more damaging. The situation was in other respects topsy-turvy. Parnell's election manifesto turned into a terrible blunder; for he had handed between 25 and 40 seats to the tories, and every one of these would now mean a vote against home rule. Besides, it had injured or irritated great numbers of liberals, and rendered it very much harder for Gladstone to convert his party. Fundamentally, however, Parnell had made a worse mistake than that. All through his career, in practising *oderint dum metuant* towards the English politicians, he had forgotten that there was an England behind them. He had never tired of saying that he held himself responsible to his countrymen only, and did not in the least care what the English thought or said about him; his whole attitude expressed a deliberate hatred towards their nation, which was not unnaturally returned. Moreover some features in the Irish revolution—the shooting from behind hedges, the hideous maiming of animals, the boycotting, and secret murder clubs—had been peculiarly repugnant to English-men's common instincts. If their short memories could have amnestied such things, the dynamite outrages at Westminster and the Tower that very year were there to prevent oblivion. To concede home rule to Parnell seemed like handing over Ireland to a king of the ogres.

For Gladstone his son's indiscretion had destroyed all the fruits of his own costly reticence. He saw precipitated the very con-juncture which he wished to avoid. But he steeled himself to go on. His hardest task was with his leading colleagues—Harting-ton, Chamberlain, Bright, Harcourt, Selborne, and James. They had an indisputable grievance. Yet they could allow much for the veteran's tactics; they knew it was second nature to him to feel his way, to hide his further objectives, to keep surprises up his sleeve. Perhaps if he had brought them privately together and explained with candour, not only what he had concealed, but why he had concealed it, they might have yielded. He never did. One difficulty was that his reticence had not been impartial; he had told to some more than to others. In fine, he handled them badly; of those six only Harcourt came over.

His worst error related to Chamberlain. He entirely under-rated his importance, hiding the truth from him after he had confided it to others, under circumstances which rendered con-cealment very like deception. Yet it was Chamberlain who destroyed his scheme. It was not merely that he made by far the most powerful speeches against it. The hostility of the con-servatives could be discounted; so could the estrangement of Hartington and the whigs; but that of the radical leader could not be. His following all over the country was exceedingly large; and his attitude threw against the bill, when it came to polling, hundreds of thousands of the very voters who otherwise would have felt bound by Gladstone's lead. Yet here it may be that no tact could have averted the schism. Chamberlain was not merely acting in pique; and he certainly was not seeking his self-interest, which lay plainly in following the party ticket. The sharp line which he drew between his own proposals for devolution and Gladstone's for home rule may or may not convince us, but it was sincere. Against giving Ireland anything to be called a parlia-ment he really was a conscientious objector.

A few days after the queen's speech Hicks Beach on behalf of the government gave notice of a Coercion Bill. Next day

(27 January 1886) ministers were defeated on an English agrarian amendment ('Three acres and a cow') moved by Chamberlain's henchman Jesse Collings. Lord Salisbury resigned the following morning; and Gladstone formed his third cabinet (3 February) amid a general confusion. It was no secret now that he was converted to home rule, but it remained very uncertain what his Home Rule Bill would be like. Hartington and Goschen declined all offers, and Sir H. James, the previous attorney-general, refused the lord chancellorship—said to have been never before refused in modern times. Chamberlain joined the administration, but very doubtfully; and he only took the presidency of the local government board. Sir William Harcourt became chancellor of the exchequer, and Hugh Childers home secretary, their previous positions being thus exchanged. Morley, who in unwonted divergence from Chamberlain was the strongest home ruler in his party, entered the cabinet as chief secretary for Ireland; while Lord Rosebery, then a mediator between whigs and radicals, went for the first time to the foreign office.[1] Dilke was not included because he had been made co-respondent in a divorce case the trial of which was to open nine days later. Perhaps the most impressive convert to home rule was Lord Spencer. Eight months before he had headed opposition inside the earlier cabinet to Chamberlain's council scheme. Now he had become convinced that no 'firm' government of Ireland was feasible, since he saw the success of his own interrupted and lightly thrown away even by a conservative ministry.

Events in the drama moved fast. On 26 March 1886, when the Home Rule Bill was before the cabinet, Chamberlain and Trevelyan, the two leading radicals, with some minor ministers, resigned. On 8 April amid phenomenal public excitement the bill was introduced by Gladstone in a masterly 3½-hour speech. Its plan was to set up an Irish parliament and executive in Dublin, which should have powers of legislation and control over all but

---

[1] According to Lady G. Cecil (*Life of Robert Marquess of Salisbury*, iii (1931), 225), Queen Victoria vetoed Granville's return to it, and also exacted from Lord Rosebery a promise that he would continue Lord Salisbury's policy. The first would be an exercise of the prerogative well recognized and illustrated in other instances. The second would not. Lord Crewe, however (in *Lord Rosebery* (1931), i. 259–62), puts a good deal of water into Lady G. Cecil's wine, averring that Granville that 'not only Queen Victoria but all his senior colleagues believed that foreign affairs ought to pass into younger and stronger hands', and of Rosebery that his motive for continuity was that 'he and Gladstone both felt that their predecessor's policy had been prudent'. Granville went to the colonial office instead.

reserved subjects. The chief categories reserved were those affecting the Crown, peace and war, the defence forces, foreign and colonial relations, customs and excise, trade and navigation, post office, coinage, and legal tender. One-fifteenth of the charges in the United Kingdom budget for 'imperial' purposes (i.e. debt interest, defence expenditure, and some other heads) was to be defrayed by Ireland; the rest of the revenue raised there (subject to a large charge in the early years for the constabulary) would be at the disposal of the Dublin parliament and government. To safeguard the Irish minority, the new legislature was to consist of two 'orders'—in effect, a chamber and a senate, the latter about half as numerous as the former and including at the start the 28 elective Irish peers. But there were not to be two houses; the 'orders' would form but a single chamber; though they could vote separately when desired, and each had a suspensory veto over measures brought in by the other. No Irish members were to sit at Westminster unless summoned thither for the special task of revising the Home Rule Act. Future Irish judges would be appointed by the Irish government, paid by the Irish exchequer, and enjoy security of tenure on terms exactly analogous to the English. There were to be full rights of appeal from the Irish courts to the judicial committee of the privy council in London, which was also to be the forum for deciding whether any act of the Irish parliament or government was *ultra vires*. An essential part of the policy, though cast in a separate bill, was a plan for simultaneously buying out the landlords. Of all those details the one most criticized was the exclusion of the Irish members from Westminster. Sick as they were of Irish obstruction, many Englishmen at first liked this. Later it was seen to destroy the stability of the whole scheme; since Ireland could never be held long under a British parliament, which would fix her taxes and pocket about 40 per cent. of the proceeds, but in which she would be unrepresented. On 27 May, when it was too late, Gladstone offered to reconsider this feature.

The measure never reached the lords, but on sixteen days in the commons it was debated at very high levels of eloquence and argument. Gladstone spoke five times with compelling power. Hicks Beach most ably directed the conservative opposition, to which new force came from the side of Ulster. But the fate of the bill rested with the liberal dissentients. The leaders of their opposite wings, Hartington and Chamberlain, happened to be two of the very strongest parliamentary debaters known in modern times, and each intervened with crushing effect. Possibly an even deadlier blow was struck outside. The only survivor of the great figures coeval with Gladstone, John Bright, made no speech; but a week before the fateful division he wrote a short weighty letter of condemnation. About 1 a.m. on 8 June 1886 the second reading was defeated in a full house by 343 votes to 313. Some 93 liberals voted in the majority.

It was not a wide margin of defeat, nor did Gladstone yet despair. A month earlier the National Liberal Federation had declared on his side, and save in Chamberlain's Birmingham territory most of the party's local associations did likewise. He decided to dissolve; and in July the liberals and Parnellites, who seven months before had appealed against each other to the electors, engaged as allies in a common campaign. On the other side the conservatives gave support to the dissentient liberals. But it now appeared how much more anti-home rule the country was than the house. Three hundred and ninety-four seats fell to the victors (316 conservatives and 78 dissentient liberals); the vanquished had but 276 (191 liberals and 85 nationalists). Gladstone resigned at once, and Lord Salisbury returned to office with a composite majority of 118.

So ended the most dramatic thirteen months in modern English party history. The consequences went farther than then appeared. The liberals, hitherto normally the dominant party and expecting to be still more so on the widened franchise, were for the moment disrupted and defeated. No one foresaw that, excepting one brief triennium, their defeat would last nineteen years.

The parliament elected in December 1885 is notable as being the first since 1832 in which the British two-party system was broken up by the appearance of a permanent third party, allied to neither of the others, and strong enough to prevent either of them from having a working majority without it. Had Gladstone been unwilling to concede home rule, his alternative would have been to agree with Salisbury on a truce for the purpose of joint opposition to Parnell. But such an alliance could not have lasted long, since the recent conservative flirtation with the Irish party had destroyed faith in a disinterested anti-Parnellite front. And another dissolution, bringing back Parnell in undiminished strength, would probably have renewed the same arithmetical problem.

How this would have been resolved, it is idle to speculate; for Gladstone, by embracing home rule, did at least restore the two-party system. In form and spirit the Irish remained a separate organization; but in fact down to 1914 they were linked with the liberal party as being the only one from which they could expect home rule. Moreover it resulted from their having a national instead of a doctrinal basis that, though solid, they could not expand. The '86 of '86' proved to be their high-water mark.

Little noticed by the magnates of politics, the seed of a much more radical challenge to the system was sown during this very period. Following the failure of chartism, socialist ideas became nearly extinct in England for a quarter of a century, though the greatest socialist of the period, Karl Marx, was living as an exile in London nearly all the time. In the seventies the exiles were reinforced by many from France after the fall of the Paris commune, and towards 1880 they began to make contacts with the London radical clubs. In 1881 the Democratic (afterwards Social Democratic) Federation was founded by H. M. Hyndman, an ex-conservative journalist and stockbroker, who had studied Marx in a French translation. It became the first modern English socialist body; and when in 1883 William Morris joined it, his fame as a poet and art-craftsman brought it for a while a number of pioneers in art or ideas. At the end of 1884 he left it and founded the Socialist League; and meanwhile in January of that year another set of men, very young and still obscure, but brilliantly gifted, had founded the Fabian Society. In the winter of 1885-6, when trade was bad, the Social Democratic Federation leaders organized meetings and marches of the unemployed. On 7 February 1886 a meeting held by them in Trafalgar Square led to considerable disorder, and windows were broken in Pall Mall. For this four notable men—H. M. Hyndman, John Burns,[1] H. H. Champion, and Jack Williams—were prosecuted at Bow Street; but in April an Old Bailey jury acquitted them

[1] B. 1858 in London of Scottish descent; went to work at ten; at fourteen, engineer's apprentice; learned to speak on the temperance platform, passing thence to trade unionism; early member of the Social Democratic Federation; prominent in London open-air agitation, 1886-7; and in the Dock Strike, 1889; L.C.C. 1889; M.P. 1892; president of the local government board, 1905-14; president of the board of trade, 1914; resigned at the outbreak of the European war.

after a four-day trial. On 21 February a monster concourse of 50,000 in Hyde Park was broken up by the police.

Similar unemployed disturbances occurred in Manchester and elsewhere. And the more seminal London movements had also their counterparts in the provinces. Edward Carpenter[1] (later to become the author and composer of *England, Arise!*) began his propaganda in Sheffield the same year that Morris became a socialist. A branch of the S.D.F. was formed in Glasgow in 1884. A special stirring was that in the coal-fields. Before the Franchise reform of 1884 very few miners had votes; then they were virtually all enfranchised; and very soon they began to talk of putting up candidates of their own instead of voting for the squires and carpet-baggers who had hitherto represented most of their constituencies. One of the first to think thus was a young ex-miner at Cumnock, who in 1886 after years of effort succeeded in launching an Ayrshire Miners' Union. His name was James Keir Hardie, and we shall hear of him later.[2]

As yet, however, labour in parliament meant trade-union officials elected as liberals. The first to become a minister was Henry Broadhurst, originally an Oxfordshire stonemason; whom Gladstone made under-secretary at the home office in 1886.

[1] See p. 161.
[2] B. 1856 in Lanarkshire, son of a ship's carpenter; at seven went to work in Glasgow; employed in coal-mines from ten to twenty; learned to speak on the temperance platform, passing thence to trade unionism; dismissed and boycotted by employers, was in 1879 elected a miners' agent; in 1880 moved to Ayrshire to organize miners there; in 1886, first secretary of the Scottish Miners' Federation; in 1888, first secretary of the Scottish Labour party; M.P. 1892–5; first chairman of the I.L.P. 1893; M.P. again, 1900–15; chairman and leader of the parliamentary labour party, 1906 and 1907; d. 1915.

IV

ECONOMICS AND INSTITUTIONS, 1870–86

AFTER Waterloo the populations of what are now the four chief western countries had been approximately:

France (1821)	30·4 millions
Germany (lands of the subsequent Reich, 1815)	21 ,,
United Kingdom (1821) . . .	20·8 ,,
United States (1820)	9·6 ,,

Thus France still had a very long lead, though she was by no means such a disproportionate giant among nations as she had been in the later seventeenth and eighteenth centuries. The United Kingdom was much farther behind in reality than the table suggests, for nearly a third (6·8 millions) of its total lived in Ireland, whose population, whether in peace or in war, was in the main a source of more weakness than strength. Germany, too, was still subdivided into a large number of separate sovereign states.

After the Franco-Prussian war the order was as follows:

Germany (1871)	41 millions
United States (1870)	38·5 ,,
France (1872)	36·1 ,,
United Kingdom (1871) . . .	31·8 ,,

to which United Italy must now be added with a population (in 1871) of 26·8 millions. The reversal of positions between France and Germany had been accentuated by the transfer of Alsace-Lorraine; but France had fallen to third place before that. Germany passed her about 1851, and the United States about 1868. The United Kingdom did not pass her till 1890;[1] and it is important to remember throughout the period of the previous chapters that France, not England, was and always had been the larger of the leading liberal Powers in nineteenth-century Europe—hence the heavy setback to European liberalism after her overthrow at the hands of Bismarck. The United Kingdom had fallen behind Germany in consequence of Ireland; whose population (partly through the Famine but chiefly through emigration to the United States) had not merely stopped growing, but actually

---

[1] Even then France, by Mulhall's reckoning, had over 11 per cent. more men capable of bearing arms (M. G. Mulhall, 4th ed. (1899), *Dictionary of Statistics*).

declined to 5·4 millions. But the island of Great Britain had risen from 14 to 26 millions, of which 22·7 were in England and Wales; a remarkable performance, seeing that in the same period it had colonized Australia and New Zealand and sent a very large outflow to North America.

Ten years later the same tendencies had gone still farther and the order then became:

United States (1880)	.	.	.	.	50·1	millions
Germany (1880)	.	.	.	.	45·2	,,
France (1881)	.	.	.	.	37·6	,,
United Kingdom (1881)		.	.	.	35·2	,,
Italy (1881) .	.	.	.	.	28·4	,,

The bearing of these figures on the risk of a French *revanche* against Germany is obvious. Yet Bismarck did not feel safe till he had formed the Triple Alliance of Germany, Austria-Hungary, and Italy, which at its inception in 1882 had a combined census population of 111·4 millions. The next largest fighting and diplomatic unit in Europe was Tsarist Russia with a population on this continent (very difficult to mobilize) of 87 millions. Within the United Kingdom Ireland had fallen to 5·1 millions; Great Britain was 29·7 millions (less than 1½ millions over Italy); and 26 millions were in England and Wales, showing a density of 446 per square mile, the highest in the world except Belgium. When Gladstone first proposed home rule in 1886, the Irish population was smaller than when Pitt passed the Act of Union. Great Britain, on the other hand, had come near to trebling hers; so that the risks to be apprehended from a decontrolled Ireland were immensely less than they had been during the French wars. But English opinion was slow to grasp this.

Population in England and Wales during the decade 1871–81 still grew rapidly. The increase over the ten years reached 16·9 per cent.; it was 19·63 per cent. in the towns and 7·42 per cent. even in the country. The mean birth-rate[1] for the decade was 35·4 per thousand and for the quinquennium 1881–5 it was 33·3. By comparison the French birth-rate during the latter period

[1] The *recorded* birth-rate had been rising gradually since the forties, and the highest point, 36·3, was reached in 1876. But the rise, which was in all slight, is believed to be explained by gradually improved registration. Birth registration was first enforced under penalty in 1873. There is no evidence that the birth-rate ever changed appreciably before 1877. What had quickened the growth of population was the fall in the death-rate. (Cp. Harold Wright, *Population* (1923), pp. 101–6.)

was 24·7, and the highest of the German birth-rates (that in industrial Saxony) was 41·9. The slight drop shown above in the English rate meant more than then appeared; for the sequel showed it continuous. It started from the year 1877, when a prosecution of Bradlaugh[1] and Mrs. Besant[2] for publishing a Malthusian pamphlet served to give methods of birth control their first really wide advertisement in England. Its significance was masked for some time by the lower British death-rate; which, at 21 per thousand for the United Kingdom in the decade 1871–80, contrasted markedly with 24·3 in France and 27·1 in Germany. In 1886, the last year in the series that we are considering, the excess of births over deaths was in England and Wales 13·3, in Germany 10·8, and in France 1·4.

The result of all this was that England throughout the period of our first three chapters still had both the courage and the difficulties of a rapidly growing community. If families of ten or twelve children were no longer so common among the business and professional classes as they had been a generation earlier, families of six or eight were still normal, and the modern one-child or two-child family did not, as a type, exist. And while population grew, wealth grew considerably faster. According to an estimate by Sir Robert Giffen, the wealth of Great Britain in 1875 was £8,548 millions, but in 1885 it was £10,037 millions. The relative position of the western countries may be gauged more or less by the figures of their external trade.

Foreign Trade in £millions
(Mulhall's figures)

	1870	1880	1889
United Kingdom . .	547	698	740
France	227	339	311
Germany . . .	212	294	367
United States . . .	165	308	320
Belgium and Holland .	136	237	310
British Colonies . .	128	203	298
Italy	66	91	94

[1] See above, p. 67. This prosecution had much to do with the animus shown against him at Westminster.

[2] Annie Wood, b. in London of Irish parents, 1847; married Rev. Frank Besant, 1867; separated from him, 1873; associated with Bradlaugh as freethinker and radical for about ten years; joined the Fabian Society, 1885, and became one of the essayists; transferred her interest to theosophy, 1889; settled in India as theosophist leader and became prominent in Indian nationalist movement; d. 1933.

At the climax (about 1870) of the period of unparalleled prosperity, which began with the Californian and Australian gold
discoveries towards the end of the forties, British trade had
reached its relative zenith. The above table gives some idea of
its extraordinary lead. It will be seen that it largely exceeded
the trade of France, Germany, and Italy put together; and if you
added to it that of the British colonies, you could throw in that
of the United States on the other side and still beat the combination. By 1880 neither of those things held good; and though the
increment of British trade was a very large one, it was much less
than the increments of French and German added together, and
not much more than the American alone. Any doubt that we
were relatively losing ground is completely removed by the 1889
figures, which show a German increment approaching double
the British and a Belgo-Dutch increment equalling the German.
Nevertheless even in 1889 British trade greatly exceeded that of
the two next countries put together.

The expanding modern production, of which all these growths
were an expression, was essentially based on expanding facilities
for transport. Just as in the beginning it had been the port of
Liverpool which gave rise to the Manchester cotton industry and
not vice versa, so it was the English invention of railways which
enabled the United States to become a great nation and later
rendered possible the pivotal iron and steel industry of Germany.[1]
Before railways America could only be colonized effectively near
the coast or up the rivers; and down to Pitt's day the European
Powers valued a good sugar island like Jamaica or Guadeloupe
much above slices of the unprofitable, because inaccessible, mainland. It had been the railways which opened up the prairies,
and now it was the steamers which brought the prairie wheat
into the markets of Europe. To provide rails, engines, and
engined ships new methods had to be discovered for producing
cheaply in sufficient quantities first iron and then steel; and these,
too, England successively invented and pioneered.[2]

The iron age and the earlier railway age lie just behind this volume; but the steel age and the age of the triumphant steamships
come right into it. Bessemer's process, the first for producing steel
cheaply on a large scale, had been patented in 1856; but it was

[1] To bring Germany's ores to her coal required an overland haul of 150 miles.
[2] In what immediately follows I am much indebted to the second volume (1932)
of Prof. J. H. Clapham's masterly *Economic History of Modern Britain*.

only in the seventies that steel really began to oust puddled iron. Of pig-iron, the basis of them both, the output in Great Britain exceeded that of all the rest of the world at so late a date as 1871. Of puddled iron, a craft-product in which she held a long lead through the number of her skilled puddlers, she seems to have produced something like 3 million tons a year in 1872–3. Thereafter there was a drop during the great depression; in 1882 the figure was as high as 2·8 millions again; but from 1884 it dropped permanently owing to the growing substitution of steel all round. Yet steel itself until the middle eighties was subject to a similar British primacy. Down to 1879 both the large-scale processes for making it—the Bessemer converter and the Siemens-Martin open-hearth—could only use iron obtained from non-phosphoric ores; and, the principal sources of such ores being Sweden and Spain, they could very cheaply be shipped in the one case to Middlesbrough and the north-east coast, in the other to South Wales and Barrow-in-Furness. But the French and German coal-fields, being inland, could not advantageously get them; and the abundant native ores within their reach were all phosphoric. It was an Englishman, Sidney Gilchrist Thomas,[1] who discovered how to make steel out of phosphoric iron by a method applicable to either converter or open-hearth; it was at Blaenavon and Dowlais that the first trials were made; and it was at the Bolckow-Vaughan works in Middlesbrough that success (1879) was proved. One sometimes hears it said reproachfully that foreigners were left to utilize this English invention. But the reason is that they stood to gain most. It was a minor point for England to use her native ores, though most of them are phosphoric; but a major point that she lost her peculiar advantage. On the other hand, the discovery created a gigantic German steel industry which would not have been possible without it; and this, which by 1895 had a larger output than the British, played a very important part in predisposing Germany to aggressive war and enabling her after 1914 to sustain and prolong it. Also it had much to do with the curtailment of Great Britain's trade by German com-

---

[1] B. 1850 in London of a Welsh father; educated at Dulwich College; at seventeen became a clerk at Marlborough St. police-court; transferred to Thames police-court, which he did not leave till 1879. Studied metallurgy at South Kensington and experimented in a backyard; found the theory of his discovery, 1875; first patent, 1877; final success, 1879; died of consumption, 1885. His coadjutor was his cousin, Percy Gilchrist, afterwards F.R.S., an ironworks-chemist in South Wales.

petition from the middle eighties onward; for in the long previous period of her uncontested supremacy metallurgy had been the very heart of her success.

The British railway systems changed over from iron to steel in the seventies; the North-Eastern ceased buying iron rails in 1877.[1] Their lay-out had by 1870 been completed in its main features. But to the 15,620 miles then existing some 2,285 were added by 1880, and another 2,150 by 1890. These extensions were mostly minor lines, though they did much to open up the more secluded counties. But on major routes some of the largest works were then carried out; in 1886 the Severn Tunnel was opened, and about the same time the Forth Bridge was begun. Generally speaking, however, the big advances in British transport between 1870 and 1886 were not internal but external. If the country owed much to metallurgy, it owed yet more to the sea; and now, as the two joined forces, British shipbuilding and shipping reached an extreme pre-eminence. For most of the period construction was in iron, not steel, because iron was cheaper; and to this was due our continued large output of iron down to 1884 after the railways had ceased to use it. Wooden ships and sailing ships were still built, but iron and steam steadily encroached. The fastest sailing-ships of the sixties (down to the celebrated *Cutty Sark* of 1869) had been 'composites' (wooden walls on an iron frame), and this fashion was not extinct in the early eighties.[2] But iron sailing-ships had also been largely built since 1860; and the launch of the famous *Loch Garry*[3] (1875) confirmed iron as best till about 1884, when steel superseded it. For steamers iron had come in decisively, when the screw superseded the paddle; but the fuel consumption of all the earlier steamers was so high that for voyages of any length they were almost confined to passengers and light valuable freight. The use of compound engines[4] in a series of improved forms reduced fuel consumption between 1863 and 1872 by one-half, and the

[1] Clapham, op. cit., p. 53.

[2] The conservatism of the admiralty used 'composite' structure even with steam propulsion till quite a late date. One of the author's earliest memories is the launch of a 'screw composite gunvessel' of 950 tons (H.M.S. *Racer*) at Devonport in 1884. Such vessels were not ill suited for prolonged absences 'showing the flag' in distant seas, as their coppered bottoms fouled less than iron.

[3] Both the *Cutty Sark* and the *Loch Garry* are illustrated in R. J. Cornewall Jones's *The British Merchant Service* (1898) at p. 236.

[4] Chiefly the invention of John Elder of Glasgow (1824–69), a great genius suddenly cut off. See *D.N.B.*

tonnage saved from coal became available for goods. This was one of the main factors in the sudden flooding of Europe by cheap American wheat a few years later. Meanwhile the supersession of sails by steam is shown in the following table:

Tonnage on the British Register

	Sail	Steam
1870 . .	4,580,000	901,000
1875 . .	4,200,000	1,900,000
1881 . .	3,690,000	3,005,000
1885 . .	3,400,000	4,000,000

The tonnage of new ships built in the United Kingdom from 1871 to 1880 inclusive was: sail 1,390,000, steam 3,190,000. Remarkable as a productive effort in relation to the resources of the period, it implies an even steeper increase in the volume of seaborne trade, since each steamer could make many more voyages than a sailing-ship in the same time. The opening of the Suez Canal in 1869 caused the downfall of the China tea-clippers, fastest of sailing craft.[1] The speed of steamers took a jump in 1881 with the advent of the triple-expansion engine.[2] This was soon afterwards fitted in the Cunard Company's first all-steel vessel, the *Servia* of 3,900 tons register, 10,500 horse-power, and speed of 17¼ knots. Divided by transverse bulkheads into twelve water-tight compartments and lit by incandescent electric lights,[3] she marks the beginning of transatlantic travel as we now know it. But in 1884 the sisters *Umbria* and *Etruria* of 8,127 tons, 14,500 horse-power, and 19½ knots' speed carried it still farther. The *Umbria* crossed the ocean outwards in 5 days 22 hours.

Behind metallurgy and shipping alike stood coal. In the decade 1871–80 Great Britain did not, as in all previous decades of the nineteenth century, raise more than half of the world's coal supply. But she accounted for 1,305 million tons out of 2,855 million. In the nine years following the figures showed a lower proportion—1,461 million out of 3,785 million. The relative drop was chiefly due to the expanding production of two

---

[1] R. J. Cornewall Jones, *The British Merchant Service*, pp. 235–6.

[2] The idea had been patented by Normand in France in 1871 and by A. C. Kirk in England in 1874. But it never succeeded till Kirk's engines were fitted in the s.s. *Aberdeen* in 1881.

[3] The first British vessel to be so lighted (June 1881) was the Inman Line's *City of Richmond*.

foreign countries—the United States and Germany; but there may have been some sagging in native efficiency. British coal production was 373 tons per miner in 1871; in 1881 it had risen to 403 tons; and in 1891 it was down to 358 tons.[1] With the miners' trade unions, which grew much stronger during this period, the policy of regulating the output of coal in proportion to the demand for it at the current price had always remained a leading principle;[2] and occasions for asserting it were now frequent. The rivalry of the coal-fields abroad helped to make them so, though less by direct sales competition than through the creation of competitive metallurgies. Our export of coal itself, always the highest in the world, rose rapidly at this period; 12 million tons in 1870, 19 millions in 1880, 29 millions in 1889. The prudence of increasing it had already been questioned by W. S. Jevons[3] upon long-view grounds; but for a country needing many bulky imports it possessed the great merit of providing outward ships with bulky cargoes. During the seventies the general introduction of mechanical fans enabled mines to be sunk deeper; while better equipment for winding and haulage made it practicable to drive the underground 'roads' much farther from the shaft. But England did not lead in these inventions; they came from abroad.[4]

The vigour displayed by the English of that age in the fields which we have briefly reviewed was matched by them in many others. The country regarded itself as 'the workshop of the world' —a phrase then universal, which expressed not an aspiration, but a fact. The comparative trade figures quoted above, astonishing as they are, do less than justice to it; for the export trade of the United States was as yet almost entirely in food and raw materials; whereas the great bulk of British export values was in manufactured goods. Coal was the only raw material which we sold in very large quantities; our copper, tin, and lead outputs, which earlier in the century were important, had been supplanted by the far more copious foreign ore-fields. Our leading export manufactures were still the textiles, in which we had pioneered the industrial revolution a century before. In the five years 1880–4 the average annual value of our goods sold

---

[1] Professor Clapham's figures; Mulhall's reckoning gave lower results.
[2] S. and B. Webb, *Industrial Democracy* (1897), p. 447.
[3] *The Coal Question* (1865).
[4] The fans from Belgium, an invention of first-class importance.

abroad was £234 millions; yarns and textile fabrics accounted for £108 millions of it, and, among them, cotton for £76 millions. If the backbone of our foreign trade was Lancashire cotton, the backbone of our cotton sales was the market in India and China. But we still sold large quantities to the United States, Germany, and central Europe, as well as to the Levant. So much were we on top, that a considerable part of our outward trade was in effect (though seldom directly and consciously) financed by our own capital lendings. Many of these were misplaced and lost; yet in 1885 Sir Robert Giffen estimated the then total of our foreign investments at £1,302 millions. Professor Clapham computes that about £1,000 millions of this had been accumulated in thirty years, despite a total cessation during the bad triennium 1876–8.[1] Great Britain's position as a creditor nation caused little embarrassment to the exchanges, since with her free trade market she was at all times ready to accept payment in goods.

Yet to any one now looking at the period certain seeds of weakness are apparent. English higher education was much inferior to German, not at its high points, but in the mass; and Germany thus steadily acquired long leads over us, first in the chemical and then in the electrical trades. The United States, again, offered a more open career to talent. Many English industries were now in the second or third or even fourth generation of the families that had founded them; the results were old plants in the factory, nepotism in the management, and a disinclination to hustle for new inventions. Clever English workmen, who saw no chance of rising high in the businesses where they were employed, emigrated to America, founded firms there, and in a few years were manufacturing on a very large scale. That is the history of many cases in the minor industries.[2] So, too, with inventors; Graham Bell was a Scotsman, born, educated, and domiciled in Edinburgh till he was twenty-three; but he invented the telephone (patented 1875) in Boston. The time was passing when a great foreign pioneer with ideas to exploit would settle in England to exploit them, as the elder Brunel had in 1799, or William Siemens in 1843. Ludwig Mond's founding of his alkali works at Winnington in Cheshire (1873) was perhaps the last case of this kind.

---

[1] Clapham, op. cit., p. 237.
[2] e.g. the American leather glove industry is said to have been largely developed in this way by workmen from the factories in Somerset.

Between 1870 and 1886 occurred two financial crises, each followed by an industrial and commercial depression. The first began on the Continent in 1873 at Vienna, and soon spread over central Europe. It had been preceded by an orgy of company flotation in Austria-Hungary and Germany, and a post-war building mania in the latter. Simultaneously had come a railway boom in the United States, a rise of prices everywhere, and a prevalence of strikes for higher wages. Then supervened certain monetary factors, notably the demonetization of silver by the new German Empire and by the Latin Union (both in 1873), which was equivalent to a contraction of the world's gold-supply. When the strain developed, the City and the Bank of England, still sobered by the Overend and Gurney collapse of 1866, were well prepared to meet it. Prices of coal and iron remained fairly high through the winters of 1874 and 1875. But early in 1876 the slump became general, and for three years English industry suffered the brunt of the great depression. The failure of the City of Glasgow Bank in 1878 was something like a climax. From the end of that year industry improved; though the agricultural depression, which had been added to it in 1878, went on steadily deepening. The second crisis started in 1882 in Paris; where the collapse through over-speculation of a great banking house (the Union Générale) paralleled closely the panic of 1866 in London. But it was succeeded in 1883 by a continued fall in prices, which lasted three years and at its climax in 1886 produced, as we saw in our last chapter, serious rioting in London and elsewhere. This slump of the eighties, following so soon after that of the seventies and linked to it by the unlifted depression in agriculture, gave Victorian courage and optimism the severest shock that it had yet received. Among its by-products were a Lord Mayor's Fund (memorably maladministered); a circular from Chamberlain at the local government board to the local authorities urging relief works (an experiment chiefly valuable for its negative results); a royal commission 'on the Depression in Trade and Industry', which buried itself under the pile of its own blue-books; and a hot stirring of social thought, which will be touched on in our next chapter. Soon after Lord Salisbury's second government got into its stride, the sky cleared; and before the end of 1887 trade was working towards another boom. But England was not the same afterwards. There was 'never glad confident morning again' in the outlook for the workshop of the world. It is symptomatic that the word 'unemployed' used as a noun is first recorded by the *Oxford English Dictionary* from the year 1882; the word 'unemployment' from 1888.

An industrial and commercial change which, steadily developing throughout these sixteen years, had deep silent effects on the whole tone and fabric of English life, was that from the individual captain of industry to the limited company. The Companies Act of 1862 had been followed by a rush of new issues, averaging £120 millions a year over three years. But after the Overend and Gurney failure (directly resulting from this) the figures fell away sharply to £28·8 millions in 1867, and did not again pass the £100 millions until 1872.[1] Thenceforward, however, the conversion of firms into companies proceeded rapidly. At first it was aimed more at limiting liability than at divorcing the ownership from the management of factories and works. But, as time went on, it had increasingly the latter effect. There were irresistible advantages; the technology of the day demanded larger and larger aggregates of capital, and the new system rendered it possible to obtain them. It also provided some antidote to the evil of nepotism, where wealth descended to heirs in the form of a factory which they were personally unfitted to run. Yet it made a profound breach with our tradition in that it legalized irresponsible wealth. Hitherto accumulated riches in England had taken one of two principal forms. The oldest, land, had for centuries carried with it the public duties of a justice of the peace. It also implied an intelligent co-operation with the farmers, whose fixed capital the landowner in great part provided; and it was the almost invariable practice of English squires to reside for a large part of the year on their estates.[2] When the industrial revolution introduced a rival wealth and gave a new meaning to the word employer, most of the individual manufacturers, ironmasters, and mine-owners developed a similar attitude of patriarchal leadership towards their employees. They lived among them; knew them personally from boy to greybeard; were interested in their families; and, though often raking an inordinate profit off the fruits of the joint enterprise, were yet not unconscious of its joint character, deploring nothing so much during

[1] Ellis T. Powell, *The Evolution of the Money Market* (1915), pp. 395–6.
[2] To the difference in these respects between England and Ireland the agrarian troubles of the latter were partly due. Lord Carnarvon, a typical good English landlord, was frankly scandalized during his viceregal tour of West Ireland (1885) by the rent-drawing absenteeism which he found.

a depression as the necessity to discharge hands. This was not so in all industries, nor in all places. Most of the labour in the great ports was casual; the employers had no personal relation to it; hence London, Bristol, Liverpool, and Glasgow became early notorious for the brutality and violence of their mobs. Lancashire, again, before industry settled there, was a thinly peopled county; to a considerable extent both employers and employed came to be immigrants without local roots; and so its work-people were driven early to develop self-helping class activities, such as trade-unionism and co-operation. On the other hand, the cloth industry, whether in the west of England or the West Riding, conformed very generally to the conditions described above, and so did most of the English industries south of the Trent. The different types may be illustrated from the coal-fields. Those which especially produced coal for export and for large-scale smelting—that is, in particular, South Wales, Durham, and Scotland—were early developed under large concerns with little personal relation between masters and men. In those, on the other hand, composing what came later to be known as the English federated area, employment much longer remained personal and considerate. To go from, say, the Rhondda Valley to Penistone was to breathe a different moral air. Down to 1914 this was visibly reflected in the number and character of labour disputes.

The spread of the company system throughout English industry was relentless but gradual. Reckoning from 1872 it took about thirty years to complete.[1] Patriarchalism disappeared. The owner-entrepreneur disappeared also. Property passed to shareholders concerned only for dividends; control was exercised on the shareholders' behalf by boards of directors, nominally elected by them, but in fact mainly co-opted, often representing only financial, social, or personal 'pulls' and devoid of any specialized understanding of the firm or even of the industry. Thus for the alert individual carrying his business in his head came to be

---

[1] It was in 1902 that Alfred Baldwin converted his Stourport ironworks into a company. That had been one of the very last important individual firms. The often-quoted speech which his son, Mr. Stanley Baldwin, delivered in the house of commons on 5 March 1925 describes the social aspects of the change in a very moving manner. For the collectivist implications inherent in company ownership, see a brilliant passage in Dicey's *Law and Public Opinion in England during the Nineteenth Century*, pp. 246-7. Dicey's illustration is from a railway company, but the principle is the same.

substituted a collectivity finding safety in rules and records. The profession of accountancy acquired a totally new importance; and the invention of the typewriter[1] was one of many mechanical devices helping in the same general direction. Similar and parallel changes invaded banking. Down to 1866 there were still a large number of private banking firms; but the Overend and Gurney failure gave a strong stimulus to their conversion into limited liability companies. Already during the seventies there was a marked tendency to amalgamate these into bigger units, thereby reducing overhead costs and pooling resources against emergency. Here too the change spelled progress for forces which would not be denied. The type of bank evolved was much safer for depositors, and it could lend on a scale commensurate with that of company-owned business. Yet the old factors of local knowledge and personal confidence in character became correspondingly weakened. Advances and overdrafts were determined more by formal rules and less by individual judgement and responsibility. All this made it harder for the innovator without capital to forge to the front in industry, and gradually blunted the spear-point of individualist initiative, which had hitherto opened the new ways for England.[2]

A consequence of the company developments was the rise into visible prominence of a rentier class. It had its beginnings some decades earlier, when the advent of the railway companies had widened the hitherto narrow field of interest-bearing investment. Now it received even wider stimulus, and whole towns sprang up to house the comfortable families of those who had retired to 'live on their income'. Bournemouth practically dates from 1870, when the railway first reached it; it became a borough in 1890. Eastbourne started a little earlier; it was incorporated in 1883. In contrast with the higgledy-piggledy hideousness of Victorian industrial cities, these homes for the well-to-do were the tardy harbingers in England of what is now called town-

---

[1] The first practicable one was patented in America in 1867. Taken over by the Remington Company in 1873, it soon crossed the Atlantic; though English business was too conservative to adopt it generally till the nineties.

[2] It is perhaps not irrelevant to note, that down to the beginning of 1933 the United States, which from 1880 onwards more and more took Great Britain's place as the torch-bearer in industry and the home of an individualism offering the freest career to talent, retained in its banking system (for evil as well as good) a very large number of small local personally conducted banks.

planning. In other respects their contribution to the nation's general culture has been less, perhaps, than might have been expected.

While British industry thus continued to display an astonishing vigour, qualified only towards the end of the sixteen years by certain hints of decline, British agriculture, which till then had almost as conspicuously led the world, was thrown overboard in a storm like an unwanted cargo. We have briefly told the political story of this in Chapter II.

What occasioned the sudden and overwhelming invasion of Europe by American prairie-wheat in the late seventies? Three causes, which by accident came together. First, railway expansion. In 1860 the United States had approximately 30,800 miles of railway (about thrice the British mileage at the same date). By 1870 this had become 53,200 miles, and by 1880 about 94,200 miles. These prodigious growths were mainly across prairie; and the railways, in order to encourage farmer-settlers, undertook to carry their crops for less than cost over a series of years. The consequence was a land-rush followed by very cheap grain-freights. Secondly, a sudden abundance of cheap ocean-going steamer transport resulted, as explained above, from improvements in marine engines. The cost of sending a ton of grain from Chicago to Liverpool water-borne was £3 7s. in 1873, £2 1s. in 1880, and £1 4s. in 1884—a cheapening equal to 9s. 9d. on every quarter of corn for water-freight alone. The third and decisive factor was agricultural machinery. The peculiarity of the prairie-farmer's position was that he could have as much virgin land as he wanted, but it was next to impossible to get any hired labour. No manures were needed; no intensive culture was worth while; the land itself was his asset, and the more he cropped, the bigger his return. But he had to do his work himself, and the limit of his extension was set by what machines would enable one pair of hands to perform. Under so strong an urge it is not surprising that the United States from 1840 or earlier led the way in inventions of agricultural machinery; and perhaps the single most epoch-making one of them all was the self-binder attached to the reaping-machine, because it enabled the latter to be worked by one man instead of two. The first commercially successful type was the Locke wire binder brought out in 1873, and immediately adopted on a most extensive scale. In principle it meant doubling every prairie-farmer's crop, and already by 1878 its effect was enormous.[1]

With the Law of Diminishing Returns on its back, no agriculture in densely populated, highly farmed Europe could possibly meet prairie prices upon level terms. It was not a question of efficiency; European agriculture was far more efficient. It was a question of the bounty of virgin Nature. By 1879 every country west of Russia faced the alternative—to put on a tariff or lose the best of its wheatfields. And every wheat-growing country chose the former, save the two densest and most industrialized—Great Britain and Belgium. The blow which struck the British farmer could not have fallen at a worse time. From 1875 to an extraordinary culmination in 1879 he experienced bad wet summers. Apart from the cheapening of wheat, there was a world monetary depression under which meat and dairy prices fell considerably. Moreover in 1877 occurred the last British visitation of rinderpest; 1879 brought an outbreak of liver-rot in sheep, by which several millions were lost; and 1883, a terrible epidemic of foot-and-mouth disease, which was only less catastrophic for cattle.

In 1877 English wheat averaged 56s. 9d. a quarter; but for the rest of the century it never again came within 10s. of that figure. In 1878 it dropped to 46s. 5d.—not an unusual price in a good year with a large crop, but damaging in a bad year with a small one. That was one of the deadliest features of the new imports; they not merely modified but destroyed the old inverse relation between home prices and home yields. So the figure went on dropping, till in 1886 it reached 31s. a quarter. By 1885 the British area under wheat had shrunk a million acres, or about 28½ per cent. The loss was really greater, for the first to be abandoned were the heavy rich 'three-horse' lands, which bore the biggest crops but cost most to cultivate. The barley area dwindled greatly also. Our dependence on foreign cereals grew by leaps. In the decade 1831–40 we had imported 2 per cent. of the grain that we consumed; in the decade 1861–70 the percentage was 24; in the nine years 1880–9 it was 45—for wheat it was 65. Contrary to what has been often supposed, the fall in

---

[1] The Appleby machine, which among other improvements substituted twine for wire, was patented in 1879. With its famous tying device known as the 'Appleby knotter', it was perhaps the most ingenious agricultural machine of the nineteenth century.

grain production was not compensated by a growth in the number of animals. There was some substitution of cattle for sheep,[1]
but little or no net increase; nor is this surprising, since it is now
well recognized that land in a rotation under the plough yields,
in addition to its grain-output, as much animal food as if it was
permanently under grass. As for farming employment, the 1881
census showed 92,250 fewer labourers at work than in 1871.
Many went into town slums as 'general' labourers—the bottom
class of the urban proletariat, which increased by 53,496 in the
same period. Many more emigrated—nearly a million persons
left England and Wales in that decade.

The period of this chapter closes with the ruin still in progress;
its cruellest time fell in the nineties. Englishmen born in the
twentieth century may find it hard to realize what it meant; so
unimportant has farming long become in the nation's life. But
down to 1880, despite all the marvellous expansion of mining
and manufacture and metallurgy, agriculture retained a kind of
headship. It employed incomparably more people than any
other single industry. With its fortunes those of the rest still
largely fluctuated; a good harvest quickened trade all round, a bad
one slowed it. More than a century of keen practical research
and experiment, for which nobility and even royalty shared the
credit with commoners, had lifted its technology far ahead of
most farming on the continent. Its breeds were the best, its
cropping the most scientific, its yields the highest; its virtually
universal[2] substitution of horses for oxen for all purposes of
farm traction typified visibly its specialization for quality and its
application of superior force. Its wages, though low to our eyes,
were the highest agricultural wages in Europe, and represented
a distinctly better standard of material comfort than that of
most of the self-employed peasantry in similar European latitudes. Much the same may be said of its housing conditions.
Its worst remaining employment abuse—the gang system—had
been finally exposed and almost suppressed in the sixties. Joseph
Arch's agricultural trade-union movement, launched in February 1872 and prudently conducted by dissenting lay preachers,
succeeded in raising wages over wide areas by 1s. 6d. or 2s. a

---

[1] Sheep between 1878 and 1882 actually decreased by over five millions in four
years.
[2] Oxen ploughing could still be seen in 1889 on at least one Dorset farm where
they had never been given up, but only as a curiosity of individual conservatism.

week, and in some cases by 3*s*. or 4*s*., besides improving hours and conditions.[1] It suffered a defeat in 1874, but would probably have recovered itself, had not the beginnings of the depression followed in 1875. After 1877, when tens of thousands of workers were discarded yearly, wages fell by as much as they had previously risen, and more.[2] Farmers themselves sank into ever increasing embarrassments; bankruptcies and auctions followed each other; the countryside lost its most respected figures. Those whose pride in, and conscience towards, the land was greatest, suffered most; for the only chance of survival was to lower farming standards all round. Across the stricken field strange birds of prey flitted; speculators who bought populous corn-lands for conversion into uninhabited sheep-runs; or 'pirate' tenants, who went from one farm to another exhausting the soil by a policy of taking without giving. Adjustments, as time went on, were made; but always upon the basis of withdrawing both capital and men from the land. For twenty years the only chance for any young or enterprising person on the countryside was to get out of it. The motto over the door of Dante's *Inferno* might have been truthfully posted at the entrance of a typical English village.

So was consummated the urbanizing of a nation, which till a century before had possessed only one great city, and whose traditions of popular culture were almost entirely rural. England, being now 'the workshop of the world', staked her future upon continuing to be. With the outlook as it then appeared to her, she could probably have done no other. Yet even at this moment other nations were developing policies incompatible with her ideal. Not only during the eighties did the menace of rival 'workshops' first come in sight, but the tariff-exclusion of British goods entered on a new phase. Cobden, while believing in free trade for Great Britain regardless of what other countries might do, had nevertheless expected her example to be contagious. So down to a point it was. But when France and Germany each decided on protection for their farmers, their manufacturers naturally claimed corresponding treatment. Thus industrial and agricultural tariffs grew side by side, each demanding to be raised whenever the other was. At the same time the

---

[1] Hasbach, *History of the English Agricultural Labourer* (1894), English version (1908), p. 280; cp. p. 284.

[2] Royal Commission on Agriculture (1881). *Evidence*, Q. 58,559; cp. Q. 61,264.

spectacle of British wealth derived from industry made other countries anxious to rear infant manufactures of their own; and they could only do so by barring out British goods. This policy had been practised in varying degrees by the United States since Alexander Hamilton's day; but there was now an agitation greatly to extend it, which led, in 1890, to the McKinley Tariff. Excepting New South Wales and the Cape, even the colonies to which we had but recently given self-government raised fast-growing walls against us.

The sacrifice of agriculture led to a general fall of rural rents, heaviest where there had been most arable, lighter where there was less, and nil or negligible in a purely pastoral area like Snowdonia. Coupled with the rent-war in Ireland, this began the economic dethronement of the landowners. Till 1880 they had remained the richest class. Lord Beaconsfield, writing to Queen Victoria in 1878, observed that 'the Duke of Bedford is the wealthiest of Your Majesty's subjects; his income absolutely exceeding £300,000 a year'. Part of the duke's rents came from his Bloomsbury estates, but a large part from agricultural land. The decisive changes in the relative importance of landed and commercial wealth occurred after 1886; but already by that date the position of the former was severely shaken. Nor could political headship long survive economic defeat.

An interesting achievement of technology, which belongs to this period, was the import of frozen and chilled meat. It cannot be said to have greatly injured the British farmer, assuming that he had to face competition from foreign meat imports in any case. But it notably humanized the trade, and enabled New Zealand and Australia to obtain a share in it which would otherwise have been scarcely possible. Down to 1882, when the first frozen New Zealand mutton reached London on board the s.s. *Dunedin*, the home production of meat for a fast-growing population had been stationary over nearly twenty years, but the foreign imports had risen rapidly.[1] Some of the import trade was in canned meat, but the great bulk was in live cattle. Their largest source was the United States, but other very large sources were Denmark and Holland; none yet came from any country south of the equator. The first man to manufacture ice by artificial process on a commercial scale was James Harrison, an

---

[1] Yearly averages, 1861–70: home, 1,036,000 tons; imported, 131,000 tons. Year's totals, 1882: home, 1,090,000 tons; imported, 654,000 tons.

Australian;[1] but when he tried shipping a meat cargo in 1873, it was spoiled through insufficient care and he was ruined. Another Australian pioneer, T. S. Mort, was similarly ruined in 1876, though not till he had helped to advance the idea. Where they failed, some French engineers succeeded; and in May 1878 the s.s. *Paraguay* landed 5,500 carcasses of mutton from Buenos Aires in perfect condition at Havre. On the top of this epoch-making[2] feat, its authors tried to raise capital in France for the new industry. It is very significant that they could not; the French public at that date would not subscribe to such an object. Thus it was that the profits of the *Paraguay*'s lesson were reaped for the British flag; and on 2 February 1880 the s.s. *Strathleven* arrived in London from Sydney and Melbourne with 40 tons of beef and mutton. A lamb was sent to the queen, a sheep to the prince of Wales; the meat had an excellent press; and the future of the business was assured. Two years later, by the enterprise of Thomas Brydone, the *Dunedin* brought New Zealand into it, with wonderful results for what till then had been a rather struggling and backward colony. Within another ten years New Zealand was exporting two million frozen carcasses a year; within twenty years, four million.

The new method supplemented the shipping of live animals, but did not supersede it for a long time. They continued to arrive in increasing quantities from the continent and North America and (after 1885) from the Argentine. The peak year for live cattle was 1890 (642,747); for live sheep 1895 (1,965,470). Apart from the horrible cruelties which on the longer routes were incidental to the sea-voyage, particularly when it was stormy, the great drawback to this method was that it so often brought cattle diseases into our island. On this ground an Order of 1892 (never revoked) stopped the shipping of live slaughter-animals from the continent; Argentine live stock were prohibited in 1900, and again, after a brief lifting of the ban, in 1903. United States swine were banned in 1910; and by 1913 the intake of live North American cattle had dwindled to below 15,000. Thus the refrigerating method conquered the field; and,

[1] About 1850: British patents 1856 and 1857. Harrison was from Glasgow, Mort from Bolton; both were born in 1816, and both had emigrated to Australia in 1838.

[2] Small consignments of chilled beef had been sent over successfully by T. C. Eastman from New York since 1875. But it was a different and much easier proposition on that short non-tropical route.

given the problem of feeding our dense population from overseas, has solved it very remarkably. A calculation made by R. E.
Turnbull[1] in 1912 showed that, whereas in 1880 our supply of
meat to a population of 34·77 millions worked out to 102 lb.
a head (home-grown 68 lb., imported 34 lb.), in 1910 for a
population of 44·85 millions the figures were 114 lb. per head
(home-grown 63 lb., imported 51 lb.). The aggregate supply
of home-grown meat had increased by 20·1 per cent., showing
that the importations, though they had driven down the price
of bullocks by about $1\frac{1}{2}d.$ per lb. and of sheep by about $2d.$, had
in no sense destroyed the industry. So their effect differed essentially from that of the grain imports.

At this point something must be said of the navy, which stood
guard over all these fast-growing economic commitments overseas.
The period witnessed a growing rivalry among naval nations in
the passage from wooden walls to steel gun-platforms. Great
Britain had so much the largest and costliest fleet that she was
never left long behind; but it is rather noticeable, in view of her
great technological lead in civil life, that she originated none of
the main nineteenth-century naval changes. Neither armour nor
turrets nor breech-loaders, neither mines nor torpedoes nor submarines, were British ideas. The Service did not favour invention.

Armour was first used in the Crimean war by the French;
the first turret was that of the American Federalist *Monitor*,
which fought the Confederate *Merrimac* in March 1862. Great
Britain's first ironclad, the *Warrior*, had been completed in 1861.
She was an advance on the French pioneers in that she was built
of iron instead of being a wooden structure with iron plating.
But she was a full-rigged steam-and-sail ship with three masts
and a bowsprit, and carried her guns on the broadside, where
each had a very limited arc of fire. The example of the *Monitor*
was copied for coast defence in the *Prince Albert* (1866), and attempts were then made in the *Monarch* and *Captain* to adapt the
idea to ocean-going vessels. But the conservatism of the navy
insisted on making them into full-rigged three-masted ships with
high poop and forecastle besides other superstructure; and the
tragic, though not unnatural, result was that on 7 September

[1] J. T. Critchell and J. Raymond, *History of the Frozen Meat Trade* (1912),
pp. 320–2.

1870 the *Captain* capsized and foundered with nearly all hands in a gale in the Bay of Biscay. The immediate reaction from this disaster was to revert to broadside ships for the high seas and confine 'monitors' to home defence; but after a year or two the correct inference was drawn, which was not to go back on turrets, but to abandon sails. The *Devastation* (1873), which embodied this logic, was the first warship in the navy with a modern silhouette. She carried two turrets, and only a single stumpy iron mast for observation and signalling, her funnels and other top-hamper being placed with it amidships between the turrets. Her armour was carried on the turrets and in a belt on the waterline; the rest was undefended. She and her sister, the *Thunderer*, provided the general pattern followed in fighting ships for over thirty years.

The prime factor was guns. But our navy between the Crimean war and 1886 was in the singular position of having to go for its guns to the war office (owing to the abolition of the board of ordnance at the former epoch). Friction resulted and it became clear that in war the army would be served first and the navy would have to be content with what was left over. Yet not till 1886 did an inter-departmental committee recommend that the navy should keep its own war stores and design its own ordnance. Meanwhile, as we saw in Chapter I, the artillery branch of the army was in the hands of reactionaries with a passion for muzzle-loaders, and they imposed their views on the navy at a time when naval ordnance elsewhere was progressing faster than military. The muzzle-loaders were most inefficient; at a famous trial 'duel' between two anchored monitors at Portland in July 1872 the navy's crack gunner missed his opponent's turret at 200 yards. Woolwich was still unconvinced, and it was not till ten years later that the first heavy breech-loaders were mounted in the British navy (on the *Conqueror*, completed 1882). Meantime the muzzle-loader was brought to its furthest development in an 80-ton gun (christened the 'Woolwich Infant'), of which four were mounted in the *Inflexible* (1881). These monsters threw a projectile of nearly 1,800 lb., but their range and accuracy were very limited, as the necessity for drawing the gun back into the turret to reload kept the barrel extremely short. The *Inflexible*, although the largest vessel (11,880 tons) yet built for the navy, was in some other ways an anachronism, being brig-rigged with two masts and enormous yards to carry sails. If felled in action they would not only have done deck-damage, but might probably have fouled the propellers. Yet they accompanied her into the bombardment of Alexandria, where mercifully the Egyptian gunners missed them. The chief lesson of that engagement was the disadvantage of black powder. The British warships had to interrupt their fire for quite long spells in order to let the smoke clear. This gave a direct impetus to the search for smokeless explosives.

In 1886 appeared the *Collingwood* (9,500 tons), first of the 'Admiral' class. She was the earliest battleship built throughout of steel, though iron remained for ten years more the backing in the steel-faced 'composite' armour-plates. The *Collingwood* had two pairs of 46-ton breech-loaders, each mounted in a barbette (i.e. fixed open-topped turret); but she also had amidships a considerable 'secondary' armament of unprotected 6-inch guns and light quick-firers. This remained a feature of battleships for the next twenty years, though as time went on shields and other protection were introduced for their gun-crews. Their object was to beat off torpedo-boats, which had gradually become a serious menace with the development in the seventies of the Whitehead torpedo. Other early precautions against them (besides nets) were double-bottoms and water-tight compartments; the *Inflexible* had 135 of the latter. The development of gunnery at this stage first brought into controversial prominence Captain John Fisher, afterwards Lord Fisher of Kilverstone. In 1883 he was appointed to the *Excellent*, then the Gunnery School at Portsmouth. He found firing practices still being carried out with smooth-bores! He substituted modern quick-firers.

Although the tonnage of these battleships seems small by twentieth-century standards, it represented a vast increase on the cost of wooden navies. 1886 was only a quarter of a century from our earliest ironclad; yet the difference between the *Collingwood* and a three-decker was like that between an express train and a stage coach. Nor were the new vessels permanent assets like the old; each fresh type was speedily outclassed. Our naval estimates, which were £9¼ millions in 1870, had gone up to practically £13 millions by 1886. The only Power that we built against was France, with a fleet much smaller than ours but usually ahead in novelties. The third naval Power in Europe was Italy; who was traditionally pro-British, and after the Tunis episode anti-French. Naval inventions were chiefly French or American, save for those of the gunmakers—Krupp in Germany and (less important) Whitworth and Armstrong in England.[1]

If we turn now to the government of this island in the same period, we shall see behind the wavering fortunes of parties and cabinets two steady tendencies—democracy and bureaucracy. Both comparatively new, they developed together. The starting-point of the one was the 1867 franchise reform. The other, in its modern shape, may be referred back to the institution of the Civil Service Commission in 1855; though it derived much from the reform of 1870, which for the first time made public competitive examination the normal entrance to a Whitehall career.

Gladstone's 1868–74 government, despite its reforming reputation, had only a limited accord with either tendency. The rising radicalism in the town constituencies, which since 1867 inspired the liberal party's biggest battalions, was already collectivist by instinct. But in the cabinet its single representative was the ageing individualist Bright; unless Stansfeld, who came in at the bottom in 1871, may perhaps be deemed one. Hence all the ministry's main legislative achievements—Irish disestablishment, judicial reform, the abolition of purchase in the army, elementary education, and the ballot—could be squared with individualist principles. Yet three of them—the judicial, military, and educational reforms—followed that trend towards a more efficient state, which was likely (as the whigs who opposed Cardwell divined) to enlarge the state's borders. But since enlargement remained unconscious or reluctant, neither Gladstone nor his colleagues gave it enough thought. The spheres, where positive and constructive statesmanship was most called for, were those of local government. In 1870 the very term was but a dozen years old, having been invented in 1858 by a conservative, C. B. Adderley.[2] And the thing which it described remained chaotic,

[1] Whitehead was also an Englishman, but he invented his original torpedo at Fiume in 1866.

[2] B. 1814; educated privately and at Christ Church, Oxford. Inherited large estates round Birmingham, including the site of Saltley, which he started town-planning as early as 1837. Vice-president of the education committee of the privy council and president of the board of health, 1858; under-secretary for the colonies, 1866–8; chairman of royal commission on the sanitary laws, 1868–71; president of the board of trade (but not in the cabinet), 1874–8, when he retired with a barony as the first Lord Norton. He was a direct descendant of Oliver Cromwell; a keen Evangelical; and much interested in colonial as well as local government. He took part with Gibbon Wakefield and Lord Lyttleton in founding the church colony

rudimentary, corrupt—altogether behind the needs of the community.

The only nation-wide scheme of local authorities was that of the boards of guardians administering the 1834 Poor Law. For the rest, the counties were still ruled by the justices of the peace in quarter sessions; and in the urban areas responsibility for such primary services as paving, cleansing, lighting, or drainage devolved sometimes on a municipal corporation, sometimes on an improvement commission, sometimes on a local board, sometimes on a London vestry; not unfrequently being divided between two of these bodies. The 1868–74 government itself added yet another *ad hoc* authority—the school boards, which were set up in most areas under its 1870 Education Act. At the centre there was an equal lack of co-ordination. Poor Law came under a distinct department; but it came alone, and the president of the poor law board rarely had cabinet status. Public health since 1856 had been partly under the medical department of the privy council (with Dr., afterwards Sir John Simon, the famous pioneer of sanitation, at its head), and partly under the local government section of the home office. This last was directed by Tom Taylor, a well-known figure in Victorian letters and art-criticism; who, although he did not become editor of *Punch* till 1874, had already written some proportion of his hundred stage-plays and, for all his sterling qualities of heart and head, must be confessed very far from the modern ideal of a hard-worked departmental chief.

Hence though sanitary administration was at that time better understood in England than anywhere else, its practice remained very inadequate in the towns, while in rural districts it barely existed. It was not a party question; the opposition was that of 'interests'. Possibly the liberal party included more of the few enthusiasts among its rank and file. But as between the party chiefs the balance was the other way round; Disraeli expressed a concern in sanitation quite exceptional among the politicians of his day; whereas Gladstone showed none at all. Indeed the blind eye, which he consistently turned towards the importance of local government, explains some of the gravest gaps in his statesmanship, and in its effect on history may be accounted a national misfortune.

at Canterbury, New Zealand; and New Zealand's autonomous constitution was drafted at his house.

Before leaving office in 1868 Disraeli had appointed a commission on the sanitary laws, which came to be presided over by C. B. Adderley, and it reported in 1871. Stansfeld had then just become president of the poor law board in succession to Goschen, whose ambitious bill to set up representative government in parishes and counties had been dropped, after opposition, through Gladstone's lack of interest. The scheme of organization advocated by the commission fell into two halves: a single supervising authority at the centre, and a single local health authority in each area at the circumference—in boroughs the municipal corporation, in other populous areas a local board, and in country districts the board of guardians. Increased powers were also recommended for the authorities, and important extensions of sanitary law. Stansfeld carried in two successive bills the commission's scheme of organization; but his proposals to extend the sanitary law were resisted, and he had to jettison practically all of them. His constitution of the local government board left much to be desired; for of the three bodies which went to compose it he allowed the poor law board to obtain a dominant, almost an exclusive, position. The effect was bad, because the traditions of that board were entirely negative and restrictive. Set up to guard against extravagance in the granting of poor relief, it had imbued its officials with the idea that Whitehall's sole duty towards local authorities was to prevent them from doing what they ought not. But at this time what the local authorities, other than boards of guardians, really needed from the centre was positive stimulus, enlightened guidance, and constructive advice based on research. Dr. John Simon's department was ready to give these, and possibly Tom Taylor's section might have been; but the first was most unwisely subordinated, and the second virtually disappeared when Taylor shortly afterwards left. Nobody who has experienced an amalgamation will wonder at the poor law board's preponderance; for Stansfeld started with it as his own titular department, and the rest were for him outside accretions. Yet it is difficult to over-estimate what the country lost through having its local authorities down to 1914 placed under a central department constantly on the alert to hinder them and rarely, if ever, to help. The much greater progress made by Prussia between 1870 and 1914 on many sides of local government administration was associated with an almost opposite relation between centre and circumference.

It speaks volumes for the public spirit surging up in England at that time that so much municipal development nevertheless went forward. Stimulus came gradually through the franchise reform of 1867, which in towns gave most municipal voters a vote for parliament also. Narrow and often corrupt cliques, kept in power at the town halls by electoral apathy, could not survive the new public interest. The radical city of Birmingham showed the way, and the celebrated mayoralty of Joseph Chamberlain (1873-6) not only transformed its civic life, but held up the torch of example to municipalities far and wide. As Chamberlain himself put it, the town was 'parked, paved, assized, marketed, Gas-and-Watered, and *improved*—all as the result of three years' active work'.[1] While it was still in progress came 1875—Disraeli's *annus mirabilis* of social reform—bringing the great Public Health Act. This for the first time armed the English municipalities as a whole with most of the powers which had hitherto proved useful when obtained by some of them under special acts. In the same year the first of Cross's Housing Acts introduced a new method of housing reform. Till then there had only been Lord Shaftesbury's two acts of 1851, permitting local authorities to supervise common lodging-houses (and in some cases procure their erection), and the Torrens Act of 1866, enabling them to compel the owners of individual insanitary houses to put them in proper condition. Cross's acts were the first authorizing what are now called clearance schemes; they empowered local authorities to condemn, demolish, and reconstruct whole areas. Chamberlain in 1875-6 carried through at Birmingham the largest project of this kind hitherto attempted. It covered between forty and fifty acres, and required a special local act, in whose passage the conservative president of the local government board co-operated with the radical mayor. The great thoroughfare known as Corporation Street resulted.

The second Cross Act and a second Torrens Act were both passed in 1879. Even so, the feeling grew that far too little was being done. In 1881 there was a select committee of the house of commons; in 1882, another Act; in 1883, a pamphlet by G. R. Sims, *The Bitter Cry of Outcast London*, moved the queen and shook even the party politicians. The outcome in 1884 was the famous Royal Commission on Housing, in which the prince of Wales, Cardinal Manning, Lord Salisbury, Goschen, Cross, Torrens,

[1] J. L. Garvin, *Life of Chamberlain*, i (1932), 202.

Jesse Collings (representing Birmingham), and Henry Broadhurst (representing trade unionism) sat with others under Dilke's
chairmanship. Their report in 1885 was followed by yet another
act. Meanwhile the local authorities had begun to attack the
worst slums. In London between 1876 and 1884 the Metropolitan Board of Works undertook schemes which displaced
22,872 persons and rehoused 28,352. The weak feature in them
(paralleled elsewhere) was that the board never provided the re-
housing itself, but merely offered the sites for sale on the condition
that they should be so used. But for the existence of philanthropic
bodies like the Peabody Trust, the effects would have been even
worse than they were. Yet the individualist preference for avoiding public enterprise, wherever possible, died hard.

Though municipal enterprise in Birmingham under Chamberlain struck the imagination most, the great cities of northern
England were moving even earlier. Manchester opened up
Deansgate—its equivalent to Corporation Street—under an act
obtained in 1869. In the same year it appointed its first medical
officer of health; Birmingham's was not appointed till 1875.
Liverpool had anticipated them both as far back as 1847. The
Manchester town hall, completed in 1877, was at that date unequalled for size and convenience among the municipal buildings of Europe. At Liverpool the greatest of the city's features,
its monumental granite-walled docks, received their most important additions during this period at the hand of the Mersey Dock
and Harbour Board. The Liverpool Municipality in the early
eighties showed itself particularly active in slum-clearing. Bradford's Italianate town hall and exchange date from the seventies.
All these cities (and with them, notably, Glasgow) began now to
embark upon one type after another of municipal trading—
water, gas, trams, electricity. The common feature of these was
that the services concerned, whether in private or in public
hands, were 'natural monopolies'. In London at this period they
were without exception left to be exploited by companies; which
in some cases (especially water) were unequal to their task and
grew distinctly unpopular. In the great provincial cities, where
municipalization became increasingly the vogue, it had not been
identified in the minds of its promoters with any collectivist principle. They were simply empirical Englishmen facing public
needs, and trying to meet each of them specifically in what
appeared the most practical way. Only as the period of this

chapter was ending did the young intellectuals of the Fabian Society seize on the process, christen it 'municipal socialism', and base on it a philosophy of politico-economic evolution.

Its progress was much quickened by what was really a revolution in municipal finance. In September 1880 the Liverpool Corporation, under a special act, achieved the first successful flotation of a consolidated municipal stock. The municipal statesman chiefly responsible was Sir W. B. Forwood; the amount subscribed was £2 millions. Birmingham had tried to make such an issue in 1877, and failed. But now she followed hard on Liverpool's success, and her issue had a novel feature—it was authorized, not by a private bill, but by a provisional order, which saved much expense. Of the door thus thrown open to municipal enterprise the towns were soon eager to avail themselves; and their stocks proved very welcome to prudent investors. Thirty years from the start the amount of local government debt in the United Kingdom stood at £600 millions.[1]

A weak point in municipalization at this stage, as indeed in many other activities of the time, was that being the work of men, most of whom had received little or no cultural education, it was too often deficient in any sound feeling for beauty or even amenity. Some of the causes and consequences of this will be discussed more fully in the next chapter; but it is pertinent here to point out that the failure was partly due to the non-interference theory of government. In the eighteenth and early nineteenth centuries the centre left everything of that kind to the circumference, and the circumference meant the justices of the peace, i.e. country gentlemen who had been educated at Oxford or Cambridge and rounded off their novitiate by a tour on the continent. The result was to evolve during several centuries perhaps the most beautiful countryside in the world. But it was a different thing leaving beauty and amenity to a circumference manned by self-made speculative builders, contractors, manufacturers, merchants, and shopkeepers, who had gone as boys into business after very brief and utilitarian schooling. If the centre had conceived its functions in less purely negative terms, its more educated personnel might have done much to control ugliness, and to champion amenity as well as sanitation in the reform of the Victorian towns.

At Whitehall several important changes fall within this period

[1] R. H. Gretton, *A Modern History of the English People*, i (1912), 29.

besides the birth of the local government board. The reforms of
the army and war office have been sketched in Chapter I. When
Queen Victoria accepted the principle that the commander-in-
chief must be responsible to the government and not to herself
personally, she renounced one of the last moot points in personal
rule. She continued, however, to feel and speak as if the army
belonged to her in some special way, and fought successfully to
maintain her cousin, the duke of Cambridge, as commander-in-
chief till 1895. Therein she did the nation a disservice. Nobody
has ever accused the duke of serious corruption, but he had nearly
every other disqualification for his post, and his unremitting
opposition to Wolseley's reforms was far from ineffectual. In
the civil departments the growth of bureaucracy and state activity progressed together. The home office, for instance, was
concerned in 1871 with a consolidating Factory and Workshops
Act, in 1872 with a fresh Mines Act, in 1875 with a Food and
Drugs Act, in 1878 with another Factory and Workshops Act,
and in 1883 with a further act affecting certain trades. Each of
these measures involved increases of staff. Chamberlain, again,
at the board of trade, with his Patents Act and Bankruptcy Act
and his revival of the board's commercial department, added
considerably to its personnel. The first woman to receive a post
of any importance in the civil service was probably Mrs. Nassau
Senior (daughter-in-law of the economist), who was appointed
a poor law inspector by Stansfeld in 1872. She did not live to
hold it long, and the precedent was not repeated till 1883, when
Dilke as president of the local government board appointed
several women inspectors. He urged Harcourt at the home office
to do the same, but was not listened to.

In 1885, when Gladstone's second administration was nearing
its end, the separate Scottish office was created, with a minister
(normally of cabinet rank) at its head. Its real author was Lord
Rosebery,[1] and its idea was a bureaucratic devolution. The work
of the home office, the local government board, the privy council's education department, and certain branches of the board of
trade, was in each case, so far as it affected Scotland, taken out
and assigned to the new department. Since debates on the Scottish Vote in the house of commons came by a sort of courtesy to
be left to Scottish members, Scotland did thus obtain some of the
substance, without the form, of home rule.

[1] Lord Crewe, *Lord Rosebery* (1931), pp. 168, 172, 242.

As the British state grew more democratic, it was natural that the class-organizations of the workers should gain further freedom of development. Already since 1825 trade unions had enjoyed in England a degree of liberty which they were denied in France till 1884 and in Germany till 1892. But the exact quantum of it had been left vague by parliament, and was the subject of oscillating decisions in the courts. The 1825 act did not define what a criminal combination was, but in two sections it declared that certain combinations were not to be penalized—those, namely, whether of employers or employed, which had as their sole purpose the fixing of wages or hours. Strictly construed, the words of these sections, while they allowed collective bargaining, did not confer a right to strike or lock out; but in leading cases the courts had expressed or implied that a strike within the same limits of purpose would not be criminal. Yet much remained prejudicial or doubtful: (1) the allowance did not extend to many ordinary trade-union objects—e.g. the limitation of apprentices or the restriction of overtime; (2) the act, in its third section, penalized the use of 'violence', threats', 'intimidation', 'molestation', and 'obstruction', and it was far from clear exactly how much the last words covered and what, if anything, in ordinary strike practice fell outside them; (3) the position of trade unions in regard to holding their property and enforcing their agreements was prejudiced by their being bodies which acted 'in restraint of trade', and, while it would be too much to say that they were wholly outlawed by the courts, their footing remained extremely precarious. On all these points there was recurrent divergence among the judges; some, like Mr. Justice Crompton,[1] clinging close to the older and narrower view, which members of the enacting parliament had doubtless held in 1825; others, like Sir William Erle, the chief justice of the common pleas, taking a rather different line and recognizing that 'the Common Law adapts itself by a perpetual process of growth to the perpetual roll of the tide of circumstances as society advances'.[2]

The case of *Hornby* v. *Close* (1867)[3] brought things to a crisis. It was there held that a trade union, as an illegal combination, could not protect its funds by registering as a friendly society.

---

[1] In the famous case of *Hilton* v. *Eckersley*, decided in 1856 (106 R.R. 507).

[2] Sir W. Erle's *Memorandum on Trade Union Law* to the Report of the Trades Unions Commission, 1869.

[3] L.R. 2 Q.B. 153.

The decision was negatived by a special act passed in 1869; but meanwhile a royal commission on trade societies had been appointed. Erle was the chairman, and among its members the most hostile to the trade unions was J. A. Roebuck[1] and the most sympathetic, Thomas Hughes[2] and Frederic Harrison.[3] The last two, with Professor E. S. Beesly,[4] played for some years a very important part in reconciling leaders of the political world to trade-union claims. On the side of the unions the principal figures were George Odger,[5] of the London Trades Council; William Allan,[6] secretary of the Amalgamated Society of Engineers, and Robert Applegarth,[7] secretary of the Amalgamated Carpenters and Joiners. The commission reported in 1869, the Majority Report being less unfavourable than had been expected, while that of the Minority (signed by Hughes, Harrison, and Lord Lichfield) was an extremely skilful statement of the trade-union case. Its main points were embodied in the Gladstone government's Trade Union Act of 1871; but to the chagrin of the trade unions this was coupled with a Criminal Law Amendment Act, which re-emphasized the 1825 Act's third section and 'under the specious guise of protecting public rights prohibited all incidents

[1] 1802–79: originally a chartist and radical, was at this stage a whig, and later became a follower of Lord Beaconsfield.

[2] 1822–96: author of *Tom Brown's Schooldays* (1856). Educated at Rugby and Oriel College, Oxford; barrister and (after 1882) county court judge; liberal M.P. 1865–74. Associated with F. D. Maurice and Charles Kingsley as a 'Christian Socialist'.

[3] 1831–1923: for many years leader of London Positivists. Educated at King's College School and Wadham College, Oxford; conveyancer, equity barrister, and author.

[4] 1831–1915. Contemporary with Harrison at Wadham College, Oxford, and, like him, became a leading positivist. Professor of history at University College, London, 1860–93; long editor of the *Positivist Review*.

[5] By far the ablest mid-century Labour politician. B. 1813, in west Devon, son of a Cornish miner; shoemaker by trade, settled in London; became prominent member of the Ladies' Shoemakers' Society, and as such took a leading part in the London Trades Council from its formation in 1860; succeeded George Howell as secretary in 1862, and held office till 1872. Between 1868 and 1872 made five unsuccessful attempts to enter parliament as a labour candidate; at Bristol in 1870 retired rather than split the liberal vote, but at Southwark in the same year persisted and polled 1,400 votes more than the defeated liberal. President of the general council of the (First) Labour International in 1870; d. 1877.

[6] The first secretary, 1851–74, of the Amalgamated Society of Engineers; famous for the prudent administration and financial skill whereby he caused that great trade union to be during the nineteenth century a model for the movement generally. See S. and B. Webb, *The History of Trade Unionism* (1894).

[7] Secretary of his union, 1863–71; a close disciple of Allan. See A. W. Humphrey, *Robert Applegarth* (1914).

of effective combination'.[1] One of the features of Disraeli's reforming zeal in 1875 was the repeal of this obnoxious act and its
replacement by a Conspiracy and Protection of Property Act,
which legalized peaceful picketing and laid down that a combination of persons concerned in a trade dispute might lawfully
do any act which was not punishable if committed by one person. Thus collective bargaining and its incidents were finally
legalized.

The first meeting of the Trades Union Congress had been held
in 1868. It was not, however, till its third meeting, held in March
1871, that it elected the 'Parliamentary Committee', destined
for the rest of our story to figure as the annually chosen political
executive of the movement. The trade unions, when it started,
were still confined to skilled workmen, and organized on the craft
basis, not the industrial. So it was even in an industry like coal-
mining; the unions were practically limited to the skilled coal-
getters at the face. The membership being relatively small, they
could choose their leaders from personal knowledge of their
characters; and usually they chose well. As the quarter-century
of good trade drew to its climax, this type of trade unionism became strong enough to carry through with success a number of
'prosperity' strikes for shorter hours or higher wages. The most
historic is the five months' strike of 9,500 Tyneside engineers in
1871 for a nine hours' day. It was unofficial, and disapproved
by William Allan,[2] but it succeeded. In January 1872 the nine
hours' day was generally conceded in all the chief engineering
establishments of the kingdom. Later in that year came an
epidemic of strikes—by builders and by agricultural labourers,
who succeeded; by gas-stokers and by Metropolitan police, who
failed. But in 1873 the onset of the great depression began;
70,000 iron-workers in South Wales struck against a 10 per cent.
wage-reduction, and were defeated. In the succeeding years of
slump down to 1879 the unions fared very badly; in some areas
(such as South Wales, where there was another desperate strike
in 1875) they were almost effaced. This period of defeat shook
the complacency of the craft unions, and made their younger
members more susceptible to the revival of socialism in the early

---

[1] C. M. Lloyd, *Trade Unionism* (1915), p. 25. For a detailed discussion see **R. Y.**
Hedges and A. Winterbottom, *The Legal History of Trade Unionism* (1930), ch. iv.

[2] It was run by a local 'Nine Hours' League', whose secretary, John Burnett,
became general secretary of the A.S.E. in 1875 following Allan's death.

eighties. But their officials kept the old courses; and the rise of the 'New Unionism' falls beyond the period which we are now considering.

On the other side of proletarian organization, the co-operative movement, these sixteen years witnessed a steady growth. The Co-operative Wholesale Society had commenced business (in Manchester) in 1864. The profits on trading first exceeded £5,000 in 1871; first exceeded £10,000 in 1880; and first exceeded £20,000 in 1886.[1] Such increases reflected a corresponding expansion in the trade of the affiliated retail societies.

General wages, with few and slight set-backs, had risen steadily from 1850 to 1874. Mr. G. H. Wood, taking the chief occupations of the country together and allowing, not only for the wage-movement in each, but for the process of labour transference from worse-paid to better-paid trades, calculated[2] that from a base-line of a hundred in 1850 wages rose to 156 by 1874; and that by 1886, despite the two historic slumps in the twelve-year interval, they had not fallen lower than 148. Prices had risen sharply between 1850 and 1856, and again between 1870 and 1873; but from the latter date their fall was very much greater than the fall of wages, so that the mass of workers (though not, of course, all individuals or even all trades) lived still on a rising plane of prosperity and comfort. But they would be less conscious of it than when the rise was visible in money form.

Reviewing the period as a whole, it is important to realize that in spite of the relative falling-back in the race with other nations, the ruin of agriculture, and the dawning menace to our export trade, this was a time of great and many-sided advance in the nation's general standards of living. Education, at last universal, was moving, as we shall see in our next chapter, on many sides. Sanitation and the paving and lighting of streets spread rapidly, and beginnings were made with slum clearance. The actual hours of labour were shortening; and what the continent still calls 'the English week', i.e. the half-holiday on Saturday, became more general. There were changes in the habit of taking holidays; the rise of watering-places for the working-classes in the north and midlands began in the seventies; Black-

[1] Percy Redfern, *The Story of the C.W.S. 1863–1913* (1913).
[2] G. H. Wood, 'Real Wages and the Standard of Comfort since 1850', in *Journal of the Statistical Society*, vol. lxxii (1909), pp. 91–103.

pool was made a borough in 1876. In Lancashire[1] working people began to go away on 'trips'—to Blackpool, Windermere, Llandudno, and elsewhere; in the eighties these were common, in the seventies they had been rare. There was also a marked improvement in the behaviour and manners among people of the manufacturing towns. The streets were safer. At the same time taxation weighed lightly, especially on the working-class;[2] rents and rates were low; building costs were extremely low. A good four-roomed cottage, which was built in a large Lancashire town in 1870-1 and stands to-day almost unimpaired, cost only £90. But houses erected in the same district for the same class in 1886 were rather larger and better—perhaps 20 per cent. A similar expansion went on in industry; the cotton mill built in 1886 was larger than that built in 1870, and its new machines were bigger and more efficient. Work on them was rather harder and 'speeding-up' had already begun; but actual earnings were higher.

A rich country, while it remains at peace and its people are employed, grows insensibly more rich. The thrift and energy of the mid-Victorians were bearing their fruit. No costly war taxed British resources, nor had done since 1856. Unemployment during the great depression of the seventies caused more suffering to individuals than during the post-war period of the twentieth century, because there was no state unemployment insurance; but its total mischief was on a far smaller scale. The tide of material progress flowed up all sorts of creeks and inlets. Here is one illustration: the National Gallery, founded in 1824, increased the number of its pictures between 1870 and 1890 by 50 per cent.

[1] I am indebted for much in this paragraph to Mr. Joseph Owen, whose recollections of Oldham in the early eighties are precise and vivid. His also is the calculation about the National Gallery.

[2] Prof. Clapham (op. cit. ii. 463) summarizes the effect of certain estimates made by Leone Levi in 1884 as showing 'that the average wage-earner with a family, who had paid out 16 per cent. of his income in taxes in 1842, paid only 7¼ per cent. in 1882'.

V

MENTAL AND SOCIAL ASPECTS, 1870–86

DICKENS died in June 1870; Grote in 1871; John Stuart Mill in 1873. No one familiar with the main currents of Victorian thought can miss the break which these three deaths mark. Each in his different way they had been pioneers of the democratic idea before it was realized. Now, as realization dawned, they quitted the stage. Of their greater contemporaries Carlyle and Tennyson survived till 1881 and 1892 respectively; but from neither was any further creative impulse forthcoming, though the writings of both were in the seventies and eighties at the pinnacle of their fame and influence. Browning, who died in 1889, had only a very select public until the eighties; but he too had shot his bolt—*The Ring and the Book*, which ended his ascending effort, appeared in 1869. Darwin's last great work, the *Descent of Man*, was issued in 1871; and Clerk-Maxwell, the other greatest English man of science then living, published his *Electricity and Magnetism* in 1873, six years before his early death. Let us add that Livingstone died in 1873; Brassey, the greatest English entrepreneur of the railway age, in 1870; and Wheatstone, the English inventor of the telegraph, in 1875.

These examples suggest, what is indeed the case, that round about 1870 occurs a watershed in English life.[1] The race of giants, who had rendered the first half of Queen Victoria's reign so memorable, had passed or was passing; Gladstone was alone among them in making history right through to 1886 and even beyond. As we shall see in due course, a middle and then a younger generation succeeded them; but though there were great men in each, it is obvious that giants were much fewer, and on the whole of less stature. Why they should have been, at a time when population was larger and education more advanced, may well afford food for thought.

New fashions in ideas and conduct were not popularized then so quickly as now; and down at least to the queen's first jubilee in the year following the sixteen with which this chapter deals, the mass of her subjects, high as well as low, lived much the same

---

[1] A famous passage in the essay prefixed by Bagehot in 1872 to the second edition of his *English Constitution* makes this point very well; though, referring only to the political front bench, he dates the division five years earlier.

mental life as they had done when the Prince Consort died. At the core of it was religion. No one will ever understand Victorian England who does not appreciate that among highly civilized, in contradistinction to more primitive, countries it was one of the most religious that the world has known. Moreover its particular type of Christianity laid a peculiarly direct emphasis upon conduct; for, though it recognized both grace and faith as essentials to salvation, it was in practice also very largely a doctrine of salvation by works. This type, which had come to dominate churchmen and nonconformists alike, may be called, using the term in a broad sense, evangelicalism. Starting early in the eighteenth century as far back as William Law, author of the *Serious Call*, coming down through the Wesleys and Whitefield, Johnson and Cowper, Clarkson and Wilberforce and the Clapham 'Sect', great schoolmasters like Thomas Arnold and Charles Wordsworth, great nobles like the Greys on the whig side and the philanthropic Lord Shaftesbury on the tory, not to mention many nineteenth-century preachers and divines, it became after Queen Victoria's marriage practically the religion of the court, and gripped all ranks and conditions of society. After Melbourne's departure it inspired nearly every front-rank public man, save Palmerston, for four decades. That does not mean that they were all Evangelicals in the sense of being bigots for the low church, as Shaftesbury and Cairns were—Bright was a quaker; Gladstone and Selborne and Salisbury were pronounced high churchmen; Livingstone, like many another, was reared in Scottish presbyterianism. But nothing is more remarkable than the way in which evangelicalism in the broader sense overleaped sectarian barriers and pervaded men of all creeds; so that even T. H. Huxley, the agnostic, oozed it from every pore of his controversial writing, and Cardinal Newman, the convert to Rome, composed in *The Dream of Gerontius* a poem of pure catholic orthodoxy, to which nevertheless no Irish or continental catholic could have given its peculiar flavour at that time, nor any one, probably, who had not breathed from early life the air of evangelical England. Even Disraeli, by nature as remote from it as Palmerston, paid every deference to it in politics, and conformed to all its externals in Hughenden church.

The essentials of evangelicalism were three. First, its literal stress on the Bible. It made the English the 'people of a book', somewhat as devout Moslems are, but as few other Europeans were. Secondly, its certainty about the existence of an after-life of rewards and punishments. If one asks how nineteenth-century English merchants earned the reputation of being the most honest in the world (a very real factor in the nineteenth-century primacy of English trade), the answer is: because hell and heaven seemed as certain to them as to-morrow's sunrise, and the Last Judgement as real as the week's balance-sheet. This keen sense of moral accountancy had also much to do with the success of self-government in the political sphere. Thirdly, its corollary that the present life is only important as a preparation for eternity. Exalted minds in abnormal moments may have reached that feeling in all ages, and among primitive peoples it has often moved mass enthusiasms. But the remarkable feature of evangelicalism was that it came so largely to dispense with the abnormal; made other-worldliness an everyday conviction and, so to say, a business proposition; and thus induced a highly civilized people to put pleasure in the background, and what it conceived to be duty in the foreground, to a quite exceptional degree.[1] A text from the Epistle to the Hebrews, 'He endured as seeing Him who is invisible', has often and very aptly been used to commemorate General Gordon. It might equally have been applied to Livingstone's lonely heroism in midmost Africa, to Gladstone laying daily before God the issues of right and wrong in national politics, to Shaftesbury championing oppressed classes who could never conceivably reward him, to Clarkson and Wilberforce in an earlier day climbing their 'obstinate hill' to end the slave trade and slavery; and no less truly, though on a lower spiritual plane, to the common conscientious Victorian:

> Staid Englishman, who toil and slave
> From your first childhood to your grave,
> And seldom spend and always save—

---

[1] In the preface to his *Sermons* John Wesley says: 'To candid reasonable men I am not afraid to lay open what have been the inmost thoughts of my heart. I have thought, I am a creature of a day, passing through life as an arrow through the air. I am a spirit come from God and returning to God: just hovering over the great gulf; till, a few moments hence, I am no more seen; I drop into an unchangeable eternity! I want to know one thing—the way to heaven; how to land safe on that happy shore. God himself has condescended to teach the way; for this very end he came from heaven. He hath written it down in a book. O give me that book! . . . Let me be *homo unius libri*.' Written in 1747, that passage expresses the religion of most English people between 1840 and 1880, not only in its Bible-worship, but even more in its business-like other-worldliness.

And do your duty all your life
By your young family and wife.[1]

This is not the place to evaluate Victorian evangelicalism on religious or theological grounds. But to ignore its effect on outward life would be to render much of the period's history unintelligible. It is often now accused of being gloomy, but it seemed less so at the time to its votaries; who for their self-denials had compensations not visible to their latter-day critics. Certainly, however, it was anti-hedonistic. To-day's passion for pleasure would have shocked it profoundly. Its own corresponding passion was for self-improvement; and perhaps there never has been an age and a country in which so many individuals climbed to outstanding excellences or achievements of one sort or another across the most discouraging barriers.

This religion was sustained by a vast amount of external observance. The evangelicals set relatively little store by sacraments; to communicate only twice a year (the practice of the prince consort and Queen Victoria) was quite normal even in the church of England. But they spent a remarkable amount of time on organized prayer, praise, and preaching. The pulpit dominated. In typical English villages in the seventies and eighties practically all the inhabitants above infancy attended either church or chapel every Sunday, many of them twice or even three times. The children also went twice to Sunday schools.[2] Apart from cases of necessity, the only exceptions to this universal worship would be, here and there, a few known village ne'er-do-wells. In addition the chapels held prayer-meetings during the week, and the church often a regular weeknight service—both numerously attended. In the towns of moderate size there was almost as much strictness, though different regions showed a prevalence of different sects. Thus in many of the Lancashire manufacturing towns a low-church anglicanism predominated; in their Yorkshire equivalents, dissent. This was reflected in politics, where parts of Lancashire developed a conservative and Yorkshire a liberal tradition. Local distribution varied similarly among dissenters themselves; e.g. primitive methodists would preponderate in some regions, and wesleyans in others. Only in the dozen largest English cities were there considerable areas,

[1] Clough, *Dipsychus*, Scene V.
[2] Of three successive lord chancellors—Lords Cairns, Hatherley, and Selborne —each taught in a Sunday school nearly all his life.

whose growth neither church nor chapel had ever overtaken, and extensive 'heathen' populations who attended no place of worship. In London these areas and populations were of enormous size, and from the middle of the century onward much devoted but quite inadequate missionary effort was spent on them by both anglicans and nonconformists. But public worship was not all; a great feature of the period was the almost universal practice in the upper,[1] middle, and lower-middle classes of family prayers. The observance, too, of Sunday was almost a religion in itself. No games of any kind were ever played on it; no field-sports indulged in; no entertainments given, public or private. Even books were censored for the day; novels were banned; you might only read the Bible or serious, preferably religious, works. Thus sermons had large sales,[2] and so did 'magazines for Sunday reading'. It is easy now to see the ludicrous side of these restraints; but they had another. The habit of setting apart one rest-day in the week for religion and serious thinking deepened the character of the nation. And some high peaks of literature—the Bible, *Paradise Lost*, and the *Pilgrim's Progress*, for instance—became extremely familiar to very wide classes who to-day would never read anything on that level.

By 1870 the religion which we have been describing had attained its maximum influence in England, and, though very strongly entrenched, showed some first signs of decline. It was sapped from three sides—the anglo-catholic movement (then called ritualistic, and earlier tractarian) within the church, the freethinking movements outside it, and thirdly the cult of hedo-

[1] In September 1868 William Cory, Eton master and poet, visited the second Lord Northbrook (soon afterwards viceroy of India) at his large country-house in Hampshire as one of a distinguished house-party, and wrote down deliberately for the benefit of posterity a complete time-table and record of the doings of a particular day. But for one item, it might have been written yesterday, so conservative are country-house habits. The exception is that at 9 a.m. the host assembled his guests, family, and servants in the library and personally read prayers to them, including a chapter from the Old Testament. Cory records this without any suggestion that it was strange conduct in a peer (*Letters and Journals of William Cory*, p. 253); and there are reasons for thinking that it remained usual until about 1886. Probably the laxer standards promulgated by the prince of Wales (Edward VII) and his set helped to hasten its obsolescence; which began at the top of society and worked downwards.

[2] By far the largest were those of the sermons of C. H. Spurgeon (1834-92); who throughout this period drew enormous congregations to the Metropolitan Tabernacle, and who, if native eloquence and wide popular appeal be the test, must be ranked among the greatest English preachers of any age.

nism, which grew with the growth of facilities for luxury. The first of these was almost entirely a movement of the ordinary clergy, not of the episcopacy or the laity; and, apart from any question of its spiritual appeal, it is obvious that it met a peculiar professional need of the anglican clergy at this time. During the later eighteenth and early nineteenth century there had been little or no doctrinal difference between most of them and most of the dissenting ministers. The vantage-ground which they enjoyed over these rival practitioners was legal, since the state inflicted heavy civil and educational disabilities on the latter and their flocks. But between 1828 and 1871 all these disabilities were repealed, and in the latter year even the ancient universities were thrown open. Unless anglicanism redeveloped some convincing doctrinal difference, its clergy would have difficulty in maintaining any exclusive professional position.[1] Here the new movement came directly to their aid. By placing again in the foreground salvation through grace, grace received through sacraments, and sacraments only valid if administered by episcopally ordained clergy, it supplied exactly what the profession needed. Hence it is not surprising that, though the bishops were cold to it and the laity, as a rule, fiercely hostile, the rank and file of the clergy, including many of the ablest, came round to it more and more. By 1874, as we saw in Chapter II, it had gone so far that a Public Worship Bill designed to curb it was introduced by the archbishop of Canterbury and passed with the support of Shaftesbury and Disraeli. In the following years this measure was not left idle; in 1880 alone the incumbents of five different parishes were prosecuted under it, and at least one was sent to prison. But the effect of prosecutions was much less to crush the movement than to sharpen its anti-evangelical character.

Freethinking, in the Voltairean tradition, had maintained itself in a corner of the English radical movement since Tom Paine's day. The last and perhaps greatest leader in that succession, Charles Bradlaugh, we have already met as a politician in Chapter III. His religious vogue was at its height in the seventies and eighties, but he scarcely touched the more educated

---

[1] Nothing could better illustrate their situation and attitude than the case of *Keet* v. *Smith*, decided on final appeal by the judicial committee of the privy council in January 1876. The claim was there put forward that a wesleyan minister could not lawfully be described on his tombstone as 'the Reverend'. It was actually affirmed by the chancellor of the diocese of Lincoln and, on appeal, by the dean of arches, but negatived by the judicial committee.

class. Far more formidable as creators of opinion were two highly cultured men, who—in quite different styles—were probably the ablest controversialists writing in the English reviews of that epoch. These were the poet, literary critic, and educationist, Matthew Arnold, and the biologist, T. H. Huxley. The refined rapier-play of the first and the terrific bludgeon of the second were alike actuated by a spirit at bottom evangelical; and if official evangelicalism had possessed any elasticity, it might have kept them within its fold. But that was just what, in its organized forms, it did not possess. Bound by its view of the verbal inspiration of the Bible, it could not listen calmly to any one who disbelieved the miracle of the walls of Jericho or the story of the Gadarene swine. Consequently during this very period the writings of these two men were potent, and perhaps decisive, in creating an intellectual breach between it and the rising generations.

In the hedonistic movement the leading social influence was that of the prince of Wales. Reacting against a strict upbringing, he had already launched out upon a 'fast' life in the decade succeeding his father's death. But at first his example influenced few, for he was not widely liked; in 1871, soon after a divorce case in which a penitent respondent had named him among her adulterers,[1] he was hissed even on the Epsom race-course. But his illness at the end of that year wrought a revulsion in his favour; and after it he became for the rest of the century the unrivalled leader of London Society. His charm and kindliness, so unlike any of his remembered predecessors, made him immensely popular, and the least things that he did were noted and copied. Thus the fact that he always lived a life of good-natured self-indulgence could not be, and was not without far-reaching social effects. Not only were many of his sex laxities common knowledge, and his extravagances in betting and gambling[2] a

---

[1] The corroboration brought against him in the form of letters was inconclusive, and the court accepted his denials.

[2] Much attention was drawn to this a little later by the Tranby Croft case (1891), in which the prince was shown to have instigated and taken part in the playing of baccarat by a large mixed house-party (including army officers, some young), with counters representing £10 each. After it he told Archbishop Benson that he 'never gambled', defining gambling as the staking of higher sums than one can afford (E. F. Benson, *King Edward* (1933), pp. 159–60). But it seems that he did so, even within that definition; and the common belief was that he contracted very large debts, and leaned heavily on certain millionaire financiers, who were members of his inmost circle. To their aid in 1901 it was attributed that 'for the first time in

matter of daily observation, but in minor ways he set himself to wear down a tradition which he disliked. Thus in the eighties he opened one of the first breaches in Sabbatarianism by giving Sunday evening dinner-parties at Marlborough House. Later he sponsored and perhaps invented the 'week-end'. In the twentieth century this institution is so familiar that few realize its late appearance in the nineteenth. It was scarcely possible while Sunday was religiously observed. Many of the prince's innovations were far from welcome to the queen; but her method of allotting the royal duties, which was to devolve all the social side upon him while closely retaining all the political side for herself, rendered him, and not her, the leader and exemplar of London.

A culminating phase in the Victorian cult of the Bible was the making of the Revised Version, which falls exactly within this period. Though initiated by the anglican church, it was a national enterprise. In 1870 the convocation of the province of Canterbury passed a plan and appointed a revision committee, which in turn appointed two 'companies' of revisers, for the Old and New Testaments respectively. But the co-operation of the other Christian bodies was then sought, and none excepting the Roman catholic church declined it. Further a revision committee on parallel lines was set up in the United States, so that the whole English-speaking world was brought in. The revision of the New Testament took ten years; that of the Old Testament, fourteen; and the complete Bible in the new version was on sale in 1885.

It is disappointing to record that in spite—or perhaps because —of all this many-sided effort the new version was not a success in the sense of obtaining wide acceptance. To some extent it fell between two stools. Its extreme conservatism did not save it from offending lovers of the familiar text; while its novelties were much too pinched for those who wanted a translation up to modern standards.

The abolition of the newspaper tax in 1855, preceded in 1853 by that of the tax on advertisements and followed in 1861 by that of the duty on paper, had charted a course for the British press from which it did not deviate during these sixteen years. The leading type was the penny morning paper. It was exemplified in 1870 by the whole of a very flourishing provincial daily press and

English history' (as his private secretary put it) 'the heir-apparent came forward to claim his right to the throne unencumbered by a penny of debt'.

in London by the *Daily Telegraph* (City of London conservative), the *Standard* (Salisburian conservative), and the *Daily News* (liberal); to whose ranks the *Daily Chronicle* (liberal) was added in 1877, while the *Morning Post* (aristocratic conservative) came down in 1881 to the same price. Above them stood *The Times*, sold at 3*d.* and ruled till 1877 by J. T. Delane, its greatest and most fortunate editor.

These penny dailies conformed very much to one character. Originally modelled on *The Times*, they catered distinctively for the upper and middle classes, and almost exclusively for the male reader. Though, as a rule, they earned comfortable profits, their ownership was not primarily commercial, and the newspaper world was about the last quarter in which any one then would have looked for a millionaire. Nearly all of them were family properties. Their controllers were usually well-educated middle-class people, cautious rather than ambitious, seeking no new worlds to conquer, valuing their papers chiefly for the political and social influence which accrued through them, and disposed in most instances to view the proper exercise of this influence very seriously as a sort of personal trust. On the contents side they were overwhelmingly political. They gave some space to business and religion, and some to racing and cricket; while for 'human interest' they relied largely on sensational law cases, and brought leaders of the bar and bench into a brighter limelight than ever before or since.[1] But the staple was politics, especially speeches; and proceedings in parliament were reported and read all over the country at full length. The way in which the news-matter was handled would to-day be thought incredibly dull and matter-of-fact. Headlines were few and paragraphs long. But the reader was at least fairly given the facts, on which he could form his own judgement. Editorial opinion was more or less confined to the leading articles; which were written by the highest-paid men in the office, or occasionally (though always anonymous) by good writers outside.[2] Propaganda was made by open argument; not, as in the twentieth century, by the doctoring of news.

[1] The Tichborne case, whose successive civil and criminal proceedings stretched in portentous length from May 1871 to February 1874, probably interested the public more than any other English trial since the impeachment of Hastings.

[2] Many of those in the *Standard* were contributed by Lord Salisbury, or, at a later period, written to his directions by Alfred Austin, afterwards poet-laureate. George Meredith at different times lived largely by leader-writing.

Behind the daily papers a great influence was wielded by the monthly and quarterly reviews, which everybody in the governing classes read, and to which all the best writers of the day contributed. Their vogue was more nation-wide than that of the London dailies, since they were not, like the latter, ousted in the provinces by provincial organs. At this period perhaps their extreme high-water mark was reached in the *Fortnightly Review* under the remarkable editorship (1867–82) of John Morley. Any one turning over its back numbers may well marvel at the galaxy of the most brilliant Victorian talents which it then displayed month by month.[1] The articles were few and long; they amounted to small treatises; and the components of many of the more famous mid-Victorian books first appeared in this form. Besides the monthlies two weekly reviews had in the period great importance—the *Spectator*, which was strongly liberal till the home rule split, but then went liberal unionist, and the *Saturday Review*, which as the brilliant organ of an intellectual conservatism numbered among its writers Lord Salisbury and Sir Henry Maine.

This dignified phase of English journalism reigned unchallenged till 1886 and indeed beyond. Yet the seed of its destruction was already germinating. In 1880, ten years after Forster's Education Act, a branch manager of a fancy-goods business, named George Newnes, became aware that the new schooling was creating a new class of potential readers—people who had been taught to decipher print without learning much else, and for whom the existing newspapers, with their long articles, long paragraphs, and all-round demands on the intelligence and imagination, were quite unsuited. To give them what he felt they wanted, he started in that year a little weekly, well described by its name *Tit-Bits*. It was a complete success in its way; but nobody then had any inkling how far that way would lead.

---

[1] Its essay contributors during the first two years of this chapter's period included (besides Morley himself) Mill, Helen Taylor, Bagehot, Herbert Spencer, Huxley, Tyndall, Galton, E. A. Freeman, James Gairdner, Frederic Seebohm, Goldwin Smith, Fawcett, J. E. Cairnes, Sheldon Amos, James Sully, E. S. Beesly, Frederic Harrison, Moncure Conway, Justin McCarthy, the second Lord Lytton, Sir A. C. Lyall, Leslie Stephen, Edward Dowden, Sidney Colvin, D. G. Rossetti, and Walter Pater; among distinguished foreigners were Mazzini, Von Sybel, Castelar, Laveleye, and many Frenchmen. These names give a good idea of intellectual currents in the early seventies, covering, as they do, nearly all the best prose-writers than active, excepting Newman, Matthew Arnold, and Froude. In the same period it published well-known poems by George Meredith and William Morris, and a novel by Anthony Trollope.

Education during this period advanced notably at its two opposite ends—in the elementary schools and in the universities. The 1870 Education Act ordained that, for the first time, a school should be placed within the reach of every English child. Until the schools for which it provided were in being, it was not practicable to make attendance everywhere compulsory; but in 1880 this was done. The initial task was a battle with illiteracy. While three million children were learning the '3 R's', further refinements had to wait; there would not, in any case, have been teachers to impart them. A system of 'payment by results', originated by Robert Lowe, enabled the central authority to standardize a curriculum which was effective within the limits.

The popularly elected boards, which ran the new schools, might naturally have developed into bodies of very wide significance. At the first school board election for London the poll was headed by Dr. Elizabeth Garrett, and among others elected were Huxley, Lord Lawrence of the Punjab, W. H. Smith, 'Hang Theology' Rogers,[1] and Miss Emily Davies—a striking combination. But religious wrangles between anglicans, Roman catholics, and dissenters soon blighted much of the promise. Dissenters were suited by the religious instruction in the publicly provided board schools; anglicans and still more Roman catholics were not. The core of the difficulty was over buildings, the cost of which for the voluntary (i.e. sectarian) schools fell on the voluntary (i.e. religious) bodies. The church wanted to keep a large proportion of the schools, but it could not afford to provide good new buildings. Consequently it opposed their being provided by the school boards either; and its representatives on those bodies were often driven into an attitude indistinguishable from obstruction. The squabble went on all over the country. Most school board elections were fought over it. It was perhaps inevitable under the terms of the 1870 act; but it cannot be said to have been fortunate either for the boards or for education or for religion.

---

[1] Rev. William Rogers (1819–96) was instrumental in founding more non-state schools than any other Victorian. Appointed perpetual curate of St. Thomas's, Charterhouse, in 1845, he began with schools for ragamuffins, and continued with primary schools of several types. Becoming rector of St. Botolph's, Bishopsgate, in 1863, he turned his attention to secondary education, and pioneered a number of middle-class schools. As a governor of Alleyn's Charity, he took a leading part in the changes which enabled Dulwich College to become the great school which it now is.

Other flaws in the 1870 system developed as time went on. 'Payment by results' became cramping. A still deeper mischief was the lack of liaison between elementary, secondary, and technical education, so that the first remained a mere 'schooling', starved of liberal or even vocational developments. For all this, the elementary teachers wrought a great work within their own sphere; so that in the general election of 1886, which closes the period, out of 2,416,272 votes cast in England and Wales only 38,547 were those of illiterates.

On the university side some steps of great moment were taken during these years. Already Gladstone's Order in Council of 4 June 1870 directing that all entrance appointments to permanent situations in the civil departments of the state (excepting the foreign office and posts requiring professional knowledge) should be filled by open competitive examination, had given at the top a new stimulus to university teaching. But the England of 1870 was extraordinarily deficient in university equipment. In proportion to population the number of students was far less than in the leading foreign countries, or in Scotland. The ancient universities of Oxford and Cambridge were still virtually closed to dissenters and Roman catholics by religious tests; and the cost of their residential system put them largely beyond the purses of the middle-class rank and file. Two modern universities—those of London and Durham—had been founded in the thirties; but Durham remained small, and London, apart from the teaching organization of two colleges, was little but an examining and degree-giving board. The constitution of the latter had, however, this advantage, that if anybody chose to start a college anywhere in the country, he could by sending his students in for the London examination obtain for them full and free access to a reputable university degree. A number of colleges run on these lines gradually made their appearance in the more important provincial centres; of which Owens College at Manchester (founded 1850) and Mason College, Birmingham (founded 1875), were perhaps the leading examples. Their objects were to provide local university institutions standing in the same relation to the local day-school system[1] as Oxford and

---

[1] The earlier of these colleges were in their inception little more than day-schools themselves. Professor Spenser Wilkinson (*Thirty-Five Years*, ch. i) records how in 1867 he went to Owens College at the age of 14. He stayed there six years, when, after passing his London B.A. examination, he proceeded to Oxford as an undergraduate.

Cambridge had to that of the boarding schools, and also to secure curricula in new modern subjects of vocational value. But prior to 1871 the institutions which taught for the London University degree had generally, too, a sectarian motive. The dissenters, whom Oxford and Cambridge banned, found here alternative homes. Thus even educated England was divided into two nations, one of which—that from which fiery nonconformist preachers were drawn—laboured under a sense of grievance and disinheritance. The Tests Act of 1871[1] removed the grounds for this; it enabled non-Anglicans to take part on equal terms in Oxford and Cambridge; and gradually, though not in one generation, the old bitterness faded out of dissent.

A few years after this epoch-making act the modernization of the two ancient universities was completed, for the nineteenth century, by the royal commission of 1876, the Universities of Oxford and Cambridge Act 1877, and the work of the commissioners appointed under it. The main effect (continuing the direction taken in 1854) was to give the two universities a clearer footing as distinct from their constituent colleges, to render the endowments of the latter more freely available for purposes of learning, and so to open doors for widening and modernizing curricula. The same decade saw the starting of university extension. This missionary movement, which began from Cambridge in 1873, and in which Oxford did not become very active till 1887, gave a new meaning to adult education in England; the system eventually developed within the present century by the Workers' Educational Association derives from it. It supplied a further stimulus to the founding of local colleges in large centres of population on the lines already explained. Then in 1884 was born the first of the more modern English provincial universities, the Victoria University. Its constitution was federal; it embraced colleges which had been separately developed at Manchester, Liverpool, and Leeds. Hitherto they had utilized the examinations of London University; now they had an examining and degree-giving authority of their own. Fortunately the new body did not yield to the temptation to make its degrees too easy, but set a courageous example, which benefited the whole subsequent development of the provincial universities.

Even more revolutionary were the changes pioneered at this time in the education of women. In the first half of the nineteenth century English families who sent their boys to school usually kept their girls at home under governesses. University education for women scarcely existed in any shape until Queen's College, London, was opened in 1848. The subsequent leaders in the reform and expansion of girls' schools were two women who combined vision and courage with practical capacity in a very high degree—Frances Mary Buss (1827–94) and Dorothea Beale (1831–1906). Both were Victorian evangelicals, with the strong, almost ascetic, sense of personal duty which that implied. Miss Buss had started the North London Collegiate School in 1850; and she handed over the property in it to a body of trustees in 1870, thus founding the first public day-school for girls, which she continued to direct till 1893. Miss Beale had in 1858 been appointed headmistress of the Cheltenham Ladies' College, a proprietary boarding-school founded four years earlier. Both of them had in 1865 given evidence before the Endowed Schools Inquiry Commission, whose reports on the education of girls attracted wide attention in 1869. The seventies opened, therefore, with a strong current in their favour; and following Miss Buss's transfer of her property the Girls' Public Day-Schools Company was launched, and began establishing first-grade girls' day-schools throughout the country, avowedly taking the North London Collegiate School as their model. The opening under local auspices of the Manchester High School for Girls (1874) marks something of an epoch for the north of England. The development of girls' boarding-schools on Miss Beale's model came somewhat later.

The greatest difficulty which confronted these pioneers was the extreme dearth of suitably educated women to appoint as teachers. There were scarcely any women university graduates from whom to recruit. London University alone had thrown its examinations and degrees open to their sex. This eventually, however, had the important effect that all the provincial colleges, which under London's aegis developed nuclei of university life up and down the country, took women on the same terms as men; and the Victoria University, when formed, continued doing so as a matter of course. But the seventies saw the movement brought for the first time to the doors of Oxford and Cambridge. In 1869 Emily Davies[1] founded Girton College at Hitchin; in 1871 Newnham College, chiefly through the agency

[1] Sister of the well-known Broad Church clergyman, J. Llewelyn Davies.

of Henry Sidgwick, was opened in Cambridge itself with Anne Clough (a sister of the poet) as its first head. In 1872 Girton was removed to Cambridge. Oxford's turn came a little later; Lady Margaret Hall was founded in 1878; both it and Somerville College were opened in 1879. St. Hugh's dates from 1886; and St. Hilda's was started in 1893 by Miss Beale as the Oxford end of a teachers' training college which she had long been running at Cheltenham. The members of these six bodies were not admitted as members of either university, but they were allowed to attend lectures and take the degree examinations. After a while a few began to appear high in the class lists. In 1887 Miss Agneta Ramsay was placed above the Senior Classic at Cambridge, and three years later Miss Philippa Fawcett was placed above the Senior Wrangler.

For good or for evil, the movement conformed girls' and women's education as closely as might be to the curricula, the methods, and the organization which had grown up in England for boys' and men's. The idea of developing any system more distinctively feminine, with curricula and aims of its own, was driven out of the field. It is true that in 1883 Thomas Holloway, who had made a fortune by selling patent medicines and determined to devote it to philanthropy, was inspired by memories of Tennyson's *Princess* to build Holloway College as the nucleus of a separate residential women's university. It was a generous initiative, but found no imitators; and the new institution, being obliged to come under London University for its degree examinations, had perforce to run its teaching programme into the usual moulds.

However, the first problem of all education, male or female, was at this period, it may be said, one of numbers. Before 1870 the majority of those who, in the interests of the community as well as their own, required a certain standard of formal education, were not getting it. Those whose needs were elementary became, after 1870, the concern of the state. But higher education was still left to institutions, endowed or other, which the state did not bring into existence, and whose many gaps it made few attempts to fill. Extremely little public money was spent on anything but elementary schools. Yet before the seventies neither the schools nor the universities in England afforded, for example, any widely extended facilities for the study of those sciences from which the industrial revolution had sprung, and which were needed for every step of its progress. Until Clerk-Maxwell was appointed professor of experimental physics at Cambridge in 1871, no front-rank figure in any natural science except geology had, as such, held a post either there or at Oxford during the nineteenth century. So far as teaching or co-operative study in such subjects had been available at all, it was supplied by the Scottish universities,[1] by the Royal Institution in London, by the more recently established School of Mines, or by 'mechanics' institutes' and local scientific (then usually termed 'philosophical') societies in various industrial towns.

Thus though between 1800 and 1870 England contributed a great many discoveries in science and technology, most of those who made them were comparatively self-taught men, owing little to schools and nothing to universities, unless the Scottish. And this lasted into our period, both of whose two most important scientific inventions—that of basic steel-smelting and that of the incandescent electric lamp—were made by men of this type. Of Sidney Gilchrist Thomas, the classically educated police-court clerk who revolutionized the steel industry by experiments conducted in the back-yard of a small suburban house, we have spoken in Chapter IV. Sir Joseph Wilson Swan (1828–1914), who invented the incandescent electric lamp,[2] was even more self-taught. Not only was he a key inventor in a number of fields (in photography he discovered the carbon process, bromide printing papers, and much else, and was the first to produce, in 1877, really rapid and practicable dry plates; while through his invention of a squirted filament for his lamps he became also the first progenitor of artificial silk), but some of these fields

[1] Sir William Thomson, afterwards Lord Kelvin (1824–1907), had been professor at Glasgow since 1846, doing scientific work of the utmost value for industry. Edinburgh also had a notable record for teaching and research in many branches of science. Clerk-Maxwell, who was a product of Edinburgh and (for mathematics) Cambridge, held his first professorship (from 1856) at Marischal College, Aberdeen.

[2] The incandescent electric lamp was independently invented by Swan in England and by Edison in America, but the Englishman was decidedly prior. Edison's successful experiment was made on 21 October 1879. Swan had not merely made his lamp in 1878, but exhibited it at a meeting of the Newcastle Chemical Society on 18 December of that year. After the two men's interests had been amalgamated in the Edison and Swan Company, the company for legal reasons decided to rely on Edison's patent, which had been taken out earlier. For that purpose Swan's priority was inconvenient, and it had to be ingeniously glossed over. But see for the facts the fully documented *Memoir* (1929) of Swan by his son and daughter. Swan's filaments were also much more practical than Edison's, which were soon abandoned.

required peculiarly wide and deep scientific knowledge. Yet he had left school at 12, and at 14 had been apprenticed in a Sunderland druggist's shop; and it was as partner in a similar business in Newcastle that he embarked on his career of discovery. To the high technical accomplishment and wide intellectual culture which he eventually won, no educational institution contributed anything.

One of the anomalies of the Victorian age in England is that, while it abounded in great literature (including poetry, history, oratory, essays, religious works, scientific exposition, novels, indeed nearly every type except stage drama), it was in the arts of everyday life remarkably unsuccessful. Architecture, decoration, furniture, and the allied art of costume touched between 1860 and 1880 a sort of nadir. The period was bad for them everywhere in western Europe, but worst in England; and it is the memory of this visible ugliness, perpetuated in so many monuments of the age's wealth and generosity, which more than anything else has since damned the Victorians. Had their art been merely starved or unenterprising, it might have been less disapproved. But instead it was costly, flashy, pretentious, insincere, preferring new ways (or archaisms) which nearly always proved ugly.

It is common to regard this as evidence of defects in the Victorian soul; and to some extent it may be. But the simpler, and possibly even complete, explanation seems a more material one. The amazing progress in technology, which England achieved during the two middle quarters of the nineteenth century, revolutionized the basis of all the arts which produce material objects. Take, for example, building. In the main it is ruled, and always must be, by the law of cheapness; it has to aim—on the average and consistently with the standards of accommodation and permanence required—at keeping the cost of a structure as low as possible per cubic foot. Before the invention of railways this was achieved by using materials obtained on the spot—local varieties of stone and slate in the areas with quarries, local bricks and tiles in the brick-field districts, with other domestic variants such as thatch for roofs, and timber, wattle-and-daub, or cob for walls. These local materials always harmonized with each other and with the landscape; and since the same things had been used in the same places for a great many generations, codes of sound tradition had been evolved for their employment, which persisted and developed whatever the architectural fashions—Gothic, Tudor, Renaissance, or Classical—of succeeding centuries might be. In the special circumstances of England (its long peace and order, its diffusion of prosperity and culture, and a certain native bent of the people towards craftsmanship) this yielded results of peculiar beauty. On the eve of railways, it seems broadly true to suppose, any one viewing most of the country might scarcely have found an ugly house in it. Plenty were insanitary, dirty, overcrowded, or in gross disrepair; but that is another matter.

These conditions the railways destroyed; for by enabling heavy materials, for the first time,[1] to be freely distributed at low cost all over the land, they abolished the cheapness of local materials, and substituted that of national ones. The cheapest walling was found to be brick; the cheapest covering, a low-pitched roof of North Wales slate; all towns, wherever situated, and (though much more gradually) nearly all villages became invaded by this unnatural combination. The fact that it broke all tradition and was in itself ugly, could not avail against the law of cheapness. It argues no special vice in the Victorians that they succumbed to it; probably the men of any other age must equally have done so. But that was not all. At the same time came cheap iron (and then steel), cheap foreign softwoods, cheap cement, cheap glass, and the possibility, through machinery, of cheapening every kind of repetitive ornament. Within a few decades the whole basis of building structures was revolutionized. In a sense the builder gained many new freedoms; he could attempt all sorts of things which before were out of the question. Sudden emancipations, like that, exhilarate those whom they befall. But they seldom produce beauty; almost inevitably, for the time, they destroy it. For its craft formulas all have to be worked out afresh; and as they have usually resulted in the past from the slow maturing of a tradition, so a labour of time is needed for their reintegration.

Thus is explained alike the Victorian ugliness and the Victorian exhilaration—that self-complacent enthusiasm of the sixties and seventies—which their bad art renders preposterous, yet which sprang from exactly the same source. What happened

[1] Save for a few decades and to a limited extent by canals and rivers; which in certain industrial districts had already begun the mischief.

to building happened also to the other applied arts. In furniture the revolutionary fact was spring-upholstery, rendered possible by the cheapening of metal springs. The Victorians had devised a seat which made all pre-existing seats seem uncomfortable. In their zeal for the new invention the traditions of beautiful chair-design evolved during the seventeenth, eighteenth, and early nineteenth centuries were heedlessly scrapped. Upholstery seemed so good that you could not have too much of it; and about 1870 the furniture of a fashionable drawing-room showed scarcely any surfaces but silk or plush, and scarcely any forms but those of jelly-bags. Here in the conflict between design and upholstery, between beauty and comfort, men had stumbled unawares on one of the major antinomies—one which we are far even yet from having solved. The immediate effect on the Victorians was such an all-round surrender of design that they lost nearly all sense of form and proportion even in dealing with non-upholstered things. In the matter of decoration generally the most formidable among a host of new and confusing factors was the facile multiplication of ornament by machinery. For us machine-made ornament is a by-word. But to the generation which invented the machinery it seemed an illimitable hope. Here, if anywhere, the Victorians were exhilarated.

Two secondary influences rendered the rot even worse than it need have been. One was the Gothic Revival, which in the seventies reached its height. It did harm, not so much because of any vice inherent in Gothic, as because it supplied an additional cause of breach with the living tradition at a time when it was important to keep hold of every scrap of tradition which the new technology permitted to be retained. The other was the numerical dominance of a class of uneducated rich. The landowners and clergy, whose tastes set the standard of consumers' demand in earlier reigns, had been the educated leaders of a stable society. But the self-made men, to whom the industrial revolution brought sudden riches, were in a very different case, as were the new mercantile and business classes generally. The framework of higher English education, before the change began, had been designed to cover only quite small numbers. It expanded, but far less rapidly than population and wealth and machine-made goods. By 1870 the lag had grown prodigious; and the demand which English architects and designers of all kinds had to satisfy was very largely that of untaught persons.

Thus it has come about that if one traverses one of the many English towns which during the nineteenth century expanded outwards in concentric rings, the ugliest zone of building will be found to lie between 1860 and 1880, and oftenest in the later of those two decades. The same stigma will be found attaching to the period by any one who looks through volumes of illustrated papers to obtain an idea of costumes, decorations, and the outward appearance of society.

Yet amid dominant ugliness a revolt began. Its greatest leader, the poet and art-craftsman, William Morris (1834–96), was a man who would have been memorable in any age, and greater perhaps in one which did not so inevitably throw his work into attitudes of dissent from the world around him. Perhaps few men with a keener sense of craftsmanship, or greater natural gifts for giving effect to it, have ever lived. The original firm of Morris, Marshall, and Faulkner, in which there were seven partners (the others being the painters Burne-Jones, Rossetti, and Madox Brown and the architect Philip Webb), had been started as early as 1861; but its productions had been on a very limited scale, and except wall-papers and a small amount of furniture, were mainly designed for churches. It was in 1875 that Morris became sole proprietor and manager, in the same year that he made himself an expert in dyeing and thus opened the way to a notable production of printed and woven fabrics. In 1877 he began tapestry weaving; in 1879 he started weaving carpets and rugs; in 1881 the scale of his output warranted his opening a really large and well-equipped works at Merton Abbey. It must not be supposed that at any time he supplied any large part of the general market; but towards the end of our period his example began to influence the firms which did, and a gradual rebirth of design resulted. On the taste of the upper classes he acted as a strong purgative. No one so effectually disillusioned the Victorians of their blind enthusiasm for machine products; and his famous apophthegm, 'Have nothing in your house except what you know to be useful or believe to be beautiful', did more than anything else to sweep away from Victorian living-rooms the senseless litter of manufactured knick-knacks with which they had till then been encumbered.

The architecture of public buildings took a turn for the better about the same time. In London the ill-planned and unreal Law Courts by G. E. Street (built between 1868 and 1882) and at Oxford the buildings of Keble College by William Butterfield (chapel completed 1876) represented the last ambitious kicks of the more aggressive Gothic revivalists. The Oxford Examination Schools by T. G. Jackson (1882), discarding Gothic for English renaissance, afford one of the first large examples of the return to styles more congruous with modern needs and capacities. But perhaps the typical architect of these sixteen years is Alfred Waterhouse, whose Manchester Town Hall (1877) was still an orthodox, though very skilful, essay in Gothic, but who subsequently worked his way to modified styles, showing a much greater sense of reality.

Turning to the great plastic arts of painting and sculpture, we find them also embarrassed and confused at this period by new conditions set up through mechanical inventions. Down to the advent of photography their starting-point had always been representation. The only way to obtain a likeness of anything or anybody was to get some one to draw it or model it. For artists other than decorative designers this had been the immemorial basis of their activity, upon which everything else, however vital, was in a sense superstructure. Photography destroyed it. The sun was made able to reproduce any actual optical image far more accurately and certainly than the most skilful hand could. With such a rival it became useless to compete. So art had to orient itself anew—to get away at all costs from exact representation, and to concentrate upon things which photography could not do. This need was realized and faced in France a whole generation earlier than in England; and hence from the middle of the nineteenth century the decisive rise of French painting to primacy. But London in 1870 was unaware of it. The body with highest official prestige, the Royal Academy, was following leaders like Leighton and Millais, whose whole bent was representation. That even this had been so much narrowed down to pictorial story-telling may be explained by the circumstance that drawn illustrations for journals and books formed the economic standby of all rising English artists.[1] Aside from this popular current, G. F. Watts's best portraits of eminent men date from the years under survey; so do many of his allegorical pic-

[1] It was not till the early nineties that this was largely taken away from them by the development of the process-block for printing from photographs. Illustration seems to have had less economic importance in France, though some great artists there, e.g. Daumier, reflect its influence.

tures. The only painters outside the Academy conspicuous as a group were Rossetti and his allies. Rossetti's original work with the brush was really over before 1870; though the publication of his poems in that year (and of the further volume in 1881) brought him to his maximum vogue. But the painter with most influence inside this period over people of taste and high culture was Burne-Jones. At the Grosvenor Gallery, which from 1877 for about a decade gave exhibitions eclipsing the Academy's, his pictures were for such people events of real moment; and they were so because, far more than many painters of greater accomplishment as such, he was able to create and evoke a world of his own, a world of high and rare spiritual values. Burne-Jones had known William Morris since they were Oxford undergraduates,[1] and they were closely associated through their joint lives. Yet, in spite of much give-and-take between them, Burne-Jones's peculiar spiritual note was not Morris's, and appealed to a different, a more aristocratic class.

The earliest school developed in reaction against the photograph in France was that of the impressionists. Their art had long been established there, when its challenge was first forced upon London in 1874 and 1877 by the American artist, Whistler, who had studied in Paris. Against his *Nocturnes* (including *Old Battersea Bridge*), shown in the latter year at the Grosvenor Gallery, English taste reacted with violence. Ruskin[2] accused him of 'flinging a pot of paint in the public's face', and a famous libel action resulted. The conflict may seem surprising and the critics merely stupid, until we grasp the key; which was that hitherto painting in England had always been conceived on a representational basis, so that its votaries were unequipped to see what wilful divergence from this might be aiming at. Gradually, however, the impressionists became understood; though it was not till 1886 that they were able to collect their forces in the New English Art Club and present an organized front to the Academy.

Of the two best (though not most fashionable) English sculptors in 1870, the greatest, Alfred Stevens, died in 1875. The other,

---

[1] They entered Exeter College together in 1853. Burne-Jones, it may be noted, though often popularly classed with the Pre-Raphaelites, had never belonged to their brotherhood, and his art bears little relation to their tenets.

[2] In *Fors Clavigera*. Whistler obtained a verdict. Note that he, Morris, and Burne-Jones were of the same age within a few months. Ruskin was fifteen years older.

Thomas Woolner, who had once been Rossetti's ally, joined the Academy in 1871, and in 1877 became its professor of sculpture. His statue of Mill on the Embankment in London shows the doomed art of representation at a high level, using the common-place for significant forms, while exactly adhering to an historical record of how the subject looked and dressed. Two other sculptors, who came to the fore in the eighties, were Hamo Thornycroft and A. W. Gilbert; the *Gordon* of the one in Trafalgar Square (1885) and the *Eros* of the other at Piccadilly Circus (a later work, not unveiled till 1893) have always ranked high among the few good outdoor sculptures in London. Unfortunately none of these men typified the prevalent sculpture of the period; which was as bad as the buildings and furniture.

An art, in which a real English revival began at this time, was music. In 1875 died Sterndale Bennett, till then probably the most gifted English composer since Purcell, though sadly sterilized by life in non-musical England. His work at the Royal Academy of Music was nevertheless a seed-sowing; and after 1870 four men—Parry, Stanford, Mackenzie, and Sullivan—by their compositions and teaching formed the beginnings of an English school. By far the greatest musician among them was Parry; and he was in a personal position, moreover, to effect a much-needed improvement in the social and intellectual status of musicians in his country. Any one reading George Eliot's *Daniel Deronda* (1876) may see how even down to that time, as for most of two centuries before, the English upper class held music in Roman contempt as a field for foreigners and ill-bred underlings. But Parry belonged to the upper class himself; he was educated at Eton and Oxford; he was a man of fine presence, social gifts, and high all-round culture.[1] At the same time good musical teaching was extended beyond the Academy. In 1880 the Guildhall School of Music was started; and in 1883 the Royal College of Music (with Parry and Stanford as professors) opened a very important chapter indeed.

England had long been a lucrative visiting-ground for famous foreign musicians. But in this period there were several who laid her under a higher debt by helping materially in her musical

[1] See *Mary Gladstone: Her Diaries and Letters*, edited by Lucy Masterman (1930), for many vivid pictures of music invading the governing class (as exemplified by the Balfour, Lyttelton, and Gladstone families) and of Parry's part in this. The book is also a document for the influence of Burne-Jones.

rebirth. Foremost among these was the violinist Joachim, with whom may fitly be named the pianist Clara Schumann, the composer's widow. These two more than any others revealed to Englishmen the difference between great music and mere virtuosity. In a different field Hans Richter rendered a similar service. He became famous in England in 1877, when there was a three-day Wagner festival at the Albert Hall—Wagner himself held the baton part of the time, but Richter was the real conductor.[1] His subsequent visits did much to create an intelligent interest in orchestral music. Very much, too, was done by Sir Charles Hallé,[2] pianist and conductor, who from 1858 had organized a permanent orchestra in Manchester, and from about 1870 took it regularly to Edinburgh, Leeds, Birmingham, Bristol, and other cities. Meanwhile the cult of Handel's *Messiah* and Mendelssohn's *Elijah* continued—on a basis as much religious as musical; and this was an era of famous oratorio singers— Sims Reeves, Santley, and others.

On a lighter side of music Sullivan won a place for himself by his collaboration with W. S. Gilbert in a series of comic operas; which, though owing something to Offenbach, opened a genuinely English vein. *H.M.S. Pinafore*, the first of real note, appeared in 1878; the most successful, the *Mikado*, dates from 1885 and ran for nearly two years. The greater merit in this historic partnership was Gilbert's, and the operas have always specially appealed to people not otherwise musical. Yet Sullivan had a real gift for popular melody; though little of his prolific and ambitious output in other fields is now remembered.

It is not proposed here to attempt a literary history of the period, but only to indicate general currents in thought and letters. Of these the returns of the *Publishers' Circular* tell us something. In 1870 by far the largest group of new books published were 811 on religious subjects. The next largest— 695 'juvenile works and tales'—included many more of a religious cast. 'Novels and other fiction' came fifth on the list with 381 volumes—just below 'history and biography' (396) and just above 'poetry and drama' (366). By 1886 novels had leaped into

---

[1] This was the earliest introduction to England of Wagner's mature work. When Covent Garden two years before had first heard *Lohengrin* (then 27 years old), it was welcomed as 'typical Wagnerian opera'. The *Ring* was not played in London till 1882.

[2] Originally Karl Halle, born and trained in Germany, he received his English knighthood in 1888.

the first place with 969 volumes—a significant increase of over 150 per cent. Religion still led all the rest, but its fall to 752 volumes betrays the weakening hold. That poetry and drama had fallen to 93 volumes, while 'belles-lettres, essays, and monographs' had risen from 249 to 479, corresponds to a tendency on the aesthetic sides of literature for criticism to supersede creation. On the scientific sides the most noticeable growth is in books on economics and trade; which rose from 119 to 246, reflecting the many-sided destruction of economic complacency by the depressions of the late seventies and early eighties.

Novels at this period still invariably made their first appearance as books in three-volume editions (at 31s. 6d.), which were bought almost solely by circulating libraries. But now for the first time a sharp difference developed between those meant for the multitude and those designed for the intelligent reader. Down to and including George Eliot, all the great English novelists had been best-sellers. But George Meredith, whose four greatest books appeared in these years,[1] never reached a large public. Henry James, who came to Europe in 1869 and published his first notable novel in 1875, made an equally restricted appeal. Thomas Hardy, whose earlier masterpieces also appeared now,[2] had a broader vogue. But he was never a best-seller in the widest sense. Much the same is true of R. L. Stevenson; his *Treasure Island* (1883) and *Kidnapped* (1886) enjoyed almost the fullest popularity; but no other of his best books reached so far.

Most of the best-sellers are now forgotten. Perhaps the most successful was Mrs. Henry Wood; her first book *East Lynne* (rejected by Meredith in his capacity of publisher's reader) had appeared in 1861; but between then and her death in 1887 she produced over thirty novels, which had an enormous aggregate sale. In popular books the growing influence of the woman reader began to be felt. All the best English novels of the nineteenth century were aimed at a masculine taste; even George Eliot was a woman writing primarily for men, just as surely as Arnold Bennett in the Edwardian era was a man writing primarily for women. Adoption of the feminine outlook by the best writers is a phenomenon confined to the twentieth century.

---

[1] *Harry Richmond* (1871), *Beauchamp's Career* (1875), *The Egoist* (1879), and *Diana of the Crossways* (1885).
[2] *Far from the Madding Crowd* (1874), *The Return of the Native* (1878), and *The Mayor of Casterbridge* (1886).

But already in the seventies and eighties there was a trend towards it in the popular novel. The eighties, however, developed also a masculine fashion in romantic adventure, of which the outstanding success was Rider Haggard's *King Solomon's Mines* (1885). Stevenson, in the books mentioned above, contributed to and benefited by this current.

The output of poetry, after its brilliant phase between 1830 and 1870, collapsed almost suddenly. Tennyson and Browning each published a series of senile volumes, containing, besides a little gold, most of the dross that their detractors now fasten upon. Swinburne's publications sank not much later into the same category. Morris's *Sigurd the Volsung* (1876) and Patmore's *Unknown Eros* (1877) and *Amelia* (1878) alone represent in the later seventies the upper level of their authors; and in the early eighties Morris's few socialist poems and Carpenter's *Towards Democracy* (1883) stand out over a thin crop of obviously minor work.

English history at this time made signal advances. Stubbs was regius professor at Oxford; his *Select Charters* appeared in 1870, and his *Constitutional History of England* in 1874–8. Freeman, who succeeded him in the Oxford chair in 1884, completed his *History of the Norman Conquest* in 1879. S. R. Gardiner published the last instalment of his *History of England 1603–1640* in 1882, and the whole work was issued in ten volumes the next year. J. Gairdner, plodding away as a clerk at the record office throughout this period, was now at the height of his vast editorial productivity; the *Calendar of Letters and Papers of the Reign of Henry VIII*, in which as collaborator or editor he took a part all through, poured out most of its twenty-one volumes during these years; and his great three-volume edition of *The Paston Letters* appeared in 1872–5. These are all books which it is now difficult to conceive the body of English history without; and taking them together their advent implied an enormous addition to the accurate and vivid knowledge of our island's past. In its rather different fashion, as an original and very brilliant piece of learned popularization, J. R. Green's *Short History of the English People* (1875) was also outstanding; so were the twelve volumes of Lecky's *History of England in the Eighteenth Century*, the first six of which appeared between 1878 and 1887. Yet a further influence was Acton, who in 1886 helped to found the *English Historical Review*. One way and another the intelligent citizen, anxious to learn what the real history of his country had been, had far better means of doing so in 1886 than in 1870. In this respect few, if any, periods of equal length have been more fruitful.

Parallel rises in the level of learning became discernible in many other fields. The study of English law had since Selden's day been too much divorced from the universities, with serious risk to its intellectual bases. But the publication (1861) of Maine's *Ancient Law*, in which it was approached from the side of history and comparative jurisprudence, had begun a revival of academic interest; and following the appearance in the early eighties of a band of brilliant law teachers,[1] both Cambridge and Oxford developed important law schools. The traditional subject of English education, classical scholarship, received a new impulse about this time towards Hellenism; stimulated partly by the German archaeologists,[2] and partly by a large growth in the number of persons taught to read Greek with facility. A performance of the *Agamemnon* of Aeschylus at Balliol College in 1880 (with F. R. Benson as Clytemnestra) started a fashion, which soon became widespread among learned bodies, for acting Greek plays in their original language. Jowett's translation of Plato (1871) similarly pioneered an endeavour to make Greek ideas more widely available to English theorists.

On the borders of speculative thought attention was attracted by the men of science, and by the conflict (real enough at the time) between science and religion. Tyndall delivered his famous Belfast Address[3] in 1874, and Huxley's activity in the reviews was incessant. In the field of philosophy itself the leading figure in popular estimation was Herbert Spencer, a self-taught journalist of genius, who owed nothing to universities. But the teaching of T. H. Green at Oxford in the seventies and the publication of his principal works after his early death in 1882 established in England much higher standards of philosophical attainment. Whatever be thought of the English Idealist school, which Green did so much to found, they at least conceived their task as one for fully trained and organized professionals, not for gifted but isolated amateurs. On the political side Green's teaching was notable as providing a theory of the state which, in oppo-

---

[1] A. V. Dicey was elected to a chair at Oxford in 1882, and Sir Frederick Pollock to another in 1883; F. W. Maitland to a readership at Cambridge in 1884.

[2] In 1874 Schliemann published his *Ancient Troy*; in 1877 Olympia was excavated and the *Hermes* of Praxiteles discovered; in 1880 the great frieze at Pergamos came to light.

[3] Reprinted in the 5th edition (1876) of his *Fragments of Science*.

sition to the individualism of Mill and Spencer, justified the new trends towards collectivism in public affairs.

Among the wider currents of political thought were two—imperialism and social reform—of which the first subsequently became dominant from 1886 to 1901 and the second ruled from 1905 to 1914. Each implied a positive view of the state, and they were not necessarily opposed. But, though combined by Disraeli at the outset, they proved rivals in the sequel; only a few people took much interest in both. Imperialism in the seventies was to some extent a revulsion away from Europe. The continent between the Crimean and the Franco-Prussian wars had swollen its armies to such a scale that Great Britain, which at the former epoch played an important military part among great Powers, was revealed at the latter as completely outclassed. We recorded in Chapter I the shock which this administered to public opinion. When he looked overseas and called in new worlds to redress the balance of the old (as by bringing Indian troops to the Mediterranean), Disraeli applied a real salve to his countrymen's wounded pride and alarm. After his death the single influence which did most to develop the imperialist idea was the very powerful and popular book *The Expansion of England*, by Sir John Seeley, who from 1869 to 1894 filled the chair of modern history at Cambridge. Seeley, who was a specialist on the rise of Prussia and the career of Napoleon, was a believer in the beneficence of rule by the strong. But the full harvest of his sowing was not reaped until the period following this.

Social reform had its roots in evangelical philanthropy—Disraeli learned much from Lord Shaftesbury. This philanthropy was still very active in the seventies. To take three examples, it was in 1870 that Dr. T. J. Barnardo opened the first of his great homes; between 1870 and 1875 that 'Hospital Sunday' and 'Hospital Saturday' were successively established in Birmingham, Manchester, Liverpool, and London;[1] and in 1878 that the Rev. William Booth, after thirteen years' evangelical mission-work in the east end of London, founded the Salvation Army.[2]

---

[1] 'Hospital Sunday' in its primitive form as started by Canon Miller of Birmingham goes back to 1858. But it was its adoption in Manchester by the Rev. John Henn in 1870 that really set the ball rolling.

[2] Its name dates only from 1880. 'Armies' were noticeably common about then; thus a 'Blue Ribbon Army' (teetotal) had a great vogue from 1878; and in 1883 a 'Skeleton Army' was formed to fight the Salvationists. The Boys' Brigade, also, dates from 1883.

Not formally religious, yet born directly under Lord Shaftesbury's star, the Charity Organization Society was built up from 1869 onward, and did much to bring order into the chaos of sporadic alms. But the slumps of the late seventies and early eighties, disturbing the complacency of all classes, started a more radical current, anxious not merely to relieve symptoms, but to remove causes. Only a small left wing took part in that rebirth of socialism which we recorded in Chapter III; but milder enterprises were widespread. Perhaps the most fruitful in after-effects was the foundation of university settlements. The first important settlement, Toynbee Hall, dates from 1884. Arnold Toynbee (1852–83), after whom it was named, typified the new prickings of youth's social conscience.

In social life the feature of the period is the rise of the suburban middle class. Originally the typical gentlefolk were landowners and their relatives. The earlier founders of industrial wealth had sought to be like them; they bought land and horses, built country houses, laid up wine in cellars and grew grapes in conservatories, and, if in London, sought a patent of gentility in admission to one or other of the jealously guarded social clubs. But already in the seventies the new class was becoming numerous enough to form habits and standards of its own. After 1878 the downfall of agriculture and the pinched fortunes of the country landlords quickened the process.

Nothing is more characteristic of it than the development of organized games. This, which on any reckoning may rank among England's leading contributions to world-culture, has been far more recent than is often realized. The English landed society did not pursue games but sports. Its recreations were shooting, fishing, hunting, coursing, and horse-racing; beside these the little unorganized cricket and football, which its members might play at school, were of small account. Archery was the only widespread aristocratic sport involving competitive scores; tennis was rare, lawn-tennis unborn, and golf a peculiarity of Scotsmen.

Some dates may bring the change into perspective. The types of football now popular were only two out of many which had been played rather informally at different schools or colleges. The laws of the Association game were first formulated (based on the practice of Cambridge undergraduates) in 1863; the first real international match was played between England and Scotland in 1872; England *v*. Wales followed in 1879, and England *v*. Ireland in 1882. Rugby football was the game which happened to be in vogue at Rugby school, when a wave of popular interest in that school followed the publication (1857) of T. Hughes's *Tom Brown's School Days*. The senior London Rugby club (Blackheath) dates from 1860; the English Rugby Union (the governing body for England) was founded in 1871. In that year England first played Scotland; in 1875, Ireland; and in 1880, Wales. Association football soon became very popular in the manufacturing towns as a spectacle attracting gate-money; the natural result was professionalism, which crept in about 1880 and was recognized by the Association in 1885. By contrast the Rugby Union fought hard for the principle that the game should be played for the game's sake, and banned all professionalism within its clubs, though a good deal developed outside them.

Cricket, long before our period, had entered the professional stage. But the gate-money was then small, and it was an amateur, Dr. W. G. Grace, who first made watching cricket a popular craze. Born in 1848, the period 1870–86 marks the zenith of his amazing prowess. A further great stimulus followed the advent of the Australians; their first visit to English cricket-fields was in 1878; and as they beat eight out of their twelve opponents (including a strong team from the M.C.C. itself), its regular repetition became assured. Cricket is a game which specially lends itself to reporting; and it was the first to obtain—at this time—considerable space in the newspapers.

Where football and cricket differed from shooting and fishing was that the best matches, whether for player or spectator, could only be held at main centres. The suburb-dweller and the professional man were on the spot for them; the landowner with his broad acres was not. Besides, they were on a club, not an individual or a family, basis; to take part as of full right you needed no ground of your own. Football, however, is for youth, and for male youth only; it was the discovery of games suited to older ages and both sexes that completed the change. Lawn-tennis was quite literally an invention; its begetter, a Major Wingfield, took out a patent for it in 1874 under the name of Sphairistike. But it was rapidly modified; in 1875 a committee of the M.C.C. drew up rules for it; and in 1877 a committee of the Wimbledon

All England Croquet and Lawn Tennis Club[1] made more or less final revisions. It enabled every good-sized suburban garden to match the resources of a great country house; and it introduced a new type of graceful athleticism both for men and for women. Golf was a rather later growth. Played in Scotland from time immemorial, it was in England confined to a few Scotsmen until the founding of the Westward Ho and Hoylake clubs in 1864 and 1869 respectively. In the seventies it made slow and in the eighties rapid progress; but it was not till after 1885, when women came to be admitted to play on the main links (previously the clubs had confined them to special 'short' links), that its full possibilities as a suburban pastime gradually opened up. Almost contemporary, and closely parallel in its social and physical consequences, was the introduction of cycling. In the period under review ladies could only ride tricycles, for bicycles were still of the 'spider' type with a very high front wheel and a very low back one; the 'safeties', which, among other advantages, made it possible to ride in skirts, only succeeded in the latest eighties. Yet even the earlier sort produced a marked effect. Till then it had been normal for every gentleman to ride horses; in the country there was often no other convenient way to keep in touch with friends. But for such purposes a bicycle was much more efficient,[2] while it saved the cost of grooms and stabling and could be stored on the smallest premises. Well-educated men of slender means, such as the expanded schools and universities were multiplying, found it just the thing for them. Thus it began the revolution which in our own century the motor-car has consummated.[3]

The rise of the educated suburban class had broken down by 1880 the exclusiveness of upper-class society in and round the great towns; though in the counties it fought hard to maintain itself till the end of the century. In London even clubland gave

---

[1] It had originally been a croquet club, but in that year it annexed lawn-tennis, and began the famous series of championship meetings which has continued ever since.

[2] The extreme limit for a day's visit by horseback was about fifteen miles; the usual one, about six. The bicycle doubled each of these.

[3] An interesting contrast between old tastes and new is furnished by those close contemporaries and near neighbours, A. J. Balfour and Lord Rosebery. Balfour was an enthusiast for lawn-tennis, golf, and cycling, but he cared little for shooting, hunting, or racing. With Rosebery these likes and dislikes were exactly reversed. It is in keeping that on the intellectual side Balfour had a passion for music and for contemporary painting, while Rosebery, indifferent to either, nourished an eighteenth-century taste on classical prose.

way. Some of the older clubs remained small and select as ever, but larger numbers and more open doors became usual. The foundation in 1883 of the National Liberal Club and the Constitutional Club marked a double innovation. For they were the first ever formed with political party membership as an express qualification, and also the first with no personal or social basis.

Games and cycling were the chief influences modifying men's costume in this period. In the seventies that of a gentleman in London, or on full-dress occasions elsewhere, was still what it had been in the early fifties—a black frock-coat, top-hat, and wide tubular trousers sweeping the ground at heel but rising in front over the instep. Men, however, had long ceased to play cricket in top-hats; and they no longer wore black frock-coats on mountain walks, as Ruskin is depicted doing in Millais's portrait of 1854.[1] For town and Sunday wear the variation of a 'morning coat' with tails increased its vogue, though never in London thought equally full-dress. More important was the development, for provincial and country use, of an early form of lounge-coat presaging the universal dress of to-day. The prince of Wales seems particularly to have favoured it; popular photographs of him thus clad had appeared even in the late sixties. But by the early eighties it had a much stronger footing. By then, too, cycling had introduced a new type of loose short breeches fastened with a buckle below the knee; they were usually worn with a buttoned-up coat modified from a shooting-jacket and known as a 'Norfolk' jacket. Similar breeches replaced the long trousers originally worn for playing football, and were themselves replaced in the late eighties by open 'shorts', originally introduced for running and jumping. Long trousers of white flannel, which had become standardized for cricket, were adopted for lawn-tennis. But the greater emphasis on agility in the new game helped to make them shorter, freer, and more workmanlike; and their cut seems to have reacted beneficially on the over-long trousers till then fashionable in daily wear. Altogether the progress made by men's costume in the upper and middle classes between 1870 and 1886 was very marked in the direction of lighter, shorter, freer, and more hygienic forms; and with it came eventually some lessening of the ugliness which in this as

[1] A messenger from the foreign office once found Lord Salisbury rabbit-shooting in a frock-coat, but that is recorded as a personal eccentricity.

in other spheres was worse before 1880 than after. In the working class the chief tendency of the time was towards abandoning old garbs distinctive of trade or occupation. It was now that the country labourer gave up his smock frock; and in the towns workmanlike corduroy and fustian, though still prevalent, began to lose ground.

Women benefited much less. The crinoline, which they had long thought their worst enemy, ceased to be fashionable about 1868, though photographs show it worn in 1870 or later. But it continued to be the object of dress-design, not to follow natural forms, but to pervert and distort them; and costume so inspired, whatever its vogue at the time, will always seem ugly and often ridiculous to posterity. Perhaps the silliest-looking distortion ever invented was the bustle, which was in fashion from 1870 to 1890. But the most serious evil was the constriction of the body by corsets of steel and whalebone designed to alter all its natural proportions and in particular to produce the narrowest possible wasp-waist. In the seventies skirts trailed on the floor for a yard or so behind the wearers and had to be held up out-of-doors with one hand. In the eighties they were shortened to just off the ground, probably under the influence of the new games. Women wore bustles and tight corsets even when playing lawn-tennis; but they could not have worn skirts which required holding up. As it was, their clothing remained for all purposes a great physical handicap.

It is important, however, to remember that the sway of fashion over women was much less universal then than now. Dressmaking was still quite an individual business, and few clothes worn in any class were ready-made. Women of taste and intelligence could find a style that suited them and keep to it with but limited regard to fashion's dictates. A notable instance was that of the Morris and Burne-Jones circle; their women wore loose dresses of richly coloured material falling in straight lines and only constricted by a natural girdle. In that case the prompting was aesthetic; in others a hygienic or a sports motive ruled. Similarly the mass of working women all over the country, though of course aware of fashion, were not tied as now to its extravagances. They had their traditional modes of dressing; and though they shared with their richer sisters such burdens as unhygienic underclothes, they were not obliged to trail their skirts on the floor, or to ruin their constitutions by wasp-waisting. Fashions not only ruled less, but changed less often. There was no one able, like the controllers of dressmaking to-day, to decree each year some slight innovations with the sole object of rendering last year's dresses unwearable.

In the social habits of the time the leading feature was domesticity. Urbanization had as yet scarcely affected English traditions in this respect. In the upper and middle classes families were big, and social entertaining was done almost entirely at home. Houses, rooms, tables, dinner-services, joints, and helpings all averaged a good deal larger than to-day; and older people commonly exercised their hospitality with a cohort of sons and daughters round them. Domestic servants were plentiful and cheap. Any well-to-do married man, if he was not to inherit a paternal mansion, usually aimed at establishing himself as soon as possible in a house which would last him for the rest of his life. One of its features would be a cellar, in which he would systematically lay down wines.

The working classes, both in town and country, were too poor to entertain much in their houses; for social gatherings they looked rather to the chapel or the public-house. Nevertheless, save among the submerged slum-dwellers, the cult of home held them strongly. A fair indication is the immense popularity at this time of the song *Home, Sweet Home*, which despite its mediocre words and music became for the seventies and eighties a second National Anthem, simply because of the idea which it expressed.

The sex-morality of the period corresponded. Divorce, though it had been obtainable at law since 1857, was still held unspeakably disgraceful. It was not till 1887 that Queen Victoria would allow even the innocent party to a divorce-suit to attend her court.[1] In the previous year one of the most rising men in politics, one for whom many prophesied a premiership, had been driven into the wilderness because he was co-respondent in a divorce-suit. This case of Sir Charles Dilke is the more striking because the judge at the divorce trial (12 February 1886), while granting a decree *nisi* against the respondent, dismissed with costs the petition against Dilke as co-respondent, and observed that 'there is no evidence worthy of the name as against him'. In fact there was none but that of the respondent herself. Nevertheless, because he had not gone into the witness-box to deny the charges

[1] *The Queen's Journal*, 10 May 1887.

a fierce agitation broke out. To quell it and enable himself to give evidence, he reopened the case by moving the queen's proctor to intervene. In the event this proved very bad tactics. The court held him to be no longer a party but only a witness, so that at the trial (16–23 July 1886), when the charges were renewed, he could not take issue against them as affecting himself. Thus he suffered the damage of their renewal without gaining any chance of reply. Whether he really was guilty or not may never now be settled. The point of significance to note is that a leading statesman could be ruined politically by a charge of adultery, even though the court had held there to be 'no evidence worthy of the name' against him. He was left out of the cabinet while the first trial impended; lost his seat before the second; and remained exiled from politics for six years. This tragedy of Dilke's will help us to understand the greater tragedy of Parnell four years later.

A school of recent writers, concerned to paint the Victorians as hypocrites, has suggested that behind a façade of continence their men were in fact profligate and over-sexed. Religious restraints, it argues, did not really check physical impulse. The view may, like any other, be backed by particular instances. But as a generalization it misunderstands the age. The religion-ruled Englishmen then dominant in the governing, directing, professional, and business classes spent, there can be little doubt, far less of their time and thought on sex interests than either their continental contemporaries or their twentieth-century successors; and to this saving their extraordinary surplus of energy in other spheres must reasonably be in part ascribed. Probably at the bottom of society there was a greater amount[1] of coarse prostitution than now, just as there was of drunkenness, of physical squalor, and of ruffianly crime. Progress in all those respects from the bottom upwards has been persistent, though intermittent, for a century. But it is very significant that when well-to-do Victorians gave way to vice they commonly went to Paris to indulge it; also that there was a white slave traffic from England to Paris and Brussels, but little or none in the opposite direction. The Criminal Law Amendment Act of 1885 for the first time made such trafficking a criminal offence; and by raising the age

---

[1] W. T. Stead, who in 1885 ran a famous newspaper campaign against vice and in the course of it rashly committed acts which brought him to the dock of the Old Bailey, estimated in his speech in his own defence that there were 50,000–60,000 prostitutes in London. But he was a sensationalist, not a statistician. A reasonable estimate would seem to be perhaps a third of that figure.

of consent from 13 to 16 and that of abduction from 16 to 18 it notably extended the legal protection of women.

A very memorable movement falling almost entirely within this period was the agitation against the Contagious Diseases Acts. These acts (passed in 1864, 1866, and 1869) had adopted for eighteen garrison or dockyard towns the system of registering, licensing, and medically examining prostitutes in vogue generally on the continent. At first the policy was unopposed; but when its advocates wanted to extend it to the whole country, there began in 1869 a counter agitation to repeal the acts. After fourteen years' effort the repealers in 1883 carried a resolution in the house of commons. In April 1886 a repealing statute became law.

The agitation was important: first, because it saved England from a bad system of vice-regulation, which is now at last being widely abandoned on the continent itself; secondly, because it greatly advanced the idea of a single standard of virtue for men and women; and, thirdly, because it powerfully stimulated the more general movement for women's rights. Its heroine was Mrs. Josephine Butler;[1] its hero, James Stansfeld. Mrs. Butler, a lady of exceptional altruism and eloquence, compelled public attention for years to unsavoury evils the mere mention of which by a woman brought obloquy. Stansfeld showed almost greater self-sacrifice. In the first Gladstone administration he had been a cabinet minister, and a high place in politics was marked out for him. But in 1874 he abandoned it all that he might give his parliamentary experience and influence unreservedly to this then failing cause. Only after twelve years, when repeal had passed the house of commons, did he consent to join a cabinet again.[2] One may doubt whether the history of any modern country can present a similar case of a front-rank statesman throwing up his ambitions for a thankless crusade of mercy in so rewardless and repellent a field.

[1] 1830–1906. Her father, John Grey, had worked with Clarkson, the emancipationist. Her husband was the brother of Dr. Montagu Butler, the celebrated headmaster of Harrow and Master of Trinity College, Cambridge.

[2] He took Chamberlain's place following the resignation of the latter in March 1886 over home rule.

VI

LORD SALISBURY'S PRIME

ON the morrow of the 1886 election the conservative leaders still doubted the scope of their victory. Their party had a majority of 40 over Gladstonians and Parnellites combined; but it would be placed in a minority of 40 on any division where the 78 liberal unionists supported Gladstone. Thus the casting-vote, which belonged to the Parnellites in the last parliament, was transferred to the liberal unionists in this; and Lord Salisbury's first step was to press Lord Hartington as their leader to accept the premiership. Only after his firm refusal[1] was the framing of a conservative cabinet put in hand.

It differed in only a few respects from its predecessor. Sir Michael Hicks Beach, though he had in turn led the house and the opposition with much credit, declined to lead the house again. He felt, as he afterwards frankly put it,[2] that Lord Randolph Churchill, though his junior by twelve years, was his 'superior in eloquence, ability, and influence', and that 'the leader in fact should be leader in name'. Lord Randolph thereon insisted that Sir Michael should become Chief Secretary for Ireland, on the ground that he 'could only honourably give up the Leadership by taking what was at that moment the most difficult position in the Government'. Lord Iddesleigh became foreign secretary that Lord Salisbury might be freer for his task as premier; though it was understood that he would retain a special oversight over his old department. A minor appointment of some importance was that to the local government board of C. T. Ritchie; for which Lord Randolph, who was much interested in the reform of local government, was partly responsible. A less fortunate choice, in which the tory democrat was also concerned, was that of Mr. Henry Matthews[3] as home secre-

---

[1] His private reasons were: (1) that Chamberlain, with whom Lord Salisbury declined to sit in any joint ministry, would, with his following, slide back to Gladstone; (2) that his own section would be too small to escape the charge of subjection to the conservatives, and probably neither he nor Sir H. James could be re-elected in their constituencies. Different reasons were given in public. See Lady Gwendolen Cecil, *Robert Marquess of Salisbury*, iii (1931), 310; Bernard Holland, *Life of the Eighth Duke of Devonshire* (1911) ii. 170–1.

[2] W. S. Churchill, *Lord Randolph Churchill* (1906), ii. 125.

[3] B. 1826, son of a Ceylon judge. Educated at Paris University and University College, London. Barrister, 1850; Q.C. 1868; M.P. 1868–74 and 1886–95; home

tary. He was a successful conservative barrister, who by Chamberlain's aid had been elected for East Birmingham. In the sequel he did more, perhaps, to render the government unpopular than any other minister.

By far the most important of these changes was the elevation of Lord Randolph himself. Aged only 37, he was the youngest chancellor of the exchequer and leader of the house after Pitt. From the age of 31 his rise had been meteoric. On public platforms his party had no equal to him; in the election fight against home rule he had been its mainstay throughout the constituencies. He seemed predestined to be prime minister at no distant date; and, as indicated above in Chapter III, might but for the events of the previous year have stepped into Disraeli's place already. Yet ere 1886 ended, from his sudden eminence he fell sheer.

The queen's speech was read on 19 August. An uneventful session of the new parliament lasted till 25 September. Parnell introduced a Tenants' Relief Bill, which was rejected by 297 votes to 202; and the government set up a commission under Lord Cowper to inquire into Irish rents and land purchase. Public attention, exhausted by the home drama, was diverted to a drama abroad. We shall see later on in this chapter how, following the abdication of the first prince of Bulgaria, the anti-Russian party in that country declared it independent. In the European crisis which accompanied these events, Lord Iddesleigh at the foreign office continued the Disraelian tradition of hostility to Russia, but with a lack of foresight and intelligence, of which Lord Randolph Churchill complained bitterly to the prime minister in private letters of 4, 6, and 30 September. Outwardly the cabinet were harmonious; and the new leader of the house earned golden opinions, not least from the queen.

On 2 October he delivered at Dartford a speech which was a manifesto. At home it outlined a great programme of reforming bills; in the Balkans it foreshadowed an exertion of British influence on the side of the Central Powers—not, however, in the Disraelian cause of Turkish integrity, but in that of the freedom of the Balkan peoples. The speech marks his political zenith; and though there were tory mutterings against its boldness, at

secretary, 1886–92. As he was a Roman catholic an arrangement was made whereby the ecclesiastical patronage of the home office was exercised by the first lord of the treasury. Created Lord Llandaff in 1895 and died 1913.

the conservative party conference on 26 October the orator fully vindicated himself. But then followed in the background a cabinet struggle over the forthcoming budget. Churchill evolved a comprehensive scheme which altered nearly every existing tax and added several new ones. He was to obtain £4·5 millions from extra taxation (about two-thirds of it by increasing death-duties and house-duties) and £8·4 millions from saving (£4·5 millions by lowering the Northcote Sinking Fund, £2·6 millions by stopping the old local government grants, and £1·3 millions by direct economy). This would change an estimated deficit of £400,000 into a surplus of £12·5 millions; and with it he proposed: (1) to lower the income-tax from 8d. to 5d.; (2) to lower the tea duty from 6d. to 4d.; (3) to take 4d. a lb. off tobacco; (4) to give, on a new system, local government grants totalling £5 millions. A treasury surplus of £730,000 would be left over. Such in outline was this radical budget. Doubling the local government grants would permit of a really large reform in that sphere; the tea and tobacco remissions ensured a popular appeal; while the lowered income-tax conformed to the best economic thought of the day. With a budget of only £94·5 millions such boons seemed heroic.

The cabinet accepted in principle, but hitches arose over the direct economy of £1·3 millions. Lord Randolph hoped to squeeze it from the admiralty and war office. Both were very reluctant, for the war-cloud in Europe had forced soldiers and sailors to make up arrears, and moreover the year had an extra day—it was leap year. Lord George Hamilton for the admiralty made some approaches, but W. H. Smith, the war minister, persisted in refusal. On 20 December Churchill wrote to Lord Salisbury, saying he must resign unless Smith were overruled. The premier replied on the 22nd declining to overrule Smith. Churchill treated the letter as a final acceptance of his own resignation, which it clearly was not, and we know now was not meant to be.[1] He sent a rejoinder on that basis; and burned his boats by publishing his resignation in *The Times*.

Why did he take this step which, since nobody of consequence rallied to him, ruined his career? Not because he need have.

---

[1] The evidence of a letter written by Salisbury to Hicks Beach on 21 December seems conclusive. See Lady Victoria Hicks Beach, *Life of Sir Michael Hicks Beach* (1932), i. 300, and W. S. Churchill, *Lord R. Churchill*, ii. 236. Neither prints the text, but its tenor is evident from Hicks Beach's reply.

The £500,000 or so, which at the outside he may have expected from Smith, could have come at a pinch from the estimated Treasury surplus. Further, from Lord Salisbury's refusal he was by usage entitled to appeal to the full cabinet, which would almost certainly have arranged some compromise. His resignation was a calculated repetition of tactics which he had practised with signal success in May 1884. Then, at the height of a struggle for the conservative machine, he had resigned the chair of the Council of the National Union, and a surge of popular feeling in his favour had swept him back to it in a fortnight. Clearly he expected the same thing now; for indeed the conservatives without him had not one strong debater in the commons save Hicks Beach, who was busy with Ireland. But he forgot that, since the budget discussions remained a cabinet secret, his public would have nothing to go on. In fact they were quite mystified, and scarcely a dog barked on his behalf.

Salisbury's letters had shown great patience towards him so far; but the rupture brought relief as well as embarrassment. 'Did you ever know', he is reported to have said, 'a man who having got rid of a boil on his neck wanted another?'[1] He again offered the premiership to Lord Hartington, who again refused it; but it was settled by way of compromise that Goschen, who stood a little to the right of the other liberal unionists, should join the government as chancellor of the exchequer. This was a great reinforcement, for Goschen was a first-rate debater and also a financier of European fame. But it did not balance the loss to nascent radicalism within the conservative party. Lord Salisbury wrote on 30 December[2] that 'the two circumstances which made it especially difficult to work with' Lord Randolph 'were his resolution to make the interests of his Budget overrule the wishes and necessities of all the other Departments, and secondly his friendship for Chamberlain, which made him insist that we should accept that statesman as our guide for internal politics'. Nine years later the same guidance was to be welcomed by Salisbury himself in the great unionist coalition; but for the present it could only be exercised from the outside. The immediate result of Churchill's downfall was to set Chamberlain thinking about liberal reunion. On his initiative and at Harcourt's sug-

---

[1] Lord Ullswater, *A Speaker's Commentaries*, i. 188.
[2] In a private letter to Sir James Fitzjames Stephen (Lady Gwendolen Cecil, *Life of Robert Marquess of Salisbury*, iii (1931), 336–7).

gestion a 'round table conference' of five[1] explored the avenues to it at a series of meetings. They failed; but one of the liberal unionist leaders, Trevelyan, went back to Gladstone unconditionally. Later, on 5 April, Chamberlain had a long private discussion with his old chief. But it ended without result, and was never repeated.

The early months of 1887 piled up troubles for Lord Salisbury. Goschen, who had much inner knowledge of the European chancelleries, had insisted on Lord Iddesleigh's being removed, against his wish, from the foreign office.[2] On 12 January, after the old man had taken leave of his staff, he died suddenly of syncope in Lord Salisbury's room and presence—a tragedy which gave rise to much cruel comment. On 27 January the house of commons met, but without a chancellor of the exchequer, as Goschen had lost his by-election the day before. No remedy could be found but to elect the liberal unionist for a conservative stronghold—St. George's, Hanover Square. Finally at the beginning of March Hicks Beach, the seemingly indispensable Irish chief secretary, was threatened with loss of eyesight and had to resign his office. The fate of the government hung in the balance.

But from that moment it rallied. W. H. Smith proved an unexpected success as leader in the commons. Then a new star of the first magnitude flamed out on the conservative horizon. A. J. Balfour, Lord Salisbury's nephew, promoted to Hicks Beach's unenvied succession as Irish chief secretary, suddenly revealed himself in that office as possessing courage and resource of a very high order together with consummate gifts for parliamentary debate. Though wearing a different mantle from Lord Randolph Churchill's, he swiftly and effectively replaced him as the young and dazzling standard-bearer for his party's combatants. Once more they had a spokesman who could stand up in the commons against Gladstone. This was the last blow to Churchill's hopes of recovery; and it was a strange irony which caused it to be dealt by one of his former fourth party associates.

Before we carry the political story farther, we must take

[1] Chamberlain, Trevelyan, Harcourt, Morley, and Lord Herschell. See J. L. Garvin, *Life of Joseph Chamberlain*, ii (1933), 277–94.

[2] Lady G. Cecil, *Robert Marquess of Salisbury*, iii (1931), 340. The public reason given for Lord Salisbury's return to the foreign office was that his office of first lord of the treasury was needed in order to provide a conservative leader of the house of commons in the person of W. H. Smith.

account of the event which more than any other makes 1887 memorable. The year brought Queen Victoria's first jubilee. A wave of personal loyalty and patriotism swept the country, whose depth it is perhaps difficult for any one not then living to realize. The future, of course, was not visible; men did not know that the queen had nearly fourteen years more to reign, nor could they perceive, as we now can in our longer perspective, that the speed of the nation's ascent was slackening and its day had passed the noon. The half-century since 1837 seemed to them, as it does not to us, a completed era—one of beneficent material progress quite unexampled in history; one, too, in which a noble rebirth of moral idealism had won continuing victories for freedom and justice and the humanizing of life, both at home and abroad.

The celebrations contained features memorable in themselves. On Jubilee Day (21 June 1887) the queen went in procession from Buckingham Palace to Westminster Abbey to attend a thanksgiving service, accompanied by princes, potentates, and envoys representing virtually every nation. Among these the most observed individual was her son-in-law, the Crown Prince Frederick of Germany—already menaced by disease, though few then suspected that he had less than a year to live; but as a class the most conspicuous were the Indian princes. On the same evening bonfires were lit on almost every hill of any size or note between Land's End and Shetland, the signal for starting them being given from the Malvern Hills. In the next month the queen held three great reviews—of the volunteer corps at Buckingham Palace, of the army at Aldershot, and of the fleet at Spithead. It was the last which chiefly impressed the world. Great Britain stood then near the apex of a long period of unchallenged naval supremacy, by which all the development of her trade and empire had been conditioned; and here, as never before, was its visible embodiment. Yet by twentieth-century standards the tale of the Spithead Armada seems surprisingly small. Apart from torpedo craft, troopships, and many still humbler[1] vessels, there were only thirty-five fighting ships, of which nine were unarmoured. So rapid was later naval growth.

Besides these central displays every locality in the land had its festival. In the cities these were on an imposing scale; and often great works were undertaken as permanent memorials. At the

---

[1] e.g. a 'paddle frigate' and six 'training brigs'.

other end, some thousands of country parishes each organized a free tea, at which all the separate elements in the old hierarchized life of rural England—gentry, farmers, shopkeepers, labourers, rich and poor, church and chapel—sat down for once in equality together. It was the swan-song of that life before its final break-up.

The Jubilee's main effect in politics was Imperial. All the self-governing colonies sent their prime ministers to London, and at the suggestion of the Imperial Federation League advantage was taken of their visit to combine them in consultation with the heads of the home government. This 'Colonial Conference', though the actual decisions which it reached were not very important, proved a great starting-point. All subsequent colonial or imperial conferences descend from it. The mere coming together of the empire's premiers—each not an ambassador but a principal—evolved a new organ, and went some way to meet the immediate need; which, as Lord Salisbury told the delegates, was 'to form neither a general Union nor a Zollverein, but a Kriegsverein—a combination for purposes of self-defence'. The conference drew stimulus from the alarm felt by the colonies at the new overseas ambitions of the European Powers, and also from the growing British imperialism focused in London by the successful Colonial and Indian Exhibition of the previous year. The profits from the latter went to the Imperial Institute, which was founded in South Kensington as a national Jubilee memorial.

The League just mentioned (founded in 1884) formed the chief nursery of imperialist thought at this early stage. W. E. Forster had been its first head; Lord Rosebery, W. H. Smith, Froude, J. R. Seeley, and James Bryce were among its supporters; and it enrolled some of the best-known colonial statesmen. But its members could never agree on a positive policy; and in 1893 it broke up.

It was fortunate for the Salisbury government that throughout 1887 party controversy was still dominated by Ireland. For in this way their doubtful liberal unionist supporters, particularly Chamberlain, were brought steadily into closer alliance. The defeat of Parnell's Tenants' Relief Bill in the previous autumn had been followed by renewed evictions, which Hicks Beach in vain tried to discourage. The reply from the Irish side was the famous 'Plan of Campaign'. Circulated throughout Ireland on

20 November, it called on the tenants of each estate to organize; to treat with the landlord as a united body, standing or falling together; and if their offers of rent were not accepted by him, to pay the money instead into a campaign fund. Its chief promoters were William O'Brien and John Dillon; Parnell privately disapproved. At first its spread was remarkable; but soon the resulting evictions created a turmoil worse than any since 1882. Lord Salisbury had to abandon all hope of governing by the ordinary law. The first business brought before the commons, when they reassembled in January 1887, was an amendment of their rules, allowing the closure to be carried by a bare majority on the motion of any member, provided the Speaker consented and at least 200 members voted for it. Thus forearmed, the government was able to pass a new and drastic Crimes Act. Skilfully piloted by Balfour in his new capacity, it was helped on the day of second reading by the publication in *The Times* of a facsimile letter dated 15 May 1882, i.e. nine days after the Phoenix Park murders, purporting to be signed by Parnell and condoning the murders. Parnell at once denounced this in the house of commons as a forgery. But it looked very genuine; and the series of articles on 'Parnellism and Crime', in which it appeared and which contained other reputed secret letters by Irish leaders, had a profound effect on English public opinion. To get the bill through committee the government had to innovate still further in the restriction of debate, with a 'guillotine' resolution (which Gladstone did not oppose) fixing a time-limit beyond which clauses were to be put without amendment or discussion. Meanwhile Lord Cowper's Commission had reported advising certain concessions to Irish tenants. These were embodied in a companion measure. Both bills became law before parliament rose; and Balfour, with coercion in one hand and relief in the other, stood foursquare against the Plan of Campaign. In August the National League was 'proclaimed'. A sort of 'war' lasting nearly three years began, during which Ireland was once more convulsed by rebel lawlessness and dragooned by arbitrary authority.

This was wholly undesired by Parnell. He had realized too late the need for appeasing English popular opinion and allowing the bugbears of moonlighting and cattle-maiming to be forgotten. But he could not stop men like O'Brien and Dillon, any more than Hicks Beach had been able to hold back Lord Clanricarde and the other eviction-forcing landlords. Before long blood flowed. On 9 September, at the opening of a prosecution against O'Brien, a crowd of 8,000 persons had collected at Mitchelstown, in County Cork. While Dillon was haranguing it a scuffle broke out with the police. Driven back by numbers to their barracks, they thence opened fire on the mob, killing one man and mortally wounding two others. A coroner's jury found wilful murder against the county inspector and five constables. But none were brought to trial; five months later the Queen's Bench in Dublin quashed the verdict on technical grounds. It was Gladstone, and not any of the Irish leaders, who coined the grim watchword 'Remember Mitchelstown'; which for long remained current among home rulers in both islands. Other fatalities followed elsewhere.

In the house of commons Balfour fought Parnellites and Gladstonians alike with unfailing resource. In Ireland his aim was to hold the scales fair; yet in practice he rather tilted them towards the landlords. He was less critical than both Carnarvon and Hicks Beach had been of the intransigence shown by absentee rack-renters, since in face of the Plan of Campaign's challenge to legality it had to be his prime care to enforce the law. Whoever defied it went to prison; at one time it was the Lord Mayor of Dublin; at another, the English poet, Wilfrid Scawen Blunt. But the victim who gave most trouble was O'Brien, who refused to wear jail clothes and wrung special privileges for political prisoners.

In connexion with his case occurred the famous episode of 'Bloody Sunday' in Trafalgar Square on 13 November 1887. The Commissioner of Police, Sir Charles Warren, was anxious to put an end to the use of Trafalgar Square for open-air meetings, which since 1884 had become very popular with London radicals and socialists. For about a month before 'Bloody Sunday' the Social Democratic Federation had off and on been holding meetings in the Square. Warren alternately permitted and prohibited them; but the more the police interfered, the larger the meetings became. The meeting for 13 November was summoned in defiance of a prohibition, and its object—to 'demand the release of William O'Brien, M.P.'—was chosen so as to attract Irish besides Radical militants. The socialists tried to baffle the police by approaching in many different bodies from all sides.

Some were dispersed by baton charges in Holborn, the Strand, and Parliament Street; but many reached the side of the Square, and rushes were made. Heading one of them, R. Cunninghame Graham, M.P.,[1] and John Burns were arrested. The police fought hard and long against superior numbers, till Foot Guards and Life Guards came up, and the latter with their horses cleared the Square. No shot was fired, and the Riot Act was not read, though a magistrate came prepared to read it. There were over 100 casualties. Two out of the crowd afterwards died of injuries; the police also suffered severely. Cunninghame Graham and Burns were convicted at the Old Bailey in the following January and sent to prison for six weeks. Others, having elected to be dealt with summarily, had at Bow Street received longer sentences.

The affair is worth recording as the most considerable *émeute* in London during the latter half of the nineteenth century. Bitter memories of it lasted in the working-class districts for over twenty years. Much odium fell on Warren, who was indeed largely to blame; and much on the home secretary, Matthews, who was already unpopular in parliament. That it had no sequel may be ascribed to a rapid trade improvement. This, which did much to ease the government's task for the next three years, seems to have been monetary in origin. It followed the sudden inflow of South African gold. During 1887 the Rand first showed what it could do. In May its gold output had been 887 oz.; in December it was 8,457 oz. The effect was that of a mild but sufficient inflation.

In the ding-dong fight between Balfour and the Irish Nationalists, alike at Westminster and in Ireland, Parnell took little active part. But he remained the undisputed leader of his people; and with his fortunes those of home rule rose and fell.

We have seen that in April 1887 *The Times* published in facsimile a most damaging letter ascribed to him, which he declared in parliament to be a forgery. He brought no action at law, an omission which some attributed to his disdain for English opinion and others to a sense of guilt. But later an Irish ex-member, whom *The Times* attacked, sued the newspaper for libel; and at

---

[1] B. 1852, son of a Scottish laird; educated at Harrow. M.P. 1886–92; defeated candidate twice later. After his political career was over, he became (from 1895 onward) a well-known author. D. 1936.

the trial of the case (*O'Donnell* v. *Walter*) on 2 July 1888 counsel for the defence, Sir Richard Webster,[1] produced other incriminating letters which Parnell was alleged to have written. Unable to ignore the charge longer, but disbelieving that he could get justice from a Middlesex jury, the Irish leader asked to have the authenticity of the letters inquired into by a select committee of the house of commons. The government declined, but brought in a bill setting up a special commission of three judges to investigate the whole of *The Times* charges. The commissioners were Sir James (afterward Lord) Hannen, Mr. Justice Day, and Mr. Justice (afterwards Lord Justice) A. L. Smith. They met in September 1888.

Now these letters were clever forgeries. They had been bought in good faith by *The Times* after submission to a handwriting expert. The vendor had in turn bought them from one Richard Pigott, a disreputable Irish journalist. Pigott forged them with his own hand. It was not till February 1889 that he entered the witness-box; but there he speedily broke down under cross-examination. He absconded abroad; posted a full confession to *The Times*; and when the British police tracked him to Madrid with a warrant for his arrest on a charge of perjury, blew his brains out. These sensational events caused a strong revulsion of popular English feeling in favour not only of Parnell but of his cause. His brilliant counsel, Sir Charles Russell, himself an Irishman,[2] created the public impression that there had been a cut-throat conspiracy against the honour of the Irish nation by traducers who did not stick at forgery. This was not wholly true; for the one actual villain had been Pigott, and his sole motive was money. But it appealed overwhelmingly to the latent English love of fair play; so much so that, when the Commission reported nearly a year later (2 February 1890), entirely exculpating Parnell, but establishing grave charges against Davitt, Dillon, O'Brien, and the Irish leaders generally, the acquittal almost wholly diverted attention from the blame. *The Times* was mulcted in the enormous sum of £250,000 for the whole cost

---

[1] 1842–1915; educated at Charterhouse and Trinity College, Cambridge; attorney-general in all Lord Salisbury's governments until 1900, when he became lord chief justice and took the title Lord Alverstone; resigned 1913. At this time law officers were entirely free to accept briefs in private suits.

[2] 1832–1900; born at Newry; educated at Trinity College, Dublin; called to the English Bar 1859; attorney-general, 1886 and 1892–4; lord chief justice, with title Lord Russell of Killowen, 1894–1900.

of the inquiry. It had already paid £30,000 in acquiring the material for its articles.

For a brief while Parnell touched a new top-point. In December 1889 he visited Gladstone at Hawarden. Had there been a dissolution in the first half of 1890, there can be little doubt that the veteran statesman would have been returned with an overwhelming home rule majority. Balfour's coercion was not popular. The revelation of forgery sapped confidence in the whole case against home rule. The government had been consistently losing by-elections ever since it started, and its original majority of 114 had dwindled by 1890 to 70. But suddenly the disclosure of an episode in Parnell's private life brought down his career and his cause together.

On 17 November 1890 the Divorce Court granted a decree *nisi* to Captain O'Shea in a suit against his wife, in which Parnell was the co-respondent. There was no defence. The facts of Parnell's relation with Mrs. O'Shea are given elsewhere.[1] We have seen also in the case of Dilke the stigma attaching to adultery in Queen Victoria's reign, and how it would operate to prevent a man from becoming a minister of the Crown. In this instance the shock to opinion was severe; for though the bare fact that a liaison between Parnell and Mrs. O'Shea existed had been well known to his leading Irish colleagues for many years, and to some front bench liberals also, the general public were quite unprepared to learn of it.[2] Yet the situation was not on all fours with Dilke's; Parnell had no present prospect of becoming a minister and kissing the queen's hand; moreover he belonged to no English party and held himself responsible to his country-

[1] Appendix B.
[2] In February 1886, when Biggar and Healy tried to prevent Parnell from procuring the by-election candidature of Captain O'Shea at Galway City, Biggar publicly stigmatized Mrs. O'Shea as 'Parnell's mistress'; and though the phrase was kept out of the papers, it circulated among Irish politicians. It had already been used by Harcourt to cabinet colleagues in 1882 after the Kilmainham Treaty. The Gladstone Papers at the British Museum show that from that time onward Gladstone had a considerable, though intermittent, correspondence with her, using her as his regular channel of private communication with Parnell. But this may be naturally explained, since he knew her as the niece of his former colleague, Lord Hatherley; and the scanty evidence available all suggests his unawareness of the liaison. One of his private secretaries, Sir George (then Mr.) Leveson-Gower, can remember venturing (with the approval of his uncle, Lord Granville) to warn the prime minister that rumours were prevalent; but Gladstone (who shared with many mid-Victorians a particular aversion to hearing or repeating scandal) treated them as idle gossip. He scouted the idea that a man in Parnell's responsible position could be guilty of an intrigue so incompatible with it.

men only. He decided to retain the leadership, and at first nearly all his leading colleagues except Davitt backed him. The day after the decree was pronounced, John Redmond presided over a meeting of the National League in Dublin, attended by at least seven other prominent M.P.s, which pledged its support by acclamation. From America Dillon, O'Brien, Harrington, and T. P. O'Connor cabled in the same sense; and two days later both Healy and Justin McCarthy expressed their public agreement in the Leinster Hall.

But on the following day the National Liberal Federation met at Sheffield; and though nothing was said in public, it was privately represented to the front bench in the persons of Morley and Harcourt that English nonconformists could not continue any association with the Irish party unless it changed its leader. This line was quite a sincere and natural one for religious Victorians to take. The persons chiefly responsible for focusing opinion upon it were the Rev. Hugh Price Hughes, one of the most influential ministers in the Wesleyan Connexion; W. T. Stead, in the *Review of Reviews*; and E. T. Cook, in the *Pall Mall Gazette*.[1] The feeling at the National Liberal Federation was reported to Gladstone; and just a week after the decree, on the eve of the meeting of parliament, he penned a letter to Morley for the latter to show next day to Parnell. In it he sufficiently, though obscurely, indicated that, unless the Irish party changed its leader, he would himself cease to lead the liberals.[2] Privately apprised of this, the Irish chief could still without loss of dignity or eventual authority have laid down his command for an expiatory period. But Morley on the morrow was unable to see him until after the Irish party's meeting had in ignorance[3] re-elected him leader. He was now entirely obdurate. Gladstone, Morley, Harcourt, and their chief whip, Arnold Morley, took counsel together in despair. They sent the

[1] Cook was a political journalist of great sobriety and sagacity. The other two might not unfairly be termed demagogues, but each had taken a particular concern in crusades against sexual vice in London.

[2] The operative words were: 'The continuance I speak of' [i.e. that of Parnell in the Irish leadership] 'would not only place many hearty and effective friends of the Irish cause in a position of great embarrassment, but would render my retention of the leadership of the Liberal party, based as it has been mainly upon the presentation of the Irish cause, almost a nullity.'

[3] They had received, it is true, a message from Gladstone through Justin McCarthy, but its vagueness concealed its import. For the whole episode see Morley, *Life of Gladstone* (1903), bk. x, ch. 5; Barry O'Brien, *Life of Parnell* (1899), ch. 22.

letter to the press; and its contents became known in the house that night.

Whether this hasty publication was wise or necessary is one of the most debated points in Gladstone's later career. In itself it transformed the letter. From being a private advice to Parnell it became a public ultimatum to the Irish party to choose between him and Gladstone. A man of Parnell's temperament could never accept such dictation; and it confronted all his colleagues with an instant and cruel dilemma. Should they, at English bidding, depose their brilliant national leader or should they, by retaining him, sacrifice all chance of home rule just when its ship seemed coming into port? By their inability to agree on embracing either loss, they eventually, as we shall see, incurred both.

The details of their schism belong to Irish rather than English history. Before anything had been decided Parnell issued (29 November 1890) a long manifesto to the Irish people. On the principle that the best defence is counter-attack, he circumstantially though unplausibly charged Gladstone with wishing to pare down and betray home rule. It completed for many of his colleagues the conviction that Parnell had become impossible.[1] On the following day a new and, as it proved, decisive weight was cast into the scale: the Irish episcopacy intervened. Placed in a hard strait they had hitherto kept silence, while the English nonconformists thundered and the English Cardinal Manning wrote imploring them to put morality above politics. But once wielded, their power proved immense. On 1 December the Irish members at the house of commons met in Committee Room No. 15, and for twelve memorable days debated the case there. Parnell made a clever attempt to divert the odium to Gladstone and snatch the Anti-Parnellites out of his hands. He actually induced them to join with his own following in a mischief-seeking deputation to the Liberal leader. But Gladstone's reply out-

---

[1] Dillon, W. O'Brien, and T. P. O'Connor were (as mentioned above) in America, and read the manifesto there before they had taken sides. The last-named wrote a year later: 'It throws a very curious light on Mr. Parnell's mind, that he should have thought that such a manifesto was likely to bring intelligent, or generous, or honourable men round to his views. . . . Indignation, disbelief, disgust, despair were so quickly and clearly roused, that we rushed out to the first station from which it was possible to send a cablegram, and announced to our colleagues that from this time forward we were to be counted among the opponents of Mr. Parnell's leadership' (T. P. O'Connor, *Life of Parnell* (1891), ch. 9). Of the delegation in America Harrington alone dissented.

flanked him; and eventually the party broke up, 44 seceding under McCarthy and only 26 remaining with Parnell. Almost immediately afterwards a by-election at Kilkenny permitted a trial of strength. Parnell had a good candidate, and fought desperately for him in person. But he was beaten (22 December 1890) by nearly two to one. In only one district was the parish priest on his side, and only in that district had he a majority.

The story of 1891 is soon told. Parnell continued to fight, and in doing so impaired his health, which had long been uncertain. O'Brien and Dillon, who had escaped from Ireland the previous August after warrants were out for their arrest, returned from America to northern France, where a fruitless episode known as the Boulogne negotiations developed between them and Parnell. Eventually they returned to Ireland, went to prison for five months, and emerged as anti-Parnellites. Two more by-elections were fiercely contested—North Sligo in April, Carlow in July. In both Parnell was beaten, though not so heavily as at Kilkenny. In June he married Mrs. O'Shea—a natural step, but one which deepened the hostility of the bishops and priests. On 27 September, while suffering from rheumatism, he addressed an outdoor meeting in the rain. Returning to England gravely ill, he went home to his wife at Brighton; the rheumatism affected his heart; and on 6 October he died. The unforeseen tragedy softened enmities only for a moment; but amid nation-wide mourning his countrymen buried him in Glasnevin cemetery close to the grave of O'Connell.

Parnell as a political tactician had excelled all his antagonists and allies save Gladstone only. Indeed if we take Peel, Palmerston, Disraeli, and Gladstone as the four supreme parliamentarians of Queen Victoria's reign, Parnell comes nearest their stature among the rest. Brief though his career was, it stamped an ineffaceable mark; as Gladstone said, he did 'for Home Rule something like what Cobden did for Free Trade—set the argument on its legs'.[1] He had scarcely any Irish features; he was almost typically an English aristocrat; the haughtiness and reserve, which sat so well on him, were those of a 'milord'. But in him, as in those closely contemporary aristocrats, Lord Randolph Churchill and Lord Rosebery, there were also traits of the spoiled child; and it was these which politically undid all three of them. Had his death been followed by a prompt reconciliation, the

---

[1] Morley, *Life of Gladstone* (1903), bk. x, ch. 5.

Irish, while losing their leader, might possibly have retrieved their cause. But the savage feuds, which he sowed so recklessly among his followers in the last ten months of his life, kept them fiercely apart. Their strife alienated all onlookers, and brought balm to the Salisbury government. The first three years of Balfour's chief secretaryship had been mainly given to the unpopular tasks of coercion. But as time passed and coercion triumphed, he could deal more in remedial measures. The creation of the Congested Districts Board and the construction of light railways in the west brought him a real popularity. In 1891, while the Irish members were rending each other, he was able to pass a valuable Land Purchase Act with the help and approval of all of them. Thus the parties drifted towards the General Election of 1892 in a very different posture from that of 1889-90. There was now no prospect of an overwhelming home rule majority.

Let us revert to other sides of this administration's story; and first to that in which its head was most largely absorbed—foreign policy. Here the principal achievement of the period was the peaceful partition of Africa.[1]

The scramble for the Dark Continent began in the seventies. The travels of Livingstone, Speke, and H. M. Stanley, the three great Victorians who withdrew the veil from most of its immemorial secrets, had disclosed not only mighty rivers, vast forests, and immense unorganized territories capable of supporting far more people than they contained, but the appalling horrors of the slave trade, human sacrifices, and cannibalism. Expeditions partly commercial and partly humanitarian began to multiply. In 1876 King Leopold II of Belgium convened at Brussels a Geographical Conference designed to co-ordinate them; which, besides drawing up certain declarations, created an 'International Association for the Exploration and Civilization of Central Africa', with its seat at Brussels and the king as president. The new body's first expeditions all started from Zanzibar, and were wrecked by tsetse-fly and malaria. But in 1877 Stanley completed the three years' traverse of Africa, in which, after mapping the two greatest lakes, he journeyed down the Lualaba to Nyangwe and thence traced the Congo to the sea.

[1] For fuller details see especially J. Scott Keltie, *The Partition of Africa*, 2nd edition (1895); Sir H. H. Johnston, *The Colonization of Africa* (1913); Demetrius C. Boulger, *The Reign of Leopold II* (1925).

He declared that 'the Power which makes itself mistress of the Congo must absorb, despite the Cataracts, all the commerce of the immense basin which expands itself behind that river'. But he found London (where Lord Beaconsfield was then absorbed in the Eastern Question) completely apathetic; and soon he was invited to Brussels and entered King Leopold's service. The result was the formation of the 'International Association of the Congo', which beginning in 1879 founded what became the Congo Free State and is now the Belgian Congo. Meanwhile French exploration worked down from Gabun to the right bank of the great river. In 1881 De Brazza hoisted the flag of the Republic at Brazzaville on the north side of Stanley Pool; in the following year the French Congo was definitely constituted. These enterprises, together with the French conquest of Tunis (1881), set the ball rolling elsewhere, and now for the first time Germany took an effective hand. Her shipping and trading classes had long desired colonies; but it was not till after 1882 that Bismarck fell in with their wishes. Another Power much affected was Portugal, which, besides owning large strips of the African coast-line, had shadowy claims to a great deal more, and was disposed to revive them when she saw that they were valuable.

Great Britain's position was that, while in the field of private enterprise her explorers and traders led all others, in the field of state action, whether under Beaconsfield before 1880 or under Gladstone after that date, the opinion prevailed that we had quite enough African territory and had better acquire no more. Even in South Africa, where our concern was especially great, we waited till Germany annexed the important contiguous area which came to be known as German South-West Africa, though at any time down to 1882 it could have been ours for the taking. That we nevertheless obtained a large share in the eventual division was chiefly due to three individuals—Sir William Mackinnon, Sir George Taubman Goldie, and Cecil Rhodes—and to the three chartered companies with which they were respectively associated—the British East Africa Company (1888), the Royal Niger Company (1886), and the British South Africa Company (1889).[1] To the first the empire owes what are now Kenya and Uganda, to the second what is now Nigeria, and to the third what are now Southern and Northern Rhodesia. Among

---

[1] The dates are those of the charters. The companies were in each case formed rather earlier.

them the figure which most struck the British imagination was Rhodes—an English clergyman's son, who went out young to South Africa, made a fortune in Kimberley diamonds, returned to read at Oxford, went back to take part in Cape politics and Rand gold development, and in 1890 became premier of Cape Colony. Rhodes, who was an enthusiast for Imperial Federation and in 1888 sent £10,000 to Parnell for Irish home rule, became in the early nineties a symbol of the imperialism of that epoch; and he looms larger in history than either Mackinnon or Goldie. Yet the actual additions which they made to the Empire have proved, down to the present, more important than his. Goldie, a Manxman (his father was speaker of the house of Keys), was an officer in the Royal Engineers, who in 1879 formed the United African Company to amalgamate all British trading interests on the Niger. The result was to defeat a commercial invasion of the Lower Niger by subsidized French firms; and five years later they sold out to the British combine. In 1885 the Powers were notified of a British protectorate over the portion of the Guinea coast between the old British colony of Lagos and the new German colony of the Kameruns; and in 1886 Goldie's enterprise was given a charter, as the Royal Niger Company, to control the territories up the Niger from its confluence with the Benue to the sea. But he also negotiated treaties with the Muhammadan Emirs much farther inland, and thus earmarked their lands against the Germans and French. The total area which he eventually brought under the British flag exceeded that of France and Germany combined—a great achievement, but not made possible until the vast upstream areas of the Niger 'bend', though originally opened by British enterprise, had fallen irrevocably under French sway. Mackinnon was a Scottish merchant, ultra-religious and interested in missionaries as well as trade; he had subscribed a quarter of the original small capital to King Leopold's venture; though later the king bore all its expenses. On the east side of Africa, where the Sultan of Zanzibar had shadowy rights over an enormous coast-line, the Germans showed great activity under the lead of Dr. Karl Peters, who formed a German East African Company and obtained a charter for it. It was Mackinnon and his associates who counter-developed British claims, first through an East African Association and later through their chartered company. Hampered by an 1886 agreement between Lord Iddesleigh and Germany, he was nevertheless able in May 1887 to get an important concession from the Sultan. In the spring of the same year Stanley, largely financed by Mackinnon, started on his famous expedition through the forest north-east of the Congo 'bend' to relieve Emin Pasha, who was still holding Egypt's equatorial province against the Dervishes. He went armed with authority to conclude treaties with chiefs in the region of the Nile lakes, whereby they put themselves under British protection. When he finally emerged on the east coast two years and a half later, he carried a bundle of these treaties, which formed the main starting-point for British territorial rights in that region.

Beside these private adventurers three government servants may be fitly named—Sir John Kirk (1832–1922), Lord Lugard (1858–), and Sir Harry Johnston (1858–1927). Kirk, after gaining fame as a co-explorer with Livingstone, was for twenty years British agent and consul at Zanzibar. He misconceived the future of tropical East Africa as one of Arab rule with British permeation; but to his unique local knowledge and influence all British enterprise in those quarters was indebted. Lugard, after a brief but brilliant period as administrator for the British East Africa Company, found his life-work in British West Africa, whose whole administrative development was moulded by his genius. Johnston, a most many-sided man—explorer, administrator, linguist, naturalist, artist, and author—took a leading part in one East African area after another during several decades.

Colonial development through private enterprise, by and at the expense of chartered companies, proved afterwards to be only a stage and not a lasting one. Yet without it we should never have obtained our African empire. To suppose that its acquisition was a work of prescient statesmanship would be to falsify the facts. In France from the late seventies and in Germany from the early eighties politicians came to see things from that standpoint; but Beaconsfield and Iddesleigh, Gladstone and Granville, were blind to them. Fortunately Salisbury saw farther, though not very far. As late as 1892 he is found complaining in a letter that the French in the regions under their influence sought exclusive commercial privileges for themselves, as though it were not essential to their whole scheme to do so.

The diplomatic side of these developments began with Granville and Dilke. In February 1884 they concluded a convention with Portugal, of which Dilke (then under-secretary for foreign affairs) was the author. By it the old and shadowy claims which Portugal had over the coast astride the Congo estuary were, in return for certain concessions, recognized by Great Britain on a generous scale. Three parties at once took umbrage—France, Germany, and King Leopold; they declared, very reasonably, that the status of the Congo could not be settled by any two nations over the heads of the rest. It was just at this time that Gladstone's Egyptian policy had made Great Britain dependent upon Germany's goodwill at Cairo, and Bismarck did not mind treating Granville with a certain roughness. In June the British government withdrew the Dilke Convention; and in November a full-dress Conference met at Berlin, where Bismarck presided over representatives of fifteen governments. It secured universal recognition for the Congo State (which the United States, France, and Germany, but not Great Britain, had recognized before it met); and by an exchange of territory with Portugal gave it an adequate access to the sea. It also prescribed freedom of navigation and commerce in the Congo basin, and made a number of important declarations. The five years following this witnessed the height of the scramble. It is almost surprising that the rivalries of the Powers, though productive of critical situations, did not bring them to blows; but in fact a war in Europe was the one extreme that they all shunned. Two personalities in particular wielded a restraining force—Bismarck and Lord Salisbury. But it was not till after Bismarck's fall that the worst risks of conflict were brought to an end by the agreements of the year 1890.

Those signed by Great Britain were three—that of 1 July with Germany, that of 5 August with France, and that of 20 August with Portugal. Taken together they form the most positive achievement of Lord Salisbury's diplomacy. Perhaps it is an index of their general fairness that none of them pleased majority opinion in either of the signatory countries. Viewing all the transactions together in the broadest way as a European partition of Africa, one sees certain anomalies. Of six Great Powers only three obtained valuable portions; it might have eased matters later if Austria-Hungary had participated, and still more if Italy had obtained something worth having. Of the successful three, Great Britain, on the whole, having regard to the very preponderant part that her exploration and commerce had taken in opening up the Dark Continent, scarcely received more than her share. Germany secured three large territories and one small one; they were valuable, but less than the British, far less than King Leopold's or the French, and less than corresponded to Germany's position in Europe. Had Bismarck seen what King Leopold saw at the time when King Leopold saw it, he might have secured for his countrymen nearly everything of value in tropical Africa; and later history would have been different had he done so. As things were France was the first Great Power to perceive what was afoot; she early planned her objectives and pursued them in a spirit of frank aggression.[1] Her reward was to obtain a predominant share. It is perhaps not generally realized that the colony known before the war as the French Congo had alone a larger area than all Germany's African colonies put together.

With Germany and with Portugal the British treaties of 1890 effected fairly complete settlements. Portugal had been in collision with British diplomacy over Mashonaland and Nyasaland and the Zambesi basin. She dreamed of creating a Portuguese belt right across Africa from her eastern to her western colony. But the titles which she put forward were, as Lord Salisbury said, 'archaeological'. From neither of her coastal strips had she effectually penetrated those inland areas, which had been opened up by British enterprise working from south and north. On this Lord Salisbury stood firm, and in January 1890 ended three years' wrangling by an ultimatum. The agreement of August, completed next year by a convention (11 June 1891), closed the controversy and confirmed Mashonaland and Nyasaland to Great Britain, while at the same time placing within Portugal's

---

[1] A good example was her acquisition of Madagascar. Everything that Europe had done for its people (and that was a great deal) had been done by British traders and missionaries. France had no footing there at all. But to the French expansionists of the Third Republic the island appealed as a desirable stepping-stone between their African and their Indo-Chinese empires. So in 1879 they picked a quarrel with the native government; in 1882 they claimed a protectorate over part of the island; in 1883 they extended their claim to the whole island and bombarded Tamatave; and in the following two years they conducted an intermittent war, which ended in the establishment of a *de facto* protectorate. During all this Granville can scarcely be acquitted of flagrant weakness; though it must be remembered that in the earlier stages, when the French aggression could most easily have been arrested, he was hampered by the need for France's co-operation in Egypt. The most that he left it possible for Lord Salisbury to do was to keep an opening in the island for British trade; and after the French declared a formal annexation in 1896, even that disappeared.

sphere of influence areas much larger than her eastern colony had hitherto embraced.

The negotiation with Germany was of a different order, for here there was no doubt about the other Power's effective activity on the spot. The early attitude of Great Britain to German colonial expansion had been grudging; and even in a case like South-West Africa, where her own long neglect had been conspicuous, she yet put in futile claims as soon as the German claim materialized. But Bismarck's sharp reprimand to Granville, and our new need for German support in Egypt, reversed all that; and for some years German enterprise, especially in East Africa, benefited not only by the energy of its own government but by the yielding disposition of ours. Lord Salisbury, however, was not deaf to men like Goldie and Mackinnon; and when the great adjustment was made in 1890, Great Britain gained on both sides of Africa. On the east the island sultanate of Zanzibar, a great bone of contention, became a British protectorate. The sphere of British influence in tropical East Africa (substantially what is now Kenya Colony and the Uganda Protectorate) was mapped in such a way as to bar German ambitions towards the Upper Nile, and undo a great deal that the pushing Dr. Peters had already done towards realizing them. On the west the incessant hostility, with which Germany since 1884 had menaced and harassed Goldie's enterprise, was brought to an end. A direct negotiation between Goldie and Berlin followed, ripening in 1893 to a formal agreement, which granted the Germans a narrow strip from their Kamerun colony up to Lake Tchad. To this they had no prior title, but Goldie was glad to see them there, because they barred a French encircling advance from that side. A similar but much narrower extension (known as the 'Caprivi strip') was conceded under the 1890 Agreement to German South-West Africa, connecting it with the upper waters of the Zambesi.

How did Lord Salisbury obtain this balance of African advantages from his negotiation with Germany? By a small but important cession in Europe. The tiny island of Heligoland, commanding the sea-approach to the mouths of the Elbe and Weser and the coast of Holstein, had been annexed by us from Denmark in 1807. But for this it would have gone to Prussia with Schleswig-Holstein. Germany since 1887 had been constructing the Kiel Canal, and did not wish a point controlling

its western outlet to remain in the hands of another Power. The
Heligolanders preferred British rule. But they were very few,
and we had long ceased to make serious naval use of the place;
so Lord Salisbury saw no objection to trading it—an idea about
which Chamberlain had sounded Herbert Bismarck in the previous year. Many of his countrymen disapproved, while equally
most Germans thought they had a bad bargain. Few then
realized on either side that, besides England's renouncing a
naval asset, Germany acquired one. Yet the island when fully
fortified became afterwards the keystone of her maritime position, for offence as well as defence.

What shaped British policy here was not foresight about
the future value of Kenya or Uganda, but our desire to keep
foreigners out of the valley of the Nile. Achieved thus at high
cost in regard to Germany, it was only achieved nine years later,
again at high cost, in regard to France. The Anglo-French
Agreement of 1890 was of limited scope. Under it we purchased
French recognition of our Zanzibar protectorate by recognizing
France's position in Madagascar. We also admitted some of her
large Central African claims; while Goldie's company was confirmed in its claims over the Sokoto kingdom, which now forms
a large part of Northern Nigeria. Viewed as a bargain, it was
unfavourable to us. But at least it helped to stabilize the map.

During these years the general orientation of the Powers underwent some important changes.[1] The pivot round which Europe
revolved was, as long as he remained in office, Bismarck. We
noted in Chapter III how in 1879, following his estrangement
of Russia at the Congress of Berlin, he had made an alliance with
Austria-Hungary; and how in 1882 it became a Triple Alliance
by the accession of Italy. Both alliances were secret. But in the
meantime by a treaty of 18 June 1881 signed at Berlin he renewed
a *Dreikaiserbund* between Germany, Austria-Hungary, and Russia. Its first article provided that if one of the three Great Powers

---

[1] For fuller details see especially G. P. Gooch, *History of Modern Europe 1879–1919*
(first edition, 1923); A. F. Přibram, *England and the International Policy of the European
Great Powers* (1931) (which contains a useful list of the chief German books on
Anglo-German relations at this time) and *Secret Treaties of Austria-Hungary* (1920),
vol. ii; and J. A. Spender, *Fifty Years of Europe* (1934). Documents will be found
mostly in Přibram's *Secret Treaties of Austria-Hungary*, vol. i, or in the great German
publication *Die Grosse Politik der europäischen Kabinette* (1922–6), the most important
items of which may be consulted in English in the four volumes of E. T. S. Dugdale's *German Diplomatic Documents* (1928–31). Much primary evidence is given
also in biographies, particularly in that of Lord Salisbury by Lady G. Cecil.

were at war with a fourth,[1] the other two would observe benevolent neutrality and localize the conflict. This also was secret.
Relations between Bismarck, Austria-Hungary, and the Tsar
were thus regulated by two secret treaties; but the Tsar knew
only one of them, while the point of the other was turned towards his breast.[2] Save as against Great Britain (who till after
the Penjdeh incident, early in 1885, was still regarded as Russia's
natural adversary), the renewed *Dreikaiserbund* was indeed of
small use to him. For his other potential adversary was Austria-
Hungary herself; and in the event of his clashing with her he
could not tell how Germany would act. However, he was not
long left uncertain.

In September 1885 Eastern Rumelia revolted from Turkey
and proclaimed her union with Bulgaria. The separation of the
two in 1878 had, it will be remembered, been imposed by Lord
Beaconsfield against the keen opposition of Russia. But now she
as keenly opposed their union, because in the interval an anti-
Russian party had come to the top in Bulgaria. Lord Salisbury's
first instinct was to abide by the Beaconsfield policy. But from
different standpoints Queen Victoria and Sir William White,
our extremely able ambassador at Constantinople, induced him
to reverse it; and in this he was joined by Austria-Hungary.
While the Powers were thus divided and punitive measures hung
fire, King Milan of Serbia pressed a demand for territorial compensation, and on refusal invaded Bulgaria. But at Slivnitza
(17-19 November 1885) the Bulgars were completely victorious.
Austria-Hungary intervened to save Milan from total ruin; but
Bulgaria's right to nationhood had been established. The Tsar,
however, though foiled, was not reconciled; and there followed
in August 1886 the kidnapping of the Bulgarian sovereign, Prince
Alexander, by Russian agents. It cowed him into abdicating,
but did not cow the anti-Russian Bulgars. Under their leader,
Stambulov, they rejected the Tsar's nominee for their vacant
throne, and looked about Europe for a substitute. Meanwhile
war threatened; opinion in Russia became very anti-German;

---

[1] By a special proviso this stipulation was only to apply to a war between one of
the three Powers and Turkey 'in the case where a previous agreement shall have
been reached between the three Courts as to the results of this war'.

[2] Austria-Hungary's obligation was to aid Germany if attacked by Russia;
Italy's, to aid her if attacked by France; Germany's reciprocated each of these.
The obligation on the three Powers to make war together only arose if one or more
of them were attacked by *two* Powers.

and in January 1887 Bismarck obtained from the Reichstag an increase in the German army. To dispel these clouds he concluded in June of the same year a secret 'Re-insurance Treaty' with Russia, providing that if either of them were at war with a third Power, the other would maintain benevolent neutrality. In all Bismarck's tortuous record, this has been perhaps the most criticized phase. True there was a special stipulation implying that if Russia attacked Austria-Hungary Germany need not stand neutral;[1] but not many will agree with Bismarck that this entirely cleared him of bad faith. If it is added that since 1883 both he and Austria-Hungary had a secret defensive alliance with Rumania against Russia, the inconsistency of his obligations may be seen. But the worst tension was yet to come. The Bulgars induced Ferdinand of Coburg to become their prince, and in August 1887 he went to Sofia and took up his task. The Tsar wanted to turn him out. But the demand, if conceded by the other Powers, would have meant that Bulgaria became Russia's subject; and Lord Salisbury supported Austria-Hungary and Italy in demurring to it. As a last resource to avert a Russo-Austrian war, Bismarck in February 1888 published the Austro-German treaty of 1879. This showed that if he were forced to come down from the fence, it would be on the Austrian side. A few weeks later Russia gave way. Austria-Hungary emerged as the dominant Power in the Balkans; Rumania was secretly her ally; Bulgaria and Serbia were both openly her clients. Germany and Italy (who renewed the Triple Alliance in 1887) stood beside her; and Great Britain stood behind. The 'Liberator' of 1878 had not a useful friend in the picture.

It was these events which threw Russia into the arms of France. The approach was tentative; first came contracts for French munitions; next, the floating of Russian loans in Paris. But the Re-insurance Treaty still linked Germany and Russia together; Bismarck still did his best to appear pro-Russian; and M. de Giers, the Russian chancellor, was undoubtedly pro-German. The decisive breach followed Bismarck's dismissal by the Emperor William II in March 1890. Before he fell he had obtained the Emperor's consent to the renewal of the treaty. But his successors at once jettisoned it. The formal responsibility was that of the new chancellor, Caprivi; but the deciding influence was

---

[1] Nor Russia, if Germany attacked France. See text in Přibram, *Secret Treaties of Austria-Hungary* (1920), ii. 275.

that of a high official in the German foreign office, Baron von Holstein. This powerful and secretive man, who owed everything to Bismarck but had thrown him over just in time, became for the next sixteen years the master hand in German foreign policy, directing the major decisions of successive chancellors and foreign secretaries.[1] In August 1891, following an historic visit of the French fleet to Kronstadt in the previous month, an *entente cordiale* between Russia and France was put in writing. From that time the Dual Alliance existed in embryo; though the military convention which virtually completed it was not, owing to the Tsar's personal reluctance,[2] signed till December 1893. An early fruit of the French loans was Russia's Trans-Siberian Railway, commenced in 1892.

These events, we see now, made a turning-point for the world. What was Lord Salisbury's share in them? In 1885 by supporting a united Bulgaria he had reversed the policy of Britain under Beaconsfield. But he was little criticized for it, since both Russia and Austria-Hungary reversed theirs. Seven years before he had personally doubted if Turkey were worth propping; and the interval had convinced him that nation-building in the Balkans was a more hopeful barrier to Russia's advance on Constantinople. There were some, notably Lord Randolph Churchill (as also Sir Robert Morier, our ambassador at St. Petersburg), who preferred ceasing to bar it altogether, and coming instead to an understanding with the Tsar, whereby he should purchase our complaisance in the Near East by calling off his menace in Central Asia. Such was not Salisbury's view. Aiming at peace, he regarded France and Russia as the two aggressive Powers. France had since 1879 pursued a policy of violent and unscrupulous expansion overseas; since 1882 she had everywhere edged her knife against England; during 1887-9 she underwent the

---

[1] Little was written about Holstein in Germany before the War, but he now figures in a large literature. His influence on decisions is attested by his memoranda in *Die Grosse Politik*. The best English summary of his character and career is Dr. G. P. Gooch's long essay in *Studies in Modern History* (1931). For a detailed hostile portrait see Johannes Haller's biography of Philipp zu Eulenburg (English translation by Ethel Colburn Mayne, 1930). Holstein, though very able, was a psychopathic case; circumstances and predisposition together had made him in his personal career an aggressive intriguer and blackmailer of sinister type; and the reflection of his temperament in his country's diplomacy had a considerable effect on European history.

[2] Probably enhanced by the inopportune outbreak of the Panama scandals, which convulsed France at this juncture.

strange fever of Chauvinism evoked by General Boulanger. Russia's restless ambitions had been broadcast by Penjdeh at the beginning of 1885 and by her threats to Sofia at the end of it. The British statesman, therefore, debarred by the Egyptian entanglement from standing quite alone, was drawn into general support of the Powers of the Triple Alliance. In 1887 he went farther, and in February signed an agreement with Italy for the maintenance of the *status quo* in the Mediterranean, Adriatic, Aegean, and Black Seas. Italy pledged herself to support British interests in Egypt, and Britain to protect the Italian coast-line from the French fleet. Soon after Austria-Hungary joined the pact, making it triple.

Though secret it was known to Bismarck. As the year wore on, he sought to extend it, not by joining in, but by procuring the signature of a treaty. Eight articles pledged the three Powers in more detail to uphold the *status quo* in the Near East, with particular reference to Bulgaria and the Straits. But Salisbury's suspicions were aroused by Bismarck's determination to keep Germany outside; and it was to allay them that Bismarck wrote to him on 22 November 1887 a famous personal letter. In it he declared that Germany, Austria-Hungary, and England were now contented, peaceful, and conservative nations, while France and Russia were potential aggressors;[1] and affirmed that the preservation of Austria-Hungary was 'a necessity for Germany'. But he went on to explain that Germany also needed, so far as it could be obtained, an understanding with Russia; since by no other way could she avoid the danger of a war on two fronts. Though friendly at every point, the letter offered no solid base for an Anglo-German alliance; as Lord Salisbury's reply shows that he saw. What then of the triple Mediterranean treaty? It was signed on 12 December 1887. The British Premier's

---

[1] 'L'Autriche, de même que l'Allemagne et l'Angleterre d'aujourd'hui, appartient au nombre des nations satisfaites, "saturées" au dire de feu le prince Metternich, et partant pacifiques et conservatrices. L'Autriche et l'Angleterre ont loyalement accepté le *status quo* de l'Empire allemand et n'ont aucun intérêt de le voir affaibli. La France et la Russie au contraire semblent nous menacer: la France en restant fidèle aux traditions des siècles passés qui la montrent comme ennemie constante de ses voisins, et par suite du caractère national des Français: la Russie en prenant aujourd'hui vis-à-vis de l'Europe l'attitude inquiétante pour la paix européenne qui caractérisait la France sous les règnes de Louis XIV et de Napoléon Ier.' The whole text will be found in *Die Grosse Politik*, iv. 376–80, and in *German Diplomatic Documents*, i. 345–8; also, with Lord Salisbury's reply conveniently annexed, in J. V. Fuller, *Bismarck's Diplomacy at its Zenith* (1922), pp. 329–35.

qualms about it seem to have been overcome by Bismarck's informing him of the contents of the 1879 Austro-German alliance. They scarcely could have been had he been aware also of the Re-insurance Treaty, under which the German Chancellor had just promised Russia benevolent neutrality in the event of her advancing upon the Balkans and the Straits.

However, the new treaty, involving grave war possibilities for Great Britain, remained in force for five years.[1] It was not known outside the chancelleries concerned until 1920. Questions asked by Labouchere at the time in the house of commons were turned aside. In 1889, a year after William II's accession, Bismarck went farther. He made a firm and distinct offer of an Anglo-German alliance. But it was to be an alliance against France only. He still declined to bind himself in any way against Russia. Therefore Lord Salisbury—who felt that the equivalent of France's danger to Germany was not France's danger to us but Russia's—did not accept. This was all that divided Great Britain at the time from acceding as a fourth member to the Triple Alliance. The two sides felt abundant friendliness, but they could discover no means of driving an equal bargain. An alliance that did not bind Germany against Russia would give Britain too little; one that did would cost Germany too much. And then in March 1890 the young emperor dismissed his chancellor.

When Bismarck had described Germany as a 'saturated' Power with no ambition of her own that could lead to war, he was giving an honest account of her policy as he himself shaped it. The vast expansions which afterwards became her aims, whether by land at the expense of Russia or overseas at the expense of England, were not present to his mind. Yet the elements out of which both the aims crystallized were already at work. We see the one implicit in the growing rivalry of Austria-Hungary with Russia for the Balkans; the other in the forces which so suddenly made Germany a colonial Power. The first compelled Bismarck, contrary to all his prepossessions, to take sides against Russia; while the part to be played by Austria in the land-expansion of 'Germanism'[2] slowly defined itself. With the second the veteran statesman from 1882 onwards had similarly to comply; but he was careful to break no bones over it, and neither then nor at any

---

[1] Lord Rosebery in 1892 allowed it to lapse.

[2] i.e. *Deutschtum*, a concept to which the broadening ties between Berlin and Vienna gave a growing importance from this time.

other time can one conceive him as supposing that (in William II's phrase of 1896) 'Germany's future lies on the water'. Consequently his removal from office was, in effect, the removal of a restraining influence. This was not at first apparent on the British side, towards which the new chancellor, Caprivi, was by way of displaying friendliness. It was with him that Salisbury negotiated the African settlement of 1890. In 1891, when the Triple Alliance was renewed for the second time, there was a protocol registering the desire of the signatories to bind Britain more closely than ever under the Mediterranean treaty. Two months later the German foreign secretary, Marschall, saw Lord Salisbury. But the latter, though he would have reciprocated a binding promise from Germany to stand by Britain against Russia as well as France, still declined to incur new obligations for anything less; and from such a promise Germany still held back, for the reasons given in Bismarck's 1887 letter.

It has been sometimes said in England that after Bismarck left the stage of international diplomacy Lord Salisbury succeeded him as the leading actor on it. This is in no sense true, either of the period 1890–2, which we are now considering, or of that after his resumption of office in 1895. He never took, as Bismarck habitually did, the guiding initiative in European affairs. His situation did not allow it. The statesmen of the monarchical Powers objected constantly that he served a parliament and could not bind future parliaments; thus both secrecy and permanence were in peril.[1] So, except for his Mediterranean pact, he remained isolated outside the secret treaties; and yet, owing to the Egyptian entanglement, whose diplomatic consequences he unceasingly deplored, he never had isolation's full freedom. Once he made a convention with Turkey (signed 22 May 1887) providing under certain conditions for the evacuation of Egypt in three years; but France and Russia dissuaded the Sultan from ratifying. Temperamentally, too, it was not Salisbury's bent to scheme ahead like Bismarck. He was content to meet situa-

---

[1] Cp. the memorandum of Sir Philip Currie on his conversations with Bismarck, 28–30 September 1885; where the latter 'complained that any treaty with England was uncertain, since, when there was a change of Ministry, it might not be considered binding'. Sir Philip argued against this but 'Prince Bismarck still demurred. Austrian statesmen had been convinced by Mr. Gladstone's repudiation of his predecessor's policy in 1880, that no trust was to be placed in England. The same thing might happen again.' (Lady G. Cecil, *Life of Robert Marquess of Salisbury*, iii (1931), 259.)

tions as they arose. Hence he can scarcely be ranked in the first flight of international statesmen, though his place must be extremely high in the second. Personal respect for his massive wisdom and calm temper was nearly universal abroad.[1] Backed by the very long lead of his country's fleet and the formidable record of her small army, he enabled her amid successive dangers to hold her own for the time being better than her position otherwise warranted.

His government's chief domestic achievements fell in the spheres of finance, local government, and education. After Balfour his most successful colleague was Goschen.

Few chancellors of the exchequer, if any, have come to that office with more previous financial experience. But his earlier budgets repeated, though cautiously, the ideas embodied in Lord Randolph Churchill's draft. Lord Randolph was to raid the Northcote Sinking Fund for £4·5 millions; Goschen's first Budget raided it for £2 millions. Lord Randolph was to reduce the income-tax from 8d. to 5d. Goschen reduced it to 7d. in 1887 and to 6d. in 1888. Lord Randolph was to take 2d. off tea; Goschen did so in 1890. The smaller reduction on tobacco he made at once. Lord Randolph was to increase the amount of central subventions to local government by £2·4 millions; Goschen (who had special knowledge of local government) went farther, increasing it in 1888 by £2·9 millions, and in 1889 and 1890 finding still larger amounts. All this suggests the continuing influence of treasury officials. But whereas Lord Randolph's schemes involved forcing economies on his colleagues, Goschen was successful in defraying a rising expenditure. Beside the expansion of local government there were increases in the army and navy estimates and a special naval building programme (1889), and £2 millions for free education (1891). While helped in his task by a trade improvement, he resorted also to small new taxes. He shared Gladstone's dislike of the income-tax, but he believed that the only way to avoid undue reliance on this and a few other big imposts was to reverse to some extent the Gladstonian policy of sweeping away lesser ones. Not all his proposals went through; a 'wheel and van' (promptly nicknamed 'veal and

[1] Not quite: Holstein, e.g., had a rooted objection to his 'intolerable personality'. See many passages quoted from him by Dr. G. P. Gooch, *Studies in Modern History* (1931). The Emperor William II also disliked him.

ham') tax in 1889 raised a clamour like that against Lowe's
match duty, and had to be abandoned. The most important
which he carried was an estate duty of 1 per cent., to fall on
estates, real or personal, exceeding £10,000. This, which was
introduced to meet the extra naval expenditure of 1889, proved
a foundation on which Sir William Harcourt five years later
built bigger things.

But Goschen is best remembered for his conversion of the
national debt in 1888. It seemed a very large operation by
nineteenth-century standards, though the immediate saving in
interest was no more than £1,400,000, and the ultimate only
twice that amount. In it he dealt with three blocks of 3 per cent.
stock: (1) £166 millions of 'New Threes'; (2) £69 millions of
'Reduced'; (3) £323 millions of 'Consols'. The first could be
and were redeemed at par without notice; on the other two,
which could only be redeemed with notice and in large sums,
he offered a small premium of 5s. per cent. for immediate conversion and a commission of 1s. 6d. per cent. to agents. The
uniform new Consols which he created in substitution bore 2¾
per cent. interest; but it was to become 2½ per cent. after 15
years. The postponed drop proved subsequently of great importance; for by the time it came gilt-edged interest rate had moved
back again upwards. The whole scheme went through parliament unchallenged, save for the proposal to pay commission;
against which Gladstone, with but little support, divided the
house. Much of the credit for its success belonged, outside the
treasury, to the then governor of the Bank of England, Sir Mark
Collet.

Goschen was also concerned in the reform of local government. In 1870-1, just before Stansfeld succeeded him as president of the poor law board in the first Gladstone administration,
he had worked out a scheme which covered the rural areas on
ambitious lines. But his bills raised much outcry from the landowners, who for centuries had governed the counties as a non-
elected oligarchy through quarter sessions; and Gladstone, never
interested in local government, dropped them. Accordingly the
government of counties and parishes still remained unreformed,
when under the act of 1884 household suffrage was extended to
their inhabitants. This made large changes inevitable; for neither
party could afford to oppose the demand that those who now
had votes for parliament should likewise have votes to elect their

local rulers. Lord Salisbury's president of the local government
board, C. T. Ritchie, was responsible for the main measure, the
Local Government Act 1888. By it, for the first time, were created
county councils, 62 in all, each of the historic shires having one,
and some of the larger ones more. By it, too, was created the
divorce between counties and county boroughs; the latter being
the larger boroughs (normally those over 50,000 population),
which were in effect taken out of their counties and treated each
as a county in itself. This severance is sometimes criticized, and
it certainly has involved drawbacks as well as more obvious
advantages; but it followed the best foreign precedents, notably
that of Prussia. In London the large area, which since 1855 had
been made a unit for some purposes under the Metropolitan
Board of Works, was constituted as a county with a council like
the rest; and the area of the City Corporation (though that
ancient body retained very large autonomy) was included in the
county and represented on its council by four members. Broadly
speaking, the powers handed over to the councils covered the
administrative (as distinct from the judicial and licensing) functions of quarter sessions, the most important being highways and
bridges; in London they included all the powers of the previous
board of works. The police of London, outside the City, remained under the commissioner appointed by the home office;
but in the other counties their control, being considered to have
both administrative and judicial aspects, was handed over to a
Standing Joint Committee of Quarter Sessions and the County
Council. Any borough, however, which had mustered 10,000
population by the 1881 census, was allowed to retain a separate
police force, controlled by its own council through the Watch
Committee. The franchise for county councils was closely assimilated to that for borough councils. Women, if unmarried, might
be electors in both cases, but not be elected in either.

Helped from Goschen's side with not inadequate grants, the
scheme made a good start. In London Lord Rosebery became
the first chairman of the council, and the second was Sir John
Lubbock.[1] All over the country administration was quickened,
and new public activities opened up, now that there were responsible bodies to undertake them. Parliament soon began adding
powers. In 1889 it passed the Technical Instruction Act, making
the county and county borough councils the authorities for that

[1] The notable scientist and banker (1834–1913), in 1900 created Lord Avebury.

subject; and in the very next year Goschen was able, by passing on to them the windfall of the 'whisky money', to provide the wherewithal for a most important educational progress.[1]

But the educational reform which most interested politicians was the abolition in 1891 of school fees in elementary schools. At a Carlton Club meeting a year earlier, Lord Salisbury had won over his doubting followers by a cogent party argument. They must, he said, settle the problem, because otherwise, 'if their opponents should obtain a majority in a future Parliament, they would deal with it in such a manner that the voluntary schools would be swept away'.[2] In other words, the conservatives were obliged to make elementary education free everywhere, lest the liberals, by making it only free in the publicly provided board schools, should place the church schools at a hopeless disadvantage. No doubt less opportunist motives had their weight in the cabinet. Sir W. Hart Dyke, who as vice-president of the council had charge of education, was an intelligent and progressive minister.

Other measures of reform were a Factory Act 1891, a Tithes Act 1891, and a Small Holdings Act 1892. The first was the tardy response of the home secretary, Mr. Matthews, to a wave of industrial unrest which was greatly exercising the public conscience. It raised the minimum age for employing children in factories to 11, and fixed the maximum hours of labour for women at 12, with 1½ for meals; it also nibbled at the evils of sweating and sub-contracting. The other two acts resulted from the constitution, for the first time, in 1889 of a Ministry (then called Board) of Agriculture. The Tithes Act made tithes payable by the owner and not the occupier of land, so that the cattle

---

[1] See Chapter X. The history of the whisky money is curious. The Local Government Act, 1888, as originally introduced, contained provisions to transfer liquor licensing from the justices to the county councils, arming the latter with compulsory powers to close redundant public-houses and a special revenue to compensate the licence-holders. Unfortunately this fell between two stools; the liquor trade disliked compulsion and the temperance party denounced compensation. The clauses were therefore dropped. But Goschen had reduction of licences very much at heart, and the alarming growth of drunkenness during the prosperity years 1887-90 impelled him to try again. In his Budget of 1890 he put an extra 6d. a gallon on spirits, and with this and a third of the beer duty formed a new fund for compensating licence-holders. Again the same union of opposites defeated the plan. As, however, the money had already been voted, he persuaded parliament to pass it on to the county councils for technical education—another subject in which he took a particular interest.

[2] Annual Register, 1890, p. 81.

and other movables of a tenant occupier could not be distrained on. This for about three decades virtually abolished those incidents of distress for tithe which during a long previous period had caused recurrent bad feeling on the countryside; it was only after 1919, when so many tenants bought their farms, that the union of occupier and owner in one person revived the possibilities of distress and with them the old bad blood. The Small Holdings Act was the first of its kind. Well-meant but over-cautious, it proved in the sequel a dead letter.

From some standpoints the most important domestic event during these six years was the London Dock Strike of 1889. Like many other disputes in the same period it was a 'prosperity strike'. That is to say it was a case, not of workers with high standards being forced to lower them on account of trade depression, but of workers with low standards revolting against their continuance in the face of swelling and obtrusive prosperity. And it occurred at a time when the educated and reflecting classes had but lately come to realize how very low many working-class standards of life still were.

The dockers struck to obtain a standard wage of 6d. an hour. That spoke for itself. It was well known that their work was hard and their casual earnings extremely precarious, since far more 'stood by' in the Port than could ever be employed simultaneously. Public sympathy, therefore, was with the men; who then, perhaps, represented with their families the largest single mass of chronic poverty in the Metropolis. The strike started at the West India Docks, in the south dock, on 14 August 1889. Its author was Ben Tillett,[1] an English-born Irishman from the lower strata of the working-class, who two years before had begun organizing first warehousemen and then dockers. But his principal helpers were Tom Mann[2] and John

[1] B. 1860 at Bristol; no regular schooling; a street arab; went to sea for five years; worked as a tea-cooper in the Monument Tea Warehouse. Organized warehouse-men, 1887; helped to run a dock strike at Tilbury, 1888. After the 1889 Dock Strike he became secretary of the Dockers' Union, and for over forty years was a prominent figure in the trade-union world and, more intermittently, in political labour organizations. Sat in parliament as a labour M.P. 1917–24 and 1929–31.

[2] B. 1856 near Coventry, son of a colliery clerk; worked in the pit at 9 years old. At 14 became a foundry apprentice at Birmingham, where he attended evening and Sunday classes, and became a vegetarian, a Swedenborgian, and a speaker on temperance. At 21 moved to London; worked at Thornycrofts' (famous Thames builders of torpedo-boats); and at 25 joined the A.S.E. After 1882 he worked in

Burns,[1] both skilled workmen and members of the Amalgamated Society of Engineers, then known as the 'aristocracy of Labour'. This co-operation typified a new phase in British trade unionism. Hitherto it had been mainly a craft movement, confined to the minorities of skilled workers in certain trades. Now it was to organize the unskilled majorities, and in that task members of the older and more exclusive unions were to play a missionary part of great importance. After a month's struggle public opinion proved too strong for the dock companies. They conceded the main demand, the 'docker's tanner'. Several mediators took part in the settlement, notably the veteran Cardinal Manning.

The dockers' victory and the trade boom together gave trade unionism a decisive stimulus. Even older societies like those of the miners were much affected. But its most striking feature was the organization of unskilled labour. Not only the Dockers' union, but the Gasworkers' and General Labourers' and the Workers' were built up at this period. The 'New Unionism', as it was called, had two novelties. It organized men by the industries which employed them rather than by the crafts which they exercised; and it preached political as well as industrial action. Its leaders were conscious socialists; and they sowed much of the seed from which ten years later the Labour party germinated.

Let us take a glance at the liberal opposition. Individually their great leader still dwarfed every other member of parliament. But his position after 1886 was materially changed. As we saw in Chapter I, there was no class division between the parties in the days of his duel with Disraeli. The line of cleavage was vertical, not horizontal—

> Beneath each banner proud to stand,
> Looked up the noblest of the land.

The great whig potentates, such as the dukes of Bedford, Devonshire, Westminster, and Argyll, were socially and territorially a match for anything that the other side could produce, even

the Henry George movement for land nationalization; in 1885 he joined the Social Democratic Federation; in 1893 he became the first secretary of the Independent Labour Party. Later he at one time kept a public-house; but the bulk of a long and very varied career was spent in England, Australia, and elsewhere as a revolutionary agitator, first on syndicalist, and latterly on communist lines.

[1] See above, p. 100, n. 1.

though (as the country was again reminded in 1884) the house of lords had a permanent conservative majority. After 1886 all this ceased. Excepting Lords Spencer, Ripon, Rosebery, Kimberley, and Granville, virtually the whole whig peerage left Gladstone over home rule. So did a large majority of his upper-class and upper-middle-class supporters everywhere. In exclusive clubland (which still had much political importance) the three chief liberal clubs of that time—Brooks's, the Reform, and the Devonshire—were rent by the schism. At Brooks's it resulted in an orgy of mutual blackballing, only quelled in 1889, after it had gone to great extremes, by a speech from Lord Granville.[1] London society, following the known views of the queen, practically ostracized home rulers.

The result was to push the Gladstonian party into radicalism. But it was radicalism with a difference. Chamberlain, the foremost leader of that school, had thrown Gladstone over, and drawn its capital, Birmingham, with him. Both London and Lancashire had voted heavily against home rule, while many London radicals went off as socialists. Hence the radicalism dominant behind Gladstone was that of districts hitherto in the background, and particularly of Wales and Scotland. Over and above its alliance with the Irish, the liberal party came very visibly to depend on the 'Celtic fringe'. This lasted down to 1914, and save in the landslide election of 1906 the party never again won an English majority.

At Newcastle in October 1891 it took a step which had lasting consequences. This was the formal adoption (by the party in conference first and by Gladstone in a speech immediately afterwards) of a long list of policies, the 'Newcastle Programme'. Home rule led the way, followed by church disestablishment in Wales and Scotland, local veto on the sale of intoxicating liquors, 'one man one vote' (i.e. abolition of plural franchise) and triennial parliaments. Bids for the rural vote figured at much length, including reforms in the land laws, the creation of district and parish councils, and new powers to acquire land for allotments or other public purposes. The chief sop for trade unionists was Employers' Liability (for accidents); but there was, too, a vague formula about limiting hours of labour, and a still vaguer one about payment of members. The programme was criticized by its opponents as an attempt to make a majority by combining

[1] A. D. Elliot, *Life of Goschen* (1911), ii. 116–18.

minorities, and thus carry a string of measures none of which stood a chance on its own merits. The answer of its authors was that it represented the application to multifarious problems of a single consistent body of liberal principles. There was truth in both contentions; tactics and principle had each a share. But in the long sequel most liberals regretted the over-wide commitment. For they could not disown its items, though many permanently alienated important sections of the community.

Towards the end of this parliament two important changes occurred among the government's supporters. On the same day as Parnell, died W. H. Smith; who in January 1887 had taken Lord R. Churchill's place as leader of the house of commons. Though no orator, he filled the post to general admiration, and his name has passed into a by-word for the kind of success which can be achieved in parliament by sterling character without the aid of eloquence. He was succeeded in the leadership by Balfour. Two months later the liberal unionist leadership in the same house also changed hands. Lord Hartington, on his father's death, went to the lords as eighth duke of Devonshire, and was succeeded in the commons by Chamberlain. This benefited the unionist alliance by harnessing to it more closely the most independent of the anti-Gladstone liberals. But already on 25 November 1891, speaking at Liverpool by Lord Salisbury's side, he had renounced the last hope of liberal reunion.

The 1892 session was short, and soon after midsummer Lord Salisbury advised the queen to dissolve. His majority was by then 66. The general election in July substituted for it a home rule majority of only 40 (liberals 273, Irish home rulers 81, and independent labour 1, as against conservatives 269 and liberal unionists 46). Ministers did not resign before parliament met, but on 11 August they fell to a vote of No confidence moved by H. H. Asquith. Thus Gladstone obtained his fourth innings as prime minister, but in a much weaker position than ever before.

VII

A LIBERAL INTERLUDE

THE interlude of liberal administration from 11 August 1892 to 24 June 1895 was only half the length of a normal government's life in those days; and the two cabinets which filled it were paralysed for want of any real majority either at Westminster or in the constituencies. Yet as a break in what else would have been over nineteen years of continuous conservative rule it had much importance. It kept the two-party system alive, and enabled a number of men to obtain ministerial experience and status whose services were available when the country at last tired of conservatism and called for an alternative government.

The prime minister upon taking office was but four months off 83. His vigour considering his age was extraordinary, and he could still dwarf rivals in debate. But he could not be what he had been, and the outlook before him was bleak. Only one thing detained him in politics—his duty, as he conceived it, to settle Ireland before retiring. Less than two years earlier he had well-grounded hopes of a majority enabling him to do so. Now the effort seemed nearly hopeless, but he would not shirk it while a chance remained. If he failed there could for him be no third attempt.

His tried lieutenants were Harcourt (chancellor of the exchequer), Morley (Irish secretary), Rosebery (foreign secretary), Herschell[1] (lord chancellor), and Campbell-Bannerman[2] (secretary for war)—each holding the post which he had held six years earlier. But the most successful, as it turned out, were two newcomers to the cabinet, both nonconformists. The elder of them, H. H. Fowler[3] (local government board) had entered parliament

---

[1] B. 1837, son of a clergyman; educated at University College, London, and at Bonn; barrister, 1860; M.P. 1874; solicitor-general, 1880–5; lord chancellor, 1886 and 1892–5; d. 1899.

[2] B. 1836 at Glasgow, where his father was for three years Lord Provost. Educated at Glasgow and at Trinity College, Cambridge; M.P. 1868; financial secretary, war office, 1871–4 and 1880–2; secretary to the admiralty, 1882–4; chief secretary for Ireland (not in cabinet), 1884–5; secretary for war, 1886 and 1892–5; prime minister, 1905–8; d. 1908. Inherited great private wealth.

[3] B. 1830 at Sunderland, the son of a Wesleyan minister; educated at St. Saviour's School, Southwark; settled as solicitor in Wolverhampton; mayor, 1863; M.P. 1880; under-secretary, home office, 1884–5; financial secretary, treasury, 1886; president of local government board, 1892–4; secretary for India, 1894–5; chancellor, duchy of Lancaster, 1905–8; lord president of the council, 1908–10; created Viscount Wolverhampton, 1908; d. 1911.

late in life after being mayor of Wolverhampton, where he held a position like Chamberlain's in Birmingham. On his showing during these three years he might have risen very high indeed, but his party's long exile from office frustrated him; by 1905 he was an old man. The other, H. H. Asquith,[1] was a barrister of 40, who had never been even a minor minister. He became almost at once the most brilliant home secretary within living memory.

Two other points should be recorded regarding the composition of this ministry. One is that for the first time the premier made it a condition that incoming ministers should resign all directorships of public companies. This salutary rule was waived by Lord Salisbury in 1895, and by Balfour following him; but it was restored by Campbell-Bannerman in 1905, and has been observed since. The other matter concerns the monarch's prerogative. H. Labouchere[2] was a leading radical M.P. whose status in the liberal party fully warranted his inclusion in the cabinet. But he owned a periodical which had been given to commenting on the royal family in a way which Queen Victoria deemed scurrilous. So she laid it down to Gladstone that, though he need not exclude Labouchere from all preferment, he must not bestow on him any which would render the queen liable to meet him personally. This, of course, effectively excluded Labouchere from the cabinet and from any other post which Gladstone could have offered him without insulting so important a person. The queen was exercising a royal prerogative which under her and her predecessors was well established; though it is difficult to conceive a king in parallel circumstances excluding any one from the cabinet to-day.[3]

Gladstone's premiership lasted till 3 March 1894. His main concern was the Second Home Rule Bill. Introduced in

[1] B. 1852 at Morley, in the West Riding; family congregationalists; educated at Fulneck Moravian School, City of London School, and Balliol College, Oxford; barrister, 1876; M.P. 1886; home secretary, 1892–5; chancellor of the exchequer, 1905–8; prime minister, 1908–16; created earl of Oxford and Asquith, 1925; d. 1928.

[2] 1831–1912; educated at Eton; for ten years in the diplomatic service; M.P. 1865–1906; editor and proprietor of *Truth*.

[3] Labouchere, who guessed what had happened, tried to drag it to light; but Gladstone loyally took the responsibility, and kept the queen's name out of his explanations. In recent years, however, letters have been published placing the facts beyond doubt. See *The Letters of Queen Victoria*, 3rd series, ii (1931), 150–1, and P. Guedalla, *The Queen and Mr. Gladstone* (1933), ii. 437–40.

February 1893, it passed its second reading on 21 April by a margin of 43 votes, and its third reading on 1 September by 34. It had then occupied the commons for no less than 85 sittings. Its veteran author had piloted it in person, speaking early and late in endless tourneys of eloquence against a most formidable opposition. Its deadliest critic was Chamberlain. For pure oratory the palm went to a speech by John Redmond, leader of the Parnellite minority among the Irish. Its fame helped towards his rise later.

The bill had been drafted by a cabinet committee consisting of Gladstone, Morley, Spencer, Herschell, Campbell-Bannerman, and James Bryce.[1] It differed from that of 1886 in providing that Ireland should send members to the imperial parliament. But they were only to vote there on matters of Irish or imperial concern. As in the earlier measure, army, navy, customs, trade, and foreign relations were excluded from the scope of the Irish legislature. The supremacy of Westminster was affirmed in the preamble. The bill shared with that of 1886 the defect of virtually ignoring Ulster; though Belfast, as before, protested with vehemence.

In the house of lords the second reading was proposed by Lord Spencer and opposed by the duke of Devonshire. The latter prevailed by 419 votes to 41, and the bill dropped dead (8 September 1893). Gladstone wanted to take up the challenge and dissolve. But his colleagues objected; and the turn of public opinion, plainly more relieved than indignant, upheld them against him. All his long effort since 1886 might seem fruitless. Yet we can now see that, whether for good or evil, it was not. The Home Rule Bill of 1886 had been only a flash in the pan. The commons had rejected its bare principle; its details were not reached. Had it lacked a sequel for nineteen years, there might never have been one. But the bill of 1893 went through all stages in the elected house. It emerged a complete measure which, but for the veto of the house of lords, would have come into force.

[1] The distinguished historian, jurist, and writer on political science, who from 1880 to 1893 was Regius Professor of Civil Law at Oxford, and had published *The American Commonwealth* in 1888. B. 1838 at Belfast; educated at Glasgow (High School and University) and at Trinity College, Oxford; barrister, 1867; M.P. 1880; under-secretary for foreign affairs, 1886; chancellor of the duchy of Lancaster (with seat in cabinet), 1892–4; president of the board of trade, 1894–5; chief secretary for Ireland, 1905–7; British ambassador to the United States, 1907–13; created viscount, 1914; d. 1922.

It was almost bound to be revived if and when a majority of the nation took the view that the lords used their veto unfairly.

The eighteen months during which this measure was the main care of the government were not uneventful in other ways. They witnessed a swelling of the imperialist tide which had been rising ever since the 1887 Jubilee. Cabinet ministers were divided about it. At the outset in 1892 they were asked for a decision on Uganda. By the Anglo-German Treaty of 1890 it had gone to Great Britain, which devolved it on the British East Africa Company. But the company was now in financial straits, and the question was whether the government would retain or abandon the territory. Rosebery was for retention; Harcourt for abandonment. As a compromise Sir Gerald Portal was sent out to advise. Eventually he reported in favour of retention, and in 1894 (after Rosebery had become prime minister) a British protectorate was declared.[1]

The pole-star of that period's imperialism was not, however, in East Africa, but in South. Rhodes was the magnet which drew men on. Since 1890 he had been premier of Cape Colony; since 1889, when he obtained a charter for the British South Africa Company, he had been its managing director and used it to bring under the British flag vast territories of the Transvaal. Kimberley's diamonds and the Rand's gold shed their glamour round him. Shares in the Rand mines had become a leading subject of speculation on the London Stock Exchange; 'Chartereds' followed in their wake. In October and November 1893 events occurred which impressed the public imagination still further. South of the Zambesi the Chartered Company's territory comprised two main areas—Mashonaland and Matabeleland. The former had been occupied and brought under white administration; in the latter the warlike Matabeles, a dreaded offshoot of the Zulus, were ruled by their own king, Lobengula. After much friction the Company declared war on him, and in two months a small force of mounted police under its civilian administrator, Dr. Jameson, completely crushed the Matabele power and conquered the country. The campaign was really little more than an early demonstration of the effect of machine-

---

[1] See Lord Lugard, *The Story of the Uganda Protectorate* (1901). As Captain Lugard he was the company's administrator in Uganda (1890–2), and (Sir Harry Johnston, *The Uganda Protectorate* (1902), i. 233) 'effected very wonderful things with very small resources'.

guns; but memories of Isandhlwana and Rorke's Drift only fourteen years earlier made it seem an exploit of fantastic brilliance. Even Jameson's head was turned by it; with consequences that will concern our next chapter.

In the summer of the same year occurred the 'Mekong' crisis between Great Britain and France. The subject was Siam, which France was visibly aiming to annex. In May she had declared war on her victim, and on 20 July served an ultimatum demanding huge cessions. But Lord Rosebery met her in this quarter with greater firmness than Lord Salisbury had shown before, or was to show later. On 31 July France agreed with Great Britain to maintain Siam as a buffer state, and the immediate tension was relaxed. Final adjustments, however, were not reached until 1896; when Salisbury gave away much that Rosebery had defended.

In domestic legislation the most important subject dealt with besides home rule was local government. We have noticed before,[1] how the extension of a popular franchise to the countryside necessarily quickened the demand for elective local authorities there. The conservatives had only partially met it in 1888 by the act creating county councils. Upon bodies administering so large an area as a county poor men could seldom afford to sit, and the new councils tended to be manned by almost the same class as the old quarter sessions. So there arose—and was embodied in the Newcastle Programme—a renewed liberal demand for elective parish councils. To the nonconformists, who were strong in rural England, it particularly appealed, because such administrative functions as had hitherto attached to the parish were in the hands of the churchwardens and vestries.

When, therefore, H. H. Fowler introduced in 1893 what became the Local Government Act 1894, it was generally known as the Parish Councils Bill, and as such encountered considerable opposition. But its author was assiduous, prudent, and tactful. He put a great many things into his bill, and was content to lose some, if he could pass the rest. The commons spent 38 days on the measure before it went to the lords; 619 amendments were actually moved and dealt with; Fowler spoke over 800 times, but never moved the closure. There followed a severe wrangle with the lords, the bill going to and fro thrice between the houses, before the government (1 March 1894) passed it with the lords'

[1] p. 202, *supra*.

amendments. It did not effect a village revolution; for, though about 6,880 parish councils were set up under it and on paper they wielded wide powers, an opposition amendment, which had restricted their ordinary spending to the equivalent of a three-penny rate, caused most of the powers to be little used. But on other sides the reform reached far. Following an act passed by Stansfeld in 1872, the sanitary authority outside the boroughs had come to be, as a rule, either a 'local board' in the more populous areas, or the board of guardians on the countryside.[1] Fowler straightened this out into the system of urban district councils and rural district councils which has since obtained. The new bodies had and used fuller powers than the old, and were more democratic. In the elections for them two great innovations were made in favour of women. The liberals in 1882 had admitted single (but not married) women to vote (if otherwise qualified) for town councils. The conservatives six years later followed exactly the same course for county councils. But the Fowler Act of 1894 not only removed the ban on marriage; it laid down that women qualified to vote were qualified to be elected as well. It was the first clear sign-post towards their eventual emancipation.

In the same month of February 1894, in which it rejected home rule and crabbed the reform of local government, the house of lords killed (by inserting a contracting-out clause) an Employers' Liability Bill which Asquith had piloted. These were all the government's important bills to date; and as the lords in the previous six years had never touched a conservative measure, the partisan use of their powers began to be undisguised. In the debate of 1 March over the mutilation of Fowler's proposals Gladstone pointed this out. The differences between the houses, he said, had in the present year created 'a state of things, of which we are compelled to say that in our judgement it cannot continue'; and the controversy, 'when once raised, must go forward to an issue'.

This utterance, more truly prophetic than it may have seemed at the time, was Gladstone's finish in parliament. Earlier on the same day he had held his last cabinet. On 3 March 1894 he resigned. The motive alleged to the queen and the public was the state of his sight and hearing. More operative ones were the

---

[1] But fifty-four of the more populous areas were still governed by 'Improvement Commissioners', appointed under pre-1875 local Acts.

decision against dissolution, which had ended his personal chance of dealing with Ireland, and a cabinet controversy about expanding the navy, over which he found himself in a minority against his old friend Lord Spencer, the first lord. So the last of his four governments ended. It was 61 years since he had delivered his maiden speech in the commons, and 52½ since he was sworn privy councillor. No one ever quitted the front rank in British politics with quite so long a record behind him.

When a prime minister resigns, the monarch under our system need not ask his advice as to his successor; though if asked it will, it seems, like other advice, be binding. Queen Victoria did not ask Gladstone's in 1894. Had she done so, he would have nominated Lord Spencer. But of her own volition she chose Lord Rosebery. Both choices excluded the man who in the eyes of the liberal rank and file was the natural successor—Sir William Harcourt.

The truth was that Harcourt had made himself intolerable to all his colleagues by his overbearing behaviour in cabinet. Even Morley, the anti-imperialist, preferred the imperialist Rosebery. But the public did not know that. Rosebery said afterwards that the right course would have been to insist on Harcourt's trying to form a cabinet first; after his failure there could be no talk of his having been supplanted. As it was, such talk persisted with a virulence which blasted the new premier's authority.

One may doubt whether in any case he could have led his party long. He had come to the front as the Prince Charming of politics—young, handsome, rich, eloquent, candid, and popular. His appeals to public spirit pleased everybody. Rich and poor were ready, as they always are, to fall in behind a manifest favourite of fortune. Only the previous year, when the country was suffering grievously from a long coal stoppage in the old 'federated' area (Yorkshire, Lancashire, and the Midland counties), it was he of all ministers, the foreign secretary, who had been asked to settle it and had triumphed.[1] But he was fatally lacking in party aptitudes. Succeeding to his title as a minor, he had never been apprenticed in the house of commons. Few men could speak so eloquently on a public platform, yet none so seldom woke party applause. Thus the fighters in his own camp never liked him, and least of all the dominant nonconformists;

[1] See p. 299 below.

in whom as a whig aristocrat and an owner of race-horses he inspired instinctive distrust. Besides he was nothing if not an Imperialist. And already dislike of the aggressive note, which Imperialism came to strike in the nineties, was driving the majority of liberal stalwarts in an opposite direction.

His very first speech as premier on the address betrayed the amateur. He quoted from Salisbury and endorsed the words: 'before Irish Home Rule is conceded by the Imperial Parliament, England as the predominant member of the partnership of the Three Kingdoms will have to be convinced of its justice and equity.' The anger among home rulers was intense. They actually defeated the government next day in the commons. How was England, they asked, a 'predominant partner'? Why was an English majority necessary to carry home rule? In vain a week later at Edinburgh the premier explained that he had intended no more than a platitude—more English votes would be needed if the cause were to prevail. He could not silence his critics. Perhaps he did not deserve to.

His government lasted not quite sixteen months. From first to last the house of lords gave its bills no quarter, and intimated a virtual veto on the whole of its legislation. In so acting it succeeded on the short reckoning. The electors had little use for Gladstone's government now Gladstone had left it; they entirely refused to share the indignation of ministers who, fearful of dissolving, brought forward one foredoomed measure after another to 'fill up the cup'. But on a longer view the lords' tactics (which went completely counter to Disraeli's wisdom) may be differently estimated. A second chamber could never hope to perpetuate its powers if it used them solely and indiscriminately against one of the two parties. Still less could it hope to keep effective the edges of its weapon for defeating Irish home rule if it blunted them by hacking blindly at every other bill it saw. *Nec deus intersit, nisi dignus vindice nodus* was the adage that Lord Salisbury forgot. Nobody then in politics had a stronger belief in a second chamber than Rosebery; and his words in criticizing the house of lords, distasteful as they were to Queen Victoria, show a far deeper sense of its true interests[1] than the deeds of the conservative leaders. Nemesis followed slowly, but it was bound to come.

---

[1] See especially his Memorandum to the queen of 7 April 1894 (printed in Lord Crewe's *Lord Rosebery* (1931), ii. 451-4) and his letter to her of 1 November 1894 (ibid. ii. 461-3).

In this situation the only legislative sphere left open to the government was the budget; and here in 1894 Harcourt as chancellor of the exchequer scored its sole parliamentary success. His death duties of that year, completely superseding Goschen's of 1889, rank with the major events in British fiscal history. The immediate motive, as in Goschen's case, was naval; the Spencer building programme, which Gladstone had resigned rather than endorse, had somehow to be paid for. Harcourt put a penny on the income-tax, 6d. a gallon on spirits, and 6d. a barrel on beer. But that was not enough. By the advice of Sir Alfred Milner,[1] chairman of the board of inland revenue, who was the real creator of the new impost, he decided that, to fill the gap, the state should take substantial toll of the capital wealth left by deceased persons. For this purpose he brought all forms of property, landed or other, for the first time into one reckoning; and having thus obtained a pooled value for the total estate passing on a person's death, graduated his main tax according to the size of the pool, and not to the amounts drawn out of it by particular beneficiaries. The immediate revenue for which he allowed from this source was only £1 million, and the ultimate only £4 millions.

But he had done something much beyond raising any particular sum of money. He had established a great new direct tax; comparable to the income-tax, yet quite independent of it, and capable like it of being augmented automatically, and almost

[1] B. 1854 at Giessen (Hesse-Darmstadt); educated at Tübingen, at King's College, London, and at Balliol College, Oxford; barrister and liberal journalist; joined *Pall Mall Gazette* under Morley, 1881; assistant-editor under W. T. Stead, 1883; private secretary to Goschen, 1884–9; through him appointed under-secretary for finance in Egypt, 1889–92; chairman of the board of inland revenue, 1892–7; high commissioner for South Africa, 1897–1905; governor of Cape Colony, 1897–1901; governor of the Transvaal and Orange River Colony, 1902–6; member of the war cabinet, 1916–19; colonial secretary, 1919–21; created baron 1901, viscount, 1902; d. 1925. His father, Karl Milner (b. at Neuss 1830; d. at Tübingen 1882), was of German nationality, had a German mother, and only spent six years of his life (1861–7) in England; but Alfred, whose mother was British, and who after her death in 1869 settled in England in his sixteenth year (his father shortly remarrying in Germany), was able to opt for British nationality under a statute of 1773 (repealed in 1914), because his grandfather had originally been English. The circumstances, however, that his father, three uncles, and many cousins were Germans settled in Germany, and that he began life with a German upbringing besides going to a German school, are of serious historic interest. For in most of its salient virtues and defects his temperament conformed far more to a German than to an English type. See Hansard, v. lxxvii. 593 (home secretary's statement); also articles in the *Daily Chronicle* (24 December 1915), the *Star* (4 January 1916), and the *New Age* (30 May and 20 June 1901).

indefinitely, by simple turns of the screw. It was this very quality in the income-tax which Gladstone so disliked; his thrifty instinct saw in it, truly enough, a standing temptation to increased public expenditure. Thus it is not surprising that in private the veteran disapproved the new death duties. Inside the cabinet their adversary was Lord Rosebery. Otherwise they were uniformly opposed by the conservatives on the ground (which became truer in the sequel than it was at the time) that they victimized the landowning class; and almost uniformly hailed with enthusiasm by liberals and social reformers as a first step towards obtaining for the community a more adequate contribution from the rich. What neither side made much account of, though today it may appear the most distinctive feature of the policy, was that under it for the first time the state took *capital* and spent it as if it were *income*. Had it used it instead to wipe off capital liabilities or to build up capital assets, the effect on the individuals mulcted might have been the same, but that on the nation's wealth would have been quite different. This, however, showed more clearly later, when the screw had been given its turns. Meanwhile Harcourt's prophecy that no matter how the conservatives might denounce his tax, their chancellor of the exchequer would never forgo it, has been consistently verified.[1]

A little less than a month after the budget passed, the prime minister had a success in quite another field. His horse *Ladas* won the Derby. The victory was immensely popular on the Turf. But it did Rosebery no good with his party. Apart from the large section in it which regarded racing as tainted, there were many who thought, not unreasonably, that a prime minster bearing the responsibilities of an empire ought not to be distracted by sporting anxieties. Rosebery, however, went his way. Next year, while he was still prime minister, he won the race again (with *Sir Visto*). Such double luck was at least unique.

Foreign affairs underwent some pregnant changes at this time.

[1] It is worth noting briefly how far the process of screw-turning has gone. At the bottom of the scale the graduation remains as Harcourt left it on estates up to £5,000. But beyond that the differences are enormous. Harcourt's highest rate of tax was only 8 per cent., and was only paid on estates of over a million. To-day 8 per cent. begins after £18,000, while the rate after a million is 40, that after £1¼ millions is 42, that after £1½ millions is 45, and that after 2 millions is 50. There are 33 separate rates on to-day's scale; there were only 12 on Harcourt's. The average annual receipts for the five years ending 31 March 1934 were £77,627,303 from death duties, of which the estate duty (Harcourt's tax) yielded an average £68,440,646, and in the last year £75,488,476.

Rosebery on taking the premiership had given the foreign office to Lord Kimberley,[1] Sir Edward Grey remaining under-secretary. But the new head kept close to the old, and direction was unaltered. On 16 July 1894 Great Britain signed a treaty with Japan providing for the abolition after five years of British consular jurisdiction. No other European Power had yet made this gesture of trust in the modernization of the Mikado's realm, and it was much appreciated. The following month brought war between Japan and China over Korea. The Chinese façade crumbled almost at a touch. In a swift series of victories on land and sea the islanders drove their opponents from Korea, overran the Liao-Tung peninsula, and in November captured the great fortress-harbour of Port Arthur, which dominates the Gulf of Pe-chi-li and the sea-approach to Peking. By the Treaty of Shimonoseki (15 April 1895) the Chinese were forced to cede these areas, as also the island of Formosa; but thereupon a group of three European Great Powers—Germany, Russia, and France —intervened, and ordered the victor to give back the Liao-Tung peninsula and Port Arthur in the name of the integrity of China. Deeply mortified, Japan complied. But the fact that Great Britain stood away from the intervention was very favourably noted by her. China, unforeseeing, felt grateful to the Russians, and gave them a railway concession across Manchuria which shortened their line to Vladivostok. She was fast falling into the position of Turkey—a sick empire with jealous vultures waiting to divide the carcass.

Turkey herself outraged civilized opinion by a series of massacres in Armenia, of which news first came through in July 1894. They were similar to the 1876 atrocities which cost her Bulgaria, but on a larger scale. Yet this time they cost her nothing, and she repeatedly resumed them with impunity. British opinion was deeply moved. Lord Kimberley took every step possible short of committing his country to single-handed military or naval action. Thanks to him a commission of inquiry (January to July 1895) forced the facts to light; and in May a scheme of reforms was presented to the Porte by Great Britain, France, and Russia. But the sultan temporized and evaded as usual, while

[1] B. 1826; educated at Eton and Christ Church, Oxford; succeeded as 3rd baron Wodehouse in 1847; Irish viceroy, 1864–6; created earl of Kimberley, 1866; lord privy seal, 1868–70; colonial secretary, 1870–4 and 1880–2; Indian secretary, 1882–5 and 1886; president of the council and Indian secretary, 1892–4; foreign secretary, 1894–5; d. 1902.

Russia refused to admit any kind of coercion. Still worse was the attitude of Germany. Seeing that Great Britain, who for over forty years had enjoyed the most favoured position at Constantinople, risked losing it by her efforts to save the Armenians, she decided to supplant her by supporting the sultan in his infamous conduct. It was done gradually (for the tragedy, as we shall see, dragged on for years), and with complete success.[1]

This cynical action of Germany belonged to a scheme of new and arrogant ambitions which will be noted more fully in the next chapter. The foreign office was as yet more aware of them than the public. In parliament the acute question was: Should Great Britain act single-handed, or confine herself to trying to move the Concert of Europe? Radicals favoured the former course; and even before the Rosebery government fell, there were the seeds of a revolt against its chief on that issue.

The weakest government may have its triumphant days, and even this had some. One such was marked by Fowler's great speech on the Indian cotton duties (21 February 1895); which has since been oftener cited, perhaps, than any other to prove the thesis that oratory in the commons can turn votes. Others were due to Asquith, whose early debating prowess was admired on all sides. Asquith was also one of three ministers who achieved notable administrative progress in their departments. The others were A. H. D. Acland, the education minister (of whose work more will be said in Chapter X), and Campbell-Bannerman, at the war office. The latter's main success was in a single point; he procured the compulsory retirement of the duke of Cambridge from the post of commander-in-chief. That vigorous man but ultra-reactionary officer had remained to the last a great obstacle to progress in the army. He was now 76, the same age as his cousin the queen, who still strongly backed him. Campbell-Bannerman, who behind an exceptionally genial exterior half concealed great strength of will, overcame both their oppositions. He also baffled the queen's desire to put her son, the duke of Connaught, in the vacant place.

Strangely enough, on the very afternoon (21 June 1895) when he announced the decision to the house of commons, Campbell-Bannerman was the occasion of the government's fall. Cordite

[1] How she had, two years earlier, employed the Egyptian lever to stop British firms from competing with German for railway concessions in Asia Minor, is told in Viscount Grey's *Twenty-Five Years*, i. 9–10.

had then not long come into the army's use as a smokeless pro-
pellent explosive; and the war minister on a 'snap' vote was
censured (quite unjustly) for not having procured enough of it.
Next day the cabinet debated whether to resign or dissolve parliament. Only four (Rosebery, Harcourt, Ripon, and Tweedmouth[1]) were in favour of the first course; but their will prevailed.
So the liberals went out of office, and Lord Salisbury came in.
Recent speeches had already indicated that the liberal unionists
would join him; and he formed a cabinet including five of them.
The general election followed in July, and the new government
obtained a majority of 152 over the opposition (340 conservatives and 71 liberal unionists against 177 liberals and 82 nationalists). Gladstone did not stand; Harcourt and Morley both lost
their seats. The common term 'unionists' became now generally
applied to both sections of the government combination, though
they retained separate party machines.

Why did the general election of 1895 show such a turn-over?
Partly because the policy of 'filling up the cup' instead of dissolving had impressed the nation as timid and futile. Partly
because certain of the liberal measures—notably two successive
Local Veto Bills introduced by Harcourt—had been widely unpopular. But mainly because England (though not Scotland,
Wales, or Ireland) had now been caught up into currents of
political feeling and doctrine—those of expansive imperialism—
with which the unionists were ready to comply, and most of the
liberals were not.

The wave of imperialism began to be dominant from the time
of the conquest of Matabeleland, i.e. from the end of 1893. It
appeared on the surface to overcome and displace the currents
of social unrest, crusading philanthropy, and incipient socialism,
which in 1892 were still running strongly enough to carry two
socialists and many liberals into parliament. Yet before the setback came, the socialistic forces had achieved an advance which
was never lost.

In 1891 a famous strike at the Manningham Mills, Bradford,
had made that place for the time being the leading centre of

---

[1] Edward Marjoribanks, b. 1849; educated at Harrow and Christ Church, Oxford; M.P. 1880; liberal whip, 1886–92; chief whip, 1892–4; succeeded as second
Lord Tweedmouth, 1894; member of cabinet as lord privy seal and chancellor of
the duchy of Lancaster, 1894–5; first lord of the admiralty, 1905–8; lord president
of the council, 1908; d. 1909.

labour politics in the industrial north; and a Bradford Labour
Union was formed with 3,000 paying members. At the 1892
election this body came near returning Ben Tillett for East Bradford against a sitting liberal manufacturer. Other labour unions
sprang up elsewhere, and a special stimulus was the return to
parliament for West Ham (South) of J. Keir Hardie, the avowed
leader of the movement to withdraw trade-union officials from
the liberal camp, to which most of them still resorted. In January
1893 a national conference of labour and socialist organizations
was held at Bradford, with Keir Hardie in the chair, to co-ordinate these local and sporadic efforts under a national organization. The result was the formation of the Independent Labour
Party. Lord Snowden has recently characterized this as 'the
most important political event of the nineteenth century'.[1] On
any reckoning it was a great starting-point. For the first time
a popular socialist party was founded in England on thoroughly
English lines, deriving from and appealing to what were then
the natural channels of working-class expression in the industrial
areas, viz. the trade unions and the nonconformist chapels. Compared with the incurable exoticism of the Social Democratic
Federation or even the middle-class cleverness of the Fabian
Society, the 'I.L.P.' represented an enormous advance towards
making practical socialism a genuine popular issue.

Nevertheless the early years of the new organization were not
prosperous. It failed to achieve any mass-conversion of the trade
unions, and settled down to an uphill process of enrolling individuals and organizing branches. Though the weakness and
dissensions of liberalism after Gladstone retired gave it some
recruiting opportunities, on the whole it suffered more from the
common submergence of the left by the popularity of unionist
imperialism. Keir Hardie lost his seat in 1895, and there was no
compensating win elsewhere. Two things alone saved it over
these difficult times. One was the almost incredible self-devotion
of its rank and file, fired by an idealism like that of religious
evangelists. The other was the stupid and grudging attitude of
the local liberal associations. Each was run, as a rule, by a group
of middle-class people, who had no use for a candidate without
funds; and so, though organizations like those of the miners
could buy their way into liberal seats, they were closed to individual gifted aspirants. Even when the latter would otherwise

[1] Viscount Snowden, *An Autobiography* (1934), i. 53.

have preferred to work through the liberal party, they were apt to be forced back on the I.L.P.[1]

Even apart from Gladstone's exit, the short 1892–5 parliament witnessed considerable changes in the political personnel. On 24 January 1895 died Lord Randolph Churchill after long suffering from a slow malady which did not prevent his speaking in parliament, though with sad loss of power, down to March 1894. With Parnell dead and Lord Rosebery soon to retire, only Balfour remained from the previous decade's most glittering quartet. Among the conservatives no brilliant new light shone out. But on the liberal side at least three ministers emerged who were fated to go very far—Campbell-Bannerman, Asquith, and (much noticed already, though only an under-secretary) Sir Edward Grey. And on the back benches appeared another man of destiny. When Asquith, as part of 'filling up the cup', brought forward a Welsh Disestablishment Bill (for whose second reading Chamberlain voted), it was ably criticized on the score of inadequacy by a young Welsh nationalist who had entered the house in 1890 at a by-election. Black-haired, blue-eyed, Welsh-speaking, addicted to picture-phrases, using English with great wit and fluency, but with the air of a foreign language, this young man seemed then an incarnation of the Celtic spirit. His name was David Lloyd George.

[1] Cp. the case of Ramsay MacDonald, for which see his very explicit letter of 1894 to Keir Hardie on joining the I.L.P. (printed in W. Stewart's *J. Keir Hardie* (1921), 92).

VIII

THE ASCENDANCY OF CHAMBERLAIN

LORD SALISBURY's third cabinet was certainly one of the strongest that has ever held office in Great Britain, a fact not the less remarkable because it laboured under three disadvantages. First, its chief, as in his former administration, combined the foreign office with the premiership—never a good plan. Secondly, it was a coalition, and one in which the smaller party contained proportionately far more men fit for high office, so that there were inevitable heart-burnings—the big conservative battalions grudging each liberal unionist promotion, while liberal unionists in not a few instances saw posts, for which they were the best candidates, filled by conservatives for party reasons. Thirdly, the strongest and most popular man, as it proved, was a liberal unionist, and as such debarred not only from being premier but even from leading the house of commons. Fine tact and skill on the part of Salisbury and Balfour alone surmounted this last difficulty. They allowed Chamberlain 'usually the power of a co-Premier and on some rare occasions more'.[1]

The initial allocation of offices was unexpected. The duke of Devonshire was offered the foreign office, but preferred to be lord president of the council. Chamberlain was invited to be chancellor of the exchequer, and chose instead the colonial office. Goschen did not thereupon resume the chancellorship (apparently because he was alarmed by the unorthodoxy of Balfour about bimetallism—then a rising topic), but went to the admiralty. James, who wanted the lord chancellorship, and certainly had strong claims, was denied it because the conservative ex-lord chancellor, Halsbury, could not be displaced; but he joined the cabinet as chancellor of the duchy of Lancaster with a peerage. Yet another liberal unionist, the fifth marquis of Lansdowne, who had been both governor-general of Canada and viceroy of India, came in as war secretary. He obtained that department, because (as noted above[2]) he had, like Campbell-Bannerman, been in it long before under Cardwell. But it was a bad choice; for the war office at the time needed strong treatment, and Lord Lansdowne's abilities were much more on the diplomatic than on the administrative side. Lastly, the

[1] J. L. Garvin, *Life of Chamberlain*, iii (1934), 7.   [2] p. 16.

chancellorship of the exchequer, after both Chamberlain and Goschen had refused it, was given to Sir Michael Hicks Beach. Apart from Balfour, he was now the only debater fit to fight in the first rank whom the conservative party possessed in the house of commons.

The colonial office had hitherto a very low status. There was general surprise when Chamberlain went there. But a great head will magnify any department, and by taking this he placed himself on the crest of the rising imperialist wave. He had wanted it for more than ten years, impressed by the opening which it offered for tasks of constructive development. His view, expressed in public before as well as after he became secretary of state, was that the colonies, or many of them, were 'undeveloped estates'. He told the house of commons on 22 August 1895 that he was prepared to consider and submit to the House

'any case which may occur in which by the judicious investment of British money those estates which belong to the British Crown may be developed for the benefit of their population and for the benefit of the greater population which is outside'.[1]

This was a sharp departure from the *laisser-faire* policy which had till then ruled our colonial administration. Though even to-day it may be true that Great Britain during the past hundred years has devoted to the development of her colonies proportionately less public money than other colonizing Great Powers, a great deal of leeway was made up under Chamberlain's initiative. Not all the colonial sphere fell under his department; notably British East Africa, which by a decision of the Rosebery government was taken over from its Chartered Company for £250,000 and transferred to the Crown on 1 July 1895, was assigned to the foreign office, and so remained for a few months short of ten years. But in tropical West Africa he was continually active. The construction of railways and ports, and the promotion of schools of tropical agriculture and tropical medicine, were among the chief forms which his policy took. Subsidies were also given to establish new steamship lines, notably to the long-neglected West Indies.

Right at the outset a decision had to be made about Ashanti, whose king, Prempeh of Kumasi, still carried on the slave-raiding and human sacrifices which Wolseley in 1874 had forced

---

[1] Hansard, 4th series, xxxvi. 642.

his predecessor, Kofi Karikari, to renounce. Lying right across the approaches from the British Gold Coast to the interior, the Ashanti warriors made progress in trade or civilization impossible. Chamberlain induced the government to send a military expedition under Colonel Sir Francis Scott; and after a march of three weeks from the coast Kumasi was occupied without fighting (17 January 1896). Prempeh was deposed, and exiled to the Seychelles; no successor was appointed; and the Ashanti chiefs were placed under British guidance, a garrison of Hausas being left at the capital. These well-drilled black troops had formed the bulk of Scott's force, and the losses by fever were less than in 1874. But among them unfortunately was the queen's son-in-law, Prince Henry of Battenberg, who had joined the expedition as a volunteer.[1]

The most anxious problem before the new colonial secretary lay in South Africa, where affairs in the Transvaal were working up to a crisis. We saw above[2] how that republic was left after the London Convention of 1884. In 1886 occurred a development which Wolseley had forecast as likely, but the British government had left out of account. A goldfield of extraordinary richness was discovered on the Witwatersrand. Foreigners, mostly (but by no means all) British subjects, flocked in to exploit it; and year after year, as the mines developed, their population grew. Johannesburg became a great city. The attitude of the Transvaal government under Kruger towards the new-comers— 'Uitlanders' as they were called—was from the first uncompromising. 'We will not exclude you,' they said in effect, 'but this is our country, and if you come here to seek wealth, it must be entirely on our terms. They are that you shall have no votes and no rights, and we shall so tax you, both directly on the mine profits and indirectly by enormous duties on imported mine-requisites, that a large part of what you get will pass to us.' The Uitlanders preferred coming even on this footing to not coming at all; and Kruger treated their doing so as justifying any hardship that he might care to put on them. 'They need not have come,' was his refrain, 'but having come they must abide the consequences.' 'You need not have admitted them,' was the

---

[1] He was brother to Prince Alexander, the first sovereign of Bulgaria and victor of Slivnitza, and also to Prince Louis, who was first sea lord at the admiralty when war broke out in 1914. He had married the queen's youngest daughter, Beatrice, who was her mother's chief personal stay in old age.

[2] p. 69.

British retort later on, 'but having admitted them, you must treat them justly.'

The upshot was that the treasury of the Transvaal, which had been the poorest, soon became the richest in South Africa. Kruger's ambitions rose. He bought extensive armaments. He had glimpses of a Boer paramountcy. From Europe he engaged clever Dutch civil servants; and these 'Hollanders', as they were called, naturally strengthened the anti-English bias to which they owed their posts. They helped him to coquet with European Powers, particularly Germany. Here there was an obstacle in the 1884 Convention, which debarred the Transvaal from treating with foreign governments, other than that of the Orange Free State, except through Great Britain. Notwithstanding it, he made contacts with Berlin; and on 27 January 1895, addressing a *Kaiser-Kommers*[1] held by German residents in the Transvaal, he publicly indicated their purpose.

Two earlier episodes had some bearing on his attitude. The first went back to November 1884, when a British force of 4,000 men under Sir Charles Warren put an end to obstinate Boer encroachments in Bechuanaland and compelled respect for the frontier fixed nine months earlier by the London Convention.[2] This hemmed the Transvaal on the west; while later the Chartered Company's acquisition of Rhodesia hemmed it on the north. The second episode was a treaty regarding Swaziland and Tongaland made by Lord Ripon with the Transvaal in December 1894. Under it, after years of dispute, Kruger obtained Swaziland as a protectorate; but Tongaland, the coastal strip between it and sea, was earmarked by Great Britain. He had been much set on getting a port of his own, and this final exclusion from salt water mortified and rankled with him intensely.[3]

---

[1] i.e. a convivial meeting to celebrate the German emperor's birthday.

[2] The minister who had impelled the Gladstone cabinet to this resolute action was, curiously enough, Chamberlain. His interest had been stirred by the famous Birmingham congregational minister, Dr. R. W. Dale (1829-95), whose own zeal had been enlisted on behalf of the Bechuanas by a great missionary, the Rev. John Mackenzie.

[3] In July 1895 he told Garrett, the editor of the *Cape Times*: 'I always said it [Swaziland] was nothing save as a way to the sea. I said that all along, and it was well understood. And now they no sooner give it to me than they take away altogether the only thing that made it worth having—the way to the sea' (Sir E. T. Cook, *Edmund Garrett* (1909), 211). Five years earlier he had told the same interviewer: 'If England works together with me in that way [i.e. by conceding him

Over against Kruger in South Africa stood as his main adversary Cecil Rhodes. Then the 'Colossus' of politics and finance, he led not merely the British but the Cape Dutch; whose party, the 'Bond', made him premier at Capetown, and who resented Kruger's hostility to the Cape's trade. Rhodes, besides being managing director of the Chartered Company, had large interests on the Rand; and his brother Frank was a leader of the Johannesburg Uitlanders. At Westminster he had friends in all camps, but his favourite on the front benches was Lord Rosebery; and he seems to have preferred his government to any other. Under it he had been negotiating with the colonial office for Bechuanaland. His company coveted all that it could get. But its minimum need was a strip along the Transvaal frontier, in order to carry the Capetown–Kimberley railway up to Rhodesia. It already ran north as far as Mafeking, and the area up to that point—known as 'British' Bechuanaland—had been promised to the Cape government, of which he was head.

So Chamberlain's initial autumn in office confronted him with three problems—first, Rhodes's claims to Bechuanaland; secondly, a dispute with Kruger over trade across the Vaal; thirdly, an agitation, growing for some time past, among the Rand Uitlanders. As to the first, he carried out the promise that the Cape should have 'British' Bechuanaland; but of the Bechuanaland Protectorate beyond it, which Rhodes claimed for the Chartered Company, he refused to concede more than the narrow strip for the projected railway. This was because three Bechuana chiefs, of whom Khama was the leader, came to England, and petitioned against being placed under chartered rule. In the conceded strip, however, the company was granted policing rights, as elsewhere in its territories. The dispute with Kruger arose from the desire of the latter to discourage imports through the Cape in favour of imports through non-British Delagoa Bay—the Portuguese harbour whose railway to Pretoria was opened on 8 July of that year. He first held up traffic

a port], I will do everything to work together with England and with the colonies. I will come into a Customs Union; I will give free leave for railways to be built, wherever it will pay any one to build them; I will do my best to make the South African States in one; I will do everything together with the colonies, for I believe their interests are the same as the interests of this country' (op. cit., 207). Garrett's theory was that a final settlement could have been obtained by a bargain on these lines. Yet if Kruger were in earnest about coming into a Customs Union and 'making the South African States in one', it is a little difficult to see for what he so much wanted a port of his own.

on the railway from the Vaal to the Rand, and then, when an ox-wagon service was organized instead from the south bank, closed the 'drifts' (i.e. fords) on the river. These were breaches of Article XIII of the 1884 Convention; and Chamberlain, having Cape opinion behind him, dispatched on 3 November 1895 a veiled but unmistakable ultimatum. Kruger gave way.

Meanwhile the Uitlanders in Johannesburg were almost ostentatiously conspiring to rebel. A petition signed by over 35,000 of them in August had been rejected. Their wrongs and claims had for a year been occupying Chamberlain's predecessor, Lord Ripon; who that summer in sending out a new high commissioner, Sir Hercules Robinson,[1] had said that 'what he most feared, was a rising at Johannesburg'.[2] Chamberlain, therefore, fully expected one, and after consulting Lord Salisbury had approved a plan to meet it; which was that on its outbreak the high commissioner as representative of the paramount Power should travel to Pretoria, and mediate between Kruger and the rebels.[3]

Rhodes, however, unknown to either Chamberlain or Robinson, had quite a different scheme. It was to assemble as large a force of mounted police as the Chartered Company could muster at a 'jumping-off ground' on the newly acquired strip. Dr. Jameson,[4] the company's administrator, was to command them, and on a signal they were to make an armed dash for Johannesburg. This, of course, meant pure filibustering; and as against a state, like the Transvaal, with which we were at peace, it was utterly indefensible.

At the brink of crisis an event occurred which warped the whole British situation. On 17 December 1895 Grover Cleveland, president of the United States, sent a message to Congress. It was virtually an ultimatum to Great Britain. The subject was the boundary between British Guiana and Venezuela, about which negotiations had long been in progress between London and Caracas. Venezuela was claiming on historical grounds a

---

[1] 1824–97; created Lord Rosmead in 1896. He had already before (1880–9) been governor of Cape Colony.

[2] J. L. Garvin, *Life of Chamberlain*, iii (1934), 58.

[3] Ibid., 59–63.

[4] Leander Starr Jameson, b. 1853 at Edinburgh; in medical practice at Kimberley from 1878; Chartered Company's administrator from 1891; led the raid which ended in his surrender, 2 January 1896; elected to Cape parliament, 1900; premier of Cape Colony, 1904–8; created baronet, 1911; died 1917.

large part of British Guiana, and had thoughtfully given a concession there to an American syndicate. Cleveland was within a year of the time when he must stand, if at all, for re-election. He was a gold democrat, and the tide of bimetallism, which was to sweep his party in 1896, already wetted his feet. 'Twisting the lion's tail' was still a strong card to play in American politics. In his message he announced that he would appoint an American commission to define the boundary, and impose its award upon Great Britain—by war, if necessary—in the name of the Monroe Doctrine.

This was certainly one of the most unexpected, least warranted, and least excusable steps ever taken in modern times by a Great Power. Its direct consequences need not detain us long. The message evoked a frenzy of Jingoism throughout the United States; but a chastening influence was exerted by a catastrophic fall in American stocks. British opinion displayed restraint from the start. It became obvious that, while an Anglo-American war would still be the most popular of all wars in America, in England it was viewed as fratricidal. Cleveland appointed his Commission; but it was composed of prudent men, and Lord Salisbury accepted its invitation to supply it with documents of the British case. Meanwhile Chamberlain, who had an American wife, was active behind the scenes; first using as intermediary the veteran Lord Playfair[1] (also married to an American), and later, in September 1896, visiting the United States and interviewing Cleveland's secretary of state, Olney, in private. The result of these talks was the Treaty of Washington (2 February 1897), by which the question was referred to arbitration. The award (promulgated on 3 October 1899) confirmed all the principal British claims.

But the indirect consequences went much farther. The Cleveland message laid bare the isolation of Great Britain. Had war resulted, it might have been 1779 over again, with Germany heading a hostile Europe against us. Already in October there had been a wrangle between London and Berlin over Germany's support of Kruger.[2] The message was perhaps decisive in confirming the Wilhelmstrasse's anti-British orientation. It may, too, have helped to precipitate Rhodes's action, for since Kru-

---

[1] See above, p. 25, n. 4.
[2] For documents of it see *Die Grosse Politik der europäischen Kabinette*, xi (1923), 5–15.

ger's *Kaiser-Kommers* speech the German peril weighed especially with him. But it also helped to divide and unman the Rand plotters; since among them were not a few Americans and Germans, and a doubt was opened up if Great Britain's could be the winning side. At the last moment they were paralysed by a dispute whether in revolting they should hoist the British or the Transvaal flag. On 27 December Robinson cabled to Chamberlain that the movement had collapsed. Next day Rhodes at the Cape said the same to Sir Graham Bower, the imperial secretary. All this time Dr. Jameson had been waiting in the corridor north of Mafeking in pursuance of Rhodes's design. From Johannesburg and even from Rhodes's factotum, Dr. Rutherfoord Harris, he received discouraging messages. But none came from Rhodes himself; and on the evening of 29 December the 'Raid' was launched.

Jameson had 350 Chartered police with him at Pitsani, and 120 Bechuanaland police placed under his orders joined him on the road. With this body of 470 mounted men, 8 machine-guns, and 3 pieces of artillery, he planned to reach Johannesburg, 180 miles distant, before the Boers could stop him. Apart from the criminality of the enterprise, it was an absurd miscalculation of force, only to be explained by the Chartered men's misvaluing of their Matabele victories. 'If Isandhlwana could be wiped out by machine-guns,' they seem to have reasoned, 'why not Majuba too?' Events soon undeceived them. Near Krugersdorp on their fourth day out the raiders were halted by deadly fire from invisible Boers. Next morning (2 January 1896) they were manœuvred at Doornkop into a complete trap; and on a promise that their lives would be spared, laid down their arms. Their captor was Commandant Cronje. They had about forty casualties, including sixteen killed; the Boer casualties were under ten.

Till 29 December Chamberlain had had no inkling that anything like the Raid would happen. Receiving then a vague report that it might, he cabled strongly to Robinson against it—repeating his monition in the most emphatic terms when news of the start reached him thirty-six hours later. Following the first cable Robinson had a courier sent after Jameson; who overtook him when two days out, and ordered him in the queen's name to desist, but he refused. Following the second, he issued a drastic proclamation against the raiders. Meanwhile Chamberlain himself sternly denounced them to the Chartered Company, and telegraphed a direct repudiation to President Kruger. These steps he took while the result was still in the balance, and in defiance of the company's attempt (by publishing a faked letter alleging that women and children had been in danger at Johannesburg) to make the raiders popular heroes. Stronger prima facie proof, that he neither foreknew nor favoured nor condoned that particular crime, he could scarcely have given.

Rhodes's guilt was obvious, and he resigned the Cape premiership. But the day after Jameson's surrender produced a new complication—the celebrated 'Kruger telegram'. The German emperor cabled to the Transvaal president (3 January 1896): 'I sincerely congratulate you that, without appealing for the help of friendly Powers, you with your people, by your own energy against the armed hordes which as disturbers of the peace broke into your country, have succeeded in re-establishing peace and maintaining the independence of your country against attacks from without.'[1] Though sometimes afterwards ascribed to a random impulse of the Kaiser, this message, implying Germany's right and intention to interfere in the Transvaal contrary to the 1884 Convention, was in fact a most deliberate act of state.[2] It is now known that it emanated from a conference held by William II, at which the chancellor, foreign minister, and three others were present. Nor did it stand alone; orders were sent to ship colonial troops from German East Africa to Delagoa Bay, whence with a naval detachment from three German cruisers already lying off Lourenço Marques they were to go by rail to Pretoria. Had they done so, war could scarcely have been avoided; but the Portuguese stood firm and refused transit.

Down to this telegram the wider English public, nettled by fourteen years of persistent French opposition in every quarter of the globe, had assumed that Germany under Queen Victoria's grandson was Great Britain's friend. The disillusionment was keen, and an explosion of anger shook the nation. The government promptly manned and sent to sea a 'flying squadron' capable of crushing any other navy afloat, as navies then were. German statesmen felt they had gone too far. They veered to

---

[1] See the German text in *Die Grosse Politik*, xi (1923), 31.
[2] As originally described to Sir Valentine Chirol, *The Times* correspondent, by Marschall von Bieberstein, then foreign secretary. See Chirol's letter to *The Times* of 14 November 1922.

an apologetic tone. But the anti-English policy, whose theorist was Holstein,[1] was not abandoned; and at home from the emperor down they used the 'flying squadron' as a new and potent argument for creating a great German navy.

The telegram worsened the South African sequel of the Raid. It blunted British repudiation of Rhodes and the Raiders. Following the fiasco Sir Hercules Robinson hastened to Pretoria —in no position now to mediate with a high hand. Kruger used him to obtain the unconditional surrender of the Johannesburg rebels. Their leaders were put on trial in the Transvaal; four (including Rhodes's brother) were condemned to death, and fifty-nine to various periods of imprisonment with fines of £2,000 each. Chamberlain with difficulty got the death sentences commuted, and the others partially revised. Meanwhile the Raiders had been handed over to the British government; and Jameson with the officers of his force stood in the dock at Bow Street. Sent for trial 'at Bar' before three eminent judges,[2] they were convicted and properly sentenced. But the effect on opinion abroad, and especially in the Transvaal, was more than cancelled by a fever of London enthusiasm for the accused. Although in the main a reaction against the Kruger telegram (and chiefly metropolitan at that), it helped foreigners to view the whole nation as Jameson's accomplices. Already on 4 March a pro-Kruger candidate, Marthinus Steyn, had been elected president of the Orange Free State against J. G. Fraser, the leader of the moderate party. A year later (17 March 1897) Steyn signed at Bloemfontein a treaty of offensive and defensive alliance with the Transvaal.

The deeper problems of the Raid's authorship were referred to a select committee of the house of commons. Chamberlain himself was a member, and the opposition representatives included Harcourt, Campbell-Bannerman, and Labouchere. The committee sat five months; heard Chamberlain, Rhodes, and a multitude of witnesses; and reported in July 1897, severely censuring Rhodes, but entirely acquitting Chamberlain and the colonial office.[3] This finding was supported by Harcourt and Campbell-Bannerman, and indeed by the whole committee save Labouchere and an Irish member. But there was a fatal flaw

---

[1] See his memorandum of 30 December 1895 (*Die Grosse Politik*, xi (1923), 67–9).
[2] The lord chief justice (Lord Russell of Killowen), Baron Pollock, and Mr. Justice Hawkins.
[3] Though the imperial secretary at the Cape and another official were censured. The Report (Cd. 311) is still the most valuable document for the Raid episode.

in it. The company's agents, in their anxiety to shelve inquiry, had put about that certain telegrams, sent from London to Capetown before the Raid, contained evidence that Chamberlain had been involved. Before the committee 44 telegrams were produced out of a series of 51, but 7, which it was implied were the incriminating ones, were by Rhodes's order expressly withheld. The committee failed to compel their production, and thereby rendered possible the charge that its members hid the truth to shield Chamberlain. To most Englishmen it was a sufficient answer that men like Harcourt and Campbell-Bannerman were assenting members of the committee. But to foreigners this only made the affair more sinister. Both front benches, thought the Boers of the Transvaal, were in league against their liberties. The impression was deepened by the ensuing commons debate, when, after Harcourt had spoken powerfully for the colonial secretary, that statesman rose at the end, and while defending the government's decision not to follow up censuring Rhodes by punishing him,[1] slipped in the grievous overstatement that the Colossus had done nothing affecting his 'personal position as a man of honour'.

What was the truth here? A primary duty of the select committee had been to clear up to the satisfaction of reasonable men, whether at home or abroad, the responsibilities of the British government. Why, by acquiescing in the mystery of the telegrams, did it fail to do so? Again, when Chamberlain signed the committee's report, he subscribed to a most proper censure of Rhodes. Why did he virtually unsay it in his house of commons speech? Sinister explanations were current among well-informed people at the time. It was said that the committee had been influenced by some secret communication from a very high quarter. It was said that Chamberlain made his whitewashing speech under duress, and that a liberal member of parliament sat in the house of commons with the telegrams in his pocket, ready to read them if he did not toe the line. The first story may now, in all its forms, be dismissed, in face of the very categorical denials by Lewis Harcourt, who in 1897 had acted as his father's secretary and knew everything that he knew.[2] But the second

---

[1] Rhodes's enemies demanded that (1) his name should be struck off the roll of the privy council; (2) his company's charter should be revoked.

[2] See A. G. Gardiner, *Life of Sir William Harcourt* (1923), ii. 429 n. (written statement) and 434 (statement in letter).

may still be true. Harcourt himself regarded Chamberlain's speech as having done nearly all the mischief.[1] He thought also that Chamberlain, while he had a clean sheet in regard to the Raid, had not one in regard to the preparation for a rising in Johannesburg, and that this privity rendered him liable 'to something in the nature of "severe pressure"' by Rhodes and his friends.[2]

Was this so? 'My case is', wrote Chamberlain to the permanent head of his Department, 'that while I knew all about the revolution, I knew nothing of anything so mad as Jameson's raid.'[3] What did his 'knowing all about the revolution' cover? The full text of the missing telegrams remains unpublished, but the quasi-incriminating passages in them can now be read.[4] None suffices to rebut the otherwise overwhelming evidence that he did not foreknow the Raid. But more than one would have made an ugly impression if printed at the time; and it seems scarcely doubtful that Dr. Rutherfoord Harris, who was their chief author, had deliberately worded them (and some of their fellows in the Blue Book) with an eye to subsequent blackmail.[5] For sanctioning the vile use made of them the blame is Rhodes's; but why did Chamberlain sit down under it? There are other documents printed by his biographer which may suggest that he feared the alternative. Thus on 18 December 1895, after the Cleveland message, he had written to the head of his department to discuss whether, and in what way, that complication might affect the timing of the Johannesburg revolt. His conclusion was that 'either it should come *at once* or be postponed for a year or two at least'; and he asked that a certain high official of the colonial office should communicate this to Rhodes's agent in London, Maguire. This was done; Maguire cabled to Rhodes, with whom were Beit and Harris; and Beit at once wired to Johannesburg 'urging instant flotation new Company'. Chamberlain himself more than a year later made the marginal comment: 'I have no doubt that Beit and Harris were influenced by Maguire's telegram'.[6] In short, Downing Street had done something very like pulling the trigger; though without really knowing what trigger it pulled.

[1] Ibid., 433.   [2] Ibid., 430 n.
[3] J. L. Garvin, *Life of Chamberlain*, iii (1934), 115.   [4] Ibid., 110–11.
[5] So Lord Salisbury wrote (5 September 1896) of 'the monstrous libels which have been invented against Chamberlain, and *for which proof has been to a certain extent manufactured*' (Lord Newton, *Lord Lansdowne*, 141).   [6] *Life of Chamberlain*, iii. 72–4.

Chamberlain might have done better to defy Rhodes and let the facts come out. They were after all less heinous than might at first appear. The Transvaal's was not a friendly government; short of being actually at war it could scarcely have been more hostile. The British Uitlanders, whom Kruger oppressed, formed half of the country's white male population; and a British minister could not be expected to lack sympathy for them. Nor did the rebels really contemplate killing Boers, or 'levying war' save in a technical sense; their idea was merely for a dramatic move to enable the high commissioner to intervene. But the result of leaving undetermined the degree of Downing Street's complicity with Rhodes was to cause Dutch South Africa to surmise much worse guilt. It believed Great Britain to have backed the Raid; and the belief was a main stage on the path to eventual war. The Transvaal Boers, who before had been pretty equally divided between Krugerism and progress, were now united by their fears and suspicions. In 1893 Kruger had been re-elected president by 7,854 votes against 7,009 cast for his progressive opponent. In February 1898 he polled 12,858 votes, and his two progressive opponents could not muster 6,000 between them. Nor was the mischief confined to his republic. Before the Raid Rhodes had enjoyed the support of the Dutch in Cape Colony and the trust of those in the Orange Free State. Owing to the Raid he forfeited both. Owing to the proceedings of the select committee and Chamberlain's unhappy speech Great Britain forfeited them likewise. The cause of unity and reconciliation between the two white races in South Africa received an incalculable setback.

A minor result of the Raid was a most formidable native rising (April 1896) in Matabeleland, now denuded of its mounted police. After murdering isolated settlers, and approaching but recoiling from Bulawayo, the Matabele settled down to guerrilla warfare, for which parts of the country, especially the Matopos, were extremely suitable. It was in this campaign that Colonel R. S. S. Baden-Powell (afterwards to become founder of the Boy Scouts) first attracted wide notice by his talent for scoutcraft. Eventually Rhodes himself, with only a few companions, entered the Matopos, parleyed with a number of the chiefs, and by the force of his name and personality persuaded them to surrender. Though the effect of what he achieved was then, and has since been, exaggerated, it was a brave act; and reminded Rhodes's countrymen that, despite his colossal and criminal blunder, he was a great man.

Let us turn back a little to other fields. The government, when it took office, had resolved to distinguish itself by social reform. Chamberlain was to show the way, and Lord Salisbury was now convinced of the wisdom of following him.

Chiefly perhaps because Chamberlain became diverted to imperial concerns, not very much came of it. The single big measure was the Workmen's Compensation Act 1897. This made handsome amends for what the lords had done in 1894 when they hamstrung Asquith's Employers Liability Bill;[1] for Chamberlain's principle was a better one than Asquith's. He cut loose from the intricacies of the English law about 'negligence' and enacted squarely that the accidents which occur to workmen in an industry must be paid for by the industry, like any other of its working costs. Not a few conservatives called this 'revolutionary', but they had to give way. The act as passed did not extend to seamen, domestic servants, or agricultural labourers, though the first of these categories especially needed it. But by subsequent acts within ten years they were all brought in.

Compensation for accidents was the first step in a policy to insure the working-class population against the main risks which darkened and deranged their lives. The next in Chamberlain's mind was to ward off pauperism in old age. Since 1889, when the German Reichstag passed its famous 'Law of Insurance against Old Age and Infirmity', this problem had come fast to the fore. In 1891 Charles Booth (who may be regarded as the father of Old Age Pensions) read an epoch-making paper upon it.[2] In 1892 Chamberlain came out with a scheme of his own—the first front bench man to produce one. The liberal government of that year met it by appointing a Royal Commission on the Aged Poor with Lord Aberdare as chairman and the prince of Wales a member. Its Report (1895) exposed many evils, but recommended no remedies, advising a further inquiry on extended lines. Accordingly in 1896 the unionist government appointed a Committee on Old Age Pensions with Lord Rothschild as chairman. It examined over a hundred schemes; disapproved them all; and reported in the negative (1898). Chamberlain at once got yet another inquiry on foot—this time

---

[1] See above, p. 214.   [2] *Journal of the Royal Statistical Society*, liv (1891), 600–43.

by a select committee with Henry Chaplin[1] as chairman and Mr. Lloyd George an active member; and in 1899 it reported recommending an actual scheme.[2] A departmental committee was then appointed to ascertain the cost; but by the time its Report appeared in 1900 the expense of the South African war precluded acting on it. Thus the second step in Chamberlain's policy was never achieved within Queen Victoria's reign, nor, as it afterwards turned out, by his party at all; nor was any other large reform brought before parliament in its stead. An Education Bill of 1896 had to be abandoned. An Agricultural Rates Bill of the same year became law. Passed near the end of the second and worst phase in the catastrophe of British agriculture, it remitted one-half of the farmer's rates. It was the first important example[3] of that 'derating' principle which parliament in 1929 adopted on a far wider scale.

The liberals were in no state to quicken this slow pace. The Armenian question, which began to divide their party before it lost office, did so much more afterwards; for the massacres were repeated and prolonged. Lord Salisbury followed the line taken by Lord Kimberley, and vainly urged the Powers to collective action. But the keener liberals desired Great Britain to act single-handed, and among them, in his retirement, was Gladstone. After the Cleveland message and the Kruger telegram the sultan, with Germany strongly courting him, threw fears to the winds. Butchery followed butchery. The most terrible of all began on 26 August 1896, after some Armenian bomb-throwers had perpetrated an insensate crime at the Ottoman Bank in Constantinople. For three days and nights a wild orgy of massacre went on in the streets of the Turkish capital under the eyes of thousands of horrified foreigners. This dreadful atrocity, in which 6,000 Armenians perished, recalled Gladstone to the platform; and on 24 September, three months before his 87th birthday, he made at Liverpool his last speech, pleading for isolated action. Its chief result was unintended; ten days afterwards Lord

---

[1] 1841–1923; educated at Harrow and Christ Church, Oxford; M.P. 1868; chancellor of the duchy of Lancaster, 1885; president of the board of agriculture, 1889–92; president of the local government board, 1895–1900; created viscount, 1916. A picturesque survival in parliament of a much earlier type of M.P. Sobriquet: 'The Squire.'

[2] 5s. a week, under strict conditions, to needy and deserving poor over 65.

[3] Smaller ones may be found in the Public Health Act 1875, s. 211(6), and the adoptive Public Libraries Act 1892, s. 18(1) (c). A much earlier one is in the adoptive Lighting and Watching Act 1833, s. 33, tit. *Gas*.

Rosebery, finding himself 'in apparent difference with a considerable mass of the Liberal party on the Eastern Question and in some conflict of opinion with Mr. Gladstone', resigned the liberal leadership. A stronger man would not have so acted, but his sensitive nature had been stung past bearing by pin-pricks. Following the regular usage in the liberal and conservative parties, the ex-premier was succeeded by different leaders in the two houses—Lord Kimberley in the lords and Sir William Harcourt in the commons. But the exceptional standing of the latter gave him virtually the leadership of the whole party; though he was not destined to retain it long. At the end of 1898 he too threw up his post in a sulk. Morley followed him by withdrawing from 'the formal councils of the heads of the Liberal party'; and the succession lay between Campbell-Bannerman and Asquith. The whips offered it to Asquith; but, as he was then a practising barrister dependent on his earnings at the Bar, he preferred that it should pass to Campbell-Bannerman.[1] The appointment, though no one knew then, carried the premiership seven years later.

The year 1897 was that of Queen Victoria's second, or Diamond, Jubilee. The 1887 programme having been an unqualified success, it was thought well, so far as the queen's strength allowed, to go through it again. But a good thing repeated is seldom quite so good the second time; and on the whole this was true of the two Jubilees. The queen herself by the later date had become aged and fragile; neither the nation nor the governing classes in it felt any longer the same self-confidence about their position; and imperialism, which was again the leading note in the celebrations, no longer commanded universal assent, compromised as it now seemed to many by a rising passion for aggression and conquest. The people's enthusiasm for the sovereign, however, was as unanimous as ever.

---

[1] A letter to the present writer from Asquith's eldest son Raymond, dated from Asquith's house 22 December 1898, reads: 'The Whips lunched here the other day and *offered my father the leadership*; but he defers to C.-Bannerman, being a poor man and dependent on his practice at the Bar. From a pawky letter, which he has received from C.B., I gather that the latter will take it with a little pressing.' This, though not the common version of what happened, is, it is believed, the correct one. The popular myth, that Asquith was 'passed over' as too imperialist, has been based on an anachronism. No such division between him and Campbell-Bannerman in regard to imperialism existed to any important extent until after the outbreak of the South African war. Technically the whips were not in a position to make an 'offer', the decision resting with the ex-cabinet ministers in the commons, i.e. Asquith, Campbell-Bannerman, Fowler, and Bryce. But practically, in all the circumstances of this case, they were.

Repeating 1887 meant repeating the Colonial Conference, and this was perhaps the most important result of the occasion. The first conference had not been conceived as inaugurating a series; and although what is known as the second had been held at Ottawa in 1894, it originated as a business gathering to debate Pacific cables, and only by courtesy went on to discuss the fiscal preference ideas, in which its hosts, the Canadian ministers, happened to be interested. The British government was represented at it neither by a minister nor even by an official, but solely by Lord Jersey,[1] an ex-governor of New South Wales. The 1897 conference, presided over by Chamberlain and attended by the premiers of eleven colonies,[2] was an altogether bigger affair. By resolving that in future conferences should meet at intervals, it went far to convert the experiment into an institution; though its members again separated without fixing any period for their reassembly. The previous ten years had brought out the fact that 'uniting the Empire', which in a vague way was everybody's aspiration, might follow three quite distinct lines of development—political, military-naval, or commercial. The first meant providing the empire with some common machinery for determining policy; so that, for example, a question of peace or war might be decided, not merely by the British parliament at Westminster, but by a body in which the colonies had a voice and by whose decision they might be bound. The second meant envisaging the problem of empire defence as a whole, and determining what military or naval contributions each part should make to it. The third soon tended to narrow itself to schemes for fiscal preference.

Chamberlain, who presided, opened the conference with a speech stressing the first line. He suggested a council of the empire to which the autonomous colonies might send 'representative plenipotentiaries', and which 'might slowly grow to that Federal Council to which we must always look forward as our ultimate ideal'. But the colonial statesmen were unpersuaded. Courtesies apart, that was not their ideal. What each colony treasured most was its own self-government; and they feared lest a federal body might encroach on it. Perhaps they were right, too, if they suspected that, under no matter what forms,

---

[1] The seventh earl (1845–1915).
[2] Canada, Newfoundland, New South Wales, Victoria, South Australia, West Australia, Queensland, Tasmania, New Zealand, Cape Colony, and Natal.

the direction of foreign policy, and of high policy generally, must remain in British hands; while a federal form would lessen their freedom to dissent from it. So without even broaching a resolution on Chamberlain's lines they passed one declaring that 'the present political relations between the United Kingdom and the self-governing Colonies are generally satisfactory under the existing condition of things'. Only New Zealand (Richard Seddon) and Tasmania (Sir E. Braddon) dissented. This resolution dispelled for ever the dream of imperial federation; though not all the dreamers at once awoke from it.

On defence there was also a difference. The admiralty preached the high strategy of a single navy; fleets defending the empire must be viewed as a whole, and the fate of any given colony might be settled by operations many thousand miles away. Similarly the war office sought the interchangeability of military units. Only a little was achieved in either direction. The premier of Cape Colony offered unconditionally the cost of a first-class battleship.[1] But the Australian colonies who in 1887 had undertaken a rather modest annual contribution (£126,000) to the cost of a special squadron in the Pacific, were content to confirm it. Their naval outlook remained local; they wanted more ships in their own waters.

While the home government was thinking of federation and defence, the colonies took far more interest in fiscal preference. Not that they would look at an imperial Zollverein. Chamberlain had already expounded the case for one in his Canada Club speech (25 March 1896). He had explained that while the colonies might for revenue purposes retain a great many non-protective duties even against their fellow members of the empire, actual protection must within the empire disappear. But in most of the colonies protection had even then developed too many vested interests for that to be acceptable. Preference was their alternative. It was a scheme greatly in their own favour; for while their markets for imports were still relatively small in proportion to Great Britain's export trade, a preferred footing in the British import market, the largest in the world, would have sufficed for virtually all they had to sell.[2] Great Britain's free-

[1] The offer was made without authority from his parliament, and later had to be withdrawn. An annual naval contribution was substituted.

[2] Chamberlain himself had said at the Canada Club that the foreign trade of the United Kingdom was 'so gigantic in proportion to the foreign trade of the

trade system was another obstacle; and yet another were treaties in force with Germany and Belgium, which debarred even the Dominions from giving, if they wished, a preference to the mother country. A resolution was passed in favour of denouncing these treaties; and on 28 July they were denounced. A unilateral preference of 12½ per cent. given by Canada on the 23 April previous could thereupon be regularized.[1]

Meanwhile very important issues had been raised for our tropical empire in West Africa. Early in the year Sir George Goldie, the head of the Royal Niger Company, had performed a remarkable feat. At the head of company forces organized and commanded by himself (it must be remembered that he was originally, like Gordon and Kitchener, an officer in the Royal Engineers), he had overthrown the Arab emirs of Ilorin and Nupe on both the banks of the Niger above its confluence with the Benue. In the history of his chartered company this was comparable to the conquest of Matabeleland in that of Rhodes's, though in reality a much finer military exploit. But forward movements by the French were now afoot, which threatened the entire future value of the British West African settlements, at any rate west of the Niger.

France's expansion was governmental and military, not, like ours, made through trading companies. She had large native forces commanded by French officers, and her policy over a period of years had been to push them across the hinterlands, so that the British coastal bases were left without roots. She had done this to our old settlement on the Gambia, completely sterilizing it. She had followed suit with Sierra Leone; and now she was encroaching in the same way on the hinterlands of the Gold Coast and Lagos. We had agreements with native chiefs in these areas, but they availed nothing against actual occupation by French military forces. On the French side the foreign minister, Hanotaux, resolutely backed the invaders. The British foreign minister, Lord Salisbury, now past his best, was much less reso-

---

Colonies, that the burden of an arrangement of this kind would fall with much greater weight on the United Kingdom'. (J. Chamberlain, *Foreign and Colonial Speeches* (1897), 169.)

[1] Of this conference, which may be said to have wiped finally off the page of practical politics (*a*) imperial federation and (*b*) an imperial Zollverein (i.e. 'Free Trade within the Empire'), only a bare summary was published at the time (Cd. 8596 of 1897). Of the full shorthand note, which still exists unpublished, a few passages will be found in J. L. Garvin, *Life of Chamberlain*, iii (1924), c. liv.

lute to stop them. Here Chamberlain stepped in with decisive effect. He organized a 'West African Frontier Force' on French lines—Hausa troops and British officers—and placed it under the brilliant command of Lugard to do what the French had been doing. An interminable Niger Conference had begun in Paris, and lasted nine months—from the autumn of 1897 to midsummer 1898. Nearly all that time French and British expeditions were hoisting their rival flags over the length and breadth of large areas, which, though conceded to Great Britain by the 1890 Agreement, had since been penetrated by France. It was much to the credit of the officers on both sides that no armed collision occurred. At last on 14 June 1898 an Anglo-French Convention ended the dispute. The lines between French and British in West Africa were drawn substantially as they are to-day. France was assured of northern hinterlands enabling her to link up effectively her domains in West, North, and West-Central Africa. Great Britain gained most of the territory in which the recent marching and countermarching had gone on; in other words, she recovered most, though not all, of what it had been open to her to occupy after the Agreement of 1890. It was far more than she would have done but for the intervention of Chamberlain.

A more severe conflict with France was soon to follow. It arose out of decisions taken in the year 1896. March in that year witnessed the most serious defeat of white men by black that has ever occurred on African soil, when an Italian army of 30,000 men under General Baratieri was overwhelmed by the Abyssinians at Adowa. Following it the Italians at Kassala were heavily attacked by the Sudan dervishes, and to relieve the pressure Great Britain consented to make a diversion up the Nile.[1] The British Sirdar of the Egyptian army, Sir Herbert Kitchener,[2] had long laid his plans to reconquer the Sudan, and this was his opportunity to embark on them. Cromer was hostile; leaders in the cabinet, including both Balfour and Chamberlain, were diffident; and Great Britain had to advance the capital expendi-

[1] The Italians eventually decided to abandon Kassala, which in December 1897 was handed over to an Egyptian force under a British officer.

[2] B. 1850; in 1870 served as volunteer in the French army of the Loire; entered Royal Engineers, 1871; on Palestine survey, 1874–8; notable service in Sudan, 1883–5; governor of the Red Sea Territories, 1886; Sirdar of the Egyptian army from 1890; created baron, 1898, after victory of Omdurman; in South African war, chief of staff to Lord Roberts, 1900, and commander-in-chief, 1900–2; viscount and O.M. 1902; commander-in-chief in India, 1902–9; British representative in Egypt, 1911–14; earl, 1914; war minister, 1914–16; drowned on service, 1916.

ture, since France and Russia vetoed Egypt's raising it. But in
the event Kitchener's rare blend of strategy and economy got
past obstacles. His method was to advance by short stages up
the Nile, building a railway as he went. Most of his troops were
Egyptians, but they were stiffened by the presence of British
units. When it came to fighting he made large use of machine-
guns. In September of that year he captured Dongola; about a
year later he occupied Berber; in April 1898 at the Atbara river
he defeated in a pitched battle an army of 18,000 dervishes, of
whom about 2,500 were killed and 2,000, including their commander, taken prisoners. From this it was but one step to Khartoum; and as soon as his railways were ready and the Nile
had risen he started. On 2 September 1898 a dervish army
commanded by the Khalifa in person was defeated outside Omdurman, with a loss of about 10,000 killed. Omdurman and Khartoum were immediately occupied and the Egyptian and British
flags hoisted side by side. A long-prepared, boldly planned, and
finely executed effort had reached its goal. But three days later
a vessel from the south brought news to Khartoum that six white
men flying a strange flag held a post up the White Nile at Fashoda.

These men were Captain Marchand and his French officers,
commanding a small detachment of Senegalese troops. Like
Kitchener they had started their expedition in 1896. On 28
March 1895 the British government, through the mouth of Sir
Edward Grey speaking in the house of commons, had announced
that 'the advance of a French expedition under secret instructions right from the other side of Africa' into the Nile valley
'would be an unfriendly act and would be so viewed by England'.
In spite of this emphatic warning the Marchand expedition was
secretly sent off in the following year; and after marching 2,800
miles in about twenty-four months and surmounting great hard-
ships, they reached Fashoda early in July. There Kitchener in
person found them on 18 September 1898. An admirable diplomatist at all times, the British commander treated the French-
man with extreme courtesy, but handed him a written protest,
hoisted the British and Egyptian flags, and left an Egyptian
garrison on the spot.

The matter was thus transferred to the foreign offices, and for
some months Great Britain and France stood on the brink of war.
Hanotaux had been replaced at the French foreign office by
Delcassé, but the new minister represented no change of policy.

It was only a minor relaxation, when on 4 November the French agreed to instruct Marchand to quit Fashoda. For he had left behind him a string of posts through the Bahr-el-Ghazal, and France claimed to retain them; which would have given her a corridor of territory and a river of her own right through to the White Nile. These claims Great Britain declined to admit,[1] and in effect defied her to fight for them. After taking some months to make sure that neither Russia nor Germany would back him, and that contrary to expectation Lord Salisbury could not this time be squeezed, Delcassé (15 February 1899) gave way. An Anglo-French Convention (21 March) fixed a line (roughly the watershed between the Nile and the Congo) beyond which Great Britain would not seek territory or influence westwards, nor France eastwards. Though popular feeling in France had been rendered intensely anti-English, this agreement and that about the Niger ended most of the competitive friction between the governments; and with the advent of Paul Cambon as French ambassador in London their relations took a turn for the better. Meanwhile Great Britain, more solidly established in the Nile valley than ever before, had almost unawares put far away from herself the possibility of that early evacuation of Egypt which till a few years before her leading statesmen had sincerely desired.

We must turn back to South Africa, which during the lifetime of this government was never far out of the picture. In March 1897 Sir Hercules Robinson (who had become Lord Rosmead) was recalled, and a new high commissioner sent. This was Sir Alfred Milner,[2] who till then had been chairman of the Board of Inland Revenue. When not in an official position he had always been a liberal; but his experience in Egypt, where he took part in a most beneficent phase of British rule[3] under Lord Cromer, had made him also a convinced imperialist. He went to South Africa with the good wishes of all parties, and not least of the Opposition. Yet in one respect his was not a good appointment. He had the gifts and temperament of a first-class administrator. But he lacked those of a diplomatist.

Just before he started, a conflict had developed with Kruger

---

[1] They were rendered the more sinister, because France had been intriguing with Menelek of Abyssinia, the victor of Adowa.

[2] See above, p. 217, n. 1.

[3] Which he afterwards described very ably in *England in Egypt* (1892).

over two new and tyrannical aliens laws, whose repeal Chamberlain demanded. The president was not ready to fight, and he gave way. But he spent the year arming. The war material imported through Delagoa Bay rose from £61,903 in 1895 to £256,291 in 1897. Over £1½ millions was spent on forts at Johannesburg; heavy guns were mounted, and German artillery officers engaged. Over £70,000 was allocated for the secret service maintained by the Transvaal in the adjoining British territories. Asked in August by the prime minister of Natal what was the motive of his enormous armaments, Kruger replied: 'Oh, Kaffirs, Kaffirs—and such-like objects'.[1]

Milner spent his first ten months studying the situation. He travelled over the colonies, learned Dutch, and saw every one that he could. Much would depend on the Transvaal presidential election in February 1898. As we have seen, it resulted overwhelmingly in Kruger's favour. The old man followed up his triumph by trampling on the Transvaal judicature, dismissing its head, and making himself virtually a dictator. Milner, the workings of whose mind may be traced almost from day to day in the *Milner Papers*, now became deeply alarmed. He wrote to Chamberlain that 'there is no way out of the political troubles of South Africa except reform in the Transvaal or war. And at present the chances of reform in the Transvaal are worse than ever'.[2] In a notable speech at Graaff-Reinet (1 March) he warned the Cape Dutch that the cause of strife lay not in the British policy but in Krugerism, and they must exert their influence against the latter if they desired peace. He obtained but a limited response. What above all kept the Dutch aloof was the re-emergence of Rhodes. The 'Colossus', though fallen from his ministerial pedestal, was too big a personality not to have resumed unofficially the leadership of the British element in South Africa. But all sections of Dutch opinion combined now in an invincible distrust of him; and when, for instance, on his return after the Raid Inquiry he gave out his slogan: 'Equal rights for all civilized men south of the Zambesi', the effect was to render suspect a claim whose justice more than half of them would otherwise support. In April 1898 he recovered his place on the board of the Chartered Company, which Chamberlain in 1896 had forced him to resign.

[1] Cecil Headlam, *The Milner Papers*, i (1931), 58.
[2] Ibid., i. 221.

As 1898 wore on, another hope appeared. There was a chance that by an arrangement with Portugal and Germany Great Britain might acquire Delagoa Bay. It was assumed (though in the light of what we now know it seems very doubtful) that, if this happened, the Transvaal would accept the completion of its encirclement without fighting. But it fell through. At the Cape elections in the autumn the Sprigg ministry, which had succeeded Rhodes's, was defeated by the Dutch party, the 'Bond'. A ministry was formed under W. P. Schreiner, himself a moderate man of high ideals, but entirely dependent on the votes of extremists (14 October 1898).

In November Milner went home on leave, and during his absence an event occurred at Johannesburg which incalculably increased the tension. An English workman, one Tom Edgar, was shot dead by a Boer policeman in circumstances which Uitlander opinion (quite justly, on the reported facts) regarded as constituting murder. The policeman was arrested, released on nominal bail, tried for manslaughter two months later before a jury of Boers, and not merely acquitted, but commended by the presiding judge. This episode transformed the character of the Uitlander unrest. Hitherto it had been controlled by the capitalists. Now a mass agitation ran away with the workmen; and the harsh violence which the Boers proceeded to use towards it only increased its momentum. A petition from British subjects on the Rand to the queen received 21,684 signatures in a few weeks. It was sent home on 24 March; and when it reached Downing Street the government faced a sharp dilemma. Either they must take it up; which, if Kruger persisted in flat defiance, might mean war. Or they must decline it; which would mean notifying all loyal British subjects in South Africa, and indeed overseas generally, that the mother country washed her hands of them. They delayed decision for several weeks, but on 9 May they took up the petition. They were no doubt stiffened by the famous 'helots' dispatch[1] from Milner, which had reached them a few days earlier giving chapter and verse for the Uitlanders' grievances.

[1] Printed six weeks later as no. 78 in Cd. 9345 of 1899. 'The spectacle', wrote Milner in it, 'of thousands of British subjects kept permanently in the position of helots, constantly chafing under undoubted grievances and calling vainly to Her Majesty's government for redress, does steadily undermine the influence and reputation of Great Britain and the respect for the British Government within the Queen's Dominions.'

The full details of negotiation between this point and the outbreak of hostilities five months later are too intricate to be traced here. New light on them has been thrown by quite recent publications.[1] The effect of these has been to dispel the myth that a bellicose Chamberlain drove a reluctant cabinet into war. The documents show that the cabinet was indeed reluctant, but so was the colonial secretary. He had, as we shall see later on, been taking a leading part in European affairs, and was fully alive to the grave risks of a colonial war-entanglement. Moreover his training as a business man had given him a strong bias towards negotiation. He never failed in patience or diplomatic resource during these months. The person who did was Milner. The high commissioner had made up his mind (and his view cannot be lightly ignored, for he formed it on the spot and was a good judge of facts) that the Transvaal's helm was set for an independent United States of South Africa under Dutch auspices, and that Kruger, with the wind of Afrikanderdom in his sails, was most unlikely to abandon the goal under any pressure short of military defeat. Therefore, while constrained to negotiations by Chamberlain, he did not approach them with hope or zest.

Four stages may be briefly distinguished. The first, after the British government had accepted the Uitlander petition, was a direct conference at Bloemfontein between Milner and Kruger (31 May–5 June 1899). Here was perhaps the best hope of peace, for the moderate Dutch of the Cape and the Free State brought considerable pressure to bear on the Transvaal extremists. But Milner appeared at his worst; his clear super-civilized mind lost patience with the tedious and devious obstinacy of the Arcadian president; and after five days he broke off the talks. A cable from Chamberlain urging him not to, and suggesting new lines of negotiation, reached him just too late. The second stage saw a long discussion of various obscure and complicated franchise bills in the Transvaal legislature, while the Cape Dutch leaders renewed their moderating efforts; until Chamberlain (27 July) offered an olive-branch in the form of a proposal for joint inquiry into the bills by British and Boer delegations. The Dutch in the Cape parliament welcomed this, but Kruger would not listen

---

[1] i.e. Cecil Headlam's *The Milner Papers*, vol. i (1931) and J. L. Garvin's *Life of Chamberlain*, vol. iii (1934), to which may be added E. A. Walker's *Lord de Villiers and his Times* (1925). The chief Blue Books are Cd. 9345, Cd. 9404 (Bloemfontein Conference), Cd. 9518, Cd. 9521, and Cd. 9530, all of 1899; also Cd. 369 and Cd. 420 of 1900.

to them. Then, thirdly, came new and much more liberal proposals, made (13 August) to the British agent through the Transvaal state attorney, Jan Christiaan Smuts.[1] These, as they stood, seemed to end the dispute, but Kruger went on to add conditions which he knew the British government could not accept; and on 2 September he withdrew the offer. The fourth stage consisted of a final offer by Chamberlain in moderate and conciliatory terms (8 September); which, though approved by the Cape Dutch leaders as well as by what were soon to be called the 'pro-Boers' in England, was rejected in a few days. A last attempt by Chamberlain (22 September) to keep the door open met with no response. Nor did a conciliatory speech (30 September) by the much-trusted duke of Devonshire. Both sides turned to moving troops.

It must be added that throughout these years a dispute had persisted, first by itself and then as a bitter flavouring in the main discussions, about the word 'suzerainty', which was used in the preamble to the 1881 Convention, but not repeated in the Convention of 1884. The British government maintained that the preamble governed both conventions (the second revising the first in respect of its articles only). No less a person than Sir Edward Clarke, solicitor-general in Salisbury's previous government, held this British interpretation to be wrong. But Chamberlain was not pedantic about it; he disclaimed any wish to read into 'suzerainty' more than the 1884 Convention itself contained. It is difficult to say how much mischief the word bred; but Sir Henry (afterwards Lord) de Villiers, the Afrikander chief justice of the Cape, who worked as hard to save peace as any one, thought that through its effect on Kruger it was of capital importance.[2]

Should the war have been avoided? The liberal party at home became divided between those like Morley who thought so (the 'pro-Boers') and those like Lord Rosebery who thought not (the 'liberal imperialists'); Campbell-Bannerman inclining to the former camp, and Asquith to the latter. The cleavage rent the

---

[1] Now General Smuts. He was then only 29 years of age.

[2] 'In 1884', he wrote, 'when the President went to England, he informed me that he intended to have the suzerainty abolished, and he afterwards informed me with great satisfaction that his object had been accomplished. The real cause of all the subsequent trouble was the substitution of the 1884 Convention without inserting the suzerainty from the 1881 Convention.' E. A. Walker, *Lord de Villiers and His Times* (1925), p. 180 n. Lord Bryce also thought the 1884 Convention a mistake (*Impressions of South Africa*, Preface to 3rd edition (1899), xxi).

party for a long time; but there were eventual compensations. The fact that the 'pro-Boers' had been numerous and courageous helped much in the reconciliation of the Transvaal seven years later. The fact, too, that the leaders of the I.L.P. and the young radicals stood together on difficult and unpopular anti-war platforms rendered easier that measure of general co-operation between them which under the Campbell-Bannerman and Asquith governments was fruitful in social reform.

But History, to the question posed above, has since found no certain answer. It is easy to argue after the event that the risks and losses of the long struggle were disproportionate to the Uitlanders' grievances, and that the Transvaal must eventually have reformed itself when Kruger, who was old, should die. But Kruger, even when broken and in exile, lived till 1904; and if Great Britain had left her oppressed nationals unchampioned until then, she might by then have looked in vain for any loyal nationals in South Africa. Much more than the details of the case for redress was involved in her accepting the Uitlander petition. It concerned the whole future of the Dominions, and can only be judged in the light of whatever value we may think that they (and particularly the Union of South Africa) possess, as Dominions, for Great Britain. Probably, however, no government could have let the petition drop. Nor after it was accepted is it easy to see much room for improvement in the British handling, save at the Bloemfontein Conference. Chamberlain worked well, though seriously and undeservedly handicapped by the suspicion of his personality, with which party feeling in England had infected South Africa.

There remain two wider factors. Though the cabinet of Great Britain was not bellicose, a large and noisy section of her people undoubtedly were. London imperialism, in particular, had developed during the nineties a swaggering aggressiveness; it grew markedly worse after the victory of Omdurman. If Jameson had become a hero by atoning for Isandhlwana, what of Kitchener, who had retrieved Khartoum? And what remained to complete the trilogy but to undo Majuba in like fashion? It is often said that this temper caused the war; and it may be true, though not in the most obvious sense. It did not affect Whitehall; the exceedingly strong combination of Salisbury, Chamberlain, Balfour, and Hicks Beach was one much above yielding to mob-clamour. But it did affect Pretoria. If the Boers became united by the mistaken conviction that a British government wanted their blood, it was largely because they heard a British public calling for it.

But secondly, the Boers were not thinking of defence only. There was a strong aggressive element on their side. They had sound military reasons for expecting to win, and but for an early error in large strategy might well have done so. They went into the fight as a new War of Independence, necessary to give birth to a new United States. At what point the party of action acquired irrevocable control cannot be known. But for the Boers as a nation of horsemasters the ideal time to begin a war was as soon as the seasonal rains renewed the veldt grass—no earlier and no later. It is significant that the war did begin exactly then; and possibly, or even probably, none of the Boer proceedings after the Bloemfontein Conference had any other purpose.[1]

On 27 September the Free State publicly threw in its lot with the Transvaal. The effect was that the Boers could place in the field a combined force of about 50,000 mounted infantry. They had rifles and ample ammunition for 80,000, and hoped to reach that figure later by enrolling Cape Dutch. Against them Great Britain had at that date in South Africa no more than 14,750 regulars. It is true that on 8 September the government had ordered up 10,000 troops from India who reached Durban on 8 October. Even then the Boers were nearly two to one, with a much greater superiority in artillery; the main British reinforcement—a field force of 47,000 men from England—not having been authorized by the cabinet till 29 September. These facts explain why, though both sides had drafted ultimatums, the Boers (on 9 October) got theirs in first; and also why the pith of it was a demand for the withdrawal of troops and stoppage of reinforcements. The priority of their ultimatum did not really imply aggression; for, if war were to be, they naturally could not wait for their enemy to reinforce himself. But the Krugerish truculence with which it was phrased gave them all the air of aggressors; and it helped enormously to consolidate opinion against them, both in Great Britain and in the colonies. The latter, to whom the mother country's championship of her overseas nationals made a special appeal, were kindled with a new solidarity, and vied in offering contingents of fighters.

[1] In particular, the episode which began on 13 August seems only intelligible on this ground.

The thirty-two months' war which followed had five successive phases, three of which fall within this chapter. The first was that of Boer invasion, which may be regarded as closing with the surrender of Cronje (27 February 1900). The second was that of organized Boer resistance to British invasion, and it ended (October 1900) with the occupation of Komati Poort and Kruger's flight into Portuguese territory. The third (which lasted till March 1901) was that in which the Boers developed guerrilla warfare, before the British had evolved any plan for meeting it.

The British disasters in the first stage would have surprised no one, had the military data been studied beforehand. But because the British army had then no general staff, and even the intelligence department at the war office was starved and made of small account, there was a complete lack of foresight on the British side. The two republics formed a large salient, walled in by mountain ranges and giving the Boers the advantage of interior lines. Outside it nearly all the country people of Cape Colony (save part of the eastern province) were Dutch, and so were the border settlers in Natal. This meant that advancing Boers need fear little for their communications, while the advantage in intelligence and facilities for surprise were always on their side. Their armies of highly mobile marksmen were ideal for the peculiar terrain, which they understood how to utilize perfectly. Their Krupp guns were far better than the types then used by the British artillery. Add their initial superiority in numbers; and the question is seen to be, not why they won battles, but why they lost the campaign. The explanation is strategical. Their right course was to contain the three immobilized British forces at Kimberley, Mafeking, and Ladysmith; hold the Natal passes defensively; and sweep Cape Colony with their main effort. Had they done so, there was little to stop them till they reached Cape-town; and with the entire country to win back and an enemy doubled by rebels, Great Britain might well have seen best to make terms, especially in view of probable foreign intervention. All this did not happen, because the Boers dallied over fruitless and unnecessary sieges of Kimberley and Ladysmith, and directed their larger effort to Natal. For the latter mistake the motive was political; they aimed to annex Durban, which would have suited them ideally as their seaport.[1]

[1] Curiously enough, the much maligned intelligence department at the war office

The first fighting was in northern Natal. Sharp actions took place at Talana Hill and Elandslaagte, and an advanced British brigade had to fall back with heavy losses on Ladysmith, the British centre of operations, where Sir George White commanded the Natal Field Force. While Transvaalers and Free Staters converged on him from three sides, White struck out, but with less than no success; the brigade on his left fell into a trap at Nicholson's Nek, where two battalions of infantry with a battery of guns had to surrender (30 October). Two days later the rest of White's force (now about 10,000 men) was completely invested in Ladysmith, though not before some indispensable naval guns had been railed into the town from Durban. But for these it would have been defenceless against the Boers' Krupps. Meanwhile two other sieges were in progress—Kimberley, where a large civil population (including Rhodes) increased the anxiety of the garrison; and Mafeking, a small town skilfully defended by a small force under Col. R. S. S. Baden-Powell. The Boers dissipated their strength most unwisely on these places; at the start no less than 10,000 under Piet Cronje invested unimportant Mafeking.

By this time the main British army was reaching Capetown with Sir Redvers Buller as commander-in-chief. The kernel was an army corps in three divisions commanded by Generals Gatacre, Clery, and Lord Methuen. Buller at once broke it up. Gatacre with a brigade was sent to the north of Cape Colony; Methuen with a large division was ordered to relieve Kimberley; and Clery with most of the rest was dispatched by sea to Natal, whither Buller himself soon followed him. Methuen was the first engaged. Pressing north he fought three actions—Belmont, Enslin, and Modder River—and won his ground each time, but each time incurred many casualties and inflicted few. Then followed 'Black Week'. On 10 December Gatacre was defeated at Stormberg, losing 719 men and two guns; on the 11th Methuen was disastrously repulsed by Cronje at Magersfontein losing about 950 men; and on the 15th Buller, advancing to the relief of Ladysmith with four brigades of infantry, a mounted brigade, and six batteries of artillery, was signally outfought by Louis Botha at Colenso on the Tugela River, and retired after losing ten guns and 1,100 men. The only son of Lord Roberts was killed in

had as early as 11 June 1896 drawn attention to the probability that this motive might govern their strategy. (Royal Commission on the South African War: *Report* (1904), p. 158.)

endeavouring to save the guns. Buller was so unnerved by his defeat that he actually signalled to White that he should surrender Ladysmith, and cabled to the cabinet proposing its abandonment. White replied that he did not intend to surrender. The cabinet's reply was to supersede Buller in the chief command. The bereaved Lord Roberts was appointed generalissimo, with Lord Kitchener as his chief of staff.

The nation was sobered, but resolute in this ordeal. Queen Victoria set a notable example. When Balfour referred to the disasters, she cut him short with: 'Please understand that there is no one depressed in *this* house; we are not interested in the possibilities of defeat; they do not exist.'[1] To meet the need for larger forces militia, yeomanry, and volunteers were invited to serve, and did so with great readiness. The colonies offered additional contingents. On 6 January 1900 the Boers committed the folly of trying to storm Ladysmith, and incurred casualties they could ill afford. Meanwhile in the north centre of Cape Colony, which they ought to have swept, two of their best leaders, Christian De Wet and De La Rey, were baffled round Colesberg by an inferior force under General French, the sole British leader to succeed thus far. Buller, reinforced by a division, made his second attempt on the Tugela; but was again badly out-manœuvred; and after losing some 1,700 men (chiefly on the tragic hill Spion Kop) retired once more (24 January 1900). A third attempt by him, at Vaal Krantz, was equally unsuccessful (5 February).

But now Roberts was moving, and at once he strikingly illustrated what genius can do to reverse a military situation. Rejecting entirely Buller's strategy of piecemeal objectives and scattered units, he organized one large force, appointed French to command the cavalry, and aimed for the heart of the Free State, Bloemfontein. First feinting as if to move by Colesberg, he achieved instead an unopposed concentration between the Orange and Modder rivers. This made the Boers suppose his objective to be Kimberley, and Cronje entrenched his men to block the route again at Magersfontein. But Roberts was content to send French with the cavalry by a long detour to relieve the diamond town; with his main force he left Cronje alone and struck east. He had scarcely begun the cross-country movement when the whole of the transport collected for it, 178 waggons, was captured by Christian De Wet (13 February). With charac-

[1] Lady G. Cecil, *Life of Salisbury*, iii (1931), 191.

teristic daring Roberts refused to be diverted; he cut down his men's rations, but pressed on. Kimberley having been relieved on 15 February, Cronje was in danger of envelopment, when he tardily left his stronghold. But French on the north headed him, and in a few days he was brought to bay. Digging himself in behind the banks of a dry river bed at Paardeberg, he bloodily repulsed a series of frontal attacks ordered by Kitchener, who was directing Roberts's advanced divisions. But the meshes of the net drew round; and, despite a bold diversion by De Wet, 4,000 Boers were still with Cronje when on 27 February he surrendered. On the following day Ladysmith was relieved, Buller's fifth attempt succeeding, where his fourth a fortnight earlier had failed.

The war now entered its second phase. The Boers were on the run, and on 13 March Roberts marched into Bloemfontein. Here he was again astride a railway; but the month was nearly out before a line of supply could be organized along it. In the interval the Boer generalissimo, Joubert, died, and was succeeded by Louis Botha, an abler man. De Wet resumed the raiding of which he proved such a master, and on 31 March at Sannah's Post ambushed a mounted brigade and some guns within a few miles of Roberts's head-quarters; soon afterwards he scored successes at two more places bewilderingly remote from each other. Delayed by these and other difficulties Roberts did not start north till 1 May; but before the end of the month he had traversed the length of the Orange Free State (which was declared annexed on 28 May), and on 31 May he entered Johannesburg. Five days later he occupied Pretoria and liberated 3,000 British war prisoners. Kruger had already left, going east down the railway which led towards Delagoa Bay. The relics of the main Transvaal army under Botha retreated east after him, and on 9 June Roberts defeated it at Diamond Hill.

The main advance of the British naturally eased the situation for them elsewhere. On 17 May after a 217 days' siege Mafeking was relieved, an event which caused more pleasure in England than any other during the war.[1] On the same day as Diamond Hill Buller invaded the Transvaal from Natal through Laing's Nek. But soon afterwards the Free State Boers, inspired by De Wet, broke out into such widespread guerrilla warfare that the main line of communication was threatened. Over a month went

---

[1] The crazy and rather unlovely carnival, by which the news was celebrated in London streets, gave rise to the word 'mafficking'.

in dealing with this, but Generals Archibald Hunter and Rundle gradually hunted the guerrillas into a corner, and on 29 July Prinsloo, with no less than 4,000 of them, surrendered. Roberts then advanced east along the Delagoa Bay railway, while Buller converged towards the Eastern Transvaal from the south. On 27 August at Bergendal the last organized Boer army (under Botha) was beaten and dispersed. On 30 August the remaining British war prisoners were freed. On 11 September Kruger crossed over into Portuguese territory; on 25 September the British occupied the last station on the railway, Komati Poort. On 25 October a formal ceremony for the annexation of the Transvaal took place at Pretoria. The war was thought to be over, and nobody imagined that more than half its duration and its cost in money (though not in lives) were yet to come. Roberts and Buller both went home. Kitchener was left, as commander-in-chief, to clear up the guerrillas.

But in November and December the Boers' new kind of war-fare flared up into a wide conflagration. De Wet (who had only just escaped capture in Prinsloo's host), Botha, Kritzinger, Hert-zog, and De La Rey each severally inflicted serious local reverses on the British. Kitchener had not sufficient mounted men. On 22 December it was announced that 30,000 more would be sent. But the queen's reign ended before any clear plan had been devised for using them.

During the South African war Great Britain felt her isolation acutely. She had no ally and scarcely a friend. It was an un-covenanted mercy that, although for thirty-two months she had, as it were, one hand tied behind her back, no group of Powers attacked her. To understand her situation we must briefly review foreign developments since the triple shock of the Cleve-land message, the Raid, and the Kruger telegram.

Anti-British tendencies in official America were largely over-come in the third year after President Cleveland's outburst through the sympathy shown towards the United States by Great Britain, alone among the European Powers, during the Spanish-American war (April–August 1898). The British attitude ren-dered impossible a collective anti-American intervention, which might else have been started by Germany and would have been widely popular on the Continent. There was a particular in-cident at Manila, where the British naval commander interposed his ships between the American and German squadrons to discourage high-handed action by the latter.

But Great Britain's standing in the Old World did not become easier with the passage of time. The other five Powers were now linked in their combinations, the Triple and the Dual Alliance; and though the terms of these were secret, and Germany in particular seems as yet to have been far from realizing the definiteness of the tie between France and Russia, they already created a problem. Two courses were possible for the isolated sixth Power, and both were tried. One was to blur the sharpness of the rival alliances by preaching and practising the Concert of Europe—six friendly Powers working together, not two rival alliances drawing apart. Another was to win a footing for Great Britain in one or other of the camps. If both efforts failed (as both at this time did), there was nothing left but to reduce the country's risks as far as possible by negotiating wide settlements of actual and potential disputes. Even that was always done at a disadvantage; which is partly why 'graceful concessions' were so much in Lord Salisbury's line.

The difficulty of making the Concert a reality had been shown since 1895 by the case of Armenia. It was further illustrated in 1897 by those of Crete and Greece. February of that year saw the landing of Colonel Vassos in Crete with 1,500 Greek troops and orders to hoist the Greek flag in defiance of Turkish sovereignty. From then until September 1898 the island was a source of perpetual trouble to the Powers, though, unlike Armenia, it was quite small and accessible, and any one of them singly could have settled it in a few days. Lord Salisbury, as representing the strongest fleet in Cretan waters, was allowed the lead. Through 1897 he preserved the Concert, but largely at the cost of its refraining from any timely action, so that in April Greece and Turkey drifted into a ridiculous war, in which a Turkish army under Edhem Pasha heavily defeated the Greeks at the Miluna Pass and occupied Thessaly. The Powers intervened to regulate the peace, and it was due to Salisbury's firmness that Turkey only obtained a very slight rectification at the Aegean end of her frontier, and the plain of Thessaly was not retroceded to her. Germany, now fixed in the role of Turkey's protector, with her late foreign minister, Marschall,[1] established as ambassador at Constantinople and soon to become all-powerful there, had

[1] Count Bülow succeeded him at the German foreign office in 1897.

adhered thus far to the Concert; but in March 1898, while the future of Crete was still undetermined, she left it, followed by Austria-Hungary. The remaining Powers continued to differ and delay, until in September a Moslem outbreak at Canea not only massacred some hundreds of Christians, but killed and wounded a few British soldiers and sailors. On that the British admiral took firm action; and two months later the four Powers ejected all Turkish troops and officials from the island. They then (November 1898) appointed Prince George of Greece to govern as high commissioner.

Germany in 1897 passed some momentous cross-roads, and took turnings which were to render it eventually impossible for either Britain or Russia to be on her side. In June Admiral Tirpitz became minister of marine, an office which he held without interruption down to the European war. Peculiarly adroit at manipulating the press and the Reichstag, and more unfailingly supported by William II than any other of his ministers, this masterful specialist incarnated the idea of creating a great German navy which should ultimately dispute sea-power with the British. The first outcome of his appointment was a Navy Law of April 1898, planning to add within 6 years 12 new battle-ships, 10 new large cruisers, and 23 new small cruisers to the modest totals of 7, 2, and 7 vessels, which Germany as yet possessed in those respective categories. Almost simultaneously she began to throw herself across the path of Russia. Her wooing of Turkey received demonstrative expression from the Kaiser during the Turco-Greek war of 1897, and in 1898 he made a sort of state journey to Constantinople, Damascus, and Jerusalem, delivering flamboyant pro-Turk and pro-Moslem speeches. Already in virtue of concessions dated 1888 and 1893 a German group (with the Deutsche Bank at its head) had built railways in Asia Minor starting from opposite Constantinople, first to Angora, and then to Konia. Vast projects were now shaped for extending the Konia line to Bagdad, and later for prolonging it to Basra, with an extension to some port on the Persian Gulf, and branches, right and left, to Aleppo, Urfa, Khanikin, and other places. This was the 'Berlin–Bagdad' scheme; and by creating a vast German belt west-to-east across Turkey, it would block the Russian dream of an expansion north-to-south into the Mediterranean. British opinion did not dislike it in the nineties, when as yet it was more obvious that it would keep the Tsar out of Constantinople than that it would let the Kaiser into the Persian Gulf. As the idea and the concessions widened by successive stages, the German interests repeatedly sought British financial participation on a minority basis; and it was not till 1903 that the last of their offers was refused.

These new ambitions of Germany on sea and land were stimulated by the rapid growth in her population, her military and industrial strength, and especially her steel output. Before 1897 was over, she launched yet another adventure. During the previous year, Tirpitz, then commanding a squadron in the Far East, had been secretly ordered to examine the Chinese coast for a site for a 'military and economic base'. He recommended the harbour of Kiao-chau, in Shantung, as the only 'unappropriated pearl' worth having.[1] In August 1897 two German missionaries were opportunely murdered in the Shantung province; and in retaliation the coveted harbour was occupied. Part of the heavy indemnity demanded was a lease of it for ninety-nine years, which China granted by treaty (5 January 1898). Germany thus gained a first-class foothold in the Far East. But she let loose the scramble for Chinese territory, which the leading scramblers had so sternly rebuked in the case of Japan two years earlier.

Lord Salisbury at this very time had on foot an approach to Russia. Tired, it may be, of depending in Egypt on a Germany, whose bullying manners became more and more insupportable,[2] and holding since as far back as 1877 that our great mistake had been to reject before the Crimean war Tsar Nicholas I's proposals for a partition of Turkey, he submitted in January 1898 a detailed offer to St. Petersburg. It was to settle all subjects of difference between the two Powers on partition lines, with a view to a full entente. The temper roused by Kiao-chau wrecked this far-seeing proposal; and Russia, who had unwillingly assented to Germany's act, seized the still more valuable harbour of Port

---

[1] A. von Tirpitz, *Erinnerungen* (1919), p. 62.

[2] This quite peculiar feature of Germany's post-Bismarck diplomacy is admitted by German historians. Cp. Erich Brandenburg, *Von Bismarck zum Weltkriege* (1924), 111: 'Die Art, wie die deutsche Politik stets sofort das gröbste Geschütz spielen liess, war den englischen Staatsmännern höchst unsympathisch. Sie waren rühigere und geschäftsmässigere Formen des diplomatischen Verkehrs gewohnt und gegen Drohungen sehr empfindlich'. So Chamberlain (J. L. Garvin, *Life*, iii. 334) observed to Salisbury in 1899: 'The policy of the German Empire since Bismarck has been always one of undisguised blackmail.' While in part it was probably parvenu arrogance (Demosthenes notes something similar about the Thebans after Leuctra), it may perhaps also have been accentuated through the personality of Holstein.

Arthur (with Ta-lien-wan added) as compensation. Great Britain thereupon, after entering a strong protest, obtained a lease of Wei-hai-wei, and France took Kwang-chau-wan in South China; but these were very far from equivalents.

Salisbury's approach to Russia was followed by the similar approach to France, which resulted in the Niger settlement, though its wider effects were spoiled by Fashoda. Otherwise all the attempts made by Great Britain to escape from her isolation during this period were in the nature of approaches to Germany. Two such were made—in 1898 and 1899. The mover in the first on the British side was Chamberlain, with whom, in this matter, the duke of Devonshire strongly sympathized. On the German side Baron Eckardstein of the German embassy played the initial part, with the ambassador, Count Hatzfeldt, continuing. Lord Salisbury consented to Chamberlain's advances, though never sanguine of their success. Probably to him, as to the duke of Devonshire, the drawbacks of isolation were most visible in China; where Lancashire risked losing one of its largest markets, if Russia or other conquering Powers absorbed the country.

Chamberlain offered a definite alliance, and the conversations lasted over most of March and April.[1] Their failure was probably made certain by the fact that the Navy Bill was then going through the German legislature. The Kaiser was infatuated with his naval programme; but, directed as it was against the British monopoly of sea-power, there would have been no case left for it, if Great Britain and Germany had become allies. In the end the British advance was both snubbed and betrayed. The talks had been held under pledge of secrecy on both sides; yet on 30 May William II, writing to the Tsar, with signal perfidy revealed their story.[2] Three days before he had written an equally wild letter to Queen Victoria, petulantly attacking her prime minister.[3]

[1] For documents see *Die Grosse Politik*, xiv (1924); Eckardstein, *Lebenserinnerungen und politische Denkwürdigkeiten* (1919)—the English version (1931) is called *Ten Years at the Court of St. James*'; and J. L. Garvin, *Life of Chamberlain*, iii (1934). Messrs. G. P. Gooch and H. Temperley's invaluable *British Documents on the Origins of the War*, which become available from 1898 onward, throw no direct light on this affair, as it was not transacted through the British foreign office; but they are indispensable for Lord Salisbury's approach to Russia.

[2] Text in Walter Goetz, *Briefe Wilhelms II. an den Zaren*, p. 309.

[3] Its text and Salisbury's defence and the queen's very able reply are all in *Queen Victoria's Letters*, III. iii (1932), 375–82.

In August Russia recalled attention to herself through the issue by Tsar Nicholas II of an invitation to all governments to take part in a conference, which should consider 'the maintenance of universal peace and a possible reduction of excessive armaments'. The result was the first Hague Conference held next year (18 May to 29 June 1899). Beyond a revision of the laws of war, its only outcome was the establishment at The Hague of a Court of Arbitration, to which disputing nations might voluntarily resort—a quite important first step. But the Russian proposal, that for five years all armies and military budgets should be limited to their existing size, received no support. Germany killed it by asking how armaments could be defined, and pointing out that Russia, without adding a man to her paper strength, could immensely increase it for practical purposes by building railways. The United States wished to propose the immunity of private property at sea, but Great Britain refused to discuss the subject.

Meanwhile, in June 1898 had arisen the hopeful chance of acquiring Delagoa Bay from Portugal. But in July Germany violently objected, with the old threat to take the anti-British side in Egypt. This destroyed the prospect; but there followed (30 August 1898) an Anglo-German treaty, in which for a hypothetical large share of the Portuguese colonies, should Portugal ever dispose of them, Germany renounced her interest in the Transvaal. Her promise did not prevent her twelve months later, as soon as the South African war became imminent, from extorting still further blackmail in the shape of a bargain abandoning British rights in Samoa. But in November 1899 the Kaiser came to Windsor for the queen's eightieth birthday, and Chamberlain launched a second time his proposal for an alliance. William II and Count Bülow affected to receive it favourably, and suggested that he should publicly advocate a triple combination of Great Britain, Germany, and the United States. Chamberlain did so in a much-criticized speech at Leicester on the day after the Kaiser's departure. But in the following week the German government allowed a fierce outcry to develop in its controlled press; and when Bülow met the Reichstag, he threw Chamberlain over.

Shortly afterwards, at the turn of the year, British cruisers seized the *Bundesrath* and two other German mail-steamers suspected of carrying contraband to the Boers. Germany was prompt with her bullying protests, phrased even more offensively than usual. The British government quickly gave satisfaction, but the incident was exploited in lurid fashion by Bülow and Tirpitz to win support for a new Navy Bill. This measure (passed 12 June 1900) actually doubled the scale of naval strength adopted two years before, and eventually, though not immediately, played a decisive part in worsening Anglo-German relations.

For the time they were good, to the extent at least that repeated suggestions by Russia for a pro-Boer intervention were not entertained in Berlin. And later in 1900 events caused Germany to give, as it were, hostages to Great Britain. An anti-foreign movement broke out in China; where the so-called 'Boxers' murdered the German minister in Pekin, and besieged the rest of the foreign diplomatic corps in their legations. An international relief force was organized with contingents from all the Powers. Japan, Russia, France, and Britain could each draw on forces from areas relatively near; and it was in fact the British and Japanese who first relieved the legations. The Kaiser, as having been especially insulted, burned to send a strong representation of the German army; but it would have to go from Europe, dependent on British coaling-stations and within the power of the British navy. Eventually he did send a large contingent,[1] which, though too late to help in the relief, took very severe punitive measures. This situation not only secured Great Britain for the time against any risks from Germany, but it led to an Anglo-German Convention (16 October 1900) to restrain foreign territorial aggression in China and maintain the 'open door' for trade. Early in December 1900 President Kruger, who had come to Europe seeking support for the Boers, and had been officially received in Paris by President Loubet, went to Germany expecting a similar welcome. He was notified that the emperor would not receive him—a rebuff which went far to blight his prospects.

Thus it was that Great Britain passed through the most dangerous phases of the South African war without being subjected to a foreign intervention, which public opinion in France, Germany, and Russia alike would have overwhelmingly approved.

[1] Under the veteran field-marshal, Count von Waldersee, who was made nominal generalissimo of the international contingents.

Within the empire these closing years of the queen's reign witnessed two developments of high importance. One was the voluntary dispatch of contingents to South Africa by all the self-governing colonies outside it. They were sent the more enthusiastically, because the issue at stake in the war, as the colonies conceived it, was whether Great Britain should stand up for her overseas nationals. The only case in which there was any holding back at first was Canada, where there was some disposition among French Canadians to ask whether a British war was necessarily a Canadian one. The prime minister, Sir Wilfrid Laurier, being himself a French Canadian, could not ignore this feeling, but ultimately helped towards overcoming it. Canada sent from first to last about 8,400 men; the Australian colonies, 16,463; and New Zealand, by herself, no less than 6,000. Thirty thousand volunteers were raised in South Africa; but the Schreiner government at Capetown, kept in office by Dutch votes, gave no help. Its negative, though legal, attitude exasperated Milner, who wanted the home government to suspend it. Chamberlain very wisely refused.

The other development was the federation of Australia, which was completed when the British parliament passed the Commonwealth of Australia Act 1900. The coming together of the six Australian colonies had been advocated with growing momentum since 1883. Its motives were nationalist. Australians felt that they would be a greater people if they faced the world as a combined continent; they felt, too, that they would have more security against possible European aggression, such as they fancied to be foreshadowed by France's presence in Tahiti and Germany's in Papua. Further, they wanted a continental government to deal with the problems of their tropical north, which was too vast for any single colony to tackle, while its suitability for Asiatic colonization menaced the ideal of a white Australia. Homogeneous as the Australians were in language, blood, law, institutions and traditions, a unitary rather than a federal solution might have been thought natural. But, apart from the question of its size, the country had been settled and organized in colonies each separately approached from the sea; and there was extremely little trade or intercourse between them. Accordingly a system of true federalism was set up, with federal and state parliaments alike, and important functions for the governments responsible to each. A Zollverein, which elsewhere has often preceded and paved the way for a federation, was here included as its corollary. Conceivably the scheme would have worked better in the long run had the states each retained their tariff freedom.

The constitution had been drafted by the Australian federal convention (1897–8) and by negotiations between the six Australian governments. There was no question of the parliament at Westminster wishing to teach them their business; yet a point for dispute was found, concerning the right of final appeal to the judicial committee of the privy council. The act which federated Canada in 1867 had retained it, and the chief justices of the Australian colonies all desired its retention now. But the Australian statesmen did not, and they refused to admit any amendment of their draft. A compromise was finally reached, providing that the appeal should be retained, 'except in the cases where Australian interests alone are concerned'. Obviously centrifugalism had the best of this bargain, and the chance (for what it was worth) of developing a supreme court for the whole empire disappeared. The queen signed the Commonwealth Act on 9 July 1900—a memorable date even in so great a career as that then nearing its close.

Domestic interests languished in parliament during these years; save the London Government Act,[1] there is scarcely a statute of any note after 1897. May 1898 brought (in his 89th year) the death of Gladstone. His last illness was painful, but its prolongation summoned sympathy and gratitude from all over the world, and silenced for a while the peculiar bitterness with which party rancour had assailed him since 1886. Salisbury and Balfour pronounced memorable orations over an opponent, with whom each had in private not a little in common.[2] Yet the national mourning for him carried no political repercussion; the aged prophet had indeed 'died in his enemies' day'. Both its creeds affronted his; not only the militant imperialism then rising towards its war climax, but the collectivism, whose less noisy, yet deeper, currents were destined ere long to carry politics into a new ocean. To-day, as we gaze backward into the nineteenth century, we see some British statesmen with greater gifts for constructive policy than his. But we see no parliamentarian equal

[1] p. 297 below.
[2] Salisbury shared in particular his devoted churchmanship; Balfour (who in early life seemed not far from becoming his son-in-law), much else.

to him, and no public financier superior; nor any man in the high places of state who possessed a richer culture of mind and soul, or had a deeper perception of what the dignity of human nature consisted in. The house of commons did for him much, but he also did much for the house of commons; as Balfour very truly said on this occasion, 'he raised in the public estimation the whole level of our proceedings'. There have been potent figures in that assembly since; but none has known how to rivet, as he and Disraeli did, the attention of the whole country from day to day.

In 1900 two very important events occurred—the foundation of the labour party in February, and a general election in early October, at which the unionists renewed their mandate for another term of years. We saw in the previous chapter, how in January 1893 the 'Independent Labour Party' was formed, and how, although christened a 'party', it never became much more than a socialist propaganda-society—one among others, though the most popular. The body formed in 1900 was not so ambitiously christened, and did not assume its present name until 1906. But it was, from the start, a party in the real sense. Far more than the I.L.P., it was what Keir Hardie, the I.L.P.'s first leader, had been aiming at since 1887. Yet without the I.L.P.'s preparation of the ground, it could scarcely have come into being; and for many years afterwards the two bodies played parts complementary to each other. The great lock-out of engineers in 1897 had been followed in 1898 by the election of G. N. Barnes, a member of the I.L.P., to be general secretary of the Amalgamated Society of Engineers, then still the premier trade union. Other I.L.P. men were becoming prominent in the Trade Union Congress about the same time; and the startling performance of the German socialists in the 1898 Reichstag elections (where they polled 3 million votes and won 50 seats) was also not unnoticed. So in 1899 the congress by resolution decided to call a conference of delegates from 'Co-operative, Socialistic, Trade Union, and other working-class organizations' to 'devise ways and means for the securing of an increased number of Labour members in the next Parliament'. The co-operators could not come, but delegates of the three socialist societies and over half a million trade unionists conferred (27–28 February 1900) in London at the Memorial Hall in Farringdon Street. What they set up was called the 'Labour Representation Committee' (L.R.C.); its secretary was an I.L.P. delegate,

J. Ramsay MacDonald; and on its membership special representation was secured for the socialist as well as the trade-union bodies.[1] Deeply significant was the consent of the unions to a levy, even though only of 'Ios. per annum for every 1,000 members or fraction thereof'. An amendment carried by G. N. Barnes helped the socialists by enacting that candidates to be run for parliament need not be working-men, provided they were 'sympathetic with the needs and demands of the Labour movements', and their candidatures were promoted by an affiliated body. A still more vital amendment was that carried by Keir Hardie, defining what the committee was to aim at. It was to establish 'a distinct Labour Group in Parliament, who shall have their own Whips and agree upon their policy, which must embrace a readiness to co-operate with any party which for the time being may be engaged in promoting legislation in the direct interest of Labour, and be equally ready to associate themselves with any party in opposing measures having an opposite tendency'; further, no member of the group must oppose an L.R.C. candidate. This resolution was remarkable both for its omissions and its stipulations. On the one hand it made a clean departure from the socialist habit of relying on the adoption of dogmas, and left the party free to shape its policy as it went along. On the other, they were to have whips of their own and be quite distinct from the unionist and liberal parties, with or against either of whom they must be willing to work impartially, as the 'direct interest of Labour' might dictate. Keir Hardie had prophesied since the eighties, that a living party thus acting together in parliament would focus labour aspirations in a way that no amount of theoretic propaganda could do. The future was to prove him right.

The new body had not time to do much in the 1900 elections, and only returned two candidates to parliament. Keir Hardie was one. The other, Richard Bell of the Amalgamated Society of Railway Servants,[2] was really a liberal, but his union insisted on his running under 'L.R.C.' auspices. The next year, however, was to raise an unexpected issue, than which none could have been devised more apt to give the new body life.

The same month which saw the birth of the L.R.C., witnessed

[1] On a committee of twelve the socialist bodies had five seats, though the trade union membership represented was about twenty times theirs—a remarkable recognition by the trade unions that it was not sufficient merely to count heads.

[2] Precursor of the National Union of Railwaymen, which absorbed also some smaller societies. See below, p. 300.

the reunion of the Parnellites and the anti-Parnellites at Westminster. All the groups of Irish nationalists combined under the leadership of John Redmond. The full effects were not felt at once. Sympathy with home rule had fallen to a low ebb in Great Britain, and nationalist glee over Boer victories sent it still lower.

The general election of early October was the work of Chamberlain. History knows it as the 'Khaki' election, because the dissolution was quite frankly an attempt to capitalize the emotions of military victory in terms of votes for the government. High-minded students of politics, irrespective of party, were inclined at the time to regret it, as derogating from the best traditions of fair play in the English political game. But the precedent was followed in 1918, and perhaps always must be in similar circumstances. If it was new in Chamberlain's day, one may reply that such circumstances had not previously arisen since the franchise was democratized. The nearest parallel was the situation when Lord Beaconsfield returned from the Berlin Conference; and the results of his omitting to dissolve then can scarcely have been absent from his successor's mind. The real drawback to the Chamberlain procedure is, that ministers seeking a mandate on a sole 'Khaki' issue cannot afterwards claim one for contentious measures in other fields. This may not prevent their adopting them, but electoral resentment is apt to accumulate if they do, with such consequences as were seen in 1906 and 1922. Already in 1900 the unionist administration was not popular; its majority had fallen from 152 to 128 since it took office. Even Khaki failed to recover more than three seats on balance.

After the election Lord Salisbury reconstructed his government. Now near the end of his 71st year and ageing rapidly, he at last gave up the foreign office. Lord Lansdowne succeeded him there, with happy results; and the war office was transferred to St. John Brodrick, the hero of the cordite amendment, which had turned out the Rosebery cabinet in 1895. Another veteran, Goschen, left the ministry altogether, and his place at the admiralty was filled by Lord Selborne.[1] Among half a dozen other changes, C. T. Ritchie became home secretary, and George Wyndham became Irish secretary without a seat in the cabinet.

[1] The second earl, son of the famous lord chancellor, whom he succeeded in 1895. B. 1859; educated at Winchester and University College, Oxford; undersecretary for the colonies, 1895–1900; first lord of the admiralty 1900–5; high commissioner for South Africa, 1905–10. He was Lord Salisbury's son-in-law.

Wyndham was the most brilliant young conservative who had appeared since Balfour, but he was not destined to be equally fortunate.

Queen Victoria saw the century out, but died on 22 January 1901. The war probably shortened her life, for she devoted much energy to its tasks—visiting wounded, comforting widows, seeing off regiments, counselling courage and energy to her ministers and generals, and handling with equal tact and firmness her difficult grandson, the German Emperor. She showed herself again in London, and in April she even visited Ireland and stayed twenty-two days at the Viceregal Lodge. She had been moved thereto by the prowess of her Irish regiments, and she was well received; though so late a visit could scarcely undo the effects of her long years of absence from Irish soil. All these exertions told on her; in the summer her health began to fail; and for the rest of the year she suffered increasingly from insomnia and repulsion for food, though as late as mid-November she reviewed colonial troops.

The shock of her death struck the nation at a dark hour, when it had just discovered that the war, presumed to have been won, was still not in sight of an ending. Men felt that a great epoch had closed. The sky of England had been clouding for years before; what with the collapse of the country-side, the new-born social unrest in the towns, the waning of religious faith, and above all the sense of an uncontrollable transition to the unknown—the feeling that the keys of power were blindly but swiftly transferring themselves to new classes, new types of men, new nations. The queen's death focused it all. It is true that few credited her with much influence in state affairs; her grasp and capacity in that hidden field were as much underrated by the general public as those of her son were overrated afterwards. But the reverence with which her subjects had come to regard her was a real factor in their lives. In a degree unapproached by any of her predecessors save Queen Elizabeth, she had made herself a national talisman.

IX

ECONOMICS AND INSTITUTIONS 1886–1900

FOR the period under review in this chapter the populations of the western Powers were measured by two sets of censuses —those of 1890–1 and 1900–1. The processes of change, which we noted at work before in the vital matter of their relative man-power, were stretched very much further. The first set gave the following results:

United States (1890)	62·6 millions
Germany (1891)	49·4 ,,
United Kingdom (1891)	38·1 ,,
Great Britain, 33 millions	
Ireland, 4·7 millions	
France (1891)	38·3 ,,
Italy (1891)[1]	30·3 ,,

But ten years later the showing was still more drastic in the same senses:

United States (1900)	75·9 millions
Germany (1900)	56·3 ,,
United Kingdom (1901)	41·9 ,,
Great Britain, 37 millions	
Ireland, 4·4 millions	
France (1901)	38·9 ,,
Italy (1901)	32·4 ,,

What here most leaped to every eye, was the tiny absolute increase, and consequent relative decline, of France. Her figures were even lower than the tables show, for on both occasions her enumeration included much over a million foreign residents, not available for military service and some other purposes. People began seriously asking whether she would not before long have to be written off as a Great Power. When Lord Salisbury in a celebrated speech of 1898 alluded to 'dying nations' (for which term probably Turkey and China were the chief candidates in his mind), it is significant that a great many people on the Continent took him as referring to France, and Paris protested loudly on that assumption.

On the other side, Germany's increase seemed to pursue its course unabated, and by 1901 her numerical military superiority over France had become absolutely crushing. Consciousness of this had a marked psychological effect. From 1871 down almost to Bismarck's dismissal in 1890, her first pre-occupation had been

---

[1] Estimated; no census was taken between 1881 and 1901.

the risk of losing a return duel with France. But it now became obvious that that Power alone could never again stand up to her. The minds and hands of the Wilhelmstrasse were freed to incur risks with others. Thus while the Iron Chancellor had made it his first principle to preserve harmony with Russia and, subject to it only, sought also the friendship of England, the emperor who dismissed him had by 1898, as we have seen, adopted two new and grandiose policies bound in the long run severally and simultaneously to antagonize both Powers.

The increase within the British Isles, though by 1890 it had carried their native population past that of France (a thing that would have seemed unbelievable in any previous century), appeared nevertheless modest beside Germany's. This was due to the continuance of an actual decrease in Ireland. In the second half of the nineteenth century the population of Great Britain went up from 20·8 millions to 37 millions, but that of Ireland went down from 6·5 millions to 4·3 millions. As suggested before, this had a bearing on home rule; which at the middle of the century would have meant putting nearly a quarter of the people of the United Kingdom under a Dublin parliament, but at the end, less than one-ninth.

But in England and Wales, which now had become numerically, at all events, so very much the predominant partner in the Kingdom, the growth of population, though still exceedingly rapid, had assumed a totally new character. The birth-rate was falling continuously, but a fall in the death-rate more or less kept pace with it. We noted the beginning of this process in Chapter IV, but it now became much more marked. A table will best exhibit it.

| | Average Annual Rate per 1,000 | | |
Quinquennium	Births	Deaths	Natural Increase
1871-5 . .	35·5	22·0	13·5
1886-90 . .	31·4	18·9	12·5
1891-5 . .	30·5	18·7	11·8
1896-1900 .	29·3	17·7	11·6

If we take the decade 1891-1900 we shall find that the 'natural increase', here shown as a rate per thousand, yielded an average figure for England and Wales of 357,977 additional persons every year. The net population did not rise to that extent, because of migration, which in the same period took away an annual average of 109,585 persons. Of these, it is worth noting, 60,023 went to the United States; 15,974 to Canada and Newfoundland (a good many of whom would soon pass into the United States); and only 10,319 to Australia and New Zealand put together. So much stronger was the American magnet than any other.

Most authorities are now agreed that by far the largest (though not the sole[1]) cause of the fall in the English birth-rate since 1877 was that people learned to use contraceptives. If (as certainly was the case) the first to learn were the more educated classes, and if the practice only gradually worked its way down into the working classes, being earliest adopted by those of them (such as textile workers) among whom there was a large amount of remunerative employment for married women, we should expect to find any fall in the birth-rate due to it distributed unequally over the community in accordance with this unequal progress of the new factor. Data to discover statistically, whether this had really occurred, were not available before the census of 1911; but a return then obtained enabled the relative fertility of marriages in different classes and among certain main groups of workers to be ascertained for the previous fifty years. The accompanying table exhibits some of the results worked out on this basis by Dr. T. H. C. Stevenson,[2] then Superintendent of Statis-

Total fertility of marriages in various classes at various dates, as measured by the total of births, and expressed in percentages of the corresponding rates for all classes jointly.

Date of Marriage	Upper and Middle Class	Higher Intermediate Class	Skilled Workmen	Lower Intermediate Class	Unskilled Workmen	Textile Workers	Miners	Agricultural Labourers
1851–61	89	99	101	99	103	94	108	105
1886–91	74	87	100	101	112	90	126	114
1891–96	74	88	99	101	113	88	127	115
1896–1901	76	89	99	101	114	86	125	114

tics at the General Register Office. The first horizontal line of figures maps the distribution of fertility among the various classes

[1] Another cause, e.g. was the tendency among women to defer marriage to a later age than before. This also affected the professional more than the working classes, and among the latter those in trades of predominantly female employment.

[2] See especially his long paper in the *Journal of the Royal Statistical Society*, vol. lxxxiii (1920), pp. 401–444. The above table is extracted from the fuller one given by him at p. 416.

in pre-contraceptive days. Contrary to frequent conjecture, we see that the differences in fertility were then inconsiderable, apart from a material deficiency in the highest class and a much smaller one among the textile workers. But the other lines[1] show the development for the first time of a very marked class differences, corresponding closely to the spread of contraceptive practices. The more successful and prosperous classes fell rapidly behind in their contribution to the future personnel of the nation. Such a strong and growing tendency to non-survival among the fittest stocks is not known to have before occurred in England, at any rate since the Reformation.

Apart from its ultimate eugenic bearings, it showed psychological and social effects almost at once. Members of the professional and business classes marrying within the nineteenth century had normally been brought up in large families, seven or eight being usual numbers, and only higher ones attracting attention. But from about 1890 they did not themselves, as a rule, intend to have more than two, or at most three, children.[2] It meant that for the average young man in these classes the upbringing of a family became less of a principal life-task; it did not strain his energies so rigorously and exhaustively as before: more margin was left for personal luxuries, and for distractions from work; the 'pace' might quicken, but the 'drive' slackened; actual office-hours tended to shorten, and at the very end of the century room began to be made for week-ends. It also meant smaller houses, smaller rooms, smaller tables for meals. The diminution in scale was not so great as it has since become; but if you compare the houses built for married members of the educated and professional classes in the nineties with those built for their parents in the mid-Victorian decades, it is very unmistakable. The tendency was encouraged by a rapid falling-off in the supply of domestic servants. This began in the eighties and during the nineties became acute. Domestic servants are in all countries and for obvious reasons drawn almost entirely from the countryside; and their supply depends on the balance between rural and urban population, which in England, as we shall see, had by now become thoroughly inverted.

[1] The slightly less differentiation in the last line may be explained by the fact that marriages contracted in the latter years had not by 1911 had time to develop their differences fully.

[2] The designed restriction to a one-child family, which is now so common, scarcely occurred till two decades later.

When the 1901 census was being taken, Chamberlain had the idea of ordering, on the basis of contemporary colonial and imperial censuses, a tabulation for the whole British empire. Owing to the counts in South Africa being postponed (in consequence of the war there) until 1904, this was not completed and published till 1906. But with that exception it represents things as they stood at the death of the queen. The white population of the empire was shown to be 54 millions; which was, it will be seen, 2·3 millions below the total recorded for Germany in the previous year. Australia had 3·8 millions; New Zealand, 816,214; and British North America, 5·6 millions. Canadians in 1866 had forecast to Dilke that their population would be 10 millions within 10 years; here it was, 34 years later, at only just over half that figure. The main reason was the suction and superior attraction exerted by the United States. The natives of Canada enumerated there by the 1900 census were no less than 1,181,255, while only 127,899 natives of the United States were enumerated in Canada. It was this drain of population which led Canadian statesmen at imperial conferences from 1894 onwards to press their demand for imperial preference. They saw that a manufacturer, e.g. in Buffalo, U.S.A., had privileged access behind a tariff to 75 million customers inhabiting the United States, while a similar manufacturer in Toronto would only have similar privileges in regard to 5·4 million customers in Canada itself. Their idea was to make competition between the two less unequal by enlarging the Toronto man's privileged market to include Great Britain, and, if possible, the whole empire. Their weak point was that they had already given him protection, not only against the United States, but against Great Britain. And while he firmly refused to forgo this, there was no chance of forming a real British Zollverein on all fours with the American and German ones.

Aggregate wealth in Great Britain still grew fast, but less fast than before. We saw in Chapter IV that Sir Robert Giffen computed its total in 1885 at £10,037 millions. That estimate was based on the income-tax returns for 1884–5; and an estimate for 1895, identically computed on the income-tax returns of ten years later, shows a total of £11,393 millions.[1] Giffen himself by the same method had reached totals for 1865 and 1875 of £6,114

---

[1] Fabian Tract No. 7, 5th edition (1896): the work of Sydney (now Lord) Olivier.

millions and £8,548 millions respectively. A simple subtraction infers, on these four figures, that our wealth grew by £2,434 millions in the decade following 1865; by £1,531 millions in the decade following 1875; and by only £1,314 millions in the decade following 1885. Remembering that the increment is not a percentage but an absolute figure, one might have expected it to keep on expanding in proportion as it had a fast-widening field of population and industry to grow on. Its actual shrinkage is certainly remarkable, even allowing for the falling price-levels of the period.

A brighter light on some of the facts and problems involved is thrown for the years covered in this chapter by a famous Blue Book[1] of 1903, which, in endeavouring to review the trade development of Great Britain and her principal rivals since the middle of the nineteenth century, found the fullest statistical evidence available from about 1880 onwards. Its findings were in some respects re-assuring. It showed that during the forty years 1860–1900 the mass of British workers had very substantially improved their economic position. The index-number representing the general price-level in the United Kingdom stood at the same figure in 1860, 1871, and 1878. Expressing this figure as 100, we find that between 1860 and 1871 it fluctuated but slightly; that between 1871 and 1878 it rose to and fell from a sudden peak of 119 in 1873; but that after 1878 it zigzagged heavily down to a zero of 70 in 1896, from which it only rose to 83 in 1900 at the peak of the South African war. Conversely in the case of wages, if the figure representing the general wage-level in 1900 be expressed as 100, we find that wages in 1860 were only 68 per cent. of it, while in 1875 and again in 1890 they were 90 per cent. Between 1860 and 1875 they rose gradually with a high peak of 96 in 1873; but between 1875 and 1890 they sank again, and fluctuated a little above or below 85 for most of the fifteen years. From 1890 to 1897 the figure kept close to 90; but it made the climb to 100 by steady rises during the last three years of the century. It is natural to attribute at least part of the improvement in money wages from 1890 onwards to the successful London Dock Strike in 1889 and the numerous other 'pros-

[1] *Memoranda, Statistical Tables, and Charts prepared in the Board of Trade with reference to various matters bearing on British and Foreign Trade and Industrial Conditions* (Cd. 1761); edited by Mr. (now Sir) H. Llewellyn Smith. Ordered in connexion with the fiscal controversy described below in Chapter XI, it is generally known as the *Fiscal Blue Book* of 1903.

perity' strikes during the decade which followed it. If we combine the price and wage movements together in order to find the movement of 'real' wages (i.e. of wages in terms of what money would buy), we may calculate that as between 1860 and 1900 they had improved about 77 per cent. Roughly a quarter of this forty-year progress was made in the last ten years. Comparing 1860 and 1890 the improvement in 'real' wages at the latter date works out at about 57·5 per cent.

The position disclosed in regard to the country's chief industries and markets was by no means so favourable. Whereas in the mid-Victorian period Great Britain's exports had consisted chiefly of manufactured articles, the sales of her leading lines in these were now stationary or falling off; largely in consequence of the hostile tariffs which protectionist policy was deliberately setting up against her in one country after another. Baffled thus she was paying her way by greatly increased exports of machinery (which would subsequently enable the foreigner to do without her manufactures), of ships (which would enable him to do without her shipping), and of coal (i.e. of an irreplaceable natural asset, yielding her far greater economic advantage if used for her own steamers, blast-furnaces, and factories than when shipped in a crude state to run those of other nations). Plainly such were makeshifts, and no permanent programme for a 'workshop of the world'.

The accompanying table[1] reveals the situation.

Value of certain principal classes of British Exports

(In thousand £)

	To All Countries		To Ten Principal Protected Countries	
	1880	*1900*	*1880*	*1900*
Cotton Goods	75,564	69,751	15,990	13,840
Woollen and Worsted	21,488	21,806	13,526	11,475
Linen	6,814	6,159	4,895	4,052
Iron, Steel, and other Metals . .	32,000	37,638	17,626	15,171
Machinery and Mill Work . . .	9,264	19,620	5,797	10,892
Coal, Coke, &c.	8,373	38,620	4,822	23,349

Here we see, legible enough, the early effects of rising foreign

---

[1] Based on pp. 23-4 of the *Fiscal Blue Book* (Cd. 1761 of 1903). Figures for exported ships and boats are not available; they were only brought into the returns from the year 1899, in which they already stood at the high level of £9,897,000.

tariffs upon Great Britain's trade. They markedly reduced within their areas the sales of her textiles and similar consumable manufactured goods. On the other hand they stimulated the demand for her coal and machinery. Foreigners who were starting new factories behind tariff walls, required machines to equip them with; and down to 1900 they came chiefly to England for them. Where (as in Italy and Spain and the Baltic) they lacked coal, they would buy her coal too. Given this demand for machinery abroad, it naturally paid her to supply it rather than leave it to be supplied by others. And machines in themselves were a lucrative export, embodying more skilled labour in proportion to material than the rails relied on by the mid-Victorians. Yet there was this profound difference. Every time we built a railway abroad, we could expect more trade as its sequel. But every time we sold a machine, we must look for less. We were equipping our customers to cease buying from us.

The tariffs which wrought these effects were not then of long standing. Substantially the whole change falls within the last quarter of the century; and it was in particular from the eighties onward that the consequences came home to British trade. Germany first made her tariff really protectionist in 1879. Russia followed with general increases in 1881 and 1882; France and Austria-Hungary in 1882. In the ensuing years one country after another built its walls still higher—in 1884, Russia and Switzerland; in 1885, Germany; in 1887, Russia and Austria-Hungary; in 1888, Italy. American policy fluctuated a little according to the party in power, but the McKinley tariff of 1890 and the Dingley tariff of 1897 placed the United States among the most highly protected nations. Our own colonies fell in with the tendency. Canada and Victoria adopted high tariffs in 1879; and though New South Wales remained on free trade till 1900, an early result of the Commonwealth Act of that year was to make the whole of Australia protectionist.

Comparing British basic industries with those of the United States and Germany, we find that in 1900 at the end of the period the United Kingdom raised 225 million tons of coal, the United States 240, and Germany 107.[1] The American output had passed the British for the first time in the previous year, but we still raised more than double Germany's. Part of the reason lay in our mounting coal exports. These had now a special justification,

---

[1] A. D. Webb, *New Dictionary of Statistics* (1911), p. 86.

since they furnished our ships with bulky outward cargoes corresponding to the bulky imports of grain, timber, and forage, which our swollen population and ruined countryside combined to render necessary. And for them we retained two decisive advantages—the nearness of our coalfields to the sea and the excellence of our steam-coal for bunkering ships. It was otherwise with the iron and steel industry. There our last special advantage had disappeared with the discovery of the Gilchrist-Thomas process, recorded in Chapter IV; and the accompanying table[1] tells the story of our sinking to third place. We continued,

Steel Production

(In thousands of tons)

Years	United Kingdom	Germany	France	U.S.A.
1890	3,579	2,195	670	4,275
1896	4,133	4,745	1,160	5,282
1900	4,901	6,260	1,540	10,188

it is true, for a little longer to lead Germany in the production of pig-iron; it was not till 1903 that she passed us there also. But considering the primacy, which steel had by 1900 attained as the universal material for rails, engines, ships, metal bridges, tools, machines, guns, armour, and engineering generally, the fact that two other countries alone produced much more than three times the British steel output implies a quite fundamental departure from the economic relation between our island and the rest of the world, as it had been in the heyday of the Victorian 'workshop'. Nor was our recession in scale only. Germany and the United States made their steel with newer, larger, more efficient units of plant than ours, and fairly outclassed us under most aspects. In 1900 we imported 283,075 tons of German, Belgian, and American steel;[2] in 1902, 533,808 tons; and the amount grew fast later.

The Lancashire cotton industry remained our largest single source of export. But the change in its outlook was becoming fundamental. It may be seen from the altered figures[3] for consumption of raw cotton by manufacturers.

[1] Figures from the same, p. 353.

[2] The return includes an unspecified but probably small amount of manufactured iron.

[3] From p. 443 of the *Fiscal Blue Book* (Cd. 1761 of 1903), which based them on Messrs. Ellison & Co.'s *Annual Review of the Cotton Trade*.

Consumption of Raw Cotton: Annual Averages

(In millions of lb.)

Years	Great Britain	Continent of Europe	United States
1871-5	1,228·6	856·6	524·7
1896-1900	1,686·5	2,251·9	1,572·1

Plainly there was ceasing to be a market for British cotton piece-goods either in Europe or in the United States; and in fact by 1900 our shippers were driven to rely overwhelmingly (save for the finer counts) on the markets of India, China, and the Levant. It only needed that Asia should develop cotton-mills in her turn (she had already started), for Lancashire to reach the predicament which was in fact reached twenty years later. Wool fared better, because a more considerable part of our woollen cloth exports were (and still are) of a class bought by foreigners from motives of fashion and luxury, and capable thus of over-leaping even the high tariff-walls of the United States. British consumption of raw wool rose from an annual average of 307 million lb. in 1870-4 to one of 715·6 million lb. in 1895-9—a strikingly greater proportionate expansion than in the case of cotton.

Shipbuilding remained one of our most progressive industries; but from the accompanying table it will be noticed how the proportion built for export rose from the eighties onward. Steel now superseded all other materials; as early as 1887 out of 289,000 tons of new steamers, 257,000 were steel-built. No great change

Tonnage of Shipping Built in the U.K.: Annual Averages

Years	For British Owners	For Foreign Owners
1870-4	396,380	67,129
1875-9	399,929	35,612
1880-4	567,663	101,400
1885-9	431,950	83,732
1890-4	617,061	118,508
1895-9	593,454	176,298

developed in the character of up-to-date merchant vessels during the years 1885-1900; though there was a constant tendency to increase their size, and in the late nineties German high-class passenger liners made their competition felt. In 1897 the North German Lloyd steamer *Kaiser Wilhelm der Grosse* took away the

Atlantic 'blue ribbon' from the Cunarders who were holding it at the time[1]—it had always hitherto been held by British-built ships. In 1894 Sir Charles Parsons, inventor of the turbine, had a small vessel fitted with a turbine engine; but the extended use of such engines for shipping did not begin till about ten years later.

Great Britain succeeded in retaining to the end of the century a very large proportion of the world's carrying trade. The accompanying table is only for vessels entering or cleared at British ports, but it supplies a fair index of the state of things.[2] We see reflected in it a British preponderance, that culminated in 1888, and only a slight relative decline afterwards. Thus the island kept its unique lead on the seas long after it had lost it in the factories.

Proportion per cent. of British to Total Shipping Entered and Cleared in the Foreign Trade of the United Kingdom

Years	Entries	Clearances
1880–4	71·7	71·6
1885–9	73·1	73·2
1890–4	72·4	72·3
1895–9	70·5	71·1

Internal transport underwent little change. The great Forth Bridge was completed in 1889. But only one conspicuous railway extension belongs to these years—the bringing to London of the Manchester, Sheffield, and Lincoln Railway (re-christened the Great Central Railway, and now forming the most westerly section of the L.N.E.R.) and the opening for it (March 1899) of the last metropolitan terminus, Marylebone. The same year saw the amalgamation of two railways, which till then had competed for the traffic of Kent—both non-paying concerns and heavily over-capitalized. They were the least profitable and least efficient lines running into London, but their complaint was one from which virtually all British railways suffered in some degree. On account of it their rates, both for passengers and goods, were much higher than those elsewhere in Europe—a

---

[1] The *Campania* and *Lucania*, of not quite 13,000 tons each and good for 22 knots. The German ship was of 14,350 tons, did 23 knots, and beat their records by handsome margins. Her successors, the *Kronprinz Wilhelm* (1901) and *Kaiser Wilhelm II* (1902), carried German superiority still farther.

[2] *Fiscal Blue Book* (Cd. 1761 of 1903), p. 432.

serious handicap to business, but one from which there was
ordinarily no escape. Road competition in pre-motor days could
not amount to much;[1] though the surfaces of main roads were
notably improved after the county councils took them over.

It was partly, though not entirely, as a revolt against railways
that there was carried out now one of the two or three greatest
engineering works in all Britain—the Manchester Ship Canal.
Started in the year of Queen Victoria's first Jubilee, it was opened
by her in May 1894. A channel navigable to ocean-going ships
had to be cut across thirty-six miles of country from the Mersey
estuary to inland docks on the outskirts of the city. The vast project, resisted by Liverpool, was undertaken by a company to
which every one in the Manchester area subscribed as a matter of
local patriotism. But its finance was miscalculated, and it would
have come to a standstill had not the Manchester Corporation in
1890 advanced £5 millions on debenture. Decades passed before
any return came to the shareholders. But the benefit to the city
was almost immediate; within a few years it ranked among the
principal British ports. Trafford Park, adjoining the new docks,
became after 1900 a great industrial area.

Street traction for passengers in the growing cities of Europe
and America was being greatly improved during these years.
But the inventions were not British, and in general our cities
were behind the Continent in adopting them. The first system to
supersede horses was that of cable haulage for trams. This was
a simple but efficient American invention, which came to Great
Britain in 1884. The chief towns adopting it were Birmingham
and Edinburgh, and at the latter it could be seen working not
unsatisfactorily till far on in the present century. Next came the
electric tram, pioneered by the Siemens firm of Berlin,[2] which
gave public demonstrations of it in 1879, and opened the first
regular service at Lichterfelde in 1881. The first installation in
the United Kingdom was the Portrush Electric Railway in
Ireland (Siemens, 1883). But it remained largely experimental
till the early nineties, when two types, the trolley and the conduit, came to be adopted very widely in Germany, the Low

---

[1] There was some; e.g. the G.P.O. sent its mails to Oxford (52 miles) by horsed
vans in preference to paying the railway terms.

[2] In the ensuing years there was some rivalry between German and American
inventors about patents in this field; and in 1880 Edison at Menlo Park made a
small electric locomotive pull a trailer. But Siemens's forms proved the more
practical.

Countries, and the United States. By about 1897 such cities as
Brussels, Frankfurt, Cologne, and Berlin had grown well accustomed to using swift and convenient electric trams; while even
progressive Manchester kept its horses till after 1900, and backward London had nothing else on its council tramways north
of the Thames till 1905.

Another use of electric traction was for deep-lying underground
railways. These were pioneered in America. The first in England was the old South London Tube between the City and
Stockwell, opened as far back as 1890, with very narrow carriages
in a tiny tunnel. But the first to win real prestige was the Central
London Railway (1900), which struck the imagination of Londoners more, perhaps, than any transport change since railways
themselves.

An invention of even greater moment was being worked out in
Germany, France, and the United States. In 1885–6 a German,
Gottfried Daimler, patented the high-speed internal combustion
engine, which may be considered to have set the motor industry
moving. In 1894 the Panhard car designed in France by Levas-
sor provided the first pattern of the modern automobile, with
vertical engine in front under a bonnet and the main controls
arranged much as now. England took no share in the pioneering,
partly, though not wholly, on account of an old law, whereby
power-driven vehicles on the public roads were limited to four
miles an hour and had to be preceded by a man carrying a red
flag. This statute, which on the narrow roads of those days, encumbered as they constantly were till the fall of agriculture by
great droves of sheep, had been quite reasonable in its application
to threshing or ploughing engines on their moves from farm to
farm, was not repealed until 1896. After that date an English
motor-car industry had freedom to develop. But it scarcely
seemed in a hurry to do so; and the idea remained to the end of the
century in a sporting and experimental stage.

In none of these spheres did England make any decisive contribution to technology. At best she adopted, often with an
undue time-lag, foreign systems worked under foreign patents.
The Parsons turbine (which ultimately, among other uses,
became very important for cheapening electrical generation) and
the Dunlop pneumatic tyre (devised by an amateur for bicycles,
though destined to a wider future on the wheels of motor
vehicles) were perhaps the sole major inventions made within her

borders during the fifteen years. The fact brings home to us more perhaps than any of the trade figures quoted above, how sudden and steep had been the decline from her long industrial world-leadership.

The course of trade during these years is fairly shown by the accompanying table. It started in 1886 in the trough of a depression; rose on a boom, which reached its peak in 1890; declined gradually into another depression, whose trough was reached in 1893-4; and then rose out into another boom, which

Annual Totals of British Foreign Trade 1886–1900

(£ millions)

1886	. 618·5	1891	. 744·5	1896	. 738
1887	. 642·9	1892	. 715	1897	. 745
1888	. 686	1893	. 681·8	1898	. 764·5
1889	. 743	1894	. 682	1899	. 814·5
1890	. 748·9	1895	. 702·5	1900	. 877

was artificially prolonged and heightened by the South African war. Generally this conformed to the cyclic movement, which characterized British trade through most of the nineteenth century. In the boom of 1888-90, coincident with the increased Rand gold-output, South America as well as South Africa was prominent. The public debt of Argentina, which had been £10 millions in 1875, rose to £70 millions by 1889, and much of the inflation was spent in England on British goods. It was mainly due to over-speculation in the River Plate countries that in November 1890 the great City firm of Barings went on the rocks. The resulting crisis claims some separate attention. Nothing so grave in its kind had happened since Overend and Gurney's failure on 'Black Friday' in 1866.

Barings' liabilities were over £21 millions; and had the firm been left to its fate, the whole credit of London as a banking centre would have been shaken. That the peril was escaped was due to the vision and courage of one man, William Lidderdale, governor of the Bank of England. In 1866 the Bank had stood aside and let panic disaster take a devastating course. But under Lidderdale it came forward as the natural leader of all the financial forces in London, combining them against a common danger. The governor had only a short time in which to act before the secret must come out. He obtained 1½ millions in gold by selling Exchequer Bonds to the State Bank of Russia, and borrowed (through Rothschilds) 3 millions more from the Bank of France.

He also asked help from the chancellor of the exchequer; but Goschen refused to pledge state money for a private firm and, beyond offering to suspend the Bank Charter, would do nothing. Lidderdale then turned to the joint stock banks and greater City firms, and with lightning impetus (he headed the list at 5 p.m. on Friday and closed it before noon on Saturday) raised a guarantee fund of 7 millions. By these means panic liquidation was averted, and an immense threat to trade and industry removed. Barings was reconstructed as a joint stock company; by the end of 1894 every advance made to it from the Guarantee Fund had been paid off; and the guarantors were released from all further responsibility. High finance, through a new solidarity, had displayed a new strength.[1]

Nothing similar was attempted in 1893, when the banking system of Australia collapsed. That disaster not only crippled the colonies concerned for some years, but, coinciding with a big railway slump in America, helped to deepen the world-depression.

The change from individual to company ownership in industry and business continued to progress through these years, being nearly universal by the end of the century. Treading on its heels came now another—the formation of trusts and combines. It was less prominent in Great Britain than in the United States and Germany, because there was here no tariff to create monopolies behind; yet in many fields the movement made headway. The earliest great English amalgamation was the Salt Union (1888). The next was the United Alkali Company (February 1891), which took in no less than forty-eight firms producing soda and bleaching-powder. The Salt Union was at first successful in establishing monopoly and restoring prices to a profitable level. But it overdid price-raising, facilitated thereby the encroachments of outside production, and finally drifted into such straits that after heavily writing down its capital in 1903 it had in 1906 to yield to its competitors and come under a common sales

---

[1] Lidderdale's methods were drastic. An essential feature of his scheme was that the banks should not call in their loans to bill brokers, and an understanding was reached to that effect. A certain bank began calling in loans nevertheless. Lidderdale sent for the manager and informed him, that unless his bank were loyal to the understanding, he would forthwith close its account at the Bank of England and announce the fact in the evening newspapers. He gave him an hour to make up his mind. The manager is said to have made it up quickly (Ellis T. Powell, *The Evolution of the Money Market* (1915), p. 527).

organization with them. The United Alkali Company (which had been preceded in 1883-9 by a combination to lower output and raise prices) amalgamated all the firms using one of the two processes current for producing soda. But in the sequel it suffered heavily; in part because foreign tariffs barred the bleaching-powder, which as a by-product had made its process profitable. A far more successful amalgamation was the English Sewing-Cotton Company (1897), of which Messrs. Coats formed the nucleus, and which included fifteen firms at the start, adding others later. Soon after came other big fusions—the Calico Printers' Association (1899) at Manchester, and in the Yorkshire trade the Bradford Dyers' Association (1898) and the Bradford Woolcombers' Association (1899). These each incurred heavy early losses, though the first-named, after an overhaul, became very prosperous. A separate type of combine were the 'Alliances' which toward the end of the nineties sprang up in half a dozen small Birmingham trades, beginning with the makers of metal bedsteads. Their peculiarity was that they not merely estab-lished a monopoly against the consumer, but brought employees as well as employers into it upon an agreed basis. After a few years' very successful working they were gradually broken down through foreign competition; behind a tariff they might perhaps have lasted. The trade unions and consumer-organiza-tions each disliked them for obvious reasons; but in retrospect to-day they appear an interesting anticipation of the 'corpora-tive' idea now prevalent abroad. As the century closed, Victorian faith in free competition found decidedly less currency among business men. In the shipping world 'rings' became the rule. Even in the British steel industry, which by comparison with the huge trusts controlling steel output in America and Germany seemed an individualist chaos, several large amalgamations were at this time made.

Agriculture was ruined a second time over. After the average for wheat had sunk to 31s. in 1886 and 29s. 9d. in 1889, prices revived a little in 1890 and 1891, and such of the older and better farmers as had escaped bankruptcy regained hope. Gladstone in January 1890 said 'it was wholly out of the question to suppose that British agriculture would not always continue to be the great pursuit it had always been in former times'. Then the bottom fell out of the market once more. In 1893 the wheat price had slumped to 26s. 4d., several shillings below anything

known for a hundred years. In April 1894 one of the best farming
witnesses before the Royal Commission on Agriculture had just
been 'selling splendid wheat at 24s. a quarter in Cambridgeshire'.[1]
On 22 September the official average calculated from the returns
of 198 markets was 19s. 8d.! The average for the whole year was
22s. 10d., and for 1895, 23s. 1d. These proved to be zero figures;
thenceforward there was a gradual rise. But it was never enough
to restore confidence in good cultivation. The witness quoted
above, who farmed over 1,000 acres of the best arable in the
country, had laid down about a third of it to grass—'anything
that would not plough with a pair of horses', i.e. the richest land.
England's wheat-fields diminished by another half million acres
between 1890 and 1900, and at the latter date covered only a
little over half the acreage of 1872. They went on shrinking
down to 1914. Many other things shrank with them. In 1888 the
gross amount received by landlords from farm rents was £59
millions; by 1901 it had fallen to £42 millions. In 1897 the Royal
Commission observed in their final Report, that 'over a very considerable part of this country true rent has entirely vanished,
since the owners are not receiving the ordinary interest upon the
sum which it would cost to erect buildings, fences, &c., as good
as those now existing'.[2] Further changes came over the personnel of the farming class, as families with fine traditions, who
had just survived the first depression, succumbed to the second.
There was much dispute before the commission, whether occupants of small farms or large weathered the storm best; but
general agreement, that yeoman farmers suffered as much or
more than tenants, since they usually had a heavy mortgage
interest to pay, which could not be reduced like a rent. The
only class whose conditions improved were the labourers. For
whereas wheat prices in 1900 were only 47·5 per cent. of those in
1871, farm wages were 120 per cent. of the 1871 figure.[3] The rise
does not appear to have been determined by any cause within the
industry, but by the levels attainable in alternative occupations
outside. Hence it was accompanied by a heavy fall in the numbers employed. Between the censuses of 1871 and 1901 the male

[1] *Evidence* (Cd. 7400 of 1894), ii, Q. 17,699.
[2] Cd. 8540 of 1897, p. 28.
[3] A. Wilson Fox, 'Agricultural Wages in England', in the *Journal of the Royal Statistical Society*, vol. lxvi, pt. ii (1903), p. 60. See also his two Reports on the *Wages, Earnings, and Conditions of Employment of Agricultural Labourers in the United Kingdom* (Cd. 346 of 1900 and Cd. 2376 of 1905).

agricultural labourers (including foremen and bailiffs) in England and Wales were diminished by over one-third, while the general population increased by 43 per cent. In the last of the three decades the drop was 143,034, or 18 per cent. on the figure for 1891.[1] The townward pressure was relentless. By 1901 the population of urban districts in England and Wales was over 77 per cent. of the whole, that of rural districts less than 23 per cent. The growth in the latter since 1891 had averaged only 21,225 a year—a figure more than to be accounted for by new frills round the towns, and corresponding to a marked decline over the genuine countryside.

The royal commission was appointed in September 1893 by the fourth Gladstone government. It sat four years and made three reports. The second (in 1896) recommended by a majority the partial derating of agricultural land; and this, as we saw above,[2] was carried out. The final report reviewed the whole situation; found the chief cause of the fall of prices to be foreign competition; but offered no proposal to blunt its force. It had nothing specific to advise about rents or railway rates, though both loomed large in it. Instead it rode off on petty proposals about land tenure, tithes, dairying, small-holdings, sale of cattle by live weight, agricultural education, and so on, thereby setting a convenient fashion which served politicians down to 1914. Meanwhile as early as 1889, in the year following the County Councils Act, Lord Salisbury had created the Board of Agriculture. Unfortunately he felt obliged to place at its head country squires acceptable to the unimaginative majority of their order. Chaplin was his first choice, and Walter Long his second. These were not men from whom any constructive impulse could be expected. Nevertheless the mere creation of a department set, as it always will, a ball rolling; and by slow degrees the abler officials, with little help from their parliamentary heads, built up a centre of intelligence for the agricultural community.

The navy, upon which our policy was making the island more and more dependent, was throughout this period changing rapidly. A contemporary expert understates when he says that

---

[1] An uncertain amount (perhaps as much as 10,000) should be knocked off this figure for the fact that forty-nine militia regiments were embodied, when the census was taken. But even that leaves it enormous.
[2] p. 238.

'by 1890 the ships of 1877 had become well-nigh obsolete; and by 1900 the best ships even of 1890 were hardly worthy of a place in the crack fleets of the country'.[1] These conditions, which England could not avoid, were yet very prejudicial to her. Down to the Crimean war naval supremacy had rested on wooden ships, which took a long time to build, and which no Power had the materials to multiply indefinitely, but which, once built, were serviceable for sixty years. The effect was that Great Britain, with her large accumulation of warships, could scarcely be outbuilt by any one. But now every few years brought forth new guns, new armour, and new ship-designs, which made all existing vessels obsolete. People sometimes speak as if the twentieth-century *Dreadnought* were unique in doing this. As a matter of fact the 'Admiral' class of battleships in the eighties did it quite as much; and those of the *Magnificent* class, launched in 1895 and 1896 under Lord Spencer's programme, did so nearly as much again. Supposing, for instance, that H.M.S. *Rodney*, launched in 1884 and completed in 1888, had been set to fight a fleet comprising every ironclad launched in Great Britain down to 1881, she could, if properly handled, have sunk them all and emerged from the contest an easy winner. A single *Magnificent* would not have stood the same chance against a fleet of the 'Admiral' class; but, fleet against fleet, the victory of the later type would have been overwhelming. Every time a change like this occurred, it became more practicable for foreign Powers to build against us on level terms. We had only two special assets left—our large trained naval personnel, and our insular freedom from conscript militarism, allowing us to concentrate on the naval arm. But as soon as any continental state should have a sufficient surplusage of landpower to spare energy for a bid for sea-power, there was nothing to prevent its bidding. And that is exactly what Germany from 1898 onwards did.

The chief source of change throughout was the gun. After the over-late abandonment of muzzle-loaders, which we noted above,[2] a series of large breech-loaders were designed for the navy. The four mounted on the *Collingwood*, the first of the 'Admiral' class, were 12-inch 45-ton; but in the *Rodney* two years later they were 13·5 inch 67-ton—a type which came to form the principal armament of no less than fourteen first-line battle-

---

[1] Sir W. Laird Clowes, *The Royal Navy*, vii (1903), 68.
[2] pp. 122–3.

ships in the British service. Besides it a monster 16·25-inch 111-ton gun was designed; but with this only three ships were armed, as its use reduced the number of big guns per ship from four to two, which many held to be insufficient. All these weapons were designed to use gunpowder,[1] an explosive too quick and shattering to be an ideal propellant. Hence their heavily constructed charge-chambers, and hence, too, their very short lives—they could only be fired for a number of times so limited as severely to restrict target-practice. Not only the original 'Admiral' class, but the eight battleships laid down under the Naval Defence Act 1889 (*Royal Sovereign* class) carried these weapons. But even while the latter were being completed, a new pattern of big guns was designed to supersede them. These used cordite, a far better propellant, which made it possible to lighten the charge-chamber, lengthen the barrel, and secure much higher velocities with a lighter gun. The type most favoured had a 12-inch calibre; it originally weighed 46 tons, but was later increased to 50. The earliest first-line battleships designed to carry them were the *Magnificent* class, most of which also enjoyed the advantage of being armoured with Harveyized steel. As it had something like double the resistance of the 'compound' armour on the 'Admiral' and *Royal Sovereign* types, the all-round superiority of the new class can be seen.

These technical points explain the political history of naval affairs in the period. Its main features are the two 'scares'—that of 1888-9,[2] which led to Lord George Hamilton's programme, and that of 1893-4, which led to Lord Spencer's. The real argument was much the same on both occasions. In 1888 the 'Admiral' class (and similarly armed vessels in foreign navies) had made obsolete all our earlier ships. That rendered it necessary for us, not merely to add a unit or two, but to make a new fighting fleet. As it was we had in 1889 only five vessels carrying the heavier types of breech-loader; and at a time when strategy dictated the maintenance of two battleship fleets, one in the Mediterranean and one at home, they were not enough to go round. A disaster which occurred later (21 June 1893), when our two best battleships in the Mediterranean collided, and one (the *Victoria*)

---

[1] 'Prism brown powder', rather slower burning than the black powder of daily use, but essentially the same explosive.

[2] The 'fire behind the smoke' in 1888 was a considered official report by three admirals, expressing doubt whether the navy then reached a Two-Power standard.

was sunk while the other (the *Camperdown*) was gravely disabled, showed how narrow the margin might at any moment have become. The programme of *Royal Sovereigns* met this need for the time; but when the new cordite-firing guns appeared, Lord Spencer's advisers pointed out that once more—if we were not to run the risk that a few up-to-date foreign ships might destroy a whole obsolete British navy—it was a question of building not a ship but a squadron. Hence the second 'scare', and the Spencer programme. Gladstone, it will be remembered, was unconvinced by the arguments; and indeed to any one with the mind of an economist these repeated wholesale buildings of ships which became almost immediately outclassed could only be exasperating. Nevertheless on the outbreak of the South African war in 1899, the main thing which saved us from foreign intervention, apart from the diplomatic estrangement between our chief would-be adversaries (i.e. Germany and the Dual Alliance), was the existence of the battleships built under the Spencer programme.

In these years Great Britain came to the front in naval invention, for (it might almost be said) the first time in her modern history. The 6-inch Q.F. gun, which, discharging a 100-lb. shell, could fire fifteen aimed shots per minute, was invented on the Tyne. It was largely responsible for the growth of 'secondary' armaments, which helped to make the *Royal Sovereign*,[1] and still more the *Magnificent*, so much larger, and therefore costlier, than the 'Admiral' class had been. Another British invention was the destroyer—first exemplified in H.M.S. *Havock* (designed and built by a famous Thames-side firm in 1893). But these and most other advances were due to private enterprise. Partly for that reason they speedily became international, and England had not for long any monopoly of their advantage. The admiralty itself remained very conservative. Submarines, for instance, it totally ignored till 1900, when it ordered five small ones for experiment. It was equally backward about mines.

The changes just sketched sent up the cost of the navy enormously. The Estimates which had been under £13 millions in 1886, climbed to £21·8 millions in 1896 and to £27·5 millions in 1900. Already they strained the budget. We have seen how both Goschen's and Harcourt's Death Duties were due to them; and later we shall see other things.

---

[1] The *Royal Sovereign* (launched 1891, completed 1892) was the first battleship to cost over £1 million.

The army was a subject of much more dispute during these years. In 1888 the second Salisbury government referred the central problem of its administration and the navy's to a royal commission, over which Lord Hartington, as he then was, presided. An interim section of its Report, published in 1889, discussed and rejected a proposal to couple the two services under a common minister of defence. The army, represented by General Brackenbury, favoured the idea; but the navy opposed it. Instead, the commission suggested a naval and military council, to 'be presided over by the Prime Minister and consist of the parliamentary heads of the two services and their principal professional advisers'. This was a germ which ripened, fifteen years later, into the Committee of Imperial Defence.

In its main Report (1890)[1] the commission concentrated upon the army side, the administration of the admiralty being thought far less in need of improvement. The system at the war office was one of extreme centralization. Every matter which came up for decision, whether it concerned personnel or material, the training of troops, the promotion of officers, barracks, forts, arms, uniforms, supplies, strategy, or the distribution of forces, had to pass through the hands of a single officer, the commander-in-chief, 'who alone would be accountable to the Secretary of State even for such a matter as the defective design of a heavy gun'. The commission found nothing like this to obtain in the armies of other European Powers, and rightly condemned the system. What made it even worse, was that the old duke of Cambridge, sworn foe to all progress, was still commander-in-chief. But the commission did not say so, nor durst it dislodge the queen's cousin; it limited itself to hypothetical policies, to be adopted when he should vacate his post. The policies were: (1) to abolish the office of commander-in-chief; (2) to devolve his duties as a local commander of troops upon a general officer commanding the forces in Great Britain, analogous to the already existing G.O.C. the forces in Ireland; (3) to have at the centre five high officers each directly responsible to the war minister—viz. chief of the general staff, adjutant-general, quartermaster-general, director of artillery, and inspector-general of fortifications; (4) to form a war office council, composed of the war minister, the two minor ministers, the permanent under-secretary, and the five officers as above.

[1] Cd. 5979.

If this programme of 1890 had been carried out even so late as 1895, when Campbell-Bannerman at last ejected the obstructive duke, many, if not all, of the army's gross blunders in the South African war might have been avoided. But it was not. The keystone of its arch was the proposal to create a general staff, with a chief ranking among the five highest officers. The commission conceived the general staff as 'freed from all executive functions and charged with the responsible duty of preparing plans of military operations, collecting and co-ordinating information of all kinds, and generally tendering advice upon all matters of organization and the preparation of the Army for war'. It was to consider 'the military defence of the Empire as a whole', dealing with it 'in accordance with a definite and harmonious plan'. A general staff on these lines was already then functioning for all important continental armies, as it has since done in Great Britain for nearly thirty years; and few, if any, experts would to-day dispute the need for it. But in 1890 it was only dawning on the insular mind. A very brilliant book published in that same year—*The Brain of an Army*, by Spenser Wilkinson—was the first which clearly explained its bearing in English. Most unfortunately Campbell-Bannerman was opposed to it. As a member of the commission he signed the Report, but with a long dissenting memorandum on this very point. His arguments were that the analogy between Great Britain and the militarist Powers of the continent was misleading; that there was here really nothing for a general staff to do; and consequently there was danger lest it might make something to do. The last would seem to have been his basic objection. Just as, a generation earlier, the anti-Cardwellite whigs had wanted officers not to become too professional, lest their efficiency might grow dangerous, so now Campbell-Bannerman, apprenticed under Cardwell though he had been, instinctively shrank from giving a brain to the army, lest it might think too much.

Hence it was that in 1895, when the chance for the reform came, the war minister instead of following the commission's policy set up a new commander-in-chief in the person of Lord Wolseley. Towards a general staff no approach was made. It is true in other respects Campbell-Bannerman tried to carry out Nos. 3 and 4 of the policies listed above; but then almost immediately he left office. It was a great pity that the duke of Devonshire, whose massive practical sense had been the mainstay of the royal commission,[1] did not succeed him. Lord Lansdowne, who did, was no match for the masterful Wolseley; and the latter, under an order in council of 21 November 1895, secured that he should be 'the principal adviser of the Secretary of State on all military questions', and 'charged with the general supervision of the Military Departments of the War Office'. This policy, aptly characterized eight years later by a member of the royal commission on the South African war[2] as an 'attempt to combine the two opposing principles, of centralization in an individual soldier and devolution to a Board of soldiers, under the general control of a civilian Secretary of State', did not work satisfactorily. But even if it had, a war on the South African scale could scarcely have been handled without gross blundering, in the absence of any 'brain' to study its problems beforehand.

The result may be seen from a single sentence in the Report on the South African war by the powerful royal commission appointed to review it in 1902: 'No plan of campaign ever existed for operations in South Africa.'[3] Lord Roberts stated[4] in evidence that 'when Sir George White arrived in Natal, he had no instructions in regard to the wishes of the Government as to any particular plan of campaign, nor was he aware of any general plan of operations in South Africa'. General Symons, whom he found commanding the Natal garrison, and who seems to have been in almost incredible ignorance of the Boers' military resources, wanted to hold Dundee, while White wanted him to withdraw from it; but the governor of Natal, for purely civil reasons, came down heavily on Symons's side, and White most reluctantly yielded. Neither officer knew that the intelligence division had examined the ground beforehand, and had advised against holding, not only Dundee, but Ladysmith. Intelligence indeed was persistently starved and ignored. A little before White's arrival an instruction was sent to Symons that he had better start finding out something of what was happening on the enemy side of the frontier; and for this he was authorized to spend the oddly inadequate sum of £500. The amounts allowed for intelligence at the war office itself were tiny; even when the war was over, a witness before the commission, who admitted that

---

[1] It was not accidental that the secretary to the commission afterwards became the duke's biographer.

[2] Sir George Goldie: *Commission's Report* (Cd. 1789 of 1904), p. 147.

[3] Same *Report*, p. 23.   [4] *Evidence*, vol. i (Cd. 1790), Q. 10183.

£150,000 might be needed to do the work (including maps) properly, said he would be very glad of £20,000; for '£20,000 a year is such a very large sum in comparison with what is now spent on the Intelligence Department, that I had the feeling that, if we were to ask for it, it would be scoffed at in the War Office, before ever it got to the Treasury'. The reports of the intelligence did not go to the war minister; and in 1897 some important ones were first brought to Lord Lansdowne's notice by Chamberlain, to whose department they had come round.

The British public, which for twenty years had been accustomed to see its army perform with remarkable efficiency and success in campaigns on a limited scale against coloured forces, was amazed by the break-down. But part of the reason for it was that differences of scale, terrain, and opponents called for different methods. These having never been studied, the generals went ahead with the tactics usual on the Indian frontier—uphill frontal infantry attacks, which had done well enough against Afridis or Afghans, but were useless against armies of white marksmen armed with Mauser rifles. Only by costly lessons in the school of bitter experience was wisdom learnt. The best witnesses told the commission that our regular soldiers, town-bred for the most part and passed through the old mechanical drill, were gravely lacking in ability to think or act for themselves. Nor were the officers all that they might be. Kitchener, not their severest critic, observed: 'There appears to be too often a want of serious study of their profession by officers, who are, I think, rather inclined to deal too lightly with military questions of moment.' One reason was that down to 1899 we had still very little beyond a regimental organization. Foreign armies were organized permanently in divisions and army corps, each commanded by the officers who would command them in the event of war. But Great Britain had as yet barely the rudiments of such a system; though Wolseley had taken some steps towards one.

We shall see later what attempts were made to overcome these defects. But they fall outside the queen's reign.

Only two additions were made at this time to the departments of the central government—the Board of Agriculture (1889), which we noted above, and the Board of Education (1899), which will concern our next chapter. In these cases there was continued the bad practice, already in force for the board of trade and the local government board, of paying to the ministers at their head salaries less than half those attached to the holders of the older offices—i.e. the chancellor of the exchequer, the secretaries of state, and the first lord of the admiralty. The effect was to create within the administration two grades of cabinet ministers—those of highest standing, who held the £5,000-a-year posts, and the novices or second-raters, who alone could without infringement of their dignity be offered the £2,000-a-year posts. What made this particularly mischievous was that the departments under the lower-grade ministers were in many cases the more important for the life of the nation. Thus the local government board was fast coming to outweigh the home office; and the board of trade, which at this time combined most of the functions of a ministry of commerce and a ministry of labour, was dealing from day to day with even more difficult and vital problems of national policy than the war office. The source of the evil was that, when governments created new posts, they liked to pretend to parliament that they would be inexpensive ones. But it was exceedingly false economy, and has persisted since to a considerable extent.

The growth of bureaucracy, however, was much greater than the addition of two departments. The scope of official work was widening all the time, especially under the home office, the local government board, and the board of trade. Asquith did a good deal to develop the first-named, especially on the side of factory inspection. He appointed the first women factory inspectors— an elementary step towards efficiency which Harcourt in the eighties had refused to take. The local government board naturally expanded its personnel in order to deal with the army of new-elected local authorities set up for counties, districts, and parishes by the acts of 1888 and 1894. The board of trade grew in many directions, the most notable, perhaps, being the formation inside it (1892) of a labour department. This, which was the work of A. J. Mundella, president of the board of trade in Gladstone's fourth cabinet, was one of the last fruitful results deriving from the social idealism of the late eighties, before the imperialism of the nineties turned men's minds elsewhere.

But on the side of institutions the feature of the period was the new local government. The substitution of elected county councils for the ancient administration of counties by the justices of the peace at quarter sessions was a substitution of the democratic for the aristocratic principle. As completed six years later by the scheme of district and parish councils, it based the whole of English local government upon direct popular election. The pattern was English town government as developed since 1835 in the municipal boroughs. The counties were treated much as if they were towns of large area. No rival pattern came into the reckoning; no study had been made of foreign examples of local government: nobody ever discussed borrowing anything from the German systems, whose success was already by that time coming to be envied and copied by other northern nations on the Continent. Hence the peculiarities which had grown up in the government of English towns, and which were barely half a century old, were adopted as a matter of course for the government of all our other local areas. The new councils, like the old, had no general powers to act or to spend money for the good of their areas, beyond those which had been, or from time to time might be, specifically conferred by parliament. Their constitutions did not provide for any expert element in their membership, the place (if any) for the expert being conceived as a servant's only. Though they were in many respects to be closely controlled by the central government, the main controls were to be exercised solely from London, and not through localized central officials such as, living near the spot, could have been guided by personal knowledge. It is worth remembering that these features, which in 1888 had little more than half a century behind them but to-day have a century, were so far from being inevitable that in Europe they are practically unknown outside the British Isles.

Within the limits which English town government had already illustrated, the county and district councils made rapid and satisfactory progress. There was built up through them in the nineties a nation-wide machinery, which in later decades was to provide an increasingly efficient administration for education, for roads, and for public health. The parish councils, on the other hand, though much had been hoped from them in the rural areas, never became important. Their failure can be explained in the first instance by the severe limitation on their spending-power—normally the proceeds of a 3*d*. rate, and only to be enlarged at most to 6*d*.[1] Many people are still alive who can remember the enthusiasm with which the first parish councils were elected, and the cruel disillusionment when they found that

---

[1] In 1929 the figures were increased to 4*d*. and 8*d*. respectively.

almost everything which they had a mandate to do was beyond their purses. Opinion still varies as to whether they deserved their fate. Many argue that the parish was too small a unit for modern purposes. Others think that a distinct and promising hope of village democracy was blighted through their strangulation.

A special effect of the County Councils Act was that London acquired for the first time since its vast modern expansion a popularly elected unitary authority in the shape of the L.C.C. The new 'county' followed the boundaries fixed over thirty years before for the metropolitan boards of works, though they had in the interval become obsolete everywhere, and disproportionately so on the eastern side.[1] This niggardly and unforeseeing map has entailed growing disadvantages ever since; but it did not prevent the new body from speedily developing much corporate vigour. It was fortunate in avoiding at the outset a mechanical party division as between conservatives and liberals; the special municipal parties which were created instead—the 'moderates' and 'progressives'—succeeded nearly till 1906[2] in excluding the irrelevances of national politics. The progressives, who soon became the governing party, spread a really wide umbrella, which on the one hand attracted not a few conservatives,[3] and on the other brought in nearly all sorts of socialists—alike the intellectuals of the Fabian Society, J. Ramsay MacDonald of the I.L.P., and John Burns, who at that time had still, perhaps, the largest working-class following in London.

Thus a genuine local patriotism was aroused, which soon looked beyond the L.C.C. to the other features in the government of the metropolis. Its paving, cleansing, and public health had been hitherto left to an antiquated jumble of petty and often corrupt authorities—thirty vestries and twelve district boards—in the midst of which the ancient city corporation figured like

[1] The point may be illustrated by noting that the geographical centre of Greater London's population, as distributed during 1890–1914, was not at Charing Cross nor even at the Mansion House, but somewhere in Rotherhithe.

[2] What finally 'blew the gaff' and destroyed the system, was that in that year a large number of sitting progressives secured election to parliament as liberals for the same constituencies. Thereafter no distinction between progressives and liberals carried conviction. Hence the downfall in 1907 of the progressive régime, which never again controlled London.

[3] The brilliant Henry Cust, for instance, who from 1892 to 1896 edited the *Pall Mall Gazette* as a conservative paper, gave consistent support in it to the progressive cause.

a Triton among minnows. It was the corporation's opposition
to change which in 1884 had baffled a determined effort at
reform made by Sir William Harcourt. Harcourt's bill was for
a unified London, with a vastly expanded city corporation as its
main authority. There were to have been district councils as
well, but, although popularly elected, they would have had no
power except that which the central council conferred on them.
This measure was dropped; the County Councils Act in 1888
evaded the issue; and in 1893–4 it would have been quite beyond
Fowler's power to pass his great act had he included the metropolis in it. However, a royal commission on London government
was appointed, with Leonard Courtney as chairman, and its
Report (1895) carried the matter a stage further. Like the Harcourt Bill, it wished a great central council for London to have
the name and style of the corporation, with the lord mayor at its
head. But it laid more stress on the minor local authorities, and
urged that in the division of functions between them and the
corporation they 'should be entrusted with every duty they can
conveniently discharge'. When at last, four years later, Lord
Salisbury took up the matter, it was on the side of these minor
authorities that he came down. His London Government Act,
1899, left the L.C.C. and the city corporation where they were;
but it swept away the vestries and local boards, and in their
stead created the twenty-eight 'metropolitan borough councils',
each with a mayor, aldermen, and elected councillors complete.
These bodies were and are anomalous; for they could not have
been given the full powers of ordinary borough councils without
taking away powers from the L.C.C.—a course forbidden alike
by its undoubted prestige and by a growing public sense of the
unity of London. But within their field they were a vast improvement on the old vestries, and provided Londoners with
an important new access to public life. The chief fault of the
policy was that it perpetuated unequal financial burdens.
London, for residential purposes, is mapped into rich districts
and poor. Many of the latter were so grouped as to form whole
boroughs; and in them needs costly above the average have
since had to be met from much less than average rateable
resources. In 1904 an act was passed, which, by levying a 6d.
rate from all the London boroughs (together with the city) on
the basis of assessments and distributing it back to them on the
basis of population, did a little to lessen the inequalities.

Widely stirred by the London Dock Strike in 1889, trade-unionism went ahead through the nineties with a new impetus. Not only did it permeate fresh trades, but in main industries, such as mining and railways, it appreciably changed its character. In 1892, after the trade boom had ended, its membership total in the United Kingdom was 1,576,000. By 1900, on the top of the new boom, it was 2,022,000. That was the first time that it passed the two million mark. There was also a great increase in industrial stoppages. In 1893 some 30,440,000 days' work were lost in this way. No equal figure was recorded again for nineteen years; but the totals for 1897 and 1898 were very high as things went then. How to avoid stoppages began to be envisaged as one of the leading problems in industry.

The most famous disputes were the miners' lock-out in 1893 and the engineers' strike of 1897. The first was caused by the owners' demand for a 10 per cent. reduction in wages. It affected what was known as the English federated area, comprising all the main coal-fields south of the Tweed except Durham, Northumberland, and South Wales (where wages were regulated by sliding scales). The Miners' Federation, under whose banner the men fought, took in a number of county miners' associations, one of which—that for Yorkshire—was the third largest trade union in the country.[1] The stoppage lasted fifteen weeks, from the beginning of August to 17 November. It was one of the first in which the unions developed the tactics of inflicting shortage on the public in order to compel government intervention. In earlier disputes, when their sole aim was to put direct pressure on the employers concerned, they had wished firms or areas which were the trade rivals of these employers to remain at work. But the new tactics involved trying to stop every firm or area possible. Accordingly, though the owners' lock-out had no reference to South Wales, the Miners' Federation, whose writ did not officially run there, sought, in opposition to the local unions, to close the South Wales pits. It did so by fomenting a hauliers' strike. This was run frankly on lines of violence, the hauliers (mostly of an age intermediate between boys and coal-getters) forming 'marching gangs' which went from pit to pit stopping work and handling miners brutally. The end came when the miners of Ebbw Vale, who had been

---

[1] The Amalgamated Society of Engineers was then the largest: the Durham Miners' Association came second.

forewarned and forearmed, emerged from their pits 2,000 strong, fought a pitched battle on the mountain-side with a great army of 'gangs', and utterly defeated them.[1] The hauliers' strike then collapsed.

The stoppage, however, in the Midlands, Lancashire, and Yorkshire went doggedly on, with extremely little violence save in the last-named area. In the autumn a long-remembered tragedy occurred at Featherstone, near Pontefract. The local police had been imprudently depleted by drafts to Doncaster for the annual race-meeting, and the strikers took the occasion to attack the collieries, where imported strike-breakers were at work. At the height of the riot the police were overpowered; and while the mob were already wrecking the buildings,[2] a small body of troops stopped them by firing, with the result that two miners were killed. A special commission presided over by a celebrated judge, Lord Bowen, exonerated the soldiers and their officers from blame. The minister technically responsible was Asquith, and for years afterwards he was denounced as a 'murderer' on labour platforms. This was quite unjust, but it was not unimportant. It possibly helped to move him from the left of his party to the right centre; it certainly did much to drive a wedge between liberal and trade-unionist politics. Meanwhile, as the lock-out continued, high prices and acute shortage, especially of house coal, began to be felt in many parts of the country. If it be asked how this was possible with the South Wales, Durham, and Northumberland pits all working at high pressure, part of the answer may be found in the high British railway rates.[3] Already in October many local authorities called on the government to intervene; but Gladstone was very loath to do so, and it was not till 13 November that he invited the two parties to a conference with a minister. Lord Rosebery was deputed for the task; and four days later, after six hours' negotiation, he achieved a compromise settlement, which, though it seemed fragile, brought peace in the federated area for the rest of the century. In the South Wales area there was a

---

[1] Nobody was killed, though numbers were injured, in this remarkable combat. The Ebbw Vale men were working with the full sanction of their union, their agent being Tom Richards, one of the chief pillars of the subsequently formed South Wales Miners' Federation.

[2] The damage done was afterwards assessed for compensation at £6,000.

[3] It cost as much at that time to rail coal from the Rhondda to North Dorset as to ship it 3,000 miles to Alexandria.

hard-fought six months' strike in 1898. It ended in the men's defeat; but the building of the South Wales Miners' Federation resulted from it.

The strike of the Amalgamated Society of Engineers in 1897–8 was in its origin unofficial. Its hero on the men's side was G. N. Barnes. Several issues were involved, but the one which stood in the foreground was the demand for an eight-hour day. Against it there was organized an Engineering Employers' Federation—first on the Clyde, then elsewhere; and under a very able leader, Colonel Dyer, it became a powerful national organization. The stoppage began in July. For a long time all efforts to bring the parties together in conference were frustrated by a dispute about the chairmanship. Eventually (24 November) a conference met under the conditions stipulated by the employers, and discussed a basis of settlement drawn up by the president of the board of trade, C. T. Ritchie. It arrived provisionally at terms; but on a ballot of the men they were rejected by a large majority. The stoppage dragged on painfully past the end of the year, till on 15 January 1898 the men surrendered. The defeat of the most powerful union in the country profoundly impressed the labour world. Many were led by it to prefer political above trade-union action. Others argued that if the trade unions were to succeed in future, they must by fusion or federation build up much larger units. Movement was stimulated in all these directions.

Perhaps the most distinct tendency in British trade unionism at this stage was towards substituting organization by industries for the older organization by crafts. Examples might be seen in the miners' unions; which had originally been comparatively small associations of skilled men—the coal-getters—but now aimed to become huge all-grades mass-organizations, bringing in hauliers, datallers, surface-workers, engine-men, and every other category that might be employed at a colliery. Similarly on the railways it was the Amalgamated Society of Railway Servants— the only one of the railway unions which was open to recruit all varieties of railway employees indifferently—which now came to the fore. Its 'all-grades movement' of 1896–7 produced a considerable effect; and at the end of the century it had 60,000 members. But there were about 400,000 railway employees, and the companies denied the unions any recognition. Their attitude was uncompromising. As late as 1892 one of the directorates

went so far as to dismiss several of its men for giving evidence
before a select committee of the house of commons. But this was
resented by parliament as a breach of privilege. The offending
directors were haled before the bar of the house, and there
heavily rebuked.

The movement from trade union towards political methods
had behind it certain economic facts whose bearing was coming
to be more appreciated. Trade unionism could, as a rule, only
help certain classes of workers, and only in regard to wages and
hours. But it was not there that the need was sorest. The wages
of trade unionists in England were the highest in Europe, and
normally above a poverty line. Yet Charles Booth in 1889, on the
basis of an inquiry conducted in the previous year, published
his famous estimate that 30·7 per cent. of the inhabitants of
London lived 'in poverty'.[1] These, apart from special family or
personal circumstances, were the ranks of unskilled, casual, or
sweated labour. The 'New Unionism' had made heroic efforts
to organize some sections of them, but seldom with very encouraging results; and a large proportion appeared to be unorganiz-
able.

Again, outside the scope of trade unionism, yet oppressing its
members and contributing greatly to the discontent by which
industrial unrest was fed, there were enormous evils on the side of
housing and environment. England and Wales were better than
Scotland or Dublin; yet in England and Wales between 1891 and
1901, whereas population had increased by 12·17 per cent., the
total number of tenements had only increased by 11·51 per cent.
Housing, instead of catching population up, was still actually
falling behind it. The very blackest scandals were being lessened;
the number of one-roomed tenements containing nine persons
and upwards had fallen from 436 to 126; but fearful conditions
of overcrowding were still common. The worst area for them
was the north-east coast; in 1899 the counties of Durham and
Northumberland had respectively 34 and 38 per cent. of their
populations overcrowded, while Gateshead, Newcastle, and
Sunderland were the three most overcrowded towns. The other
areas suffering most in this respect were to be found in certain
parts of London, in Liverpool near the docks, and on the South
Wales coal-field. It is probably not an accident that, down to
1914, these (with the even more overcrowded Clyde) were the

[1] *Life and Labour of the People of London* (1902 ed.), i. ii. 21.

areas where violent revolutionary doctrines found their chief followings.

But overcrowding was not all; the incubus of past building neglects was tremendous. Pestiferous courts and alleys still abounded; dearth of sanitation, of water, of air, of sun, afflicted many hundreds of thousands of dwellings. Even above these, the typical homes of the artisans in the manufacturing towns—cottages in long rows lining mean streets, quite sanitary, but ugly, smoke-blackened, and monotonous—were apt to be starved of all such amenities as access to parks, or indeed to beauty of any sort. From the end of the eighties onward, socialist or labour representatives began to secure seats on local councils; and there they found they could immediately affect issues of this kind, vital to their class, which were out of their reach as trade unionists. Their experience formed a mainspring of the labour idealism whose advent will concern us in the course of our next chapter.

As at the close of Chapter IV, it is necessary here to add a warning against construing the economic facts too unfavourably. England in the nineties, even more than in the eighties, was in many respects losing ground. But most of the losses concerned her position in relation to other countries, or to the future; for the present, and considered absolutely, her condition was prosperous and improving. Just as her population grew despite a falling birth-rate, so her exports grew despite multiplied losses of foreign markets. It is true that in neither case did the balancing factors hold much probability of permanence; but there is a sense in which practical statesmen have no business to look too far ahead. The policies adopted during the queen's reign had lifted the English out of the slough of the forties, and enabled their teeming multitude on its narrow island to reach higher levels of economic comfort and political freedom than had ever before been witnessed on any large scale in Europe. The thing had been and still was a miracle; about which on the occasion of the two Jubilees the whole country gave expression to its gratitude and pride.

And if on some sides efficiency now slackened, on others it was tightened up. Particularly this was true of the Civil Service, which after thirty years of recruitment by public examination from the pick of the universities had improved its quality out of all recognition. It was also true of the local governing institutions, both the older ones in the towns and the newer ones which the period saw created in the counties and the districts. Here perhaps we may find the most permanent contribution of 1886–1900 to England's growth. These years equipped her for the first time with a complete modern framework for localized administration—democratic, flexible, passably honest, and capable of giving fruitful effect at the circumference to policies thought out at the national centre. Such was to prove a precious endowment for the nation, when called on to meet the demands of the twentieth century.

MENTAL AND SOCIAL ASPECTS 1886–1900

THE homogeneous England of the mid-Victorian decades broke up at the end of the eighties. In spite of its sharp divisions into classes, parties, and creeds, it had for over forty years been strongly united by fundamental identities of outlook. If we remember to give both terms a broad and not a formal sense, we may call it liberal and evangelical. The dissolution cannot be exactly dated, for it was gradual, and came earlier at the centres than at their circumferences. Queen Victoria's 1887 Jubilee was perhaps the last occasion on which enough semblance of the old unity survived to present an imposing façade.

The nineties were a period of unsettlement. The nation was out of health. It passed through a phase like an adolescence; its temper was explosive and quarrelsome; it boasted itself with the harshness of immaturity. Whole classes or strata of society were, in some degree, tasting power for the first time; and as they pushed their way out of the inarticulate and into the articulate part of the community, a kind of upstart arrogance became vocal with them. In religion, in social relations, in politics, in business, men grown contemptuous of the old ideals were stridently asserting new ones. The former clear objectives were gone, and as yet nothing took their place.

Because there was no unity of movement, the era presents very different features to different observers. To some it is the heyday of British imperialism, when the empire 'found itself'. To others, observing the early undergrowth of socialism and the memorable trade-union conflicts between capital and labour, it is the time when the British proletariat 'found itself'. Those again concerned with the fashionable surface of life and letters in London are struck by the revulsion from puritanism to raffishness, and speak of the 'naughty nineties'—the epoch of the *Yellow Book* and the Oscar Wilde case and of a more flaunting West End vice. If we look at the press revolution about to be described we may call it the age of vulgarization; but if we note how much material was being accumulated for the great educational advances of the next century, we may think of it as the dawning-hour of a new popular enlightenment. Very certainly it was a period of widening comfort; of humaner manners in the mass; of relaxation in taboos, both social and moral; and of growing mental freedom, accompanied, however, by a loss of concentration and direction.

As religion had in the preceding epoch been the backbone of English life, it is to the changes in that sphere that we may first turn. The influences separately at work to destroy the mid-Victorian evangelical unity were the same that we saw already beginning in Chapter V; which we may briefly term (though they were not the names then used) rationalism, anglo-catholicism, and hedonism. All three were much wider spread after 1886 than before. The first meant that, owing to the failure of evangelicalism to re-state its positions in conformity with either the new science or the new history (the so-called 'Higher Criticism'), a wide breach, sometimes public but far oftener tacit, was opened between it and the most educated classes. In earlier days a large proportion of the men attaining first-class honours at Oxford or Cambridge in subjects other than theology took Anglican Orders. By the later nineties such ordinations scarcely exceeded two a year. Some falling-off was to be expected, owing to the widened scope of the universities; but there were important classes, e.g. schoolmasters and fellows of colleges, whose ceasing to take Orders cannot be thus accounted for. Lay headmasters, a new phenomenon, began to be appointed at some of the public schools. Intellectual men were deterred from Orders not merely or always (though after 1886 very commonly) by doctrinal doubt, but because they no longer felt that church-going was the most central of their concerns. Not only rival interests, but rival careers were fast developing—the new civil service, the new openings in education and research, the higher journalism, and a variety of business callings, some (like electrical engineering) quite new, and others which, though old, had (like the solicitor's profession) greatly expanded in public esteem and social standing.[1]

Nonconformity, in its own sphere, receded much less during these years; but it too suffered in its recruitment of ministers from a worldly competition. Down to the eighties a gifted boy in the humblest classes found his only obvious 'escape' in the chapels; if he possessed any talent for oratory he would become a preacher, and in that way reach the goal of black-coated professional status. But from 1884 onwards a rival 'escape' appeared

[1] When Fowler entered the cabinet in 1892 he was the first solicitor to do so. He was also, it may be mentioned, the first methodist. Both facts are very significant of the change coming over England at that time.

in the labour movement. In the eighties and nineties a great many men became trade-union officials or socialist agitators (with a cabinet minister's seals of office in their knapsacks), who, had they been born twenty years earlier, would have made careers like Spurgeon's or General Booth's. To say this is not to impugn their sincerity in either case, but to recognize that human ability, like water, will rise to its level through the directest channel that may be open at any given time. The effects were of course not immediately felt; but in many great working-class areas (e.g. the South Wales coal-field) they showed themselves very markedly during the first quarter of the present century.

A time-lag operated similarly in the Anglican church, and until the end of the century the decline in its ministry was masked by the strength of the surviving elder personnel. It still possessed a very imposing bench of bishops, and its parochial clergy, not merely in fashionable town pulpits or much-noted slum missions, but as you found them quartered out over the country in the thousands of rural incumbencies, remained till then at a high average level. Often men of much distinction, who had taught as well as studied in their university, and nearly always real standard-bearers of culture, from whom high and low in their parishes could alike be willing to learn, this admirable class, with their wholesome home life and quiverfuls of well-educated children, wrought an immense social service to the countryside in their day. What eventually rendered its continuance impossible, in addition to all that has just been noted, was their economic downfall. This was an unforeseen by-product of the national decision to jettison agriculture; for the clergy's stipends were based on wheat-prices. The slump of the middle nineties, which dealt the *coup-de-grâce* to so many farms, was critical for the parsonages also; and while existing incumbents might hang on, it became nearly impossible to find successors for them of the same social and cultural standing.

Fashion among the incoming clergy at this time decidedly favoured the high church, and was in varying degrees 'Ritualist' (i.e. anglo-catholic). This was the work of certain theological colleges which the disciples of the Oxford Movement had captured, and at the head of which stood some of their ablest men. In 1885 Gladstone appointed one of them—Dr. Edward King, who had been principal of Cuddesdon—to the bishopric of Lincoln. King, though not extreme, was more of a ritualist than any bishop to whose appointment Queen Victoria had down to that time consented; and at the end of 1888 a protestant body, the Church Association, arraigned him for illegal practices in divine worship before the archbishop of Canterbury. There were no clear precedents for the authority of the archiepiscopal court to deal with such a case; and though the trial began in February 1889, the hearing did not take place till almost exactly a year later. The archbishop, Dr. E. W. Benson, sat supported by five notable bishops—Dr. Temple of London, who was to succeed him at Canterbury; Dr. Stubbs of Oxford, the celebrated historian; Dr. Thorold of Rochester, saintliest of Low Churchmen; Dr. Wordsworth of Salisbury, the learned editor of the Vulgate; and Dr. Atlay of Hereford. The practices objected to were seven; and, as the incriminated bishop admitted the acts, the only question was whether they were legal. The archbishop delivered judgement in November, finding for the defendant on five points, against him on two, and ordered that each party should pay its costs. The Church Association appealed to the privy council; but in August 1892 the appeal was dismissed.

These decisions were substantially a great victory for the ritualists. Their opponents had fought on ill-chosen ground; for to put a bishop on trial scandalized moderate opinion, and the more so because King bore a saintly character. Prosecutions became thenceforth less the order of the day; and ritualism, hitherto more or less confined to town churches, whose people could go elsewhere if they did not like it, extended its sway to places where this was not the case. Still an innovation of purely clerical origin, unpopular with most of the church-going laity,[1] it tended on the whole to disunite and diminish congregations.

The outcome of all these changes taken together was a rapid decrease in the amount of time and thought which it was customary for laymen to bestow on religion. After Lord Selborne there were no more lord chancellors who spent their Sunday leisure in teaching Sunday schools. Family prayers as an aristocratic habit began to drop out; and though in the nineties it still largely continued in upper-class or middle-class households whose heads had started it long before, you seldom found young

---

[1] Cp. Lord Salisbury: 'the High Church being backed generally by a majority of the clergy, and the Low Church by a majority of the laity' (letter of 26 January 1890, in *Queen Victoria's Letters*, III. i. 558). Though himself a high churchman he thought Dr. King went too far.

lay people starting it in new households. Actual church-going also fell off, though nothing like so much as in the twentieth century. In regard to London the case may be shown by figures. Two censuses of Sunday attendance at places of worship were taken for what became the L.C.C. area—the first in 1886, at the beginning of our period, by Robertson Nicoll for the *British Weekly*, and the second in 1902–3, soon after the period's close, by R. Mudie Smith for the *Daily News*. Nicoll's census was all done in one day, and included no services before 11 a.m.; Mudie Smith's, far more scientific, was mapped out by districts over a whole year, not missing the smallest conventicles, and it took in services at all hours. For these reasons, as well as because the population of the area had increased by half a million in the interval, the second census, had there been no decline, should have shown much the larger figures. Instead it showed a drop from a gross total of 1,167,312 attendances to one of 1,003,361. Attendances at anglican services (excluding missions) had actually fallen from 535,715 to 396,196; nonconformist attendances (excluding missions and the Salvation Army) only from 369,349 to 363,882. As Mudie Smith obtained figures showing how many persons attended more than one service, he was able to give the net number of persons worshipping. They were only 832,051 in a resident population (outside institutions) of 4,470,304, or little over two in eleven.

Fuller light regarding the religious situation in London may be obtained from the elaborate survey of it made in the years 1897–1900 by Charles Booth.[1] Many of Booth's conclusions were strongly borne out by the Mudie Smith census; e.g. that nonconformity held its men better than anglicanism, while the more ritualistic churches were particularly short of male worshippers. Both Booth and the census witnessed to the relative success of 'institutional' churches, i.e. those in which there was a strong organization catering for secular as well as religious interests. Both showed, too, that the poorest (except the Roman Catholic Irish) attended nothing save missions; and the ordinary working man did not, unless in a few special types of case, attend any place of worship at all. It must, however, be borne in mind that many conditions affecting religion in London differed greatly from those in the country at large. Not only had it always con-

---

[1] Forming the third series (in 7 volumes) of his *Life and Labour in London* (completed 1903).

tained immensely larger masses of 'heathen' than any other area, but the attendance at its churches and chapels was far less often parochial. Elsewhere people to a great extent went to worship with their neighbours; but a large proportion of Londoners, especially in the richer boroughs, scarcely had any neighbours in that sense. In particular the inhabitants of well-to-do blocks of flats, which became exceedingly numerous in the metropolis before 1900 (while scarcely to be found elsewhere in England, even in an agglomeration so huge as Manchester's), were almost wholly de-localized. It would be a mistake to suppose that the two-elevenths ratio of worshippers to population recorded by Mudie Smith was typical of England at large. He himself found higher proportions in the suburbs outside the county; and as a rule they would be higher still in the manufacturing towns, especially in the smaller ones which were strongholds of nonconformity. Yet even in the villages the falling-off had become noticeable before the end of the century. People connected it with the general break-up of rural society, the downfall of so many of the old local pillars, and the growing impoverishment of churches and chapels generally.

As a corollary of these changes, it became impossible to keep up the Victorian Sabbath. If large elements in the towns, including growing numbers in the educated and governing classes, were in no case going to spend their Sundays on religion, they must be allowed to spend them on other activities; the alternative of idle boredom, which became widespread, had nothing to commend it. Important work was done at this time by an organization formed for the purpose—the National Sunday League—towards enabling the urban demand for Sunday recreation to flow into healthy channels. It organized Sunday railway excursions at cheap rates—a matter in which it may be said to have taught the railway directorates their business; and it agitated persistently for the Sunday opening of museums and art-galleries. Victory in this last field was won in 1896, when, following a resolution by the house of commons, the state's museums and art-galleries in the metropolis were thrown open to the public on Sunday afternoons. It must not be supposed, however, that the nineteenth century ever made Sunday in England a day of pleasure in the degree that the twentieth does. The strong feeling against Sunday labour prevented it. The Victorian nobility would walk rather than drive to church, so as not to infringe the resting of their grooms and horses. This spirit, which had checked all Sunday entertaining, only yielded very slowly to examples like the prince of Wales's Sunday dinner-parties. London's hotel and restaurant life was practically in abeyance for the day during the queen's reign. There was even a strong prejudice against Sunday newspapers. They had very small circulations; the 'weekly' papers, which were so popular with the working classes, being sold on Saturday.

If we pass now to consider the press, we find ourselves before one of the turning-points in national evolution. Chapter V recorded the reign down to 1886 of an extremely dignified type of journalism, conducted with a high sense of personal responsibility, and seeking to win intelligent readers on the assumption that the rest would travel in their wake. We have now to record how in a few short years it was rivalled, defeated, and eventually almost driven out of the field, by the meteoric rise of another type, far less responsible and far less intellectual, but far more widely sold.

It is sometimes said that W. T. Stead in his editorship (1883–9) of the *Pall Mall Gazette* pioneered the downfall of the old order. But that is to mistake the scope of the change. True, the new journalism was sensational, and Stead also was. So, in their day and in their way, had been the greatest editors of *The Times*, J. T. Delane and Thomas Barnes. But Stead's sensations, like theirs, always made a direct appeal to men dealing with public affairs; even the most lurid of them, his 'Maiden Tribute of Modern Babylon' (a series of articles exposing the white slave traffic), had as its express object, in which it was successful, the passage of a measure then before Parliament (the Criminal Law Amendment Bill). The key feature of the new journalism was not sensation but commercialism. It ran its sensations, as it ran everything else, to make money, and measured them solely by the sales they brought. The indisputable pioneer of this school in daily journalism was Alfred Harmsworth, afterwards Lord Northcliffe.

We saw in Chapter V how George Newnes had started a weekly, *Tit-Bits*, catering in quite a new way for a new class of readers—the millions to whom the Forster Education Act had taught reading without teaching them what to read. They were people who only followed print painfully and with difficulty; to hold their interest it was necessary to give short words, short sentences, short paragraphs, short articles, and to put everything as far as possible in story form. Working from these premises, Newnes evolved a regular technique. He was a real inventor, and discovered not a few devices that have since been employed on a vastly greater scale. Thus he seems to have been the first to use prize competitions as a means to increase the sales of a paper; and he was the first to give his readers a free insurance, though it was only a modest policy against railway accidents. Alfred Harmsworth, who entered his office in 1885 at the age of 20, was the eldest son (by an Irish mother) of an impecunious barrister with a very large family. He had left school at 15 to struggle in the humbler paths of journalism. How much work he did for Newnes seems uncertain. But it is not disputed that through him he became aware for the first time of the new public and how to reach it. In 1888 he started the first paper of his own, a weekly entitled *Answers to Correspondents*. It was based on the idea, that, because a column thus headed was commonly one of the most-read features in a paper, therefore a whole paper so constituted would attract readers. This was a fallacy, and he might easily have been ruined by it. But Harmsworth as a projector was for nothing more remarkable than the rapid and ruthless correction of his own mistakes. He had from the first put some matter of *Tit-Bits* type in his paper; now he made that the staple, and came out as a direct rival to Newnes. Even so his venture ran near the rocks for about sixteen months, until the success of a prize scheme —a pound a week for life for guessing the value of the gold in the Bank of England on a given day—established it with a large circulation. He proceeded in conjunction with his brother Harold[1] (whose extraordinary financial genius supplied the chief business gift which Alfred lacked) to add fresh ventures to it, and build up a most lucrative business in periodicals supplying chatty un-intellectual pabulum for uneducated minds. *Answers* rose to 250,000 circulation, then deemed enormous, and five other little papers were produced along with it, the most profitable, *Comic Cuts*, being designed for schoolboys of the age at which the Harmsworths were at school.

All this would have been but a minor influence if they had not next used their sudden wealth to invade daily journalism. In 1894 Kennedy Jones, a Glasgow Irishman of semi-slum origin, then employed as reporter on an evening paper, obtained a very

[1] Since 1913 Lord Rothermere.

cheap option on the *Evening News*. He persuaded the Harmsworths to buy it and to make him editor. It proved a good bargain for both sides. Kennedy Jones was of a rough type, but he
had studied the technique of the American 'yellow' press, and
possessed the experience of daily journalism which the Harmsworths lacked. The *Evening News* was one of a few evening papers
sold at a halfpenny—i.e. half what was the standard price of a
morning one. These already reached a class which did not otherwise buy dailies. But the new methods were designed to widen it
fast. The hard work in their success was Kennedy Jones's, but
the restless imagination of Alfred Harmsworth played round it at
every point. He visited the United States to study the model on
the spot. Then he laid his plans for a morning halfpenny journal.
One such already existed—the *Morning Leader*, a small bright
radical sheet with a narrow circulation. Harmsworth's conception was nothing like that; he wanted the largest circulation in
England. By 1896 he and Kennedy Jones had matured their
scheme. The *Daily Mail*, launched in May of that year, was an
instant success. During the first twelve months its daily sale
averaged 202,000. At the end of three years it had reached
543,000. No other daily in England touched half that figure;
and the young upstart of 34, who had started practically from
nothing only eleven years earlier, stood revealed as a menace to
the whole established order of journalism. For that order lived
by advertisements and advertisements will go where circulation
goes. Harmsworth knew his advantage; and his favourite
weapon against the penny dailies was a demand for the publication of their net sales.

What sort of man, and what sort of paper, had Fortune's wheel
thus elevated? Harmsworth's best biographer, an intimate and
admirer, records that 'he knew no Latin or Greek; he had very
hazy notions of history; he was well acquainted with no modern
languages; the interest he took in science was that of a quick-
witted child'.[1] And again: 'Boyish in his power of concentration
upon the matter of the moment, boyish in his readiness to turn
swiftly to a different matter and concentrate on that. . . . Boyish
the limited range of his intellect, which seldom concerns itself
with anything but the immediate, the obvious, the popular.
Boyish his irresponsibility, his disinclination to take himself or
his publications seriously; his conviction that whatever benefits

[1] Hamilton Fyfe, *Northcliffe* (1930), p. 29.

them is justifiable, and that it is not his business to consider the effect of their contents on the public mind.'[1] Originally, apart from a born zest for news, he was only interested in newspapers as bringing money. Later he appreciated them also as bringing power. He never appreciated that they brought responsibility.

His leading characteristics were energy and ambition. Quite early he conceived a parallel between himself and Napoleon, to whom he bore some physical resemblance. He thirsted to conquer. But unlike his prototype he had no cultural uses for conquest, nor anything that in the higher sense might be called an ideal. The lack of one prevented him from becoming a revolutionary in politics, or even, like his teacher, Newnes, a liberal. But he was not really a conservative either. It was his instinct to shout with the largest black-coated crowd. But he had no Disraelian feeling for the greatness of the country's past and the continuity of her institutions. His political mentality was that of the London clerk class, among whom he lived during his formative years.

His papers bore the stamp of their uneducated founders. 'Written by office-boys for office-boys' was Lord Salisbury's famous gibe. But the public which liked them was extremely wide and by no means all poor. The business class, which had become so important in England, comprised enormous numbers of men who had not had even a secondary education. Outside the matters in which they made their money they had the minds of children. Existing newspapers ignored their naïve tastes, while assuming an amount of critical intelligence which they simply did not possess. Something very similar was true of the women in all ranks of society. Harmsworth rightly divined that the favourite paper in the boudoir and in the kitchen would be the same.

There was a sharp technical difference between the new paper and the old. The old would print telegrams and reports pretty much as they came in. The function of the sub-editor was to decide in what column and in what type they should appear, if at all, and to provide a few plain headings. But in the new his function was to re-write them. They must be condensed, re-worded, re-paragraphed, and each converted according to certain rules into a lively 'story'; after which they were given plenty of spicy and tendentious headings. The result was in

[1] Ibid., p. 106.

every way a 'brighter' paper. The mere look of the page was cheering, when the number of separate items, headings, and paragraphs on it was so much increased, and one gathered a far larger collection of stories by reading far fewer words. But the change had also a disadvantage; which may be expressed by saying that the old method served up its news raw, while the new one served it cooked. Cooking never makes news truer; and whereas hitherto the reader had been given the facts and only told what to think of them in the leading articles, now it was sought to create his opinion by doctoring the facts before they reached him. It is perhaps not easy for readers of the present day, brought up under this system, to realize what a profound innovation it was.

But indeed the whole attitude towards the reader was transformed. The old idea assumed that he was a critical politician, who watched events and would resent the paper's missing any serious news-item. All such items were therefore carefully given; and if none of them happened to be very 'bright' that was the affair of Providence, and must be accepted like rain or sun. The new idea assumed a mass of readers, whose interest in politics was slight, whose memories were short, who would never know or care if half the serious news were left out, but who day by day demanded bright stories to tickle their imaginations and to talk about. To report parliament at length, or even to report it fairly at all, was to bore and estrange them.[1] But what they asked, they must have; and if Providence did not supply exciting news, the office must not fail to make some. Hence the device of 'stunts'; about which the chief thing to note is that, though they often took the form of advocating some cause, it was seldom on its merits that the cause was espoused, but for its effect on circulation. Many of them were quite trivial; but others had far-reaching effects. For instance, it was a maxim with Alfred Harmsworth that readers liked 'a good hate'. One way to satisfy this was by exciting violent xenophobia against a particular nation; and this he did—in the nineteenth century against France, in the twentieth against Germany. Again, he realized from the start the circulation-raising properties of war. Already in 1898 the *Daily Mail* ran up its sales by its stories of Kitchener's Omdur-

[1] Few features in the new journalism were to prove of deeper political import than its abandonment of the practice, till then universal, of reporting parliament. More than anything else, it dethroned the house of commons.

man campaign. Thereafter it did all it could to render England
bellicose against the Transvaal; and, when the South African
war followed, it profited still further from its excitements. The
special train, which it was the first to charter to carry its parcels
beyond the area hitherto served by London newspapers, was
christened 'the South African train'. The lengths to which in
these days it would go for sensation, and the extent to which it
could presume on its readers' uncritical indulgence, were both
well illustrated by an incident in 1900. The fanatical Chinese
Boxers besieged the diplomatic corps in Pekin, where the white
residents (including 147 women and 76 children) had taken
refuge in the British and other legations. During weeks of sus-
pense the world was without news of them, and their anguished
relatives feared every day to hear the worst. Then one morning
the *Daily Mail* published the worst—a lurid account of a
frightful massacre. This, as appeared later when the legations
were relieved, was a pure invention, and, having regard to the
feelings of relatives, an extraordinarily cruel one. If one of the
old penny papers had done such a thing it would have been
ruined; its public would never have forgiven it. But the *Daily
Mail*'s public soon forgot. Provided it gave them the excitements that they wanted they troubled little about its veracity or
honour; and the result showed that it had rightly judged their
taste.

Only the first stage of the Harmsworth revolution falls within
these years. Till the last year of the queen's reign the *Daily Mail*
was still the sole morning paper of its kind; though in such prosperity that a landslide towards it was bound to follow. We shall
trace its extent in a later chapter.

Meanwhile Newnes, who had opened the flood-gate, had himself steered a very different course. Enriched by *Tit-Bits*, his
idea was not, like Harmsworth's, to spawn shoals of other papers
on the same mental level, but to use his money to give the public
something more educative. In 1890 he helped W. T. Stead to
start the *Review of Reviews*. In 1891 he founded the *Strand Maga-
zine*, a popular illustrated monthly (using the then new 'process-
blocks'), which was the forerunner of all such monthlies, and
did in its day a really beneficent work towards banishing drabness
from middle-class households. At the end of 1892 he intervened
in daily journalism. The *Pall Mall Gazette*, a penny London evening paper with the limited but extremely influential circulation

then open to a newspaper in that class, had long been a leading liberal organ, and since 1889 edited by E. T. Cook, one of the last and greatest 'writing editors' of the old school. An American millionaire bought it, desiring to convert it into a conservative paper and supposing, apparently, that the staff would acquiesce. Instead, under Cook's leadership they all walked out; and Newnes then engaged them in a body to run a new liberal paper, the *Westminster Gazette*, whose first number appeared at the end of January 1893. Unlike most of Newnes's ventures, this journal never shone as a money-maker. But as an organ of high politics on the intellectual plane it filled in the revival of the liberal party and during its period of pre-war rule a place of central importance. Meanwhile Cook and his colleagues were thought to have strikingly vindicated the independence of journalists.

Seven years later, however, it was again challenged. Down to the outbreak of the South African war the two London liberal morning papers, the *Daily News* and *Daily Chronicle*, took opposite roles. The *News*, edited since 1895 by E. T. Cook, was pro-Milner and supported the war. The *Chronicle*, edited by another famous writing journalist, H. W. Massingham, was pro-Boer and opposed the war. But during 1900 the politics of both papers were forcibly changed. The proprietor of the *Chronicle* squeezed out Massingham, and launched a pro-war policy; while about the same time an anti-war syndicate (originated by Lloyd George) bought the *Daily News*, and ousted Cook. Thus both editors were dislodged, and the positions of the two papers were sharply and oddly reversed—a fact to be remembered by any one studying the press opinion of that time.

Elementary education during these years was still bisected between the voluntary bodies and the school boards; and the latter were still afflicted by the religious squabbles, which did so much to lower them in public esteem. But the quality of the teachers was steadily rising; all concerned came to take compulsory education for granted; and the abolition of school fees under Lord Salisbury's Act of 1891 removed any remaining grievance of the parents. The battle against mere illiteracy was won; and it became practicable to devote more attention to problems of further education.

The first Salisbury government had set up a large royal com-

mission with Cross (then home secretary) as chairman, 'to en-
quire into the working of the Elementary Education Acts, England and Wales'. In June 1888 it issued its reports—majority and
minority. The first question confronting it had been that of the
voluntary schools. The majority believed that they ought to be
maintained, and for that their resources must be increased. They
were willing even to give them a share of the local rates. The
minority, composed of radicals and nonconformists, objected.
They particularly deprecated any payment to the voluntary
schools out of rates as 'certain, if it became law, to embitter
educational politics and intensify sectarian rivalries'. This
remained an open controversy for another fourteen years. Meanwhile, religion apart, the curriculum of the elementary schools,
once they got past the three R's, was left a good deal to chance.
The education department laid down in 1886–7 that 'the course
suited to an elementary school is practically determined by the
limit of fourteen years of age, and may properly include whatever subjects can be effectively taught within that limit'. Acting
on this principle many school boards developed 'higher elementary' or 'higher grade' schools, which possessed their own laboratories, apparatus, and special provision for drawing, and pushed
their pupils through examinations where they could earn grants
from the science and art department at South Kensington. In so
doing they largely ignored England's existing secondary schools
—the endowed grammar schools dotted over the country;
though a few big school boards—e.g. Manchester, Birmingham,
Leeds, and Bradford—did give scholarships to them. The unco-
ordinated attempt to develop secondary instruction under an
elementary school code, for children all of whom must leave
at fourteen, could not be satisfactory. 'The type of instruction,
which the higher grade schools were creating, was wanting in
breadth, and likely to confuse still further the public mind as to
what constitutes a liberal education.'[1]

'Payment by results' was another matter coming before the
Cross Commission. The minority condemned it outright; the
majority with more reserve wanted it to be 'modified and relaxed'. By the Code of 1890 this was done. In 1892, when the
liberals returned to office, Gladstone gave the post of vice-
president of the council for education, with a seat in the cabinet,
to A. H. D. Acland, who held it also under Lord Rosebery.

[1] J. W. Adamson, *English Education 1789–1902* (1930), p. 371.

Acland, whose after career was dimmed by ill health, was one of the ablest men in those two governments and, incidentally, their chief go-between in dealing with labour. He brought to his task more understanding perhaps than any previous vice-president, and his Code for Evening Schools (1893) was a distinct advance. So in its way was his drastic circular calling for reports upon the defects in school buildings; for though its immediate outcome was much cry and little wool, it did at least force to the front the problem of bad accommodation in the voluntary schools, for which, one way or other, some remedy was urgent. Later he induced Gladstone to appoint a royal commission on secondary education, with Bryce as chairman; and at the end of 1894 he was able to form in his department a special inquiries branch with Mr. (afterwards Sir) Michael Sadler at its head to investigate and report on systems and methods of education abroad. It was Sadler who, by appointing as his assistant R. L. Morant, introduced to the department the man who in a few years' time was to re-model English educational machinery.

The Bryce Commission proved a singularly fruitful one; but to understand its task we must go back a little. The leading educational feature of these years was the attempt to build up for the first time in England a national system of technical education. The starting-point was the Technical Instruction Act, 1889. Our leading industrial competitors—the United States, Germany, France, Belgium, and Switzerland—had all started from twenty-five to forty years earlier.

Technical education in modern England, like most other things, had begun with unco-ordinated private enterprise. In 1823 Dr. Birkbeck, encouraged by Lord Brougham, started the London Mechanics' Institute. By 1850 there were 622 mechanics' institutes in England and Wales with over 600,000 members. Here might have been the bases of a great system, but it proved otherwise; the institutes passed from the mechanics to the middle class. Partly it was that as yet too few artisans had had an elementary education; partly, that for too few, as yet, could a knowledge of science be of direct use. Besides technology as a subject was in its infancy. However, the movement led to the development of national examination systems; at first by voluntary bodies—the College of Preceptors (in 1853) and the Society of Arts (in 1856–7); and then from 1859 onwards by the state, as represented by the department of science and art at South

Kensington. The last, which paid government grants to schools in respect of examinations passed by their pupils, became a decidedly important body. Characteristically it was quite distinct from the department of education, though, as we have seen, a good many of its grant-earners came to be pupils in the 'higher grade' elementary schools. In 1879 a new body came on the scene, the City and Guilds of London Institute. It took over from the Society of Arts a system of examinations in 'technological subjects' (begun some six years earlier), and on these issued certificates and paid grants to schools, from funds supplied by the city companies.

Thus, it will be seen, central planning, whether state or private, was confined to examinations and grants made on them. Everything else was left to haphazard enterprise, which too often meant enterprise in the arts of make-believe.[1] The nation's requirements were not being met. At the Great Exhibition of 1851, out of a hundred different departments in which goods were displayed, Great Britain had won the palm of excellence in nearly all. But at the Paris Exhibition of 1867 she excelled her competitors in only 10 per cent. Lyon Playfair, who had been a juror at Paris, wrote a letter ascribing England's loss of ground to the fact that her competitors possessed 'good systems of industrial education for the masters and managers of factories and workshops', whereas England possessed none. A committee appointed to probe the matter confirmed his statement; but for fourteen years little came of it. In 1881 the problem was remitted to a royal commission under Mr. (afterwards Sir) Bernhard Samuelson, which reported in 1882 and 1884. It was in belated conformity with these reports that the Technical Instruction Act 1889 was passed, twenty-two years after Playfair's letter.

Besides setting up a local authority for technical education (the county, or county borough, council), the act enlarged the purview of the central authority, the science and art department. Hitherto it had only given grants for examinations passed by members of the 'industrial classes', a term defined so as to exclude any one who paid, or whose parents paid, income-tax. This restriction barred out most of the future 'masters and managers', whose need Playfair had stressed; and after 1889 it was dropped. The councils were empowered to levy a penny rate for the work;

[1] A clear picture of how it worked out will be found in H. G. Wells, *Experiment in Autobiography* (1934), e.g. at i. 173–4.

but it was the 'whisky money' of 1890[1] that really got it moving. In 1892-3 this amounted to £472,500, but by 1901-2 had reached £859,000. The local authorities also could (and did) raise large sums for new buildings by loan. In London the Technical Instruction Committee of the L.C.C. was particularly active, and under the chairmanship of Sidney Webb built up a great system for the metropolis. In Manchester the city council was enabled to develop its famous School of Technology on the lines of an English counterpart to Charlottenburg.

Thus when the Bryce Commission surveyed the field, it found two distinct sets of authorities in it. On the one hand there was the department of education, with school boards under it giving secondary education of a kind in 'higher grade' elementary schools. On the other, there was the science and art department, with the county councils under it giving technical education, much of which was secondary in character. Lastly, outside both machineries,[2] there were the grammar schools and other ancient endowed foundations, numerous but mostly small and needy, representing the only public provision for secondary education as such. To bring together these divided and partly overlapping agencies the Bryce Commission recommended forming a central education authority, to be 'a Department of the Executive Government, presided over by a Minister responsible to Parliament, who would obviously be the same Minister as the one to whom the charge of elementary education is entrusted'. Four years later this was done, and the board of education was constituted (1899) to bring under one head the old department of education and the science and art department. The Commission also recommended that the local unit for secondary education should be the county or county borough, whose council should administer it through an education committee containing co-opted members. Seven years passed before these far-seeing counsels were followed, as we shall see later on, by the Act of 1902. Altogether, if the test of a royal commission's success is that behind the evasions of governments and parties it should discern the unescapable trends of high policy, the Bryce Commission was a singularly successful one.

Elsewhere in the educational field the chief advances which

---

[1] p. 204 above.
[2] Save in so far as their curriculum was influenced by desire to earn the science and art department's grants.

concerned the state were those towards multiplying universities. The starting-points here, as we saw in Chapter V, were local colleges, whose students sat for the examinations and took the degrees of London University. We saw how in 1884 the colleges at Manchester, Liverpool, and Leeds combined to form a degree-giving university of their own—the Victoria University. In 1893 the three Welsh colleges (Aberystwyth, Cardiff, and Bangor) formed the University of Wales; in which, as in the Victoria University, women participated on an equal footing with men. Similar equality (except for divinity degrees) was embodied in the supplementary charter obtained in 1895 by the older (1832) University of Durham. In 1900 Mason College, Birmingham, obtained a charter as Birmingham University. This was the first case in which a great industrial city had a university all its own, not shared on a federal basis with other cities; and the example was not lost on Manchester and Liverpool. In 1889 parliament for the first time recognized the university colleges as an educational category by voting an annual sum for distribution between them. At the end of the century the grant was £25,000, distributed among no less than thirteen institutions, three in London and ten elsewhere in England.[1] In 1898 the University of London, fruitful parent of so many offshoots, was itself the subject of legislation. A special act of that year appointed seven commissioners, who in February 1900 issued statutes. The effect of the act and the statutes together was to give London University for the first time the framework of a modern academic organization, with a senate, an academic council, a university extension board, and eight faculties; while comprised in it as 'Schools of the University' were to be, not merely the three university colleges then receiving grants as such,[2] but ten medical schools, six theological colleges, Holloway College, the London School of Economics, the South-Eastern Agricultural College, and the Central Technical College of the City and Guilds Institution. Though the scheme was a compromise and did not go as far as some advocates of unity and centralization wished, it gave to London University more of the character of a teaching institution than it ever had before.

As yet, however, the institutions noticed in the last paragraph did not, except in the field of medicine, supply the nation with its

[1] The three Welsh colleges had a separate grant.
[2] University College, King's College, and Bedford College.

highest learning or culture. They were themselves staffed almost entirely by men from Oxford or Cambridge; and England still depended on those two ancient universities to keep her abreast of the world's advance. Similarly for her highest secondary education she relied mainly on the public schools. The quality in both cases was higher than ever before, thanks to the reforms and expansions of the seventies, and to half a century of conscientious Victorian work. But the annual output of educated persons remained too small, and could never along those lines have grown large enough. It was a growing awareness of this, that, as the century closed, made not a few thoughtful men feel the solution of England's higher education problem to be her most urgent need. It was obvious that her neighbour, Scotland, was, in proportion, far ahead of her.

An educational influence outside the schools, which made a sudden spurt during these years, was that of free libraries. As early as 1880 Andrew Carnegie, an American millionaire born in Scotland at Dunfermline, had presented a free library to his native town. Between 1886 and 1900 he founded others in Great Britain, and a retired London newspaper proprietor, J. Passmore Edwards, followed the same course.[1] In 1892 was passed a new Public Libraries Act extending the original act of 1850; and in 1894 Fowler's Local Government Act made it possible for even a rural parish to have a public library. As a result of all these things, such libraries in the nineties were rapidly multiplied.

Art now began, though with difficulty, to convalesce. Men grew conscious of the mid-Victorian ugliness, and realized in varying degrees, that it was not a matter of individual failure so much as of a general loss of direction amid the snowstorms of rapid material and social change. Art had gone astray, or, as they saw it rather, was fallen sick. Yet it was easier to become aware of the malady than to diagnose it and prescribe for it successfully. Rival diagnoses were proclaimed side by side, often with no clear sense of their inconsistency. Some, with William Morris, laid the blame on capitalism and machinery, which had killed the joy and tradition of craftsmanship and unduly divorced

---

[1] Passmore Edwards (d. 1911) erected in all twenty-four free libraries; Carnegie (d. 1919), 2,505. Most of the latter were in the U.S.A., but Great Britain benefited appreciably also.

the work of brain and hand. Back, they said, to the hand-made and the medieval, to guild crafts and 'folk' art. Out of this grew the alliance between art and socialism, and a whole theory of politics and history. Others, more on the surface perhaps, were content merely to react against the particular fashions of the recent past, and set up some other eclectic fashion in their place. So, for example, the architects of this period reacted against Victorian Gothic, and imitated English or French Renaissance instead. Others again, with Oscar Wilde, thought that the mistake of the previous generation had been to mix up art with morals, and affirmed 'Art for Art's sake'; an impulse which was far from lacking justification, but slipped too easily into the currents of the new hedonism, and proved, on the whole, less conducive to higher art than to lower morality. With the younger painters the prestige of Paris was now at last beginning to tell; and there was a strong tendency among them, if they had no particular impulse of their own, to take refuge in doing what the French had done.

English architecture towards the end of the century was dominated by Norman Shaw. His was an alert and versatile genius, constantly breaking out into new experiments and setting examples, which his fellow architects found contagious. But neither he nor they (with the possible exception of Philip Webb) got away from the notion that to give a building architectural quality involved clothing it in some form of historical fancy-dress. The prevalent style became what was known as 'free classic', but in fact was largely based on one or other of the many varieties of French Renaissance. Start along the Thames Embankment from Westminster Bridge, and you come almost immediately on New Scotland Yard (1889), which is Norman Shaw's most-praised public building. Its great merits may easily be catalogued; and yet is there any real reason why London's central police-station should look like a French early-Renaissance château (with some touches of a German castle) transported from the Loire to the Thames? Pass a little further, and you come to the large block of offices, flats, and club premises called White-hall Court (not by Shaw but contemporary), erected for the 'Liberator' building society which went bankrupt in 1892 through the Jabez Balfour frauds. Viewed from any high point within a couple of miles its sky-line is among the most effective in London; but every one who has seen the Château de Chambord knows where it comes from. It would be easy to multiply such instances. Towards the end of the century design became less imitative, and showed more concern to express the structure and the purposes of modern buildings. It would be going too far to say that their full logic was ever faced with the candour that might have created a new style. Nevertheless, English architecture at this stage became very interesting to foreign architects on both sides of the Atlantic—more so perhaps than at any time since.

One of the most ambitious public buildings in 'free classic' was the Imperial Institute, by T. E. Collcutt. In the north of England the most imposing example was the Sheffield Town Hall, by E. W. Mountford. Smaller examples of special merit are the town halls at Oxford (by H. T. Hare) and Colchester (by John Belcher). Since they were originally designed in 1899–1900 (though not completed for some years after), we should perhaps mention here the War Office (by W. Young) and the better-designed block of government buildings (by J. M. Brydon) at the angle of Whitehall and Great George Street. But they are on a different footing, since the government of the day expressly prescribed for them the 'classical' manner.

If we pass from public buildings to houses and offices, we find a distinct improvement in the homes of the well-to-do. Design was better; materials were used with a greater care for their congruity. Here the pioneer of reform had been Morris's friend Philip Webb, who was an architect of houses and not much else. He did not create a school, but the effect of his work (which he continued till 1900) was to bring upper-class house-design back to a vernacular simplicity, from which what was called 'Queen Anne' emerged. The seventeenth-century motives carried out in brick, or brick with stone quoins and dressings, which Norman Shaw rendered fashionable for mansions and large suburban houses, made some real addition to the country's stock of beautiful edifices. As much cannot be said of the dwellings produced for the mass of the people—the numerous Jubilee Streets and the many little homes christened Ladysmith or Mafeking or Omdurman. The type-unit of these continued to be a brick box with a slate lid, designed in all its parts with as much indifference to form and proportions as before; though with rising standards of room-accommodation and internal comfort.

Anglican church-building, of which there had been a steady

flow during the religious Victorian period culminating in J. L. Pearson's learned and attractive Truro Cathedral (consecrated 1887), was kept to Gothic from motives of religious sentiment. Latterly (more through the work of G. F. Bodley than of any other architect) it had gained greatly in freshness and refinement, and produced structures (like Bodley's Marlborough College Chapel, 1886) of abiding beauty. The exceptions to Gothic were a few 'basilica' churches, erected for ritualists who liked them for liturgical reasons. The Roman catholics, however, usually retained Gothic, save in the case of the modern-Italian Brompton Oratory (enlarged 1888; completed 1896–7). But when in the middle nineties they undertook the building of an archiepiscopal cathedral at Westminster, it was decided to substitute the early Byzantine style. This was done at the instance of Cardinal Vaughan, who saw the wisdom of avoiding any sort of comparison with Westminster Abbey. The appointed architect, J. F. Bentley, would have preferred it Gothic, but he accepted the decision, and giving the rest of his life to the task produced the great building which is now familiar. Founded in June 1895, its exterior, save the towers, was completed by the end of the century.

Revival in the domestic arts during this period was chiefly due to the stimulus of William Morris. His wall-papers and textiles had revolutionized commercial design; and a new type of artist-craftsman grew up in his wake. In 1888 was held the first exhibition of the Arts and Crafts Guild; and in the same year Morris began to explore yet another field—that of printing—which mainly occupied him from 1891 till his death in 1896. Opinions may differ as to the merits of the types which he designed; but of the far-reaching influence which he exerted there can be no question. From him and his collaborator, Emery Walker, it is hardly too much to say that the revival of fine printing descends. Through them England took a lead in it, which she has never since lost.

In painting the same years witnessed the tardy triumph of impressionism on this side of the Channel. The individual painter dominating the epoch was the Anglicized American, J. S. Sargent, whose work in the later nineties became the leading attraction at the exhibitions of the Royal Academy. As a portraitist he reached his summit with the *Asher Wertheimer* of 1898 and the *Lady Elcho and her Two Sisters* of 1900. His example (for, though originally a disciple of Carolus-Duran, it was as an Impressionist that he developed his personal style) made it easier for the Academy to become reconciled to impressionist painting, and one by one to win over most, though not all, of the brilliant young men who in 1886 had founded the New English Art Club. By so doing it saved itself; for, apart from Sargent, nearly all the English artists whose fame lay in the future were partisans of the newer body; and had they boycotted the old in permanence, they might have dethroned it.

Much more important to the nation, however, than any body of new painting executed at this time was its widened approach to art through the great expansion in the number and scale of its public art-galleries. Between 1886 and 1900 there were first opened in London the present National Portrait Gallery (1896), the National Gallery of British Art (1897, enlarged 1899), and the Wallace Collection (1900); the National Gallery itself received (1887) a most important extension. The state, as represented by a treasury still ruled by Gladstonian thrift, remained very stingy to art. The National Portrait Gallery[1] was built at the cost of a private individual—W. H. Alexander; and the National Gallery of British Art by another—Sir Henry Tate; the government merely gave sites. Its original grant to the National Portrait Gallery for the purchase of pictures was only £750 a year; in the case of the Tate Gallery a sum of £5,000 was assigned jointly to it and the National Gallery, out of which, in the sequel, the Tate received nothing. But when Sir Richard Wallace's widow bequeathed his marvellous collection to the nation, parliament recognized that it must be properly housed, and spent eventually £135,000 on it. So too, following the rise of technical education in the nineties, it realized that the South Kensington Museum was altogether too small, and sanctioned new buildings by Sir Aston Webb to cost £800,000. Queen Victoria herself laid the foundation-stone in 1899 of what thenceforward became the Victoria and Albert Museum. Nor did these state-supported institutions in the metropolis stand alone. A single year (1890) saw three other permanent collections opened—the City of London Corporation Gallery, the Whitworth Institute at Manchester, and the Irish Art Museum at Dublin. The municipal galleries of Birmingham, Liverpool, and Manchester became important

---

[1] The nucleus of its collection had been begun some years previously and housed in makeshift places—chiefly in the East End.

before the end of the century. But the Harcourt Death Duties had the effect, after 1894, of bringing the private picture-heirlooms of England increasingly into the market. American and German buyers early saw their opportunity; but the problem of saving the country's treasures did not become acute till the period 1900–14.

In the art of music the progress, which England had made in 1870–86, was more than continued. In 1894 the Queen's Hall replaced the old St. James's Hall as the home of orchestral music in London;[1] and round it as a nucleus a new type of concert-going public—unfashionable, intellectual, middle-class, and largely masculine—grew up to be familiar with such music and capable of appreciating it seriously. In respect of first-class concerts London was now nearly level with the main musical centres on the Continent; what kept her still below them was that she had no regular opera save the brief annual pretence of one at Covent Garden, where foreign artists were hired to perform in foreign languages at high prices for the unmusical aristocracy during the London 'season'. Outside the metropolis the chief musical event was the Three Choirs Festival, and the chief purveyor of orchestral concerts the Hallé orchestra; of which at the very end of the century no less a person than Hans Richter consented to become the conductor. But other musical centres were developing, notably Birmingham, and, for chamber music, Oxford and Cambridge.

Serious musical composition was at first chiefly in the hands of Parry and Stanford. Sullivan until 1896 continued writing light operas, and in 1900 he died. But new British composers multiplied fast in the nineties, and among them came one destined for the first rank. This was Edward Elgar, a Roman catholic organist's son from Worcester. In 1896 was produced his *King Olaf*, not a mature work, but the first from which the character of his maturity might be inferred. In 1899 came the *Enigma Variations*, a composition of European excellence, quite at the top of its class, and displaying, what no Englishman had displayed before during the nineteenth century, a complete and original mastery over the most complicated orchestration of the day. In 1900 he published his first mature oratorio, *The Dream of Gerontius*, which put him clearly at the head of English composition. It is

---

[1] The London Philharmonic Society moved there in that year; and that autumn saw the first series of Promenade Concerts.

noteworthy, however, that its English production that year at the Birmingham Festival fell flat; the choir were unequal to its difficulties. It was a German production in 1901 at the Lower Rhine Festival which revealed its greatness. Another work of note, which was first performed in its complete shape in 1900, was S. Coleridge-Taylor's *Hiawatha*. Its composer, who was then only twenty-five, and who died of consumption a few years later, was, it is worth recalling, the son of an Englishwoman and a West African negro.

Turning to literature we may as before derive some general indications from the *Publishers' Circular*. In 1887 the number of new books was 4,410; in 1899 it was 5,971.[1] In this large increase religion had no share; books dealing with it dropped from 616 to 590. On the other hand, novels and juvenile books rose from 1,201 to 1,825; history and biography from 394 to 528; economics and trade from 113 to 350; and poetry and drama from 82 to 317. Many of the writers active in 1870-86 continued into 1886–1900; but the leading notes in the later period were quite distinctive, and it brought with it some new kinds of literature.

To take the last point first, there were the clear beginnings of a revival of authorship in the English theatre. The greater Victorians never succeeded there, and the first fifty years of the queen's reign did not produce a single stage play that was literature.[2] The actor-manager reigned supreme, and neither the author nor the producer, as we now understand him, stood much chance. Plays of Shakespeare, cut and mutilated at the actor-manager's pleasure, were put on from time to time as a factor in histrionic fame; but the money—and much of the fame too—was made in performing adaptations from the French or melodramas like *The Bells* or *The Lyons Mail*, on which Henry Irving relied. But from the later eighties, influenced especially by the genius of Ibsen, certain dramatic critics began to ask for something more, and certain authors to supply it. The playwrights who deserve credit for pioneering the advance were two —Henry Arthur Jones and A. W. Pinero, the former the more prolific, the latter showing, on the whole, the higher literary quality. Pinero's admirably written *The Second Mrs. Tanqueray*

---

[1] The years 1886 and 1900 were, for different reasons, years of small and not typical output.

[2] Unless one or two of Robertson's or W. S. Gilbert's be doubtfully so claimed.

(1893) dates a real change in the public attitude; for though the furore about it owed a great deal to a fine actress (Mrs. Patrick Campbell), equal credit was given by playgoers to the author. The chief critics who fostered the movement were William Archer, J. T. Grein, and G. Bernard Shaw. The last, destined for a part of the twentieth century to become the foremost playwright in Europe, had already before the nineteenth was out published in book form no less than ten plays, many of them since perennially popular. Nothing better indicates the quality of the old theatrical régime than that it declined then to put them on. The reason was that they did not contain parts of the kind that actor-managers wanted for themselves and their leading ladies.

Another new feature was the appearance of books embodying social investigations carried out on a much larger scale and by more systematic methods than before. The first pioneer was Charles Booth, whose immense inquiry into the conditions of life in London was begun in 1886, and whose ninth volume completing the studies of *Poverty* and *Industry* appeared in 1897. The other pioneers were Sidney and Beatrice Webb, whose *History of Trade Unionism* (1894) and *Industrial Democracy* (1897) first exemplified their monumental methods of research; which subsequently from 1898 onwards they devoted to the history of English local government. In quite another field, the same tendency to throw the net of inquiry much more widely than hitherto, while crowning research with a considerable literary quality, was illustrated by J. G. Frazer's great study in comparative religion and folk-lore, *The Golden Bough* (first instalment 1890). Some very large co-operative undertakings also marked the period. Nearly the whole publication of the original *Dictionary of National Biography*, under Leslie Stephen, falls within it; and it was now that the long-incubated *Oxford English Dictionary* began, under Sir James Murray's editorship, to multiply its volumes in good earnest. The output of regular historical work, though not so epoch-making as that published between 1870 and 1886, was large and good; and some of those most distinguished in the earlier period—S. R. Gardiner and J. Gairdner, for instance—continued their productivity through the later. In the sphere of philosophy the main thing was the development of the Idealist school, going forward from the work done earlier by T. H. Green and Edward Caird. F. H. Bradley (whose

Appearance and Reality dates from 1893) and Bernard Bosanquet were the leading figures among a large number with claims to remembrance.

The striking increase, which 1899 showed over 1887 under the heading 'Poetry and Drama', was not due to drama only. There was also at this time a greatly increased publication of poetry. Some of it was famous then, and some of it is famous now; the noticeable point is that the two categories coincide so little. The poetry famous at the time as such was that by writers associated with the *Yellow Book*, or at least with the very enterprising publishers of that periodical. This was the true 'school' of the nineties, for these were the idols, before which the high-priests of advanced literary fashion in papers and periodicals daily and weekly invited the public to bow down. Alas, most of their work is to-day already almost as dead as Horne's *Orion* or Bailey's *Festus*, which had been similarly extolled half a century before. Two of the band, Francis Thompson and Lionel Johnson, have kept some readers, because they were Roman catholics and their co-religionists have preserved interest in them as such. And of others a piece here or there may survive; but on most the dust lies thick. And yet meanwhile, apart from the 'school' altogether, three great English poets were writing and publishing. One was Rudyard Kipling, whom the high-priests, however much they belauded him in other respects, could scarcely see to be a poet at all, because he did not give them 'poetic diction'. Another was Robert Bridges, who published his finest lyrical work at this time, but found so little acceptance that several of his volumes were privately printed. The third was Thomas Hardy, a born poet who had been driven into novel-writing a generation earlier by the sheer impossibility of getting his poetry before the public, and who now in 1898 published his first volume of verse, in which many of the best pieces dated as far back as 1866. It was respectfully received, because of its author's fame as a novelist; but few critics really liked it, and but for that extraneous aid it would have fallen quite dead. To our three we might add a fourth in the person of W. B. Yeats, were it not that, though he wrote in English, his quality and genius were bound to Ireland by ties lying deeper than political nationalism. The wonderful lyrics and poetic plays of his early manhood fall within the nineteenth century; his work in the Abbey Theatre at Dublin belongs to the twentieth. In 1896 appeared A. E. Housman's *A Shropshire*

Lad; a slender volume which, though well noticed from the start, was only very gradually seen to be in a different class from the other little volumes of verse then being praised by the reviewers.

In novels this is rather a between period. Earlier great authors end in it. Stevenson, writing to the last, died in 1894. Hardy's *Tess of the Durbervilles* (1891) and *Jude the Obscure* (1895) were his last great works of fiction; and Meredith published his latest novel in 1895. Their immediate successors were writers like Zangwill and Gissing, powerful and original, but not on the top level. The meteoric Rudyard Kipling poured out short stories which are classics; but the novel, though he attempted it, lay outside his genius. At the same time the differentiation between 'great' and 'popular' novelists developed; and in the front rank of the latter came two—Marie Corelli and Hall Caine—who, while of no account with critical readers, obtained enormous circulations. A novelist not easy to place exactly, whose chief books appeared at this stage, is Mrs. Humphry Ward. She might be termed, perhaps, a best-seller to the upper orders; whom she deeply interested, from Gladstone and the Cecils down. She described their mode of life with literal accuracy; and any one curious to-day to know what members of the governing class forty years ago looked like in their home surroundings, what the round of their habits and amusements was, what they read and what they talked about, may be referred to a novel like her *Marcella* as to a good photograph. No leading novelist of the twentieth century had fully established himself in the nineteenth. H. G. Wells came nearest to doing so, but his reputation then was only that of a glorified Jules Verne; his wider powers were not felt till after 1900.

Looking behind the books to the lines of thought, we shall find that the one most immediately affecting national policy was imperialism. W. E. Henley's editorship of the *National Observer* (1888–93) exerted a strong literary influence here, but the greatest was the work of Rudyard Kipling. The son of an Indian government servant, he began his career as an Anglo-Indian journalist, and his first volumes dealt almost entirely with life in India and especially with that of the British army there. But he soon travelled more widely, took the whole empire for his province and made valuable contributions to the drawing-together of Great Britain and what are now the Dominions. Beneath his thinking—and never very far down—lay the old evangelical mind, sometimes (as in the *Recessional*) rising memorably to the surface. For him imperialism was a missionary spirit; the English, a Chosen People, had a duty to rule the 'lesser breeds without the law'; he coined for it the phase 'the White Man's Burden'. Such a creed was less unplausible then than now, for the queen still reigned, and the romantic pioneering pre-eminence of the mid-century English was so recent that men scarcely realized it had passed away. But what commended Kipling's gospel in quarters like the stock exchange, not conspicuous for either religion or romance, was the British business man's need for markets. Barred from those of Europe and the United States by the growth of tariffs, he had to find others in undeveloped countries; and there seemed no more certain way of doing so than to bring these under the British flag. A windy passion for annexation swelled up, sudden and iridescent, from the conquest of Matabeleland, past Omdurman, to the South African war. But the last pricked the bubble; and neither this kind of imperialism nor Kipling's authority as a political prophet were ever the same after it.

Quite a different, but very influential, current of imperialist thought was started by C. H. Pearson's *National Life and Character* (1893). Pearson, an Oxford man, after holding posts in Modern History at London, Cambridge, and Melbourne, had gone into Australian politics and been minister of education in Victoria. There he had seen the relations of white and coloured races from an angle different from Kipling's. He believed that the white man was in imminent and deadly danger from the coloured (especially the yellow) types. What he dreaded was not so much yellow militarism (though his vision of its possibilities may appear prophetic in the light of modern Japan), but the capacity of coloured men to undercut and undersell white labour, and to make it impossible for the latter to live. By a sort of Gresham's Law the coloured worker, if allowed to enter a trade in a white man's country, was bound to oust his white competitors; yet politically and morally he never became a member of the white community, and his multiplication in it must mean its ruin. The moral was that coloured men must for the future be excluded from white countries, and those admitted in the past be squeezed out again wherever possible. The first effect of this powerful and original book was to carry to victory the 'White Australia' policy, and with that to make racial exclusiveness a leading feature in the self-governing portions of the British empire. However justified it may have been, it was a principle hard to harmonize with those on which the empire had been built up, and embarrassing for the mother country in her dual relation to the Dominions and to the great coloured dependencies.

By contrast with Kipling's mood of all-British self-confidence the fashionable literary temperament in the early nineties was exotic and downcast. It began from France, where defeat in war, relative decline in population, and the wave of shame and despair following the Panama scandals had temporarily unnerved the educated class. Wafted on such phrases as 'decadence' and *fin-de-siècle*, the mood fluttered vaguely round Europe. Among its features (as may be seen in Aubrey Beardsley's designs, which set the key for the *Yellow Book*) were a special interest in the moral decline of the ancient world, and a smacking of lips over the vices of super-civilization. In England it liked to affect foreign flavours; but there were certain earlier-established influences there—e.g. the stark pessimism of Thomas Hardy and the voluptuous aestheticism of Oscar Wilde—to which it could appeal for support. These two marked the poles that it moved between; for while the decadent waxed lugubrious over the world's decay, he found satisfaction in the thought that, since everything was so bad, he also might allow himself to be as bad as he liked. In all this there was a great deal of pose; indeed the fatal weakness of the school's literary output in England was its insincerity. The criminal conviction and sentence of Wilde at the Old Bailey in 1895 for homosexual offences tumbled a good many of its card-castles, and dealt the decadents a blow, which they may not have wholly deserved, but from which they never really recovered.

The only deep general current besides imperialism was the socialist or social-reforming demand for a crusade against poverty. It ran in all sorts of channels—part revolt and part idealism. Harcourt in 1894 wrote to Rosebery:

'You desire to avert the "cleavage of classes". The hope on your part is natural, but you are too late. The horizontal division of parties was certain to come as a consequence of household suffrage. The thin end of the wedge was inserted, and the cleavage is expanding day by day.'

Those were true words, and showed insight. We have recorded in earlier chapters the trade-union struggles and the birth of a

political labour movement. Here we must note the corresponding progression of ideas.

They started as a rule from Henry George's *Progress and
Poverty*.[1] George was not a socialist but an American land-
reformer; his gospel was the 'single tax'. But upon his catch-
word 'unearned increment', much more than on Marx's 'surplus
value', the thinking of the English socialist movement was based.
The first developments from it were the early work of the Fabian
Society. *Fabian Essays*,[2] published in December 1889, three
months after the London Dock Strike, has been called the most
important socialist document since Marx's *Capital*. And though
its pages are of much lighter texture than Marx's, it has great
significance as the earliest attempt by writers living in a parliamentary country and familiar with the working of free institutions to explain in detail how socialism could be peacefully
grafted upon them. The book sold largely, and shaped most
middle-class English socialists for at least twenty years after its
publication. Working-class leaders usually accepted its principles after their conversion; but it had not, as a rule, converted them. Far more potent as inspirers of the I.L.P. were two
American books—Edward Bellamy's *Looking Backward* (1887)
and Laurence Gronlund's *Co-operative Commonwealth* (1884). Both
were Utopias; and it is of no small consequence that popular
English socialism from its start was Utopian and idealistic, not
analytic. William Morris also published a striking Utopia, *News
from Nowhere* (1891); but though of finer literary quality it had
much less popular influence. 'Out of Henry George by either
Bellamy or Gronlund' was a true pedigree of the convictions held
by nearly all the leading propagandists who set socialism on its
feet in Great Britain between 1886 and 1900. As time went on,
they themselves produced popular books. Among these *Merrie
England* (1894) by Robert Blatchford came easily first; and it sold
over a million copies. Blatchford's high-spirited weekly, the
Clarion, was then a great propagandist force. Appealing primarily to the young thinking men and women in the clerk and artisan classes of Lancashire and the West Riding, its files mirror
admirably their hobbies and ideals—cycling, literature, music,

---

[1] Published in America in 1879; popularized in England by his lecture-visits
from 1881 onwards.

[2] Its seven authors were Bernard Shaw, Sidney Webb (afterwards Lord Passfield), Sydney (afterwards Lord) Olivier, Graham Wallas, Hubert Bland, William
Clarke, and Mrs. Annie Besant.

arts-and-crafts, 'rational' dress, feminism, vegetarianism, and back-to-the-land—all gaily jostling one another in a generous and Utopian atmosphere of socialist enthusiasm.

Socialists, however, were not the only crusaders against poverty and slumdom. Following, but often varying, the pattern of Toynbee Hall, social settlements sprang up in many poor parts of London and in several provincial cities. The first for women dates from 1887. Some, though not all, of the settlements became strongholds of the anti-socialist approach to social problems ably championed by the Charity Organization Society. All the churches increased their home missions. Among the Anglicans the ritualists were honourably prominent on this side; while the Wesleyan methodists suspended the rules of their circuit system to allow of permanent missioners at great centres. But what gained most attention was the appeal of the Salvation Army. General William Booth and his sainted wife had originally organized it as a purely religious body on revivalist lines. But working among the poorest they gradually built up alongside a network of agencies for social aid, reclamation, training, and emigration. In 1890 Booth published *In Darkest England and the Way Out*, whose pictures of urban misery shocked the conscience of the whole religious world. He was specially impressed by the evils of the urban influx from the depopulated country-side; and a leading part of his scheme was to re-educate the victims by a rural training, and emigrate them as settlers to the colonies. Dr. Barnardo's Homes also carried out emigration on a large scale.

Yet another current of thought, which should not go unnoticed, was that of Nationalism, as it developed itself in Ireland, Scotland, and Wales. In Ireland following the agrarian and political upheavals of 1878–86, there was a strong revival of the Celtic note in literature, with the poets W. B. Yeats and George Russell ('A. E.') as its foremost exponents in English, while Douglas Hyde and others worked also in Gaelic itself. In 1893 Hyde formed the Gaelic League. In Scotland a similar but smaller movement produced the poetry written by William Sharp under the feminine *alias* of 'Fiona Macleod'. In Wales the situation was different, for the native language had a far wider hold as a living tongue, and the third quarter of the century had been a creative period in its literature. Only in 1887 died Ceiriog, the greatest modern lyric poet in Welsh, unequalled throughout our islands, save by Burns alone, for his gift of writing songs whose appeal unites all classes of his countrymen. If therefore the eighties brought a new purpose in Wales also, it was not so much to keep Celtic legend alive by putting it into English, as to keep Celtic speech alive by endowing it with newspapers and books on modern and educational subjects. Three close contemporaries—Thomas E. Ellis (1859–99), Owen M. Edwards (1858–1920), and Viriamu Jones (1856–1901)—were the leaders in this work.[1] The dominant interest of them all was Welsh education, but they served it in different ways. Ellis went into parliament in 1886, and from 1894 until his premature death in 1899 was chief liberal whip. Jones, who died only two years later, had then for eighteen years been head of the Cardiff University College. Owen Edwards was content to hold a fellowship at Oxford, and from there poured out books and periodicals in Welsh, editing poets such as Dafydd ap Gwilym, Goronwy Owen, and Ceiriog, and aiming to give the Welsh country-folk enough papers and magazines in their own tongue to dispense with their reading English ones. In 1907 he left Oxford and became chief inspector of education in Wales.

It was through the influence of these men that in 1888 the Cross Commission reported in favour of bilingual teaching in Welsh schools, and of ranking Welsh with Latin, French, and German among the languages which might be taken by candidates for admission to teachers' training colleges. Both concessions—which were much overdue and had already been made by the Scottish Code in favour of Gaelic-speaking children—were granted. In the same year, when the County Councils Bill was before parliament, Ellis put down an amendment that the fifteen councils of Wales and Monmouth should elect representatives to a general council for Wales, on which the Welsh M.P.'s should also sit. But this was not pushed, the real politics of Welsh nationalism, whose home was in the chapels, being centred on Welsh disestablishment. After that had been adopted by Gladstone as a part of the Newcastle programme, any chance of the Welsh group's dividing itself from the English liberal party disappeared. But it was able increasingly to influence the party in its own directions, which were those of Nonconformity, radi-

[1] All three were early products of the 'university college' system, Ellis and Edwards having been educated together at Aberystwyth, while Jones was at University College, London. To complete their education all three proceeded to Oxford, less than ten years after it had been thrown fully open to dissenters in 1871; and it was there that they joined forces.

calism, and land reform. During the South African war the
Welsh nationalists went strongly pro-Boer. Then it was that the
still youthful Lloyd George, who at first had figured in the group
as one eloquent Celt among several, stood clearly out as a British
no less than a Welsh party leader, and revealed to all discerning
onlookers that a new force of great potency had arrived.

These various phases of Celtic nationalism roused considerable interest among English intellectuals, chiefly in circles hostile
to imperialism and attracted by social reform.

Costume in the nineties continued the evolution of the
eighties, games and cycling being the main influences which
made for shorter, lighter, less cumbrous, and less ugly clothes.
For men's wear, even in towns, the lounge coat, worn with
bowler hat in winter and straw hat in summer, ousted the top hat
and frock or tail coat, except on Sundays or in London. In the
latter the older style lasted on, serving to mark off 'gentlemen'
and the employing class generally from clerks and employees.
Any one examining, for instance, the vestiaire of an ordinary West
End club would find only top hats hanging in it. The last form of
out-door exercise, in which top hat and long coat lingered, was
riding. Men wore them to hounds over white riding breeches
and high boots down to the early nineties; but they began to disappear in Rotten Row by 1892.[1] The old working-class 'occupation' garbs fell still more out of use, artisans and workmen of all
kinds tending to dress like the shabbier clerks. The process of
standardization was helped by the advent of cheap ready-made
clothes, which even on the country-side took away, as the
nineties advanced, the livelihoods of the little village tailors.

Women's dress shed the bustle about 1890, but developed new
external uglinesses, the best remembered of which, lasting right
through the decade, were the so-called 'leg of mutton' sleeves. A
much worn style, which came in from the late eighties, was
the separate blouse and skirt. This seems to have been an outcome of lawn tennis; but the shirt-like blouses were originally
worn with stiff collars. Hats underwent a complete change, consequent on a changed mode of wearing the hair. Mid-Victorian

---

[1] 'I heard Lord Spencer tell Gladstone in 1892 at a dinner given by Arnold
Morley, M.P., that the Prince of Wales (Edward VII) begged him to ride beside
him in Rotten Row (at the request of the hatters) in a silk hat. They rode for a
week so apparelled, but could not restore the old headgear.' T. M. Healy, *Letters
and Leaders of My Day* (1928), i. 215.

women plaited their hair, and coiled the plaits in a knob at the back of their necks; with this they wore bonnets, tied under the chin in front and arched over the knob at the back. Later they wore hats held on from behind by an elastic passing (more or less invisibly) under the knob of hair. But, beginning in the eighties and becoming nearly universal for all but elderly women in the nineties, came a new way of hair-dressing ('French fashion', the term was), whereby the hair was brushed forward from the back of the head and massed on the top. This rendered the elastic impossible, and as a substitute appeared the hat-pin. It reigned thereafter for thirty years. Hat-pin hats, as we might call them, developed many varieties—now a shape like a man's straw hat, now a toque, or again a wide-brimmed 'picture' hat. But they all had this in common, that essentially they floated on the top of the head, and were only prevented from flopping off by the long pins driven through the hair. As such, they discouraged motion, and were a brake on women's otherwise considerable progress towards greater physical activity.

Fashion's chief aid to that progress was a vital change in under-clothing. This was the substitution of knickers for thick petti-coats, which came in about 1890. It began cautiously, the earliest knickers being long and frilled at the bottom; so that, if anything were seen of them, they might be mistaken for petticoats. But the change lasted, and its eventual importance was immense, not merely because it encouraged the shortening of skirts, but be-cause it vastly lessened the weight and volume of material which had hitherto cramped women's movements from the waist down-ward. It made a very real contribution to women's emancipation.

What may have helped to bring it about was the fashion for women's bicycling, which followed the advent of the safety bicycle. The first commercially successful 'safety' was the 'Rover', built at Coventry by J. K. Starley[1] in 1885, and launched on the market in the following year. J. B. Dunlop's invention of the pneumatic tyre (patented in 1888) added to its popularity; and for about a decade the English main roads were the cyclist's para-dise, after the county councils had improved them and before the early motor-cars made them hideous with dust. Women in heavy petticoats would have been much handicapped in taking advantage of them.

[1] He was the nephew of James Starley (d. 1881), the English 'father of the bicycle', to whom there is a public monument at Coventry.

In social life the single fact most prominent at the time was the movement towards a freer status for women. It pervaded all classes and took many forms. Charles Booth for instance, surveying working-class London as he studied it in the years 1897–1900, says:[1]

'There is a consensus of opinion . . . that, while there is more drinking, there is less drunkenness than formerly, and that the increase in drinking is to be laid mainly to the account of the female sex. This latter phase seems to be one of the unexpected results of the emancipation of women.'

'Emancipation' may seem now an unexpected word to encounter at a time when women had not either the parliamentary vote, or membership of the older universities, or the right to sit on a borough or county council, or admission to any of the leading professions save medicine and teaching. But in its personal and domestic aspects it was a real thing. The Married Women's Property Act of 1882 was extended by that of 1893, and between them they placed a wife in regard to her property upon the same footing (apart from any settlement on trust) as if she were unmarried. In 1891 in the leading case, *Reg.* v. *Jackson*,[2] the Court of Appeal, setting aside earlier authority, ruled that a husband cannot legally detain in his house his wife. Two years earlier Ibsen's *Doll's House* had been played for the first time in London to crowded and excited audiences, and Nora's final slamming of her husband's door echoed through social life for a decade. Moreover with the sudden change from large to small families, which, as we have seen, was brought about artificially in the educated and better-to-do sections of society, the younger married women in those sections became, as suddenly, a leisured class—not so vast a one as the married women of to-day, but unprecedented and rapidly growing. Beside them in the same social levels developed a large body of leisured unmarried women —unmarried because the oversea employment of upper-class Englishmen entailed by imperial expansion had seriously upset the balance of the sexes in those levels at home, and leisured, because so few paid employments were open to them and it was still the tradition that ladies should be maintained by their families. Much fuel was here being stacked up for the feminist politics of the early twentieth century. But as yet no one had set a match to it.

[1] *Life and Labour in London*, final vol. (1903), p. 59.   [2] (1891) 1 Q.B. 671.

The break-away from old restraints had also its bad side. Immorality in London paraded itself as never before during the queen's reign, especially in the music-halls. At their head figured the Empire Theatre, whose promenade, then a very large one, was from 1889 to 1894 universally and quite openly regarded as the regular market for the more expensive class of loose women. In the latter year it was denounced to the L.C.C. (as licensing authority for music-halls) by a lady concerned in rescue work, Mrs. Ormiston Chant. The music-hall interest, backed by certain newspapers and widely echoed in the clubs, tried to crush her with ridicule. But the plucky woman held on, fought her case single-handed before the council against leaders of the bar, and won it completely. The Empire was forced to contract its promenade to a gangway, and though the scandal revived there later, it was never again so extensive or so flaunting. Meanwhile the L.C.C., under the lead of Sir John McDougall, proceeded to clean up the music-halls as a whole. Though their proprietors resisted him, he made their fortunes; for after they ceased to be reputed 'shady', the halls drew far more money than they had before.

Another widespread feature of social life was the increase of leisure through the shortening of working hours. It affected all classes. For manual workers the Eight Hours' Day began to become practicable. It was adopted 'between 1889 and 1897 in over five hundred establishments, including the government dockyards and workshops, nearly all municipal gasworks, and a majority of the London engineering and bookbinding establishments, together with isolated firms all over the country'.[1] The government's concession in the ordnance factories was announced by Campbell-Bannerman in 1894, the admiralty following suit in the dockyards.

What with cycling and mountaineering and the cult of the open air generally, there grew up towards the end of the century a new feeling for the aesthetic side of English landscape; and, partly as an expression of it, the National Trust was founded in 1895 by Octavia Hill, with the help of Canon H. D. Rawnsley and Sir Robert Hunter. The literary influence behind this was the teaching of Miss Hill's friend, Ruskin, who had a weightier following between 1880 and 1900 than ever since. It came none too soon. Ruskin himself in mid-Victorian days had bewailed in a

[1] S. and B. Webb, *Industrial Democracy* (1897), p. 353 n.

memorable passage[1] the vandalism, by which Miller's Dale—previously among the finest sequestered rock-valleys in England—had been converted, to its irretrievable ruin, into the track of a main-line railway. As late as 1887 the same fate very nearly befell the Lake District, where it was proposed by a bill before parliament to run a railway from Ambleside to Keswick. The bill had strong support in both parties, the tellers in its favour being Labouchere, then the darling of radicalism, and J. W. Lowther (afterwards Lord Ullswater), a rising and popular tory. None of the great party captains gave any lead against it. Almost the sole front bench statesman, who realized that a national heritage was at stake, was James Bryce. But he worked unstintingly, and it was well that he did; for the Lakes were only saved from destruction by eleven votes.

[1] *Fors Clavigera*, letter 5, § 9: Ruskin also reprinted it in a footnote to *Praeterita*, III, § 86.

XI

THE UNIONIST DECLINE

Edward VII had, and seized, a great opportunity to strike the public imagination. For he was not only a king succeeding a long-widowed queen, but a brilliant man of the world succeeding a recluse. The queen had shunned pomp and publicity; but he loved them. Along with his frank amiability went a genial delight in display, a passion for uniforms and decorations, for sumptuous entertainments and processions, and big shows of every kind. For a constitutional monarch, whose duty consists more in symbolizing power than in wielding it, an important part of that duty is to exhibit the symbol to advantage before men's eyes. This King Edward understood much better than his mother.

In the result he made himself so conspicuous and popular as to create a wrong impression of his influence on policy. Many people imagined that the powers of the monarch, after dying down during Queen Victoria's widowhood, were brought alive again in the active reign of her son. The reverse was really the case. The king exerted not more but less authority than his mother, and transmitted to his successor not an enhanced but a diminished position within the constitution. The reason was that he had far less industry than she, and on the whole less ability also. The rights which Bagehot attributes to a constitutional monarch dealing with ministers—the 'right to be consulted, the right to encourage, the right to warn'[1]—depend for their effective exercise on the monarch's being willing to wade through the official papers. Queen Victoria, with tireless application, spent her days on them; her son, as a rule, preferred to spend his more pleasurably. He seldom read books of any kind. When he was just over 31 his mother wrote

that the Prince of Wales has *never* been fond of reading, and that from his earliest years it was *impossible* to get him to do so. Newspapers and very rarely a novel are all he ever reads.[2]

Ten years later, when Dilke saw much of him, he recorded that though he had 'more sense and more usage of the modern world'

---

[1] W. Bagehot, *The English Constitution* (1867), c. iii.
[2] P. Guedalla, *The Queen and Mr. Gladstone* (1933), i. 385.

than his secluded mother, he had 'less real brain power'.[1] In-discretions, which he had from time to time committed, made her reluctant that he should have access to the more confidential papers; and it was not till 1892, in his fifty-first year, that he was allowed to see (but not to keep) copies of the prime minister's reports on cabinet meetings. The deprivation may have been warranted; but it debarred him from experience. The British documents published since the war[2] illustrate the result. Not many of them bear annotations by him, and most of those are colourless or negligible. The contrast is very great with the corresponding German papers, plastered with William II's keen and knowledgeable, if often unwise, comments.

As late as 1896 the incident of the Kruger telegram had illus-trated the difference between the attainments of mother and son. The prince's reaction to it was to join in the general indignation and call for 'a severe snub'. The queen's was to compose a con-summate letter to the Kaiser, which no diplomat in history could have bettered. By the side of her ripeness in counsel and un-ruffled skill, her son's quality seemed that of a crude beginner.[3] Yet it was only five years later that (in his sixtieth year) he came to the throne. Men do not expand easily at such ages; and it would have needed an amount of hard work, which lay quite outside his habits, to endow the novice of 1896 with the more than professional expertness in diplomacy often afterwards mis-attributed to him.

Nevertheless he had in many respects great natural ability. He knew how to be both dignified and charming; he had an excellent memory; and his tact in handling people was quite exceptional. He had a store of varied, though unsystematized, knowledge gathered at first-hand through talking to all sorts of eminent men. His tastes were not particularly elevated, but they were thoroughly English; and he showed much (though not un-failing) comprehension for the common instincts of the people over whom he reigned. This was not the less remarkable be-cause, though a good linguist in French and German, he never learned to speak English without a German accent.

On 14 February 1901 he opened parliament in person, reviving

---

[1] S. Gwynn and G. M. Tuckwell, *Life of Sir Charles Dilke* (1913), i. 500.

[2] G. P. Gooch and H. W. V. Temperley, *British Documents on the Origin of the War* (1927 ff.).

[3] *Queen Victoria's Letters*, III. iii (1932), 7–9 and 19–20.

a fine ceremony of historic value, which had languished since 1861 and been totally dropped since the middle eighties. Two matters fell shortly to be dealt with, which arose out of his accession. One was the new Civil List. Queen Victoria had received £385,000 a year, out of which she had saved sums which already in 1889 totalled £824,000.[1] But the king did not intend to live in frugal retirement, as she had lived since 1861: nor did the nation want him to. Parliament therefore (advised by a select committee, on which all political shades were represented except the Irish nationalists) increased the grant by £85,000 to £470,000 a year. But it added annuities to the king's only surviving son, his daughter-in-law, his three daughters, and certain of Queen Victoria's servants, which raised the figure to £543,000; and even that was not all, for besides large contingent pensions for the queen and the duchess of York in the event of widowhood, it also undertook most of the upkeep of the royal palaces and yacht, making a total state liability in the neighbourhood of £700,000. As some set-off, it was pointed out by Sir Michael Hicks Beach that the value to the nation of the hereditary revenues surrendered by the Crown had increased during the queen's reign from £245,000 to £452,000 a year.

The other matter was the royal title. As originally borne by Queen Victoria it made no mention of any overseas territories; and Disraeli's much-opposed addition of 1876 had reference to India only. Imperialist sentiment now demanded an amending act; and eventually all British parties agreed, following the words 'of the United Kingdom of Great Britain and Ireland', to insert 'and of the British Dominions beyond the Seas'. The word 'dominions' had not then its present technical meaning; it was meant to cover everything beneath the British flag. The phrase has remained in the title ever since; though, by way of concession to the Irish Free State, 'of the United Kingdom' was removed in 1927.

The whole conduct of national affairs was still clogged by the South African war; and it will be convenient at this point to sketch its military course for the remaining seventeen months of its tedious duration. From the beginning of 1901 Lord Kitchener tentatively developed two policies—one to build chains of block-

---

[1] Report from the Select Committee on Grants to Members of the Royal Family, 1889 (Cd. 271), at p. 41. These were not all her savings from public sources, as she was believed to have made some from the revenues of the duchy of Lancaster.

houses along the railways which were his lines of communication; the other to denude the country systematically of its farms and stock, gathering the non-combatants into concentration-camps. The latter was a grim system, which only necessity could justify, and which General Weyler's then recent practice in Cuba had made odious throughout the civilized world. But the Boers, it must be remembered, fought without uniforms and in their everyday clothes, with no mark of combatancy save a rifle and a bandolier. A peaceful farmer at one moment became a belligerent guerrilla at the next, and then, by quick change, a peaceful farmer again. So long as homesteads with food, forage, and spare horses remained dotted over the veldt, it was impossible to pin him down. But it was a slow task clearing so large a country; and meantime the enemy leaders bid desperately for the initiative. In February 1901 they carried out a concerted plan, whereby Botha raided Natal, while De Wet, Hertzog, and Kritzinger separately invaded Cape Colony and sought to raise the Dutch there. These daring offensives failed. Only a few Cape Dutch rose. Kitchener was enabled by his railways to concentrate men rapidly both in Natal and in Cape Colony; and Botha, after doing considerable damage, was driven out of Natal by a large mounted force under General French. De Wet fared worse; out of 3,000 men and 5 guns which accompanied him across the Orange only half the men and none of the guns found their way back. The Boers now sought peace; and on 26 February Botha met Kitchener at Middelburg. But negotiations broke down over the question of amnesty for Cape rebels.[1]

The war then entered on a fourth phase, in which lines of blockhouses, such as hitherto had been built to guard the railways, were pushed independently across the country with wire fences to divide it into closed compartments. Only large parties of Boers could break through such a line by force; and one closed area after another was persistently 'swept', every person found in it being taken to a concentration-camp. This phase lasted till

[1] The number involved was only 200–300. Kitchener wanted to amnesty them, but Milner opposed, and the British government followed Milner. Kitchener wrote to Brodrick (22 March 1901): 'Milner's views may be strictly just, but they are to my mind vindictive, and I do not know of a case in history when, under similar circumstances, an amnesty has not been granted. We are now carrying on the war to put two or three hundred Dutchmen in prison at the end of it. It seems to me absurd and wrong.' (Sir George Arthur, *Life of Lord Kitchener* (1920), ii. 26.) The long and tragic extension of the war was a dear price for following Milner.

the end of 1901; and despite many brilliant surprises and feats of arms by Botha, De Wet, De la Rey, Smuts, Kritzinger, and others, it gradually wore the guerrillas down. But there was a shocking tragedy in connexion with it. The concentration-camps into which the Boer women and children were collected were (as often happens when military authorities deal with civilians) grossly mismanaged. Disease became rife, and within fourteen months[1] some 20,177 inmates actually died. Since the maximum population of the camps was 117,871 (in the eleventh month), it will be seen that even as a flat rate this represented an appalling mortality. But the rate during certain months was much worse; and had it continued, very few Boer children would have survived the war. It was an Englishwoman, Miss Emily Hobhouse, backed by a small but influential relief committee, who discovered and exposed their plight. She found Milner sympathetic, Brodrick politely impotent, and the military incorrigible. Baffled by their endless red-tape and hush-up, while the victims went on dying by scores daily, she gave the facts to the world; with the result that it became a party question, and the government were driven in public to evasive denials. In private, however, Chamberlain was convinced and shocked. He had the camps transferred to his own control, and speedily reformed the scandalous conditions.

This matter of the camps had a curiously far-reaching political repercussion. Campbell-Bannerman, denouncing them first outside and then inside parliament, used the phrase 'methods of barbarism'. He was severely rebuked for it from the ministerial side, but he refused to recant. The phrase travelled round the world, and reached the Boers in the field, whose previous feelings over the deaths in the camps can be imagined. They were now profoundly touched by the generosity of the enemy statesman who had faced jeers and hatred to save their children. They forgot neither it nor him. Five years afterwards, when the Campbell-Bannerman ministry conferred self-government on the Transvaal and the Orange River Colony, everything depended on whether the Boer leaders would accept and work it loyally in a spirit of reconciliation. That Botha, Smuts, and most of the rest were willing to do so was above all due to the personal feeling of trust and devotion with which the above incident had imbued them towards the British premier.

[1] January 1901 to February 1902 inclusive.

As 1901 went on, the military pressure told. In May some of the Rand mines were restarted; in July Botha sought and obtained leave to communicate with Kruger (who, however, advised continuing the war); and in December the Johannesburg stock exchange reopened. But Boer successes also persisted till the end of the year, when the war entered a fifth and final stage. The new feature was the use of the blockhouse lines not merely as fences but as lines of communication. This enabled 'drives' to be organized on a scale not practicable earlier. Escape became impossible; and despite a local victory on 7 March 1902 by De la Rey, in which Lord Methuen was wounded and taken prisoner, on 23 March, only seven weeks after the first of the new drives, the Boers sued for peace. After a very long negotiation ending in the assembly of a body of delegates (two apiece elected by thirty-two commandos still in the field) at Vereeniging, the Peace called after that place was signed on 31 May 1902. Kitchener, who had once more shown high qualities of diplomacy and statesmanship, was largely responsible for the generosity of its terms.

The war had employed on the British side from first to last a total of about 450,000 troops, of which about 250,000 were British regulars. Of these 5,774 were killed and 22,829 wounded; but in addition over 16,000 died of disease—chiefly enteric fever. The Boer losses were less accurately known, but it was calculated that they had rather less than 4,000 killed in the field. The money cost to Great Britain exceeded £222 millions. From first to last the mode of fighting, as conditioned by the terrain, had been entirely peculiar. Fifteen years later a war on the veldt would probably have been won by armoured cars; but as it was, the horsed rifleman was supreme. Thus the officers who were successful under Kitchener were nearly all cavalry officers; and by men of this type—normally its least intellectual type—the British army came to have its highest posts filled predominantly down to the European war. Having slowly learned its way into veldt tactics, it was too long haunted by them afterwards.

The principal terms of peace were the surrender of all burghers in the field with all arms and munitions; the repatriation of all who duly declared themselves subjects of King Edward VII; no proceedings to be taken against any burghers, save for certain specified acts contrary to the usages of war; English to be the official language, but Dutch to be taught in schools, if the parents wished it, and to be allowed in the law-courts; sporting rifles to be allowed on licence; military administration to be superseded as soon as possible by civil, and the latter to lead up to self-government; no special tax to be imposed on landed property to defray war-costs; a commission to be formed for repatriation; and a grant of £3 millions by the British government towards rebuilding and restocking farms.

The generosity of the last provision was entirely without precedent in the history of modern wars; though the practical case for it was strong, since the country had been totally devastated. Nevertheless, in the following August three Boer generals—Botha, De Wet, and De la Rey—came to Europe to try to squeeze further concessions. Some of their demands were very naïve—e.g. 'reinstatement of officials of the late republic in the service or their compensation for loss of office'—but the essentials were two; amnesty for the Cape and Natal rebels (which had been expressly excluded at Vereeniging[1]), and additional money. They were shown every courtesy by the king and by Chamberlain, but obtained nothing; and then went to Kruger on the continent, and launched a bitterly-worded appeal for money 'to the civilized world'. English opinion not unnaturally resented this, and an effective letter from Chamberlain evoked from Botha a partly apologetic reply.

The truth was that the Boer leaders were divided. Botha, who had been a progressive before the war, wished to be loyal to the treaty and do the best for his people under the British flag; while De Wet and De la Rey, who had before been Krugerites and still clung to the counsels of the exiled ex-president, remained at heart unreconciled. Unhappily, this division was long to continue in Dutch South Africa, nor even yet is it wholly effaced. Meanwhile, upon Milner as governor of the Transvaal and Orange River Colony fell the task of carrying out the reconstruction. It was work for which he was far better suited than for most that had hitherto engaged him in South Africa, and brought out the strong side of his remarkable administrative genius.

Just as the peace negotiations began, had died (on 26 March 1902) Cecil Rhodes—a great figure in the world's eye, though strangely compounded of virtue and guile, large vision and loose handling. Heart disease had sapped his faculties for some years,

[1] An assurance had, however, been given (and was kept) that the penalty for the rank and file should be disfranchisement only, and none of the others should be punished with death.

and his removal scarcely affected policy. But it helped to soften
rancours; and the subsequent publication of his will, with its
massive generosity and in particular its great scheme of scholarships to Oxford for young men from South Africa, the other
colonies, the United States, and Germany, added a posthumous
glory to his chequered career. His presence no longer hindered
reconciliation; though years had to pass before his memory was
amnestied.

The chancellor of the exchequer, on whom the task of financing
the war had fallen, was Sir Michael Hicks Beach, a strong conservative in party matters and an equally strong Gladstonian in
the field of finance. His careful husbandry kept the strain on
credit within narrow bounds; for though he suspended the Sinking Fund and issued four loans totalling £135 millions, he defrayed a substantial part of the war-cost by new taxation. His
1900 budget started with a large surplus, and he added £6·5
millions to it by increasing income-tax from 8*d.* to 1*s.*, and £5·6
millions by higher duties on beer, spirits, tea, and tobacco. His
1901 budget placed a further 2*d.* on income-tax, besides a duty
on refined sugar and a levy of 1*s.* per ton on exports of coal
(which in 1900 had reached a record figure of 46 million tons).
This budget is interesting as the first in our history which estimated for a higher revenue from direct taxes than from indirect;
and at the beginning of 1902 Sir Robert Giffen, then highly
regarded as an expert in such matters, published a reasoned
criticism of the tendency and a plea for 'broadening the basis of
taxation'. But the budget of that year—Hicks Beach's seventh
and last—added yet another penny to income-tax and doubled
(but later reduced again) the stamp on cheques; while its
only effort in Giffen's sense was a 'registration' duty of 3*d.* per
cwt. on imported corn and 5*d.* on flour. This was defended as a
mere revival of a Victorian duty which had been retained by
both Peel and Gladstone, and only abolished in 1869 by Robert
Lowe. But from the first its possibilities in connexion with
imperial preference were obvious to most people except its
author.

Hicks Beach's first war loan (in 1900) was for £30 millions at
2¾ per cent., repayable in ten years. It was issued at 98½ per cent.,
and subscribed eleven times over. His last war loan (in 1902) was
for 32 millions assimilated to ordinary consols—then still yield-

ing 2¾ per cent., though in 1903 to become 2½. He issued it successfully at 93½ per cent.; an index of credit comparing favourably with the 87⅜ obtained for 3 per cent. in Crimean days. These results were obtained largely at the expense of the income-tax payers, whose burden was increased by the war from 8*d*. to 1*s*. 3*d*. They bore it, however, on broad shoulders; for the yield of the tax per penny, which was put at a little over £1·6 millions for 1900–1, reached £2 millions in 1902–3. It must be noted that during these years, besides war-costs, regular expenditure on both navy and army rose fast—a matter which the chancellor criticized strongly in a cabinet memorandum of 1902.

Salisbury, too, deplored it, but perforce acquiesced. During the final eighteen months of his premiership, which lasted till 11 July 1902, he aged rapidly, and his control over policy relaxed. The remodelling of the cabinet had strengthened the following of Balfour, under whose guidance new departures were made both at home and abroad. It was he who supported against Hicks Beach the ministers that expanded the fighting services; he who prevailed on the cabinet to adopt and carry into law the great, but unpopular, Education Bill of 1902; and he who backed Lord Lansdowne at the foreign office when the latter took Great Britain out of her 'splendid' isolation and concluded an alliance with Japan. Without suggesting between uncle and nephew any divergence of which the former, at any rate, was conscious, these policies may be termed Balfourian and not Salisburian.

Surprise is still sometimes expressed that our first ally since the Crimean war should have been Japan. But the choice was profoundly natural. For what actually drove Great Britain from her isolation was not the peril during the South African war, nor the threat of the German fleet-building, but her fear of losing the China market. We saw in Chapter VIII how this fear in 1898–9 prompted Chamberlain's original efforts for a German alliance; and in Chapter IX it was shown how vital China had at that time become for the British export trade. The menace came from Russia, whose expanding empire was still seeking southward outlets and warm-water ports. Following her failure to force open the Dardanelles in 1878, confirmed by the hostility of the new Bulgaria during the eighties, she diverted the point of her pressure from the Near to the Middle East, i.e. towards India. Hence Lytton's Afghan war in 1879, hence the Penjdeh incident of 1885, and hence the Salisbury-Bismarck feelers about

an alliance in 1887 and 1889; which came to nothing because
Bismarck would not for Great Britain's sake incur risks of war
with his eastern neighbour. But Russia's approach towards
India across the roof of the world was geographically unhopeful.
Somewhere about 1890 she became aware of this, and turned
to a third field, the Far East. Here the Trans-Siberian Railway,
started by the aid of French capital in 1891, pointed to easier
possibilities, since Manchuria and northern China were without natural defences. Unfortunately, the new line of advance
threatened British interests no less than the others had, although
in a different way.

The seizure of Port Arthur in 1898 had brought Russian troops
to Liao-tung, and in 1900 they occupied the whole of Manchuria.
In that year, indeed, China, disorganized by the 'Boxer' outbreak and the European counter-campaign, seemed on the verge
of dissolution. On 16 October, as we saw above,[1] Great Britain
and Germany concluded a pact to maintain her integrity and
the 'open door' for all nations' trade. Called by the Germans the
Yangtse Agreement (because their original draft of it referred to
the Yangtse basin, though that eventually signed covered 'all
Chinese territory as far as they can exercise influence'), it provided that if a third power sought 'any territorial advantages in
Chinese dominions', these two were to discuss common action.
Great Britain attached so much value to Germany's helping her
to stop Russia that she did not make, as till then she had,[2] any
special claim for herself in the Yangtse basin. The next phase
was that the other powers, including Russia, adhered to the
pact; and the next again, that early in 1901 Great Britain ascertained the Tsar's government to be attempting two new encroachments, and inquired of Germany what she would do. The
answer was 'Nothing'; her chancellor, Bülow, declaring in the
Reichstag that the Yangtse Agreement excluded Manchuria. In
the house of commons the British under-secretary, Lord Cran-
borne,[3] retorted that the Agreement covered North China; and
certainly, had it not, Britain would have had small motive for
signing. In sum, as a co-guarantor of Chinese integrity, Germany
within five months proved a broken reed.

It speaks volumes for the extent to which French and Russian

---

[1] p. 262.
[2] Notably in a Russo-British Agreement of the previous year.
[3] Lord Salisbury's eldest son, who succeeded his father in 1903 as fourth marquess.

hostility had driven British statesmen into Germany's arms that even after this eye-opening experience their first instinct was to seek, not a new partner, but a closer partnership. The spring months of 1901 witnessed Chamberlain's third and final attempt to link London and Berlin together. There still exist two drafts of an Anglo-German convention, drawn up during May in the British foreign office, and a remarkable memorandum by Salisbury advancing various arguments against them.[1] But the main obstruction was in Berlin; and by mid-June Chamberlain wrote to Eckardstein despairing of the negotiations. Later in the year, in a speech defending the conduct of British troops in South Africa, he drew a parallel with the German troops in 1870, which was twisted into an insult by the German press. Bülow not merely permitted their violent attacks on the British minister, but in the Reichstag (8 January 1902) endorsed them.

Meanwhile another power dreaded Russia's aggressions no less than Britain. This was Japan, whose minister in London, Baron Hayashi, broached a proposal to Lord Lansdowne in April 1901, and more fully at the end of July. Her special concern was to prevent Russia from acquiring Korea. Hayashi said that his government 'would certainly fight in order to prevent it; and it must be the object of their diplomacy to isolate Russia, with which Power, if it stood alone, they were prepared to deal'.[2] Tokio, however, was divided between two policies—one as above, and the other to make a direct agreement with the Tsar. In the late autumn, when Hayashi was at last fully authorized to discuss the first, a famous Japanese elder statesman, Marquis Ito, was sent to St. Petersburg to discuss the second. But Lansdowne firmly refused to go on unless the latter mission were dropped. Ito was diverted to England, and on 30 January 1902 the alliance was signed.[3]

King Edward minuted that the German government should be at once informed, adding that 'the Emperor will be much interested in hearing the news, as he has strongly advocated a

[1] G. P. Gooch and H. W. V. Temperley, *British Documents*, ii. 66 and 68. Each side was to afford the other benevolent neutrality if at war with one power; active help if attacked by a second. Austria and Italy were to be brought in by parallel treaties. Salisbury's main objection was the difficulty of fulfilment; 'neither we nor the Germans are competent to make the suggested promises'; while 'a promise of defensive alliance with England would excite bitter murmurs in every rank of German society'.

[2] *Ibid.*, ii. 91.

[3] Full text, showing successive drafts, in *British Documents*, ii. 115–20.

close alliance between Great Britain and Japan'. This was done, and the expected response followed. But meanwhile Bülow was letting St. Petersburg know, in the friendliest way, how the Kaiser 'observed that the Agreement was a hard but not altogether undeserved punishment for the flirtation of the Russians with England, for their passivity during the South African War, their shyness towards us, their irresponsiveness to the well-meant hints of his Majesty'.[1] Such mischief-making duplicity (for William II had taken credit with both Queen Victoria and King Edward for having vetoed Russian intervention during the South African war) was habitual, as the documents now show, in German diplomacy during the Kaiser's reign. No other state quite approached it; and it would certainly have rendered an Anglo-German alliance very unstable had one been launched. Germany welcomed the prospect of a Russo-Japanese war, as likely to exhaust Russia. She did not foresee that, by closing the Far Eastern outlet, it would redirect Russia's aims to the Near East, revive her jealousy of Austria-Hungary, and render her less tolerant of the Kaiser's Berlin-Bagdad ambitions.

The king's coronation had been fixed for the last week of June, but it was postponed by a sudden illness necessitating a severe operation. As soon as recovery was completely assured, Lord Salisbury resigned. He was himself in failing health, and died thirteen months later. The sum of his premierships had aggregated 13½ years, still the longest record since the Reform Act, beating Gladstone's by over a year. His qualities as a foreign minister have been discussed above.[2] As a prime minister, it is said by his closest follower, Hicks Beach, that 'he did not exercise the control over his colleagues, either in or out of Cabinet, that Lord Beaconsfield did'; he 'frequently allowed important matters to be decided by a small majority of votes, even against his own opinion'; and 'left his colleagues very much to themselves, unless they consulted him'.[3] That implies not only good nature (which he had in abundance), but a lack of constructive aim. He did not, like Beaconsfield, plan a programme of legislative and administrative improvements, and regard his ministry as a team to get them through; he was content that his colleagues, like himself, should each in his department meet events as they occurred.

[1] *Die Grosse Politik der europäischen Kabinette*, xvii. 156.
[2] pp. 200–1.
[3] Lady Victoria Hicks Beach, *Life of Sir Michael Hicks Beach* (1932), ii. 395–63.

Critical and unsanguine by temperament, he had small faith in the value of popular reforms; and the few that he passed—the County Councils Act, free education, and the London Government Act—were only taken up when it was impossible to evade them. Hicks Beach tells us further that 'on the leading questions of Home politics of the time, such as the constitution of Parliament, local government, or Irish land, he was more Tory than his colleagues; but, though certainly no Tory Democrat, he was keen about the housing of the poor and sanitary improvement'. His generally negative attitude reflected itself in the conservative party; which under him became less forward-looking and more limited to the defence of the *status quo*.

Among his older colleagues two had some titles to succeed. For long-tested capacity in debate and in administration, no conservative excelled Hicks Beach. But he had grown out of sympathy with recent trends, and decided to quit office with his old leader, going to the house of lords as Viscount St. Aldwyn. The duke of Devonshire might have succeeded had he not been a liberal unionist. Thrice invited to be premier during the queen's reign, he was now passed over in silence, even his intimate friend, the king, offering no balm to his feelings.[1] A mightier figure than either of them, Chamberlain, was temporarily off the stage. He had on 7 July been laid up by a serious cab accident, which kept him out of parliament till the twenty-second. Thus Balfour took over with no demur from any quarter, and had little to arrange save filling the chancellorship of the exchequer. He transferred C. T. Ritchie to it from the home office—a bad choice for his government and party, as time was soon to show. A month later Lord James of Hereford followed Hicks Beach into retirement.

The new premiership lasted some months over three years. It accomplished much for the nation; but as it was followed by an overwhelming party defeat, the reproach of failure has clung to it. Balfour himself has been blamed, with little understanding. His crowning offence in the eyes of the electors was that he stayed too long in office after the need for a dissolution had become apparent. But we can see now that this course, whose domestic drawbacks were obvious, was dictated, and indeed rendered almost obligatory, by a very exceptional crisis (scantily realized by the British public) in foreign affairs.

The measures which render his period of office memorable

[1] Lord Askwith, *Lord James of Hereford* (1930), 268–9.

were five: the Education Act, 1902 (with an equivalent measure for London passed in the following year); the Irish Land Purchase Act, 1903; the Licensing Act, 1904; the creation of the Committee of Imperial Defence (1904); and the Anglo-French Convention (1904), which formed the basis of the Entente with France. Abroad there occurred the Russo-Japanese war (1904–5), and the first international crisis over Morocco (1905). Concurrent as a growing embarrassment from May 1903 onwards was the fiscal controversy raised by Chamberlain, which so split the unionist party that the cabinet, by secessions of leading members, was reduced almost to a rump. Concurrent also from 1903 was the controversy over Chinese labour for the Rand; in sanctioning which Balfour committed as prime minister his one quite indefensible mistake.

The Education Act, 1902, ranks for England and Wales among the two or three greatest constructive measures of the twentieth century. Balfour did not devise it; that was done by R. L. (afterwards Sir Robert) Morant, an official of the board of education.[1] But no statesman less dominated than Balfour was by the concept of national efficiency would have taken it up and carried it through, since its cost on the side of votes was obvious and deterrent. The act sprang from the situation described in the last chapter, under which secondary education was being developed partly by the councils of counties and county boroughs under the Technical Instruction Act and partly by the school boards under the Elementary Education Acts. Morant, starting from a keen interest in secondary education and a study of its organization in foreign countries, came to the conclusion that the school board version of it had defects that could not be put right. He also, in 1898, discovered, what nobody else knew, that it was *ultra vires* under the acts, and could be stopped by law. Just at that time a conflict was arising in London between the school board and the county council's technical education board, and Morant communicated his discovery to the secretary of the latter. The result was the bringing (1899) of a test case, and the surcharging of the school board by the official auditor, T. B. Cockerton, under seven different heads. Were the surcharges upheld, the legal basis of the higher education carried on by school boards would be gone, involving hundreds of day and evening schools up and

[1] For whose work see B. M. Allen, *Sir Robert Morant* (1934).

down the country; so the question was carried, first to the Queen's Bench Division (1900), and then (April 1901) to the Court of Appeal. Both entirely upheld Cockerton. A one-clause act was passed to legalize the schools for a year only; and in March 1902 the bill to provide a permanent solution was introduced by Balfour himself.

Through Morant's persuasion it covered not merely secondary education but elementary as well. It abolished the school boards throughout the country.[1] It made county and county borough councils the local authorities for all secondary and technical education. It gave them the same position for elementary education too, save that here the councils of non-county boroughs with over 10,000 population and urban districts with over 20,000 were to be the authorities within their areas. Moreover, it brought under the new authorities not only the board schools but the voluntary schools. By an elaborate bargain the managers of the latter, in return for providing the buildings, were to retain the appointment of teachers, while the current expenses of their schools were to be defrayed, like those of the ex-board (or 'provided') schools, out of the local rates. Public money was thus made available for the first time to ensure properly paid teachers and a standardized level of efficiency for all children alike. In the 'provided' schools 'undenominational' teaching was retained under the Cowper-Temple clause; so that the nonconformists, whom it suited, lost nothing. All local education authorities were to discharge their functions through a statutory education committee, which included members co-opted from outside the council.

As a piece of statesmanship, this measure has worked admirably; and some account of its immediate developments will be found in Chapter XV. But as an issue in politics it at once kindled fierce dispute. The anglicans and Roman catholics welcomed it, for it saved their schools, the increasing burden of which, under modern educational requirements, had reached breaking-point. But the nonconformists were furious. Their formal objection was that it would put the cost of sectarian teaching on the rates. This, though much urged, was not very plausible, since the voluntary schools had long, without protest from anybody, been drawing grants from taxes. The real grievances lay behind, and were two. One was that of the 'single-school' areas. In a large

[1] Save in London, to which the same policy was extended in the following year.

number of country parishes the only school was a church school, and the children of nonconformists had to attend it. They had hoped to see its monopoly come to an end for lack of money, and now they feared it was to be prolonged indefinitely at their own expense as rate-payers. The hardship was particularly obvious in Wales, where in some villages the parson and the school-teachers were almost the only resident anglicans. The other point—not expressed but felt—was this. The Cowper-Temple clause had, in a sense, endowed nonconformity; for its votaries got religion taught to their satisfaction at the public cost, whereas the anglicans did not. But then the anglicans tapped a bigger source of public money—the endowments of the Established Church. Dissenters, who steadily regarded the Establishment as unjust, might view their own advantageous position in the board schools as a modest set-off to it; and to them the salvation of the church schools out of the rates seemed letting the Church 'have it both ways'.

The leader outside parliament against the bill was Dr. John Clifford, a veteran baptist minister much respected by free churchmen of all types. In the house of commons it was duly opposed by all the liberal front bench; but its most eloquent critic was a back-bencher, Lloyd George, whose speeches on this subject perceptibly quickened his advance towards a place of power within his party. But the nonconformists had a voice inside the cabinet which had created a special embarrassment for the bill. It was that of Chamberlain, whose reluctant acquiescence had been obtained by the insertion of an optional clause, under which no local authority need adopt the bill's scheme unless it liked. However, in July 1902, while he was prostrated by his cab accident, the house of commons, on a free vote and by a majority of 271 to 102, cut this clause out. The nation was thus saved the folly of a patchwork covering the country with rival systems; and the bill, as Morant had designed it, became law on 20 December.

During its long and stormy passage three important personal changes had occurred. Balfour, its sponsor, had become prime minister; Lord Londonderry had been appointed by him first president of the board of education,[1] completing the till then

[1] When Sir John Gorst, who was at variance with the cabinet and had been passed over in the conduct of the bill, retired from the old post of vice-president of the council.

unfulfilled intentions of the Board of Education Act; and lastly, Morant himself, hitherto a junior official, was, as from 1 November 1902, placed at the head of the department. The act came thus to be enforced under strong leadership. Zealous nonconformists organized passive resistance on a large scale to the payment of the education rate; and in Wales the councils of counties and county boroughs refused for some time to carry out their new statutory duties. But Balfour and Morant were resourceful as well as firm, and the successive obstacles were overcome. Education almost at once took long strides forward; and though, when the general election came, there was still enough soreness to influence votes, other issues had by that time assumed much greater prominence.

The Irish Land Purchase Act, 1903, was sponsored by George Wyndham, a young intimate and disciple of Balfour, who in the cabinet reconstruction of 1900 had procured his appointment as Irish secretary. Both he and Balfour felt that, with Ireland calm and home rule off the map for the time being, a special effort should be made to heal the economic grievances, by which the nationalist agitation had been so much stimulated. In 1902 they induced Sir Antony Macdonnell, a distinguished Irish Roman catholic who had been lieutenant-governor of an Indian province and stood high in official repute, to become under-secretary, i.e. head of the Irish administration. Macdonnell took the post with a special stipulation that he should have 'adequate opportunity' to influence policy. The 1903 Land Purchase Act was the firstfruits. Irish opinion, unionist as well as nationalist, was ready for an advance in this field. In 1901 T. W. Russell, a former Irish liberal who had been a potent fighter for unionism in the North, had come out for compulsory purchase; and early in 1902 at a by-election in East Down, one of the firmest unionist strongholds in Ulster, he had run a land purchase candidate against the government and got him in. That victory probably decided the issue. A Land Conference between leading Irish landowners and the chiefs of the nationalist party, brought together by Lord Dunraven, pointed the way next. Following it the Balfour-Wyndham-Macdonnell Bill of 1903 gave, not compulsion, but something even more effective—a large cash contribution by the imperial parliament towards bridging the gap between what landlords could afford to accept and tenants to pay. Unlike the Ashbourne Act of 1885 and its successors, it dealt not merely with single holdings but with entire estates. The terms were that landlord and tenants should agree a price, and if the estates commissioners approved it, the state should add 12 per cent. The vendors received payment in stock floated on the state's credit, the purchasers paying at the rate of only 2¾ per cent. interest and ½ per cent. for sinking fund, and the period of repayment being 68½ years. The Irish peasants were always conscientious in paying their annuities, and it is fair to note that the scheme worked perfectly down to 1932; when what happened was, not that the purchasers defaulted, but that the Free State government in Southern Ireland intercepted and appropriated their payments. Meanwhile the act did solid good to Ireland by speedily bringing about nearly everywhere, in place of the 'dual ownership' set up by the great 1881 Land Act, a system of out-and-out peasant proprietorship.

The subsequent history of Wyndham's collaboration with Macdonnell was unhappy. Lord Dunraven, after the success of his Land Conference, tried to apply the same methods again. He formed a non-party association to promote 'devolution'. Ireland already, under an act passed by Gerald Balfour[1] in 1898, had elective local government on English lines; and the idea was to go further and, without giving her a legislative parliament, to create a central organ of government for certain administrative purposes. Something of this sort had apparently been mooted when Sir Antony Macdonnell took office; and in 1904 he became active in formulating a scheme and seeking assents to it. Evidently he had some measure of approval from Wyndham, and Wyndham from Balfour, though neither was expressly committed. But they had all underrated the persistence of the Irish feuds. While the affair was still in the phase of private negotiations the extremists of unionism heard about it and began a fierce agitation against Macdonnell. In the house of commons (16 February 1905) Wyndham was constrained to repudiate his action. But agitation against the chief secretary himself continued; Balfour did not dare to screen him; and on 6 March Wyndham resigned. It proved the end of his career. He was a young, chivalrous, and popular figure; and the spectacle of his

---

[1] B. 1853, youngest brother of A. J. Balfour, whom he succeeded as second earl of Balfour in 1930. Educated at Eton and Trinity College, Cambridge, where he became a fellow in 1878. M.P. 1885; chief secretary for Ireland, 1895–1900; president of the board of trade, 1900–5.

being thrown to the most unreasoning wolves in the Irish unionist pack, inevitable though it may have been under the rules of the political game as then played, drew personal discredit on the prime minister. It also extinguished any hopes that he had nursed till then of securing Irish votes at the next general election. The new chief secretary, who held office till the government fell nearly nine months later, was a safe and unimaginative tory squire, Walter Long, transferred from the presidency of the local government board.

The Licensing Act of 1904 was, like the Education Act, a case of grasping a nettle. For a generation there had been dispute as to whether or not brewers and publicans should be compensated for the withdrawal of their licences in cases where redundancy and not misconduct was the ground. Gladstone in 1880 favoured compensation.[1] But the United Kingdom Alliance was strongly against it; and there was always grave doubt as to the legal position. In 1888, when an unsuccessful attempt was made to include a compensation scheme in the County Councils Act, the law officers declared that there was a right to it; but the most learned lawyers on the other side expounded the opposite view. Finally, in 1891, in the celebrated case of *Sharpe* v. *Wakefield*[2] the house of lords judicially decided that all liquor licences were for a year only, and could be withheld at the end of it without any compensation for their non-renewal. Contrary to what might have been supposed, this did not speed up the much-needed reduction of redundant licences, but led to a kind of deadlock. They could not be reduced with compensation, and yet most justices felt it unfair to reduce them without. For, whatever the law might say, hard cash had been paid for them as property for a long time past, and the conversion of breweries into public companies had spread their ownership very widely indeed. Thus a decade went by with little or no advance.

Then in 1902 came fresh alarms. At Farnham, a place exceptionally overstocked with public-houses, a decision by the

---

[1] 'I want a frank recognition of the principle that we are not to deny to publicans as a class the benefits of equal treatment, because we think their trade is at so many points in contact with, and even sometimes productive of, great public mischief. Considering the legislative title they have acquired and the recognition of their position in the proceedings of this House for a long series of years, they ought not to be placed at a disadvantage on account of the particular impression we may entertain' (Hansard, III. ccliii. 363). This passage used to be quoted against him later, after he had adopted the local veto policy of the United Kingdom Alliance.

[2] [1891] A.C. 173.

licensing bench to refuse the renewal of six licences was upheld
on appeal at quarter sessions. About the same time it became
known that at Birmingham, where Arthur Chamberlain, the
colonial secretary's brother, was prominent in pressing for reduction, the brewers had been compelled by negotiation to surrender
over fifty licences. These events (and some others like them)
paved the way for the Balfour Act. Conceived in the spirit of the
adage that a bird in the hand is worth two in the bush, it was a
typical piece of conservative reform. It started from the common-
sense view that brewery shareholders had rights and that when
a licence was taken away not for misconduct but on grounds of
public policy, there ought to be compensation. But it squared
this with *Sharpe* v. *Wakefield* by providing that the compensation
should come, not out of public moneys, but from a fund levied on
the trade itself. This was equitable, since the closing of particular
public-houses raised the value of those left; and while it gave the
brewing trade security, it at the same time rendered possible,
without charge to the public, a gradual but beneficial reduction
of licences. As the scheme threw new responsibilities on the
licensing authority, the act at the same time transferred licensing
from special sessions to quarter sessions, and in the boroughs to
a meeting of all the justices presided over by the recorder. Balfour
was denounced by the opposition for 'endowing the trade'; and
his measure, as a 'brewers' Bill'. There were elements of truth in
both charges; and a vista of piecemeal reductions, gradually
achieved over periods of years, seemed cold comfort to enthusiasts bent on blotting out drink from whole areas by the fiat of
local veto. But the benefit, though not sensational, was practical
and cumulative; and after thirty years' working it has proved
enormous.

The Committee of Imperial Defence had existed in name
since before the South African war. But it was a mere committee
of cabinet ministers, leading a very desultory existence. Balfour
in 1903-4 made it a real addition to the organs of government.
The prime minister became its chairman *ex officio*; and those
convened included both the ministerial and the professional
chiefs from the admiralty and the war office, with the foreign,
Indian, and colonial secretaries, and the chancellor of the exchequer. But the chairman was further authorized to summon
to it from time to time, as occasion might warrant, any person
of administrative experience, whether naval, military, civil, or

imperial. More important still, its proceedings were minuted and its work carried through by a permanent secretariat with a small staff including both military and naval officers. The cabinet had still no minutes at this time, nor, indeed, until the advent of the Lloyd George government in the middle of the European war; and partly for this reason the Committee of Imperial Defence, as Balfour formed it, early became of extreme importance.

This fourth main measure did not require legislation. Side by side with its development went a series of projects for army reform. Balfour's first secretary for war was St. John Brodrick. In 1901 he had produced a scheme for six army corps—three to be complete and three to consist of *cadres* only. But in two years the army corps never got beyond paper; and meanwhile their projector was heavily weighed down by a series of committee or commission reports—on remounts, on army contracts, on the army medical corps, and finally on the South African war as a whole—revealing the gross inefficiency and even corruption which had obtained while he, first as under-secretary and then as war minister, had been the spokesman of the war office in the house of commons. At a reshuffle of the cabinet in the autumn of 1903 he got himself transferred to the India office; and the war office devolved on H. O. Arnold-Forster.[1] Soon afterwards a committee of three—Lord Esher,[2] Admiral Sir John Fisher,[3] and Colonel Sir George Clarke[4]—was appointed to advise on that department's reorganization. Their report (February 1904) was for abolishing the post of commander-in-chief and substituting an army council on the lines of the board of admiralty. It was adopted, and Lord Roberts, who had been commander-in-chief since his return from South Africa, retired. Arnold-Forster continued during 1904 and 1905 to work hard, but with only moderate success. Nobody as yet gave the army what it was most in need of, viz. a general staff.

[1] 1855–1909; orphan son of Matthew Arnold's brother William, and adopted son of his sister and her husband, W. E. Forster. Educated at Rugby and University College, Oxford; M.P. (liberal unionist), 1892; secretary of the admiralty, 1900–3; war minister, 1903–5.

[2] The second Viscount Esher (1852–1930). Held various offices which brought him into touch with the court, and was intimate with King Edward.

[3] Afterwards Lord Fisher of Kilverstone. At this time he was commander-in-chief at Portsmouth, but had recently been at the admiralty as second sea lord, and earlier had held the Mediterranean command, then the highest at sea.

[4] Afterwards Lord Sydenham of Combe.

Greater changes were made in the navy, prompted partly by the growing German challenge and partly by the emergence within the service of a high officer intensely eager for its modernization and reform. This was Sir John Fisher, who in the autumn of 1904 came back to the admiralty as first sea lord, a man of restless, forward-looking genius and strong fighting character. Lord Selborne, who appointed him, was himself an able first lord; but a few months later, when he went out to South Africa to succeed Milner, his place was taken (6 March 1905) by an even abler one, brought in by Balfour (his contemporary at Eton) from the business world. This was the third Earl Cawdor.[1]

Cawdor came direct from an eventful chairmanship of the Great Western Railway, where he had initiated policies destined to benefit that line for many decades to come. Like Fisher, he was a man who by instinct looked ahead and could see through the wall of time to what was coming up behind it; and though their collaboration only lasted nine months, the fruits were memorable. Two stand out: the redistribution of the fleet, and the laying down of the *Dreadnought* and the *Invincible*—prototypes respectively of the battleship and the battle-cruiser as they were during the European war.

Fisher perceived plainly, as a professional man, that Tirpitz's fleet was built to fight the British; and, given the intense hatred and jealousy of England felt by the German classes engaged in shipping and foreign trade and their rapidly increasing influence over German policy, he could not believe that the plan would be easily diverted from proceeding to its conclusion. For such a conflict the traditional 'far-flung' dispositions of the British navy were all wrong; and he worked at once, though by camouflaged stages, to concentrate its fighting strength in or near home waters. The practice of 'showing the flag' in remote seas was curtailed. Numbers of semi-obsolete ships—floating death-traps in wartime—were ruthlessly scrapped, saving upkeep and, in many cases, crews. A few days after Cawdor left office was made public a redistribution of the fighting navy in three fleets—Mediterranean (based on Malta), Atlantic (based on Gibraltar), and Channel (based on home ports). Hitherto there had been only

---

[1] 1847–1911; educated at Eton and Christ Church, Oxford; as Lord Emlyn (till 1898) sat in the house of commons (1874–85) without making much mark; director of G.W.R., 1890; chairman, 1895–1905; after 1905 took high rank in the unionist party, and in 1910 was one of its four representatives at the Buckingham Palace Conference.

the Mediterranean and Channel fleets, of which the former was
by far the strongest. The creation of the Atlantic fleet meant
taking half the Mediterranean fleet out of the Mediterranean.
In theory it was not taken quite out, but being based on Gibraltar
could face either way. This, however, was partly camouflage.

The other Fisher-Cawdor policy, the building of the *Dreadnought*, i.e. of a battleship which made all others then in the world
second-class, has often been criticized with too little knowledge.
In Chapter XIV below are explained the technical reasons for
designing this ship, which in their way were unanswerable. But
the strategic and international motives were no less cogent. It is
true that it deprived Great Britain of her lead in existing ships,
and involved (just as the 'Admiral' class had in the eighties and
the 'Magnificent' class in the nineties) the building of a new battle-
fleet. But it hit Germany far harder, for it entailed the complete
reconstruction of the Kiel Canal before a single ship of the new
dimensions could be taken through it. What this meant may be
seen from the fact that, though within two months of the *Dreadnought's* launch the widening was authorized by the German
Navy Law of April 1906, it was not completed till the summer of
1914, only six weeks before the outbreak of the European war.[1]
But the Cawdor-Fisher calculation went further. They adopted
a plan to lay down four dreadnoughts in 1906, four in 1907, and so
on for the present. The *Dreadnought* herself was built in close
secrecy and with entirely unprecedented speed; she was launched
in February 1906 and completed early in 1907; and it was not till
considerably later that the Germans knew enough about her to
start building themselves. Therefore Great Britain would have
had a fleet of ten, and perhaps fourteen, dreadnoughts or 'Invincibles' afloat before a single German ship of their class had been
completed; and a start would have been established which nothing
could overtake. Before such a hopeless handicap, added to that of
the Kiel Canal, the chance of inducing Germany to renounce the
race seemed a fairly good one; and it was probably the only
alternative, in the light of what we know now, to the solution of
war. But (as we shall see later) it completely disappeared when
the Campbell-Bannerman government in 1906–8, by abandon-

---

[1] A date which may have materially contributed not merely to the non-occur-
rence of the war at earlier crises, but also to its occurring when it did. Unless able
to transfer her battle-ships at will from Wilhelmshaven to Kiel, Germany could
never have exercised that control over the Baltic which in 1914–18 proved so vital
to her.

ing the Cawdor programme, threw away most of the lead which the genius of Fisher had secured for Great Britain, and encouraged Germany to try drawing level again.

Another very important step carried out under Lord Cawdor was the establishment (in October 1905) of a navy war council with the first sea lord as president, comprising the officers of the naval intelligence department, the newly established mobilization department, and the assistant-secretary of the admiralty; with power to call in other responsible officers as temporary members. This did not amount to a general staff for the navy; but in several, though unhappily not all, directions it performed the functions of one, and was a valuable advance.

Deep and lasting as were the effects wrought by the Balfour government in the fields of education, licensing, Irish land, and defence, it did something more eventful still when it brought about the Anglo-French Entente in 1904. For the result in a Europe already divided between the Triple and Dual Alliances was that Great Britain came down from the fence. And, reversing what had been the habit of her policy ever since Gladstone embroiled her with France over Egypt, she came down upon the French side.

In a memorandum written three years later a high official at the foreign office, Sir Eyre Crowe, denied that this had been intended by the British statesmen.[1] Their motive in 1904, he said, was only a desire to obliterate friction with France; they merely illustrated 'the general tendency of British Governments to take advantage of every opportunity to approach more closely to the ideal condition of living in honourable peace with all other States'. This version seems broadly correct. For, despite the non-success in 1901 of Chamberlain's last attempt at an Anglo-German alliance, Great Britain remained on terms of co-operation with Germany throughout 1902, looking to her as usual for the support which was needed in Egypt, and joining with her at the end of the year in a blockade of Venezuela. Co-operation against the Venezuelan government, partly to stop coastal outrages on shipping and partly to collect debts due to bondholders, had been originally suggested by Lord Lansdowne. The resort to blockade, however, was by the wish of Germany; to whom Great Britain's complaisance was extremely valuable, because

[1] Gooch and Temperley, *British Documents*, iii (1928), 398–520.

it diminished American apprehensions about the Monroe doctrine. Washington (under Theodore Roosevelt) even so was much stirred, until Britain readily and Germany reluctantly[1] consented to arbitration.

Now the negotiations with France had started eleven months earlier, in January of this same year, just as the foreign office was completing its Japanese Treaty, whose point was turned against France's ally, Russia. And they began with a proposal to Paul Cambon, the French ambassador, from Chamberlain himself.[2] Their scope was colonial. They were to end the clash of French and British oversea policies, an object greatly to be desired on its own account, for the friction during twenty years had been incessant and envenomed. Everything here renders improbable on the British side any anti-German implication. The side of France is another matter; for the French anglers in the diplomatic pool were just as well aware as the German that Great Britain, though an awkward fish to land, would prove a big fish if landed. Indeed, when Delcassé first sent Cambon to London shortly after the Fashoda crisis, there is reason to suppose that, mortified by the failure of Nicholas II to back them, they hoped to seek in their ex-adversary an alternative or supplementary support. The part which the ambassador subsequently played may perhaps have been a little exaggerated in his post-war recollections,[3] but it was certainly the largest one on the French side.

Anglo-French differences, when the negotiators went into them (the question did not engage Lord Lansdowne till August[4]), fell into two classes. First, a long string of local colonial disputes. In several of these (the Newfoundland fishing rights were a case in point) the French claims, resting on treaty, were of more detriment to Britain than advantage to France, and were chiefly valuable to the latter as bargaining counters, which she could not be forced to surrender without compensation elsewhere. Here was matter for tedious and intricate, but not hopeless, chaffering of the usual subordinate kind. But in the other class were two questions of very high policy—Morocco and Egypt. France's opposition in Egypt was a thorn in Britain's side, of

---

[1] For Roosevelt's high hand in this, see W. R. Thayer, *Life and Letters of John Hay* (1915), ii. 287–8.

[2] *Die grosse Politik der europäischen Kabinette*, xvii. 342, 343 n.

[3] Cf. his interview in *The Times*, 22 December 1920.

[4] Lord Newton, *Lord Lansdowne* (1929), 267.

which she must insist on being rid; yet the pang of renouncing their historic aspirations in the Nile valley was keenly felt by the French. Conversely, the barbaric sultanate of Morocco was fast falling to pieces, and France was for strategical reasons most anxious to control it; because its territory would link her North and West African possessions, and because control by any rival Great Power would gravely complicate her position. But the British admiralty were loth to see the southern shore of the Straits of Gibraltar in the hands of a Great Power; and most of Morocco's small trade was done by British merchants, who did not want it to go the way of Madagascar. In the end, however, a bargain was struck whereby Britain was to have a free hand in Egypt and France in Morocco. The problem of the straits was solved by a non-fortification clause and by reserving a northern strip to satisfy the historic claims of Spain; and that of trade by a clause to assure equal liberty of commerce for thirty years. The arrangement about Spain, which was only contingent on the event of the sultanate's breaking down, was embodied in secret articles; and in September 1904 it was completed by a Franco-Spanish Convention (also secret) to the same effect.

Before, however, any considerable Anglo-French convention stood a chance of being ratified, it was indispensable to change French feeling towards Great Britain. The outbreak of the South African war, following so shortly after the humiliation of Fashoda, had heated it to fury. No newspapers in Europe, not even the German or the Dutch, were so anti-British; and they attacked with particular indecency Queen Victoria and King Edward. Nevertheless, in March 1901, while the war still continued, President Loubet and Delcassé gave Lord Carrington, who had come as King Edward's messenger to announce his accession, very friendly messages for the king, which made a great effect on him.[1] And it was he, eventually, who won French mass-opinion over. His famous visit to Paris in May 1903 was by far the most useful of the official expeditions to foreign courts and capitals of which he afterwards became so fond.[2] In its way it was a great feat; for though the press campaign had already waned since the ending of the war eleven months earlier, yet it was a semi-hostile capital to which he went, and a most friendly one from which he

[1] Sir Sidney Lee, *King Edward VII*, ii (1927), 14–15.
[2] The tour which included it (after visits to Lisbon and Rome) was his first effort in this line.

returned. In the following July President Loubet and Delcassé came to London, and were very warmly received. As a direct result of their visit an Anglo-French Arbitration Treaty was signed on 14 October. The main treaty still needed a winter's negotiation, in which Lord Cromer bore an influential part. It was signed on 8 April 1904, and dealt with Newfoundland, West Africa, Egypt, Morocco, Siam, Madagascar, and the New Hebrides.[1]

In England it had only one adverse critic—the Germanophil Lord Rosebery.[2] As it ceded territory, the government submitted a bill to parliament, following the precedent set by Lord Salisbury over the cession of Heligoland, and thereby virtually abrogating an old prerogative of the monarch. In France it also received parliamentary ratification, though there it was a good deal censured by the leading colonial politicians. Its most immediate effects were seen in Egypt. It struck off the shackles which had hitherto cramped the great work of Cromer, and enabled the country's financial system to be changed (by a Khedivial decree) for its very great advantage. It made the Egyptian question cease to be an international problem. But in so doing it snapped the invisible leading-strings in which Germany since 1882 had held Great Britain. Bismarck's successors came to feel the loss of this hold all the more, perhaps, because hitherto they had too much taken it for granted.

Three influences soon caused the Entente (as it was now regularly termed) to become much closer, and to assume aspects of active co-operation. One—the most fundamental so far as England was concerned—was the alarming growth of the German fleet. Already in March 1903 the Balfour government had significantly decided to create a northern base for battleships at Rosyth. We have seen how in the following year Sir John Fisher, as first sea lord, began to shift the fighting weight of the British navy towards home waters. As soon as this involved reducing the Mediterranean fleet it necessitated becoming sufficiently intimate with France to entrust the French navy with the Mediterranean. A second influence in the same direction was the Russo-Japanese war (8 February 1904–23 August 1905). Para-

---

[1] Text in *British Documents*, ii (1927), 402–7.
[2] Cf. D. Lloyd George, *War Memoirs*, i (1933), 1 and 5; Lord Crewe, *Lord Rosebery* (1931), ii. 581. Rosebery denied Germanophilism, but his past was full of it.

doxically, the fact that France and Britain were allied to opposite parties induced a sort of collaboration, since the entanglement of either in the war would have dragged in the other on the opposite side. The most dangerous crisis was in October 1904, when the Russian Baltic fleet, steaming past the Dogger Bank on its way to the Far East, fired by night on a Hull trawling fleet, which it mistook for torpedo boats, killing or wounding nearly a score of British fishermen. British opinion was hotly inflamed. But Russia's amends were prompt and disarmingly complete—she apologized, paid compensation, and submitted to a Hague inquiry; and this was attributed partly to the good offices of France.

The third influence was the diplomatic action of Germany. When the Anglo-French Treaty was first announced, her chancellor, Bülow, commented on it (12 April 1904) in friendly terms; and in June, when King Edward visited the Kaiser at Kiel, the latter said that Morocco did not interest him and never had.[1] But nine months later came a swift reversal. On 31 March 1905 William II paid a personal visit to Tangier, and in flamboyant speeches proclaimed that the Sultan was 'absolutely free', that all Powers must be 'considered to have equal rights' under his sovereignty, that Germany had 'great and growing interests in Morocco', and that his own visit was to show his resolve to do all in his power to safeguard them. This was a direct military challenge to the infant Entente. Whether it held or yielded its ground, could its solidarity survive the test?

What had happened in the interval? A long series of Japanese victories had temporarily disabled France's Russian ally, and the Tsar was falling much under the Kaiser's influence. Germany had learnt about the secret articles; she had also observed France sending a mission to the Sultan with a programme of reforms, which might well be meant as a first step in 'Tunisification'. She resented that the French should rush so big a claim without consulting and 'compensating' her as, in fact, they had already compensated three other Powers—Great Britain and Spain (in the manner shown above) and Italy (by secretly recognizing her claims to Tripoli). Yet Germany was not, after all, a Mediterranean Power, and her trade interests in Morocco were trifling. Though by them she justified her interference, they could scarcely have motived it. Morocco's real value to

[1] Eckardstein, *Lebenserinnerungen*, iii (1921), 88.

her was as a wedge to split the Entente. Possibly too she had awaked more fully to the enormous strategic addition which ports near the north-west corner of Africa could make to the power of the German navy.

The Tangier policy was Holstein's, and proved a disastrous failure; for it brought Germany nothing, and it riveted instead of splitting the Entente. Yet at first it appeared successful. Germany demanded an international conference and the jettison of Delcassé; in June France gave way on both points. She was not ready to fight, and Great Britain had made no promise to fight by her side.[1] Diplomatic co-operation continued between London and Paris, but needed careful nursing. In September France and Germany reached an accord about the scope of a conference to be held in January 1906 at Algeciras. With this the last of the war dangers which had darkened the sky for nearly a year was temporarily dispersed. The Balfour cabinet, which might probably have resigned towards the end of 1904 but for the Dogger Bank incident, became now freer to do so; and all the more after Sir Edward Grey, who was heir-presumptive to the foreign office in a liberal ministry, had announced on 20 October 1905 that such a ministry's diplomacy would continue on Lord Lansdowne's lines.

On 23 August the Peace of Portsmouth had liquidated the Russo-Japanese war; and on the twelfth of that month Lansdowne had signed a new treaty with Japan. It differed from the old in that it provided for the reciprocal defence of two special interests —Japan's in Korea and Great Britain's on the Indian frontier— and that it bound each ally to aid the other, not merely if attacked by two enemies, but if attacked by one. It secured Japan against a *revanche* by Russia, and in that way enabled her to accept more moderate peace terms, though nothing was said by Great Britain as to what terms she should accept. Only a few days before (on 24 July 1905), the weak Tsar, at a private meeting with the Kaiser on his yacht at Björkö in the Baltic, had been overborne by the much stronger personality of the latter into signing a treaty of alliance, whereby St. Petersburg, and (so the terms sug-

---

[1] See *British Documents*, iii (1928) for the written (17 August 1922) statement to this effect by Lord Sanderson (formerly head of the foreign office) and its written (4 April 1927) confirmation by Lord Lansdowne. Statements in an opposite sense made by Frenchmen (notably the socialist leader, Jaurès) may perhaps be explained by the fact that King Edward, on his way back from Biarritz, had spoken somewhat ill-advisedly to French ministers.

gested) Paris also, would move in the orbit of Berlin. But neither the Tsar's own ministers nor the French would look at it; and eventually this triumph of William II's ambition had to be dropped. France was drawn the closer to her western friend because of the wavering of her eastern ally.[1]

The relative fertility of Balfour's premiership is the more remarkable because for the greater part of its term he was hampered by an acute difference over domestic policy, which split his party and deprived him of most of his leading colleagues. The issue was that of protection versus free trade, and the battle over it interested the British public at the time out of all proportion to any of the matters which we have so far reviewed in this chapter. This was partly because its protagonist was Chamberlain, whose genius compelled attention, as genius can.

To understand its origin we must go back to the earliest days of the ministry. In July 1902, between the date originally fixed for King Edward's coronation and that (9 August) when it eventually took place, there met in London the Fourth Colonial Conference.[2] Six 'self-governing colonies' were represented;[3] they held ten meetings; and they passed a resolution in favour of conferring regularly every three years. The full proceedings, like those of the 1897 conference, have never been made public, but their upshot is known. They were a profound disappointment to those who wished to strengthen imperial unity. On the morrow of their brilliant co-operation in the South African war, the colonies displayed not a co-operative but a centrifugal purpose. The explanation of the paradox (which repeated itself later after the European war) was really quite a natural one; the prowess of the colonial troops had increased their separate sense of colonial nationhood. In the two imperial directions which Downing Street wished to emphasize—political organization and defence—the colonial premiers were disinclined to

[1] Cp. what Lord Esher had written (7 September 1904): 'A secret and very intimate understanding between Russia and Germany ... accounts for the friendliness of the French towards us, as they can never have much reliance on Russia, the moment they suspect a German alliance' (M. V. Brett, *Journals and Letters of Viscount Esher* (1934), ii. 62). Throughout the war with Japan Germany ostentatiously helped Russia; coaling her fleets at sea, and enabling her to denude her western frontier of troops.

[2] The best account is still that in Richard Jebb, *The Imperial Conference* (1911).

[3] Canada, Australia, New Zealand, Newfoundland, Cape Colony, and Natal.

move. Chamberlain repeated to deaf ears his plea for a council
of the empire. Figures put before the conference, showing that
the mother country's contribution to imperial defence per head
of population was over 8½ times New South Wales's and over
14½ times Canada's, elicited nothing at all from Canada, and
from the rest almost trifling increases of naval contributions.
Only in regard to trade had the colonies any sort of imperial
policy. They passed resolutions: (1) declaring free trade within
the empire to be impracticable, but favouring the principle of
imperial preference; (2) recommending the latter to colonies
that had not yet practised it; (3) respectfully urging the home
government to consider the expediency of adopting it in the
United Kingdom.

This experience produced a great effect on the mind of Chamberlain. He was keenly concerned for imperial unity, and had
tried to approach it from more than one side. After seven
years' hard effort he found himself foiled on all of them, and
thrown back to the side of fiscal preference, where, on account
of the mother country's deep attachment to complete free
trade, it was peculiarly difficult to do anything. Could an approach be attempted through Hicks Beach's recent revival of
the 'registration' duty on corn? It was a very small impost; yet
to remit it on empire-grown corn would at least have for the
colonies a token value, as a step showing regard for their wishes.
But the cabinet were divided about it, and no decision was
taken for the time being. In the following winter Chamberlain went to South Africa, and spent some months there, visiting each of its four colonies, arranging for a customs union
between them, interviewing the leading men of all parties, and
making a series of powerful speeches. He returned in March,
a greater figure to the public than ever. But in his absence
Ritchie, the chancellor of the exchequer, had spiked his gun
by engaging the cabinet to repeal the corn-duty.

The budget of 1903, introduced on 23 April, gave effect to
this decision. Ritchie had a surplus of nearly £11 millions;
he devoted most of it to taking 4d. off the income-tax, and
argued that to drop the corn-duty was an indispensable equivalent for the indirect tax-payer. This would have been more
convincing had its imposition sent up the price of bread; but
it had not. The truth was that the duty (which brought in a
mere £2 millions) had now none but a symbolic importance;

both parties in the cabinet were thinking not of what it was, but of what it might lead to. After weeks of private altercation, Chamberlain on 15 May cast his die. A strong speech at Birmingham proclaimed his secession from free trade and his belief in imperial preference, as well as in fiscal retaliation against foreign tariffs. On 28 May he repeated and defined these views in the house of commons. They were favourably received by a large section of the unionist rank and file, but opposed by nearly all the older leaders. In the cabinet the duke of Devonshire, Ritchie, Lord Balfour of Burleigh, and Lord George Hamilton stood for free trade, and so did three very influential 'elder statesmen' outside—Goschen, Hicks Beach (now Lord St. Aldwyn), and Lord James of Hereford. As against them not a single really eminent figure supported the colonial secretary. The rest of the cabinet more or less followed Balfour and Lansdowne, who were seeking a compromise platform, on which to reconcile the disputants and reunite the party.

Through June, July, and August Balfour averted the split. Giving reasons against an immediate dissolution, he urged his colleagues to consent to differ, instancing how through many parliaments catholic emancipation had been an open question in the tory party, and so had free trade.[1] Next he put before them a policy of his own, which in September was made public in a pamphlet.[2] Nothing shows better how heated and blind the controversy had already become than the derision with which this document was hailed by Chamberlainites and free traders alike. While the latter denounced its policy as the thin end of a tariff wedge, the former with at least equal truth declared that it was not an end of their wedge at all. Yet on the side of theory it was both realistic and far-seeing; some of it had been said by Lord Salisbury as long before as 1890;[3] and of its many striking forecasts about the future only one has not been borne out by subsequent events.[4] The programme based on it was publicly launched by Balfour in a speech on 30 September 1903 at Sheffield. In brief it was that, without embarking on a general tariff, and without taxing food (which

[1] Letter of 4 June 1903 to the duke of Devonshire (B. Holland, *Life of the Duke of Devonshire* (1911), ii. 307–9).
[2] A. J. Balfour, *Economic Notes on Insular Free Trade*.
[3] Reported in *The Times*, 11 November 1890, p. 4, col. 6.
[4] Viz. the suggestion that the industry-forcing tariffs in oversea countries might, by discouraging agriculture, lead to wheat shortage (p. 23).

Chamberlain had frankly recognized as necessary to any effective imperial preference, but which Balfour opined that the country 'would not tolerate'), the government should be given power to try to force down foreign tariffs by means of retaliatory duties. Economically, much might be said for it; but politically it fell between two stools. For while it offended the out-and-out believers (like Ritchie) in 'taxation for revenue only', it yet did nothing for the empire, which had given Chamberlain his motive to disturb the *status quo*.

But before this the cabinet had broken up. On 9 September Chamberlain had written to Balfour offering to resign and go out to preach his gospel on a free platform. Balfour neither accepted nor refused; and on 14 September, at a cabinet left unaware of what Chamberlain had done, he dismissed[1] Ritchie and Lord Balfour of Burleigh. Next day Lord George Hamilton and the duke of Devonshire resigned also; but thereupon on the following day Balfour accepted Chamberlain's resignation and persuaded the duke to withdraw his. Having shed his extremists on both sides and retained the pillar-like duke, the Premier seemed for the moment triumphant. But when the four resignations were published, Chamberlain and the free traders each complained that they had been tricked into going by having concealed from them the impending departure of the other side; and the duke's position was rendered so invidious that on 6 October his resignation was announced also.

In a hard situation Balfour reconstructed the cabinet with skill. Chamberlain's son Austen[2] was made chancellor of the exchequer, and the duke of Devonshire's nephew and heir, Victor Cavendish,[3] financial secretary to the treasury; so that

---

[1] In a private letter the duke of Devonshire wrote: 'Ritchie and Balfour of Burleigh did not really resign, but were told they must go'; and in another: 'I never heard anything more summary and decisive than the dismissal of the two Ministers' (B. Holland, *Life of the Duke of Devonshire* (1911), ii. 352, 340). The public, of course, supposed them to have resigned voluntarily.

[2] B. 1863; educated at Rugby and Trinity College, Cambridge; M.P., 1892; civil lord of the admiralty, 1895–1900; financial secretary to the treasury, 1900–3; chancellor of the exchequer, 1903–5; Indian secretary, 1915–17; member of war cabinet, 1918; chancellor of the exchequer, 1919–21; lord privy seal and leader of the house of commons, 1921–2; foreign secretary, 1924–9; first lord of the admiralty, August–October 1931; K.G., 1925; d. 1937.

[3] B. 1868; educated at Eton and Trinity College, Cambridge; M.P., 1891–1908; financial secretary to the treasury, 1903–5; succeeded his uncle as 9th duke of Devonshire, 1908; civil lord of the admiralty, 1915–16; governor-general of Canada, 1916–21; Lord Lansdowne's son-in-law; d. 1938.

touch was maintained with both the opposing wings. Brodrick replaced Lord George Hamilton at the India office, being himself, as we saw above, succeeded by Arnold-Forster; and for the difficult succession to Chamberlain at the colonial office was brought in Alfred Lyttelton,[1] a nephew of the late Mrs. Gladstone and a leading barrister, without much parliamentary experience, but well able to hold his own in debate. It was a team equal to all ordinary business. Meanwhile Chamberlain, now that his hands were free, unchained a tariff agitation on the largest scale. A Tariff Reform League supplied his war-chest, followed by a Tariff Commission (with an economist, W. A. S. Hewins, as secretary) to supply facts and arguments. As the campaign developed, its scope insensibly altered. Chamberlain had begun it almost solely for the sake of unifying the empire. But the colonies could not help him directly, and the backbone of his support came from such British manufacturers as desired an industrial tariff. Protection for the empire's sake slid into protection for its own sake. Even Chamberlain's speeches very largely became appeals to save this or that 'dying' British industry.

To the liberal opposition the tariff issue was a godsend. They had not easily recovered from their split over the South African war. Towards the end of 1901 Lord Rosebery bid for the leadership again. But his speech at Chesterfield in December of that year ended any chance of his resuming it by agreement. In February 1902 he announced his definite separation from Campbell-Bannerman; and soon afterwards founded inside the liberal party an imperialist organization called the Liberal League, of which Asquith, Fowler, Grey, and R. B. Haldane became leading members. Campbell-Bannerman, however, showed no readiness to be shunted; and it was his, i.e. the more radical, section of the party, which gained most credit out of the fight against the Education Bill later in that year. But from May 1903, when Chamberlain shot his bolt, liberal differences were transcended by the defence of free trade. Here the party had strong tactical ground, and united to make the most of it. All aspects of Chamberlain's policy were acutely criticized, especially by Asquith, who followed the Tariff Reform leader

[1] B. 1857, 8th son of the 4th Lord Lyttelton; educated at Eton and Trinity College, Cambridge; notable cricketer and successful barrister; M.P., 1895–1906; secretary for the colonies, 1903–5; d. 1913.

about the country, answering each speech with a consummate debating power which did much to revive his reputation among liberals at large. But the popular cry remained that against food-taxes—'the big loaf and the little loaf'. Against it the Chamberlain counter-cry was 'Tariff Reform means work for all'. In 1903 and 1904, when there was serious unemployment, this made a strong appeal; but unluckily for Chamberlain a trade improvement began in 1905.

When the end of 1904 came, and still no dissolution, it grew evident that if Chamberlainites and Balfourites went to the electors as differing entities confronting a united free trade block, they would court disaster. Therefore in January 1905 Balfour at Manchester produced 'on a half-sheet of note-paper' a formula intended to combine them. It included duties for negotiation and retaliation, duties to stop dumping and a fresh Colonial Conference, 'unhampered by limiting instructions', to discuss 'closer commercial union with the Colonies'. These terms were accepted by the Chamberlainites, but only after nearly two months' delay, which rendered the reunion unconvincing. Even the unionist majority in the house of commons, though still large and solid enough for all other purposes, could not be relied on for a vote on the fiscal question; and when the liberals forced one, Balfour counselled his followers to abstain, and himself led them out of the house. This completed for an impatient public the impression that he had over-stayed his time.

Apart from its fiscal difficulties the government had raised against itself another issue, which alone would have caused almost any ministry to be defeated at the polls. This was the importation of indentured Chinese labour to the Transvaal to work the Rand mines.

The arguments for it were economic. There was a shortage of Kaffir labour on the Rand. The mine-owners would make larger profits and furnish the annexed Transvaal with a larger revenue, if they employed cheap Chinese coolies. But these for racial reasons could not be imported as free men; they must be not only indentured, so as to insure that they worked long enough to cover the costs of recruitment and transport, but confined by themselves in compounds and debarred even in non-working hours from the ordinary liberties of life. The mine-owners would have liked to have over 100,000 of such 'human tools'. Milner's too purely administrative mind capitulated to their pleadings; and, what was more surprising, he induced both Lyttelton and Balfour to capitulate also.

Yet on its political side the thing did not bear thinking about. Merely in itself it was a horror; for to ship tens of thousands of Chinese young men overseas to perform for long years the hardest underground toil, and coop them up for their leisure in horde-compounds with no society but each other's, meant deliberately creating, as in the sequel it did create, moral sinks of indescribable human beastliness. But principles were involved far transcending any details peculiar to the case. Canada, Australia, and New Zealand had played leading parts in winning the war. On grounds of experience they all felt most strongly against importing Chinese, and the open affront to their feelings by the mother country did the empire real harm. Deadlier still was the affront to labour. This was a time when throughout Great Britain the toiling millions, not firmly bound to any party, were awaking to their position and canvassing their claims as never before in modern history. What was the front of their demand? That labour should cease to be regarded merely as a commodity. But here in the Chinese labour scheme of the Balfour government was a reassertion of the commodity-view of labour, than which nothing could have been more plain and challenging. The workmen spoke of it always as 'Chinese slavery', and at least by Aristotle's definition of slavery they were right. What they felt in their bones, was that, if once capital were conceded the right to meet an industrial labour shortage by drawing on Asiatic cooliedom for 'human tools', all western hopes for freedom in industry would be jeopardized.

It is impossible to conceive Disraeli committing so gross a political error. Balfour committed it because, though he had more contacts than most conservatives with the liberal mind, he had none whatever with the mind of labour.[1] To do him justice, the bulk of his party were equally blind. Even after they saw the immense electoral mischief which the policy had done them, they helplessly attributed it to 'misrepresentation'. The fact was that conservatism had changed a good deal since Disraeli strove to make it the party of the common people. After the

[1] A striking picture of his unfamiliarity with it much later (1915) will be found in Mr. Lloyd George's War Memoirs, i (1933), 296.

home rule issue of 1886 caused a landslide of the propertied
interests into its ranks, it had grown increasingly to be a class
organ of those interests; and was to become even more so before
the first decade of this century was out.

Meanwhile 20,000 Chinese were at work in the Rand mines by
the end of 1904, and 47,000 nine months later. The economic
results were all that the mine-owners had wished, and the moral
evils all that ought to have been foreseen. Vice and punishment
ruled the compounds; whose inmates broke bounds, when they
could, and terrorized the veldt farms.

Organized labour in Great Britain had already a stimulus of its
own besides the Chinese issue. We saw how in 1900 it formed a
Labour Representation Committee ('L.R.C.'), combining trade
unions and socialist societies for the first time in a common party
with common finance. For a year or two its secretary, J. Ramsay
MacDonald, had a hard task to keep the new craft moving; but
then a sudden wind filled its sails and blew hard in its favour till
the general election. The source was a judicial decision—that in
the Taff Vale Case.[1]

The questions to be decided in this case were two. Could a
trade union be sued and mulcted in damages for wrongs done by
its agents? And was it also liable to an injunction? Hitherto it
had been taken for granted that the Trade Union Act of 1871
afforded absolute protection to union funds, parliament having
at that time refrained from giving a trade union either the privileges or the burdens of incorporation. But Mr. Justice (afterwards Lord Justice) Farwell, the very able High Court judge
before whom the Taff Vale Railway Company sued the Amalgamated Society of Railway Servants, answered both questions
in the employers' favour and against the trade union. His judgement was reversed in the Court of Appeal, but it was upheld on
appeal to the house of lords; and the A.S.R.S. had to pay £32,000
in costs and damages. The effect on the trade unions was frankly
disabling; the more so since an almost simultaneous case, *Quinn*
v. *Leathem*,[2] appeared considerably to extend the liability of a
strike organizer to find his acts adjudged tortious. The whole
trade union world rose up to demand remedial legislation; and
as the Balfour government at first ignored the problem, and then
(in 1903) shelved it by appointing a Royal Commission, the
'L.R.C.' rapidly became the workers' main hope. Within a year

---

[1] (1901) A.C. 426.   [2] (1901) A.C. 495.

its membership leaped from 356,000 to 861,000; and it began to win by-elections. In 1902 the liberals in the Clitheroe Division had to stand aside and see D. J. Shackleton[1] win it for labour; in 1903 at Woolwich Will Crooks[2] sensationally captured what had been a conservative stronghold; and in the same year in the Barnard Castle division of Durham Arthur Henderson[3] achieved labour's first victory in a three-cornered contest over liberal and conservative alike. These victories were not merely demonstrations; they sent to parliament to help in shaping the new party three exceedingly able men.

Here we should note, that the political sting of the foregoing judicial decisions was greatly enhanced by their being decisions 'of the House of Lords'. The peers had fancied in the seventies, that they were fortifying their house by insisting,[4] against Lord Selborne, that a court bearing its name, and indeed purporting to be it, should continue to be the final court of appeal. This policy now recoiled on them like a boomerang, and appreciably contributed to their eventual undoing.

The government's last measure of importance was the Unemployed Workmen Act, 1905. During the depression of 1904 Walter Long, then president of the local government board, got on foot in London a voluntary scheme of local unemployment committees linking up the borough councils and the boards of guardians, with a central unemployed body to supplement them for certain purposes. In 1905 Gerald Balfour, who had succeeded Long at the board, carried a bill to extend and regularize these

[1] B. 1863 at Nelson; began in a cotton-mill as a half-timer and worked there till he was 29; official of several weavers' trade-union organizations; M.P., 1902–10; chairman of the labour party, 1905; president of the Trade Union Congress, 1908 and 1909; senior labour adviser to the home office, 1910; National Health Insurance Commissioner, 1911–16; permanent secretary of the ministry of labour, 1916–21; knighted, 1917; chief labour adviser, 1921–5; d. 1938.

[2] B. 1852 at Poplar; educated partly in a workhouse; a cooper by trade. L.C.C., 1892; Mayor of Poplar, 1901; chairman of the Poplar Board of Guardians, 1898–1906; M.P., 1903; d. 1921. In his day by far the most representative English workman among the labour members.

[3] B. 1863 at Glasgow; served apprenticeship as moulder at Newcastle; became secretary of the Iron Moulders' society; Wesleyan local preacher; city councillor of Newcastle; town councillor of Darlington; Mayor of Darlington, 1903; M.P., 1903; chairman of the parliamentary labour party, 1908–10 and 1914–17; president of the board of education, 1915–16; labour adviser to the government, 1916; member of the war cabinet; home secretary, 1924; foreign secretary, 1929–31; president of the World Disarmament Conference, 1932–3; his party's chief organizer; d. 1935.

[4] See above, p. 18 and p. 39.

bodies, giving the board power to establish one in any locality upon (or even without) an application from the local council or guardians. Each of the new bodies was to keep a register of the unemployed in its area; and they might also at the cost of the rates establish labour exchanges, collect information, assist emigration or removal, and even (in the case of the central unemployed body) acquire land for farm-colonies. But they might not spend anything by way of wages or maintenance, unless public generosity defrayed it. The act was passed in August; an appeal was issued to the public in November; and being headed by Queen Alexandra, it reached £125,000 by the end of the year.

In the autumn of 1905 Lord Spencer, the 'Red Earl', who had led the liberals in the lords since 1902, and who was the only man under whom as prime minister Campbell-Bannerman might have been willing to serve, had a cerebral seizure and retired. About the same time the liberal party became exercised over Irish home rule. Campbell-Bannerman at Stirling (23 November) enunciated a 'step by step policy'—home rule was not to be lost sight of, but progress towards it was to be by instalments. Lord Rosebery at Bodmin (25 November) attacked this, and declared that 'emphatically and explicitly and once for all', he could not 'serve under that banner'. But unknown to Rosebery, Campbell-Bannerman had secured the assents of Asquith and Grey before he spoke. So no split followed; and the only result of the Bodmin speech within the liberal ranks was to cut off the prospect of Rosebery's taking office, as had been hoped, in a Campbell-Bannerman ministry.[1]

But it seems also to have affected Balfour. He was himself hard-pressed. Chamberlain (3 November) had publicly described his walking-out tactics as 'humiliating'. On 14 November the Tariff Reform leader captured the National Union of Conservative Associations. On 21 November he insisted before the Liberal Unionist Council that the Balfour policy of retaliation was impossible without a general tariff. The premier was thus brought to bay; and, inferring from the Bodmin speech more liberal dissension than in fact existed, he decided on a tactical

[1] As a matter of fact, the idea of a 'step by step' home rule policy had been put forward by Asquith himself in a letter to his constituents (1 March 1902) just after the formation of the Liberal League; which rendered Rosebery's rash attack on it in 1905 the more surprising.

stroke. Taking a leaf from Gladstone's book of 1873 and 1885, he did not dissolve but (4 December 1905) resigned. His hope was that the liberals, if called on to form a ministry without a parliamentary majority, would be torn by unresolved rivalries and by differences regarding home rule, and might already before the election set the pendulum swinging back. The trap was obvious, and many of Campbell-Bannerman's followers urged him to refuse office, as Disraeli had in 1873. But he was emphatic, that the country would never believe in the liberals, if they flinched; and in this he had strong support from Morley. On 5 December he accepted office,[1] and the long conservative domination was at an end.

One or two minor imperial episodes may close this chapter. In March 1903 was completed the Uganda Railway, 582 miles long, connecting Lake Victoria Nyanza with the sea at Mombasa. Planned originally by Mackinnon in the days of the British East Africa Company, it was begun by the British government in 1896, after the Crown had taken over the territory; and sums totalling £5,331,000 were spent on it in direct grants from the exchequer voted by parliament. Most liberals, including Harcourt and Campbell-Bannermann, originally voted against these grants; though it seems obvious now that the railway had to be built, and that unless Great Britain was prepared to build it, she could scarcely justify her occupation of the country.

Following the suppression of a ten-months' Arab revolt, which broke out after the transfer to the Crown in 1895, the coastal area of British East Africa had been in effect transformed from a protected Arab state to a province under British administration. As such it remained under the foreign office. But in 1904 there was a sharp controversy between the foreign secretary, Lord Lansdowne, and the commissioner, Sir Charles Eliot, owing to which the latter, though generally acknowledged to be in the right, had to resign. The episode drew attention to the impolicy of burdening a diplomatic department with tasks of imperial government; and in April 1905 British East Africa was transferred to the colonial office.

On the opposite side of Africa there was completed, also in

---

[1] Strictly speaking he did not, his biographer tells us, 'kiss hands', as that 'sacramental part of the ceremony' was forgotten at the time, and the king afterwards remitted it (J. A. Spender, *Life of Campbell-Bannerman* (1923), ii. 194 *n.*).

1903, a railway from the coast to Kumasi. In 1900 there had been a dangerous revolt of the Ashantis, due to the mistake of an injudicious governor; who demanded the 'Golden Stool', which he supposed to be a throne, but which really was a fetish regarded as containing the soul of the Ashanti nation. Chiefly through the steadfastness of the Hausa troops, the revolt was put down; and in September 1901 the country was formally annexed. Thereafter the building of the railway and the spread of cocoa-growing brought an era of complete pacification.

A third important African railway was that from the mouth of the Atbara to Port Sudan, connecting the Upper Nile with the Red Sea. It was opened in 1906, and, though built under the Anglo-Egyptian *condominium*, did in fact not a little towards emancipating the Sudan from Egypt, since it gave it a separate commercial access to the outer world.

Further south along the Red Sea littoral the area known as British Somaliland was in 1905 transferred to the colonial office, having been since 1898 under the foreign office, and before that since 1884 occupied as a protectorate dependent on Aden. The peace of this arid semi-desert pastoral area was broken at the end of the nineteenth century by the emergence of a 'Mad Mullah'—the fanatical leader of raiding dervish bands. The first British campaign against him was in 1900–1; there was another in 1903; and others were repeatedly called for till the Mullah's death in 1921. The motive which had brought Great Britain here was the relation of the coast to the Suez-Indian route; and costly inland operations were little to the taste of Downing Street. A later Government (that of Asquith) formally abandoned the interior to the Mullah for four years (1910–14); but this policy eventually broke down.

In Asia British activity at three points may be noted. From about 1900 onwards Russia made unmistakable attempts to get a footing in the Persian Gulf. She established consulates there, and on one occasion unsuccessfully tried to start a coaling-station. Accordingly (15 May 1903) Lord Lansdowne made a declaration that 'we should regard the establishment of a naval base or a fortified port in the Gulf by any other Power as a very grave menace to British interests, and we should certainly resist it by all the means at our disposal'. In the following November Lord Curzon, then viceroy of India, paid an official visit to the Gulf, accompanied by a squadron of warships, and held a

Durbar attended by the chiefs of the Arab coast who were in treaty relations with us. These steps made clear to all the world the position of exclusive influence claimed by Great Britain in the Persian Gulf and her intention of defending it.

About the same time Russia actively intrigued in Tibet. Various hostile acts were committed by the Tibetans on their frontier with India; and when the viceroy sent letters to the Dalai Lama, they were returned unopened. Meanwhile a Tibetan Mission to Russia was received by the Tsar and his foreign minister. In December 1904, after giving notice of their intentions to Russia, the British government sent Colonel Sir Francis Younghusband to Tibet as a negotiator accompanied by an armed force. He carried out his mission with great skill; fought his way to the Forbidden City of Lhasa (3 August 1905); imposed a treaty securing the trade intercourse and exclusive political influence, which Great Britain desired; and returned leaving Tibetan feeling much friendlier than when he came. Controversy subsequently arose between Younghusband and the then Indian secretary, Brodrick, because in certain points, about which undertakings had been given to Russia, Younghusband's Treaty conflicted with the official instructions, which had not fully reached him till it was signed. It was an error of judgement on his part; but the Balfour government thought it essential to Britain's good faith to throw him over. With the rectifications thus held necessary, the Treaty was ratified by Great Britain, Tibet, and China, and ended British anxieties in that quarter. Younghusband was eventually solaced with the K.C.I.E., at the instance of King Edward, who admired and championed him.[1]

The Anglo-French Agreement of 1904 entailed several cessions of territory, but led to one important extension. This was in the Malay peninsula. The Convention regarding Siam gave Great Britain a free hand to the west of a certain line, and in virtue of this she proceeded in the course of a few years to double her Malay possessions. This was a not unimportant step in the development of what soon after became perhaps the most successful of her tropical colonies.

[1] Sir Sidney Lee, *King Edward VII*, ii (1927), 369–71; cp. Dr. Gooch's account in *The Cambridge History of British Foreign Policy*, iii (1923), 327–8.

XII

EDWARDIAN LIBERALISM

WHEN Campbell-Bannerman became liberal leader in the commons at the end of 1898, he was not a favourite with the ardent spirits of his party. He had no notable platform gifts, being probably the least fluent speaker who has ever come to lead the house of commons. He seemed no more than an elderly, very canny, and very wealthy Scot, who was well-liked by his associates, and had earned a G.C.B. by useful departmental work. The particular sphere in which he had passed nearly all his time as a minister—the war office—was the least popular with his fellow liberals. Inverting Bismarck's perhaps apocryphal gibe about Lord Salisbury, they defined their task in 1899 as convincing the country 'that C.-B. is iron painted to look like a lath'. That he so looked, needed no argument.

Seven years later when he became prime minister, his standing had completely altered. His name was now the watchword of the radicals and the young. It was his nature, as it had been Gladstone's, to move persistently to the left. Moreover his countless trials as leader in opposition had brought to view some qualities which none of his rivals possessed in an equal degree—shrewdness, steadfast will, directness of purpose, and unselfish devotion to his party's cause. Opinion had grown, 'not only that he deserved the highest place by patient endurance and long service, but that he was the man who on the merits of his character and performance could most wisely and safely be entrusted with it'.[1]

Till the election was held, no one knew how it would turn out; and to rally round his banner as many free trade voters as possible, the radically-minded premier gave the more conservative section of his party a decidedly larger share in the cabinet than they subsequently obtained in the parliamentary majority. His only serious hitch was over the foreign office, which Grey refused to take unless the premier himself went to the lords and allowed Asquith to lead the commons. Had this been a joint demand by Asquith, Grey, and Haldane, it would have been hard to resist, for the king favoured it, and so (though this was not known) did the Vienna specialist under whose medical care Campbell-Bannerman came annually at Marienbad. But Asquith had

[1] J. A. Spender, *Life of Campbell-Bannerman* (1923), ii. 186.

taken the chancellorship of the exchequer without reserves; and he and Haldane overcame Grey's opposition, to which Lady Campbell-Bannerman would not allow her husband to submit. An offer made in the interval to Lord Cromer was declined. Two years afterwards Grey, who had been entirely conscientious in the matter, recognized that he had also been entirely mistaken.

The new ministry contained a quite extraordinary number of able men. One of Campbell-Bannerman's staunchest 'pro-Boer' allies, Sir Robert Reid,[1] became lord chancellor (as Lord Loreburn). His claim was indefeasible, as he had been liberal attorney-general seven years before, and it enabled the prime minister to refuse the post to Haldane, who took instead the war office. The other veterans of the left wing were Morley, who went to the India office, and Bryce, who became Irish secretary. With them we might almost class John Burns; who, though originally a London labour leader, had—first through prominence among the L.C.C. Progressives and then through pro-Boer activities—become very much a left-wing liberal, and who received, in an evil hour for local government progress[2], the local government board. Herbert Gladstone[3] as home secretary, Lord Elgin[4] as colonial secretary, and Lord Ripon as lord privy seal, helped to give the combination a sufficiently Gladstonian air.

But the greater weight of ability was in the 'new' men, and these only obtained junior places. No more than four besides Burns entered the cabinet—Lloyd George as president of the board of trade (the post grudgingly given to Chamberlain in strangely similar circumstances in 1880), Augustine Birrell at the board of education, John Sinclair at the Scottish office, and Sydney Buxton at the Post Office. But outside as under-secretaries or whips were Reginald McKenna, Winston Churchill, Herbert Samuel, Walter Runciman, H. E. Kearley (afterwards Lord Devonport), and F. Freeman Thomas (afterwards Lord Willingdon). Of these Churchill[5] was an ex-conservative M.P.,

[1] B. 1846; educated at Cheltenham and at Balliol College, Oxford; M.P., 1880; attorney-general, 1894–5; lord chancellor, 1905–12; earl, 1911; d. 1923.

[2] See pp. 516–18 below.

[3] B. 1854, youngest son of W. E. Gladstone. Educated at Eton and University College, Oxford; minor offices, 1881–5 and 1886; under home secretary, 1892–4; first commissioner of works, 1894–5; chief liberal whip, 1899–1905; home secretary, 1905–10; governor-general of South Africa, 1910–14; d. 1930.

[4] The ninth earl, 1849–1919; educated at Eton and Balliol College, Oxford; Indian viceroy, 1893–8; colonial secretary, 1905–8.

[5] Son of Lord Randolph Churchill; b. 1874; educated at Harrow and at Sand-

who had but recently crossed the floor on the issue of free trade. He found fortune at the colonial office, since, his chief being in the lords, he soon became spokesman in the commons for some of the government's most important policies.

The general election began on 12 January 1906, and then the full force of the country's reaction against the conservatives disclosed itself. The liberals obtained 377 seats, a majority of 84 over all other parties combined. The unionists saved only 157; conventionally classified as 132 conservatives and 25 liberal unionists, but more realistically as 109 Chamberlainites, 32 Balfourians, 11 Unionist Free Fooders, and a few uncertain. Both the Balfour brothers, with Brodrick and Lyttelton, were unseated. The Irish nationalists, now strongly organized and with few exceptions owning the lead of John Redmond, numbered 83. Last but not least—indeed the sensation of the moment—came no less than 53 labour members. Of these 29 were returned under the Labour Representation Committee to sit as an independent party. Of the other 24 a few were ordinary 'Lib-Labs', but most were the officials of the miners' unions—a body of men not yet affiliated to the L.R.C. and rather more cautiously-disposed than its leaders, yet elected like them on a decided class basis.

This overwhelming parliamentary mandate gave the liberal government complete assurance in the house of commons; and anything that could be done by administrative act they were in a strong position to do. But when it came to legislation, they had to reckon with the permanent conservative majority in the house of lords. During the ten years of unionist rule since 1895, the second chamber had, as such, lain dormant, and allowed its power of revising bills to rust in almost complete disuse. Now it was to become wide awake again, and was to re-employ that power in order, as in 1893–5, to prevent a liberal government from carrying its bills. Letters which in April 1906 passed between Lansdowne and Balfour as unionist leaders in the lords and commons respectively,[1] reveal the purely party standpoint from which they proposed to utilize the theoretical rights of the house of lords under the Constitution. Recalling the success of such tactics in 1893–5, Balfour even suggested that the house of

hurst; served abroad as an officer of Hussars; war correspondent in Kitchener's Sudan campaign and in South Africa; M.P., 1901; under-secretary at the colonial office, 1905–8; and thereafter with only a few short interruptions held cabinet rank down to 1929; re-entered cabinet, 1939; prime minister, 1940– .

[1] Lord Newton, *Lord Lansdowne* (1929), 353–5.

lords might be 'strengthened rather than weakened' by a course of bill-wrecking. But he reasoned from false analogy. The commons majority behind the liberal governments of 1893–5 was tiny, and from the outset crumbling; without the Irish they would usually have been in a minority of 40 or 50. It might be fairly questioned, how far the electorate really stood behind them for anything; and the lords, when they rejected their bills, could claim to be giving the country the benefit of a bona-fide doubt. How different in 1906, when the liberal government was fresh from winning at the polls the greatest victory on record, and had an enormous house of commons majority elected by unprecedented turnovers of votes! All that Lord Rosebery had urged in 1894 about the impolicy of allowing what should be a revising-power over the work of both parties to degenerate into a blocking-power against the work of one, was now to receive naked and unashamed illustration. The Constitution was to be exploited with no scruples regarding fair play—a course bound eventually to cause fatal collision with the fair-play instincts of common Englishmen.

In the light of post-war democracy no student can avoid asking, how practical men like Balfour and Lansdowne—the former of high and the latter of flexible intelligence—could be so short-sighted. The psychology of it was that both were aristocrats born in the purple. They belonged to, they led in, and they felt themselves charged with the fortunes of, a small privileged class; which for centuries had exercised a sort of collective kingship, and at the bottom of its thinking instinctively believed that it had a divine right to do so. Passionately devoted to the greatness of England, these men were convinced that she owed it to patrician rule. In their view her nineteenth-century parliamentarism had worked successfully, because the personnel of parliaments and cabinets was still (with a few much-resented exceptions like Bright) upper-class, and the function of the lower orders was limited to giving the system a popular *imprimatur* by helping to choose which of two aristocratic parties should hold office. Tory democracy, as Disraeli put it forward, and as it was exemplified in his 1867 franchise extension, did not depart from this view; its assumption being that the wider the electorate, the less chance it would have of behaving as anything but an electorate, and that the more the poor voted, the stronger would be the position of the popularly-revered old families as against middle-class upstarts run by dissenting shopkeepers. It was the personnel elected to the 1880 parliament which first seriously disturbed this assumption; and the shock would probably ere long have driven the whigs over to the conservatives, even apart from the home rule issue.[1] The nineteen years of unionist supremacy which we have just seen ended, may be looked on as a successful rally of the governing families to maintain their position, propped and modified by their alliance with the ablest leader of the upstarts—Chamberlain. But from their standpoint the house of commons elected in 1906 was far worse than that of 1880. Not merely were there the fifty-three Labour M.P.s—nearly all of whom had been manual workmen, and all of whom without exception had been reared in working-class homes—but a large proportion of the huge liberal contingent consisted of men with small means, and in the cabinet itself sat Lloyd George, the orphan son of an elementary school-teacher, brought up by his uncle who was a village shoemaker. To persons born like Lansdowne and Balfour (and only a little less to Rosebery) it appeared out of the question that a house of commons so composed and led should effectively rule the nation; and scarcely distinguishing in their minds between the Constitution and the dominance of their own order, they felt justified in using any resource of the former, however unfairly one-sided it might otherwise have appeared, in order to crush the challenge to the latter.

Another early pre-occupation of Lansdowne and Balfour (the latter having found his way back to the commons as member for the City of London) was the future of the fiscal controversy. Chamberlain amid the general wreckage had saved his seven Birmingham seats intact, and could count on two-thirds of the small conservative remnant elsewhere. He now was in truculent mood, proclaiming that safety lay in daring, and the whole party must swallow his policy. A compact very much in his favour was reached in letters between him and the ex-premier, and registered on 15 February at a party meeting. Had his strength remained, he well might have ousted Balfour and made himself unionist leader; but it was not to be. Sunday, 8 July 1906, was his seventieth birthday; Birmingham feted it on the Saturday with extraordinary enthusiasm; and on the Monday he made a great speech—his last. On the Wednesday he was

[1] Lansdowne himself seceded from the Gladstone government in August 1880 more than five years before the home rule split.

struck down by paralysis; and that was the end of his career. Though until July 1914 he lived on in retirement, pathetically incapacitated, it is at this point that history parts company with him. In sheer parliamentary and platform strength the country had not seen his equal since Disraeli and Gladstone. Yet an air of frustration clings round his record. As a leader, he had very high qualities, but he markedly lacked what Napoleon thought a leader's first requisite—'luck': which may or may not be a synonym for a certain final felicity of judgement. It was not merely that he never became prime minister. He was in politics for constructive aims—to 'get things done'; yet outside the colonial office work it was little that he actually achieved. In all human relations his instincts were intensely loyal; yet he helped to wreck each of the great parties in succession. Both episodes were charged to his personal ambition; yet it is obvious that in both he was acting conscientiously, against and not for his own interest. Had there been no home rule split and had he succeeded Gladstone as liberal premier, social reform might have come in England nearly twenty years sooner than it did. In that case the labour party—at least in the form which it actually took —might never have been born.

Campbell-Bannerman remained prime minister till 6 April 1908. The great triumph of his administration was his settlement of South Africa. Had it needed a bill in parliament, it would have been killed by the house of lords as his other contentious bills were; for the conservatives opposed it bitterly, and Balfour denounced its main feature—the concession of self-government to the Transvaal—in some of the least foreseeing words that have ever fallen from the lips of an English party leader.[1] But happily for the empire he was able to get it through by letters-patent, i.e. by an administrative act, for which he only needed the confidence of the house of commons. Before he took office, Milner (who despite his fine administrative work could never live down the Boers' feeling against him as the author of the war) had resigned and come home, being succeeded as governor-general by the

[1] As 'the most reckless experiment ever tried in the development of a great colonial policy' (Hansard, IV. clxii. 804). He suggested that the Transvaal would make 'every preparation, constitutionally, quietly, without external interference, for a new war' (ibid., 802). The only conservative in the house of commons who dared vote in favour of Campbell-Bannerman's policy was the then youthful F. E. Smith.

second Lord Selborne, till then first lord of the admiralty in the Balfour cabinet.[1] Selborne was a man of practical and conciliatory disposition, whom it was not necessary for the liberal government to dislodge in order to reverse the current of South African policy.

The first problem was Chinese labour. The cabinet decided that it was not feasible to annul existing contracts; but orders were sent on the morrow of the general election to stop recruiting any more Chinese. In this way the evil system came gradually to an end, though it was not till the beginning of 1910 that the last Chinese labourers left the Rand compounds. The next problem was the government of the Transvaal. Lyttelton, while he was colonial secretary, had promulgated a constitution which was a timid first step towards autonomy. Campbell-Bannerman suspended it. He persuaded his cabinet in principle, that complete colonial self-government should be granted;[2] sent out a small commission to inquire into details; announced his decision in the house of commons in July; and in December had the letters-patent issued. The policy attained historic success. Two months later, following a general election under the new constitution, General Botha became prime minister of the Transvaal with General Smuts as his principal colleague; and they led their people in a determination to do as Campbell-Bannerman had done by them, and use their liberty in the same spirit of reconciliation in which it had been granted.[3] Six months later a similar grant was made to the Orange River Colony.

The full harvest of this achievement was not reaped till after Campbell-Bannerman was dead. It was in October 1908 that a convention comprising delegates from each of the four South African parliaments met at Durban to devise a constitution for South Africa. The bill which emerged from their deliberations was (after amendments) ratified in all four colonies by the middle of 1909, and enacted by the British parliament in the autumn of that year. Then even the conservatives applauded. Many men

---

[1] Where for the short remainder of its term of office he had been succeeded by Earl Cawdor.

[2] Mr. Lloyd George, who took part as a member of the ministry, told the present writer many years afterwards, that this was entirely the veteran prime minister's own doing. He made a speech in cabinet so unanswerable as to secure at once the unanimous assent of his hearers, many of whom had till then held a different opinion.

[3] See above, p. 346. Botha himself said in 1909: 'Three words made peace and union in South Africa: "methods of barbarism".' (J. A. Spender, *Life of Campbell-Bannerman*, i. 351).

had contributed something to this great national and imperial result—among them (such are time's reversals) Dr. Jameson; who, as premier of Cape Colony when the Transvaal's letters-patent were granted, elicited from the high commissioner, Lord Selborne, a most helpful dispatch and memorandum, in which the arguments for union were mapped out. But the edifice would not have been possible without the foundation; and that was Campbell-Bannerman's.

The 1906 house of commons was at the outset a difficult body to lead. It was rich in inexperienced idealists. Radicalism and socialism alike, released from the suppressions of two decades, were radiant with sudden hopes of a new heaven and a new earth. No leader not alive to that morning glory could have carried the house with him; and that was where Campbell-Bannerman in his kindly and generous old age gave the parliament an incomparably better start than the efficient but earth-bound Asquith could have done. One marked trait in common, however, they had; both shone more in office than in opposition. Campbell-Bannerman had been particularly handicapped since 1898, because he was never able to speak with a clear authority. Now he could, he was a different man. The change appeared strikingly, when Balfour upon reappearing at Westminster attempted to repeat at his expense the logic-chopping which had served to humble him in the past. The premier retorted with a single phrase—'Enough of this foolery!'—so perfectly expressing the new house's sense that politics was a task for men and not a sport for gentlemen, that for long afterwards even Balfour's golden tongue could not win its ear.

The contentious bills of 1906 were three—an Education Bill (the chief measure of the year), a Trade Disputes Bill, and a Plural Voting Bill. The first and third were killed by the house of lords; the second got through. The history of the Trade Disputes Act, 1906, was curious. The Royal Commission appointed in 1903, with Lord Dunedin as chairman, had recently reported in favour of substantially undoing the effect of the Taff Vale and *Quinn* v. *Leathem* decisions. They did not propose to make trade unions directly immune from actions for tort, but to declare the law of agency in regard to them in such a way that actions like the Taff Vale company's would not ordinarily lie. At the same time the difficulties over *Quinn* v. *Leathem* and similar cases would be met by amendments of the law about conspiracy and picketing.

Yielding to the law officers and to legalists in the cabinet, like Asquith and Haldane, the government introduced a bill on these lines. But the trade unions (not inexcusably, for the bill as drafted was quite unintelligible to anybody but a trained lawyer) were dissatisfied. They introduced a private member's bill of their own, directly exempting trade unions from all actions for tort; and for its second reading Campbell-Bannerman himself voted. The next step was to substitute the labour bill's text for that of the government bill, where they conflicted. The lawyers protested (Asquith is said to have had his sole cabinet conflict with Campbell-Bannerman over this matter), but it was done; and the bill went to the house of lords in that form. Here, it might have been argued, was a task for a revising chamber; but the lords did not attempt it. Thinking of little but party tactics, they recoiled from increasing the hostility of organized labour towards them, and let the measure through untouched.

They did otherwise with the Education Bill. Beyond question the government had a mandate to amend the Act of 1902; and when Birrell introduced his measure, Morant, the real author of that act, who had remained head of the department, had taken care that the scheme should be such as not to injure the great educational machinery which he had set up. It was confined to an attempted removal of the nonconformist grievances. There were thoughtful anglicans who did not regard it as unworkable.[1] But a loud outcry was raised in which most of the bishops and clergy eventually joined; and when the bill reached the house of lords, it was killed by destructive amendments. From the party standpoint this was natural enough; nine-tenths of the peers were conservative, and the conservative party backed the Established Church. But it was fatal to the theoretic claim of the upper house to be a safeguard for the electorate against the lower house's exceeding its mandate. For when the commons had passed the Act of 1902, they made a revolution, for which they had no mandate; yet the lords never stirred. When, however, the commons passed Birrell's bill (by a majority of more than two to one), they had the clearest mandate imaginable; yet the lords destroyed it. The Plural Voting Bill (by which electors with a title to vote in

[1] e.g. Canon Hensley Henson, afterwards Bishop of Hereford and (since 1920) of Durham. The Bishop of Ripon (Dr. W. Boyd Carpenter) spoke in the same sense in the house of lords' second reading debate; as did the Bishop of Hereford (Dr. Percival).

several constituencies[1] would have been forbidden to vote in more than one) was likewise shelved. The formal ground alleged was that any change in the franchise ought, as in 1884, to be accompanied by a redistribution of seats. But this, of course, deceived nobody.

At the beginning of 1907 some changes were made in the cabinet. Bryce was sent to Washington as British ambassador—an appointment welcomed by all parties on both sides of the Atlantic; and in his place Birrell became Irish secretary, being himself replaced at the board of education by McKenna. The new minister introduced two bills in attempted substitution for Birrell's—the first, a one-clause makeshift, early in 1907, and the second, which was more ambitious, early in 1908; but both were withdrawn before passing through the commons. After Campbell-Bannerman's death Runciman succeeded McKenna at the board of education, and following negotiations with Dr. Randall Davidson, the exceptionally able archbishop of Canterbury, brought in yet a fourth Education Bill. This, however, though sponsored by the archbishop, was rejected by his church at a Representative Church Council meeting (3 December 1908); and being also objected to by the Roman catholics and by some of the school teachers, it had to be withdrawn. In many aspects it was the best bill of the four; and its loss was not unreasonably deplored by Asquith, then prime minister, in very strong terms. No further attempt was made in this field; and the commons' will remained frustrated.

In 1907 the chief contentious measures were a series of land bills. Land reform had been very prominent in radical programmes since the eighties, and the labour members were also intent on it. The bills introduced were four—a Small Holdings Bill for England, an Evicted Tenants Bill for Ireland, a Small Landholders (Scotland) Bill, and a Land Values (Scotland) Bill. The first two were only let through by the lords subject to such mutilations as deprived them of nearly all value. The two Scottish bills were destroyed.

Campbell-Bannerman's considered answer to the lords' tactics had already been given at midsummer 1907, when he moved a

[1] In the pre-1918 days, when totals on the register were so much smaller and different constituencies were not polled simultaneously, plural voters appreciably weighted the scale on the side of property. (It was normal for a business man to record two votes, and in such a business as a multiple shop he might record a dozen.)

resolution in the house of commons asserting that, 'in order to
give effect to the will of the people as expressed by their elected
representatives, the power of the other House to alter or reject
Bills passed by this House must be so restricted by law as to
secure that *within the limits of a single Parliament* the final decision
of the Commons should prevail'. There was here, be it noted,
nothing about the speculative problem of reforming the second
chamber's composition, but a typically English concentration on
the sole point in actual controversy, viz. the use made of its
powers. The premier explained his plan to be, that in case of
conflict between the houses over a bill, a small joint conference
of peers and commoners should sit in private; if no adjustment
were reached, the bill after an interval of six months or so should
rapidly pass the commons again; then, if necessary, there would
be another conference, another interval, another commons' passage of the bill, and another conference again. But the third
conference would be final; and the bill, if not passed in an agreed
form, would then become law in the form in which it last left
the house of commons. The root idea was not Campbell-
Bannerman's invention; it had been suggested by Bright twenty-
three years before.[1] The premier added a proviso for quin-
quennial parliaments. After three days' debate his resolution
was passed on 26 June 1907 by 432 votes to 147. The conservative peers judged it a *brutum fulmen*, and continued as before.
Three years later they were to be heavily undeceived.

   While the main party measures of the government were thus
in two successive years killed or sterilized, certain able ministers
got through ambitious legislation, which did not directly raise
party issues. The first was Lloyd George,[2] who now climbed past
the levels of brilliant criticism to those of constructive statesmanship. Like Chamberlain before him, on being relegated to an
office then thought humble, he at once proceeded to give it un-
anticipated importance. His Merchant Shipping Act, 1906, and
Patents Act, 1907, were measures on the grand scale. Both were
hailed by the opposition as semi-protectionist. For the first confined pilot's certificates to British subjects;[3] and while prescribing

---

[1] In a speech at Birmingham on 4 August 1884.

[2] B. 1863; educated at a Welsh village elementary school and at home; at 16
articled to solicitors and at 21 qualified; M.P., 1890; president of the board of
trade, 1905-8; chancellor of the exchequer, 1908-15; minister of munitions, 1915-
16; secretary for war, 1916; prime minister, 1916-22.

[3] Section 73. Cp. also Section 12 restricting the engagement of foreign seamen.

better food and accommodation under the Red Ensign in order to retain British crews, it also contained clauses compelling foreign ships using British ports to conform in some respects to British standards. Similarly the Patents Act introduced a much-needed provision compelling patentees to work their patents in the United Kingdom within three years. But these features really stood on their own merits, and did not imply in their author any conversion to fiscal protection. Other striking achievements of Lloyd George were his act (1906) for taking (for the first time in Britain) a Census of Production, and his settlement (in 1907) of a dispute between the railway companies and the Amalgamated Society of Railway Servants, in which the country had been threatened for the first time with a general railway strike. He followed up the latter early in 1908 by settling a strike of 30,000 shipyard engineers on the north-east coast. But perhaps his greatest feat was the act setting up a single Port of London Authority to amalgamate and supersede the chaos of private dock companies and wharfingers, which till then rendered impossible any planned development of England's greatest port. This had been recommended by a Royal Commission in 1902; but the task of treaty-making between the multitude of interested parties had frightened the conservatives away. Lloyd George, who here, as in the labour disputes, revealed rare gifts for negotiation, cleansed the Augean stable and provided London, none too soon, with an administration capable of bringing her abreast of the great improvements planned or executed about this time in such rival ports as Hamburg, Antwerp, and Rotterdam. The bill did not actually pass parliament till 1908, when he had been succeeded at the board by Churchill. The under-secretary, H. E. Kearley, also took a large part in it, and became chairman of the new body as Lord Devonport.

The other most active minister was Haldane.[1] His Territorial and Reserve Forces Act, 1907, was the legislative part of a great scheme of army reform extending over several years. Possessing a special knowledge of German institutions, he brought it to bear with far-reaching results on the war office. His most important step was the creation (by special Army Order) of a general staff.

---

[1] B. 1856; educated at Edinburgh Academy, Edinburgh University, and also Göttingen University; made a special study of Hegel and translated Schopenhauer (1883–6). Barrister, 1879; M.P., 1885; Q.C., 1890; secretary for war, 1905–12; viscount, 1911; lord chancellor, 1912–15 and 1924; d. 1928.

Campbell-Bannerman, who had resisted this in the nineties,[1] gave way now, because the foreign situation was so bad. The rest of the liberal war minister's reforms were subject to two conditions: that he should satisfy the radical wing of the party by getting £3 millions off the army estimates; and that he should leave untouched the Cardwellian principle of 'linked battalions', which was held sacrosanct by the prime minister. Complying with both, he went ahead and reorganized the home military forces in two lines. The first was an Expeditionary Force comprising six infantry divisions and one cavalry division (of four brigades), with artillery, transport, and medical units ready for rapid mobilization, and enough reserves to provide drafts. The second was formed by merging the non-regular non-militia categories—yeomanry and volunteers—into a single new category—the Territorial Force. In this way he arranged for 14 divisions and 14 mounted brigades, which, no less than regular divisions, were to have their own transport and medical services as part of the organization. A detail of high value was the conversion (in 1909) of the old volunteer corps at the public and secondary schools into Officers' Training Corps. It helped materially towards solving the hard problem of officering the 'new armies' during the European war.

Some points in this scheme will be considered in a later chapter. It was much opposed, though not on rigid party lines, in the commons, more especially by Brodrick, Arnold-Forster, Wyndham, and Balfour. But Haldane won through, partly by his considerable powers of persuasion, but also because it was known that all the best generals at the war office were firm on his side. He had, too, good backing from the prime minister.

Asquith's budget of 1906 was limited, of course, by the finance of the previous government. He had a small surplus; which he used to reduce the tea duty from 6d. to 5d., to repeal the export coal duty, and to add half a million to the sinking fund. His budget of 1907 showed only a little more originality. Its novel feature concerned the income-tax; it differentiated for the first time between earned income and unearned, retaining for the latter the existing rate of 1s., but lowering it to 9d. on the earned incomes of tax-payers with less than £2,000 a year. He also made a slight addition to the Death Duties in the highest ranges. In 1906 he had the advantage of a reduction of £1½ millions on the navy estimates, and in 1907 of a further reduction of nearly half a million, while the army estimates were down by £2 millions. These savings as yet went rather to debt redemption than to social reforms, but the demand for the latter steadily gathered force. In 1906 the labour party succeeded in passing a bill to enable local education authorities to provide meals for necessitous school-children; and in 1907 McKenna passed a short Education (Administrative Provisions) Bill which made it the duty of local education authorities to have the children in their schools medically inspected. The 1906 Act was important, because it brought into existence for the first time the school Care Committees, and the 1907 Act, because Morant, who was deeply concerned for the physical side of education, used it for all that it was worth, establishing a medical department under Dr. (afterwards Sir George) Newman at the board itself, and encouraging the Care Committees to develop medical treatment services following on medical inspection.

Another development, which complicated the politics of this time, was the adoption of militant tactics by women suffragists. It began just before the fall of the Balfour government, when on 13 October 1905 a liberal meeting addressed by Sir Edward Grey in Manchester was interrupted by two young girls, Christabel Pankhurst and Annie Kenney, who were afterwards convicted of assault and sent to prison on their refusal to pay a fine. The advertisement which they received encouraged them to interrupt many more liberal meetings during the election campaign; and the Women's Social and Political Union, a suffragist body formed in Manchester in October 1903, became the rallying-point of the new tactics. Its founder and head was Mrs. Emmeline Pankhurst, mother of Christabel and widow of a popular Manchester leader of the I.L.P. Its ungrudging helper and mentor was Keir Hardie. It was he who supplied the women's early lack of experience in the arts of agitation; and he who by bringing together Mrs. Pankhurst and Mrs. Emmeline Pethick-Lawrence enabled the W.S.P.U. to be established on a solid basis. The 'two Emmelines' had each great but complementary gifts, and while they co-operated (from the spring of 1906 to the autumn of 1912) the movement went ahead with extraordinary momentum. In the course of 1907, when its membership and resources were already very large, there was a split; and a number of the ablest militants seceded to form what from the beginning of 1908 was called the Women's Freedom League. The division was over internal questions—the 'autocracy' of Mrs. Pankhurst; it did not weaken the urge towards militancy.

The tactics employed in these early years were entirely directed against liberals; the logic which they expressed being that only the government could put through a Suffrage Bill, and therefore it must be opposed until it consented to do so. At by-elections every attempt was made to embarrass the liberal candidate, and no cabinet minister could open his mouth anywhere without interruptions. Friends of the suffrage, e.g. Grey and Lloyd George, were attacked no less than its opponents, e.g. Asquith and McKenna; and all sorts of devices, such as padlocking themselves to fixtures, were adopted by interrupters to prevent their removal. The tactics were carried to Downing Street and to the galleries of parliament. But at this stage little damage was done to property beyond some window breaking; and the difficult problem for the home office did not arise till later.

On the suffrage cause itself the first influence of militancy was stimulating. Later the hostilities which it aroused set the clock back. Had it not been persisted in, some kind of Women's Suffrage Bill would probably have passed the commons between 1906 and 1914. But calculations like this were almost irrelevant to most of the women concerned. What drew them together and drove them on was a spirit of revolt. The vote was not sought for any practical object, but as a symbol of equality. They were obsessed by an inferiority complex. And similarly upon politics at large their militancy had more effect than their suffragism. The means mattered rather than the end, and indeed conflicted with it. For while the vote presupposes the rule of free persuasion, the W.S.P.U. leaders proclaimed by word and deed, that the way to get results was through violence. Such doctrines are always liable to become popular, when a politically inexperienced class or classes come into the public life of a nation. Often it seems plausible then to win the game by a 'try-on' at breaking the rules. But of course if others follow suit, there is no game. The years 1906–14 in Great Britain witnessed a crescendo of rule-breaking in this sense—by labour strikers and their Syndicalists, by the house of lords and its Die-hards, by the Ulster Volunteers, by the Irish Volunteers, and by many others; until the fabric of democracy came into real danger. In that direction the W.S.P.U. set the earliest and not the least strident example;

sawing, by a strange irony, at the very bough, on which its members were demanding the right to sit.

The fates of rival or successive Suffrage Bills are of small interest now, as none of them went far. But in 1907 the new attention drawn to women's rights led to an important reform. This was the Qualification of Women Act, 1907, which enabled women, whether married or single, to sit as councillors or aldermen, mayors or chairmen, on county or borough councils, just as since Fowler's Act of 1894 they had sat on the district and parish councils which it established. Much opposition was shown in the house of lords by Lord Halsbury, Lord Lansdowne, and others; but finally the house of commons got the measure passed in its original form. A similar bill was passed for Scotland.

Members of the Campbell-Bannerman cabinet seem to have been surprised, after entering upon office, to find to what a dangerous foreign situation they had succeeded. The lull before the Algeciras Conference, fixed for January 1906, ceased as the meeting drew near. On the 10th of that month Cambon, the French ambassador, told Grey, the new foreign secretary, that his government considered the danger of an unprovoked attack to be real; as we know now that it was, since Count Schlieffen, the German chief of staff, had been urging in Berlin 'the fundamental clearing up of relations with France by a prompt war'.[1] Would Great Britain, asked the ambassador, possibly join in resisting it? And if there was even a chance of her doing so, would she allow military conversations as to the form which her possible co-operation might take? To be effective in an emergency, it would need to have been thought out beforehand.

Grey replied that he could not commit Great Britain in advance. In his opinion (and he intimated the same to the German ambassador) 'if war were forced upon France on the question of Morocco, public opinion in this country would rally to the material support of France'; but that was given as his opinion merely, and neither a promise nor a threat.[2] But the force of the argument for military conversations could not be gainsaid, and after consulting Campbell-Bannerman, Asquith, and Haldane (but not the cabinet as a whole) Grey authorized them.[3] The first was opened on 17 January between General Grierson and

---

[1] K. F. Nowak, *Das dritte deutsche Kaiserreich*, ii (1931), 308.
[2] Hansard, v. lxv. 1811.   [3] Ibid., 1812.

Major Huguet, the French military attaché in London; and thenceforward they continued till 1914.

This step made explicit a momentous transformation of the Entente. It had begun as a restoration of goodwill, based on a bargained settlement, which implied an understanding that the parties should give each other diplomatic support in realizing the advantages bargained for. France had done so for Great Britain in Egypt without serious hitch; but the British counter-support in Morocco had stumbled on the quite unexpected German intervention. By now this blackmail of Holstein's had so hardened what it was intended to weaken, that Great Britain and France were driven to face at least the possibility of carrying on war as allies, and even to concert in advance the plans requisite for a joint campaign. Moreover though it was agreed on both sides (and put in writing by Grierson and Huguet) that the conversations did not bind the governments, they yet were official; and it is obvious that two countries, each of which has unbosomed military secrets to the other, have gone far to commit themselves against fighting in opposite camps. About the same time confidential conversations took place in Brussels between the British military attaché and the chief of the Belgian general staff. These were on a different footing, being purely unofficial and not notified to either Grey or Haldane. They were expressly confined to what might be done in the event of a prior violation of Belgian neutrality by Germany. The famous Schlieffen Plan, on which Germany's violation of it in 1914 was based, had only just been adopted in Berlin (December 1905). But Schlieffen had been thinking along those lines since the turn of the century,[1] and railway dispositions on the German side of the Belgian frontier—e.g. the building of long troop-platforms at obscure country stations with little traffic—had made pretty clear what was intended.[2]

The final responsibility for the opening of the Grierson-Huguet conversations rests with Campbell-Bannerman, who had the determining voice about it. He also must be held responsible for not consulting or acquainting the cabinet. What was the reason?

---

[1] General H. J. von Kuhl, *Der deutsche Generalstab in Vorbereitung und Durchführung des Weltkrieges* (1920), 166.

[2] Records of the Anglo-Belgian conversations were unearthed at Brussels in 1914 by the Germans, who, as was natural in war-time, sought to base on them against Belgium a charge of non-neutrality. But that could not now seriously be argued.

The one which Grey gave later—that the cabinet could not be summoned—is unconvincing; and Lord Loreburn's imputation about a cabal of ex-liberal leaguers[1] seems disposed of by the prime minister's part in the transaction. Probably the motive was secrecy; the cabinet of 1906 was a large body, and leakages from its proceedings were frequent. But it was certainly a remarkable omission, not easy to reconcile with the practice of cabinet government.[2]

The Algeciras Conference, which began on 16 January 1906, proved a disappointment for Germany. Of twelve governments represented, only Austria-Hungary stood by her; Italy (whom France, it will be remembered, had compensated in advance) did not. On the other hand Russia, in spite of Björkö, stood by France; so did Spain; so did Great Britain; and so in fact, though not in form, did the United States. France and Spain obtained mandates to police the Sultanate under a Swiss Inspector-General; and though Germany was to butt into Morocco again five years later, for the present she withdrew empty-handed. A certain easing of tension followed. In the summer there was to have been held the Second Hague Conference, which the Campbell-Bannerman government desired to use for the discussion of disarmament. It was postponed for a year; but meantime the government, for a gesture, dropped a Dreadnought and a good deal else from the Cawdor programme. This was done despite plain indications from the Kaiser that he would not allow disarmament to be discussed. Undeterred by them, on 2 March 1907, the prime minister published in the first number of H. W. Massingham's then new weekly, the *Nation*, an article headed 'The Hague Conference and the Limitation of Armaments', pleading for an arrest in the armaments race and stressing at the same time the purely defensive reasons why Great Britain maintained a supreme navy. From the standpoint of a British liberal, sincerely anxious for peace, disarmament, and international goodwill, it was an admirable article. Grey had seen and ap-

---

[1] Lord Loreburn, *How the War Came* (1919), 80.

[2] One of the things which may have helped to prevent the conversations from being notified to the cabinet was that on 1 February 1906, Sir Edward Grey's wife was killed in a carriage accident near his home in Northumberland. He was thereafter away from the cabinet and the foreign office for ten days; and when he came back the Franco-German crisis was over. But it remains extraordinary that even Lloyd George was not informed of the conversations till 1911, and the cabinet as a whole not till 1912.

D d

proved it. But the effect on Germany proved irritant. Suspecting behind British diplomacy the motives which governed their own, her inspired publicists denounced the Machiavellian British premier who, at a time when Germany's navy had been put at a maximum disadvantage by the launch of the *Dreadnought*, was seeking to entice her before a Hague Conference to have the disadvantage made permanent. In vain did the British government again lop a capital ship off the Cawdor programme and offer to lop yet another, if other powers would do likewise. On 30 April Bülow announced Germany's veto on any proposals for disarmament at The Hague. At the Conference (15 June–18 October 1907) she neatly outmanœuvred Great Britain by supporting the United States against her in a proposal to exempt private property at sea from capture. Great Britain reaped no result from the discussions beyond some new 'laws of war', which proved dead letters when Armageddon came, and a plan to create an International Prize Court, dependent upon subsequent agreement about an international code of prize-law.

While the Conference was in progress, a more fateful step was taken. On 31 August 1907 was signed an Anglo-Russian Convention.[1] It had the effect of combining the Franco-Russian Alliance and the Franco-British Entente in a higher unit of co-operation. This, however, was at first not fully seen, and only in 1909 did the Triple Entente become distinctly visualized throughout Europe as the foil to the Triple Alliance. The Convention resembled that with France; it was in form a set of agreements regulating the different spheres where friction had arisen or might arise between the two countries. These were Persia, Afghanistan, and Tibet. The chief difficulty was over Persia; where social decay and political break-up had reached an advanced stage, and where Russia working from the north at lavish expense had developed all the regular antecedents of absorption, building roads and railways and supplying Russian officers to the Shah's Cossack guards. Had anything caused Great Britain to cease from being a Great Power, the Tsar would doubtless have annexed Persia at once; and with it his empire would have obtained in the Persian Gulf its much-coveted access to unfrozen seas. Great Britain had some trade, British and

---

[1] Full text in G. P. Gooch and H. W. V. Temperley, *British Documents on the Origin of the War*, iv (1929), 618–20. Negotiations regarding it fill nearly all this large volume.

Indian, in the Gulf ports, but her main interest was strategic—
to keep her rival outside the Gulf and away from the Seistan
fringe of the Baluchi and South Afghanistan frontiers. The agreement partitioned Persia along these lines into two spheres of
influence with a neutral zone between. It was criticized in
Russia by Count Witte (now prime minister there) as barring his
country's advance; and in England by Lord Curzon as giving
away to Russia nearly all Persia's best territory, including eleven
out of her twelve chief towns. To some extent the criticisms
cancel out. The spheres of influence were not to derogate from
the Shah's sovereignty, which was to be continued in both.

The Afghan and Tibetan agreements need not detain us. By
the first Russia undertook to have no political relations with the
Afghan government save through the intermediary of Great
Britain, while Great Britain affirmed her intention not to change
the political status of the country nor to take any measures there
threatening Russia. The agreement was only to come into force
with the consent of the Amir; but though this was never obtained,
its terms were kept by both parties. In Tibet they both bound
themselves not to interfere, nor to send representatives to Lhasa,
nor to negotiate save through China, Tibet's suzerain. Most of
the results of the Younghusband expedition (other than the exclusion of Russia) were soon afterwards abandoned; and the way
was left open for China to reconquer the country in 1910. Neither
about Afghanistan nor about Tibet did subsequent friction
arise. About Persia it did.

Two points require note in regard to this Convention as a
whole. In the first place it drove Russia back on the Near East
for her 'warm water'. Japan had expelled her from the China
Seas, and she now waived her approach to the Persian Gulf.
Only the Dardanelles outlet remained; and already her interest
in the Balkans quickened. Under Nicholas II it had become
almost dormant; since 1897, there had been definite Austro-
Russian co-operation in all Balkan matters; and even when, in
1903, the Macedonian Bulgars put up against the Turks by far
the biggest Christian revolt since 1876, the Tsar was content
that his foreign minister should meet the Austrian foreign
minister at Mürzsteg, and agree to a programme of 'reforms',
behind which the Concert of Europe stayed lined-up for the
next five years. That it was an inadequate programme, allowing dire misgovernment and even massacres to continue, did not

seem greatly to trouble any power save Great Britain. But when in January 1908 Baron Aehrenthal, the Austro-Hungarian foreign minister, obtained leave from the Sultan to survey a route through the *sandjak* of Novibazar whereby to link the Austrian and Turkish railway systems, Russia sharply pricked up her ears. She brought her co-operation with Austria to an end, just five months after her Convention with Great Britain. Secondly, the new Entente was an embarrassing one for a British government to sustain, because the domestic policy of the tsarism at this time was repellent to British popular opinion. After the Japanese war, as after the Crimean, Russia underwent a revolutionary upheaval; and on 30 October 1905, at the climax of a general strike which shook the whole fabric of her society, Nicholas II granted a Constitution with a Duma (i.e. elected Diet). Following that, the strike was suppressed, and the St. Petersburg Soviet arrested. But in December there was a most determined insurrection at Moscow, only crushed after desperate barricade fighting; and fierce risings among the peasantry continued through 1906 and far into 1907. The result was an orgy of counter-revolution, in which the government sanctioned ruthless barbarities. The Duma itself, though a far from radical body which might well have been utilized by a prudent ruler, was repeatedly overridden and dissolved by the weak but autocratic Nicholas. His first resort to these methods (22 July 1906) was reported in London at the moment when some of the Duma members had come there for a meeting of the Inter-Parliamentary Union. Campbell-Bannerman, on opening the latter, used the famous words: '*La Douma est morte. Vive la Douma!*' which were acclaimed by democrats all over the world. That was a year before the Anglo-Russian Convention. How he would have dealt with such a situation after it, one cannot say. But the problem was one of constant difficulty. A large left wing of the government's own supporters hated the Anglo-Russian Entente upon what, from a diplomatist's standpoint, were not grounds of foreign policy at all. So did the whole of the labour party.

Meanwhile, save for the navy question, British relations with Germany in the two years following Algeciras were good. King and Kaiser, who had been very much alienated in the period following Tangier, became seemingly good friends again, and exchanged highly successful visits to Cronberg and London. In the autumn of 1906, when Haldane was planning army reforms, he was received as a guest at the German army manœuvres and afterwards at the Berlin war office; where, though no secrets were told to him, he was courteously given every guidance in regard to published facts. A German historian has argued that this proves the 'complete guilelessness' of the German authorities towards an anti-German England.[1] That is probably putting it too high; they saw in the Göttingen-educated war minister an obvious liaison with the British cabinet, and naturally made the most of him; while their view of a British Expeditionary Force was probably what Schlieffen's had been two years earlier —that it was too small in relation to the conscript armies to turn any scales. At this same time in Russia, as the British ambassador there reported in January 1907, German influence was 'predominant both at the Court and in Government circles'.[2] Germany did not feel that her favourable footing in both capitals was appreciably changed by the Anglo-Russian Convention; nor was it, to all appearance, till the events of October 1908.

The summer of 1907 brought the fifth Colonial Conference. Seven premiers attended;[3] among them General Botha, conspicuous as a new-comer. They passed a resolution to meet every four years, and decided that the term 'Dominions' be substituted for 'Colonies' in application to self-governing units of the empire. A proposal for a permanent Imperial Council was abandoned, owing to the opposition of Canada; but it was agreed to form a permanent secretarial staff for the Conference under the colonial secretary. Nothing of importance was done in regard to defence. Five of the premiers, headed by Australia, pressed strongly for the adoption of fiscal Preference by the imperial government; but Sir Wilfrid Laurier, for Canada, and Botha, for the Transvaal, held that each government must be free to settle its own fiscal system. Laurier was in fact planning reciprocity with the United States. The insistence of the others on their demand was not very impressive, as they knew that in view of the 1906 election result no British government could

---

[1] Otto Hammann, *Deutsche Weltpolitik, 1890–1912* (1925), 158: 'Diese deutsche Unterstützung des englischen Kriegministers beweist unwiderleglich die völlige Arglosigkeit der deutschen Staatsmänner und Generale gegenüber der damaligen deutschfeindlichen Politik Englands.'   [2] *British Documents*, iv. 256.
[3] Representing Canada, Australia, New Zealand, Cape Colony, Natal, the Transvaal, and Newfoundland. The Orange River Colony had not yet its new constitution.

grant it. However it enabled Balfour to rejoin the majority of his party, by declaring at the Albert Hall (3 May 1907) that he had been converted to Preference by the colonies' zeal for it.

Arrangements for the 1908 session of parliament were made under Campbell-Bannerman as premier, but he did not live to see them through. On 12 February he made his last speech in the commons, and next day went down with serious illness. For seven weeks he left the reins to Asquith as deputy-leader; on 6 April he resigned; and on 22 April he died. It was a short, yet by no means a common-place premiership. In it he had done much to help the new democracy to find its feet, and to enable the members of a government containing almost too many talents to assess each other's worth and settle down behind acknowledged leaders. This he achieved partly by plain human qualities, and partly because he touched at once both the future and the past of progressive politics. The future, in that he warmly sympathized with the left-wing crusade against poverty. The past, in that he could still regard the two-party system as something fore-ordained by Nature, and so, when out of office, was content without trimming or embroidery to reiterate his party's well-known doctrines, confident that in due course the nation would come back to them. His was the last generation which could plausibly hold this simple faith.

King Edward was at Biarritz when he resigned, and with an odd disregard for propriety[1] summoned Asquith as his successor thither. For the only time in history a British prime minister kissed hands in a foreign hotel. The party accepted its new chief without controversy, which two years earlier it would not have done. His loyal service under Campbell-Bannerman had filmed over the old sores. But he could not for long have held the left wing, had he not at once appointed in his own place as chancellor of the exchequer Lloyd George, who had already shown himself by far its strongest leader. In other respects he markedly improved the ministerial combination. Two of the ablest under-secretaries, Winston Churchill and Walter Runciman, were brought into the cabinet as president of the board of trade and president of the board of education respectively. Lord Elgin, who had proved a deadweight at the colonial office, was advantageously replaced by Lord Crewe. Lord Tweedmouth left

---

[1] *The Times* characterized it as 'an inconvenient and dangerous departure from precedent'.

the admiralty,[1] and was succeeded by a first-rate administrator in the person of McKenna. The team thus remodelled was extraordinarily strong all round, save at the home office and the local government board.

The new prime minister was a Yorkshireman, with plenty of the shrewdness and some of the stubbornness reputed common in his native county. His type was at this time more familiar in big business than in high politics; fond of high life, but nothing of an aristocrat, and as distinct from Grey or Balfour as earthenware from porcelain; nothing of a crusader, and there differing no less sharply from Gladstone or Chamberlain or Lloyd George. Strict nonconformist origins; an orphaned upbringing in London; four successful years under Jowett at Balliol; and the building up of a solid (though never over-lucrative) position at the Bar —such had been his career before parliament. Down to becoming home secretary in 1892, he had moved chiefly in nonconformist circles, and stood on the left wing of his party. His second marriage in 1894, to a very brilliant member of the most brilliant set in high society, carried him into quite a different world; and this, together with a personal attachment to Lord Rosebery, gradually forfeited him many radical sympathies. But there was another reason why between 1895 and 1903 his political standing declined. Asquith in power was at all times a different being from Asquith in opposition, and out of proportion greater. When home secretary, when chancellor of the exchequer, when prime minister, he reached heights to which nothing in his career off the treasury bench corresponded. It was not merely as administrator, but as parliamentarian, that office exalted him. Strong in argument, but weak in imagination, his terse Latinized oratory had never in itself the magic which compels attention. But when there was attention already (as for an important minister there must be), its exceptional precision and concision told on men's ears and minds with monumental effect. From the first to the last year of his premiership he was the giant of the commons' debates. In cabinet he conceived his role as the chairmanship of a board, whose members it was his business to hold together by genial tact and judicious compromises. He

---

[1] He had just been discredited by the revelation that he had exchanged injudicious private letters with the Kaiser about the navy. He was in reality going out of his mind; and though transferred to the lord presidency of the council, had soon to resign it, and died not long afterwards.

was not the devotee of causes or ideals; he rarely looked far ahead; his concern was to carry on the king's government from day to day. He was now 56 and at the height of his powers.[1]

The domestic record of 1908 had only one feature to distinguish it from those of 1906 and 1907. The budget, which Asquith, who had framed it, introduced in person, showed once more a modest surplus. Nearly half was again due to Haldane, who had pulled down the army estimates by yet another £2,354,000 (almost £4½ millions since he took office). It was now too risky to squeeze the navy estimates as well, but only £900,000 was put back on them. Most of the surplus went to reduce the sugar duty from 4s. 2d. per cwt. to 1s. 10d. In the light of nine months later this costly remission of ¼d. per lb. seems hard to justify. It reflected the party's haste to remove all food taxes as quickly as possible, in order that if the Tariff Reformers came into office they should not find any which they could abolish in substitution for their tax on corn. But (and here came the year's novelty) a small sum of £1,200,000 was devoted to a scheme of non-contributory Old Age Pensions—to start on 1 January 1909 only. So tiny was the beginning of that policy of mitigating poverty by direct state payments, which has since attained such vast dimensions. Unlike succeeding social schemes, it was non-contributory. The scope was narrow; the pension was only 5s. a week, and did not begin till 70; and an income of no more than 10s. a week disqualified for it. In imitation of the income-tax's penalties on marriage, the pension for two old married people living together was thriftily cut down to 7s. 6d. The case for old age pensions had really been overwhelming since Charles Booth revealed it nineteen years earlier; but they had been so long talked about without anything being done, that much enthusiasm prevailed at the prospect of their starting. The lords were unwise enough to tamper with the Old Age Pensions Bill; but when the lower house asserted 'privilege', they desisted.

The main government measure for the year was a large-scale Licensing Bill. It was well framed, and attracted non-party

---

[1] One of the most living sketches of his personality is the brief one by Prince Lichnowsky, who four years later became German ambassador in London. The prince brings out both his *bon-vivant* side and his easy competence in affairs—'he treated all questions with the cheery calm and assurance of an experienced man of business, whose good health and excellent nerves were steeled by devotion to the game of golf'. (*My Mission to London, 1912–14*; English translation (1918) of a German original circulated, but not published, in 1916.)

support, especially from the religious bodies. And there was room for it; for the Balfour Act of 1904, though a great measure in its way, was all too slow in its operation to reduce the then monstrous evil of intemperance—how monstrous, it is perhaps difficult for the present generation to realize. But the liquor trade naturally took up arms, and the conservatives in the commons espoused their cause. What would the lords do? In October the king summoned Lord Lansdowne, and urged on him strongly the impolicy of rejecting the bill.[1] A few of the very ablest peers, including Lord St. Aldwyn, Lord Cromer, Lord Milner, and Lord Balfour of Burleigh, shared the king's opinion. But a party meeting decided on rejection, and the bill was killed on second reading; though the bishops voted for it, and the Archbishop of Canterbury gave memorable expression to the consternation of thoughtful non-party men. The lords had been confident that their action would be popular outside; but there was not, in fact, much mob approval.

Yet the outlook for the government as its third year closed was cheerless. Its members recognized, as every one must now, that the lords were breaking the spirit, though not yet the letter, of the Constitution. The root-idea of British parliamentarism, as it had developed, was that each party in turn, if it obtained a mandate for its purposes from the electors, should have reasonable freedom to carry them out. A second chamber, that openly sought to confine the rights of government to one party and deny them to the other, no matter what commons majorities that other had, was in effect holding up the Constitution's working. But how could it be effectively brought home as an issue in a general election? Trade in 1908 was bad; and in electoral matters it is an observed phenomenon, of which politicians by then were aware (though Gladstone in 1874 and Beaconsfield in 1880 had not been), that bad trade throws votes against the government in office. By-elections were going in the opposition's favour. Tariff Reform made converts every day. The unionist peers expected 1895 to repeat itself; and so it might have done, could they have kept their heads. But their action over the Licensing Bill showed that they had already lost them.

Meanwhile the international sky had darkened. In July 1908 the Young Turk party, which had organized in Salonica a

---

[1] Lord Newton, *Lord Lansdowne*, 368.

'Committee of Union and Progress', carried out an armed revolution against the Sultan Abdul Hamid, and compelled him to grant Turkey a Constitution. Its immediate effects were hopeful; the race-war in Macedonia was suspended; and Great Britain took the lead in claiming for the reformers a fair chance. But Russia and Austria-Hungary, who were temporarily reconciled, saw things in a different light. Neither wished the Sick Man to make too good a recovery. On 15 September their respective foreign ministers, Isvolsky and Aehrenthal, met and struck a bargain. Russia was to obtain the opening of the Dardanelles, and Austria-Hungary to annex Bosnia and Herzegovina. Both aims were in conflict with existing treaties. It was Isvolsky's intention to consult other signatory powers; but before he could do so, Aehrenthal brusquely announced his government's annexation of the two provinces. It was notified diplomatically to the powers on 5 October; and on the same day Prince Ferdinand of Bulgaria proclaimed his country's complete independence, and took the title of Tsar. Crete followed suit, and demanded incorporation with Greece.

These actions gave a violent shock to Turkey and to Serbia. Turkey's rights over the provinces, as over Bulgaria, were indeed shadowy; but she could not afford to admit their unilateral abrogation. Serbia was still more injured; for her hope of incorporating those Serb lands in a larger unity seemed finally barred out, and failing it she must at least seek some alternative outlet to the sea. Sir Edward Grey took his stand on the Declaration, which both Russia and Austria-Hungary had signed at the London Conference of 1871,[1] that 'no Power can liberate itself from the engagements of a Treaty nor modify the stipulations thereof, unless with the consent of the Contracting Powers by means of an amicable arrangement'. He demanded another Conference, and secured the assents of Russia and France.[2]

---

[1] p. 5 above.

[2] Isvolsky wanted to make it a condition that Great Britain did not oppose the opening of the Straits. King Edward (J. A. Spender and Cyril Asquith, *Life of Asquith* (1932), i. 247–8) urged the cabinet to give way to him, in order to save his face at St. Petersburg. But they preferred to reply, that the Straits question should not be raised at this juncture; that, when it was, there must be a *quid pro quo*; and that the proper one would be a right of ingress to the Black Sea for other powers: whereupon Isvolsky dropped the topic. King Edward was particularly sore about the annexation, because only two months earlier he had visited the Austrian emperor at Ischl and the latter, while affecting candour and intimacy, had not breathed to him a word about it.

Aehrenthal refused his. Germany was awkwardly placed; for, as between Austria-Hungary and Turkey, the one was her only powerful friend, and the other her special protégée, on whose goodwill all the Berlin-Bagdad dreams depended. Her Kaiser 'was beside himself' when he heard of the annexation, and called it 'a robber attack against Turkey'.[1] But her dilemma had to be determined in Austria's favour, for the alternative was isolation among the powers. So she too opposed the Conference; and by 5 November was acting so mischievously that the British government 'could form no theory of the German policy which fitted all the known facts, except that they wanted war'.[2] War dangers lasted for over five months. In January Austria settled with Turkey, by a payment of money and by returning to her the *sandjak* of Novi-bazar; but as Serbia was not compensated likewise, her grievance became only the more inflamed. Since 1903, when King Alexander II, the petty Caligula who closed her Obrenovitch dynasty, had been assassinated by Russian partisans, she had been ruled by King Peter Karageorgevitch, a devoted Russophile. Russia had therefore to stand by her; and when in March Austria threatened Serbia with an ultimatum, the peril of an Austro-Russian war arose precisely as in 1914. But on 23 March 1909 Germany intervened at St. Petersburg with a polite but unmistakable ultimatum of her own; and Russia, not as in 1914, abruptly climbed down. This was the succour, of which the Kaiser boasted at Vienna in 1910 in his famous 'Shining Armour' speech.

The Bosnian imbroglio was not made less perilous by two grave incidents, which were contemporary with although outside it. One was the Kaiser's *Daily Telegraph* interview; the other the Franco-German Casablanca dispute. In his interview (published 28 October 1908) the Kaiser painted himself as the Anglophile ruler of an Anglophobe Germany. He claimed to have refused the request of France and Russia to join with them in saving the Boer republics; and to have supplied Queen Victoria with a plan of campaign, which 'as a matter of curious coincidence' was very like that adopted later by Lord Roberts. These assertions, by which he had often sought privately to ingratiate himself with royal or ministerial personages in England, had a very different effect when blazoned to the widest public. Germany

---

[1] Otto Hammann, *Deutsche Weltpolitik, 1890–1912* (1925), 183.
[2] Lord Newton, *Lord Lansdowne*, 371.

was swept by two rages at once—against Great Britain and against the Kaiser. Strong demands were made in the Reichstag that the conduct of foreign affairs must not be carried on by the Kaiser over the chancellor's head. The results were the resignation of Bülow (deferred till the following summer), and a blow to the Kaiser's controlling prestige over the German military leaders, from which it never recovered.

The Casablanca dispute was Franco-German. It arose over a question about German deserters from the French Foreign Legion, who had been harboured by the German Consul. Things came very near war when Austria-Hungary, who wanted Germany's strength reserved for the Bosnian quarrel, intervened to cool them down. There was a reference to the Hague Tribunal; and in February France and Germany signed a Morocco Agreement, recognizing the 'special political interests' of the one and the 'commercial and industrial interests' of the other.

While they were still in the thick of the crises, the British government made alarming discoveries about the navy. By departing in and since 1906 from the Cawdor programme, they had deprived their country of its great lead over Germany, and encouraged Tirpitz to redouble his efforts. In 1908 he had laid down 4 'all big-gun' ships to Great Britain's 2, and in 1909 he was to lay down 4 more. Further he had enabled the German establishments so markedly to expand their capacity, that they could accumulate guns, armour, and other requisites beforehand, and thus complete the ships long before the expected time. In that case, as the admiralty became aware in the winter of 1908, the British navy might for a few critical months find itself actually inferior to the German in its number of Dreadnoughts.

McKenna's answer as first lord of the admiralty was to ask for 6 Dreadnoughts on the 1909 estimates. His idea was that the same number should be laid down in each of the two years following, making 18 in all. He was strongly opposed in the cabinet by Lloyd George and Churchill, who within that body were the protagonists of social reform, and who maintained 4 to be sufficient. The strife between 6 and 4 was healed by an Asquithian compromise; 4 were to be laid down at once, and 4 contingently upon need being shown. Both sides accepted this. But in order to explain it to parliament, ministers had publicly to state what was known about the German power to accelerate. Then Tirpitz admitted before the Reichstag's Committee that the power existed, though he denied his intention to use it. Public opinion in England felt that national safety could scarcely be rested on a foreign rival's expression of intentions; and amid a rising scare agitation (with a music-hall refrain, 'We want Eight, And we won't wait') it was decided to lay down all 8 at once. The admiralty thus got 2 more out of hand than it had asked; but in each of the two next years McKenna had 5 laid down, so that he reached his original total of 18 in 3 years. It was these 18 ships, which in August 1914 gave Jellicoe's Grand Fleet the margin of Dreadnought superiority which it had.

The navy badly upset the finance of the year. It already was a little unstable, since Asquith when starting old age pensions had provided for them in one quarter only, and this year they must cost four times as much. Adding the extra Dreadnoughts meant that a total of over £15 millions would have to be found by new taxation. It seemed a vastly bigger sum than it would to-day, being indeed without precedent. Even the masterful Hicks Beach in 1900, with a war to defray and in a period of exceptional trade-boom, had put on new taxes to raise no more than £12·1 millions.

Such was the genesis of Lloyd George's famous 1909 budget. Out of difficulty he created opportunity. The lords' destruction of liberal bills had seemed thus far to be wearing the government down. They were in the position of a blockaded city, whose supplies must steadily run out, so long as it remains powerless to shake off the blockader. Only a direct counter-offensive could save it.

A conservative writer with long experience in his party's central office has described and analysed Lloyd George's budget campaign as a masterpiece of political strategy, a classic example for the student of that art.[1] In effect it was so; though it is impossible to say how far it was planned ahead, and how far it was evolved, as the events proceeded, by the instinct of a born fighting-man.

The budget itself cast a wide net. Undeterred by the size of his task, the chancellor had proceeded to add to it. England's roads, for instance, had for some years been developing a deplorable state of dust and mud, thanks to the new motor traffic; a

---

[1] Philip G. Cambray, *The Game of Politics: A Study of the Principles of British Political Strategy* (1932).

board, therefore, was to be set up to finance their improvement, and for it the budget provided £600,000 a year out of special taxes, to be levied on petrol and on motor licences. This starting of the Road Board proved an unqualified national boon. So did the assignment of a modest £100,000 to found a national system of labour exchanges. Less important in the sequel, yet striking in conception, was the creation of the Development Commission with an income of £200,000 a year to spend on developing country life and natural resources. Yet another minor novelty was the introduction of children's allowances for payers of income-tax. True, the abatement of income for taxation was only £10 for every child under 16, and was only granted on incomes under £500. A new principle was none the less asserted.

The requisite new revenue was to be obtained as follows. Death Duties were made to yield £2·5 millions more (£4·4 millions in a full year) by raising the scales on estates between £5,000 and £1 million. Tobacco was to yield £1·9 millions more, and spirits £1·6 millions. Liquor licence duties were increased to bring in £2·6 millions extra per year. Raising the income-tax from 1s. to 1s. 2d. would produce (after allowing for the new abatements) £3 millions; and super-tax was created for the first time, fixed at a low rate, and estimated to bring in from the incomes above £3,000 a modest total of half a million more. Such, with £650,000 added to stamp duties and £3 millions knocked off the sinking fund, were the measures which met the deficit. But beyond them were others, not estimated to yield above £500,000 in the current year, but put forward as an eventual source of growing revenue to meet the growing demands of the state. These were the Land Value duties—a duty of 20 per cent. on the unearned increment of land value, to be paid whenever land changed hands, and also a duty of ½d. in the £ on the capital value of undeveloped land and minerals. It is still disputed, what the fiscal value of these taxes would have been, had they ever been carried out as intended; and it is obvious that quite different considerations apply to the first and the second of them. But their political value proved immense, both as slogans and as irritants. For they involved making a complete valuation of the land of Great Britain. To this the classes that owned it, with the peers at their head, violently objected; and the more violent they were, the more the democracy became persuaded that they objected for sinister reasons.

Setting the land taxes on one side and viewing the rest of the proposals with a post-war eye, it may be difficult to understand why they caused such soreness. The amounts taken were by subsequent standards so small, that similar tax-payers to-day, if mulcted by no more than them, would think themselves lucky beyond belief. The brewers, who had just prevailed with Lord Lansdowne to kill the Licensing Bill, might indeed groan to see how the chancellor had hit back at them; but none of the other victims had any reason for surprise. Why then were the conservatives so much inflamed? For a number of reasons. First, the Tariff Reformers seem to have agreed in their hearts with Lloyd George that, if the budget went through, it might remove the revenue motive for a tariff; they therefore wished at all costs to stop it. Secondly, it was feared as the thin end of a socialist wedge—the more so when it was found that the labour party's budget expert, Philip Snowden,[1] had previously advocated a budget very much on Lloyd George's lines. A third, and very real, factor was the sensationalism of the Harmsworth Press. Lastly, the author of the budget himself could wish nothing better than that his conservative opponents should present themselves as a party of angry rich men trying to dodge paying their fair share to the nation; and they, leaderless and tacticless, walked blindly into his traps.

Their lack of leadership was due to the fiscal controversy. The great Duke of Devonshire had died in the previous year, yet four indubitable Nestors still sat in the house of lords—Lord St. Aldwyn, Lord James of Hereford, Lord Cromer, and Lord Balfour of Burleigh. But because they were free traders, they were not listened to. The official leader, Lord Lansdowne, as an ex-whig and a Balfourian, lacked the prestige of being either a true-blue tory or a 'whole hog' Chamberlainite; while yet he was himself too much subject to the prejudices of property[2] to be able to use his eyes unclouded by the dust of conflict. In the other house Balfour might have done so, but he, again, had lost most of his authority through the fiscal differences. He was painfully trying to recover it by wooing the extremists; and during the process the last thing he could afford was to appear as a curbing influence.

---

[1] Created viscount, 1931. His ascetic form and caustic eloquence had led many conservative M.P.s at that time to regard him (absurdly enough) as a sort of Robespierre.

[2] As he especially showed in regard to Ireland (where he was a large landlord), not only in 1881, when he seceded from Gladstone, but even so late as 1916, by his veto on the Carson-Redmond settlement.

A real leader, had any such been in charge, could not have failed to impose at this juncture tactics of patience and restraint. The pendulum was swinging hard towards the conservative side; they had only to wait and be prudent for the next election to bring them a majority; and then they could rearrange budget, second chamber, and everything else to their liking.

Instead, they did exactly what Lloyd George desired. In the commons they took up positions against the budget, which allowed of no compromise. At party demonstrations they committed themselves to fight it without quarter. They even tied themselves to a special organization—the Budget Protest League. Then the chancellor turned on them, and delivered over the country a great series of speeches, every stroke in which drew blood. That at Limehouse (30 July) is the best remembered, but it was only one of many. There had been nothing like them since Chamberlain's campaign for the 'unauthorized programme' in 1885. But Lloyd George had a weapon in his armoury which Chamberlain lacked—ridicule; and by turning the laugh against his adversaries he completed their loss of self-control. With skill he kept the peers in the foreground, constantly presenting them as the protagonists of monopoly and privilege, so that long before their leaders had decided to reject his budget he was fore-armed against their doing so. Behind the scenes he had difficulties in the cabinet. More than one colleague recoiled before his audacities. But Asquith stood firm by him there; and also in parliament and in the country rendered the budget's cause a peculiar service by the calm weight of his approval, as coming from an acknowledged financial purist.

So the struggle went forward, and it began to be mooted, whether the lords would reject the budget. Though attempts were made to argue otherwise, it could not really be disguised that this would be unconstitutional. There had been no precedent for such a course for over 250 years; and the whole basis on which parliamentary government had been built up during that long period, was that, while the house of commons had power through the purse to halt a ministry's career and force a dissolution, the house of lords had not. If the rejection came about and were acquiesced in by the nation, the control of the executive by parliament must pass from the elected to the hereditary chamber. That was scarcely a plausible transfer in the twentieth century, and it seems almost incredible now, that a great party should have hoped for popular acquiescence. Lord Lansdowne had originally intended not to oppose the Finance Bill in the upper house.[1] But by September the pressure upon him for rejection became (as Lord James recorded at the time) 'irresistible'.[2] Balfour was swimming with the stream already; and Lansdowne by 2 October[3] was no reluctant convert, despite the earnest warnings of such cooler heads as the four Nestors already mentioned, and others like the fourth earl of Onslow and the second earl of Lytton. King Edward in vain counselled caution. He was most anxious that the lords should pass the budget; and even asked Asquith to sanction his trying to bribe them by the promise of a January dissolution. The prime minister had perforce to reply that after only four years in office the government could not justify a dissolution to its party; and he might have added that to concede one to the lords' threat would be to give away the very principle at stake.[4]

The immediate sequel is soon told. The budget passed the commons on 4 November 1909 by 379 votes to 149. It was rejected on second reading by the house of lords on 30 November by 350 to 75. Two days later Asquith moved and carried in the lower house (by 349 votes to 134) a resolution: 'That the action of the House of Lords in refusing to pass into law the financial provisions made by this House for the service of the year is a breach of the Constitution and a usurpation of the rights of the Commons.' That made a January general election inevitable, and all parties girded themselves for such a contest as had not been paralleled since 1886, nor equalled even then. Far more than the merits of the budget itself, the issue on the platforms was the veto of the lords; and they had committed themselves to fighting for it in the most unfavourable postures, as palpable constitution-breakers and as rich men trying to evade taxation. A feature of the election was that for the first time (through an amendment of the house of commons' Standing Orders on Privilege) the peers in person were allowed to take active part. In the nineteenth century they had never been.[5] But their sudden liberty

[1] Lord Askwith, *Lord James of Hereford*, 300.
[2] 'The agents, the organizations, and the Licensed Victuallers' Trade all demand it. They know nothing of, and care nothing for, Constitutional Law.' (Ibid.)
[3] See his letter of that date to Lord Balfour of Burleigh, printed in Lord Newton's biography at pp. 378–9.
[4] J. A. Spender and Cyril Asquith, *Life of Asquith*, i. 257–8.
[5] It had sometimes been a grave party handicap; e.g. at the 1880 election, where

was not wholly a help to them; it had in some cases the disadvantages which the act permitting a prisoner to give evidence is generally allowed to have entailed for the prisoner.

At the polls the unionist party was heavily defeated. A calculation in January 1909, based on the evidence of by-elections, had given them a majority of about 100 in the event of a dissolution at that time. Now they were in a minority of 124; so that opposing the budget and defying the constitution had cost them well over 100 seats. None of the other three parties, however, had unreserved cause for satisfaction. The figures were: liberals 275, labour 40, Irish nationalists 82, unionists 273; so that in this parliament, unlike the last, the liberal government would depend on Labour and Irish support. For the labour party this was particularly embarrassing. Despite having effected a consolidation in 1909 between the Miners and the main body, it had lost a dozen seats on balance; and many of its followers wanted it to seek recovery by separating itself more sharply from the government in the division lobbies. But that was just what it could not henceforward afford to do; on the contrary, it must cast many reluctant votes to avoid defeating the ministry. The Irish had an even more instant difficulty. In 1909 they had opposed the budget and voted against its second reading, though they abstained on its third. The reason was indeed almost trivial; the budget had raised the excise duties on spirits by £1,200,000, and a marked feature of the nationalist party was its financial dependence on distillers and publicans. But now the same budget confronted them on the threshold of the new parliament, and unless they voted for it, the parliament might break down.

These embarrassments were less real than they looked on paper, because the three parties with their joint majority of 124 (one of the largest since 1832) were solidly united on behalf of two causes. They all wanted to deal with the house of lords on Campbell-Bannerman lines, i.e. not by altering its composition, but by defining and limiting its power of veto. And they all wanted to give home rule to Ireland. About this the liberals had been comparatively apathetic in 1906, but quite a new feeling had come to pervade their ranks since the brilliant success of Campbell-Bannerman's policy in bestowing self-government on the Transvaal. Their slogan now was 'to make Redmond the

the forced abstention of Lord Beaconsfield, Lord Cranbrook, and Lord Salisbury deprived the conservatives of their three most powerful speakers.

Irish Botha'. And indeed he had many qualities for the part. He led a united party which comprised 70 out of the 82 Irish members; his dignified eloquence expressed a generous and conciliatory temper; and, unlike Parnell, he had, apart from the Irish grievance, a warm admiration for England and Englishmen. Had their hand been extended to him as it was to the Boer leader, he would have grasped it in the same spirit. Apart from what they might desire, however, he had, as we shall see in our next chapter, one flaw in his prospect, which Botha had not.

Following the election the natural thing was to pass the budget, but for this the Irish votes were wanted, and Redmond wished to have a Veto Bill first. Then followed several hitches. The first was over the so-called 'guarantees'. It was strongly held by most liberals, as well as by the Irish, that for settling a question so plainly referred to the country as this of the house of lords had been, one general election ought to suffice; and consequently that, if the lords attempted further resistance, the king should sanction their being coerced, as in 1832, by the creation of new peers. And it was generally assumed that Asquith had obtained 'guarantees' to that effect from King Edward before dissolving parliament. But on 21 February 1910 the prime minister told parliament that he had received no such guarantee, nor even asked for it. Most of his followers thought this improvident of him; but they settled down eventually on the assumption that things must be governed by the 1832 precedent, if the occasion arose. In point of fact the king had thrown the precedent over, and notified Asquith (on 15 December 1909), that he would not create new peers till after a *second* general election.[1] This meant altering the scales heavily in the lords' favour; and, if it had been disclosed by events in Edward VII's lifetime, might have had very serious effects on the relations between the monarchy and the popular parties. Fortunately it remained a secret till long after.

The other hitch was in the cabinet itself. When its chiefs drafted a bill on Campbell-Bannerman lines, Sir Edward Grey, still a Roseberyite by conviction, objected that it must also include the reform of the house of lords. He even made a public

[1] Five days earlier Asquith had said at the Albert Hall meeting which opened his party's campaign: 'We shall not assume office, and we shall not hold office, unless we can secure the safeguards which experience shows us to be necessary for the legislative utility and honour of the party of progress.' It was the conflict between this public announcement and King Edward's subsequent secret intimation which occasioned the 'guarantees' hitch.

speech saying that 'to leave the policy of reform of the Second Chamber—to leave all the ground unoccupied for the other side' would result in 'disaster, death, and damnation'. His obstinate scruple was at last overcome by giving the bill a preamble beginning: 'Whereas it is intended to substitute for the House of Lords as it at present exists a Second Chamber constituted on a popular instead of a hereditary basis, but such a substitution cannot immediately be brought into operation.' A preamble like that, of course, enacts nothing. It is only a *vœu*; and its value in this instance may be judged from the fact, that during the subsequent quarter-century liberal, conservative, and labour ministries all held office for substantial periods, besides a variety of coalitions, and not one of them introduced a bill to carry the matter farther. However it contented Grey, and the cabinet moved forward.

It was decided to pass through the commons in the first instance, not the bill, but a set of three resolutions embodying its principles. The first dealt with money bills; the second with bills other than money bills; and the third with the reduction of the life of a parliament from seven to five years. Asquith's handling of them in the house was masterly, and though he could not undo his failure to obtain 'guarantees' before the last dissolution, he assured the house categorically that he should obtain them before the next.[1] The resolutions were all passed by 14 April 1910 (with majorities varying from 98 to 106); and following the last the Parliament Bill itself was introduced and read a first time. On 27 April (with a majority of 93, which included 62 Irish) the budget was passed also. The next day it was sent to the house of lords, and they let it through without a division. Parliament adjourned for a short holiday; and the prime minister went to Gibraltar in the admiralty yacht.

Suddenly, while they were all away, a curtain fell. King Edward died (6 May 1910). He had paid his usual spring visit to Biarritz; but a short while after his return suffered from spasms of heart-asthma, to which he had long been liable. In the first week of May their severity caused alarm; but he continued to get up, to dress, and even to receive visitors; he did so even on the day of his death. His final collapse was a matter of hours, and the nation, which only one bulletin had prepared for it, was utterly

---

[1] 'In no case would we recommend Dissolution except under such conditions as will secure that in the new Parliament the judgement of the people as expressed at the election will be carried into law' (Hansard, v. xvi. 1548).

stunned by the news. In the presence of death disputes were hushed, and the universal feeling was that for a while party strife should be suspended.

So, with nothing settled save the budget, the reign closed. Personal memories of Edward VII have transferred to it something of the king's own character and atmosphere. Men think of the decade as one of calm and contentment, of pomp and luxury, of assured wealth and unchallenged order. Court splendours apart, it was none of those things. It was an era of growth and strain, of idealism and reaction, of swelling changes and of seething unrest. At home, politics had never been so bitter; and abroad, the clouds were massing for Armageddon.

One Imperial matter may here be briefly recorded. The agitated parliament of 1909 found time to pass the Indian Councils Act of that year, introduced by Lord Morley in the upper house. Hitherto the legislative councils in India, both at the centre and in the provinces, had been purely nominated bodies. The new act made them for the first time partially elective; and it enlarged their scope, while still withholding from them any binding power over the executive governments. It also enlarged the executive councils, into which a few Indians were introduced. These cautious steps forward were taken through the hearty co-operation of the liberal secretary of state with a notable conservative viceroy, the fourth earl of Minto. Though their sponsor declined to admit it, they were in fact a first approach to the idea of a self-governing India.

XIII

HEADING FOR CATASTROPHE

KING GEORGE V ascended the throne in his 45th year. He had only become heir-presumptive in his 27th, a circumstance of some advantage to him, since he had been enabled for fifteen years to follow a professional career in the Navy. Since then he had visited widely the British Empire overseas, and studied the personalities and problems of the chief countries composing it. But he had not shared his father's responsibilities in dealing with party issues at home, and possessed no inner familiarity with their intricacies. He created at once an impression of goodwill and impartiality; and there was a strong popular feeling that he should be given a fair start.

When his father's funeral was over, he sounded the leaders on both sides as to whether they would be willing to call a truce, and try to settle their controversy by a round-table conference. Balfour at once expressed readiness, but the government did not jump at the proposal. Later, the conservative rank and file objected, and both Balfour and the king cooled; but the government came round to the idea, seeing that the alternative, an almost immediate general election, would be highly unpopular. Eventually on 16 June 1910 eight politicians—four from each major party[1]—met at 10 Downing Street behind closed doors. The Constitutional Conference held twenty-one sittings and was in being for nearly five months. On 10 November its failure was announced; but any disclosure of what happened was expressly withheld. Nor did documented evidence become available until the publication long afterwards of certain biographies.[2] From these, which supplement each other, a clear view of the episode may be obtained. The negotiators did not cling to the plan of the Parliament Bill, but explored a wide field; yet what

[1] The ministers were Asquith, Lloyd George, Birrell, and the Earl of Crewe; the opposition leaders, Balfour, Austen Chamberlain, the Marquess of Lansdowne, and the Earl of Cawdor. Though the minor parties were not directly represented, Birrell provided a liaison with the Irish Nationalists.

[2] Lord Newton, *Lord Lansdowne* (1929); J. A. Spender and Cyril Asquith, *Life of Asquith* (1932); Denis Gwynn, *Life of John Redmond* (1932). It should be added, however, that more than one parliamentary journalist obtained and published at the time fairly detailed accounts, which, though they could not then be verified, prove now to have been generally accurate. See notably Harry Jones, *Liberalism and the House of Lords* (1912), pp. 209–16.

in the end divided them was not so much any general constitutional theory as the particular desire of the conservatives to block Irish home rule. Provisional agreement was reached that no Finance Bill was to be rejected by the house of lords, unless a joint committee of the houses decided that there was 'tacking' (i.e. avoidable inclusion of non-financial matters); that other bills might be rejected by the second chamber, but that, if one was rejected two years running, a joint sitting of the two houses should be held to determine its fate; and lastly that the representation of the lords in the joint sitting should be so scaled down, that a liberal government with a commons majority of fifty would be able to pass its bills. But (and here was where the conference failed) the conservatives wished to except from the joint-sitting scheme certain bills or classes of bills, which they variously termed 'constitutional', 'organic', or 'structural', and to have these made subject to a referendum. The liberals would consent to this for bills affecting the Crown or the Protestant succession or 'the Act which is to embody this agreement'; but they would not go further, and particularly refused to include in the excepted category Irish home rule. For the conservatives, on the other hand, home rule was what had chiefly motived their demand for a special class of bills; so at this point they broke the conference off.

In the light of all subsequent events it is difficult not to regret their action. On the purely constitutional side much agreement had been arduously reached. The joint-sitting scheme, which originated with Lord Ripon, represented a considerable liberal concession, since under it a liberal bill could only be enacted with a commons majority of fifty, and often only after a year's delay; whereas any commons majority, however tiny, could make a conservative bill law at once. In regard to the Irish question itself there was at this very moment an influential move[1] inside the conservative party for settling it by agreement on a basis of federal home rule. The promoters were, as tariff reformers, anxious to clear Ireland out of their road; and they saw, as the liberals did, the unique opportunity which the Redmond-Botha conjuncture afforded. But Lord Lansdowne, who dominated the conservative side of the conference, was the last person to give effect to their views. For while his interest in tariff reform remained tepid, his views about Ireland remained narrow and

---

[1] Voiced especially in the columns of *The Times* and the *Observer* newspapers.

obstinate, being those of a Southern Irish landlord who had never forgotten the Land League. Had a leader less inelastic on this subject been in charge, the conference would have succeeded.

During its course the boldest of its members tried to reach agreement by widening the field for it. A proposal was made by Lloyd George to Asquith for an actual coalition with the conservatives, with a view to carrying out not merely agreed second-chamber and home-rule policies, but an agreed development of agriculture, an agreed system of national military training (on Swiss lines), agreed social reforms, and even (after a fair and judicial inquiry into the fiscal system) an agreed policy about the tariff. Asquith approved, and imparted the scheme to Crewe, Grey, Haldane, and Churchill, who approved also. It was next broached to Balfour, and he, with Lansdowne, Cawdor, Curzon, Long, and Austen Chamberlain, distinctly inclined towards it. But then strong, semi-occult forces lower down in the conservative party secured its rejection; though Lloyd George tried to placate them by offering to remain himself outside the government.[1]

The failure was followed by negotiations between the premier and the king. When Asquith had declared, on 14 April, that he would not recommend another dissolution 'except under such conditions as will secure that in the new Parliament the judgement of the people, as expressed in the election, will be carried into law', he was relying on assurances from King Edward, to which King George had not been a party. The latter now endorsed his father's position, but stipulated that parliament should not be dissolved before the house of lords had had an opportunity of pronouncing on the Parliament Bill. Accordingly the bill was introduced there, and the lords on second reading 'postponed the consideration' of it, using the time afforded to them to pass counter-proposals of their own. It will be convenient at this point to fix what the rival policies were.

The Parliament Bill embodied three main propositions: (1) 'Money Bills', as defined by it, should, under certain conditions, become law without the consent of the house of lords, the decision whether a particular bill complied with the definition being left to the Speaker of the house of commons; (2) other bills, if passed

---

[1] D. Lloyd George, *War Memoirs*, i (1933), 35–41. See also the memoir of Lord Balfour in *The Times* (20 March 1930), and J. A. Spender and Cyril Asquith, *Life of Asquith* (1932), i. 287.

by the commons in three successive sessions and rejected each time by the lords, should then become law, provided two years had elapsed between the bill's first introduction[1] to the house of commons and its final third reading there; (3) five years should be substituted for seven as the maximum duration of parliament. The scheme was that of Campbell-Bannerman's 1907 resolutions with but two differences: (a) Campbell-Bannerman's proposal for a conference between the houses (conciliatory but not arbitral) was dropped; (b) the three successive sessions, in which a bill must be passed by the commons, need not be sessions of the same parliament. Lord Lansdowne's alternative plan, as approved by the lords after two days' debate, virtually accepted the Parliament Bill's proposal about money bills, save that the decision which that measure gave to the Speaker would be transferred to a joint committee of the two houses, with the Speaker as chairman having only a casting vote. Other bills, if passed by the commons and rejected by the lords in two successive sessions with an interval of not less than a year, were to have their fate determined by a joint sitting; but if the difference between the houses 'relates to a matter of great gravity and has not been adequately submitted for the judgement of the people', it should be sent to a referendum. This scheme, though in vaguer and less defined form, reproduced, it will be seen, the conservative proposals at the Constitutional Conference. The supporter who lent most weight to it was Lord St. Aldwyn; since it was known that he had not taken part in rejecting the budget or the Licensing Bill.

As between the two programmes, the liberal made the readier electoral appeal. It had been before the country since 1907 and was well understood. The conservative scheme as presented to the public wore the air of a vague improvisation; the only feature in it that could be caught hold of was the referendum. Yet even from the standpoint of the liberals it had really some advantages—notably the reduction of the waiting-time from two years to one. Few, however, until later the Home Rule Bill showed it, foresaw how mischievous a long waiting-time might prove.

Meanwhile, on Lord Rosebery's initiative, the house of lords had also passed resolutions in favour of changing its composition. Rosebery, who had preached this for a quarter of a cen-

---

[1] When the bill was in committee in the following year, the government amended this date to that of the second reading.

tury, never had any success with it until after the electoral rebuff to the peers in January 1910. But in March he had induced them to endorse the principle, that 'the possession of a peerage should no longer, of itself, give the right to sit and vote in the House of Lords'. Now (17 November 1910) he carried: 'That in future the House of Lords shall consist of Lords of Parliament: (a) chosen by the whole body of hereditary peers from among themselves and by nomination by the Crown; (b) sitting by virtue of offices and of qualifications held by them; (c) chosen from outside.' This was a good deal more liberal than the only reform scheme hitherto carrying any official authority—that of a committee presided over by Lord Cawdor in 1908, which had recommended a second chamber with about seven-eighths of its membership drawn from the hereditary peers. But the country was quite unimpressed. It saw that the lords only voted with Lord Rosebery, after they had lost the last election; and shrewdly surmised that, if they won the next, they would have little more use for his schemes.

On 18 November, while these debates were in progress, Asquith announced a dissolution for ten days later. The step had not been taken without misgiving; the rank and file still argued it unnecessary, and more than one minister feared for the result. There was the swing of the pendulum—since 1832 no ministry in office had ever won three elections running; moreover the spring delays, King Edward's death, and the five months' truce had all weakened the strong popular current. The man who overcame these tremors was the Master of Elibank,[1] the chief liberal whip, whose ability gave him an influence over the cabinet such as few whips had before exercised. The conservatives on their side knew that they could not win by merely defending the house of lords. Was advocacy of tariff reform or opposition to home rule to be their mainstay? They decided for the latter, and fought the election almost wholly upon it. Redmond, who had just been raising funds in America, was denounced as the 'dollar dictator', and the government as his venal tools. On 29 November Balfour announced his willingness to submit tariff reform to a referendum—a shelving of Chamberlainism which won him back some Lancashire seats.

[1] Alexander Murray (1870–1920), eldest son of the first Viscount Elibank; educated at Cheltenham; in the colonial office 1892–5; M.P. 1900; Scottish liberal whip, 1905–10; chief liberal whip, 1910–12; created Lord Murray of Elibank 1912.

Yet when in December the country was polled, the result (Liberals 272, Labour 42, Irish 84, Unionists 272) was extraordinarily close to that of the previous January. The liberal and labour parties together had exactly the same majority over the Unionists as before, viz. 42; but the Irish had gained two seats, so that the whole majority for the Parliament Bill and for home rule was 4 more (126) than it had been. Nothing could in its way have been more decisive. Any further election was out of the question. The situation permitted to the king no further doubts as to what his duty might be in the event of the upper house continuing to defy the lower; and Asquith, who had wavered too often in the previous ten months, recovered his firmness. Political excitement in the country, which for fifteen months had been intense (nourished not only by two election campaigns, but by the long series of full-dress debates in both houses, in which virtually every leading figure took part) now rapidly waned. The people regarded the issue as settled, and only wanted the dispute wound up as quickly as possible.

Continuing his father's practice King George opened the new parliament in person; and on 21 February 1911 the prime minister introduced the Parliament Bill. It passed its first reading after two days' debate by a majority of 126, and its second eight days later by 125. The committee stage, which was held under a 'Kangaroo' closure, allowing every amendment of substance to be discussed, was not ended till 3 May; and on 15 May the third reading was passed by 121, the prime minister receiving a very exceptional ovation from his followers. In this session, indeed, he had appeared at his best, constantly dominating debate by the dignity, clearness, and terse force of his argument and no longer (as he had done in 1910 and was to do still more in 1912–14) weakening the effect of firm phrases by irresolute action. Meanwhile the lords were again discussing their own reform. Lord Balfour of Burleigh, an enthusiast for the referendum, introduced a bill to bring it into constant use; but this after two days' debate was shelved. Next came a bill moved by Lord Lansdowne, for which, as it proposed to restrict the Crown's right to create peers, an address to the Crown and the assent of the latter were necessary, before it could even be discussed. It was competent for ministers to advise the Crown to withhold assent, but they naturally decided to put no obstacle in their opponents' way. The scheme, which is still of some theoretic interest, was for a second chamber of about 350 'Lords of Parliament'. Of these 100 were to be elected by the hereditary peers from among those of their number possessing certain scheduled qualifications; 120 were to be chosen by M.P.s—grouped for the purpose into electoral colleges on a regional basis; and 100 were to be nominated by the Crown on the recommendation of the government in proportion to the strength of parties in the house of commons. The balance would be made up by Princes of the Blood, a diminished episcopal bench, and law lords. All the first three classes were to be appointed for twelve years, subject to triennial retirements. The scheme marked an advance as being the first to provide serious representation in the second chamber for other parties than the conservative. But that party would still on Lord Lansdowne's own calculation have retained a small majority there in 1911, although there was one of 126 against it in the house of commons. The house of lords passed the second reading without a division, but with every sign of a general disapproval; to which two dukes and half a dozen other peers gave particular expression.

On 23 May the Parliament Bill reached the house of lords. Lord Crewe, who till March had led the small liberal party there with much ability, was temporarily invalided by overstrain. The bill was piloted by the veteran Lord Morley, who in the previous year had retired from the Indian secretaryship and become lord president of the council. Over six weeks, only broken by a brief interval for the king's coronation, the lords debated it, passing a long series of amendments in the committee stage, which lasted till 6 July. Their policy was not to reject, but to send it back to the commons transformed.

Nobody, however, expected that the commons would accept the changes, and the question of ultimate surrender was only postponed. If Lord Lansdowne thought to ease it by delay, he misreckoned. In June a 'no surrender' movement was started among the peers. Its first mover, Lord Willoughby de Broke, was a young man better known in hunting circles than in politics; but he was speedily joined by the veteran ex-lord chancellor, the earl of Halsbury, then 84 years of age, with the prestige of a great judge, though in politics he had always been a narrow and bitter partisan. On the third reading of the bill in the lords (20 July), these two made speeches breathing ultimate defiance; and the applause with which they were received gave due notice to Lord Lansdowne, that he would have difficulty in preventing his house from committing suicide. The rebel movement, which a liberal paper christened 'Die-hard' and which accepted the name,[1] was early reinforced by the three sons of the great Lord Salisbury; the youngest of whom, Lord Hugh Cecil, had already outdone all his party in the commons' debates by the fanatical quality of his opposition to the bill. They drew into the revolt their brother-in-law, Lord Selborne, whose more tolerant temperament seemed less in place there.

The effect of Lord Lansdowne's amendments to the Parliament Bill was nothing less than to substitute for it the policy of his counter-resolutions, including the referendum. It was unthinkable that a government which had just won two general elections against the lords and passed its bill through the commons by a majority of 121, could accept such a reversal; and Lansdowne, who must have known that, showed once more poor leadership in committing his party so far to an untenable position. Two days earlier he and Balfour had been privately informed by Lloyd George on behalf of the government of the pledge to create peers obtained from the king in the previous November, and of ministers' reluctant determination to secure their bill by that means, if no other were left.[2]

Next day, therefore (21 July), Lansdowne convened at his house the unionist peers, and read to them a letter from the prime minister (procured by arrangement for this purpose), which stated the government's intentions and the king's consent. But again he failed as a leader.[3] He had made up his own mind to the less theatrical course dictated by obvious prudence; and if he had enjoined it on his party and told them that he would resign unless it were followed, the rebels would have had an uphill task. Instead he fumbled and asked for expressions of opinion, giving them the very opportunity which they wanted. Both the two unionist whips deserted to them, and the situation might well have drifted to catastrophe, if a younger man had not stepped in and retrieved it. This was Lord Curzon. It was he who organized the anti-Die-hard peers; and he who induced Balfour (hitherto silent and giving even less of a lead than Lans-

---

[1] They were also called 'Ditchers' (as wishing to die in the last ditch), while the Lansdowne section were called 'Hedgers'.

[2] Lord Newton, *Lord Lansdowne*, 417.

[3] As his biographer admits: Lord Newton, *Lord Lansdowne*, 423.

downe had) to write three days later a letter to Lord Newton throwing his weight against the Die-hard revolt. He too, organized an unofficial committee, which proceeded to explore the strength of the two factions, and, finding that the seventy-five peers supporting the government would certainly be out-voted by the Die-hards, induced a number of unionists headed by Lord Winchelsea and Lord Camperdown to sacrifice them-selves when the need should arise by voting for the bill. But Lord Lansdowne to the end characteristically refused to advise, or even to condone, this course, though it was obvious that the result which he desired could not be attained without it.

Meantime on 24 July the friends of the Die-hards in the com-mons, headed by Lord Hugh Cecil, howled down the prime minister in a scene then without precedent. This seems to have suggested to the unionist leaders that they might satisfy the rebels and reunite the party by moving a vote of censure on the government for its dealings with the king. Nothing, however, resulted from the debate, save a masterly exposition and defence by Asquith. The commons having rejected the lords' amend-ments, the final debate in the upper house took place on 9 and 10 August. Its drama has rarely been surpassed in parliament; for the result remained in doubt till the division, though Lord Morley had expressly intimated that rejection must be followed by 'a large and prompt creation of peers'. Finally the bill was passed by 131 to 114, some 29 unionist peers voting with the government, besides both archbishops and 11 out of 13 bishops.

Thus was consummated the Parliament Act: the most decisive step in British constitutional development since the franchise extension of 1867, to which, in some sort, it might be regarded as a corollary. In the last analysis the lords had no one to blame for it but themselves. Lord Beaconsfield in 1880 had warned his successors that 'no conflict must be permitted between the two Houses, unless something substantial is to be gained there-by'.[1] When they bargained over franchise extension in 1884 or rejected home rule in 1893, they acted in accord with his advice. But when they afterwards made it their regular annual practice to reject all the controversial bills of liberal governments, they plainly were courting Nemesis. In the accident of its permanent control over a second chamber having such large powers of rejection in the abstract, the conservative party held a one-sided

[1] Lord Balfour, *Chapters of Autobiography* (1930), 126.

advantage, which could not be theoretically justified to a democracy. Prudently restricted to rare and picked occasions, it yet might have lasted on. Used indiscriminately to hamstring a government with a huge popular majority like that of 1906, it revealed an anomaly past tolerance. Even so, on the swing of the pendulum, the peers might, as the saying is, have 'got away with it', but for their open breach of the constitution in holding up the 1909 budget. From that false step they could scarcely have recovered, even if they had been stronger in debate. But the government commanded much more effective artillery, whether in parliament or on the platform.

Now that a quarter of a century has passed, any one re-reading those famous debates in the light of subsequent history may be surprised by two features. One is the extreme exaggeration of the fears expressed by the conservatives about the consequences of the bill if passed. It is usual for parties to be extravagant in denouncing measures which they dislike, and by dint of repeating their extravagances to become convinced of them. But here the gap between conviction and reality was abnormal. The other curious feature is the depth of the liberal leaders' aversion to creating peers. Nothing shows more plainly, how unrevolutionary was their temper, for a large creation of peers would have helped them enormously. Asquith's papers contained, and his biographers have printed,[1] a draft list of about 250 suggested liberal peers. They were a very strong body, and in proved character, intellect, business, and public activity certainly outweighed the then existing house of lords, if a score of leaders in the latter were deducted. Had their creation gone through, the liberal government, being in control of both houses, could have passed Irish home rule, Welsh disestablishment, and a reform of the second chamber all in one session. With the Die-hards doing their utmost to bring this about, there seems something paradoxical about the conservatism of the liberals, who toiled to prevent it from happening.

As for the king, though he was criticized with asperity by Lord Hugh Cecil, nobody has shown how else he could have acted. Any alternative course (e.g. accepting Asquith's resignation and sending for Balfour) would have meant an immediate third general election. But at this, as was admitted on all hands, there was no prospect of obtaining a different result, and its interposi-

[1] J. A. Spender and Cyril Asquith, *Life of Asquith*, i. 329–31.

tion would have been most unpopular. Compared with the 1832 precedent, the 1911 threat to create peers was more and not less warranted. In Lord Grey's case there had been only one election; in Asquith's there had been two. Moreover Lord Grey's bill had only reached second reading in the upper house, while Asquith's had gone through all its stages there.

After the Bosnian crisis closed at the end of March 1909, there had been a *détente* in Europe. Some months later the replacement of Bülow by Bethmann-Hollweg as German chancellor (July 1909) brought a friendlier tone into Anglo-German relations. Following King Edward's death in May 1910 the Kaiser came to London for the funeral, and created an exceptionally good impression by his sympathetic attitude.

The crux now between Britain and Germany was the German fleet. Its alarming increase had necessitated the McKenna programme of the British admiralty; and the cost of that programme had been what immediately motived the 1909 budget, with all its consequences. Down to the Bosnian crisis Germany had persistently refused to discuss limitation, and treated any suggestion about it as little short of a hostile act. But after that her attitude changed. Calculating, it would seem, that the settlement of March 1909 had only postponed an inevitable Russo-Austrian war, in which she must herself take part, she aimed to secure in advance the neutrality of Great Britain. For this she was willing to bargain in terms of fleet limitation; and discussions in that sense went on from July 1910 till May 1911. But nothing came of them, because the German foreign office, as in Holstein's[1] days, over-rated Great Britain's complaisance and played too unyielding a game. The naval concessions that they suggested were trifling—temporary retardations at most. On the other hand they demanded an exclusive political entente. Grey on behalf of Great Britain was willing to offer a non-exclusive one, which should complete but not destroy the circle of goodwill represented by the ententes with France and Russia. But he was not willing to throw the French and Russian ententes over.

Meantime England was growing nervous about her defence.

[1] Holstein had fallen from power in April 1906, but down to his death in May 1909 he exercised (through Bülow and Kiderlen-Wächter) a certain influence on affairs. In his last interview with Bülow he urged him to conclude a naval agreement with England **before resigning the chancellorship** (Prince Bülow, *Denkwürdigkeiten*, ii. 468).

Lord Roberts on 23 November 1908 had put forward in the house of lords his demand for conscription. It could not be acceded to, not merely because liberal sentiment disliked it, but because its adoption would have precipitated war. But, as we have just seen, in 1910 leading ministers and ex-ministers on both sides were not averse to joining in a programme which included the Swiss form of national military training. In that year Admiral Fisher, the strongest champion of the 'blue water' school, ceased to be first sea lord. And in July 1909 the French-man, Blériot, had made the first aeroplane crossing of the Channel. In January 1911 Asquith was induced by Haldane to appoint the sub-committee of the Committee of Imperial Defence, which produced the famous 'War-Book', in which there was worked out for each Department every detail of what it should do in the event of war, all necessary proclamations or orders in council being kept ready in type. The War-Book was constantly revised till August 1914, when it proved of inestim-able value.

Till midsummer 1911 general relations with Germany re-mained good. In May the Kaiser visited London for the unveil-ing of the Queen Victoria Memorial. In June his son, the Crown Prince, attended King George's coronation. But at the end of that month the German government, at the instance of Kiderlen-Wächter, its foreign secretary, took a step which shook Europe. This was the dispatch of the German gunboat *Panther* to Agadir in Morocco. The resulting crisis was not less serious than those of 1905–6 and of 1908–9.

Since the Franco-German Morocco agreement of February 1909, France had given a widening interpretation to the 'special political interests', which the agreement allowed her in that country. In April 1911 there was a crisis at Fez, the Moroccan capital, the Sultan being threatened by the advance of a Pre-tender with a native army. The French accordingly marched a force there with—as they announced beforehand to the Signa-tory Powers—the object of protecting the European residents. Sir Edward Grey accepted that motive, but others might well be suspected; and Spain proceeded to make a parallel expedition within her sphere of influence. Berlin said little; but Kiderlen-Wächter seems early to have made up his mind that the Act of Algeciras was dead, that French absorption of Morocco was inevitable, and that the only thing left for Germany was to obtain compensation. According to the assumptions of pre-War diplomacy, these were not unreasonable views; but to give effect to them by brusquely sending a warship to seize a Moroccan port conformed to the worst traditions of post-Bismarck violence and blackmail. Britain was doubly alarmed, both by the threat to France, to whom in Moroccan (though not in other) matters Grey held himself under a formal obligation to give diplomatic support, and by the prospect of a German naval base on the Atlantic coast of Morocco, which the admiralty deprecated most strongly. On 3 July the British foreign secretary told the German ambassador that he considered the situation so important that it must be discussed in a meeting of the cabinet; and next day he notified as the cabinet's decision, that 'we could not recognise any new arrangements that might be come to without us'.

To this communication the German government replied with silence. Seventeen days elapsed. It was learned from Paris that the French government was being pressed for an impossible amount of 'compensation' in the Congo region; and from Morocco that the Germans at Agadir were landing and negotiating with the tribes. The German press was clamouring for Moroccan territory, and it looked as if the solution which Great Britain least desired might shortly be presented to her as a *fait accompli*. On 21 July Grey saw the German ambassador and pressed him for an answer. But he was still 'without instructions'. That evening Lloyd George was to speak at a Mansion House dinner; and with the approval of Asquith and Grey, but without any wider consultation of the cabinet, he there gave public warning to Germany of the risks which her government was running. After referring to Great Britain's influence in Europe and recalling how it 'has more than once in the past redeemed continental nations, who are sometimes too apt to forget that service, from overwhelming disaster and even from national extinction', he went on:

'I would make great sacrifices to preserve peace. I conceive that nothing would justify a disturbance of international goodwill except questions of the gravest national moment. But if a situation were to be forced upon us, in which peace could only be preserved by the surrender of the great and beneficent position Britain has won by centuries of heroism and achievement, by allowing Britain to be treated, where her interests were vitally affected, as if she were of no account in the Cabinet of Nations, then I say emphatically that peace at that price would be a humiliation intolerable for a great country like ours to endure.'

This, of course, was a contingent threat (or rather counter-threat) of war. The impression widely current abroad was that the cabinet had drafted it, and chosen the leading radical and Germanophile for mouthpiece to show the unity of the national front. But this was not so; the initiative was Lloyd George's own; and the most valid criticism of the step was, that in a matter of peace and war three ministers, however eminent, ought not to act over the cabinet's head.

The effects were good. Germany was enraged, but the German government was recalled to a sense of realities. It disclaimed interest in the coast of Morocco. It lowered the extravagant demands which it had made for Congo 'compensation'. But negotiations about the latter continued at Paris, and had yet to pass through difficult stages. In September war seemed so near that the South-Eastern Railway was quietly patrolled. At the worst stage in the middle of that month panic assailed the Berlin Bourse, and there was a run on the German banks. Kiderlen-Wächter unbent further, and a Morocco Accord was signed on 11 October. The whole tangle, including the Congo 'compensation', was straightened out by treaties of 3 and 4 November. The *Panther* was withdrawn not long after.

So ended the Agadir crisis—the third within six years, in which Germany had brought war near on account of Morocco. Once more her action had drawn closer the tie between France and Great Britain. A foreign office minute of 2 November 1911, which was read by Grey to the cabinet a fortnight later and received that body's approval, defines what it now was.[1] A British government needed to have public opinion behind it before it could support France. If France took the aggressive line, there could be no British support for her; but if she were the victim of aggression, British public opinion would enable it to be forthcoming. And the text shows that military support was implied, 'immediately and at the outset'.

The war preparations led to a curious conflict in London between the war office and the admiralty. The former was moved by Sir Henry Wilson, then director of military operations, the latter by Sir Arthur Wilson, who early in 1910 had succeeded

[1] Gooch and Temperley, *British Documents*, vii. 602.

Fisher as first sea lord; but each of the two cabinet ministers involved, Haldane and McKenna, stood firmly by his professional adviser. The plan of the soldiers was to send six divisions to France as soon as war was declared, and they asked an assurance from the admiralty that they could be transported by a certain date in September, if occasion arose. The sailors replied that no such assurance could be given, unless preparations were made, which would at once be interpreted abroad as steps to war. McKenna declined to make such preparations; while Haldane criticized the admiralty's unpreparedness and argued its need for a general staff. Asquith inclined to the war office view; but he characteristically shrank from pushing it home by appointing Haldane to the admiralty. He took five weeks to think it over, and then at the beginning of October made Winston Churchill, who had been home secretary, and McKenna, who had been first lord, change places. Both men did well in their new offices; though it was a curious reversal since 1909, when McKenna had been the champion and Churchill one of the two chief opponents of a forward naval policy. But the new broom at the admiralty did not sweep clean. Faced with the strong opposition of Sir A. Wilson to 'the whole principle of a War Staff for the Navy', Churchill decided to shelve the question 'during his tenure'. Soon afterwards Wilson retired, and the formation of a 'Naval War Staff' was announced. But its functions were purely advisory, and its role subordinate. It did not develop into a general staff. Nor had the navy one when the European war broke out; and to this some of its serious shortcomings may be attributed.

Agadir had a direct repercussion abroad in another sphere. Italy had long been preparing to seize Tripoli. Already before Algeciras she had purchased the assent of France to her doing so; and when the *Panther*'s spring was announced, she determined to hold back no longer. After completing her plans she declared war against Turkey (29 September 1911) on trumped-up charges. Turkey was now ruled by the Committee of Union and Progress, who had alienated the liberal Powers by reverting to policies of Ottomanization and massacre. Germany was once more her only friend, and once more, as in the Bosnian case, could not help her against the wishes of an ally. The war therefore was very one-sided; and since Italy had full command of the sea, she could pluck her prize with very little interference. For naval purposes she also occupied Rhodes and the adjacent islands; and this occupation became permanent.

The Tripoli war had in turn a repercussion. For just as Agadir had inspired it, so it inspired the Balkan war of 1912. And since the Balkan war laid the powder-train for the European war, one may view the final catastrophe as descending directly, though at several removes, from the *Panther*'s voyage.

The reader may have observed that the two first months of the Agadir crisis—July and August 1911—coincided with the final crisis over the passing of the Parliament Act. The day on which Lloyd George spoke at the Mansion House was the same day on which the importance of the Die-hard movement revealed itself at the Lansdowne House meeting. But those months were critical in yet another way; for they witnessed the onset of the gravest strike movement that till then the country had known. To understand its origins and character we must go back a little.

Although the election of fifty-three labour members to the 1906 parliament had startled the upper classes, it under-expressed the strength of labour and socialist opinion in the country. The British system of single-ballot elections has its counterpart in a system of two parties, against which it is extraordinarily hard for a third party to assert itself, because its candidatures 'split the vote'. In the pre-war years this told heavily against the labour party (as in the post-war years it has against the liberals); and it gave their followers the impression that they were not getting a fair deal. The course of the 1906 parliament, after its first year, left little scope to the labour members; and in the election of January 1910, instead of recording an advance corresponding to the increased acceptance of their propaganda, they lost a quarter of their seats and dropped to forty. A converging influence was that of the Osborne case. The Walthamstow branch of the Amalgamated Society of Railway Servants had resented the levying of compulsory contributions by that union for labour party purposes. Through their secretary, W. V. Osborne, they sued for an injunction in the Chancery Division. Mr. (afterwards Lord) Justice Farwell granted one, holding that it was illegal for a trade union to provide for parliamentary representation by means of a compulsory levy, even though its rules had been altered to permit it. The decision was upheld (28 November 1908) by all three judges in the court of appeal, and (21 December 1909) by all five judges in the house of lords.[1] After the latter date injunctions were obtained restraining a number of unions from continuing a compulsory levy. Some sixteen M.P.s found their salaries cut off. Attempts were made to replace compulsory levies by voluntary, but with poor results.[2]

All this set up a current away from parliamentary to trade-union action, and towards a new fashion in trade-union ideas imported from France and called Syndicalism.[3] Syndicalist doctrine had two features which specially concern us here: (1) considering the trade union and not the state to be the germ of future democratic organization, it taught that trade union leaders should influence parliaments, not from inside by becoming M.P.s, but from outside by 'direct action'; (2) regarding the class-struggle as war, it relied frankly on violence, elaborating such special tactics as the 'sympathetic' strike, the 'lightning' strike, the 'staying-in' strike, and 'sabotage', all leading up to the general strike. In varying forms and with fluctuating fortunes these doctrines played a considerable part in the British labour world from 1910 to 1926. They were helped at the start by a period of rising prices and stationary wages. They derived further stimulus from the action of the house of lords in rejecting the budget. 'If the peers', it was a common saying in trade-union branches, 'may sabotage the Constitution for their own purposes, why may not we?'

The new spirit became conspicuous in the latter part of 1910. In July there was a four-day railway strike in the Newcastle district, started and run by local men against the wishes of the union's head office, upon an occasion whose triviality suggested deep-lying unrest. On 3 September a general lock-out nearly

[1] (1910), A.C. 87. It illustrates the darker side of trade unionism, that the A.S.R.S. thereupon closed the Walthamstow branch and expelled Osborne and another from membership, confiscating their eighteen years' contributions and terminating their benefits.

[2] The Amalgamated Society of Engineers took a vote of its 107,499 members as to whether they would voluntarily subscribe one shilling each, and only obtained 5,110 favourable replies.

[3] *Syndicalisme* merely means trade unionism; the full French phrase for what the English called 'syndicalism' was *syndicalisme révolutionnaire*. American revolutionary trade unionism, as preached and practised by the 'Industrial Workers of the World' (founded in 1905 and generally termed the 'I.W.W.'), had at this time less influence in England than French; though some leaders, e.g. Mann, drew inspiration from it.

took place in the Lancashire cotton industry, following a reckless strike over the question whether a single grinder should do certain technical work on his machine. It had got as far as the stoppage of 120,000 workers, when the board of trade settled it. About the same time began a great lock-out of boilermakers on the north-east coast. This affected all the ironworkers employed by the Federation of Shipbuilding Employers; lasted fourteen weeks; cost the Boilermakers' Society £100,000 in strike pay and the workers £800,000 in lost wages; and ended in the men's defeat. Its cause was the breaking by local members of an agreement made by the Boilermakers' Society on their behalf; and the revolt throughout was almost as much against the union's head office as against the employers. Presiding that autumn at the Trades Union Congress, James Haslam vainly protested against indiscipline, and stressed its injury to collective bargaining. In October an event occurred in France, which was much observed in England. This was the French railway strike, which paralysed the Nord and État systems, and abruptly cut off all Channel and North Sea ports from Paris and southern France. It was quickly crushed by the government's[1] arresting the organizers and issuing a military mobilization order covering railway servants and engine-drivers; a device which, as English railwaymen noted, could not be repeated in England. Then in November in South Wales, where the Miners' Federation had only just averted a stoppage of the coalfield in the previous March, a local strike of 30,000 men (mainly employed by the Cambrian Coal trust) broke out in the Rhondda and Aberdare valleys in sympathy with a handful of miners dissatisfied over the rate of pay on a particular seam. On 7 November at Ton-y-pandy miners attacked the pithead and stopped the ventilating machinery; and thereupon a riotous mob looted and terrorized the place for three days. Police brought from Swansea and Bristol proved insufficient in face of the numbers. The chief constable of Glamorgan asked for troops; and 200 Hussars and two companies of infantry were sent from Salisbury Plain. But Churchill, who was then home secretary, had them stopped at Swindon, and telegraphed on the 9th to the men urging them to

---

[1] Curiously, the three leading ministers in it—Briand, Millerand, and Viviani—had not very long before been the three most brilliant leaders, after Jaurès, in the French socialist party. This further discredited parliamentarism in the labour movement.

cease rioting. They did not, and the troops had to go on, as did a body of Metropolitan constables. But next day the riot burned itself out. Churchill was much attacked over this episode by the unionists in parliament. His delay, though it sacrificed property, almost certainly saved life; but it may be that more drastic action would have checked the rise of strike-violence in the two following years.

A lull ensued, and 1911 was nearly half through, before the dispute occurred which precipitated the others. This was the seamen's and firemen's strike. Seamen and firemen were generally regarded at that time in the trade-union world as the most helpless and down-trodden of organized workers. On 14 June 1911 they struck for higher wages and overtime rates; and on 24 June at Southampton the shipping magnates conceded their demands.[1] The effect on restless workers in other trades was electric. 'If even the seamen can win', they asked, 'why not we?' Sporadic strikes followed, particularly among low-paid labourers[2] in engineering works. But the obvious repercussion was on the dockers. On 27 July the Port of London Authority granted 7d. an hour instead of 6d. to the dockers employed by it. Thereupon those employed (already at 7d.) by the shipping companies demanded 8d. On 1 August they all came out; 20,000 port workers were idle, and over 20 ocean liners were held up. Sir Albert Rollit was invited to arbitrate, and awarded the 8d. Subsidiary disputes with lightermen, coal-porters, and others were settled by the board of trade; and on 11 August at midnight the strike ended to the all-round satisfaction of the men. Meanwhile the London Carmen's Trade Union had come out, and (as is difficult to prevent in carmen's strikes) there was much violence. But on 11 August they, too, secured a settlement in their favour; just in time for the government to countermand the sending of 20,000 troops to London. Parallel dock strikes at Liverpool and Manchester were not so quickly successful. At Liverpool there was savage rioting. Troops were called in; on 15 August they had to fire, and two men were killed. Some railway porters had struck to help the dockers; the dockers stayed out to secure reinstatement for these allies; and then the whole A.S.R.S., which was itching to strike on its own account,

[1] The settlement at Liverpool came three days later; but there and at Manchester there was a complication over dockers and carmen, who had struck in sympathy.
[2] See p. 515 below.

became drawn in. On 15 August (the day of the firing) the four railway unions decided to call out their men at 8 p.m. next day.

After a discussion in the house of commons, however, they agreed first to meet the prime minister at the board of trade on the 17th. Asquith asked in what their grievance consisted; they replied, in the failure of the railway companies to observe the spirit and letter of the 1907 agreement. The prime minister rejoined by offering a royal commission to investigate this at once; but in regard to the threatened stoppage he mounted the high horse, and said the government could not allow a general paralysis of the railway system. Probably his reason was that the country then stood in almost hourly danger of a war with Germany. But the railway leaders knew nothing of it, and received the worst possible impression. Retiring in anger, they gave the signal; and England found herself for the first time in the throes of a general railway strike. It was not universal; one of the (then nine) great English railway systems, the London and South-Western, was unaffected; but inside a quadrilateral bounded north and south by Newcastle and Coventry, and east and west by Hull and Liverpool, industrial England was completely paralysed. Troops were freely used to overawe disorder; in London they camped in the parks. The only very bad rioting was at Llanelly, where shops and a train were looted; soldiers fired killing two men, and five more men perished by an explosion among the freight.

Meanwhile Asquith had wisely handed over the reins of negotiation to Lloyd George. The latter persuaded the parliamentary labour party to withdraw a vote of censure, and brought its leader, Ramsay MacDonald, into the conference. On Saturday night, 19 August, at 11 p.m. the strike was settled on terms of immediate resumption and reinstatement; the conciliation boards to meet at once to settle questions in dispute, and a special commission to investigate forthwith the working of the scheme of 1907.[1] Settlements followed of the Manchester carters' dispute and the Liverpool dockers; and the month ended more quietly. It had been one of the most eventful in the history of the British proletariate, on whose outlook it left lasting traces. Among factors which quickened the pulses of revolt, besides the contemporary example of the Die-hards in parlia-

[1] Two board of trade officials played leading parts in this settlement—Sir H. Llewellyn Smith and G. R. (afterwards Lord) Askwith.

ment, was a run of exceptional weather. The summer of 1911 was the hottest in England since 1868. The shade temperature in London commonly went over 90° F. during the earlier days in August; on the 9th it touched 97° F.; and a long drought was not broken till the 21st. Till then the sweltering town populations were psychologically not normal.

But the strike impulse continued. In October the Miners' Federation of Great Britain, which now covered all the coal-fields, altered its rules to make it possible to call a general coal strike. On 20 December a strike in an Accrington weaving-shed against the employment of two non-unionist weavers led a week later to a lock-out affecting 126,000 workers. It was only settled on 19 January 1912, by a truce which left the status of non-unionists undecided, after £1 million had been lost in wages and £250,000 drawn in strike pay. Meanwhile the miners took a ballot on a general strike for minimum wage-rates; and the return on 18 January showed more than a two-thirds majority for, all districts except Cleveland supporting. Notices were given to stop work after 29 February. A national conference between owners and miners followed, and on 6 February reached deadlock. On the 22nd Asquith met the parties separately, but effected nothing. On the 28th the government proposed a minimum wage in each district to be fixed by district conferences, at which a government representative should be present and should decide failing agreement. Two-thirds of the owner-interests agreed, but those of Wales and Scotland would not. Nor would the Miners' Federation; which had put out a schedule of specified minima for the various districts, and refused to abandon it. So on 1 March, to the number of about 850,000, the men came out; and ten days later it was estimated that 1,300,000 workers in other industries had been thrown idle. The government continued conferring with the parties, but made no headway, and on 15 March Asquith announced that it would bring in a bill to set up a minimum-wage machinery on the lines of its pre-strike proposal. The bill soon followed; and after criticisms by the Welsh and Scottish owners, it was opposed on second reading by Balfour and Austen Chamberlain, and carried against them by 348 to 225.[1] But in committee the miners pressed to insert minimum figures—5s. for datallers and 2s. for boys. There was a new and fruitless conference over the point.

[1] Only three unionists voted for the bill, and only one liberal against.

On the report stage the unionists withdrew their opposition; but the miners' leaders, to save their faces, urged the '5 and 2' to the bitter end. Without this and against them, the bill was carried by 213 to 48, the unionists abstaining. Not without difficulty was it passed through the lords; but, once enacted, it proved a complete success. The men started returning to work; the Federation took a ballot; only 244,011 favoured continuing the struggle, while 201,013 voted for dropping it; and the strike was called off.

If the strikes of the previous year had shown the advantages of combination on a large scale, this coal strike illustrated its drawbacks. The Miners' Federation was an unwieldy stiff-jointed body; tied to its voted programme and schedules, it lacked freedom and flexibility to meet opportunity half-way. Moreover, once so large a human mass had been laboriously set in motion towards a strike, nobody could prevent its occurring, even after it had become superfluous. In the result the miners gained a good deal; but they could have had it all before the stoppage.

Next followed the 1912 London dock dispute, which revealed another weakness of mass-action—the difficulty of inducing a mass to keep its head and consolidate its gains. In August 1911 the London dockers had triumphed at the cost of little effort or hardship. Jericho had fallen to the blast of a trumpet. Nothing would now persuade the hotter heads but that it must do so again, and that there was no virtue like trumpeting. Peace was constantly threatened. The employers prepared to meet a challenge; and in May 1912 it came. A man, who was normally a foreman and held a foreman's ticket, worked as a hand without a union ticket. The Transport Federation (in which the dockers, stevedores, lightermen, and carmen were now combined) made a very exaggerated protest, and on 23 May called out 100,000 men to compel submission in this single case. Their folly was soon apparent. Sir Edward Clarke was appointed to hold an inquiry, and reported in part against them. Numbers of their members resented being called out, while the employers at once started organizing a considerable dock service by 'free labour'. The government proposed a joint conference, and the employers refused; then it proposed a joint committee, and after postponing their answer for days they refused that also. The Port of London Authority came to the fore in the person of the chairman, Lord Devonport, and insisted on the men's surrender. In the middle of June Asquith made a strong effort to resume negotiations, but the Authority was adamant. For six more miserable weeks the dispute dragged on. The labour party in parliament kept urging the government to intervene, but ministers saw no ground, and a mid-July attempt at mediation failed. On the 23rd a labour motion demanding intervention was rejected by 255 to 58; and on the same day the L.C.C. decided that it could not feed the dockers' school-children during the holidays. At the end of the month the strike collapsed.

This abject failure, following the very limited success of the miners, put an end for the time being to the strike-ferment in England. It had lasted round about two years, and the workers saw that they must give it a rest.

The year 1911 brought a good deal of legislation besides the Parliament Act. There was a Shops' Act, which introduced the principle of a legal weekly half-holiday; a Coal Mines' Act, which consolidated and amended the law of its subject; a comprehensive Copyright Act, which arose out of the Berlin Copyright Convention (1908) and the report (1909) of a committee appointed to advise on harmonizing the United Kingdom's law with it; a Small Landholders' (Scotland) Act, which created a Scottish Board of Agriculture and enacted much of the bill rejected by the lords in 1907; an Official Secrets' Act, rendered necessary by the growing extent of German espionage; and a first Aerial Navigation Act empowering the home office to prohibit the navigation of aircraft over prescribed areas. Besides these measures there was Payment of Members and the great National Insurance Act.

Payment of members had ranked officially, though vaguely, as a liberal policy for twenty years, having been mentioned in the tail of the Newcastle programme. But it was the Osborne decision and the resulting plight of the labour party, which at last brought it to the fore. On 10 August 1911 (the day on which the lords passed the Parliament Bill) the house of commons, after comparatively little discussion, established it by a mere financial resolution on the basis of £400 a year for each member. The legitimacy of the procedure was debated three days later; but three modern precedents were cited for it; the earliest and most interesting being from 1833, when the state's first grants to aid elementary education had been established in this way.

The National Insurance Bill had been introduced by Lloyd George while the Parliament Bill was still in the commons. But only after the latter had been made law was time found in an autumn session to push the former through parliament. It was a vast contributory scheme to insure the whole working population against sickness, and certain sections of it against unemployment; modelled on the working of the German Law of 1889, in that compulsory contributions were collected from employers and employed by means of stamped cards (a device till then untried in England); but differing, in that the great English friendly societies, which had covered much of the less difficult ground on a voluntary basis, were, with the trade unions, brought in as 'approved societies' to administer the money benefits for their members. More is said elsewhere about its bearings on the organization of national welfare.[1] Here we only record the politics of its passage. It was bitterly opposed by the unionists, and, but for the change wrought by the Parliament Act, would certainly, like all the main liberal measures preceding it since 1905, have been killed by the house of lords. The immediate practical result of the lords' defeat was, not merely that any bill could be carried against them under certain conditions in three sessions, but that a great measure of national utility like this was enacted in a single session, whereas previously it could never have been enacted at all. Unable to destroy it in parliament, the opposition tried hard to wreck it in the country by furiously fomenting every popular prejudice or professional alarm which so vast a scheme was bound to encounter. Duchesses visited the Albert Hall to exhort the public not to 'lick stamps'; mistresses organized domestic servants in the same crusade; wage-earners of every kind were urged to resist the deductions from their wages as a monstrous oppression by the government. In addition, it was sought to make political capital out of the anxieties of the doctors, whose livelihoods were bound to be greatly affected, one way or the other, and without whose co-operation the act could not possibly be worked.

All these manœuvres eventually failed; but they helped to debase the currency of politics. The conservatives slid a stage farther down the perilous slope of 'direct action' and refusal to be bound by the rules of constitutional politics, on which they had been unnaturally launched by the lords' rejection of the

[1] Below, pp. 519-20.

1909 budget. At the same time their attempt to represent the insurance scheme as a sort of plundering of the poor drove Lloyd George by way of counterblast into his famous '9d. for 4d.' phrase[1]—a line of retort easily slipping into crude bribery of the electorate. The two dangers thus exemplified were the basic ones for democracy—faction and corruption; but at the moment the former was by far the most immediate. The Insurance Act did not buy votes for the government of the day, but like the other greatest social reform of the century, the Balfour Education Act, it lost them. The currents towards faction were specially swollen at this time by the sensationalism of the popular Harmsworth newspapers. Alfred Harmsworth himself, since 1905 Lord Northcliffe and since February 1908 controller also of *The Times*, was nearly always on the side of violence in public affairs. He saw events and policies in terms of the headlines which would sell his papers; he was ignorant of history, indifferent to English political tradition; and yet he exerted over the party that ought to have conserved it a masterful sway, which the parliamentary leaders were at once too proud to confess and too weak to curb.

The unionist party was indeed much disorganized. After the final humiliation over the Parliament Act it turned upon its chief. 'B.M.G.' (Balfour Must Go) was a slogan started by tariff reformers, who disliked him on fiscal grounds; but it soon became the expression of a wider discontent. The last straw was a blunt speech by the Duke of Bedford at Luton on 6 November 1911. Two days later Balfour resigned the leadership, which he had held in the commons for twenty years. His fall was the penalty for several years' weak and unwise leading; for which, however, Lansdowne, who did not fall, had been more to blame than he. The rivals for his succession were Walter Long and Austen Chamberlain, and as the partisans of neither would accept the other, agreement was found by their both standing aside for a third candidate—Andrew Bonar Law.[2] The new

---

[1] 4d. was the proportion of the weekly insurance stamp deducted from the employee's wages. In addition, the employer paid 3d. and the state's contribution was valued at 2d. more; so that the whole value which went to insure the employee was 9d. Lloyd George's expression was first used by him at Whitefield's Tabernacle on 14 October 1911.

[2] B. 1858 in New Brunswick, Canada, his father being a Presbyterian minister and both parents Scottish. Brought to Scotland as a boy, and finished his education at Glasgow High School. In business in Glasgow as an iron merchant; M.P. 1900; parliamentary secretary to the board of trade 1902–5; leader of the conservatives

leader was a good debater, and for the purpose of controlling his party's wild men had the advantage over Balfour of being an unimpeachable tariff reformer. But he had all his spurs to win; had never even held cabinet office; and from any standpoint was a personage of much smaller calibre than the previous leaders who had moulded conservative policy since 1832. What the party most needed at this juncture was a strong hand and cool brain to bring it back to realism and a sense of proportion. But the most that Bonar Law could hope, was to restore some ultimate central authority over his various extremists by backing them for the present unconditionally; and the latter was his line down to the outbreak of the war. Following the usual rule among parties in such cases, he was elected to leadership in the commons only, with Lansdowne holding a parallel position in the house of lords.

Shortly afterwards the lords rejected a bill in circumstances which, unlike those of other cases since 1905, were entirely appropriate to the action of a revising Chamber. This was the Naval Prize Bill. We saw how the Hague Conference of 1907 agreed to setting up an International Prize Court, subject to subsequent agreement as to the code which the court should administer. On 4 November 1908 a conference of experts met in London, and after sitting on into 1909 drew up such a code in 71 articles, known as the Declaration of London. It embodied British doctrine on one important matter—'continuous voyage' —but its most striking feature was a triple classification of seaborne goods as either absolute contraband, conditional contraband, or absolute non-contraband. Most raw materials were put in the third class, where they could not be touched if carried in neutral ships; while food was put in the second, confiscable if for a military or naval destination. In November 1910, before any attempt had been made to ratify the Declaration, the Glasgow and Edinburgh Chambers of Commerce published detailed protests against it; and the foreign office retorted with a counter manifesto. In March 1911 the Declaration was debated for three days in the lords; after which the Association of Chambers of Commerce carried a resolution against it by a large majority. The government, however, went ahead and embodied it in a Naval Prize Bill. But this they were only able to get through the

in the coalition ministries of Asquith and Lloyd George, 1915–21; prime minister 1922–3; d. 1923.

commons with majorities on second and third reading of 70 and 47, though their everyday majority for other purposes exceeded 100. Having regard to the weak commons' support, the strong mercantile opposition, and the lukewarmness of the admiralty, the lords were well within their rights in rejecting it; and the subsequent course of the European war showed them to have thereby rendered a service to the country. Yet the real faults of the Declaration were curiously different from those chiefly found with it. It prejudiced Great Britain, not by increasing (for no change of rules could increase) her pre-existing insular liability to have her food supplies cut off, but by diminishing her right to use her naval power to deprive an enemy of raw materials. Thus, if in force, it would have rendered inapplicable one of the chief forms of pressure which in 1918 brought Germany to her knees.[1]

To the record of 1911 belong two other matters of foreign policy. In 1899 a general arbitration treaty had been signed at Washington between the then secretary of state (Richard Olney) and the British ambassador (Sir Julian Pauncefote), but the Senate had refused to ratify. On 19 December 1910 President Taft made a speech declaring America's readiness to submit to a properly constituted arbitral tribunal any issue that could be settled by arbitration, 'no matter what it involves, whether honour, territory, or money'. On 13 March 1911 Sir Edward Grey, speaking in a debate on naval expenditure, took up and welcomed the president's utterance. His speech met with wide approval on both sides of the Atlantic; but in point of fact it was not till 1914 that a general arbitration treaty between the two countries was made. Meanwhile, as in anticipation of it, the Anglo-Japanese treaty was revised, and a clause inserted, that neither party should be obliged by the alliance to go to war with any third Power, with which it had a treaty of general arbitration. The intention was to exempt Great Britain from siding with Japan against America.

The second matter had reference to Persia. The effect of the Anglo-Russian Agreement had been to hold up Russia's advance there. This was seen and resented by Russian agents on the spot,

[1] It is impossible now to read the Declaration without astonishment at the failure of its authors to visualize either the importance of raw materials in modern war, or the vital military uses to which many non-military articles might be put. (Barbed wire, for instance, was to be only conditional contraband.) Yet most jurists favoured it; though one of the most eminent, the late Professor T. E. Holland, did not.

who, as was the way in the Russian service, often acted on their own impulse contrary to their official instructions. Hence arose a number of vexatious intrigues and aggressions; and Grey was hard put to it to reconcile his pro-Russian policy with his desire to see Persia maintained as a buffer State. She had at this time embarked on an experiment in parliamentary government, in which a radical group of English and Irish M.P.s took great interest. Their generous zeal was restrained by no compunction for the Anglo-Russian Entente; on the contrary, they hated the Entente and approved of the Persians all the more, if they crossed its plans. Grey could neither satisfy nor ignore them; and, had he not been a remarkable parliamentarian, might easily have come to grief in the commons.

His most difficult period was from May to December 1911, when W. Morgan Shuster, an American nominated by President Taft, was treasurer-general to the Persian government. Shuster may have been an able financier, but politically he courted failure from the start. He ostentatiously ignored alike the *de facto* position of Russia in northern Persia and the terms of the 1907 Agreement, and asserted the Persian government's right to ignore them too. This gave him obvious and immense popularity with the Persian politicians, but of course was no basis for achieving anything but a fire of straw. The fire burned for rather over seven months; and then the second of two Russian ultimatums (29 November 1911) required his dismissal. Grey had previously let St. Petersburg know that Great Britain would not oppose the demand; for indeed Shuster had been only less troublesome to her than to Russia. The Persian parliament refused to give way. But the regent dissolved it, and Shuster left the country. Russia not only stipulated, with Grey's approval, that Persia should engage no more foreigners without Anglo-Russian consent, but sent in troops and demanded an indemnity—direct steps to a permanent occupation. Here Grey drew the line. He told the Russian ambassador (2 December) that if such a course were persisted in, the Entente would end, he himself would retire, and there would be a new orientation of British policy. The Russians took the warning in time; and agreement was maintained with less difficulty thereafter.

The opening months of 1912 were shadowed by the coal strike, but when it was over the stage was set for bringing in the liberal measures to which the veto of the lords had been a barrier for the past two decades. On 11 and 12 April respectively were introduced bills for Irish home rule and Welsh disestablishment. In the event of the lords' still opposing them to the bitter end, the time-table under the Parliament Act would permit their becoming law in the summer of 1914.

The third Home Rule Bill differed from those of 1886 and 1893 in being inspired by a federalist conception. Ireland's situation within the British Isles was no longer viewed as unique save in point of urgency; and the measure offered her was so framed that similar treatment might afterwards be given to Scotland, Wales, or England. For the present, however, a single British parliament at Westminster was to remain the Imperial parliament, and to it a reduced representation of forty-two Irish members was to be sent. The Imperial parliament's authority was to remain supreme; and a fairly exact picture of the home rule parliament's relation to it may be obtained by looking to-day at the constitution of Northern Ireland. For the Act of 1920, under which the parliament of Northern Ireland was set up, reproduced textually for two Irish parliaments (of which only the Northern came into being) the main provisions which the Act of 1914 had prescribed for one; and the successful working of the present Northern Irish constitution has disposed of the criticisms directed against the original bill on its technical side. As to federalism, it has to be remembered that the principle was much more widely esteemed in the world before the European war than, for various reasons, it has been since; and of the five great federal systems—the American, German, Swiss, Canadian, and Australian—three were Anglo-Saxon. There was some theoretic support for the federal idea among English unionists.

As between 1912 and 1886, however, the greatest change was not in the bill, but in the Ireland for which it was designed. In 1886 the country had only just emerged from the worst throes of its agrarian revolution. Class-war and nationalist upheaval had gone together; but the native Irish, while they had overthrown the ruling 'English garrison' in the centre, south, west, and north-west of the island, were still themselves rebels, not rulers. A quarter of a century later the agrarian problem had been solved. First the Land Courts under Gladstone's 1881 Act, then the enterprises of Balfour's Congested Districts Board, then the series of Land Purchase Acts culminating in Wyndham's, and lastly the work of Sir Horace Plunkett and the Irish Agricultural Organization Society, had transformed the rack-rented tenants of the old days—half serfs, half outlaws—into prosperous self-respecting small farmers. Moreover, since Gerald Balfour's Act of 1898, establishing county and district councils, they had in local affairs grown accustomed to self-government. Their political leaders, the Irish national party, had also changed. Not in personnel, for most of them before 1890 had been Parnell's lieutenants; but in outlook, for they had breathed the air of Westminster so much longer. John Redmond was Parnell's closest follower and inherited his mantle; but where Elijah had been Anglophobe, Elisha was Anglophile. Nor in that was he alone.

So much was gain from the standpoint of the practical home rulers, but other changes were not. The Irish parliamentary party no longer consisted of young men, and had acquired some of the weaknesses of a vested interest. Jealous and rebellious youth outside its ranks in the Irish labour movement, the creamery movement, the Gaelic League, the (still very obscure) ranks of Sinn Fein, and the secret councils of the Irish Republican Brotherhood, kept semi-hostile watch, eager to make the most of anything that might be charged against the party as a betrayal of the Irish cause. The Irish leaders knew too little of these men and movements;[1] and took more direct note of the little group of their own dissidents headed by T. Healy and W. O'Brien. But they were aware that nationalist opinion, after being baulked of home rule for a quarter of a century, was in no mood to assent to its being whittled down. On the other hand the large British-descended colony in north-east Ulster, where alone there was a protestant community comprising all classes—tenant farmers and proletariate as well as landowners and employers—had since 1886 acquired a much stronger self-consciousness. Parnell down to the first Home Rule Bill hardly realized that 'Ulster' existed.[2]

[1] Redmond remained in amazing ignorance of them down to Easter 1916 (Denis Gwynn, *Life of John Redmond* (1932), 456–7). Dillon, more a revolutionary by instinct, knew more, and therefore was usually concerned to dissuade the broader-minded Redmond from steps which might have overstrained nationalist loyalty to him.

[2] A memorandum of 6 January 1886 from him to Gladstone (addressed in form to Mrs. O'Shea) is preserved among the Gladstone Papers at the British Museum, in which with reference to 'the concession of a full measure of autonomy to Ireland' he observes that 'the Protestants, other than the owners of land, are not really opposed to such concession'. So completely did he then ignore the problem of a non-landowning Ulster opposition.

But the controversy over that bill and the propaganda of some English unionist leaders (especially Lord Randolph Churchill) made the community of which Belfast was the capital much more aware of itself as a separate entity. Fresh life returned to the traditions of warfare and deadly faction-feud between catholic natives and protestant settlers from the seventeenth century down; and within the Ulster fold liberals and conservatives, presbyterians and Orangemen, joined forces together, with the conservatives and Orangemen very much on top. There were periods between 1886 and 1906 when this united front was temporarily broken;[1] but from the moment that a government friendly to Redmond took office at Westminster, the ranks were closed. The great growth of Belfast, due to its shipbuilding, fortified the local pride of the northern protestants and their resolution not to be put under Dublin, a city smaller than their own. There, then, lay the obstacle to making Redmond 'the Irish Botha'. The nationalist leader did not feel strong enough with his own people to take home rule for anything but the whole of Ireland. But the Ulster protestant community refused to come in. Unless, therefore, he could either over-persuade them or get parliament to force them, he could not obtain home rule in a form which he could afford to accept. He put his faith in a combination of these methods.

So late as 1910, when there was the movement among unionists for a federal settlement, persuasion might probably have prevailed, had the good offices been forthcoming of the English unionist party. Redmond was ready to give the Ulstermen almost any 'safeguards' short of actual exclusion, and Balfour and Lansdowne could have driven a strong bargain for their Belfast clients on those lines. But at an early stage the Irish unionists sought to commit their party to the opposite course—that of stimulating Ulster's opposition as a means of defeating home rule. On 27 February 1910 Sir Edward Carson[2] accepted an invitation to lead them as a group in the house of commons, and from then on this masterful man increasingly imposed his will on his English colleagues.

[1] Especially during T. W. Russell's agitation for compulsory land purchase (1902), which the presbyterian farmers supported and the Orangemen opposed.
[2] B. 1854 at Dublin; educated at Portarlington School and Trinity College, Dublin; Q.C. at Irish Bar, 1889; at English, 1894; M.P. 1892; solicitor-general for Ireland, 1892; solicitor-general, 1900–5; attorney-general, 1915; first lord of the admiralty, 1917; member of the war cabinet, 1917–18; lord of appeal 1921–9; d. 1935.

Carson was a Dubliner with no roots in Ulster at all, and it was only on 31 January 1911 that he presided for the first time over a meeting of the Ulster Unionist Council. In the following autumn, a month after the passing of the Parliament Act, he held on 23 September at Craigavon a review of the members of Ulster unionist clubs and Orange lodges, and to an audience of 100,000 people announced what thenceforth was the Ulster programme. They were not merely to defy Dublin's home rule but to prepare an alternative, and be ready, 'the morning home rule passes, to become responsible for the government of the Protestant Province of Ulster'. Two days later their delegate meeting appointed a commission to draft the constitution for a provisional government. With the New Year they went a step farther, and, having on 5 January 1912 complied with the law by seeking and obtaining permission from the local magistrates, began drilling a Volunteer Force. This was three months before the introduction of the bill. On the eve of it, on 9 April, a review of 80,000 Ulster Volunteers was held, and four men—Sir Edward Carson, Lord Londonderry, Bonar Law (now unionist leader in the Commons), and Walter Long—took the salute.

Had the prime minister looked the issues fairly in the face, he might early have come to two clear conclusions. The first was that it was out of the question to impose home rule on the Ulster protestants. A large organized community desirous of staying under the British parliament could not be forced against its will under a Parliament of its hereditary enemies. Any idea of using a commons majority for such a purpose meant ignoring the deeper foundations on which alone democratic constitutionalism can rest—respect for minorities and for the subtle boundary which divides government by freedom and consent from that by dictatorship and violence. Had the bill originally recognized this or been early conformed to it, it would have at once cleared the political air. Secondly he should have taken immediate steps to make the organization of 'private armies' in Ireland illegal and to put them down. For this he had sufficient warrant in Irish history itself. But the policies hung together; you could scarcely enforce the second without the first. Yet the first was much less difficult than it looked; for Redmond's 'whip-hand' over the liberals was limited. He could not turn them out without letting the unionists in, which for him would have been a fatal prospect. Moreover, his situation had this great advantage over Parnell's in 1886, that he need not vote with the liberals to give them a majority. It sufficed that he should abstain.

Unfortunately it was not Asquith's bent to face issues promptly. Driven to bay, he would act with vigour; but the habit, which grows on most prime ministers, of postponing decisions and trusting that time will untie the knots, obtained an altogether excessive hold on him. A phrase which he several times uttered early in 1911—'wait and see'—was afterwards not unfairly made his nickname. Thus it was that down to 1914 he still had no clear policy, but remained poised on equivocations, waiting for something to turn up. In his own mind he knew that he could never 'coerce Ulster'; and indeed he was probably one of the least enthusiastic home rulers in his party. Yet officially he stood committed to a bill from which Ulster was not excluded. So he durst not suppress the Carson movement, but had to treat it with a weak tolerance which nobody, least of all Carson himself, could ever mistake for magnanimity. His attitude behind the scenes towards Redmond was even worse; it was one of complete unreliability.[1] A bolder course could have run straighter, and would have been at once more honourable and more helpful. The Irish leader himself could not make the concession to Ulster, for his people would not have let him. But if he could have represented it to them as something which the government imposed on him against his will and without his acceptance, he might then have directed their minds to their true task—that of winning Ulster's eventual adhesion by consent.

The matter was discussed in the cabinet, where at least three leading ministers—Churchill, Lloyd George, and Grey—saw early that the Ulster protestants were the crux, and that they could not be coerced. But it was decided otherwise, and when in committee on the bill (11 June 1912) a back-bench liberal, T. C. R. Agar-Robartes, moved an amendment to exclude the counties of Antrim, Armagh, Down, and Londonderry, Birrell at once intimated that the government could not accept it. Thus a great opportunity was fatally missed; though even so the amendment was defeated by only 61 votes, in contrast with the majority of

[1] Redmond was a very systematic archivist; he not only kept every letter that he received and a copy of every one that he wrote, but invariably made a written note of interviews immediately after their occurrence. Thus the evidence regarding his dealings with Asquith, as set out by his biographer, is singularly complete. It shows Asquith, whose career elsewhere exhibited so many features of greatness, at his weakest and worst.

101 which on 9 May had carried the second reading.[1] The fact was that at this stage, apart from the strength of nationalist sentiment for an indivisible Ireland, the leaders of all parties (and not least Carson himself) were under the delusion, that Ireland without the Belfast area could not pay its way, so that exclusion would prohibit home rule. There was also, even at this stage, a great difficulty over Tyrone and Fermanagh. These counties, in addition to Agar-Robartes's four, contained very large blocks of the essentially 'Ulster' population, but they also contained slightly larger numbers of catholics. And the difficulty of partitioning them was very great, since the rival populations were intermingled in layers.[2]

But if the British liberals erred in ranging themselves behind the full demand of one of the Irish factions, the British conservatives committed themselves no less unfortunately in regard to the other. For Carson to preach and organize rebellion in Ulster was one thing; he was an Irishman and, though he had been a law officer in the Balfour government, did not implicate the English party. The serious commitment was made by Bonar Law. We have seen how at the first review of the Ulster Volunteers he was one of those who took the salute. By words as well as by his presence he there gave the movement his support; and before long he was making speeches quite as violent as Carson's, directly countenancing, and by 13 November himself uttering, incitements to mutiny in the army. A more experienced leader would scarcely have done so. But Bonar Law, not a strong man at any time, was in a weak position; and violent courses are the easiest for a politician so placed. On 27 July 1912 speaking in England at a great party demonstration at Blenheim Palace he said: 'I can imagine no length of resistance to which Ulster will go, which I shall not be ready to support, and in which they will not be supported by the overwhelming majority of the British people.' In these words, which he reaffirmed afterwards as 'the Blenheim pledge', the driver simply threw the reins on the horse's neck. It is difficult to imagine a Disraeli or a Peel, a Salisbury or a Balfour, so abdicating control. To pledge a great English party to follow

---

[1] A point to notice about the second-reading majority is that it included one of 39 among the members representing Great Britain. In 1893, on the other hand, there had been a British majority of 14 against the bill, and in 1886 one of 94.

[2] The division was really vertical rather than regional, the protestant settlers occupying the lower-lying and more valuable land.

a small Irish faction wherever it might lead would hardly have appealed to any of them.

Thus launched, the quarrel pursued a course in 1912 and 1913, whose details are little worth tracing. Carson, be it said, gave much prudent care to the hard task of preventing riots in Belfast; and one of his most theatrical devices, the signing (September 1912) of the Ulster Covenant, was contrived for this purpose as a safety-valve. On 25 October 1912, at Ladybank, Asquith appealed earnestly for a compromise settlement. But one of his conditions—'nothing must be done to erect a permanent or insuperable bar to Irish unity'—implied that any exclusion of Ulster must have a fixed time-limit; in which form it would, of course, be useless from the Ulstermen's standpoint. Over this and over the question of areas all progress towards agreement was held up. By the end of 1912 the Ulster issue had become the sole serious ground of unionist opposition to home rule; and it so remained through 1913. The scandal of the conservative defiance to law grew steadily greater, and exerted an unsettling influence throughout the whole community. But the government remained powerless to deal with it; and the Irish nationalist leaders still blindly repeated that the Ulster attitude was 'bluff'. Meantime under the usual conditions of obstruction and guillotine the Home Rule Bill passed the commons by large majorities in two successive sessions, and was twice rejected by the lords.

In the heat of this struggle the unionist party's enthusiasm for tariff reform again melted. At a great party demonstration on 4 December 1912 Lord Lansdowne had officially withdrawn the plan of submitting food taxes to a referendum, and had suggested a duty of 2s. per quarter on foreign corn. Twelve days later Bonar Law also declared for food duties. But these decisions roused keen opposition among the unionists of Lancashire and Yorkshire. A memorial was organized asking the unionist leaders to agree not to impose food taxes without a second general election; and in a letter dated 13 January 1913 Bonar Law on behalf of both of them accepted the terms. It is not usual for British party leaders to swallow such a public rebuff; they did so to clear the ground for Carson.

Two other factors contributed to the domestic unsettlement of these years. One was the Marconi affair; the other, a new phase of suffragist militancy. The first arose out of a scheme for an 'Imperial wireless chain'. It had been recommended by the sixth Colonial or (as it was now called) Imperial Conference, which met in 1911 and was largely occupied with defence matters. In March 1912 the postmaster-general (Herbert Samuel) accepted, subject to subsequent ratification by parliament, the tender of the Marconi Company. Wireless telegraphy was then still open to experiment; the prospect of such a big contract not unnaturally sent the company's shares soaring; and it was no less to be expected that people interested in rival wireless systems (of which there were four) should agitate against the postmaster's decision. The terms of the definite agreement were put before parliament in August, but their consideration was deferred till October; and meanwhile rumours appeared that certain ministers had corruptly influenced the bargain in order to make money out of Marconi shares. A French paper named the postmaster-general and the attorney-general (Sir Rufus Isaacs[1]) as culprits; but on their bringing a libel action it at once capitulated, apologized, and paid costs. So when the contract came up for ratification (11 October 1912), the house of commons sent it to a select committee to inquire into the conduct of ministers and the technical aspects of the bargain. The latter part of the inquiry was delegated to an advisory committee of experts under Lord Parker of Waddington, a famous patent judge; and they reported that 'the Marconi system is at present the only system of which it can be said with any certainty that it is capable of fulfilling the requirements of the Imperial chain'.

The inquiry about ministers raised more controversy. The postmaster-general was acquitted; but three others—Lloyd George, Sir Rufus Isaacs, and the Master of Elibank (who had since left the government for quite different reasons)—were shown to have held shares, not in the British Marconi Company, with which the Post Office was concerned, but in a parallel one formed for the United States. There was no question of their corruptly influencing the decision; for their earliest purchases of shares were made more than five weeks after the tender's acceptance had been announced to the public. On this the committee were unanimous, as also in finding that there was no case of

---

[1] B. 1860; educated at University College School and in Brussels and Hanover. Q.C. 1898; M.P. 1904; solicitor-general, 1910; attorney-general, 1910–13; lord chief justice (with peerage as Lord Reading), 1913; on special missions to the United States, 1915 and 1917; ambassador at Washington, 1918; viceroy of India, 1921–6; foreign secretary, August–October 1931; d. 1935. He was the first attorney-general to be made a member of the cabinet.

ministers having used any privileged knowledge to buy stocks which they knew, and the public did not, must rise. But other points invited criticism. A brother of Sir Rufus Isaacs was the secretary of the British Marconi Company, and had originally offered him the American Marconi shares; though he declined them then, and only subsequently took them off another brother. It was these shares which formed the first purchases of all three ministers; and but for the relationship between the attorney-general and the secretary of the company, the offer of them could scarcely have come their way. Again, though the American and British companies were quite distinct, and though the Majority Report of the select committee held reasonably enough on the evidence that 'the ministers concerned, when entering into the purchases, were all bona-fide convinced that the American company had no interest in the agreement', it is pretty obvious that the Minority Report was also right in claiming that such an interest existed and was 'material, though indirect'.

The committee were divided; the liberal majority acquitted the ministers, while the conservative minority led by Lord Robert Cecil found that the original purchases were a 'grave impropriety', and that the ministers, for keeping silence about them in the debate of 11 October, were 'wanting in frankness and in respect for the House of Commons'. Isaacs and Lloyd George, while asseverating their good faith, freely owned their error of judgement, and to the house of commons (18 June 1913) expressed regrets for it. The house eventually had before it two amendments to an original motion and an original amendment. The one, moved by an influential liberal back-bencher, accepted the ministers' expressions of regret, acquitted them of acting otherwise than in good faith, and reprobated the charges of corruption. The other, propounded by Bonar Law with the rasping violence which at that time he affected, expressed 'the regret of the House' instead of accepting that of the ministers, and if carried would have entailed the resignations of them both. But the former was adopted on a party vote. This was a bad conclusion to an episode unfortunate throughout. A smoke-screen of rumour and press innuendo had disturbed the public with suggestions of serious corruption. They were found to be baseless, and it was important that parliament without distinction of party should dispel them; for corruption is a real danger, and to sanction cries of 'Wolf', when no wolves are there, is not at all the way to keep such dangers off. In ordinary times the conservatives would have met the need. It gave an alarming measure of their frayed temper and weak leadership, that they stuck instead to party vendetta.

Suffragist militancy had entered on a new phase in June 1909, when an imprisoned militant went on hunger-strike. As she obtained her release, her example was soon widely followed. The authorities after a while countered by forcibly feeding the prisoners through tubes—a difficult and sometimes dangerous operation till then practised chiefly in lunatic asylums. About the same time the militants, whose heckling of ministers had been made very difficult, took to a new tactic, destroying property to advertise their claims. At first it was confined to window-breaking, but even so gave the authorities much trouble. 'The argument of the broken pane', declared Mrs. Pankhurst characteristically some years later, 'is the most valuable argument in modern politics.' A constant round of excitements, imprisonments, and now hunger-strikes, had brought a great many militants into a psychopathic state, where it was not easy either to save society from them or them from themselves.

After a six months' crescendo the W.S.P.U. called a truce for the first 1910 election, and this on various grounds was extended till the following November. Meanwhile suffragists of many schools and parties came together and evolved a 'Conciliation Bill', intended to combine them all. The combination was for the time effected, but at the cost of giving the bill a very pro-conservative cast;[1] and after passing second reading by 299 votes to 189, it was by 320 to 175 referred to committee of the whole house, i.e. shelved. A violent episode of militancy in November was succeeded by a truce for the second 1910 election, which again lasted till the following November. During 1911 a modified Conciliation Bill passed second reading by 167 majority; and though the government refused further time for it in that session, Asquith in June promised to find 'a week or more', and to raise 'no obstacle to a proper use of the closure', if it passed second reading again in 1912. For a while this contented the W.S.P.U.; but after an

---

[1] As Miss Sylvia Pankhurst says with truth and point: 'it made the mistake of flouting the interests of the political party in power, which alone could ensure its passage' (*The Suffrage Movement* (1931), 338). The cross-issue between suffragism and democracy played a great part at this time, strong believers in women's suffrage like Lloyd George and Ramsay MacDonald being unwilling to give it in a form which would only enfranchise single women with property, for the most part elderly and conservative.

interview with the prime minister on 17 November it declared
war again. The new campaign consisted almost entirely of widespread attacks on property (chiefly window-breaking, though
arson was tried in a few cases), followed by hunger-strikes in
prison, when the culprits were found and convicted. These were
profound errors; they exasperated parliament; and when in
March 1912 the Conciliation Bill came again for second reading,
it was defeated by 14 votes. In July the government introduced
a democratic Reform Bill, which, though believed capable of being
amended to include women, was, as drafted, for men only. The
W.S.P.U. had consequently to decide whether the militancy
which had failed should be called off or intensified.

The decision to intensify was that of Christabel Pankhurst.
From July 1912 she began a yet more violent policy—the organization of secret arson. Using her influence over her mother,
Mrs. Pankhurst, she drove from the Union the Pethick-Lawrences
who opposed this newest militancy; and establishing herself outside the jurisdiction in an office in Paris, proceeded for two years
(save for short truces) to organize a campaign of crime. Arson in
many forms was the staple; letters in pillar-boxes were set on fire;
many empty houses (some very large), public and private pavi-
lions, boat-houses, a grand-stand, a railway station, and a school
or two, were burned down; later, bombs were exploded, pictures
in public galleries slashed; the British Museum and the Tower
attacked; golf greens and Kew orchid-houses destroyed; telephone wires cut; and hundreds of false fire-alarms given. These
offences engaged a number of women and went on all over the
country. They were too serious to tolerate, yet very difficult to
stop or punish; for those sentenced regularly went on hunger-
strike, and forcible feeding was an ugly affair, about which public
opinion grew uneasy. It was not till the middle of 1913, when
McKenna, then home secretary, passed the 'Cat and Mouse' Act
(enabling him to release hunger-strikers, so that they should not
die on the government's hands, and to rearrest them afterwards
practically at pleasure), that the authorities regained the upper
hand in the struggle. Nevertheless it went on; and continued to
do much to foster the vogue for die-hard anarchism, while doing
less than nothing to help women's suffrage.

That cause had a gleam of new hope, when the government
promised to accept any feminist amendment which the commons
might make to its Reform Bill. Three alternatives were put down

for the committee stage in January 1913, and the passage of one
or other seemed assured, when the Speaker caused universal
surprise by holding that they were out of order and the bill could
not be passed with them. This affected not only the amendments
to enfranchise women, but one by the government to enfranchise
a new class of men; so eventually the measure had to be withdrawn and a mere Plural Voting Bill substituted. Meanwhile the
madness of the later militancy was throwing thoughtful friends of
the suffrage back on the constitutional suffrage societies; and the
scale of their propaganda grew rapidly. In the year 1913 those
combined in the National Union of Suffrage Societies spent over
£45,000[1] in a well-organized propaganda, whose effect was
beyond question considerable.

After the Agadir crisis there was a considerable revulsion
among the parties supporting the government against the newly
disclosed extent of Great Britain's commitments to France. The
radical formula was 'allies to none and friends to all'—an excellent one, if it were practicable. Hitherto, as we have seen, it had
not been; Grey's attempts to make a friendship with Germany on
a footing similar to those with France and Russia had foundered
over Germany's insistence that to join her he must leave them.
The British government now determined to try once more. At
the end of 1911, as a friendly gesture, they mooted lowering their
standard in battleships from 2 : 1 against Germany to 16 : 10.
Word came to them through a great financier, Sir Ernest Cassel,[2]
that the Germans would like to see a British minister at Berlin.
Haldane was on the point of visiting the country on some university business. He knew its ways and language, and the Kaiser
liked him. So he was detailed for the task, which in February
1912 he discharged with his customary ability.

Tirpitz, the Grand-Admiral, was clever at extracting from
events the moral that Germany needed a larger fleet. He had
exploited Lloyd George's Mansion House speech in that sense,
and a Navy Law of 1912 was the result. Haldane did not discuss
it, but he brought back a copy of the draft, and also Berlin's conditions for a political agreement. They were, as before, that England should promise benevolent neutrality in any war. The

---

[1] Dame M. G. Fawcett, *The Women's Victory and After* (1920), 55.
[2] He and Albert Ballin, the German shipping magnate, had been semi-officially
negotiating about the naval question, off and on, for some years.

British cabinet then offered an alternative—a formula of mutual friendship and non-aggression. But the Germans insisted on adding: 'England will therefore as a matter of course remain neutral if war is forced upon Germany.' Since Germany's wars were always 'forced upon' her, this was the old formula again, whose acceptance would terminate the Entente. But, as Asquith observed in his cabinet report to the king, 'if there had been no Entente at all Great Britain would have been bound in her own interest to refuse it', since it would 'have precluded us from coming to the help of France, should Germany on any pretext attack her and aim at getting possession of the Channel ports'.[1] Nothing therefore came of the Haldane mission, and the British government had to resign itself to building against Tirpitz's new programme, which was formidable indeed. Later in the year a further defensive step was taken. We saw above how, beginning in 1904, the admiralty utilized the Anglo-French Entente to transfer the fighting strength of the navy from the Mediterranean to the Atlantic and the North Sea—a policy which greatly lessened the cost of meeting the German menace. After being extended by degrees it was now pushed to its conclusion, the British battleships assuming first-line responsibility for the Atlantic and Channel, while the French assumed that for the Mediterranean. Had there been an Anglo-French Alliance, nothing could have been more rational; but there was not. Therefore on 22 November 1912, after consultation with the cabinet, important letters were exchanged by the foreign secretary and the French ambassador, putting on record that the military and naval consultations must not be held to tie either government's hands; and a special clause noted that 'the disposition of the French and British fleets respectively at the present moment is not based upon an engagement to co-operate in war'. No verbal caveat, however, could quite undo the logic of the facts. Moreover, the same letter contained an undertaking that, if war threatened either, the two governments would consult; and this (inserted at the wish of Poincaré) was new as a formal commitment.

But soon a new quarter engaged the attention of Europe. Under the impact of Italy's Tripolitan war the Young Turk régime at Constantinople began to totter. There were several military mutinies and semi-revolts, and in June the Moslem Albanians, on whom the Sultans were wont to rely as ultra-

---

[1] J. A. Spender and Cyril Asquith, *Life of Asquith* (1932), ii. 68.

loyalist, broke out in rebellion, not against Turkey, but against the régime. They won a considerable battle near Mitrovitza, and proceeded to overflow wide areas coveted by Serbia, Greece, or Montenegro. The Monastir garrison mutinied in sympathy; and on 17 July 1912 the Young Turk leaders resigned, and a government of different complexion succeeded them.

Unknown to any Power but Russia the Christian states of the Balkans had ere this formed alliances. The idea had been mooted for some time past,[1] but the obstacle was at Sofia. The clever, shifty Tsar Ferdinand was at bottom pro-Austrian (or rather pro-Magyar); and thanks to him the anti-Russian and anti-Serb tendency continued to rule the country after popular opinion had moved the other way. But in March 1911 he had to accept a pro-Russian cabinet; and after Italy attacked Turkey in the autumn, Bulgaria and Serbia drew together.[2] They were united by the Ottomanizing policy of the Young Turks, whose anarchy and massacres in Macedonia menaced the interests of both. On 14 March 1912 Bulgaria signed a treaty with Serbia, and on 29 May with Greece. Serbia and Greece also signed a treaty, and there were understandings with Montenegro. The critical pact between Bulgaria and Serbia[3] had a secret annex, which (with a military convention soon following it) pointed towards early war for the conquest and partition of European Turkey. Its conclusion was not a little due to the Russian minister at Belgrade, Hartwig; and it provided that in certain problems of the partition which it left unsettled the Tsar should be arbiter. It was communicated to that monarch by a Bulgarian deputation on 7 May, and well received by him; but his foreign minister, Sazonov, strongly enjoined caution and delay. Officially Russia was at this time still in agreement with Austria-Hungary to prop up Turkey.

But then came the Albanian insurrection, the Young Turk break-down, massacres at Kotchani and Berana, and the Albanian seizure of Üsküb. After six weeks of growing agitation, the Balkan Allies mobilized on 30 September 1912, the Turks follow-

---

[1] e.g. there was a Greek military proposal to Bulgaria in August 1910: Gooch and Temperley, *British Documents*, ix, pt. i (1933), 199.

[2] The first interview between the two premiers was on 11 October 1911, just twelve days after Italy declared war on Turkey.

[3] The texts of the various treaties and conventions made by Bulgaria before the war will all be found in I. E. Gueshoff, *The Balkan League* (English version by C. C. Mincoff, 1915).

ing suit next day. The Powers, who had been fencing with the Porte about 'reforms' in the usual fashion, made last-minute efforts to stop war. On 10 October Russia and Austria issued a Joint Note stating that, if it occurred, they would 'tolerate at the end of the conflict no modifications of the present territorial *status quo* in European Turkey'. Undeterred, the four Allies declared war on Turkey on 18 October. They were speedily victorious in every field. Turkey's main army in Thrace was crushed by the Bulgarians in the battles of Kirk Kilisseh (22–3 October) and Lule Burgas (28–9 October); her main Macedonian army by the Serbians at Kumanovo (27–8 October); while the Greeks, the weakest of the three main Allies, had defeated another force at Elassona. Macedonia was speedily swept clear of Turks; Salonica fell to the Greeks on 8 November, and Monastir to the Serbians ten days later; while in Thrace the Ottoman army, leaving Adrianople to be invested, fell back on the Tchataldja lines for the defence of Constantinople. There a Bulgarian assault was repulsed on 17 November, the first check to the Allied progress.

These victories pleased all lovers of freedom, because they liberated a large area of mainly Christian population from the hideous misgovernment of the Turk. But they also set a slow-burning match to the powder-barrels of Europe; and it is important at this stage to see how and why. Behind the strife of local forces stood the vital interests of Great Powers—those of Russia, on the one hand, and those of Austria-Hungary and Germany on the other.

Russia had her immemorial quest for a warm-water access to the sea. Foiled elsewhere, she was now concentrated on seeking it at what anyhow was the best point for her empire, the Bosphorus and Dardanelles. 'Freedom of the Straits' under a weak Turkey was her immediate object; the reversion of Constantinople when the Turks collapsed, her further goal. Her method of approach was to dominate the Balkan peninsula through its Slav inhabitants; and her chief obstacle to it, the mutual jealousy of Serbs and Bulgars. For non-Slavs, like the Greeks and Rumanians, she had much less regard, though naturally she preferred to have them on her side. Her primary fear was of Austria-Hungary. British opposition was now relaxed (though not expressly waived). But the 'ramshackle' bulk of the Dual Monarchy lay as a Great Power on the flank of the advance; and for its disintegration hardly less than that of Turkey the Pan-slavist idea was worked.

Austria-Hungary's outlook was mainly defensive, though she had also certain appetites—e.g. that (which set her against the Greeks) for Salonica. Her concern was to keep the Balkan States small and weak, that they might not divide and despoil her. For two of them had large irredentas within her borders. Transylvania, though diversified by German and Magyar colonists, was really a Ruman country; and in the Banat of Temesvar, Croatia, Southern Dalmatia, and Bosnia-Herzegovina were comprised more Serbs than in Serbia herself, besides the natural sea outlets, of which the small kingdom was deprived. The other Southern Slavs in that Monarchy were nearly related; while the Czechs in the north were extremely Russophile. The two ruling races, the Austro-Germans and Magyars, were mutually hostile, and only held together by fear of Russia and desire to dominate the other elements—both passions being peculiarly strong among the Magyars. The Balkan policy of the Monarchy was to maintain Turkey, as a bulwark against Russia and the Slavs generally; to keep Serbia small and land-locked, and, if a chance offered, to fall on and crush her; and to work towards Salonica by economic penetration. There was an alliance with Rumania, but, owing to Transylvania, no cordiality. The sole Balkan people friendly to Austria-Hungary had been the Bulgarians; for they had not an irredenta under her flag. But her long failure to prevent Turkey from massacring their fellow Bulgars in Macedonia and Thrace had driven them at last, despite Magyar-loving Tsar Ferdinand, into the arms of Russia and Serbia; with the results that we have seen.

These results, then, were not merely a triumph of Christian liberators over Turks, but a victory for Russia in the Balkans, and a blow for Austria-Hungary. But behind the latter stood Germany, the 'brilliant second' who in 1908–9 had enabled her to defy Russia and put down Serbia in the Bosnian crisis. Germany could not afford to desert Austria, her one firm ally in Europe; and besides she had interests and ambitions of her own. We saw earlier how the Berlin-to-Bagdad idea was started in the nineties, and evolved towards that of creating a solid block of German influence from the Baltic to the Persian Gulf. In this gigantic conception key parts were assigned to Austria—cast out from Germany proper, but remaining a spear-head of 'Germanism' among her subject races; to the Magyars—who were brought to love Berlin as much as they hated Vienna; and to the Turks— won over by two decades of able and unscrupulous work to regard Germany as their one true friend and the German army as the only model for Ottoman fighters. Minor parts were reserved for Rumania or Bulgaria, of which the Kaiser (who was apt to think in terms of crowned heads) preferred the former for personal reasons. The strong point about this conception was that it called for no use of ships, but only that of armies and railways, in which Germany was already supreme; and had she taken the one task at a time, and not alarmed England by building Tirpitz's premature and provocative fleet, she might have put herself into a position of such power and wealth, that the trident would subsequently have fallen into her lap. But all these prospects dissolved like dreams, if once a permanent block of united and Russophile Slavdom were to dominate the Balkans, followed, as it must be, by Russia's own advent on the Golden Horn. The conflict between the two thrusts—the Russian north to south and the German west to east—was absolute.[1] And it needs to be clearly grasped, because it was what motived the war of 1914.

What special concerns had the British government in the issue? Directly, none; indirectly, several. In the first place, if war came France would be drawn in under the terms of the Dual Alliance; and her participation would at once raise questions—even if there had been no Entente—of the Channel ports and of oversea possessions. But secondly, there was the even more fundamental fact of Germany's naval challenge. Could the island-Empire stand passively aside and see the mastery of the Continent pass to the one Power which already threatened it on the element by which it lived? Thirdly, there was the special and neutral interest which Britain, as the world's greatest trading and financing nation, had in peace.

Grey showed wisdom and skill in this crisis. He kept in the foreground the consideration last mentioned, and so far won the confidence of both sides, that they agreed to deal with the situation, as it developed, through a conference of ambassadors meeting in London under his chairmanship from December onwards.

---

[1] Though as late as 1911 so little appreciated by Bethmann-Hollweg, that for transitory reasons he was ready to concede the Straits to Russia. The arguments of Marschall von Bieberstein against this course are well worth reading: *Die Grosse Politik*, xxxiii (1926); see especially pp. 224–5, 230–1, 243–5. Bethmann-Hollweg had not much knowledge of foreign affairs.

After a second failure of the Bulgarians before Tchataldja (which all the Powers really welcomed, since none of them desired a Bulgarian occupation of Constantinople), an armistice was signed there on 3 December, from which only the Greeks stood out. On 16 December the peace delegates met in London; and till the last week in January 1913 two conferences proceeded side by side—that of the belligerents agreeing terms of peace and that of the ambassadors revising them. The Powers had let lapse the threat of 10 October against territorial modifications, and recognized that in a broad way what the Balkan Allies had won they must be allowed to hold. The chief exception concerned the Adriatic. There the Serbians had pressed through Northern Albania to the coast and occupied Durazzo and Alessio. Inland farther north the Montenegrins were blockading Scutari, which for economic reasons they were desperately eager to annex. Farther south the Greeks coveted Valona, but, when they shelled it on 3 December, had been warned off by Austria-Hungary and Italy. The Albanians themselves had declared their independence on 28 November. Austria, backed by Germany, insisted that all these places must go to them, the Montenegrins be kept to their mountains, and Serbia be still excluded from the sea. On the other side Russia, backed by France, stood up for her Slav protégés. The Germanic Powers were dour and sore; they felt that Russia had stolen a very long march on them. Some aggrandizement of Serbia they could not veto, but at least at all costs they must keep her from the Adriatic.

Now here the British foreign secretary followed a remarkable course. His professed attitude at the conference was that of the honest broker. But in fact he threw his weight strongly on the side of Germany and Austria.[1] The other Entente Powers were displeased, considering, perhaps rightly, that the Central Powers had been caught off their guard and would have swallowed worse terms without a rupture. Grey, however, was anxious not merely for present but for future peace. He wanted to prove to the Central Powers that, so far from scheming to 'encircle' them, Great Britain, wherever they were the threatened party, would do her best to secure them fair play. Here was his opportunity to ratify by deeds the assurance which he had often proffered in words. He took it in a manner that could not be overlooked. His

---

[1] As recognized by Prince Lichnowsky, who was present as German ambassador: *My Mission to London*, 10–11.

gesture, as we shall see, was lost on Germany; but if, on the balance of forces within her, she had really been a peace-loving Power only plagued by 'encirclement', it would not have been. In that sense it supplied an acid test.

The effects on the Balkans were not good. In their plan to divide the conquered territory, the Balkan Allies had shared Albania between Serbia and Greece. Of Macedonia a north-west corner was to go to Serbia, and a southern belt to Greece, but the main mass of the country, which was ethnically Bulgar, was assigned to Bulgaria. When Serbia and Greece found Albania barred to them, they began to claim compensation from Bulgaria, which, since it meant surrendering her kith and kin, she was very loth to give. The dispute was interrupted by a Young Turk revolution at Constantinople. It caused a resumption of the war. But the Ottoman luck was out; their beleaguered fortresses—Adrianople, Yanina, and Scutari[1]—had to capitulate; and at a resumed London Conference peace was signed (30 May 1913) leaving Turkey nothing in Europe but the small area between Constantinople and the Enos-Midia line. Then Serbia and Greece banded themselves firmly against Bulgaria; and after the Tsar had in vain offered mediation and both sides had moved round their armies, the second Balkan war began with a Bulgarian offensive on 30 June. In its opening phase it was very unlike the first, for both sides had learnt the value of trenches; they dug themselves in, and brought each other almost at once to a standstill. But then Rumania, which had earlier received compensation for passivity, moved into the war claiming more. Her large fresh army marched down on the undefended rear of exhausted Bulgaria, and Tsar Ferdinand had to submit. Peace was signed at Bucharest (10 August 1913). What Rumania herself took was not immoderate,[2] but by her action large parts of Macedonia containing Bulgar population went to Serbia and Greece, while Bulgaria was almost cut off from the Aegean again, and even lost Adrianople to the Turks, who filched it back in her extremity. Serbia came out of the two wars a much larger state than she went in, even though some of her new subjects were not willing ones. Moreover, her troops were considered by

[1] The dispute over this place came nearest to wrecking the Ambassadors' Conference; but by a mixture of threats, money, and naval blockade its Montenegrin captors were got out of it without actual military measures.
[2] About 3,250 square miles and 340,000 inhabitants.

good judges to have excelled any others on the field of battle, and their artillery, which was French, had given better results than the Krupp guns of their adversaries. These results so distressed Austria-Hungary, that a day or two before the Bucharest Treaty was signed she secretly invited the support of her Allies, Germany and Italy, in an attack on Serbia, which she defined as 'defensive action' involving the *casus foederis*. Italy refused to regard it in that light; and for the time the project dropped.[1] Otherwise the European war might have been anticipated by eleven months.

But the Austrian attitude, though serious, was not the gravest new fact for Europe. Austria had a fire-eating chief of the general staff, Conrad von Hötzendorf, who habitually urged war on any suitable pretext. She had also early in 1912 lost her foreign minister, Count Aehrenthal, and taken as his successor Count Berchtold, a man much more pliable to Conrad's impulses. But in the last resort she could never plunge without the backing of Germany; and this, though difficult to refuse, could not be taken for granted. Graver, then, than any effect on Vienna was the effect of the Balkan events on Berlin. It is clear that in January 1913 a decision was there taken, that war between the Triple and Dual Alliances had become inevitable, and that Germany's business was to prepare for it instantly and bring it about when she was ready—in her time, not in her enemies'. For in that month were formulated plans, which in March became printed bills for the Reichstag, not merely to augment the army's annual intake of conscripts from 280,000 to 343,000 (by including all hitherto exempted fit men), and to make corresponding increases of officers, non-commissioned officers, horses, guns, &c., but to raise for non-recurring military purposes a capital levy of 1,000 million marks. Germany, it must be remembered, was already before this taxed to the utmost. She was not a rich country compared with England or France; she had scarcely any money to spare for foreign investment; her mushroom industries were in few instances on a lucrative basis apart from state orders. So painful had grown the pinch of taxation that the Reichstag was almost mutinous. Yet here was a project to pile on top of it in one year 1,000 million marks—a sum equivalent in gold for the foreign exchange to about £50 million sterling, but in German domestic

[1] These facts were first disclosed by Giolitti, then Italian prime minister, in the Italian Chamber on 5 December 1914.

values very much more. No statesman in Europe had ever before dreamed of raising by extra taxation, in one year and during peace, so enormous an extra sum as this then seemed. Lloyd George's 1909 budget, which convulsed British politics and society, was only for an addition of about £15 millions. It looks plain in retrospect (though confused for contemporaries by smoke-screens) that if such a supreme sacrifice were imposed for war-making, the war would have to be made, since it could not possibly be imposed twice. And the decision shows all the starker against the background of the conciliatory and reassuring treatment which Germany and her Ally were experiencing at this very time from Grey in the London Conference.

Who made the decision at Berlin? The general staff.[1] How far they carried with them, save for immediate steps, the Kaiser or the civil authorities, we need not inquire, beyond noting that everything material done by the latter fitted into the military plan. For what date was the war designed? There are reasons for thinking that from the inception the date worked towards was the beginning of August 1914. Early August was well recognized as the proper (almost the obligatory) season to choose for launching a war, because it was that at which the German army had most fully digested its conscripts, and had a maximum strength of trained men.[2] It was arranged that the war levy should be collected by instalments, to be spent at once as they came in;[3] and the last was to be in before midsummer 1914, so that by August of that year the army would be completely equipped. The widening of the Kiel Canal, for lack of which Germany's dreadnoughts were still unable to use that route between the North Sea and the Baltic, was to be completed just in time for the same date. An extra argument for that date was early supplied by the French. In answer to Germany's increase of her peace-time effectives they could not, like her, conscribe a margin of hitherto exempted fit men, because they had none. Instead, they lengthened the period of each conscript's service from two years to three. This was calculated to make them much

---

[1] For a fuller discussion of the relation at this time of the rival German authorities, see Appendix C, section 2.

[2] It also allowed sufficient time to deal with Russia before the winter, after crushing France, under the Schlieffen time-table, in six weeks.

[3] Which incidentally facilitated payment, as big steel or munition firms could pay in a large cheque to the levy, and receive it back the same day in payment for war material.

stronger by August 1915, but in August 1914, owing to the difficulties of the change-over, actually weaker.

What was the reaction of British statesmen to these portents? They took surprisingly little account of them. In August, almost at the very time when Austria-Hungary was sounding her Allies about immediate war, Grey allowed the Ambassadors' Conference to close down, on the assumption that there was no more occasion for it. It was a pity; for it was the one place in Europe where the six Powers could meet round a table, and it brought together some, e.g. Great Britain and Austria-Hungary, which knew very little of each other's standpoints and had few other opportunities of learning.[1] Nor was another controversy long in coming. In November the Young Turks appointed General Liman von Sanders, the successor of General von der Goltz at the head of a German Military Mission, to command their 1st Army Corps at Constantinople. The Russian foreign minister, Sazonov, not unreasonably objected to this as equivalent to posting a German garrison on the Bosphorus. He wanted a strong note from the Triple Entente, but Grey demurred, and a verbal inquiry at the Porte was substituted. In the end by a compromise General Liman resigned the 1st Corps and became instead 'Inspector-General' of the Ottoman Army. The change was more titular than material; and Liman at Constantinople was worth a great deal to Germany after the outbreak of the European war.

But during most of these months the British cabinet seems to have centred such attention as it could spare for foreign affairs round a single point—the immediately vital one for Great Britain; viz. the threat of the German Fleet. Despite all previous rebuffs, Churchill (26 March 1913) proposed a 'naval holiday'. Germany was due to lay down two capital ships in the twelve months, and Britain four; why not let the six stand over? In the autumn (18 October 1913) he repeated the offer in more detail; but German pronouncements on it were all adverse. There were in truth some solid objections; e.g. the need to provide continuous occupation for plants and workmen. While attempts to conjure the threat failed, Grey tried patiently to mollify the threatener by reaching peaceful settlements of outstanding Anglo-German questions. He was here much helped by the German ambassador, Prince Lichnowsky, whose personal goodwill was beyond

---

[1] As Mr. J. A. Spender has acutely observed: *Fifty Years of Europe*, 388–9.

doubt and who was well seconded by his immediate subordinate, Baron Kühlmann. Two very large pieces of negotiation were carried through. One was a revision of the 1898 agreement about the reversion of the Portuguese colonies in Africa; the other comprised parallel arrangements with Turkey and with Germany about the Bagdad railway, Mesopotamia, and the Persian Gulf. The first was embodied in an Agreement initialled in August 1913; the second, so far as Germany was concerned, in a Convention of June 1914. Owing to delays by Germany, neither had been signed when the European war broke out; and it is still uncertain how far Berlin cared about them save as baits which might help to keep Great Britain neutral in that event. Yet they were very favourable to Germany, representing the liberal government's fixed idea of overcoming her hostility by kindness.

Anxious as the British ministers were, partly for financial reasons, to persuade her to stop building against them, they remained slow, partly for the same reasons, to face the naval consequences of her refusal. Though Rosyth's defences had never been completed and the insecurity of its site[1] was recognized, it was not till 1912 that they decided to make Cromarty and Scapa Flow defensible. Yet by August 1914 not one of the three places had been rendered secure; and Jellicoe's Grand Fleet was to spend many perilous months at the beginning of the European war keeping constantly at sea, because it had no safe harbour to lie in. In the winter of 1913–14 a strong party in the cabinet became so much impressed by the friendliness of Lichnowsky and Kühlmann that they urged cutting down the naval estimates. Lloyd George at the exchequer led this movement, and early in 1914 the conflict between him and Churchill reached such a pitch that it seemed as if one or other must resign. Asquith's genius for compromise alone kept them together.

During 1912–13 central and southern Ireland were convulsed by a succession of strikes and lock-outs centred round a body called the Irish Transport Workers' Union. This was a syndicalist organization by no means confined to transport, run by two leaders of opposite and complementary types—James Larkin, a voluble, loud-voiced, large-limbed Irishman, who liked fighting for its own sake without deeply studying what it was about, and

[1] Inland of the great Forth Bridge and liable to be cut off from the sea by its demolition.

James Connolly, a small, silent, remorseless desperado, compact of courage and scheming. Their violent methods at first scored many successes. But then the employers rallied, and a lock-out, which began on the Dublin tramways in mid-August 1913, spread to most of the other districts and firms where the union had members. All through the rest of the year it was bitterly fought on both sides; and in January 1914 the union's effort collapsed.

The struggle had consequences beyond itself. It created a cleavage between the Irish nationalist party and the Dublin workers, driving the latter over to Sinn Fein;[1] and it brought into existence for the first time in southern Ireland a 'private army' similar to the Ulster Volunteers. This began as quite a small affair, formed to keep the strikers out of mischief; but before the dispute was over, its example gave rise, as we shall see, to a political body. In the same January the British trade-union world witnessed a 'Triple Alliance' for the first time between the railway workers, the transport workers, and the miners. The immediate object was to synchronize the expiry of their agreements, so that disputes, if any, might be synchronized also. But it was really a victory for the syndicalist idea.

The autumn of 1913 had seen also the first moves towards a compromise on the Home Rule Bill. On 11 September, after it had twice passed the commons and twice been rejected by the lords, a letter in *The Times* from Lord Loreburn, the ex-lord chancellor, urged a policy of special treatment for Ulster. In the cabinet two years earlier, when Lloyd George originally proposed this, Loreburn, a doctrinaire radical, had been its leading opponent; but now he recoiled from the consequences. About the same time Bonar Law and Lansdowne put forward a demand, backed by four eminent unionist lawyers,[2] that the king should force a dissolution by dismissing Asquith. Such a course would have been legal, just as the lords' rejection of the budget in 1909 was legal; but, if not so flatly unconstitutional as that was, it would have been even more disastrous. The sole modern precedent—William IV's dismissal of Lord Melbourne in 1834—was the reverse of encouraging. But now to make the Crown the unionists' agent for the purpose of cancelling the Parliament Act

[1] Whence their later prominence in the rebellion of Easter 1916 under the leadership of Connolly, who was executed for his part in it.

[2] Lord Halsbury, Sir William Anson, Professor A. V. Dicey, and Mr. (afterwards lord chancellor) Cave.

would have been incalculably more serious; it would have brought the Monarchy right down into the arena, not merely of party, but of faction, and have created a breach between it and the rising democracy scarcely possible to repair. Fortunately an unanswerable memorandum from Asquith to the king[1] put the idea out of court. Meanwhile the king took advantage of the peace-current started by Loreburn's letter. At Balmoral in September conversations took place between Churchill and Bonar Law; and later, writing from the same place, Asquith arranged to meet Bonar Law himself. At their interviews (14 October and 6 November 1913) Bonar Law gave as his terms 'the permanent exclusion of the four north-eastern counties "plus perhaps Tyrone and one other", with an option of inclusion at some later date, if these counties so decided'.[2] A settlement on this basis might have avoided much subsequent evil; though even if Asquith had accepted, it is doubtful whether Bonar Law could have implemented his offer. Lansdowne in particular, whom he had not consulted, and who was habitually deaf to reason in Irish matters, might probably have played a wrecking part in the name of the southern unionists,[3] as he afterwards did in 1916. However Asquith, as he told Redmond later, 'gave no countenance whatever to this idea'.[4] Nor did the cabinet, but lent ear instead to an ingenious alternative suggested by Lloyd George. This was to amend the bill by postponing its coming into force in the Ulster counties for five years. The idea was, not to procure the Ulstermen's consent, but to spike their guns; since it was thought that they could neither go to war in 1914 to prevent something which would not happen till 1919, nor keep up their organization five years longer to resist at the later date. But even about this no decision was reached and (in deference to Redmond) no announcement made. From mid-December to mid-January Asquith conducted an extremely secret negotiation with Carson; but as none of the fancy safeguards which the prime minister elaborated could divert the Ulster leader from his plain demand for exclusion, nothing came of it.[5]

[1] Printed in J. A. Spender and Cyril Asquith's *Life of Asquith*, ii. 29–31.
[2] Ibid. ii. 35.
[3] See his letter to Carson of the following day, given in Ian Colvin, *Life of Lord Carson*, ii (1934), 220–2.
[4] Denis Gwynn, *Life of John Redmond* (1932), 234.
[5] The curious documents of this episode are printed in Ian Colvin, *Life of Lord Carson*, ii (1934), 262–71.

While the parleys proceeded in private, in public Carson grew bolder and Bonar Law more violent than ever. On 28 November at Dublin the latter made an unmistakable appeal to the army to disobey orders when the time came. The political attitude of army officers, as Asquith had told Redmond eleven days earlier,[1] was already a grave matter. They were overwhelmingly unionist, and as a class drawn to a very disproportionate extent from the Anglo-Irish gentry, the 'garrison', whose unionism was hereditary. Lord Roberts, the last commander-in-chief, was Anglo-Irish; so was his predecessor, Lord Wolseley; so was the director of military operations, Sir Henry Wilson.[2] The first and last named were active partisans. Roberts chose the Ulster Volunteers' commander-in-chief for them. Wilson was in frequent contact with Bonar Law, and appears to have been in the habit of betraying official secrets to him.[3] Both in advising Carson's Volunteers and in fostering the idea among army officers that they should 'refuse to coerce Ulster', he took a leading part, quite impossible by any ordinary standards of honour to reconcile with the holding of his post.[4]

Three days before Bonar Law's Dublin speech a meeting held in that city with Professor John Macneill, one of the founders of the Gaelic movement, and P. H. Pearse,[5] a Gaelic teacher, as its principal sponsors, had formally launched a movement to enrol Irish Volunteers. Redmond distrusted the men and disliked the movement; but it grew very fast in spite of him. Asquith thereupon allowed Dublin Castle to perpetrate a characteristic folly. Till the end of 1905 there had been an embargo on import-

[1] He said that 'his information from the War Office with regard to the attitude of the Army was of a serious character, pointing to the probability of very numerous resignations of commissions of officers in the event of the troops being used to put down an Ulster insurrection. Some of the authorities estimated the number of these resignations as high as 30 per cent. He did not believe in this figure, but he was satisfied that there would be a number of resignations' (Denis Gwynn, *Life of Redmond*, 235–6).

[2] It is often supposed that the chief of staff, Sir John French (afterwards Earl of Ypres) was also Anglo-Irish, but in point of fact he had no nearer connexion with Ireland than his great-grandfather. His mother was Scottish. He was not a partisan.

[3] See the reference in Bonar Law's letter to Carson of 24 March 1914 (Ian Colvin, *Life of Lord Carson*, ii. 351).

[4] The evidence is that of his own diaries, quoted in Sir Charles Callwell's *Field-Marshal Sir Henry Wilson: His Life and Diaries* (1927), i. 137–47.

[5] In the Easter rising of 1916 he was first 'President of the Irish Republic' and afterwards executed. In 1913 he was secretly carrying out a mission in Ireland for the Fenians of the United States.

ing arms into Ireland, which the Campbell-Bannerman government took off as unnecessary. On the formation of the Ulster Volunteers it might well have been re-imposed, but was not. Now that Dublin formed Volunteers, it at once was. The inference drawn inevitably in Ireland reacted not only against Asquith but against Redmond, and in weakening him made more difficult the approach to any reasonable compromise.

After two months of discussion and negotiation, Asquith on 9 March 1914 (when moving for the third time the second reading of the Home Rule Bill) made known the government's proposals regarding Ulster. A White Paper gave the details, but the substance was that any county might by a majority of its parliamentary electors, vote itself out of home rule for six years. This, it will be seen, was a modified form of the earlier Lloyd George idea. In respect of its county basis it was very unfair to the Ulstermen. There were only four counties which as such were certain to yield them a majority—Antrim, Down, Armagh, and Derry; yet South Down, South Armagh, and parts of West Derry were much less truly their territory than large parts of Tyrone and Fermanagh. They also had good reason to resent the time-limit. The theory of it was that before it expired the electors of the United Kingdom would have been twice consulted,[1] and if they twice ratified Ulster's inclusion she would have no grievance. But in fact, of course, to make the inclusion of Ulster the sole issue at a general election in, say, 1919 would have been scarcely possible, and if possible, most undesirable. Carson therefore had equity on his side in demanding that there should be no time-limit upon Ulster's right to stay outside the Dublin parliament until she was persuaded to come in.

The proposals brought less than no immediate gain; for they were violently rejected by the unionists, and at the same time were so unpopular in Nationalist Ireland as further to weaken Redmond. Meanwhile the army trouble drew nearer. Lord Willoughby de Broke, leader of the Die-hards against the Parliament Bill, put about the idea that the house of lords should refuse to pass the Army Annual Act, thus depriving the government after 30 April of any disciplined force. The unpatriotic recklessness of such a course—at a time when Germany was making such war-preparations as Europe had never witnessed before, and when, with France, Russia, and Austria-Hungary

[1] i.e. not later than December 1915 and not later than December 1920.

all responding towards the limit of their inferior resources, the world almost visibly drifted towards catastrophe—may, in retrospect, take the reader's breath away. Yet such was the insularity of British politics and the temporary loss among unionists of any sense of proportion, that most of them jumped at the idea. Bonar Law became its leading advocate, and even talked over Sir Henry Wilson, who seems, if only on this occasion, to have become conscious of some conflict between his political intrigues and his professional duty. The cabinet therefore resolved to act, while yet there was time. It appointed a sub-committee which on 12 March sanctioned naval and military decisions. Churchill started transferring the Atlantic Fleet from the coast of Spain to the Isle of Arran, and Seely,[1] who in 1912 had succeeded Haldane as war minister, sent instructions to Major-General Sir Arthur Paget, commander-in-chief in Ireland, to concentrate and reinforce the troops in Ulster at a number of strategic points.[2] Churchill at Bradford on 14 March made a speech reflecting the government's new-found firmness.

Then on 20 March ensued the fateful episode at the Curragh. Paget had boggled about carrying out even his preliminary instructions. He came to London, and obtained from Seely a concession. Any officers whose domicile was in Ulster might, in the event of their units being ordered north, be allowed for the present (on giving their word of honour that they would not join the Carsonites) to 'disappear'. It was unwisely granted, since it implied admitting that something like civil war was in contemplation; but the unwisdom was greatly increased by Paget's clumsiness. Instead of quietly finding out who the few Ulster-domiciled officers might be and apprising them individually, he summoned a conference of all his general officers, and through them broadcast to the whole of the officers of the Curragh a notification that (a) those with an Ulster domicile might 'disappear'; (b) those without such a domicile should, if they were not prepared to undertake active operations against Ulster,

[1] B. 1868; educated at Harrow and Trinity College, Cambridge; served with Imperial Yeomanry, 1900–1; M.P. 1900; under-secretary for the colonies, 1908–10, for war 1911; secretary for war, 1912–14; distinguished service in the European war; under-secretary for munitions, 1918, for air, 1919. Cr. Lord Mottistone, 1933.

[2] What the plan was, to which these steps would have led up, was never disclosed; but Mr. Colvin (*Life of Lord Carson*, ii. 331–2) prints a detailed account from some papers which reached the Ulster Unionist Council 'through a trustworthy channel'. He does not name the 'channel', but it is perhaps unnecessary to look beyond Sir Henry Wilson.

send in their resignations, when they would be dismissed the army. Conferences took place later between the brigadiers and their colonels, and between the colonels and the officers of their regiments; and at the end of the day Paget telegraphed to the war office that the brigadier (General Hubert Gough[1]) and 57 (out of 70) officers of the 3rd Cavalry Brigade 'prefer to accept dismissal if ordered north'. Some colonels and many other officers in the infantry took similar action; and there is no doubt that in certain cases a good deal of pressure was put on individuals to offer their resignations with the rest.

The war office next ordered Gough and his three colonels to Whitehall. There on 23 March they proceeded to negotiate with the government, being covertly advised on every step by the government's own servant, Sir Henry Wilson. Parliament met the same day for the first time since the 'mutiny'[2] of the 20th, and the indignation of the government parties boiled over. The action of the officers was intensely unpopular in the country, and the foremost spokesmen on behalf of outraged democracy were labour leaders—John Ward[3] of the Navvies' Union, and J. H. Thomas, of the Railway Servants. Yet while the M.P.s protested, the heads of the war office were selling the pass. The cabinet had agreed to a memorandum in three paragraphs, the second of which ran: 'An officer or soldier is forbidden in future to ask for assurances as to orders which he may be required to obey.' In direct defiance of this Gough and his officers persisted in demanding a written assurance that they would not be called on 'to enforce the present Home Rule Bill on Ulster'. Seely, to appease them, with the approval of Morley, weakly added two more paragraphs, which he and the chief of staff and the quarter-master-general initialled; and when Gough asked whether they meant what he wanted, the chief of staff, Sir John French, initialled a written statement that they did. Gough returned victorious to the Curragh, where he had an ovation from his officers, and all resignations were withdrawn.

[1] Afterwards Sir Hubert Gough, commander of the Fifth Army in the European war.

[2] Strictly there was no mutiny, for the officers concerned disobeyed no order; they were offered an option to take a certain course, and took it. Yet if it be mutiny to conspire to paralyse from within the disciplined action of an army, unquestionably there was such a conspiracy, although the actual officers at the Curragh were not its authors.

[3] Who afterwards rendered the nation great service during the European war, where he organized and commanded, as colonel, a Navvies' Battalion.

The government majority was now, and with reason, thoroughly roused. So was the country, and there was reason to believe that, had Asquith then dissolved, the unionist party would have been swept away. But a government cannot be so irresponsible as the opposition under Bonar Law had become; and the prime minister had the foreign situation in his eye. A 'purge' of the old army caste was warranted on political grounds, and might probably in a few years have meant greater army efficiency; but for the time it would disorganize the Expeditionary Force. Seely and the two generals who initialled Gough's document had, of course, to resign; and in place of the former Asquith executed the heroic gesture of becoming war minister himself. His followers supposed that this betokened a drastic policy, such as only a prime minister could put through; in fact, it heralded a policy of surrender, such as only a prime minister could put over. He did not touch even the arch-offender, Sir Henry Wilson.

The Curragh episode, thus handled, disarmed the government. A month later, on 24 April, a second episode, the Larne gun-running, enabled the Ulster Volunteers to become armed. They had perhaps five or six thousand rifles before, and a limited stock of ammunition. But on this occasion they landed 30,000 rifles and bayonets and 3 million rounds. The affair was well organized by their chiefs, who mobilized a large force with remarkable secrecy, and were able without active violence to hold up all the police and coastguards of a wide area. It could hardly have been managed but for the palpable inefficiency into which Birrell, during his seven years' tenure of the Irish secretaryship, had allowed the Royal Irish Constabulary to lapse. Though it greatly altered the perspective in the Ulstermen's favour, one of its more immediate effects was probably not anticipated by them. This was a rush on the part of nationalists, especially in Ulster, to join the new National Volunteers. Soon they outnumbered the Carsonite force,[1] and continued to grow rapidly. So far there had been not a little friction between them and the parliamentary party. But early in June Redmond officially took over their leadership, and nationalism presented externally a united front.

In face of the menacing growth of these rival 'private armies'

[1] By the middle of May they were over 100,000, of whom one-third were in Ulster (Denis Gwynn, *Life of Redmond*, 307).

in Ireland Asquith continued to vacillate and play for time. On 26 May the Home Rule Bill completed its third passage through the commons, but it was not till 23 June that the government introduced in the house of lords their Amending Bill—still on the lines announced in March. A week later the most determined effort at settlement, which had yet been attempted, was made by Lord Murray of Elibank. Going to and fro between the parties with the concurrence of the king and the help of Lord Rothermere,[1] he brought to Redmond two days later the most practical terms to which the unionist leaders had yet consented. They were to exclude by plebiscite, not individual counties, but a selected area, which was that of to-day's Northern Ireland minus South Armagh, South Fermanagh, and possibly South Down. There was to be no time-limit, but an option to the area to rejoin the rest of Ireland by plebiscite at any time. Were this offer accepted, Bonar Law and Carson undertook to cease all opposition to home rule, to abandon all intention of repealing it if their party came into power, and to 'support and encourage the Irish Parliament in every way possible'. Here was perhaps the fairest chance ever offered to Ireland of reconciliation on a basis of freedom for both factions and coercion of neither; and had it been accepted it is difficult to think that in the event the partition would have survived the European war. But Redmond could not accept; Asquith's policy, or lack of policy, had too much weakened his authority. Besides, one of his strongest personal convictions was the unity of Ireland. He would sacrifice almost anything to avoid partition. Perhaps he sacrificed too much to that object.[2]

The chance passed and never really recurred. On 18 July King George (acting, as he was careful to state, on the prime minister's advice) summoned a conference of party leaders to attempt settlement. Eight attended (21 July)—Asquith and Lloyd George for the liberals, Bonar Law and Lansdowne for the conservatives, Redmond and Dillon for the nationalists, and Carson and Craig for the Ulster unionists. The king opened with a speech, and then asked the speaker (J. W. Lowther, afterwards the first Lord Ullswater) to take the chair. A better chairman could not have been wished, but there was small chance of succeeding in the clash of parties across a table where

---

[1] Whose brother, Lord Northcliffe, was not consulted in this matter.
[2] In 1918 it may be fairly said that he gave his own life for it—in vain.

under far more favourable conditions so expert a negotiator as Lord Murray had just failed. The conference lasted three days, and met on the fourth to wind up. Its time was given chiefly to arguments about the geography of exclusion in Northern Ireland, and particularly in Tyrone; but the disagreement remained much wider than that.[1]

On the day that it ended, the cabinet discussed its failure, and decided for the time being to 'wait and see'. As the members rose to go, the foreign secretary gravely claimed their attention; he had serious news. It was the text of the ultimatum sent by Austria-Hungary to Serbia the day before.

Two days later a fresh turn came to the Irish situation. After the Ulster gun-running it would have been prudent (since no steps were to be taken to disarm the Ulstermen) to remove the ban on importing arms. To continue it was to turn the ill-gotten Carsonite armament into a state-protected monopoly. Yet this was what Asquith and Birrell did. The natural result followed. On Sunday 26 July the National Volunteers carried out at Howth a gun-running on the Ulster model. The law being unaltered, it was the duty of Dublin Castle to stop it; and the assistant-commissioner of police, a Mr. Harrel, called out soldiers as well as police for the purpose. There was a scuffle on the road. The Volunteers got most of their rifles away, but Dublin was furious at the seeming discrimination between them and the Ulstermen. On marching back through the city the soldiers were stoned by the crowds, and at Bachelors' Walk they turned and fired on them. Three civilians were killed and thirty-eight injured—half of them seriously.

This shooting has its niche in Irish history. Asquith, horrified after the event, appointed a committee of inquiry under Lord Shaw of Dunfermline, which found fault with Harrel for calling out the troops. Then the European war caused parliament to forget it. But Ireland never did.

In the late spring of 1914, as the fateful August drew nearer, preparations in Germany for a war at that date had grown still more definite. The 1,000-million-mark levy was being duly collected and spent; the widening of the Kiel Canal, carried out to

---

[1] A brief account of it is given by Lord Ullswater, *A Speaker's Commentaries*, ii. 162–4; the fullest is in Denis Gwynn, *Life of John Redmond*, 336–42. The more summary sketch in Ian Colvin, *Life of Lord Carson*, 415–18, confirms the latter.

time. Now measures of another class were put in hand. At the peak of the Agadir crisis in September 1911 what had curbed Germany was financial panic and a run on the banks. That this should not recur when the war came, gold must temporarily be amassed in advance, and steps were accordingly taken that German firms should get in, as far as possible, all moneys due to them abroad. It could not be done without considerable disturbance of the London money market. The strain was first felt in the latter half of February, when the discount rate in the open market, which had been $1\frac{11}{16}$, was rapidly forced up to $2\frac{15}{16}$. In the course of March conditions eased again, and in April the rate fell back to $1\frac{3}{4}$. But in May the demand for gold became again abnormal, and the rate returned to $2\frac{15}{16}$. This lasted till near the end of the half-year, when the demand once more fell towards normal. As a result, the gold reserve in the Reichsbank on 15 July was a record for Germany.[1] The supply of silver was likewise exceptionally high. When the war came at the end of that month, it was found that Germany had collected nearly everything owing to her from her prospective enemies, while leaving her debts to them outstanding. It is significant that the main operations which by the beginning of August had produced this temporary situation—a situation which obviously could not have been maintained for long—were carried out before the assassination at Serajevo, chiefly in the month of May.

On the 12th of that month the German and Austro-Hungarian chiefs of staff had an interview. They did not meet often, and Moltke, the German, seems (perhaps wisely) to have been reticent towards his Austrian colleague, the fire-eating Conrad. In previous communications, of which we have record,[2] since the first Balkan war, the German staff's line to the Austrian is that the great war must come and the two Allies will wage it together, but it must not come *now*; they should complete their preparations and wait for the proper occasion. But at this May interview Moltke agreed with Conrad that the time was at hand: 'every delaying means a lessening of our chances'.[3] And they went on to discuss some details. Conrad wanted to know (it is

---

[1] Gooch and Temperley, *British Documents*, xi (1926), 205. The war-chest of gold coins at Spandau had simultaneously been increased by over 70 per cent.; but that, since it was a permanent hoard, has no particular bearing on dates.

[2] e.g. Moltke's letter to Conrad of 10 February 1913 (*Die grosse Politik*, xxxiv. 352; translated in Dugdale's *German Diplomatic Documents*, iv. 160).

[3] Baron Conrad von Hötzendorf, *Aus meiner Dienstzeit*, iii (1922), 670.

significant that till then he had not been precisely told) how
long Moltke's campaign against France would last, before he
could join Austria with large forces against Russia. The answer
was: Six weeks.

Anglo-German negotiations for the Mesopotamia treaty were
then nearing completion between Grey and Lichnowsky. Behind
them the Berlin foreign office still nursed the hope that Great
Britain might stand out of the struggle, as Napoleon III had
stood in 1866. 'On our side', Moltke told Conrad, 'I am sorry
to say they persist in awaiting a declaration from England that
she will be neutral. That declaration England will never give.'
The general staff disagreed here with the foreign office. Intend-
ing under the Schlieffen Plan to violate Belgium comprehen-
sively, they felt sure that Britain must come in, and had made
their calculations on that footing.[1] They believed the war would
be too brief for her blockade to tell; while their view of her small
expeditionary force is sufficiently shown by their instruction to
the German admiralty in August not to risk any vessels trying
to stop it.

France and Russia, not knowing what was intended about
Belgium, felt less sure than Moltke that the German foreign
office would fail in its wooing. The intimacy between Grey and
Lichnowsky alarmed them. Neither during the London Ambassadors' Conference nor later in the Liman crisis had they
received from Great Britain all the support which they expected.
Partly to assuage their uneasiness, King George, when in April
he paid a state visit to Paris, took Sir Edward Grey[2] with him.
The meeting was extremely cordial and showed the Ententes
to be still in vigour. To suggestions from Paris and St. Petersburg, that they should be turned into Alliances, Grey opposed a
firm negative. But he accepted (subject to the approval of the
cabinet, which in due course followed) a proposal put to him by
the French foreign minister, Doumergue, that Russia should
be informed of the military and naval arrangements between
France and England, and that an Anglo-Russian naval convention might be negotiated on parallel lines. The negotiations
could not, for geographical reasons, have much naval value;

[1] General H. J. von Kuhl, *Der deutsche Generalstab in Vorbereitung und Durchführung des Weltkrieges* (1920), 189. 'Wir rechneten', says Kuhl, 'unbedingt mit England als Feind.'
[2] Grey as foreign secretary had never left England before.

their significance was as a gesture. Begun in May, they were kept very secret, and had not been completed when the war broke out. But as confidential correspondence between the Russian Embassy in London and its foreign office in St. Petersburg was regularly communicated to the German government by an embassy official, Berlin soon became aware of their inception. The news synchronized there rather unfortunately with an anti-Russian war scare, the pretext for which was a proposal put before the Duma to raise the Russian peace effectives from 1,240,000 to 1,700,000 in answer to the German increase. The scare, wrote Bethmann-Hollweg to Lichnowsky (16 June 1914), had hitherto been confined to 'extreme pan-Germans and militarists', but 'His Majesty (this is *very private*) has now identified himself with this school of thought'.

At the end of that May Mr. Wilson, who had been rather over a year in office as President of the United States, sent his personal confidential agent, Colonel House, to Berlin to interview the Kaiser and the heads of his government regarding the possibilities of an international peace pact. House, who was a keen cool observer, saw all the leading personalities there; and then, travelling via Paris, had similar interviews in London. The record of his experiences is very informing. In Germany during the last days of May and the first of June he found the 'militaristic oligarchy' supreme, 'determined on war', and ready even to 'dethrone the Kaiser the moment he showed indications of taking a course that would lead to peace'. House's reaction to what he saw and heard was one of sheer consternation. Reporting it in London, he 'could talk of little except the preparations for war, which were manifest on every hand'.[1] But when he discussed his pact with Asquith or Grey or Lloyd George,

'the difficulty was that none of these men apprehended an immediate war. They saw no necessity of hurrying about the matter. They had the utmost confidence in Prince Lichnowsky, the German Ambassa-

---

[1] Burton J. Hendrick, *Life and Letters of Walter H. Page* (1922), i. 296, 299. This impression of Colonel House's was not in the least unique. The fever of German war-preparation was far too intense to be hidden on the spot, and the present writer heard the same from other good observers. One of them, Mr. George Renwick, then the very able Berlin correspondent of the *Daily Chronicle*, pointed out to him privately as early as December 1913, that the date on which all signs clearly converged was the beginning of the following August. But Mr. Renwick's editor, who was in frequent and reassuring contact with the attractive Kühlmann, viewed his correspondent's evidence much as Asquith and Grey viewed House's.

dor in London, and von Bethmann-Hollweg, the German Chancellor. Both these men were regarded by the Foreign Office as guarantees against a German attack; their continuance in their office was looked upon as an assurance that Germany entertained no immediately aggressive plans. Though the British statesmen did not say so definitely, the impression was conveyed that the mission on which Colonel House was engaged was an unnecessary one—a preparation against a danger that did not exist.'[1]

Here is indeed a most valuable record of the mind of British statesmanship on the eve of world-catastrophe. In the matter of judgement it was astray—chiefly through its natural and habitual but quite erroneous assumption that a German chancellor was tantamount to a British prime minister.[2] Bethmann-Hollweg, a weak man in a very weak position, was not really a 'guarantee' for anything. But on the moral side the British ministers showed well. Their sincere 'will to peace' could not be mistaken. Colonel House, and through him President Wilson, were always afterwards aware that, whoever had been the warmongers, the British were not.

By midsummer all the stars in their courses worked for the Central Powers. With a strange simultaneity Great Britain and France appeared temporarily paralysed together—the one by the climax of Carsonism,[3] the other by the feuds culminating in the Caillaux-Calmette murder. The only thing lacking was a *casus belli*; and a few days later that too was supplied.

On 28 June the Archduke Francis Ferdinand, heir-apparent to the crowns of Austria and Hungary, was murdered by Serb irredentists at the Bosnian capital, Serajevo. The assassins were Austrian subjects, but their conspiracy had been hatched on Serbian soil. Few tears were shed either in Vienna or in Budapest for the Archduke; who had been extremely unpopular with both the dominant races in the Monarchy. But it was decided to utilize his murder as the pretext for attacking Serbia. The first thing was to get Germany's approval; and for this the aged Emperor Francis Joseph wrote an autograph letter to William II. On 5 July, just a week after the crime, the Kaiser answered promising his full support. No doubt it was the reply expected;

[1] *Ibid.* 298. Cp. also Prof. C. Seymour, *The Intimate Papers of Colonel House*, i. (1926), c. 9, especially pp. 267–70.

[2] See below, Appendix C, section 2.

[3] For the impression made by Carson's movement on Berlin see J. W. Gerard, *My Four Years in Germany* (1920), 91.

for only eight months earlier (26 October 1913) when discussing Serbia with Count Berchtold, the Austro-Hungarian foreign minister, he had himself suggested the bombardment and occupation of Belgrade, and concluded: 'you may rest assured that I stand behind you, and am ready to draw the sword whenever the lead you take makes it necessary'.[1] He was due to start next day on his annual cruise in Scandinavian waters, and was careful not to arouse suspicion by changing his plans. But before he went, he summoned the chiefs of the war office and admiralty to Potsdam, and warned them of the coming danger.

Nobody indeed in Vienna or Berlin could have desired a better jumping-off ground for the decisive war. A Serbian issue suited Vienna, because it united Magyars and Austrian Germans. A Serbian regicide issue was particularly good, because it revived the strong prejudices felt against Serbia in England and elsewhere on account of the murder of King Alexander in 1903. These were good points for Berlin, too, but still better was the fact that the issue was Austro-Russian and not Germano-French. The German general staff could trust its own people much better than its Allies, and it was far preferable that Germany should be in the posture of fighting for Austria against the dragon of Slavdom than that Austria should be in the posture of fighting for Germany. Viewing it all round, the *casus belli* afforded was so marvellously trim and timely, that it would have been a miracle if those who had loaded their weapon for the beginning of August had been kept from using it to pull the trigger.

At first there was no hurry. The occasion had been slightly premature. After William II had given his *carte blanche*, Austria hid her intentions for eighteen days. Then events moved swiftly as to a time-table. On 23 July Vienna's ultimatum was presented at Belgrade. It was framed as prelude to a declaration of war. 'I have never before', said Grey to the Austrian ambassador, 'seen one State address to another independent State a document of so formidable a character.'[2] It was launched with only a 48-hour time-limit, and the other Powers were not officially apprised till the next day. Moreover, a moment had been

---

[1] The record of this very important conversation will be found in *Oesterreich-Ungarns Aussenpolitik*, vii. 512–15. The reference to Germany's sword clearly went beyond diplomatic support, and implied acceptance of a European war. Mr. Spender's comment is deserved: 'In the whole series of documents there is none which may more justly be called fatal.' Unless the reply to Francis Joseph may.

[2] British White Paper (Cd. 7467 of 1914), No. 5.

chosen when the French President and prime minister were at sea returning from a visit to Russia, and would not reach Paris for five more days. Urged on all sides to be submissive, Serbia (25 July) bowed to the rigours of the ultimatum on all but two points, offering to refer even those to the Hague Tribunal or the decision of the Great Powers. It was, as the Kaiser wrote three days later to his foreign secretary, 'a capitulation of the most humiliating character'. But Austria immediately rejected it, broke off relations, and began mobilizing a portion of her army.

A stroke of singular good fortune befell Great Britain at this juncture. In the previous March the strain on the budget had led to a decision that there should be no naval manœuvres, but instead (which was much cheaper) a 'trial mobilization'. Accordingly a vast naval concentration met at Portland in the middle of July, other ships being mobilized at their home ports. On the 24th they began to disperse; but only minor craft had gone, when on the 26th, after the rejection of Serbia's reply was known, Prince Louis of Battenberg, the first sea lord (on his own initiative, promptly endorsed by Churchill), stopped demobilization. The result was that Great Britain faced the danger from the outset in a state of more immediate naval preparedness than she had ever attained before, and the indecisions of a divided cabinet were not complicated by questions about ships.

This is not the place to trace or theorize the famous criss-cross of intense negotiation which went on between the Great Powers from the morrow of the Austrian ultimatum to the first declaration of war against a Great Power; which was that of Germany against Russia on 2 August. To the question: 'Whose fault was it?' three answers have at different times and places been fashionable. That given during the war on the side of the Central Powers was: 'Russia's; she mobilized first.' That given at the same time on the side of the Entente countries was: 'Germany's; she deliberately blocked all efforts to stop Austria, till the die was cast' (this view lies behind the famous 'war-guilt' clause in the Treaty of Versailles). And thirdly, since the war ended, a theory has been developed (by German erudition in the first instance), that the culprit was Austria-Hungary, who wilfully, it is argued, ran down the steep place, dragging an innocent and reluctant Germany after her. This thesis benefited, perhaps, at the start from the circumstance that Austria-Hungary no longer exists; so that blaming her presented the conveniences found in blaming a dead person.[1]

Cases for each of these views are not difficult to construct; but their foundations are all somewhat in the air. The earthy fact was that Germany had at enormous expense been keyed-up and prepared, as no nation ever equally was before, to fight a war at that particular time, and that nobody, not even the Kaiser, durst baulk the military chiefs of the opportunity offered them. Hence the unreality of Bethmann-Hollweg's position throughout. It was not till 29 July that he first, in firm language, insisted at Vienna that Austria must exchange views with Russia. But already on the previous day Austria had declared war on Serbia and bombarded Belgrade—a step which, taken as it was without any agreement with Russia as to its limits, was bound to unchain (as in fact it did) sequences of mobilization and counter-mobilization leading unescapably to war. After that the military chiefs had little reason to fear the effect of such language by the chancellor; before that he never used it. The same is true of the Kaiser's peace-making telegrams to the Tsar. The first was not sent till 10.45 p.m. on 28 July.

Now this view has a direct bearing on the question of Great Britain's attitude during the crisis. As early as 24 July the Russian foreign minister, Sasonov, pressed strongly that Great Britain should 'proclaim her solidarity with Russia and France', and join in a triple stand against Austria's action. Six days later the French President, Poincaré, urged the same policy. Apart from the plain motives of self-interest, which would prompt France and Russia herein, their case rested on the assumption that Germany was willing, with Austria, to fight the Dual Alliance, but afraid to fight the Dual Alliance plus Great Britain. Failure to take timely advantage of this alleged German fear is still often reproached to Grey as a signal and disastrous blunder on his part. We know now, however, that so far as the German military chiefs were concerned no such fear existed. They were expecting to fight all three Powers. If, therefore, theirs was the war decision, Grey by acting as Sasonov and Poincaré urged would not have arrested it for a moment.[2] And when he had

[1] The most elaborate pleading for the third view in English, perhaps, is Professor S. B. Fay's two-volume *The Origins of the World War* (1929). An early and condensed but able presentation of the case against it is Asquith's in *The Genesis of the War* (1923).

[2] This argument does not mean that the German chancellor may not have hoped

done so and Armageddon had followed notwithstanding, there would have appeared no answer to the criticism that his plunge had made Russia and France more bellicose and forced Germany to fight to break the 'encirclement'.

But the British foreign secretary was anyhow in no position so to act.[1] The cabinet behind him was paralysed by disagreement; and the majority in it represented a much greater majority of active liberals in the country, who might not unfairly be described as pro-German and anti-French.[2] For years these elements, who had little sense of the realities beneath the surface of Europe, had been denouncing Grey for 'dragging Great Britain at the heels of France and Russia'. To seek their backing for a threat of war to help Russia save Serbia would have been a quite impossible proposition. Grey's line, if the country was to support it, had, as between the Dual and Triple Alliances, to be as non-partisan as possible. He therefore fell back on the method by which he had saved the peace of Europe in the previous Balkan crisis. He suggested, first on the 24th and more definitely on the 26th, a London Conference at which through the medium of their ambassadors the immediately disinterested Powers—Germany, France, and Italy—could get together with him to smooth out the Austro-Russian difficulty. Had the Central Powers wished to obtain Austria's satisfaction against Serbia by agreement, the plan might well have appealed to them; for London had yielded results very favourable to their side before. But, though accepted

to divert England from the war, until, as happened to Napoleon III in 1866, it was too late for her to come in. Relying on such diverse factors as Carsonism, Lichnowsky, and the Germanophile influence of the City, he might even feel sanguine of doing so. But to undeceive him earlier could not have averted the war; since his part in the decision was never much more than that of the fly on the wheel.

[1] C. P. Scott, for instance, of the *Manchester Guardian*, who was then probably the most influential liberal in the country outside the cabinet, urged on ministers on 27 July exactly the opposite policy: 'I insisted that the only course for us would be to make it plain from the first that if Russia and France went to war we should not be in it' (J. L. Hammond, *Life of C. P. Scott* (1934), 178). Lloyd George had assured him that same day that 'there could be no question of our taking part in any war in the first instance. He knew of no Minister who would be in favour of it'. The chancellor of the exchequer did, however, contemplate 'our going a certain distance with France and Russia in putting diplomatic pressure on Austria. Then if war broke out we might make it easy for Italy to keep out by, as it were, pairing with her' (ibid. 177). According to Lord Morley's *Memorandum on Resignation* (which, however, is too vague in memory about dates and sequences to be a wholly reliable authority) Grey was moved by Sasonov's words to broach his policy in cabinet, but was there at once met by a numerous opposition, led by Morley himself (*Memorandum*, 1–2).

[2] See Appendix C, section 3.

by Italy and France, the project was extinguished on the 27th
by Germany's refusal.

After 28 July the question for Great Britain increasingly
became, not how she could stop the war, but what she should do
when it broke out. On the 29th Grey warned both the German
and French ambassadors—the first not to count on the neutrality
of Great Britain, the second not to count on her intervention.
The same evening, after a Crown Council at Potsdam, the
German chancellor made a direct bid for British neutrality.[1]
He offered a pledge that no part of France should be annexed
(though her colonies might be); that Holland's neutrality and
integrity should be respected by Germany; and that, while 'it
depended upon the action of France what operations Germany
might be forced to enter upon in Belgium', yet 'when the war
was over Belgian integrity would be respected, if she had not
sided against Germany'. These terms, which pointed both to
the stripping of France and the violation of Belgium, Grey
emphatically rejected, while still appealing to Germany to co-
operate for peace. On the 30th the British cabinet for the first
time considered the problem of Belgian neutrality; and on the
same day the French ambassador, referring to the Anglo-French
exchange of letters in November 1912 and the joint discussion
there provided for in the event of a crisis, inquired what the
British government proposed to do about it. Grey asked twenty-
four hours' delay to consult the cabinet; but on the 31st he had
to report that it was still unable to 'give any pledge at the present
time'. Later that day Germany, on hearing that Russia mobilized, proclaimed *Kriegsgefahr* (a state preliminary to mobilization), and at midnight sent a twelve-hour ultimatum to St.
Petersburg demanding that the Russian mobilization should
stop. On 2 August she declared war against Russia, and on
3 August against France.

Meanwhile two urgent issues of action or abstention confronted
the British cabinet. As between France and England there arose
the problem of fleets. The Channel, it will be remembered, had
been relegated by the French to the British navy. It was therefore physically possible, if Great Britain remained neutral, for
the German fleet to steam unopposed through the Straits of
Dover, bombard the French coast, and perhaps land troops in
rear of the French forces. But such operations would not only

[1] British White Paper (Cd. 7467 of 1914), No. 85.

raise for Great Britain a question of moral obligation; conducted, so to say, on her doorstep they would, with the resultant French mine-laying, be very injurious to herself. After long debates on the afternoon of 1 August and the morning of the 2nd, Grey was authorized to inform the French ambassador that the British fleet would not permit the German fleet to operate in these waters. The step, though grave, was less so than has often been suggested. It certainly did not, as Loreburn tried afterwards to argue, 'irrevocably commit' Great Britain to war with Germany. For there is no reason to suppose that the latter would have demurred to it. She had based no plans on this back-door into France, knowing that it could not be used if Britain entered the war; and therefore she would have lost nothing by consenting to abstain from it, so long as Britain remained out.

The other issue was Belgian neutrality. Great Britain was one of its guarantors under the Treaty of 1839. She had thus a right to defend it, though not in all circumstances an obligation. It was, however, deeply rooted in her national interest. For centuries she had been concerned to prevent the Low Countries from falling under the sway of a contiguous Great Power. That was why Belgium, when made a state, had been neutralized— a policy of which Palmerston was the originator. Gladstone in 1870 had taken special steps to safeguard it,[1] and his temporary treaties with France and Prussia formed a ruling precedent. But as he proposed them after war had broken out, there was no precedent for acting while peace lasted. Even so it is surprising that the Asquith cabinet never considered the topic until 30 July. At that time most of its members were against doing anything. Morley,[2] an opponent, records the discussion as 'thin and perfunctory', and Asquith in his cabinet report that day to the king clearly indicates its non-committal outcome.[3] It has been suggested that Grey might have averted the war by announcing earlier that Great Britain would take arms against a violator. But he could not have announced such a policy down to 2 August, because something like half the cabinet were opposed to it.

It would not have availed if he had. The German general staff, as noted above,[4] in committing themselves to a plan which

---

[1] See above, pp. 3–4, and below, Appendix C, section 4.
[2] *Memorandum on Resignation* (1928), 3.
[3] J. A. Spender and Cyril Asquith, *Life of Asquith*, ii. 81. [4] p. 483.

involved violating Belgium, had foreseen the certainty of Great
Britain's intervention and discounted its consequences. They
were not going to call off their war on her account. Nor were
they going to change their plan. They had, in fact, no other;[1]
and dispositions, which involved mobilizing and moving several
millions of men at the highest possible speed from the moment
of war's outbreak, could not possibly within a few days be worked
out afresh on a totally new basis, even by the best staff in
Europe.

On the 31st Grey inquired of France and Germany, whether
they would respect Belgian neutrality, and of Belgium whether
she would defend it. France and Belgium sent affirmative replies,
but Germany objected that any answer would throw light on
her strategy. On 1 August (Saturday) the cabinet authorized
the foreign secretary to say that

'The reply of the German Government is a matter of very great
regret, because the neutrality of Belgium does affect feeling in this
country. If Germany could see her way to give a positive reply as
France has done, it would materially contribute to relieve anxiety
and tension here; while, if there were a violation by one combatant
while the other respected it, it would be extremely difficult to restrain
public feeling.'

—a formula which shows the cabinet still unready to declare
violation a *casus belli*. At noon that day Germany's ultimatum
to Russia ran out, and war between those countries virtually
began. No one doubted that it entailed war between Germany
and France. But the British government and nation were still
divided, and to an alarming extent on party lines, the liberal
newspapers crying for neutrality and the conservative for war.
Inside the cabinet the chief advocates of intervention were
Asquith, Grey, and Haldane (all formerly associated with
Lord Rosebery) and Churchill (an ex-conservative); while
against them stood at least ten radical stalwarts, with Lewis
Harcourt, old Sir William's son, pulling the wires. And there
were other factors: the bankers and financiers of the City
strong against intervention, and conservative M.P.s much less

---

[1] Bethmann-Hollweg (*Betrachtungen zum Weltkriege*, i (1919), 166) is explicit on
this: 'Unsere Militärs hatten, nach meiner Kenntnis nach langem, nur einen
Kriegsplan,' i.e. 'Our military men had, as I had long been aware, only one plan
of campaign.' The English version by Sir George Young (*Reflections on the World
War* (1920), 146) seriously mistranslates this sentence.

decided for it than their newspapers.[1] But on Sunday morning, while the cabinet were debating whether to give France the assurance about the Channel, a letter from Lord Lansdowne and Bonar Law reached the prime minister, pledging them and all the colleagues whom they had been able to consult to back the government in supporting France and Russia.[2] This sudden reinforcement doubtless helped the interventionists to carry their point regarding the Channel, though the cabinet was nearly split in the process. Burns notified his resignation, and about nine other dissidents[3] lunched together to concert further resistance. When the cabinet met in the evening, however, the opposition, as it now was, began to crumble. News had come that Germany had violated Luxemburg, and this, though not in itself held very serious, pointed to the imminent violation of Belgium, across which all but one of the outlets from Luxemburg ran. The cabinet now agreed to adopt Gladstone's principle of 1870, that a 'substantial' violation of Belgian neutrality would compel British action. Burns and Morley resigned, as next day did Simon and Beauchamp; who, however, were afterwards induced to come back.

That same evening a twelve-hour ultimatum from Germany, which for four days had lain at her Brussels legation awaiting release, was served upon the Belgian government, demanding passage for the German armies. Led by their king, the Belgians resolved not to yield, and next morning (3 August) returned a dignified refusal. The news speedily reached the British government, and King Albert telegraphed an appeal to King George, but for diplomatic intervention only; care was taken not to ask for military aid until actual violation had occurred. In the afternoon before parliament in a memorable speech Grey argued the case for intervention. He maintained that the Entente had never been an alliance; read the letters exchanged between himself and M. Cambon in 1912; and claimed that parliament was, as he had always promised that it should be when the time

[1] Lord Grey, *Twenty-Five Years*, i. 337, records that Bonar Law earlier in the week doubted whether the party would be 'unanimous or overwhelmingly in favour of war', unless Belgian neutrality were involved.

[2] The fullest account of how this letter was written, and of what preceded and followed it on the conservative side, is that given by Sir Austen Chamberlain, a principal mover in the matter, in his autobiographical *Down the Years* (1935), c. 6.

[3] Lord Morley, who was one, enumerates in addition 'Lord Beauchamp, Simon, Lloyd George, Harcourt, Samuel, Pease, McKinnon Wood (not sure about Runciman)': *Memorandum*, 15.

came, unfettered in its decision. Nevertheless for many years they had had a friendship with France; and 'how far that friendship entails obligations, let every man look into his own heart and his own feelings, and construe the extent of the obligation for himself'. He announced and explained the Channel guarantee to France; and then turned to the question of Belgium. Here the house went strongly with him, and what he might have found a hard task became an easy one.

Bonar Law announced the support of the unionists, and then a quite unexpected thing happened: Redmond, rising from the Irish benches, announced his. It was an act of signal courage. The inquest on the victims of Bachelors' Walk was being held that day; home rule was still not passed; and the Amending Bill, which was to have been introduced in the commons on 30 July, had been postponed for the war-crisis. He took his political life in his hands. Through tragic ill-faith in the war office and the persistent blundering of British statesmen, it cost him dear in the sequel. But it is difficult to overestimate what he achieved for the cause of Belgium, Great Britain, and France. By bringing the Irish into the war as free men, he incalculably stimulated the unanimity of the Dominions; and above all he rendered possible from the first the moral support of the United States. After him from the labour benches spoke Ramsay MacDonald sounding the first notes of dissent. Formally this was the voice of the party, uttered through its elected leader; but in fact, as soon became known, it was only that of a small though distinguished minority in it.

While parliament sat, a war council was held. Haldane and Grey the night before had secured from Asquith (who was still war minister as well as premier) his consent to mobilization. At 11 that morning Haldane went to the war office as Asquith's deputy, and himself put through the orders for the army, the reserves, and the territorials.[1] Thus the creator of the Expeditionary Force was also the statesman who caused it to be mobilized in time; and therein he rendered the nation a service comparable to that of Prince Louis of Battenberg in stopping the demobilization of the fleet. Neither service was made publicly known; and it is lamentable to record, that not long after, when the spy-mania newspapers were looking ignorantly about for 'pro-Germans' to hound down, these two men, for such German

[1] Lord Haldane, *An Autobiography* (1929), 274–7.

connexions as each had, were selected as victims, and before the war was ten months old the nation had been deprived of the services of each of them. At the war council of 3 August, Haldane urged sending abroad all the six infantry divisions of the Expeditionary Force. Sir John French, who was to command, supported him; but the rest of the council (which included Lord Roberts and Lord Kitchener) were afraid to send more than four, and that decision was unfortunately taken.[1]

The sands of peace now ran out fast. When the house of commons met on 4 August, Asquith read three telegrams. One gave Germany's rejoinder to Belgium's reply—a threat of force. The second announced the invasion of Belgium by German troops that morning. The third was a last appeal from the German government to condone Belgium's violation in return for an undertaking not to annex her territory. The prime minister stated that in reply the British government had renewed its demand for assurances that Belgian neutrality would be respected, and had attached a time-limit expiring at midnight.

'The House', Asquith recorded in his diary, 'took the fresh news to-day very calmly and with a good deal of dignity.'[2] Therein it mirrored the nation. London, which like other monster capitals can always produce at its centre enough idlers and frothy persons to form a mob, exhibited, it is true, some noisy scenes in Whitehall and Downing Street. But the general demeanour, through East End and West End alike, was utterly different; and in the rest of the country grave feelings alone prevailed. Very few wished the nation to enter the mêlée, but very few believed that it could any longer keep out.

At 11 p.m. (midnight in Berlin) the time-limit expired. The British ambassador, having met with a negative, had applied for his passports earlier.

The disaster which had befallen Europe had its roots since 1870 in the giant expansion and uncontrolled ambition of the new Germany. Bismarck had sown the seed, through his memorable triumphs for militarism and unscrupulous efficiency; but between 1871 and 1890 he was very careful not to water it. After his fall it grew apace, unchecked by the statesmen and encouraged by the Emperor. In the many-sided quick-changing

---

[1] Ibid. 278.
[2] H. H. Asquith (Lord Oxford), *Memories and Reflections* (1928), ii. 21.

displays of the brilliant William II two features alone never failed—arrogant megalomania and an instinctive preference for methods of violence. These, it is not unfair to say, became the national vices of pre-war Germany; and they made her an object of alarm to every leading nation save her Austrian ally.

To admit this is not to imply that the world's peace would have been assured, could any single Power have been eliminated from its reckonings. Mankind lived under a system of 'international anarchy', of which more than one Power from time to time tried to take aggressive advantage. All of them wanted to expand; and the very doctrines which had been evolved to control that tendency (e.g. the doctrine of 'compensation') often threatened as much danger as they averted. Nevertheless it was the attitude of post-Bismarckian Germany which at this time dominated the international stage, and shaped the issues that brought catastrophe.

In the case of Great Britain the reactions of policy have been well summarized by a great Austrian scholar:

'It was quite obvious to British statesmen, during the decades that preceded the World War, that England must retain her supremacy at sea; that she could not permit any Continental Power to establish a hegemony in Europe and by so doing upset the European Balance of Power in a sense contrary to British interests; and finally, that she could not allow Belgium to pass into the hands of the strongest Continental Power. Since the *fear* that Germany entertained such plans increased from year to year, British statesmen held it to be their duty to make all possible preparations to be ready to defeat such plans if Germany should one day seek to put them into operation. Hence the increase in naval armaments, the successive agreements with their allies, and hence also their endeavours to win for England new friends.'[1]

The reason for the Ententes could not be better stated. But it ought to be added that while successive prime ministers, foreign secretaries, and foreign office officials knew these things, the majority of members of the houses of commons elected in 1906 and 1910 were almost totally unalive to them. Before 1906 the relatively aristocratic parliaments were largely recruited from families with a traditional interest in foreign affairs. Palmerston or Disraeli debated such topics before a knowledgeable assembly.

[1] A. F. Přibram, *England and the International Policy of the European Great Powers, 1871–1914* (1931), 149.

After 1906 it was not so, and Grey worked under handicaps in this respect shared by none of his predecessors.[1]

Professor Příbram adds that while no British statesman desired the war, many, especially in the foreign office, held it inevitable, but Lansdowne and Grey did not. That also is true; and in so far as Grey during nearly nine years of office clung to the hope of averting war and then failed to avert it, he may, of course, be ticketed as a failure. In part he was the victim of his virtues; for just as the Campbell-Bannerman government's generously meant moderation in shipbuilding only encouraged German statesmen to think they could outbuild Great Britain, so the honourable and sincere attempts, which Grey made between Agadir and August 1914 to conciliate Germany and deprive her of any excuse for a sense of grievance, helped to foster the dangerous illusion that Great Britain would not stand by France. But at all times it was—and he knew it—his duty not only to seek peace, but to prepare against war. In the shadow of all that Great Britain suffered through entering the European war, men still often criticize as 'entanglements' those policies of Grey's, which helped to bring her in. They do not ask themselves what would have happened had she stood out. But the event made it fairly certain that in that case Germany would have conquered Europe; and when she had done so, Great Britain would have been a victim without hope or resource. If, as is the strong presumption, nothing that a British statesman could do would have averted eventual war between his country and Germany, then credit is due to that statesman who ensured that when Great Britain, France, and Russia had to fight for their lives, they stood together to do so, and did not wait to be overwhelmed piecemeal.

[1] See Appendix C, section 3.

ECONOMICS AND INSTITUTIONS 1901–14

ONE remaining set of censuses, that of 1910–11, completes the picture already drawn[1] of the divergent growths in population of the western Powers. Its results were:

United States (1910)	91·7 millions.
Germany (1910)	64·9 ,,
United Kingdom (1911)	45·3 ,,
Great Britain, 40·8 millions	
Ireland, 4·39 millions	
France (1911)	39·6 ,,
of French nationality, 38·4 millions	
Italy (1911)	34·6 ,,

The falling behind of France appears here more marked than ever. Italy is seen overhauling her, but at a rather slow pace, due to the exceptional volume of Italian emigration.

The accompanying table of large towns, though the freaks of municipal geography render it misleading in some details (e.g. Charlottenburg and Neukölln are counted apart from Berlin, West Ham from London, and Salford from Manchester),

Large Towns, 1910–11

	Over 1 million	Between 1 million and 300,000	Between 300,000 and 100,000	Total
United States . . .	3	16	41	60
Germany . . .	1	11	35	47
United Kingdom . .	1	10	33	44
France	1	2	12	15
Italy		5	8	13

yet shows very significantly the difference in urbanization, and therewith in industrial power and wealth, between France and Italy, on the one side, and the three great coal-producing countries on the other. Another comparison worth recording is that between densities of population. The United States cannot usefully be brought in, but for the rest the figures were: United Kingdom, 373 per square mile; Italy, 313; Germany, 310; France, 189. The parallelism in the first three is noticeable, but for the United Kingdom rather misleading; for Eng-

[1] See above, pp. 102–3, 269–70.

land and Wales, in which 79·5 per cent. of its population lived, carried 618 persons per square mile.

The next accompanying table shows for the United Kingdom the continued development in regard to births and deaths.[1] The noticeable points are again the gradual but uninterrupted fall of the birth-rate, due to the spread of birth-control, and the fall

Year	Births per 1,000	Deaths per 1,000	Natural increase per 1,000
1900	28·2	18·4	9·8
1905	26·9	15·6	11·3
1910	25·0	14·0	11·0
1911	24·4	14·8	9·6
1912	24·0	13·8	10·2
1913	23·9	14·2	9·7

of the death-rate, which in some years more than balanced it. The diminution of deaths at this stage occurred chiefly among young children. For a great part of the nineteenth century the infantile death-rate had been stationary. In each of the three decades which together bridge 1841–70, it averaged 154 per thousand; and the fluctuations between were not very great. But in the decade 1901–10 the average dropped to 127, and in the last year of it the figure was 105. To save life at infancy's end was the best numerical compensation for a falling birth-rate, since it did not upset the age-composition of the population. But from the eugenic point of view the compensation was imperfect; for the babies saved were, broadly speaking, those of the weaker stocks in the population, while the babies unborn were those of the stronger. Some figures published in 1907 emphasized the last point. The Hearts of Oak Friendly Society, then the largest centralized provident society in Britain, had a membership of 272,000 men recruited all over the kingdom from the thriftiest class of better-paid artisans, skilled mechanics, and small shopkeepers. It paid a 'lying-in benefit' for each confinement of a member's wife. From 1866 to 1880 the proportion of lying-in claims to membership had risen slowly from 2,176 per 10,000 to 2,472. From 1881 to 1904 it continuously declined, till in the last year it touched 1,165—a drop of over 52 per cent.[2] Apparently in this large sample of the thriftiest working-class stocks the birth-rate during twenty-four years had been halved.

[1] See above, pp. 103–4, 270–2.
[2] Sidney Webb (Lord Passfield), *The Decline in the Birth Rate* (1907), 6–7.

Emigration flowed very freely between the South African and European Wars; and partly owing to the official guidance, which Chamberlain had first made available for emigrants, a much larger proportion went to the British Dominions. During 1891–1900 they had received only 28 per cent. of the total; but during 1901–10 the proportion was just double, i.e. 56 per cent. In the year 1911 it rose to 80 per cent., remaining very high down to the War; while in the three years 1911–12–13 the gross emigration totals reached record figures. Most of the residue still went to the United States, but at the same time American farmers were moving into Canada's prairie provinces —over 120,000 Americans migrated to Canada in the year ending March 1911. As a consequence of all these tendencies the 1911 census showed far bigger Dominion increments than ever before. Canada was up to 7·2 millions, Australia to 4·9, New Zealand at last crossed the million mark, and the persons of European descent in South Africa increased to 1·11 millions. A better distribution of the white population within the Empire seemed at last on the way; and it was a peculiar misfortune that the intervention of the European War cut short the process.

At about the time when Queen Victoria died, the growth of the country's aggregate income—which in spite of cyclical trade movements had been steadily increasing in proportion to population, decade by decade, throughout her reign—came to something like a stop; and for the rest of the pre-war period 'barely kept pace with the diminishing value of money'.[1] Surveying the period 1880–1913, Professor Bowley has calculated that the national dividend increased more rapidly than the population, so that average incomes in 1913 were quite one-third greater than in 1880. But the increase was nearly all before 1900.

'Statisticians writing at or before the date of the beginning of the Fiscal Controversy (1902) could reasonably dwell with a certain satisfaction on the progress that had been made; and the slackening in the years that followed was masked by rising prices and years of good trade; but before the War it had become evident that the progress of real wages was checked, and it appears now that this check was not on wages alone.'[2]

Taking 'real' wages in 1880 as 100, he computes their average for the five years 1896–1900 at 132; that for 1901–5 at 133; that

[1] A. L. Bowley, *The Change in the Distribution of the National Income, 1880–1913* (1920), 26.   [2] Ibid. 27.

for 1906–10 at 134, and those for 1911, 1912, and 1913, at 133, 132, and 134 respectively. It is a picture of sharply arrested progress, which helps to explain the great labour discontent towards the end of the period.

What caused this check to the national productivity and prosperity? The reader who will turn back to pp. 275–8 of this volume may there find sufficient to account for much of it. It was impossible that a manufacturing country, which had come to live on exports, should find itself shut out increasingly from market after market without suffering heavily. Granted that it found new markets or developed new lines of manufacture, the changes would take time, and a good deal of capital was apt to be lost in the process. Such losses had grown common in the leading British industries, and explain the support which so many of their chiefs gave in 1903 to Joseph Chamberlain.

But at least two more factors may be traced. One was that on which Alfred Marshall, the economist, laid stress in a famous memorandum of 1903.[1] The mischief, as he saw it, was that Britain had lost her 'industrial leadership'. The very ease, with which it had been established in the third quarter of the nineteenth century, had bred subsequent lethargy and self-complacency. Many of the sons of manufacturers were

'content to follow mechanically the lead given by their fathers. They worked shorter hours, and they exerted themselves less to obtain new practical ideas than their fathers had done, and thus a part of England's leadership was destroyed rapidly. In the 'nineties it became clear that in the future Englishmen must take business as seriously as their grandfathers had done, and as their American and German rivals were doing: that their training for business must be methodical, like that of their new rivals, and not merely practical, on lines that had sufficed for the simpler world of two generations ago: and lastly that the time had passed at which they could afford merely to teach foreigners and not learn from them in return'.[2]

Marshall was by no means the first person to call attention to this. At the end of 1901 the then Prince of Wales,[3] speaking at the Guildhall after a tour to the Dominions, reported a widespread feeling there, that England must 'wake up' commercially.

The other factor was trade unionism, which, as we saw above,[4]

---

[1] Printed five years later as a White Paper (No. 321 of 1908).
[2] Ibid., pp. 21–2.
[3] Afterwards King George V.   [4] p. 298.

had acquired during the nineties quite a new importance in industry. In itself it was a healthy growth. But it early became associated in Great Britain (as in no other European country to the same extent) with a piece of mistaken economics (sometimes called 'ca' canny' and sometimes the 'loomp o' labour' theory) —the doctrine that there is only a fixed amount of employment to be had, and that, therefore, the less any worker does, the more there will be for others to do. No one who has studied British trade-union rules can be unaware that the effect of many is to increase the number of men on a job, and so to reduce output per man. Early in 1902 there was a long public argument about it,[1] the employers contending that from about 1900 onwards the tightening of trade-union control had resulted in a definite lowering of British productivity. Some of the complaints were doubtless exaggerated; but it seems significant in retrospect, that the stop in the progress of British productivity did in fact occur at that time.[2]

The arrest of growth was concealed somewhat by a marked

Sauerbeck's Index of Wholesale Prices: 1871 = 100

1901 . . 70	1905 . . 72	1908 . . 73	1911 . . 80
1902 . . 69	1906 . . 77	1909 . . 74	1912 . . 85
1903 . . 69	1907 . . 80	1910 . . 78	1913 . . 85
1904 . . 70			

upward tendency in prices. Though never getting back to the level of 1871, they travelled, it will be seen, half the way there. Was this merely a currency change, connected with the high gold output of the South African mines? The post-war reader might assume so, but it seems by no means certain; for the rise was distributed with marked unevenness over different commodities. Thus between 1900 and 1912 tin rose 57·9 per cent., zinc 25 per cent., lead only 2·4 per cent., while copper actually fell 2·9 per cent. Similarly bacon rose 50·5 per cent., but beef 13·8 per cent., and mutton only 4·2 per cent. Generally speaking, agricultural products became dearer; while coal, pig-iron,

---

[1] Beginning in *The Times* with a series of letters from representative employers in many different trades.

[2] As the first Census of Production was not taken till 1907 and the second not till 1924, there is not much statistical material to rely on. In the coal industry, however, where the progress of trade unionism was particularly marked, the output of coal per person per year, which had been 301 tons in the period 1897–9, fell to 289 in the period 1905–7; while in the United States it rose from 497 tons in 1897–9 to 555 in 1904–6.

paraffin, palm-oil, and silk were all cheaper.[1] But the result on balance was that money bought less.

The trade figures from 1905 onwards are somewhat influenced by this tendency. Reduced to the price-level of 1901, the

Trade Figures 1901–13

(in £ millions)

1901 . . 870·5	1905 . . 972·5	1908 . . 1,049·6	1911 . . 1,237·0
1902 . . 877·6	1906 . . 1,068·5	1909 . . 1,094·2	1912 . . 1,343·6
1903 . . 902·9	1907 . . 1,163·7	1910 . . 1,212·4	1913 . . 1,403·5
1904 . . 922·0			

£1,237 millions of 1911 become £1099·8 millions, and the £1,403·5 of 1913 became £1,155·7 millions. They are high totals even so. Unemployment, as measured in the returns collected from trade unions by the board of trade, averaged 6 per cent. in the decade 1901–10, as against 5·2 in the decade 1891–1900. But there was no year so bad as 1892, and no sequence of bad years like 1892–3–4. Subsequently in 1911–12–13, which were years of marked inflation, employment became exceedingly good, and the percentages out of work sank to 3·1, 2·3, and 2·6 respectively.

The period was one of much economic controversy, and was punctuated at unprecedentedly frequent intervals by the issue of Blue-books and White-papers supplying official data regarding economic conditions at home and abroad. From the last of these[2] the accompanying table is derived, comparing for the

Increases per cent. 1893–1913

	United Kingdom	Germany	United States
Population	20	32	46
Coal production . . .	75	159	210
Pig iron	50	287	337
Crude steel . . .	136	522	715
Exports of raw materials .	238	243	196
Exports of manufactures .	121	239	563
Receipts from railway goods traffic	49	141	146

period 1893–1913 (in some instances 1892–1912) how the world's three greatest industrial countries had progressed under

[1] Cp. Sir Leo Chiozza-Money, *The Future of Work* (1914), 204–7.
[2] Accounts and Papers, No. 218 of 1914: *Agricultural and Trade Development* (*United Kingdom, Germany, and United States*).

some leading material aspects. Here it is clearly shown that the pace of development in Great Britain had become slower than in America or in Germany. Yet one must remember that these were the leading three; no other large nation moved so fast; and in many ways British industry was far more solidly based than German. It owed nothing to tariffs or government subsidies; the firms engaged in it stood on their own feet. The German economic structure included not a few imposing features, which existed for military or political reasons, and could not be justified on economic grounds. But in Britain enterprises had to pass the test of paying. The national standpoints were different, and the British one, being purely economic, gave on that side better results.

Let us take for example the case of steel. We saw above (p. 277), how in 1896 the German steel output passed the British and thereafter went ahead of it. In 1908 it doubled the British (10·9 million tons as against 5·3 million). Now what did the Germans do with so much steel? They sold vast quantities of it to Great Britain. On what terms? At lower prices than it was sold in Germany. And what did the British do with it? They used it for making machinery, for building ships, for tinplate, and for other industries in which steel is a raw material. This was to their economic advantage. Their shipbuilding, for instance, led the world; and if the Germans, despite subsidies of several kinds, could never really compete with it, one of the reasons was that the British shipyards got their steel cheaper. Shipbuilding is a process of assembling materials; and the building of merchant vessels on the Tyne, the Wear, and the Clyde became thus a process of assembling German materials—not merely the bare girders and plates, but great steel forgings, like propellers and rudders. Indeed if the admiralty had not insisted on British steel for naval ships, it seems likely that the plant and capacity to produce these great forgings might before 1914 have disappeared from Great Britain altogether.

Now industries representing a higher stage of manufacture pay as a rule better than those representing a lower stage. It is more remunerative to build the world's ships than to smelt the steel for them, especially if you are to sell the steel below cost price. On the economic side Britain had the best of the bargain. The compensation to Germany was on the military side. The gigantic steel industry, which she thus uneconomically built up, proved during 1914–18 a preponderant factor in her war-strength. On the other hand, years of war passed before England could develop a steel output adequate to her fighting needs; and but for the above-mentioned policy of the admiralty she might in the critical early stages have been unable to complete large warships at all. Steel is far from being the only case in which a contrast of this kind can be traced between the British and German pre-war economics. But in studying the years 1901–14, we have primarily before us not the war-time but the peace-time effects. In spite of their 'colossal' economic developments, Germans of all classes remained decidedly poorer than Englishmen of the corresponding classes. The health of their business enterprises was much less firmly established. The world's finance ranked London at the top of the scale, and Berlin a long way down. Hence at the latter capital an 'inferiority complex' and a readiness on the part of statesmen to use military pre-eminence for economic ends. Hence also in the press and public opinion of the German commercial classes that attitude of bitter envy towards England, which Tirpitz so successfully exploited.

To the German policy of state subsidies and rebates to industry, the British state as a rule made no reply. There was one notable exception. In 1903 after the Germans had, with three successive ships, won and held the 'blue ribbon' of the Atlantic, it was decided that national prestige warranted state aid to recover it. The government accordingly gave the Cunard company a loan of £2·6 millions at 2¾ per cent. to build two turbine vessels of 25 knots. The results were the *Mauretania* and *Lusitania*, the first of which established a record unapproached in the Atlantic service. On her first trip in 1907 she regained the 'blue ribbon'; and she held it uninterruptedly for twenty-two years, her fastest crossing (4 days, 17 hours, 50 minutes from New York to Plymouth) being made in 1929. The *Lusitania*, a fine vessel but never quite equal to her sister, was destined to be sunk by a German submarine in 1915. Save for a ten years' subsidy of £40,000 a year paid (by Chamberlain's arrangement) to another company to develop direct trade between Jamaica and England, no other grants were made before the War to British merchant shipping. Yet it held its own remarkably, and on 1 July 1914 still comprised as much as 47·7 per cent. of the world's iron and steel tonnage. Germany came next with 12 per cent.; then Norway and France with 4·5 each, the United States with 4·3, and Japan with 3·9.

The first British census of production, taken in 1907, accounted for about half the wage-earners in the United Kingdom, about 38 per cent. of the home (as distinct from foreign) income,[1] and nearly all the manufacturing industry and mining. Its results took years to digest, and the Final Report[2] appeared so long after that the public never fully appreciated them. The accompanying table shows how limited even in England was the proportion of horse-power to workers employed, and how relatively low was the net value of the output per worker. Electric power was not satisfactorily recorded, but the total capacity of

	Persons employed	Horse-power employed	Net value of output per person employed
United Kingdom . . .	6,984,976	10,955,009	£102
England and Wales . .	5,808,269	9,097,869	£104
Scotland	885,403	1,397,733	£98
Ireland	291,304	259,407	£78

the dynamos owned by firms (including electric supply undertakings), which made returns to the census, was only 1,747,672 kilowatts, of which only 350,586 were as yet driven by steam turbines. About one-eleventh of the gross output was that of establishments which used no mechanical power at all. Taking what were now Great Britain's leading exports, the output of her textile factories had a net value of only £73 per head; that of her coal-mines, £127; and that of 'iron and steel, tinplate, iron tube, wire, shipbuilding, and engineering', £109. Such very low figures deserved more attention than they received.

The census of production, it is true, did not cover a most important part of the activities by which England lived. Foreign and colonial earnings lay outside it: those, e.g. from investments, from banking and discount operations, from shipping freights, or by way of foreign-paid salaries and pensions. In regard to home-produced goods a detailed attempt was made to estimate the increment of value due to marketing; but it is difficult to obtain from the returns a real measure of the value of mercantile as distinct from manufacturing activities. An

[1] A. L. Bowley, *The Division of the Product of Industry* (1919), 31.
[2] Cd. 6320 of 1912-13.

acute writer with wide business experience pointed out not long after,[1] that 'the merchants and warehousemen of Manchester and Liverpool, not to mention the marketing organization contained in other Lancashire towns, have a greater capital employed than that required in all the manufacturing industries of the cotton trade'. Within England itself it was (and is) noticeable, that the greater and richer cities were not the manufacturing but the mercantile centres—Manchester, not Oldham; Leeds, not Halifax; Cardiff, not Merthyr Tydfil. Something like this characterized England as a whole in her relation to the rest of the world. If she was no longer so much as formerly the world's workshop, she was more than ever its warehouseman, its banker, and its commission agent. And these were relatively the better-paid functions.

In productive industry few technological changes of very wide scope came at this stage to the fore. The development of ring-spinning in the United States helped to weaken the position of Lancashire; for as compared with mule-spinning, it made a much smaller demand on the skill of the operative, yet could spin the coarser counts well enough, and so was well adapted for the mills of India, China, or Japan. Coal-cutting machinery was another American invention; it was very little taken up in Great Britain—a fact which partly explains the startling divergence between the outputs per head of American and British miners. Elevators for handling large quantities of grain with a minimum of labour were also American in origin; the first English one was erected in the port of Manchester at the beginning of the century. Yet another American practice was the use of steel framework in nearly all larger buildings. Great Britain had adopted it to a considerable extent in the nineteenth century, and J. F. Bentley's was already an exceptional case when, in order to build for eternity, he excluded steel from the frame of his Westminster Cathedral. But from about 1900 onwards the proportion of steel used was much increased, and most buildings were no longer designed to hide its presence like a guilty secret.

In the world's best factory practice the most marked general change was the increased use of electrical power. This grew slowest in the United Kingdom, owing to the high price of

[1] G. Binney Dibblee, *The Laws of Supply and Demand* (1912), 47. See also pp. 50–62, where the point is more fully argued.

electricity resulting from the rabble of small inefficient electrical undertakings with which parliament had unwisely saddled the country. The only big industrial region where the difficulty was early surmounted on a large scale was Tyneside. There a number of engineering magnates clubbed together to generate a common supply for their firms; and in this way were able to sell themselves electric power at $\frac{1}{2}d$. a unit, as against figures like 6*d*. and 8*d*. which were common elsewhere. In 1905, when their success was firmly established, a Tyneside syndicate went to parliament with a private bill to enable electricity to be generated under equally favourable conditions for London. All the existing generating stations used by metropolitan undertakers were to be scrapped, and all power supplied at $\frac{1}{2}d$. a unit from two huge turbine-engined Thames-side stations to be erected at East Greenwich and Fulham respectively. This was on its engineering side a most attractive proposition; but on the political side it encountered fierce resistance, not only from existing companies wedded to their smaller and less economic stations, but from every local authority with an interest in electricity, from the L.C.C. down. Consequently the bill was rejected; and in subsequent years attempts by others (notably by the L.C.C.) to obtain similar powers proved no more successful. Parliament declined, in effect, to override local electricity authorities against their will; and the result was to hinder the cheapening of electricity in London and over a large part of the country for nearly a quarter of a century. Only in a few places like Manchester, where the statutory area for electricity was big enough to justify the erection of a sufficiently large station, could electric power be obtained before the War by ordinary British factory owners at rates comparable with the American and German.

But the greatest technological advances during these years were not in industry but in transport. We saw in the nineties the coming of the first electric trams, the first 'tubes', and the early motor-cars. For town streets in general electric trams seemed at the beginning of the twentieth century the perfect vehicle. Their speed, cheapness, and cleanness were all in admirable contrast to the only other street transport then widespread, viz. horse-drawn. Before the century was many years old almost every provincial city of any size possessed them—mostly in municipal ownership and as a rule on the overhead trolley-wire system. The L.C.C., when rather tardily it electrified its trams,[1] put in the far more expensive underground conduit system, and thereby helped to create financial difficulties for their future. But all the City and West End remained tramless, and till 1905 the only public street vehicles in the principal London streets were horse-omnibuses averaging but little over four miles per hour. To pass from electrified Manchester or Liverpool to the horse-drawn capital was to go back from a later to an earlier world. In 1905, however, the first motor-omnibuses appeared in London. They speedily drove the horse-omnibuses away, and the monopoly which they enjoyed of the rich and tramless central thoroughfares enabled them to hold their own, though their working costs remained excessive compared to those of trolley trams. The year 1905 was indeed eventful for metropolitan transport; for it also saw the opening of the Bakerloo and Piccadilly tubes, and the partial electrification of the shallow underground railways, till then worked throughout by steam. Within a few years local travelling in London became, as it never was in the nineteenth century, really rapid and convenient; but it remained much costlier than anywhere else.

These changes in urban transport had an almost instant effect on housing. They enabled people to live farther from the centres. Soon after 1900 a building boom sprang up on the outskirts of towns, and continued till 1910. The resulting movement of population was really a great social phenomenon. Seen in nearly all towns, it benefited the largest most, and London most of all. Charles Booth's great survey of the metropolitan working-class had barely completed its last volume, when its account of the distribution of the people became rapidly obsolete. The effect on the congested inner slums of east, south, and north London was like the draining of marshes. It is true that the movement went by layers, and when Poplar transferred to East Ham, Walworth to Wandsworth, or North Camberwell to Lewisham, the places left vacant might be filled from more central and crowded areas; true also, that the new houses (except those built by municipalities or trusts) took the best-off and not

---

[1] It began with those in south London, and did not run any by electricity north of the Thames till about the middle of 1905. The northern terminals of the southern lines remained completely disconnected, through the refusal of the house of lords to permit trams over the bridges or on the embankment. The lords maintained this refusal till 1906.

the neediest workers. Nevertheless, especially between 1905 and 1910, the net social gain was great. Unhappily from the latter year the building stopped. There may have been several causes, but the one most commonly assigned was the 1909 budget. Builders of cheap small houses, cutting the profit on bricks and mortar to zero, looked to recoup themselves by the increment on land. The budget's threat to this destroyed their confidence. By 1914 overcrowding was again on the increase.

Private motor-cars, though rapidly improving, did not affect as yet the siting of houses. Indeed, save for London motor-omnibuses and taxicabs, the early uses of the petrol-engine on roads were almost entirely luxurious. Cars remained costly; only rich men owned them; and as they dashed along the old narrow untarred carriage-ways, frightening the passer-by on their approach and drenching him in dust as they receded, they seemed visible symbols of the selfishness of arrogant wealth. Few things, for a decade or so, did more to aggravate class-feeling. After the 1909 budget set up the Road Board, money became available for tarring thoroughfares; and the dust nuisance, which in many places had grown intolerable, gradually disappeared. The first utilitarian purpose to which cars were widely put was the visiting of patients by doctors. But it was only after the National Insurance Act of 1911 had enriched the majority of practitioners that this use became universal.

The aeroplane was an American invention, developed in France and chiefly by Frenchmen. Neither British nor Germans were concerned in it; but after the events of 1909—the Rheims air meeting and Blériot's crossing of the Channel—the war offices of both countries took it up. By 1914 Great Britain had a few keen army aviators, but had done nothing foreshadowing her future eminence in this sphere. Germany entered the War stronger in the air than any other belligerent.

In wireless telegraphy, on the other hand, though the leading inventor was an Italian, Great Britain took the chief part in developing his invention. In 1901 the first transatlantic wireless message was sent from Poldhu in Cornwall to Newfoundland. But the feature in the invention making special appeal to Englishmen was its applicability to ships. For the first time in history a vessel crossing the ocean could maintain throughout her voyage direct communication with other vessels and with the land. In the greatest marine disaster of this period—the loss on her maiden voyage in 1912 of the world's largest ship, the White Star liner *Titanic* of 46,382 tons, through collision with an iceberg in mid-Atlantic—wireless brought a whole fleet of large vessels to the rescue. It is true that they did not reach her before she sank, and 1,635 persons went down with her. But they saved 732, who would else have probably perished in her boats.

Agriculture experienced a kind of revival. That is to say, British farmers, favoured by a small but progressive rise in prices, once more got their business on a paying basis. It was a basis, however, of diminished output from the soil.

The accompanying table[1] shows the position in regard to crops as between 1892 and 1912 in the three leading industrial countries. The German farmer, of course, was supported by a

Increases (+) or Decreases (—) per cent., 1892–1912

	Area cultivated	Wheat	Barley	Oats	Potatoes	Rye
United Kingdom .	−9	−6	−24	−2	+2	No returns
Germany . .	+8	+38	+44	+80	+79	+61
U.S.A. . .	+47	+37*	+182*	+154*	+160*	+17*

* Figures for 1893–1913.

considerable tariff (that on wheat being raised in 1906 from 7s. 5d. per qr. to 11s. 9d.), and the policy behind it was not purely economic but military. Yet his example gives some idea[2] of what the English farmer might have done had the balance between the prices of agricultural and industrial commodities been artificially maintained, not indeed where it stood from 1846 to 1877, but at levels midway between that and the post-1880 balance as determined by prairie production. A second table,[3] based on the figures immediately before the War,

Average Pre-War Production per 100 Acres of Cultivated (Arable or Grass) Land (Figures in Tons)

	Corn	Potatoes	Meat	Milk	Sugar
Britain. . .	15	11	4	17½	Negligible
Germany . .	33	55	4¼	28	2¾

[1] Figures from White Paper, No. 218 of 1914.

[2] He had lower wages to pay, but *per contra* his soil was poorer and climate (on the average) much harsher.

[3] The computation is Sir T. H. Middleton's, *The Recent Development of German*

shows the cases very clearly. Leaving the other items here to tell their own story, attention may be directed to the better showing made by meat than by milk. From the beginning of the century there was a slow upward tendency in the totals of United Kingdom cattle.[1] But the increase in Great Britain was on rather than *from* the soil. It is possible to cultivate land as a source of food, whether for man or beast; it is possible also to use it as standing-room for consumers of food grown elsewhere. The latter plan had long been adopted in England for men; it was now increasingly adopted for beasts also. Already in 1903 Balfour, when defending as prime minister before a deputation headed by Chaplin the repeal of the Hicks Beach corn duty, argued that for British farmers the purchase of corn as a feeding-stuff was more important than its sale as a crop. Of oil seeds (cotton seed, linseed, &c., used for cattle cake) the British imports in 1899 were £6·2 millions; in 1913, £12·3 millions; and other fodder imports increased similarly. It was mainly beef production, not milk, that resulted. Scotland, with her beef breeds, sent increasing numbers of calves and young stores to be raised in England; and the Irish, though they combined more dairying, developed their store cattle trade similarly. Broad English acres, which had been under the plough till the seventies and carried milking herds since, were now turned to beef-fattening. This kind of farming employed less capital and labour per square mile than any other; but a profit could be made on it. Sheep between 1901 and 1913 rose from 26·3 millions to 27·6 millions, replacing cattle on the poor pastures, to which so much former arable had fallen down; and pigs, though increasing on the whole, fluctuated violently at short intervals following the price of Russian barley.

Agricultural wages in England and Wales rose very little till 1912, when they were 4·9 per cent. higher than in 1900. Next year they jumped to 9 per cent.[2] above 1900; which even so was only just over half the rise of the price-index. Agricultural

Agriculture (Cd. 8305 of 1916). It must be understood that the figures do not indicate the produce of each crop per acre devoted to it, but are obtained by dividing the total tonnage of each product by one-hundredth of the total farmed acreage, exclusive of mountain and waste.

[1] In the thirteen successive years 1901–13, the figures (in millions) were 11·4, 11·3, 11·4, 11·5, 11·6, 11·6, 11·6, 11·7, 11·7, 11·7, 11·8, 11·9, 11·9. In most years rather more of the increase was in Great Britain than in Ireland, but the proportion between their cattle populations (about 3 : 2) remained fairly constant.

[2] *17th Abstract of Labour Statistics* (Cd. 7733 of 1915).

population continued to decline, and typical rural counties, in spite of large residential immigrations, had fewer inhabitants than in 1851.[1] Farming had ceased to be of any real consequence in the life of the nation, and the days (still so recent) when a good or bad harvest meant a good or bad season for trade in general seemed as dead as Queen Anne.

Next let us look more particularly at the condition of the poorer town classes. During the South African War national attention was drawn to it by the number of recruits rejected on physical grounds. In Manchester in 1899 out of 12,000 men offering, 8,000 were rejected right off, and only 1,200 were accepted as fit in all respects;[2] though the army measurements had just been reduced to the lowest standard since Waterloo. In 1903 an official Memorandum[3] by the director-general of the Army Medical Corps showed that during the decade 1893–1902 some 34·6 per cent. had been rejected on medical examination, besides an uncounted number known to be very large, who had not been thought worth medically examining. Following this an interdepartmental committee sat, the evidence before which gives the fullest picture obtainable of the state of things. Other important documents for it are the memorable house-to-house study of York, by B. Seebohm Rowntree,[4] and many subsequent studies of other towns inspired by its example.

British manual workers at that time fell into three broad divisions: (1) town artisans; (2) town labourers; (3) agricultural labourers. The main canker in the nation's life was the condition of the town labourers. Earlier trade unionism had ignored

---

[1] For every 100 persons living in 1851, there were in 1908: in London, 203; in 84 large urban areas, 282; in 14 rural counties (exclusive of their county boroughs), 95; in the rest of England and Wales, 184 (*Statistical Memoranda and Charts prepared in the Local Government Board*; Cd. 4671 of 1909). One of the rural counties was Devon, where Exeter, Plymouth, and Devonport were excluded, but Torquay, Paignton, Ilfracombe, Exmouth, Sidmouth, &c., were all counted in.

[2] Interdepartmental Committee on Physical Deterioration: Evidence (Cd. 2210 of 1904), 124.

[3] Cd. 1501.

[4] *Poverty: A Study of Town Life* (1901). *Unemployment* (1911), by the same author in collaboration with Bruno Lasker, throws additional light. Of similar studies made elsewhere, *West Ham* (1907) by E. G. Howarth and Mona Wilson, *At The Works* (1907—a study of Middlesborough) by Lady (Hugh) Bell, *Norwich* (1910) by C. B. Hawkins, and *Livelihood and Poverty* (1915—a study of areas in Northampton, Warrington, Stanley, and Reading) by A. L. Bowley and A. R. Burnett-Hurst, may be mentioned as among the most valuable.

them; and too little account was still taken of their distinct status. A skilled engineer (member of the great trade union then called the A.S.E.) worked in a Manchester engineering works; his weekly rate was 35*s*. 6*d*. An engineer's labourer worked by his side; he was paid 19*s*. or 20*s*. A bricklayer's rate was 38*s*.; a bricklayer's labourer earned about half that. Even in skilled industries there were often as many labourers as the skilled men; and, with or without a trade prefix, they formed more than half the wage-earners in the cities. A mass of workers engaged in transport was only slightly better off; many, like dockers and market porters, being paid at a rather higher rate, but having it offset by casual employment. In Manchester the 19*s*.–20*s*. labourer would pay 5*s*. rent for a four-roomed cottage in a mean street in one of the vast slums of that city.[1] If he drank or had many children and none earning, he would probably be driven to a hovel—back-to-back, alley-built, or otherwise insanitary—at perhaps 4*s*. With the higher cost of town living, he would really be worse off than the farm labourer earning 13*s*. 6*d*. or 14*s*., but getting a cottage and garden for 1*s*. or 1*s*. 6*d*.; and his children, owing to the environment, would grow up much less healthy. He would also be worse off than the labourer in, say, Norwich or York, where the wage was only 18*s*., but rents went as low as 3*s*. or 2*s*. 6*d*. On the other hand, he would be better off than the labourer in Newcastle, where the wages were rather lower, the rents much higher, and housing conditions appalling. The state of the labourers in that city was possibly the worst in England; it had to be seen to be believed. London was a problem, or mass of problems, by itself; earnings, rents, and costs being all higher than in the provinces. Its black patches were numerous and bad; but taking its poor industrial areas, like Poplar or Canning Town, in the mass, they were less forlorn and more civilized than corresponding areas in the northern cities. Inner London, however, was a great centre for the class which ranked even below the labourers—the 'sweated' workers, whose plight public opinion had deplored, without amending, since Tom Hood's day. Many of these last in certain trades were Jewish immigrants; but the majority were English.

---

[1] The artisan paid 6*s*. 6*d*. to 7*s*. 6*d*. for a better cottage in a better street. Slum two-roomed tenements (back-to-back) were let at 3*s*. 6*d*. The few decent smaller tenements were municipal.

The evil could be, and was, approached from many angles —wages, housing, sanitation, medical service, education, decasualization, insurance, and pauperism. Rowntree set in the foreground the money problem. Having ascertained personal and family incomes at York, he fixed a figure representing the minimum cost at which an average household could satisfy bare physical needs, and found that 27·84 per cent. of the total population (equal to 43·4 per cent. of the wage-earning class) fell below it. These figures, following on Charles Booth's looser estimate for London, made a profound impression. Politicians, generalizing from York to the nation, declared that nearly 30 per cent. of its members were living at or below the poverty line, or, as Campbell-Bannerman put it, 'on the verge of hunger'. As a piece of statistics the inference was guess-work, but in substance it corresponded to the truth. York was by no means a specially unfavourable sample of an English town.[1] Yet years went by before much was remedied on this side.

The first big step was the Trade Boards Act of 1909, carried by Churchill, when home secretary, with the object of suppressing 'sweating'. The model was an act which had been working successfully in Victoria since 1895; Dilke had been bringing in bills like it since 1898. The formation of an Anti-Sweating League in 1905 and the organization (by the *Daily News*) of a Sweated Industries Exhibition[2] in 1906 focused opinion on it. The act originally applied to only four trades, but it proved a complete success; and, being soon more widely extended, practically extinguished sweating in the old terrible sense. It hardly touched the ordinary town labourer; but his turn came with the strikes of 1911–12, of which he was the chief beneficiary. Although for the working class as a whole real wages rose little between 1901 and 1914, and although Professor Bowley has calculated that the division of the national income as between 'property' and 'labour' in 1880 and in 1913 was almost

[1] As investigations elsewhere showed. The number of people found by Rowntree in 'primary' poverty in 1901 was 15·46 per cent. of the wage-earning class in York. Investigating working-class areas in Northampton, Warrington, Stanley, and Reading in 1914, A. L. Bowley and A. R. Burnett-Hurst found 16 per cent. of the persons investigated in primary poverty—this after thirteen years in which a good deal had been done to raise that class.

[2] *Sweated Industries*, the handbook to this (compiled by R. Mudie Smith), provides one of the best records of conditions as they were before 1909. It gives exact particulars for forty-five workers at forty-three different kinds of work, with undoctored and informative photographs.

identical,[1] yet within the working class the lower-paid workers gained. While most of the artisans secured no money rises or rises which less than balanced the price-change, the labourers improved their position. New unions had grown up for them; and the old unions also, as they moved more from a craft to an industrial basis, made increasing provision for the men at the bottom. Thus in the great coal-strike of 1912 what the Miners Federation won was a minimum wage; this benefited the lowest earners, while rarely affecting the skilled coal-getter.

Closely akin to the problem of low wages was that of casual labour. The pioneer here was W. H. (afterwards Sir William) Beveridge, whose book *Unemployment* (1909) altered expert opinion. Analysing registers kept under the Unemployed Workmen Act of 1905, Beveridge found that the 'unemployed' were in most cases the casually employed. By his persuasion was passed the Act of 1909 which set up Labour Exchanges all over the country (he himself being appointed to organize them). A bill enacting unemployment insurance was drafted for 1910, but time could not be found for it. However it became law in 1911 as Part II of the National Insurance Act. This measure was one of contributory insurance against unemployment; actuarially sound, confined to certain trades, and compulsory in them. It laid no great money burden on the state, and should be distinguished clearly from the post-war 'dole', for which its machinery was utilized. It worked down to the War conspicuously well, and invited no amendment save extension.

Though the bills dealing with sweating, decasualization, and unemployment no more emanated from a cabinet minister's brain than had the 1902 Education Act, signal credit is due, as in that case to Balfour, so in these to Churchill and Lloyd George, for having as ministers brought them to the statute-book. As a rule only a minister of high intelligence, capable of discounting the discouragements of high officials and fellow ministers, will put through measures of this kind. What happens when a minister lacking those qualities holds a key position was abundantly illustrated after 1905 by the case of John Burns and the local government board. No other department bestrode so many fields where progress was needed—poor-law, municipal government, housing, town-planning, and public health. Unfor-

[1] Viz. 37½ per cent. to 'property' and 62½ per cent. to 'labour': *The Change in the Distribution of the National Income, 1880-1913*, 25.

tunately, as we saw above,[1] it had been so constituted in 1871 that its dominant tradition became that of the old poor law board—a tradition of cramping the local authorities and preventing things from being done. When Burns went there, the officials at its head included some able men deeply imbued with this spirit; and the ex-demagogue,[2] sincere and upright, but without administrative experience and lacking either the education or the kind of ability that might have saved him, fell at once under their control. The result was that for nine years, during which the home office, the board of trade, and the board of education were all helping the nation to go forward, the local government board, though it had the greatest opportunities of all, remained for the most part anti-progressive.

What was most unpopular was its handling of the Poor Law. The conservative government just before leaving office in 1905 had appointed to report on this a strong royal commission under Lord George Hamilton, naturally with a conservative majority. In 1909 it produced two justly famous reports—Majority and Minority. The Minority Report was naturally that with which most of the government's followers sympathized. But even the Majority Report was far too progressive for the minister at the head of the local government board. The Minority wanted the Poor Law 'abolished' and its work redistributed; and the Majority, agreeing that the ideas and machinery of 1834 had grown thoroughly out of date, urged an only less complete transformation. Majority and Minority alike thought that the *ad hoc* elected guardians should go; that the principle of concentrating on the main local governing authorities, adopted for education in 1902, should be adopted in this case also; that services should be specialized under expert officials, not generalized under 'poor law officers'; and that 'poor relief' in the old sense was an obsolete conception. These views had the sanction of Lord George Hamilton, a conservative ex-minister; and if any other member of the liberal government had held Burns's position, great and needed reforms would have become law. Burns single-handed fended them off, until early in 1914 he was at last sent to another post. But before his successor could do more, the war came, and then the long post-war tangle; and it was

---

[1] p. 126.

[2] 'A demagogue in the ancient and honourable sense of the word', as Bernard Shaw once called him.

not till 1929 that there were enacted—by a conservative government—those organic changes recommended twenty years earlier.

But, although less widely resented, an even worse case for the country was that of town-planning. The English system of regulating new building only by by-laws had proved its insufficiency. It secured certain sanitary and structural minima, but did not prevent the extensions of English towns from being among the meanest, ugliest, and most higgledy-piggledy in Europe. Object lessons set by private enlightenment at Port Sunlight, Bournville, Letchworth, and the Hampstead Garden Suburb struck the public imagination; and about the same time knowledge came to England of the great work pioneered in Germany by way of enabling towns to plan out their detailed development. The 'Garden City' idea, preached by Ebenezer Howard, met the 'example of Germany' idea, preached by T. C. Horsfall and others, in most hopeful conjunction; practical men took them up, and sound policies were soberly worked out, which only needed legislation to get started. Again the one man blocked the way. In 1909 Burns carried a Housing and Town Planning Act, the town planning portion of which was a masterpiece of the obstructive art. It made town planning schemes nominally possible, but planted such a hedge of deterrent regulations round them, that in ten years less than 10,000 acres were brought under planning.[1] At the same time it blocked any real town planning legislation, advocates of which were told to wait and see how the Act worked. This was almost a major disaster for England. For if, as would otherwise have happened, a real national start had been made with town planning in 1909 or 1910, all the foundation work could have been done on it in the years before 1914, when building was quiet; and after the war, when the nation needed a flood of new houses, the whole development would have proceeded on planned instead of planless lines. England to-day would be a different and a better country.

Sanitation and public health made great progress in this period, though only after 1908, when Dr. (afterwards Sir Arthur) Newsholme was appointed chief medical officer at the local government board, was much impulse to it given from the centre. Before, it came chiefly from individual medical officers

[1] The bulk of the little done was a single scheme put through for about nine square miles of Middlesex by the public spirit of a college.

of health, working as they did under conditions conducive to enterprise. The greatest feat was the sensational reduction in the infantile death-rate, and the chief agency in it was the evolution of what are now called Infants' Welfare Centres. The principle was that of reaching the individual mother, and teaching her how to rear her infant. First in the nineties came a movement in France—the *Gouttes de Lait* founded by Dr. Budin —for supplying reliable milk free to poor mothers. The earliest English milk dispensary on these lines was started at St. Helens in 1899 by Dr. Drew Harris. By 1906 there were a dozen others. A parallel move, also in the nineties, was the institution of 'health visitors', started (through a voluntary society) by Dr. J. Niven, the medical officer for Manchester, to advise and instruct mothers in their homes. This was taken up and much improved by Dr. Samson Moore of Huddersfield, whose town for some years became a sort of Mecca for those concerned in the life-saving crusade. But though these policies paved the way for the infant welfare centres, their actual prototype was foreign, being devised by a Dr. Miele at Ghent in 1903. Copied from it, the first English 'School for Mothers' was opened in St. Pancras in 1907 by Dr. J. F. J. Sykes. Its success was very great; its example spread fast; and the infantile death-rate, long so intractable, fell in a few years amazingly. The saving effects on the population figures have been noted above. An interesting point is that here, as in nearly all the social policies of this period, the leading ideas were imported from abroad. England copied, but very effectively.[1]

Of all such copyings the greatest was Part I (Health) of the National Insurance Act. Here more than in any other case at this time, the initiative seems to have come from the cabinet minister himself, i.e. from Lloyd George. The main features of the measure and its departures from the German original have been mentioned above.[2] It would have been natural to have attached its administration to the local government board (as it is now attached to the board's successor, the ministry of health); but with a régime like Burns's this was out of the question. A separate machinery was set up under four (English, Welsh, Scottish, and Irish) linked commissions, represented in parliament through the treasury. For the vast work of creating

[1] See *The Early History of the Infant Welfare Movement* (1933) by Dr. G. F. McCleary, one of its leading pioneers. [2] p. 445.

the organization the services of R. L. Morant were secured. He gathered round him the pick of the younger civil servants, and by a prodigious effort the act was launched on the appointed day. There remained a great difficulty about getting the co-operation of the doctors; but in spite of opposition organized through the British Medical Association this was obtained. In the sequel the act's greatest virtue, perhaps, was its effect on the medical profession. It at once gave the average doctor a far better income; it soon rapidly increased the nation's staff of doctors; and it brought the mass of wage-earners into a familiar contact with medical advice and treatment, to which only a minority of them were used before. Its full effects, however, on the development of the nation's health services were only seen at a later period. Another most important side of them—the medical inspection and treatment of the children in the nation's schools—had already been set going by Morant and Dr. (afterwards Sir George) Newman at the board of education. Here again the example came from Germany; first interpreted to England in work on a voluntary basis by Miss Margaret Mac-Millan.

Health Insurance and Old Age Pensions were alone among the liberal government's reforms in costing much money. Some of them positively saved it. Notably that was so with prison and penological reform. The roots of this lay farther back; they began when the home office in 1877 took over the local prisons and centralized the whole system under a Prison Commission. But the Prison Act of 1898, which repealed the rigid statutory prison rules till then in force, and empowered the home secretary to make and vary rules from time to time, rendered possible faster progress in the twentieth century. After 1906 much public interest was directed to the topic, and two acts were passed which each made epochs. The first was the Probation of Offenders Act 1907, with which the probation system in England began. The second was the Criminal Justice Administration Act 1914, under which courts were required to allow reasonable time for the payment of fines before an offender was committed to prison for non-payment. These two acts together enormously reduced the prison population, a process economical as well as humane. Other notable reforms were the development from 1908 of the Borstal system for reclaiming young criminals, and the Children Act of that year, under which imprisonment was prohibited for offenders up to 14 and strictly limited for those 14–16. A less successful experiment was that of 'preventive detention' for habitual criminals under another 1908 Act. Taken together, this great body of reforms did much, not merely to improve English criminal administration, but to humanize the outlook of English society. Their principal author, behind the parliamentarians, was Sir Evelyn Ruggles-Brise, then chairman of the Prison Commission; a man of 'humanity and insight beyond the common'.[1]

Prison reform was necessarily an affair of the central government. But in most other directions an important part was taken by the local authorities. Only now was the full value realized of the democratic machinery set up under the acts of 1888 and 1894. For many purposes touching people's daily lives it was much increased by a development exemplified in the Education Act of 1902. That act in creating the education committees made stipulations as to their composition; each was to have a part of its membership co-opted from outside the council, and each was to contain women. Both principles proved their usefulness, and came to be applied in many directions. The method of co-option rendered it possible to get public work out of suitable private people on a large scale; and hybrid bodies sprang up—Children's Care Committees, Choice of Employment Committees, Infants' Welfare Committees, and others—where this was often done to great effect. Meanwhile the volume and efficiency of regular municipal work advanced almost everywhere, and in its train the material environment of people's lives was continually being improved. To give instances at haphazard, this was a period of better roads, cleaner streets, ampler lighting, better systems of sewerage and drainage, more numerous parks, better equipped free libraries, and more efficient inspection under the Adulteration Acts and Weights and Measures Acts. These things in themselves meant a higher standard of life, irrespective of money incomes.

Change and progress nowhere showed more through these years than in the navy and army. Their leading exponent in the one case was Fisher, in the other Haldane.

Fisher's reforms began in 1902–3, when he was at the admiralty as second sea lord in charge of personnel. In 1903 the old cadet-ship *Britannia* was abolished, and Dartmouth College

[1] L. W. Fox, *The Modern English Prison* (1934), 38.

substituted—a great improvement. Fisher took advantage of it to modernize the system in many ways. His most revolutionary change was to amalgamate the training for engineer and executive officers. Till then the engineers were trained in a separate ship. Now all boys started through the same mill and specialized later.

When he came back to Whitehall as first sea lord in 1904, his earliest concern, besides lopping away obsolete units, was the redistribution of the main fleets. Till then there had for half a century been five chief commands (usually held by vice-admirals)—the Mediterranean Fleet, the Channel Fleet, Portsmouth, the Nore, and Plymouth; the last three, apart from their flagships, being really shore commands. The assumptions were that France was the possible enemy, the passage to India the chief trade-route in need of defence, and the North Sea of small naval importance. The growth of the German navy and the French Entente were rendering these assumptions obsolete, but British naval opinion was conservative, and for other reasons it was advisable to camouflage the changes. We have seen[1] how in 1905 Fisher created an Atlantic Fleet based on Gibraltar, thereby getting part of the Mediterranean Fleet out of the Mediterranean. In October 1906 a new creation was announced —a 'Home Fleet'. Six battleships, 6 cruisers, and 48 destroyers with the needful auxiliaries, were (all with full crews) to be based on the Nore; and the *Dreadnought*, then unique, was to be their flagship. This really meant that three-quarters of the big battleships—the Home, Channel, and Atlantic Fleets—would be readily available against Germany. But it was not till February 1909 that the Channel Fleet was formally incorporated in the new unit.

Fisher's other great innovation was that of all-big-gun ships— the battleship *Dreadnought* and her cruiser counterpart, the *Invincible*. We saw above[2] the strategic and political motives here—perfectly sound ones, though often since forgotten. But the primary motives were technological.[3] They arose out of startling improvements in the range and accuracy of torpedoes. Hitherto battleships carried four big guns, a number of light quickfirers for repelling small craft at close quarters, and a very large secondary armament of 6-inch Q.F. guns intended also

[1] pp. 363-4.   [2] p. 364.
[3] Admiral Sir R. H. Bacon, *Lord Fisher* (1929), 251-6, 259-64.

to be used on the enemy battleships at middling ranges. But at a certain stage the torpedo developed an effective range practically equal to that of these Q.F. guns. To fight outside torpedo range meant fighting at big-gun range only; and hence the idea of the all-big-gun ship. The *Dreadnought* could fire eight 12-inch guns on a broadside, her predecessors only four; and her superiority in firing ahead or astern was even greater.[1] Later battleships were designed to fire all their ten big guns on either broadside; and before long the 6-inch Q.F. guns came back, necessitating, of course, heavier tonnage. The *Dreadnought*, completed in 1906, was 17,900 tons; the *Iron Duke*, completed in 1913, was 25,000. The difference was accounted for partly by the *Iron Duke*'s carrying sixteen 6-inch guns; partly by her ten big guns being 13·5-inch instead of 12-inch; and partly by her engines developing 33,000 instead of 23,000 horse-power. The *Dreadnought* and *Invincible*, it should be mentioned, were the first turbine-engined capital ships in any navy, and being much faster than previous ships in their respective classes could hold their enemy at distance.

Fisher had genius, and in matters like these revealed extra-ordinary foresight. But he was also an egotist, and too apt to forget that no great service can live on one man's brains. It was not in his line to advocate or establish a proper general staff. The results of the omission were unfortunate, and not really repaired by the 'Naval War Staff' set up in 1912. After Fisher's retirement in 1910 the British admiralty had no peculiar advantage over the German in personal talent, while the latter had at the top the organization which the former lacked. Consequently when the war came, the German navy proved superior at many vital points. Great Britain had spent so much more money, that her fleet's huge lead in number of ships and weight of guns saw it through. But the Germans' gunnery and range-finders were better, and they had a far better high-explosive shell; consequently, ship for ship, they registered more hits and did more damage with them. They started the war with a large supply of very effective mines; whereas there were hardly any effective mines in the British service until (incredible as it may seem) 1917. They were also well equipped from the start with aircraft for naval scouting, whereas the British navy was not.

[1] Besides its more obvious advantages, the multiplication of big guns of uniform calibre greatly facilitated range-finding by salvoes.

This catalogue (which could be extended) is worth recalling for the light that it throws on organization, and particularly on the value of a general staff. Even Fisher would have gained by more co-ordinated thinking.

Between 1910 and 1914 some difficult special problems developed. One was that of oil-fuel. Fisher was an enthusiast for it on fighting grounds; but how, with no home or even Empire oil-wells, was a war-time supply to be guaranteed? The policy adopted was to form the Anglo-Persian Oil Company, with the state holding half its shares: a novel plan rather alarming to political purists. Another difficulty was how to provide the fast-growing navy with enough officers. A capital ship could be built in two years, but to train an officer from Dartmouth up took seven. Churchill to meet this brought in cadets at an older age from the public schools—good material, but entailing some loss of homogeneity. Yet other difficulties concerned the naval ratings. With the main fleets in home waters, they came much more into contact with working-class opinion on shore; and movements developed for better pay and a modernized discipline. In 1909 McKenna passed a not unimportant act distinguishing (on lines adopted for the army three years earlier) between prison for criminal offences and detention for breaches of rules. Questions of pay grew urgent, not merely for contentment but for recruiting. As the British and German navies expanded, it began to be an advantage for the latter that, under conscription, it was never short of men. Churchill's sensible efforts to improve the scales were a good deal hampered by the treasury and the house of commons. He justly protested against their readiness to risk fleet-wide discontent for sums which beside the costs of naval construction were trifling.

At the height of the race in warships help from the overseas Empire became very welcome. New Zealand and the Federated Malay States each contributed a battle-cruiser. Another was given by Australia, but earmarked for use in Australian waters. In Canada the Borden government in 1912–13 made a determined effort to pass a bill for the construction of three battleships; but the opposition under Sir Wilfred Laurier keenly opposed it, and procured its rejection by the Senate. In the war sequel the main contribution of the Dominions, as of India, was to be on the military side.

Nothing could better exemplify the value of thinking as a basis for action than Haldane's work for the army. It succeeded because he carefully mapped the needs before he set about meeting them. In particular he realized the prime importance of mobilization. When he went to the war office, none of the various forces could be mobilized quickly, and many could not be at all. Even the Aldershot Army Corps, which was the only large unit, was unfit to take the field without considerable delay. The cavalry lacked horses; the artillery lacked men; the regular units scattered over the country were not fully organized in divisions with the necessary staffs and commanders; and even if the infantry were brought together, artillery, transport, and hospital units would all be to seek. Behind them stood as a second line the militia; but they could not be called on to fight abroad, and the most for which their units were fit in war-time was to release the regulars from some garrison and depot duties at home. The third line consisted of volunteers and yeomanry; who, in general and with some exceptions, had no unit above the battalion, and were quite incapable of action as a mobile force.

In contrast to this, on 3 August 1914 some twenty divisions of British troops (six regular and fourteen territorial) were mobilized punctually and without a hitch, complete in all arms; besides a cavalry division of regulars, and a 7th infantry division collected not long after. A few weeks later very heavy initial casualties were made good by adequate reserves. Of the policies, by which Haldane wrought this marvellous change (chiefly in the years 1906–9), an outline has been given already.[1] With it all he saved money, and even in 1914 the army estimates were about £1 million less than in the year before he took office, although general prices had risen 18 per cent. in the interval. Some of his economies were no doubt reluctant; but the charges that he weakened the country in regard to either infantry or artillery will not bear examination.[2]

Though his main ideas were his own, Haldane's work owed something to the existence of the Committee of Imperial Defence, set up two years earlier by Balfour.[3] Balfour had derived much aid in this matter from Lord Esher, who now

[1] pp. 395–6.
[2] See an able refutation of them by the Right Hon. H. T. Baker in the *Army Quarterly* for October 1928.   [3] p. 361–2.

became one of Haldane's best helpers, being chairman of the
committee to organize the territorial force. The Committee of
Imperial Defence developed steadily its uses and importance.
Its chairman being the prime minister, when that office devolved
on Asquith, Haldane's part in it became especially prominent.
Through sub-committees a long list of war-time problems were
carefully gone through in advance; not only the duties of each
department, as systematized in the 'War-Book',[1] but thorny questions like press censorship, treatment of aliens, and trading with
the enemy, besides large aspects of imperial strategy. Summing
it all, the country became incomparably better prepared for
war than it ever had been in the nineteenth century. Many
charges can justly be brought against the Asquith cabinet of
1908–14, but not that of war-unpreparedness. That the nation
had nevertheless to do afterwards so much more than it had
bargained was not due to falling-short on its own part or on
that of its rulers.

Growth of Budgets, 1901-14

(Figures in £ millions)

Year	Revenue budgeted for	Civil services' estimates	Fighting services' estimates	Navy	Army
1901 . . .	132·25	23·60	60·90	30·87	30·03
1903 . . .	144·27	26·56	60·11	30·45	29·66
1905 . . .	142·45	28·61	63·20	33·38	29·81
1907 . . .	142·79	30·10	59·17	31·41	27·76
1909 . . .	162·59	40·37	62·57	35·14	27·43
1911 . . .	181·62	46·78	72·08	44·39	27·69
1913 . . .	195·82	54·98	74·52	46·30	28·22
1914 . . .	209·45	57·06	80·39	51·55	28·84

[1] p. 433.

MENTAL AND SOCIAL ASPECTS 1901–14

IN contrast with the last decade of the nineteenth century in England, the first decade of the twentieth showed a mood of sunrise succeeding one of sunset. Among many educated young men who came of age between 1885 and 1895, the phrase *fin de siècle* had worked like a charm. Similar young men between 1895 and 1905 reacted against it with violence. They felt themselves at the beginning, not at the end, of an age.[1]

It was to be an age of democracy, of social justice, of faith in the possibilities of the common man. There was little more room in it for Kipling's imperialism than for the *Yellow Book*'s decadence; and after the Boer war had deflated the one, as the Oscar Wilde case had earlier discredited the other, the way seemed open for new impulses of courage and idealism. The current, of course, was not confined to young people; older men had helped to start it; and exponents of many different tendencies fell in with it. Some were liberals, some socialists, many both; but there was also a strong element of implicit conservatism in the revived feeling for a traditional England.

The full force of the current was felt between 1903 and 1910. Many, indeed, of the social and legislative changes to which it led came (as the last two chapters have shown) after the latter date. But in public life there is always a time-lag between ideas and embodiments. If we look at the ideas alone, we shall see that from about 1910 their movement weakened, and a new current set in.

There was not now, as there had been in 1870, any solid core of agreed religious belief, round which the daily conduct of the nation as a whole shaped itself. Thirty years of the disintegrating influences traced above in Chapters V and X had completely destroyed the mid-Victorian evangelical unity. Creed sat lightly on the great majority in the middle and upper classes; the Bible lost its hold on them, and the volume of outward religious observance shrank steadily. At the same time the reader must not confuse in these respects pre-war with post-war. From the

---

[1] A capital description of the contrast in mood, written at the time by (as he then was) one of the prophets of the new outlook, will be found in a poem by G. K. Chesterton, beginning 'A cloud was on the mind of men'.

beginning of the new century the week-end habit developed rapidly and made serious inroads on church-going; but the far greater inroads eventually made by the motor-car had scarcely begun by 1914. Preachers of any merit still drew large and attentive audiences everywhere, and a considerable number had what might be termed national reputations. It was still altogether exceptional for a couple on whose marriage no slur rested to get married in a registry office; and a majority of middle-class people every Sunday morning still put on 'Sunday clothes' and went in them to public worship, followed often in towns in fine weather by resort to some 'church parade', where the gentlemen lifted their silk hats to one another and the ladies took note of each other's costumes. Yet the practice waned, for the young people increasingly omitted it, and there was a great difference in this respect between 1901 and 1914.

The chapels kept up their congregations better than the church of England; but the labour and socialist movement poached extensively on their preserves. Not only, as we saw earlier, did it provide careers on the platform for gifted men who would otherwise have found them in the pulpit, but the I.L.P., which made a practice of holding large indoor propaganda meetings on Sunday evenings, directly drew away the members of congregations. The ministers of the chapels, feeling the attraction which the new politics had for their people, very often went to meet it half-way. An institution which spread widely at this time was the 'P.S.A.' (Pleasant Sunday Afternoon); held as a rule in the chapel itself with the minister presiding, but, save for a short prayer and hymns, secular in character. Usually there were songs or other solo music, but the main feature was an address by a layman on a secular subject, oftenest with a bias to humanitarianism of some kind. Popular authors, travellers, politicians, journalists, or socialist propagandists were in great request for these addresses—especially the last; and it is significant of the political trend of nonconformity in these years, that while few conservative politicians were invited to speak at P.S.A.s and many liberals were not either, a leading socialist might spend practically every Sunday afternoon in them. The sects, however, differed somewhat in this respect, and the contacts of socialism were commoner and closer with the Congregational and Baptist chapels than with the Wesleyan.

One way and another the rising labour movement owed an

immense debt to nonconformity. The fund of unselfish idealism, which sustained the early I.L.P., came mostly from this source; and the methods whereby its branches were run and financed were borrowed directly by its members from their experience in religious organizations. Broadly it was due to nonconformity that socialism in England never acquired the anti-religious bias prevailing on the Continent. The church of England rendered no comparable service, for the self-helping sections of the working class were a social stratum over which it had never obtained much hold. Yet there was a socialistic school among its younger clergy, especially among the ritualists. They found their outlet mainly in slum mission work, where in dealing with classes below the self-helping level they were on the whole more successful than the nonconformists.

Outside these slum parishes, in which the pick of the young clergy graduated as curates, anglicanism began now to feel the effects of a declining recruitment. The number of ordinands continued to fall year by year, and the shrinkage of ability was perceptible. On the countryside the great race of parish clergy, as they dropped out one by one, too seldom found successors of the same calibre. Similarly on the bench of bishops, though a few very able additions were made to it at this time, the losses outweighed the gains. The church's higher statesmanship was much preoccupied with political questions—with the position of the church schools, with the unsolved problem of ecclesiastical discipline, and with the disestablishment of the church in Wales. None of these problems were very wisely handled. That of church discipline, which the rapid spread of ritualism rendered more and more controversial, was remitted by the Balfour government of 1904 to a royal commission presided over by Lord St. Aldwyn. Largely through the ability and influence of that eminent layman, the commission made in 1906 a unanimous report. It proposed the repeal of Disraeli's Public Worship Regulation Act and the reform of the ecclesiastical courts on lines already recommended by another royal commission. But its main propositions were two: that the law of the church as enacted by parliament in the rubric ought to be suitably revised by the convocations, and that when revised it should be firmly enforced, the bishops meanwhile being given further powers to enforce it. In accordance with this, letters of business were promptly issued to the convocations to take up the task; and had they performed it within a reasonable time—say a year or even two years—there seems no reason why the St. Aldwyn policy should not have succeeded. But having had the task of revision entrusted to them, the convocations in effect adjourned its performance till the Greek calends.[1] Meanwhile pending that performance the bishops, since the St. Aldwyn report had treated the existing rubric as needing revision, held themselves additionally justified in shirking its enforcement. The result was that there was worse anarchy than ever, and Lord St. Aldwyn's intentions were completely frustrated.

In the matter of church schools, and also in that of Welsh disestablishment, the anglican attitude, generally speaking, was neither magnanimous nor long-sighted. Churchmen had spent largely to create and maintain their schools, and had every right to fight hard for their continuance. But they ought to have made more effort to see the point of view of their opponents. Had they done so, they could not have failed to recognize the hardship which nonconformity suffered in the single-school areas; and instead of seeking to take advantage of it, would have sought to redress it. Effective generosity in that sense would have prevented all the bitterness from 1902 onward, and have given the church a far greater influence over nonconformists than it could ever get by educating their children against their will. Similarly in regard to Welsh disestablishment. The bill, against which all the forces of churchmanship were organized to fight tooth and nail, became law under the Parliament Act in September 1914; but being deferred during the European war, did not actually come into force till March 1920. It has proved of the greatest benefit to the anglican church in Wales, which has now far more health and vigour than it had before. Foreseeing, as any one could, that this would be so, it might have seemed the wiser line for the church's leaders to recognize frankly that the case of Wales was peculiar; that disestablishment there and in England were two entirely different affairs; that a church *of* Wales could put itself right with Welsh nationalism as the Church *in* Wales never could; and that the only thing left was to seek in an atmosphere of goodwill for a measure of financial generosity. The line which they instead took of harping on the indissoluble unity of the church in Wales and England, and denouncing

---

[1] Eventually about twenty-two years elapsed between the issuing of the letters of business and the submission of a revised prayer book to parliament.

disestablishment in the one as the thin end of the wedge for disestablishment in the other, showed an entire lack of sympathetic imagination; and the worldly party politicians, whom they got to voice it for them, did their religious authority nothing but harm.[1]

Outside the churches in this period—and to some extent inside most of them—the religious attitude regarding creeds was one of growing tolerance. To the evangelical the dogmas of his faith had seemed a condition of morality, because he ruled his own daily conduct by them.[2] A counter-intolerance was very common among the opponents of orthodoxy; they thought that any educated man who retained a creed must be guilty of at least intellectual dishonesty. With the advent of the twentieth century this tendency to hard judgements became gradually blurred and softened. At the same time people lost interest in heated arguments as to whether the Gadarene swine were possessed by devils, or whether other miracles in the Bible were to be regarded as historical. Largely, no doubt, this was due to indifference; but partly also to a new perception that the permanent values of a religion need not stand or fall with its temporal accidents. A book published in 1902, which had a very wide vogue among educated people in the ensuing years, was *The Varieties of Religious Experience*, by William James. James, who held the chair of philosophy at Harvard, and whose brother Henry, the novelist, was settled in England, examined religion from the standpoint of a student of psychology. He was perhaps less an original thinker than a prince of expositors; but he showed to great numbers of his readers something which they had never seen before, and carried their thinking about religion on to a different plane from any to which they had been accustomed. This was the starting-point in England of a popular interest in psychology—an interest which later became more concerned with questions of conduct than with religion, and even before the war had begun to disturb materially the cut and dried conceptions of right and wrong. Studies like those of comparative religion and anthropology, which, as we shall see, were notably developed at the same time, reinforced both the foregoing tendencies.

---

[1] Here again a poem by G. K. Chesterton is an apt illustration—*Antichrist*, the well-known ode addressed to (as he then was) F. E. Smith.

[2] The present writer can recall an active liberal politician saying (in 1892) that he could never vote for John Morley, because he did not see how an 'atheist' could at bottom be an honest man.

The press followed out the evolution determined in the previous period. Ownership became in all but a few cases commer-
cialized. It passed from the hands of individual proprietors, who
could treat their newspapers to some extent as a personal trust,
into those of companies or syndicates, who made public issues
of shares and had to earn interest on them. 'Twenty years ago',
the Institute of Journalists was told by its president in 1913,
'the list of the London Stock Exchange did not contain a single
newspaper corporation. Now twelve large companies, representing many millions of capital, figure in the quotations. Many
other companies are dealt with publicly in a more restricted
market.'[1] Money came before public policy under these
conditions.

The ways to make it had been discovered by Newnes, the
Harmsworths, and Kennedy Jones. To the *Daily Mail*'s technique for increasing circulation and consequently attracting
advertisers, every popular paper, it seemed, must conform or
perish. A few men early built up large newspaper businesses
from nothing, as those pioneers had done. C. Arthur Pearson,
a man of more energy than originality, worked in Newnes's
office after Alfred Harmsworth had left it; then he went out and
founded *Pearson's Weekly*, a close replica of *Tit-Bits* and *Answers*,
and developed round it, just as they had, a lucrative swarm of
little periodicals. Subsequently, still copying, he launched (1900)
the *Daily Express* in imitation of the *Daily Mail*. It never in his
time attained any solid success; but for some years he exercised
a certain force through it, particularly between 1903 and 1906,
when he made it an organ of Chamberlain's Tariff Reform
movement. The other largest concern of this kind was that of
the Hultons at Manchester. They had begun by publishing
sporting papers—a distinct line, but not very paying, because
unattractive to advertisers. But they went on to copy exactly,
like Pearson, the Harmsworth evolution; first making money
by multiplying little papers, and then launching on their
northern ground halfpenny evening and morning newspapers
modelled on the *Evening News* and *Daily Mail*.

These enterprises took away custom and advertisements from
the old-established newspapers, not merely in London, but all
over the country. The large capital resources and pushing
popular methods of the new-comers made them very hard to

[1] H. A. Taylor, *Robert Donald* (1934), p. 266.

stand up against. Many old provincial proprietors succumbed and sold out to Harmsworth, Pearson, or Hulton, as the case might be. In London a year of great changes was 1904. The *Standard* (from 1876 to 1900 under a great editor, W. H. Mudford) had flourished exceedingly through most of Lord Salisbury's period as the leading conservative party paper, drawing intimate inspiration from the prime minister. But almost from the moment of the *Daily Mail's* appearance its fortunes began to decline; and in 1904 it was sold to Pearson for £400,000, then thought a high figure. Pearson made a memorable failure with it; he changed it instantly to a paper of the new type, with the result that it lost its old readers overnight, before it could enlist new ones. It lingered moribund for some years and then died miserably. In the same year both the London liberal morning papers came down to a halfpenny. They had previously been very high-class penny political organs with circulations round about 30,000 apiece; now they were to bid for halfpenny circulations in six figures, which could only be had by copying Harmsworth-Pearson methods. For the large body of educated liberals in the south of England this was a real catastrophe. The conservatives after the *Standard's* sale could still fall back on *The Times*, the *Daily Telegraph*, and the *Morning Post*; their opponents had no morning paper of similar weight nearer than the *Manchester Guardian*. In 1906 a rich liberal tried to remove the reproach by founding in London the *Tribune* as a high-class morning newspaper. Following the great triumph of his party at the polls, he had a rare chance; but he knew nothing of journalism, and, like most who venture on it from the outside, came rapidly to grief. The lack of any London morning paper for educated liberal readers enhanced the already strong tendency for the party division in English politics to become a class division.

Meanwhile in the eventful year 1904 Alfred Harmsworth started the *Daily Mirror* as a woman's paper. It failed completely as such; but, with the wonderful agility which was half his genius, its creator switched it over to become the first of yet another new type, the cheap daily picture-paper. After its change it appealed more to women than before, and soon made enormous profits as a kind of printed precursor of the cinematographic age. Then in 1908 came the greatest stroke of all. *The Times*, in spite of the unique standing which it held in the world, had for long been half-strangled by anachronisms in the finance and constitution of its proprietary. By the end of 1907 it was at its last gasp; and the only question left was whether Pearson or Lord Northcliffe (as Alfred Harmsworth had now become) should buy it. Northcliffe won, and early in 1908 it passed into his hands. Too clever to repeat Pearson's mistake with the *Standard*, he did not affront the paper's old readers, and to the end remained aware that it was a different proposition from the halfpenny organs which he had himself founded. He sought, however, gradually to give it a more popular character, lowering its price by stages to a penny;[1] and also used it increasingly to put forward his personal opinions on public issues. Many of his changes were improvements, and it would be absurd to suggest that the able men who served him on it laboured all in vain. Nevertheless it was fundamentally a source of national weakness, that *The Times* should become a second mouthpiece for the creator of the *Daily Mail*.

But all this time the number of mouths behind the mouthpieces was growing fewer. In 1913 as compared with 1893 the proportion of newspaper readers to population had greatly increased, while that of newspapers had diminished, and that of newspaper ownerships had diminished still more. In their fierce race for circulation the halfpenny papers sought to extend their grasp ever more widely over the country. Their first means to this were trains; by going to press earlier they could catch more trains, and where this did not suffice, they ran specials. The time of going to press in London, which had been about 3 a.m., was moved forward for the early editions to 11 p.m. or earlier; the result was a hastier paper, which could no longer comment on important late news—the closing speeches, for instance, in a critical parliamentary debate, or the result of the division. The next device was to get beyond train-radius altogether by printing separately in some suitably remote city, to which the 'copy' was transmitted by private wire. The *Daily Mail* was the first to do this, when at the turn of the century it established a subordinate printing-office at Manchester. The *Daily News* copied it some years later; and other examples followed. These changes helped the process, whereby a multi-

---

[1] In 1855, when the penny press started, *The Times*'s price had been put down from 5*d*. to 4*d*.; and in 1861 to 3*d*. In February 1911 Northcliffe reduced it to 2*d*. for subscribers; in May 1913 to 2*d*. all round; and in March 1914 to 1*d*. all round.

plying mass of readers took their news and views from a diminishing band of newspaper magnates. They also extended the
influence of the capital over the provinces. Hitherto the larger
provincial centres followed each their own public opinion, often
saner and less febrile than London's. Now the passions of the
metropolis infected the whole country.

Two reassuring features may, however, be noted. In the first
place, a small number of the best penny provincial dailies held
their ground. Fortified by local advertising and entrenched in
their monopolies of local trade news, they were able in a few
instances to weather the storm better than their London contemporaries. The *Manchester Guardian, Scotsman, Yorkshire Post,
Glasgow Herald, Liverpool Daily Post,* and *Birmingham Daily Post*
became in some respects the best morning papers in the country.
But they were the survivors of a great thinning-out. Manchester
and Leeds had two penny dailies apiece; only one survived in
each instance; and other cases were similar.

Secondly, the English halfpenny papers, despite their obvious
vices, seldom sank quite so low as the American 'yellow' press,
from which they had originally been copied. Moreover from
about 1909 a distinct movement to improve them was pioneered
by the *Daily Mail* itself. Average readers were growing more
educated; it was not necessary to be so snippety or so sensational.
There was some revival of consideration for readers seeking
knowledge and ideas. A serious leader-page was developed with
signed articles by eminent writers on subjects of importance.
Here again one must beware of confusing post-war with pre-war.
The pre-war popular newspaper misplaced many values; but
it never came down to presenting a world where film stars are
of more consequence than statesmen, and where business and
politics alike become the merest sideshows to personal 'romance'.
Since the European war popular papers have been above all
shaped to attract the woman reader, but before the war they
still mainly catered for men. The reasons were, partly that
women had then no votes (and proprietors always care for
political influence); and partly that the great discovery had not
then been made, that women readers are incomparably the most
valuable to advertise to.

Halfpenny evening papers, bought largely for betting, grew
much and from many centres. But the old 'class' evening paper
catering for the London clubs fell on bad days. Two such, it is

true, were at the end of the period conducted with the greatest distinction—the *Westminster Gazette* by J. A. Spender and the *Pall Mall Gazette* by J. L. Garvin—as leading oracles for the liberal and conservative parties respectively. But they did not pay, and were only kept going by money spent on them from political motives. A cheaper way for a rich man to become a maker of opinion was to publish a sixpenny weekly review. Publications of this class became now more numerous and various than ever before, and from first to last much of the period's best writing will be found in them. But only one (the unionist *Spectator*) paid solid dividends; the rest lived on their owners' money, and their careers were apt to be brief or chequered. They took the place, in some degree, of the monthly and quarterly reviews, whose prosperity and influence after about 1904 went fast downhill, though far from reaching their post-war level.

Educational advances were very rapid after the acts of 1902 and (for London) 1903. All elementary schools being now on the rates, there was a general levelling-up of those which had lagged behind. It was a strong point in the acts that, though the managers of 'non-provided' (previously 'voluntary') schools controlled the religious education in them, they were required in respect of secular instruction to carry out any direction of the local education authority. Teachers' salaries, though far below those of the post-war period, tended to move up as the county councils established regular scales. There was a persistent campaign to reduce the size of classes and get rid of the over-sized; but the problem of buildings was involved here, and in London, where the scandalous cases were most numerous, a good many survived in the infants' departments beyond the latest years of this period.

The higher-grade schools, which had been illegally conducted by the school boards, were in most places made secondary schools. But in London the L.C.C. preferred to build new secondary schools, and developed what it had taken over from the school board as 'central' schools of a higher-elementary type. The policy of developing such schools within the elementary system came in a few years to be recommended by the board of education. The board under Morant made great exertions to increase and improve the facilities for secondary and technical education throughout the country. In 1905 the number of pupils in grant-aided secondary schools was 94,000; in 1910, it was 156,000; in 1914 it was about 200,000. Though these figures were afterwards greatly exceeded in the secondary education boom produced by the war, they represented at the time a long step towards remedying England's most obvious weakness—her dearth of higher-educated personnel. Ability, too, was recruited more widely. In 1906 the liberal government started a policy leading to a great extension of scholarships. It offered an additional grant to secondary schools which gave 25 per cent. 'free places'. The effects of this were increasingly felt from 1907.

The smaller historic grammar schools up and down the country, most of which from about 1890 had been modernized under the influence of the Technical Instruction Act, came after 1902 fully under the local authorities' umbrella as secondary schools. So did some of the larger ones, which had hitherto been members of the Headmasters' Conference; and questions of educational autonomy were raised, which led for a time to their being separated from it. The great non-local public schools, which formed the bulk of the conference, did not accept financial aid from public authorities. But they were not injured by the new competition; rather, they benefited by the educational boom; and this was the beginning for them of a period of unexampled prosperity.

The universities went similarly ahead. At Oxford the appointment (1907) of Lord Curzon as chancellor proved helpful to academic reform, in which he took a personal interest; Cambridge also made progressive changes. Both universities steadily increased the scope and variety of their provision for teaching, as well as the numbers of their undergraduates. But perhaps the most striking feature of the time was the growth of new universities. We saw above (p. 321) how Birmingham university led the way in 1900. In 1903 the three constituent colleges of the Victoria university decided to part company and form a university apiece; Manchester and Liverpool received charters in that year, Leeds in 1904. Sheffield followed in 1905, and Bristol in 1909. In addition there were by 1914 outside London six English institutions ranked as university colleges, viz. those at Nottingham, Newcastle, Reading, Exeter, and Southampton, with the Manchester School of Technology. Add the continued growth of the three colleges forming the university of Wales, and some idea will be formed of the increase at this time in local provision for university teaching south of the Tweed.

London, too, developed greatly as an educational centre, and fresh attempts were made to integrate its university organization. At the beginning of 1907 University College was formally 'transferred to' the university itself, and just three years later a similar transfer was made of King's College, excepting its theological faculty. But, among many others, the institutions containing the two largest bodies of students retained their semi-detached status as 'schools of the university'. These were (a) the group of great medical schools attached to the leading London hospitals; (b) the Imperial College of Science and Technology, in which the City and Guilds Engineering College and the School of Mines were merged. The same status was that of the London School of Economics and Political Science, which, founded on a modest scale in 1895, grew up rapidly in the twentieth century as a specialized institution for studies that the older universities had been somewhat slow to develop. Although even in 1914 it was a very much smaller institution than it has since become, it had nevertheless already attained a national, and indeed international, standing.

University extension continued, and in 1904, as a novel and vigorous offshoot of it, was born the Workers' Educational Association. The four earliest W.E.A. branches (all started between October 1904 and March 1905) were Reading, Derby, Rochdale, and Ilford. The movement, as these names suggest, cast a wide net from the first, its primary idea being that the adult working-class student must co-operate in his own education, and not be a mere listener at lectures. But it was the success of the 'tutorial class' method, originally worked out at Rochdale in 1907, which gave practical shape to this aspiration. In 1905 the W.E.A. had eight branches and about 1,000 individual members. In 1914 it had 179 branches and 11,430 individual members. Drawn largely from active workers in the trade-union, co-operative, and socialist movements, its groups were at first almost solely concerned to study such subjects as economics and industrial history. But their horizons widened as it developed.

Another form of working-class education had started, when Ruskin Hall (afterwards Ruskin College) was opened at Oxford in 1899. The idea of the founders (who were Americans) was to provide a residential training college for the future leaders that were to run the various working-class movements. Hitherto such men had been thrown to the top among their fellows, and after getting there had to pick up their knowledge and ideas as best they might. To interpose a period of residential study, even if only for six months or a year, seemed a plan sufficiently practical for a number of trade unions to subscribe to it. In the sequel it had rather unexpected results. Till then it had been usual for trade-union leaders to begin as extremists and gradually to be moderated by the contact with facts which responsible leadership entailed. Now, instead of that contact, they were thrown into a company of able young extremists like themselves for periods which, while often too short for serious study, were long enough to heat hot iron hotter. The consequence was the formation among them in 1908 of the Plebs League to urge 'independent working-class education on Marxian lines'; and in 1909 a secession from Ruskin College to a 'Central Labour College' in London, which was supported by certain unions, notably the South Wales Miners' Federation and the Amalgamated Society of Railway Servants. The number of individuals concerned in all this was not large; but as they were budding leaders, the effect on British trade-unionism was considerable. Plebs men were prominent in some of the 1911–12 strikes, and the trend towards syndicalism owed a great deal to them.

An interesting and little-known feature of this period was a revolution in the design of school buildings. From 1885 a design then evolved had become stereotyped. Its leading idea was that of a central hall, off which the class-rooms (usually with glass doors) radiated; this gave concentration and facilitated supervision. In modern practice it has been completely superseded. The idea that replaced it is that of 'an open spread-out line of class-rooms approached by corridors or open verandahs arranged to let the maximum amount of sunlight and fresh air into every part of the building'.[1] This was no impersonal or unpurposed discovery. Its features originated with Dr. George Reid, a leading authority on public health, who was medical officer for Staffordshire and based them on his hospital experience. But they might not have gone beyond a few experimental Staffordshire schools, if they had not been taken up and brilliantly developed by G. H. Widdows, architect to the adjoining education committee of Derbyshire, who applied them with great

---

[1] Sir Felix Clay, *Modern School Buildings* (1929 ed.), p. 3; cp. p. 27.

ingenuity to all sorts of varying circumstances. Between 1914 and 1922 school building was much in abeyance; but when it re-started, what these men had pioneered was found to have worked so well, that it was adopted as the normal type in new schools.

Art was still in a transition stage, but in some directions it began to feel more sure of itself. The influence of Morris and his school had banished the taste for machine-made ornament from among cultivated people, and the new impulses which he had given to craftsmanship went forward in many directions. One might instance the development of fine handwriting by Graily Hewitt, that of fine lettering on carved inscriptions by Eric Gill, that of fine printing by Emery Walker and T. J. Cobden-Sanderson in collaboration at the Doves Press, and afterwards by many others. The common trade level of design and colour in furniture and carpets had risen greatly since the mid-Victorian descent; and people of good taste and moderate means could enjoy inside their homes an environment of wholesome beauty such as it would have been very difficult for their parents to compass.

A great deal of building was done in these years, and new architects of distinction came to the front in them. They cannot be called a school, but if one takes some leading names—Lutyens, R. Blomfield, J. J. Burnet, E. A. Rickards, and E. Cooper[1]— common features can clearly be seen. Leaving behind not merely the Gothic fashion but that based on French sixteenth-century models which had succeeded it, they drew formal inspiration from the classical styles of the seventeenth and eighteenth centuries. Along a separate line the designing of houses went forward in the hands of men like Baillie Scott, C. F. Annesley-Voysey, C. R. Ashbee, and others, who followed Morris and Philip Webb in developing the Vernacular. The ground was still cumbered by some elements of tradition which had grown meaningless; but through their adherence to sound craftsmanship, structural beauty, native materials, and respect for the landscape and climate of Britain, they pointed the path to much of the best domestic architecture in post-war England. The

[1] Sir Herbert Baker did not design buildings in England at this period. He was towards the end of it appointed joint architect with Sir Edwin Lutyens for the new Delhi on the strength of his work in South Africa.

influence of a meteoric Scotsman, C. R. Mackintosh[1] of Glasgow, helped to clear away ornamental irrelevance.

Apart from big country houses (which comprise the bulk of Lutyens's best work in these years), most of the period's largest structures are to be seen in London; though what perhaps forms its single finest group of public buildings stands at Cardiff—the city hall and law courts designed by E. A. Rickards.[2] Sir Edwin Cooper's Marylebone town hall and Sir J. J. Burnet's northern elevation for the British Museum are good London examples of what the age could achieve by way of monumental effect. Two of the largest public buildings undertaken at this time were put up to public competition, and so (as is likely to happen in that case) fell to young and untried architects. The first instance was that of the Anglican cathedral at Liverpool; and the second that of the London county hall. The former, since its construction was to proceed by stages and be spread over a long period of years, was well adapted to engage a youthful genius; the latter, an immense business building which needed to be completed as quickly as possible, was not. In the one Sir Giles Gilbert Scott has been able to evolve a work of outstanding importance. In the other the result was the present county hall designed by Ralph Knott, characterized by exceptionally bad internal planning, but showing towards the Thames an imposing elevation.

A common feature of all the secular buildings just mentioned was that, while built in the American manner on steel frames and only, as it were, veneered with the traditional materials, their elevations betrayed no sign of this new and revolutionary mode of construction. Nor were their forms obviously dictated by their various functions, but by the requirements of the style to which each conformed—'style' continuing thus to be a kind of fancy-dress. The first modern public building in Great Britain, of which this could not be said, was C. R. Mackintosh's

[1] Mackintosh (1869–1928) ranks high among 'inheritors of unfulfilled renown'. In Great Britain he encountered so much disapproval that he obtained few commissions—too few to express his genius. But in Austria, Germany, France, Belgium, Holland, and Scandinavia his ideas were received with enthusiasm between 1900 and 1914, and inspired the movement known as *l'art nouveau*. He has been described by a recent critic as 'the first British architect since Adam to be a name abroad, and the only one who has ever become the rallying-point of a Continental school of design' (P. Morton Shand in *The Architectural Review*, Jan. 1935).

[2] The splendid grouping of these great edifices with others designed later by different architects seems to have started in Great Britain the idea of the 'civic centre', followed since the war at Leeds, Southampton, and elsewhere.

Glasgow School of Art (part built in 1899 and finished in 1909). Though constructed of traditional materials (stone and timber), it was, especially in its fenestration, a startling precursor of later fashions. But Mackintosh had little chance of applying his genius to steel; and it was left to Sir J. J. Burnet (also from Glasgow) to initiate by his Kodak building in Kingsway (1912) the franker treatment of steel structures on lines long familiar in their country of origin.

The improvement of design in houses began to extend downwards even to cottages. Important leads were given by some of the garden city or garden suburb developments. Their speciality was layout, not architecture. But in the first of them, Port Sunlight, it was the object of Sir William Lever[1] (its creator) to obtain from the start not merely comfortable cottages, but elevations of beauty and charm. In the earlier work at Bournville and Letchworth this aim was less prominent. But the building of the Hampstead Garden Suburb carried it much farther under the guiding genius of Sir E. Lutyens, then generally regarded as the most gifted domestic architect in the country. The development of week-end cottages for the well-to-do—an early outcome of the twentieth-century week-end habit—helped also to attract eminent designers to the cottage problem. It must not be supposed that in the spate of building between 1905 and 1910 high-class work formed any large proportion. Yet even the unarchitected 'builders' houses' caught something from example; while thanks to progressive by-laws their standards of sanitation, ventilation, and cubic air-space were steadily rising. Municipal housing schemes aimed in general (though not always) somewhat higher. The cottage estates of the L.C.C. designed by W. E. Riley take rank with the best work of the kind done in the period.

British painting still followed at a distance the progress of French. No single figure stood out, unless Sargent; who himself still changed and experimented. But the number and diversity of talents was large—possibly larger than ever before. The vogue of subject-pictures waned decidedly; portraits and landscapes prevailed; the post-war taste for still life had not begun. Impressionism was the ruling influence, but older styles held popularity, and at the other end post-impressionism struggled for a foothold. In the late autumn of 1910 the holding of the first large London exhibition of French post-impressionist pictures marked a definite

[1] Afterwards Lord Leverhulme.

stage in the development of British taste. There was keen controversy,[1] but the innovators were ably championed in the press,
and the holding of a second post-impressionist exhibition in 1912
confirmed their influence. Meanwhile the popular interest in
painting was being steadily widened and deepened by the growth
of public art-galleries. In 1903 the National Art Collections
Fund was formed, to which so many famous acquisitions have
since been due. Before long it was to have a hard task saving
British-owned masterpieces from going to the United States,
under the double urge of death duties in England and acquisitive
millionairedom in America. Holbein's *Duchess of Milan* hangs in
the National Gallery to-day, because in 1909, when the duke of
Norfolk wanted £72,000 for it and the treasury would only contribute £10,000, the National Art Collections Fund stepped in,
and found an anonymous donor of £40,000 to make up the
deficiency then outstanding. But in 1911, when an American
offered Lord Lansdowne £100,000 for Rembrandt's *The Mill*,
nothing could save it, and one of the three or four finest landscape
paintings in the world left England for ever. In 1912 other
Rembrandts only less important were sold by Lord Wimborne
to the same American for £200,000; and again nothing could
be done. The action of these wealthy noblemen in ignoring the
national loss which their sales involved may be variously
estimated. Minor art-treasures crossed the Atlantic in a stream.
Meanwhile the National Gallery, which in 1911 had been
enlarged by five rooms, received in 1912 the great Layard
Collection, the most valuable bequest till then ever made to it.

Music continued to develop rapidly. Any comparison of a
typical London orchestral programme in 1910 or thereabouts
with those of a quarter of a century earlier will show, by the form
no less than by the contents, what a long advance in musical
appreciation had been made by audiences, at any rate in the
metropolis. Even opera went ahead. It remained (all of it, that
is, which was performed with adequate orchestras) on its exotic
society-function basis; but in the last years of the period it
reached under Sir Thomas Beecham higher standards of musical
interest than it had ever had in England before. In a permanent

---

[1] Even Sargent took sides against the new-comers. Of the pictures in the first
exhibition he wrote: 'The fact is that I am absolutely sceptical as to their having
any claim whatever to being works of art, with the exception of the pictures by
Gauguin that strike me as admirable in colour—and in colour only.'

aspect, however, the chief musical events of the period are two—
the rescue and recording of English folk-song at the last moment
before universal standardized education would have obliterated
it, and the rise, headed by Elgar, of an important school of
British composers.

The first serious collector of English folk-songs had been the
Rev. S. Baring-Gould, a Devonshire country parson of the old
highly cultivated type, who besides writing some successful
novels and two of the best-known modern English hymns,[1]
published in 1889 a collection of songs and tunes obtained from
old singers in his native county. Before him it had been widely
assumed that (save perhaps on the Scottish border) the English
people, unlike the Germans, Scots, Welsh, and Irish, had no
folk-songs worth mentioning. His discoveries were quickly
followed by others in other parts of England. Collections by
W. A. Barrett, F. Kidson, and Lucy Broadwood (with J. A.
Fuller-Maitland) appeared within four years; and in 1898 the
English Folk-Song Society was founded. Yet all this was but
preliminary to the main effort. About 1903 the Rev. C. L.
Marson, vicar of Hambridge in Somerset, discovered folk-songs
among his parishioners, and in 1904 he brought down a musical
friend from London, Cecil Sharp (1859–1924), to record them.
The back parts of pastoral Somerset were then—with similar parts
of Lincolnshire—probably the most isolated in England. Sharp
recorded nearly one hundred folk-songs in Hambridge alone, and
by Marson's aid he was enabled to collect a great many more in
the regions round. Five volumes edited by Marson and himself
were the result. Thenceforward he made folk-music his life-work.
Besides songs he collected dances; and having mastered the old
dance-notation proceeded (after 1906) to launch the folk-dance
movement also. In these ways a unique and precious heritage
of the English people, both in music and dance, was saved from
extinction within the narrowest possible margin of time. In the
story of its rescue Sharp's name leads all the rest, for his wonderful
energy and enthusiasm put him easily at the head of the achievement. But the first initiatives, it will be seen, came, as was almost
inevitable in those days, from the cultivated country clergy.
Had the work been done a century earlier, it might have made
a contribution to English literature as well as to music. But
words corrupt more easily than tunes; and the versions in which

[1] *Onward, Christian soldiers* and *Now the day is over.*

they survived, at that late stage in the dissolution of English country life, were mostly of little interest save to ballad specialists.

Elgar, whom we saw completing *The Dream of Gerontius* in 1900, had between then and 1914 a period of exceptional productivity. Within it came his two other great oratorios, his two symphonies, his violin concerto, and his symphonic poem *Falstaff*. These, though differing in value, were all works on a great scale and in the grand manner; and together with the best of the many lesser works which accompanied them they formed such a body of musical creation as no other Englishman had come near achieving in the two centuries of modern music. This was well recognized in England, and receptions like that of his first symphony (performed over 100 times in two years) had undoubtedly an encouraging effect on the younger generation of English composers. Vaughan Williams's *Sea Symphony* appeared in 1910; his *London Symphony* in March 1914. Rutland Boughton, working under great difficulties without an orchestra, completed *The Immortal Hour* in 1914, and it was given that year at Glastonbury with piano accompaniment; though for proper performances it had to wait till after the war. Holst and Bax also began publication, though only with minor works. The musical idiom of all these younger composers was influenced—in some cases greatly—by the folk-song discoveries; Elgar alone, having formed his style earlier, remained unaffected by them. Another composer very active at this time, and sometimes claimed for the English school, was Delius. Of German descent, but born in Bradford and brought up there as an Englishman till manhood, he had lived subsequently in America and Germany, and since 1890 in France. Down to 1908 none of his works were first performed in England. But in that year three important ones were, two under his own baton; and thenceforward his contacts with and influence on British music became considerable.

The striking feature on the side of books was the rapid growth in their numbers following the Balfour Education Acts. It parallels the rapid spread of secondary and university education. The annual total, which we saw to have been 5,971 in 1899, and which in 1901 (during the Boer war) dropped below 5,000 works, was 6,456 in 1904, 8,468 in 1910, and 9,541 in 1913. Because the *Publisher's Circular* changed its classification, there are some important classes, e.g. novels, whose increase it is not possible exactly to determine as between 1901 and 1913. But books on science were enormously multiplied;[1] those on medicine more than doubled; history and biography rose from 438 to 933; poetry and drama from 202 to 466; and the books classed in 1901 as 'political economy, trade, and commerce', which then numbered 351, appear in 1913 to have had not less than 1,039 counterparts.

In point of literary distinction the drama easily takes first place. There now burst upon England in full flood the long-hoped-for theatrical renaissance; and the twenty years' struggle of the reforming critics and pioneers bore memorable fruit in the brilliant output of Bernard Shaw, Galsworthy, Barrie, and many others. For the first time since the age of Shakespeare the English stage led Europe in the quality of its authorship. English plays were translated into many languages, and acted in most of the leading cities of two continents.

The virile and overflowing personality of Shaw set up from the first a strong current away from the drama that creates characters to the drama that discusses ideas. They were the ideas of the time[2]—removal of inequalities between the sexes and between classes; emancipation from traditional taboos; re-apportionment within the community of the fruits of modern science and industry; re-casting of the political structure to meet modern conditions; and, amid all iconoclasms, the recurring search for some religious outlook, which should restore meaning and purpose to life as a whole. Shaw's own genius was corrosive and dissolvent; he succeeded much better as destroyer than as constructor; yet he believed himself to be most interested in the constructive side. Problems of property and marriage, socialism, imperialism, feminism, trade-unionism, Irish nationalism, syndicalism, Salvationism, and divorce—such were the typical *motifs* of Edwardian and early Georgian drama. Galsworthy, with a tidier and less discursive mind than Shaw and an outlook more definitely humanitarian, specialized also on a topic of his own, the reform of criminal justice and imprisonment. Here the great work of the home office and Sir Evelyn Ruggles-Brise, described in the previous chapter, derived material help from

[1] In 1901 'arts, science, and illustrated works' covered 310 volumes. In 1913 'science' alone accounted for 594 and 'technology' for 593. The influence of modernized education is very apparent in these figures.

[2] The stage did not merely reflect them as such. It helped powerfully to make them such.

the dramatist, whose plays *The Silver Box* (1906) and *Justice* (1910) left their mark deeply on public opinion. Barrie, less concerned with argument and more with the play of a whimsical imagination, might in another age have forborne discussions altogether. It shows the strength of the current that he did not.

Along with the rise of dramatic composition went a reform in dramatic representation. Indeed the one was necessary for the other, since the old system of actor-manager stars had been carried to a pitch where it was normally incompatible with a good drama. For the new system, which brought into the theatre as its presiding genius the 'producer', nobody in England did more pioneering work than H. Granville Barker. It was the Vedrenne-Barker management at the Court Theatre that first successfully presented Shaw; and under it all the greatest plays of his prime were given. But the old system died hard, ably incarnated by two great actor-managers—George Alexander, for whom Pinero and Henry Arthur Jones wrote notable plays, and H. Beerbohm Tree, a true showman, in whose hands the stage with built-up scenery and realistic decoration reached a sort of finality. No more typical production in that kind could be cited than his of *The Tempest* in 1904. As the actor-manager played Caliban, the piece was drastically cut in order to render the monster, as far as possible, its hero; this would have made it impossibly short, but for the very long waits requisite to shift the solid scenery, which with the *ne plus ultra* of sumptuous realism displayed the varied wonders of Prospero's isle. Shakespeare went on being so treated till 1912, when Tree staged *Othello* on similar lines. But in that year Granville Barker invaded the field, and by his productions of *The Winter's Tale* and *Twelfth Night*, followed in 1914 still more brilliantly by *A Midsummer Night's Dream*, made the old method appear obsolete. The principles now generally followed in Shakespearian production—to play the author's text with as few cuts as possible, to say the verse as verse, to facilitate changes of scene by reducing built-up scenery to a minimum and playing short scenes on an apron-stage before a back-cloth, to forgo the attempt at realistic backgrounds and concentrate upon the stage picture itself, relying mainly on costumes and lighting—were here all practised for the first time together. Barker, of course, was not their sole inventor; most of the separate ideas had come from others, notably from the actor William Poel and the stage-designer Gordon Craig. But the revolution was much more than technical, and went deeper than is now, perhaps, easily realized. It enabled Englishmen, for the first time for very many generations, to see worthily on the stage the same Shakespeare that they could read in the study; and in this way restored to them a lost heritage—almost as the rediscovery of folk-music and dancing had done.

Outside London the drama was developed at two independent centres—the Abbey Theatre in Dublin and, later, the Repertory Theatre in Manchester. Both were made possible by the generous enterprise of the same lady, Miss Annie Horniman. The Dublin theatre, while using the English language, had behind it the imaginative resources of a distinct though small nation. It produced a body of highly original literature, and formed a theatrical style of its own. The Manchester experiment disclosed rather the poverty of the English provinces in creative talent, owing to the drift of literary aspirants to London. It brought forward a number of plays by provincial writers; but only one of its successes—Stanley Houghton's *Hindle Wakes*—has since kept a permanent place.

The stage's rival, the film screen, was born in this period, but had not developed very far by the end of it. Till 1914 it was still mainly confined to a variety entertainment; its possibilities for story-telling and drama only slowly emerged. The performances, to which admissions were all very cheap, were held as a rule in small extemporized or adapted halls; and it was still debated whether 'cinema' should be spelt with a 'c' or a 'k', and on what syllable it should be accented. Such as they were, English films held their own fully against American. It was the closing of English studios during the war which gave the Americans their great subsequent lead.

Apart from the drama, the novel was now the only popular literary form. Its monopoly had grown up with the growth of women readers, who had gradually become the larger portion of the reading public, and therefore the most attractive to publishers. To an increasing extent it was coming also to be the product of women writers; though here, again, pre-war tendencies had not expanded to the post-war degree. The eminent novelists of the period—H. G. Wells, Arnold Bennett, Galsworthy, Conrad, and George Moore—were all men. But most of them were conscious of the sex of their audience. Themes of masculine adventure, such as had been prominent in the previous generation, passed now into the background; the adventure of sex, seen increasingly through the heroine's rather than the hero's eyes, took their place. Conrad is the exception; but Conrad, a foreigner who had come into English letters late in life,[1] remained in some ways a little archaic. A large proportion of the best novels reflected the keen interest of the time in social criticism and social reform. Here Wells and Galsworthy led, the books of the former rivalling the plays of Bernard Shaw in their wide effect on educated public opinion. Wells, however, was more constructive than Shaw; he not merely swept away the old cobwebs, but indirectly in his novels and directly in his brilliantly written Utopias himself spun many new ones. The preoccupation of literature with politics culminated about 1910. After the exhausting conflicts of that year, with its two general elections, a sort of fatigue set in; and in the remaining years before the war 'pure' literature, as preached by writers like Henry James and George Moore, showed distinct signs of re-asserting itself. How far it was a gain, and whether even as English prose posterity will ultimately value Moore's work above the best of Shaw and Wells, it is too early to judge with finality.

In the field of poetry there might well have been more good writers, if there had not till 1911 been virtually no audience for them. Between 1903 and 1908 Thomas Hardy published his epic verse drama, *The Dynasts*. It would have fallen totally flat but for his reputation as a novelist, and it was not until after the outbreak of the European war that its merits obtained any wide recognition. C. M. Doughty's poetry (nearly all published within this period) was neglected from start to finish. So things went on till in 1911 a much younger man, John Masefield, issued the first of his longer narrative poems, *The Everlasting Mercy*, and it achieved real popularity. Others followed from him at no very long intervals—two of more merit and almost equally popular. The excitement they set up resembled (though on a smaller scale) that over Scott's and Byron's narrative poems about a century earlier, and rendered to new poetry generally the same vital service that those had in their day—that of causing the public to take notice of it. Between then and the war a number of the younger writers secured some degree of recogni-tion; and the first volume of *Georgian Poetry*, edited by Edward

---

[1] Born a Russian Pole, he entered the British merchant service in early manhood, and rose to be a captain in it, before retiring on his success as an English novelist.

Marsh in 1912, gave them a kind of collective prestige. The appointment in 1913 of Bridges to be poet laureate had also a stimulating effect; for (unlike his predecessor) he was a poet in whom his fellow poets felt their calling honoured.

The young school then arising, though not revolutionary by post-war standards, nevertheless began a departure greater than any in verse since the Renaissance reached England. Its character (still often misconceived) may be best seen from its causes. They were scholastic. From Henry VIII's reign to the end of Victoria's nearly all the chief English poets had in boyhood been taught Latin verse, and expected from their critical readers at least a grounding in the Graeco-Roman tradition. Down to 1890 that had been the portion of all the abler boys, not only in the public schools but in the dozens of ancient grammar schools scattered up and down the country. After 1890 these last were generally modernized; laboratories were built, Greek disappeared and Latin shrank to its rudiments; chemistry, electricity, and physics were substituted. The new secondary schools started on similar lines; and early in the twentieth century, following the adoption of the school certificate system, most of the public schools themselves confined advanced classical study to a minority of their boys. The work of poets like De la Mare and D. H. Lawrence reflects the change. Theirs are clearly attempts to develop English verse as if such ideas as iambuses and trochees, anapaests and dactyls, had never existed, and the very forms of verse-music must be wrought *de novo* out of rhythms and undertones in the spoken language. These tendencies (as also the cognate tendency to be interested in no poetry but lyric) were carried much farther after the war; but, as a matter of history, they began before it.

So did a very marked alteration in the language employed for ordinary English prose. Down to about 1900 this had been influenced especially by two facts—that most readers were saturated with the Bible, and that men with more than an elementary education had been taught Latin. But the multitude of new readers out of whom the Harmsworths and their congeners made fortunes knew little Bible and no Latin, and had to be written for with a different and, save on the side of slang, much less copious vocabulary. Beginning at the halfpenny end of the press and soon spreading to novels, the new vocabulary gradually ousted the old; and, particularly by its de-Latinization, has created a distinct barrier of language between the modern Englishman and most of his country's greater literature from Milton down through Burke to Macaulay. That barrier was not so high in 1914 as it is now, but it was already there, and was growing.

Among books of learning the tendency to specialization and so to co-operative effort grew now very marked. The advance of general knowledge outstripped individual capacity, not merely in the natural sciences (where 'teams' of laboratory workers came into play), but in such fields as history, geography, or sociology. The *Cambridge Modern History* (originally planned by Acton), the *Cambridge Mediaeval History*, and the *Cambridge History of English Literature*—each parcelling out its subject among a number of specialists—appeared at this time. So did two many-volumed *Histories of England*, each the work of a team of able authors. The largest individual enterprise was the continuation of Sir J. G. Frazer's *Golden Bough*—carried eventually to eleven volumes and exerting, especially in its later phases, a profound influence on thought. Among subjects that acquired new prominence now was the academic study of English literature: Courthope, Saintsbury, W. P. Ker, A. C. Bradley, and Walter Raleigh were all active in these years. Among new subjects might be ranked the application of psychology to the study of politics, pioneered in England by Graham Wallas and W. McDougall, and earlier in France by G. Tarde. In philosophy the English idealist school had passed its nineteenth-century prime. Pragmatism, psychology, and from about 1911 the teaching of Bergson, provided alternative channels of interest; and on a more popular level the attention paid to Nietzsche and Samuel Butler was not inconsiderable.

On the whole pure philosophy lost ground as an influence on general thought, and the natural sciences, formidably abetted by the new psychology, revived their claims to be heard outside their immediate sphere. There came at this time a wave of fresh thought-disturbing discoveries. Röntgen's (1895) of the X-rays and Madame Curie's (1900) of radium and radio-activity started the great twentieth-century advances in the science of physics, in which England took a substantial part through the work, in particular, of J. J. Thomson, E. Rutherford, and F. Soddy. The atom ceased to be a rigid unit; matter was re-interpreted in terms of energy; the ultimateness of the chemical elements disappeared, and prospects were opened up of their transmutation.[1] On quite another side mathematical physics developed in the hands of Minkowski the conception of a four-dimensional world with three co-ordinates for space and one for time. Minkowski's was a daring advance from the nineteenth-century work of Riemann, and has in turn an important relation to the work of Einstein. The latter reached his 'special' theory of relativity as early as 1905, but his 'general' theory was not developed till 1915. Already, however, just as radio-activity had destroyed the postulates of the chemists, so mathematical physics was destroying those not only of Euclid but of Newton.

Hardly less thought-disturbing was the progress made in physiology and in operative surgery. Science revealed many hidden secrets in the structure and working of the human body—the functions of ductless glands and hormones, and later the function of vitamins in food. The influence, that the hormones were shown to exert over mental activity and personality, seemed ominously to extend the mastery of the body over the mind. Simultaneously Pavlov, by his study of 'reflexes', was steadily widening the areas of conduct that can be explained by un-reasoning reactions of the organism to physical stimuli. More-over, in the hands of the psychologists mind itself was being explored by scientific analysis like any other phenomenon. From 1906 Freud was working at Vienna with Adler and Jung, and gradually building up his theory of the sub-conscious. His ideas did not become widely talked about till later than that; but they were getting known before the war.

The general effect of all these discoveries was to suggest, if not a material, at any rate a mechanistic universe, and to undermine traditional beliefs in the 'soul' as an entity. Parallel to the advance of psychology was that of anthropology; stimulated both by studies of contemporary savages, like those of the Australian blackfellows by Spencer and Gillen, and by the disinterment of dead civilizations, like that of Minoan Crete by Sir Arthur Evans. Religion itself came to be seen in a new light as the result of Sir J. G. Frazer's comparative study of myths and beliefs. It was shown that, however much religions might claim to differ, their sacred narratives, dogmas, and rituals conformed to a few simple *motifs* and patterns found all over the world, and highly-developed theologies were rooted in ideas associated with

[1] Which was not, however, actually demonstrated until 1919 (by Rutherford).

primitive magic. This outlook on creeds, though it did not disprove them and was equally compatible with belief and disbelief, tended to blunt intolerance on both sides. But while it caused the standpoints of men like Bradlaugh or even Huxley to appear obsolete, it equally helped to subvert the earlier disciplines, which had employed religious sanctions to maintain high standards of ethical conscientiousness.

The varied exploits of science, and such new exploits of technology as the conquest of the air, widened the range and scope of human power. But paradoxically there went with this a growing sense of limitation and constriction. The rapid rise of populations helped it; the individual felt dwarfed by their mass; the vast urban cemeteries with their labyrinths of tombstones seemed fit end for a life as crowded, blurred, and impersonal as that of the old villages had been detached and distinct. It was the same thing with the world's geography; the map was getting filled up. Nearly everything worth exploring had been explored. In 1909 the American, Peary, reached the North Pole, and in December 1911 the Norwegian, Amundsen, reached the South. These were epic feats; and even more appealing to the imagination was the heroism of the English party under Captain R. F. Scott, who reached the South Pole thirty-three days after Amundsen, and perished in the blizzards on their way back.[1] Yet Polar exploration, after all, was a barren affair compared with what had occupied Livingstone or Stanley; it became reduced almost to an exercise in heroism for heroism's sake. The severe clashes between Great Powers over Fashoda and Morocco betoken on the international plane the same sense of constriction within a pre-empted world. In England the annexationist imperialism of the nineties died down in the following decade, not merely owing to the disillusionment of the South African war, but also because people suddenly realized that little was left to annex, and that the problem for Great Britain, with her vast and much-envied possessions, was not to get but to hold.

Chafing against the bars were many impulses of 'escape'. One was the revolt against urbanism—with the slogan 'Back to the Land'. It took many social forms, from week-end cottages to the

---

[1] A famous incident in this story, the death of Captain Oates, illustrates the shifting of moral emphasis at this time. Oates committed suicide. But because he did it in hope to save his fellows, his action was universally approved. Clergymen preached sermons in praise of it.

'simple life'; and many political forms, from passing a variety of not very successful Small Holdings Acts to penalizing with death duties the country landowners, who were regarded as blocking access to the soil. Another was the escape back to childhood, catered for by Kenneth Grahame's *Golden Age* (1895) and still more by Barrie's play *Peter Pan* (1904), the 'boy who never grew up'. *Peter Pan* and a host of boys' books exemplify yet another escape—that to the wild, to the life of the scout and the frontiersman, and the primitive sensations that civilization, in proportion as it holds sway, eliminates. Based on this was Sir R. S. S. (afterwards Lord) Baden-Powell's enormously successful invention, the Boy Scout movement. Baden-Powell's starting-point was the Boys' Brigade, in which he became interested about 1905, when it was already twenty-one years old and numbered 54,000 boys. The Brigade satisfied boys' taste for drilling and playing at soldiers; but he saw that for providing an 'escape', as also for building up a resourceful character, the scout was a much better model than the drilled soldier. His book *Scouting for Boys* (1906) was the result; scout troops were started about 1907; in 1909 no less than 11,000 boy scouts paraded at the Crystal Palace. In that year the Girl Guide movement was added by the founder. Thenceforward, despite the interruptions of the European war, the two movements each progressed, till they have gone far beyond Great Britain and been adopted in one form or another by every civilized people. We saw in Chapter V how England invented the outdoor games, lawn tennis and football, whose cult is now world-wide. The Boy Scouts and Girl Guides may count as an English contribution to world civilization hardly less remarkable; though the credit for their invention and development belongs far more to one man.

Costume continued to grow more rational and hygienic. For men the convenient lounge coat grew almost universal. Homespun tweeds came into fashion; and the wearing of grey flannels extended its range. Longer coats and top hats were on week-days practically confined to London. From 1906 onwards the morning tail-coat gradually superseded the frock-coat save for a few ultra-formal occasions; though in 1905 a frock-coat was still more or less *de rigueur* for a luncheon-party at a large London house. The sartorial habits of the house of commons elected in 1906 influenced this and other changes. Lounge coats and lower hats were still thought too informal for well-dressed gatherings; though barristers and some other professional men developed the wearing of a black lounge coat with top-hat, and a similar replacement of tails by the lounge form produced for evening wear the dinner-jacket. This last only became general, however, after 1910; and till some time after 1914 there was no rigorous division between a white-tie and a black-tie *ensemble*, such as now compels gentlemen to keep two sets of evening dress.[1]

Women's clothes for everyday wear became lighter and less restrictive. The disappearance of heavy petticoats was now followed by a reduction in whalebone corseting, as wasp waists went out of fashion. Skirts came higher off the ground than they had been within the life of any one then living; and elderly people early in the century were fond of complaining that they exposed not only the ankle but two or three inches above it. This was a real gain for activity; and though a fashion for tightening the skirt about the knee (the so-called 'hobble' skirt) somewhat offset it, the more extravagant forms of this were not universal, and their effects were soon mitigated by pleats.

Taking the wear of both sexes, but especially that of women, the greatest feature of the period was the immense development of ready-made clothes. These were so much improved in quality, that they no longer differed obtrusively from the bespoke garments worn by richer people; while their cheapness enabled all the poorer classes to raise their standards of clothing. Although it remained for the war to level up the dress of people in all classes to the democratic degree which has since been ordinary in England, a distinct start was observable some years before 1914. Its importance will not be under-estimated by any one who remembers what a cruel and unescapable badge of inferiority clothes had till then constituted.

In social life these thirteen years must indeed be recorded as years of enlightenment and progress. There went on through them a vast, silent supersession of the old snobbish class-contempts. After 1906 the hitherto ruling ranks in society, however unwise some of their political reactions may have been, realized increasingly in their private relations the need for being less

---

[1] The much earlier predecessor of the dinner-jacket was the smoking-jacket. Though coloured, frogged, and sometimes of rich effect, this was a far less formal garment, being originally not worn at dinner but slipped on in the smoking-room afterwards. In French the dinner-jacket has inherited its name—*un smoking*.

exclusive, and for meeting the trend to equality half-way. And already before 1914 the spread of education made this more possible. There resulted (as perhaps is inevitable in such cases) a decay of polished manners at the top; but against this must be set the rise in the general level.

In domestic relations there was some decrease of clannishness. Smaller families entailed fewer cousins. The progress of women towards equality stimulated a demand for reform of the divorce laws. In 1909 the first Lord Gorell, who had been president of the probate, divorce, and admiralty division of the high court, moved a motion in the house of lords which resulted in his being appointed chairman of a strong royal commission on the subject. In 1912 the commission produced two reports. The minority, consisting of an archbishop and two other strict anglicans, was against granting divorce on any ground save adultery, and consequently opposed all major changes; though they agreed that newspaper reports of divorce proceedings should be restricted, that women should be entitled to divorce on the same terms as men, and that a Poor Persons' Procedure should be introduced to render divorce no longer beyond the means of the great majority of people—recommendations which were subsequently adopted in 1926, 1923, and 1922 respectively. The majority— a very weighty body—went farther; they urged that cruelty, desertion for three years, and (with certain provisos) habitual drunkenness, incurable insanity, and a life sentence of imprisonment, should each be a ground for divorce. These recommendations corresponded to the best non-ecclesiastical opinion at the time; but it must not be thought on that account that divorce was then as lightly regarded as now. Adultery remained a ground for social ostracism; and persons divorced for it, or co-respondents, were just as liable to be driven from politics as Parnell or Dilke had been. The subsequent laxer view came in with the war as the result of war-marriages, and is one of the relatively few changes that the war may be said to have originated.

Elsewhere, and to sum up these immediate pre-war years, it may be said, so far as England is concerned, that most of the familiar post-war tendencies were already developing in them. The war altered direction less than is often supposed. It accelerated changes—at least for the time being; but they were germinating before it. It may be that some would have been carried through more wisely but for the war's revolutionary atmosphere. It may be, on the other hand, that an undistracted concentration upon home issues would itself have bred some kind of revolution—a view to which the pre-war loss of balance about home rule lends a certain colour. All that is now a matter of speculation. What is not, is the seething and teeming of this pre-war period, its immense ferment and its restless fertility.

APPENDIX A

Gladstone's Attitude to Home Rule before the General Election of 1885.

THE obvious dilemma which any student of Gladstone's evolution towards home rule has to meet is this. If he was not a home ruler till after the general election had shown that he could only obtain a majority by becoming one, the taunt of corrupt and hasty opportunism would seem justified. If, on the other hand, he was a home ruler before the election, why did he leave Parnell so much in the dark that the latter cast the Irish vote on the conservative side, and thereby, as it turned out, made the passage of home rule impossible?

We know now from overwhelming documentary evidence that the charge of corrupt haste—though in the light of the knowledge vouchsafed to them at the time his enemies can scarcely be blamed for entertaining it—was in fact entirely untrue. It remains therefore to examine the other horn of the dilemma. Why did Gladstone conceal his thoughts before the general election?

The enormous collection of the Gladstone Papers is now in the Department of Manuscripts at the British Museum. Lord Morley had them all available to him when he wrote his *Life*; but, on this episode, he did not cite some of the most significant. His account of it, while not exactly misleading, seems rather needlessly confusing. Gladstone's attitude was in reality tolerably simple. It is believed that the version given briefly above in Chapter III is correct; but the reader may welcome further detail. What follows is based mainly, it will be seen, on the unpublished Gladstone Papers; which, since the immense task of arranging them is still in progress, can only be cited at present by the dates of the separate documents. The italics used —save in two instances, which are noted—are the present author's.

The correspondence between Gladstone and Mrs. O'Shea took an interesting turn early in August. She had written and offered to send him a 'paper' by Parnell, setting forth the terms which the Irish leader would wish that the liberal leader might propose for Ireland. In reply he wrote on the 8th (the italics here and below are not his but the present writer's):

'You do not explain the nature of the changes which have occurred since you sent me a spontaneous proposal, which is now, it appears, superseded. The only one I am aware of is the altered attitude of the Tory party, and I presume its heightened bidding. *It is right I should say that into any counter-bidding of any sort against Lord R. Churchill I for one cannot enter.*

'*If this were a question of negotiation*, I should have to say that in considering any project which might now be recommended by Mr. Parnell I should have to take into view the question whether, two or three months hence, it might be extinguished like its predecessor on account of altered circumstances.

'*But it is no question of that kind*, and therefore I have no difficulty in saying it would ill become me to discourage any declaration of his views for Ireland by a person of so much ability representing so large a body of opinion. I have always felt, and I believe I have publicly expressed, my regret that we were so much in the dark as to the views of the Home Rule or National party; and the limit I assign to the desirable and allowable is one which I have often made known in Parliament and elsewhere. I should look therefore to such a paper as you describe and appear to tender as one of very great public interest.'

Here we see the formula by which he took his stand. The conservatives, who are the government, are bidding actively to prolong Parnell's alliance. He declines to 'counter-bid' against them. Therefore, though he would be glad to read Parnell's paper as 'of very great public interest', he will not negotiate on it.

This was a high-minded attitude, but, of course, of no use to Parnell; who was busy negotiating with the other side, and had seen Lord Carnarvon just a week before. He therefore did not send his paper at that time. In October, however, as the general election drew nearer, he tried again. On the 23rd, sixteen days after Lord Salisbury's Newport speech, Mrs. O'Shea wrote to Gladstone seeking to get a liberal seat in Ulster for Captain O'Shea, and at the end of a long letter slipped in the remark that she had the paper before mentioned ready whenever he cared to receive it. By return of post Gladstone replied, referring the O'Shea matter to his chief whip, Lord Richard Grosvenor, but adding as to the paper that he would 'be happy to receive' it. On the 30th Mrs. O'Shea forwarded it to him, enjoining the strictest confidence.

To this remarkable missive Gladstone drafted two different replies, which both still exist in his own handwriting. The first of them is perhaps the clearest expression of his attitude which we have. In it he says:

'*You are already aware that I could not enter into any competition with others* upon the question how much or how little can be done for Ireland in the way of self-government. Before giving any practical opinion, I must be much better informed as to the facts and prospects on both sides of the water, and must know with whom and in what capacity I am dealing.

'Further I have seen it argued that Mr. Parnell and his allies *ought to seek a settlement of this question from the party now in office, and I am not at all inclined to dissent from this opinion, for I bear in mind the history of the years 1829, 1846, and 1867, as illustrative of the respective capacity of the two parties to deal under certain circumstances with sharply controverted matters. In this view no question can arise for those connected with the Liberal party, until the Ministers have given their reply upon a subject which they are well entitled to have submitted to them.'*

This too revealing draft, to which we must return in a moment, was never sent. Instead, a second draft, seemingly made at the same time, was, as would appear from a note on it in Gladstone's handwriting to Lord Richard Grosvenor and pencil adaptations in Lord Richard's, sent in the form of a letter from Lord Richard as follows:

'Mr. Gladstone wishes me to thank you for the paper which you have sent him containing the views of Mr. Parnell on the subject of Irish Government. The important subject to which it relates *could but be considered by the Government of the day*, but all information in regard to it is of great interest to him. He will strictly observe your injunction as to secrecy: and intends to take a very early opportunity in Midlothian of declaring my [*sic*] views of the present position of the Liberal and Conservative parties in relation to Mr. Parnell and his friends, and to the policy they may propose to pursue.'

This evasive reply and Gladstone's equally evasive public utterances were all that Parnell had to go on before the general election. He held the door open till almost the last moment, and then threw the Irish vote on the conservative side.

The first draft shows plainly how Gladstone had pondered the precedents of catholic emancipation, the repeal of the corn laws, and the democratization of the franchise, and was casting Lord Salisbury for the part played in 1829 by Wellington and Peel, in 1845–6 by Peel, and in 1867 by Disraeli. This is the key to certain passages in the documents quoted by Morley—e.g. Gladstone's letter to Granville of 5 October 1885 (*Life*, bk. ix, c. 1)—which without it are almost enigmas; as also to some sentences in the Midlothian speeches. Deeply aware of the advantages accruing to the public on the previous occasions, he perhaps thought too little of the penalties which the role had in each case entailed on the player. Yet the whole situation created by the Salisbury–Carnarvon alliance with Parnell pointed to the analogy; and we know now that Salisbury and Carnarvon were themselves thinking of it.

Thus Sir A. Hardinge's *Life of Carnarvon* records (iii. 164) of July 1885, when Carnarvon was mooting his plans to meet Parnell:

'A serious discussion ensued with Lord Salisbury; the latter thought that many of the Party would be ready to accept a "forward policy", but he himself could not play Peel's part in 1829 and 1845.'

Nor was this the only occasion on which it crossed their minds. A memorandum by Carnarvon (Hardinge, *op. cit.* iii. 199) of a conversation with Salisbury on 20 November 1885 shows that the same point was raised by Salisbury then, and Carnarvon tried to parry it by saying that circumstances were different. Salisbury's reluctance to play Peel's part may be the more readily explained, if we remember (1) that he had not by that time any assured position as leader of his party, such as Peel had, and he himself acquired later; (2) that just below him stood the ambitious Lord Randolph Churchill, who was modelling his career on Disraeli, and who, despite having been to the fore in the June compact with Parnell, must have seemed obviously cast to play against his leader the part played in 1845–6 by Disraeli against Peel.

Gladstone was not wholly uninformed about what the conservative premier was thinking. In 1884 Canon Malcolm MacColl had been a go-between between the two men in the redistribution controversy. In the latter part of 1885 he tried to be one in regard to home rule. And as late as 22 December 1885 he wrote in a letter to Gladstone (G. W. E. Russell, *Malcolm MacColl: Memoirs and Correspondence*, 122):

'I found Lord Salisbury, as I gathered, prepared to go as far probably as yourself on the question of Home Rule; but he seemed hopeless as to the prospect of carrying his party with him.'

In the same letter he reports Salisbury as saying that his followers and colleagues would 'devour' him. Yet even later, on 28 December 1885, he wrote to Salisbury (*op. cit.* 126):

'The two points on which he [Gladstone] seemed to feel most strongly were that an honest attempt to settle the question in this Parliament—or rather to deal with it in this Parliament—could not be avoided without danger; and *the most hopeful way of dealing with it would be that your Government should take it up on lines which he could support as Leader of the Opposition.* This would enable you to deal with it more independently, than if you were obliged to rely on the Irish vote.'

Whatever else Gladstone wanted at that time, he obviously was not eager for office.

It remains briefly to trace the subsequent correspondence between him and Mrs. O'Shea (for Parnell) in that year. On 10 December she wrote to him to complain that she had still no reply about the 'paper', adding that she had private information that Parnell was to see 'Lord C.' in a day or two. [In the event he did not.] Gladstone replied (12 December 1885) saying:

'I am glad to hear that Mr. Parnell is about to see "Lord C." (Carnarvon, as I read it). *I have the strongest opinion that he ought if*

he can to arrange with the Government, for the plain reason that the
Tories will fight hard against any plan proceeding from the
Liberals: all or most of the Liberals will give fair play, and even
more to a plan proceeding from the Tories.'

After some other remarks he added that

'. . . no such plan can properly proceed from any *British* [*sic*]
source but one, viz. the Government of the day.'

And he closed by propounding five questions on specific points for
Parnell to answer.

On 15 December Mrs. O'Shea wrote back that she was authorized
to reply in the affirmative to Gladstone's five questions, and enclosed
a long answer from Parnell, addressed to herself and dated the 14th.
In it the Irish leader refers to details in the previous scheme, which
prove it to have been much more moderate than the 1886 Home
Rule Bill. He says that he had always felt Gladstone to be the only
living statesman who had both the will and the power to carry a
settlement that it would be possible for him to accept and work with;
adds that he doubts Lord Carnarvon's power to do so, though he knows
him to be very well disposed, and ends by saying that, if neither party
can offer a solution of the question, he would prefer the conservatives to remain in office, as under them they could at least work out
gradually a solution of the land question.

Gladstone's rejoinder was written on 16 December 1885, the day
before the first publication of his son's unlucky disclosure. In it he
shows himself still pre-occupied by the delicacy of his position:

'I do not know that my opinions on this great matter are unripe:
but my position is very different from that of Mr. Parnell. He acts
on behalf of Ireland; I have to act for Ireland inclusively, but for
the State. (Perhaps I should rather say *think* or *speak*.) [*sic*.] He has
behind him a party of limited numbers for whom he is a plenipo-
tentiary fully authorised. I have a large party behind me whose
minds are only by degrees opening, from day to day I think, to the
bigness and the bearings of the question, and among whom there
may be what the Scotch call "division courses".

'*I must consider my duties to the Government* on the one side, to Ireland
as represented by him, on the other.'

He concludes, still in very hypothetical vein:

'Supposing the time had come when the question had passed
legitimately into the hands of the Liberals, I should apprehend
failure chiefly from one of two causes.

'1. If it could be said that the matter had been settled by negotiation with Mr. Parnell before the Tories had given their reply.

'2. If the state of Ireland as to peace, or as to contracts, were
visibly worse than when Lord Spencer left it.'

Three days later, the day after his son's disclosures appeared in all the papers, came a further letter from him. In it (19 December 1885) he is still loath to give 'some development of the ideas I have so often publicly expressed', and thinks that

> '*duty to the Government* (*as and while such*), duty to my own party, and duty to the purpose in view, combine to require that I should hold my ground; should cherish the hope that the Government will act; and that Mr. Parnell as the organ of what is now undeniably the Irish party should learn from them, whether they will bring in a measure or proposition to deal with and settle the whole question of the future government of Ireland.'

On Christmas Eve Gladstone wrote again enclosing a memorandum, 'private and confidential'. It begins:

> 'My wish and hope still are that Ministers [i.e. Lord Salisbury's Government] should propose some adequate and honourable plan for settling the question of Irish Government and that the Nationalists should continue in amicable relations with them for that purpose.'

And farther on he says:

> 'The slightest communication of plans or intentions from me to Mr. Parnell would be ineffaceably[1] stamped with the character of a bribe given to obtain the dissolution of the Alliance.'

But thereafter followed a clear rupture between Parnell and the conservatives; and two memoranda from Parnell to Gladstone dated 28 December 1885 and 6 January 1886 (still addressed in form to Mrs. O'Shea and forwarded by her) mark the first steps to the Gladstone-Parnell alternative.

---

[1] The MS. has 'irrefaceably', but it is not holograph, and the word seems a slip of the copyist.

The Private Background of Parnell's Career

IT is impossible to understand Parnell's extraordinary career without some knowledge of the liaison story. Mrs. Parnell's book, which threw half-lights on it, appeared in 1914; but the main final source of elucidation (*Parnell Vindicated*, by Captain Henry Harrison), not till 1931. The chief persons involved besides Parnell were: (1) Katharine O'Shea, *née* Wood, daughter of an English baronet, sister of Sir Evelyn Wood, V.C., afterwards Field-Marshal, niece of Lord Chancellor Hatherley and cousin of Sir George Farwell, the first lord justice of that name; (2) Captain W. H. O'Shea, an Irish ex-officer of Hussars, with dashing extravagant habits, who since his marriage had squandered his money and been through the bankruptcy court; (3) Mrs. Benjamin Wood, a childless, pious, and very rich widow living in a large house and grounds at Eltham (then a Kent village), Katharine O'Shea's maternal aunt and paternal great-aunt, who had been born in 1792, but did not die till 1889. In 1880, when Parnell and Katharine O'Shea fell in love at first sight, the latter had for years ceased matrimonial relations with her husband, to whom earlier she had borne three children. By agreement she lived at Eltham in a smaller house belonging to her aunt (then already 88 years of age), and he in a West End flat which the aunt paid for; he was to visit Eltham on Sundays only, to see his children, and she in return for non-molestation was to help his career on the social side. The externals of a married state were preserved to please Mrs. Benjamin Wood. On the bounty of this aged aunt, whom the niece visited and cared for daily, the whole O'Shea family depended. Mrs. O'Shea obtained from her up to £3,000 a year, and had no hope of future support outside her will.

When the Parnell attachment was formed, the natural thing was for Katharine O'Shea to divorce her husband and marry Parnell; as he was a protestant no great difficulty would have arisen. This was not done because of Mrs. Benjamin Wood. The two lovers, who from 1881 onwards called each other husband and wife and to whom three children were born (February 1882, March 1883, and November 1884—all girls, and none now surviving), settled down to living for the greater part of the year together in the smaller Eltham house; while O'Shea, who suffered no more deprivation of his wife than before, and who had interests of his own elsewhere, put in enough visits to preserve appearances. It was the surprising longevity of Mrs. Wood which prolonged a temporary makeshift for nearly a decade. When she died in 1889 she left £144,000 to her niece. O'Shea, having for about twenty years lived on money obtained from his wife, had by then become, in effect, a blackmailer. He could have been bought off and divorced for £20,000. But the will was disputed at law by some other Woods (including Sir Evelyn Wood); Parnell's own estates were past raising any such sum on; so the money was not forthcoming, and O'Shea brought his divorce suit. One result of it was to give him the legal right of custody over Parnell's two surviving daughters, who had been born while the O'Shea coverture lasted. This was a whip-hand which he used even after Parnell's death to extort both money and silence from the widow.

The nine years (1881–90), during which Parnell's relations with Mrs. O'Shea were unknown to the world at large, were those of his greatest public influence, though not, in the main, of his greatest political activity. His haughty reserve and complete refusal to admit his political colleagues into his private life (it must be remembered that nearly all of them belonged to a different stratum of society) helped to keep the secret. Sir W. Harcourt as home secretary was probably the first minister to know that there was a liaison, for his secret service men watched Parnell constantly; and on 17 May 1882 in reference to Kilmainham he told some colleagues (Gwynn and Tuckwell, *Life of Sir Charles Dilke*, i. 445: Dilke's record says 'the cabinet', but on this there are some reasons for doubting its accuracy) that Mrs. O'Shea was 'Parnell's mistress'. In the years following the Irish leaders who fretted against Parnell's inaction often attributed it to her influence; and the rage of Biggar and Healy in February 1886, when Parnell insisted on Captain O'Shea's being candidate at the Galway by-election, was born of long resentment. Had they read a letter from Mrs. O'Shea to Gladstone in the previous October (which is preserved in the Gladstone Papers) offering to him on Parnell's behalf the Irish catholic vote in four important constituences, if only he would get O'Shea adopted as liberal candidate for an Ulster seat, they might have been still more indignant. For it shows plainly that O'Shea was using the personal situation in order to levy from Parnell political blackmail, which the latter could not choose but pay.

Mr. Barry O'Brien in his classical biography of Parnell has discussed how far Parnell's long inactivity after Kilmainham, and again after 1886, was due to the liaison. He points out that there were two other justifications for it—sound policy, and also the state of Parnell's health; but he grants that the pleasures of Mrs. O'Shea's society were a factor. To understand what sort of a factor one must appreciate the nature of the relation. Mrs. O'Shea was not a Cleopatra, nor Parnell an Antony. But whereas before 1881 his psychology had been that of an Irishman living in Ireland, who only visits England on business, after 1881 it became more like that of an Irishman who has settled in England and married an English wife.

Parnell's conduct may be variously estimated. Before he joined Mrs. O'Shea, he had to Healy's knowledge (T. M. Healy, *Letters and Leaders of My Day*, pp. 90, 93, 108–10) committed certain acts of profligacy. But his relation to Mrs. O'Shea seemed to the public in 1890 to reflect much more gravely on his character than it really did, since only O'Shea's version of it was heard in the divorce court. The incriminated pair durst not reply, because, once O'Shea had brought his action, their sole chance ever to be free from him was that he should succeed. And in order that he should, it became necessary for him to make out that he had been 'deceived' during a period of no less than nine years. It was this unmerited imputation of special and prolonged duplicity, quite as much as that of immorality, which damned Parnell with the English nonconformists.

APPENDIX C
QUESTIONS OF FOREIGN POLICY

1. *The Role of King Edward*

THOUGH the contrary is still sometimes asserted, the historical evidence seems overwhelming, that King Edward did not exercise over British foreign policy during his reign the influence often popularly attributed to him. Attributions, however, may have some importance, even when they are false; and that was the case here.

A well-known letter written by the late Lord Balfour to the late Lord Lansdowne in January 1915 (Lord Newton, *Lord Lansdowne*, 293) shows expressly what was the view of its author, and by inference that of its recipient. It was that to attribute the policy of the Entente to the king was 'a piece of foolish gossip', and that 'so far as I remember, during the years which you and I were his ministers, he never made an important suggestion of any sort on large questions of policy'. From the king's accession in January 1901 till Balfour's resignation on 4 December 1905 there was no question in foreign policy which did not pass through the hands of one or both of these two ministers; so that their testimony, even if it stood alone, would be impressive. But it does not; all the documentary evidence supports it. Messrs. Gooch and Temperley's second volume shows the genesis of the Entente clearly enough. It was the work of Cambon (primarily), Lansdowne, and Delcassé. King Edward only came in as a late, though very useful, coadjutor in the task of winning over the French people to a policy already embraced by French ministers.

Equally strong is the confirmation by *British Documents* of Lord Balfour's wider proposition. Any one reading the king's rare and brief minutes with an open mind must be struck by their relative unimportance. Nor is it in the least surprising. One can see from the volumes of *Queen Victoria's Letters* and from more than one incident in Sir Sidney Lee's *King Edward VII*, how comparatively crude his views on foreign policy were, how little he read, and of what naïve indiscretions he was capable. A single episode will illustrate the two last points. In the first August of his reign he was to meet the Kaiser at Homburg, and the foreign office furnished him with a highly confidential brief, setting out the British view of various topics on which the monarchs were expected to converse. The king—evidently without taking the trouble to read it—actually handed this confidential document over to the Kaiser. Fortunately no great harm was done, as the points involved were not of first-class importance, and the document was not uncomplimentary; but the incident speaks for itself.

The king's reputation as a diplomatist arose largely from his habit of sojourning abroad and visiting foreign courts. He had all his life enjoyed travel, and liked splendid ceremonies, and these royal tours satisfied both tastes. His usual programme, when he settled down to it, was to spend from three to six weeks at Biarritz in the early spring, seeing French ministers on his way there and back, and perhaps some Spanish royal personage across the frontier. Next, about May he would make a round of royal visits and calls, usually based on a yachting tour, oftenest in the Mediterranean; and later again in August he would go for his cure to Marienbad, commonly contriving to meet a few crowned heads or leading ministers there or by way of excursion. This programme, which was carried out every year from 1903 to 1909 inclusive, with a good many important 'extras' thrown in, enabled him to visit (besides the French President and ministers) the Kaiser, the Emperor of Austria, the Tsar, and the kings of Italy, Spain, Portugal, Greece, Denmark, Sweden, and Norway. He met the Kaiser oftener than any other crowned head; but before the Bosnian dispute of October 1908 he had paid specially assiduous court to the aged Emperor Francis Joseph. He never went to Belgium, owing to the attempt on his life there in 1900, when he was Prince of Wales. The return visits of the foreign potentates were usually arranged either for the interval between his May tour and his cure, or for that between the cure and Christmas.

Such regular rounds of international intercourse no British monarch had attempted before, nor indeed any monarch in Europe except William II. The Kaiser seems rather to have felt that his uncle was infringing his copyright; and he was the more vexed, because King Edward's visits usually left a much pleasanter impression than his own. For the king's skill and gusto on the social side were quite unmatched; as a mere emissary of friendship nobody bettered him. That was primarily how he conceived his role. He scarcely himself attempted serious diplomacy, though in certain instances important negotiations were carried on by the foreign office through ambassadors or other representatives in his suite. Some of his ministers' broader policies, it is true, corresponded to prior inclinations of his—notably that of friendship with Russia, which he had desired, off and on, ever since he visited the Russian court in 1874 for the marriage of his brother, the Duke of Edinburgh.

The main drawback to all these comings and goings was that they looked so much more important than they were. Everybody knew that, though from time to time their meetings were quite cordial, the king and the Kaiser disliked each other. The differences were largely temperamental, and first became conspicuous in the nineties during William II's yachting visits to Cowes. But the Kaiser in foreign affairs was entitled to a large measure of personal rule; his voice was

Germany's; and by a natural illusion he assumed other crowned heads to be in a corresponding position. He could never get it out of his mind that King Edward was; and that, when the king went to visit, say, the King of Italy or the Emperor of Austria, it was the director of Great Britain's foreign policy trying to seduce Italy or Austria from the Triple Alliance. Such misconceptions percolated right down through the German population, and gave rise to the baseless legend of *Einkreisung*, whereby England was held guilty of trying to 'encircle' Germany with a ring of hostile Powers. This myth, it is clear, arose directly out of King Edward's visits; but for them, it could scarcely have carried so much conviction. And in so far as it helped to create in Germany that spirit of nervousness which —in psychological alliance with the spirit of violence—helped to put the war party in the saddle, it made a definite contribution to the eventual catastrophe.

King Edward's long stays abroad had, incidentally, a domestic outcome. By removing him for large parts of each year from regular and daily contact with ministers, they made it impracticable for his wishes to be consulted in such detail as Queen Victoria's had been. This tended materially to lessen the personal influence of the monarch within the constitution.

2. *The Final Authority at Berlin 1912–14*

Just as the Germans in 1901–10 exaggerated King Edward's influence over British foreign policy by regarding him as the analogue of their own Emperor, so the liberal government and liberal party in England exaggerated the influence of the German chancellor and foreign office in 1911–14 by regarding them as the analogues of the prime minister and foreign office in Great Britain. This they were far from being.

The chancellor was, under the Emperor, the head of the civil administration of the Reich, and as such controlled the foreign office. Indeed since wide spheres of Germany's domestic administration were not federal but devolved on the federated states, foreign affairs engaged a much larger proportion of his attention than in the case of a British prime minister. Prior to Bethmann-Hollweg's advent, the holder of the chancellorship had always, save during the four years of Caprivi's tenure, been a diplomatist with ambassadorial experience.

But the chancellor did not, as the British prime minister did, control the army and navy. Although, as the Kaiser's representative in the Reichstag and the Bundesrat, it would be his duty, in conjunction with the war minister, to get the necessary monies voted and bills carried, he had a very limited voice in determining what those demands should be. For the heads of each service were, like the chancellor himself, directly responsible to the Emperor. Thus it was not in the chancellor's power to co-ordinate military or naval policy with foreign; that belonged to the Emperor alone. It is true that Bismarck himself came in effect to do so, but his authority was exceptional. Even he had trouble at times with the Prussian military chiefs, but from the foundation of the Reich his prestige was so great that he usually got his way. It was otherwise with his successors. William II was determined to be war lord, and insisted on the principle that the heads of his army acknowledged no superior but himself. He took the same line with the navy, to whose chief he habitually referred as *'mein* Tirpitz'. Hence when divergence appeared between the interests of military or naval policy, on the one hand, and those of diplomatic policy, on the other—as in the case of the German naval programme, which by 1911 had shown itself to be almost certainly incompatible with the diplomatic *rapprochement* towards England—it was always the Kaiser who decided, not the chancellor. And William II, who had an intense craving to be the hero of his armed forces, had little courage for saying 'No' to the chiefs of either.

A good illustration of this system is afforded by the general staff's adoption at the end of 1905 of the Schlieffen Plan. In its military aspects this plan (however marred in its execution by the younger Moltke in 1914) was a very great conception; and opinion in the general staff was so unanimous in its favour, that they decided to rely on it and have no other. Yet it was of the essence of the Plan that it involved violating Belgian neutrality, not merely on a fractional scale, but to the largest extent possible. It was therefore bound to provoke war with Great Britain. The general staff did not mind the prospect; the chancellor, at least when he was Bethmann-Hollweg, did. Yet the latter had scarcely a say in the matter. In the 1914 crisis, as he shows in his *Betrachtungen zum Weltkriege*, he had no alternative here but to comply with the wishes of the general staff. What they would be, he had known for a long time; and apparently the best that he could do was to multiply counter-inducements for British abstention, in the hope that when the crash came a very pacific British cabinet and parliament might perhaps keep their country out.

From 1908 onwards the dominance of the general staff over policy grew. The personal authority of the Emperor, which was the only check on it, received a shattering blow from the publication of the *Daily Telegraph* interview in the autumn of that year; and when Bülow retired in the following summer, the choice of his successor meant in itself a lessening of civilian weight in the balances. For Bethmann-Hollweg, who did not belong to the Prussian nobility, but derived from a patrician family at Frankfort, was really no more than an accomplished official in the domestic administration, the type of man who in the last analysis does not shape national decisions but complies with them. He was an expert in subjects like social policy and local government, but not in diplomatic nor in army matters, an enlightened but essentially a subordinate personality.

Subsequent international crises, in which the Kaiser rattled the sword without drawing it, still further weakened his authority over the military chiefs. There was open talk in Berlin of their preference for the Crown Prince, and of their readiness, if the father gave trouble, to make him abdicate in the son's favour. The Kaiser, who behind his bounce and bluster was very sensitive, became sufficiently aware of the army's attitude to be intimidated by it. When the first Balkan war occurred the army's displeasure found many voices. While her sovereign and diplomats were asleep, it was said, Germany's enemies had stolen a march on her. True, the army itself was unready for the challenge, but that too was the Kaiser's fault; in his enthusiasm for *die neue Flotte* he had neglected *das alte Heer*. Instant preparation must be made to retrieve the position.

The power of the soldiers was shown thereupon in their forcing on the civilians the scheme for the enormous *Wehrbeitrag* of 1,000 million marks. All the different arrangements for collecting and spending this utterly unprecedented sum converged towards a common date— the late summer of 1914. Of this the Kaiser and Bethmann-Hollweg must both have been well aware. Yet neither took any steps to fore-stall trouble at Vienna or to check it when it arose; on the contrary, when Francis Joseph wrote to him after Serajevo, the Kaiser said exactly what his general staff would have liked him to say; and the same is true of Bethmann-Hollweg's attitude at that date. What else could they do? Already in May, as Colonel House found, the mastery of the soldiers in Berlin was complete. House's evidence is exceptionally convincing, because he was armed with personal letters from President Wilson, which enabled him to pass through doors closed to ordinary diplomatists, and to watch the state of things in the highest quarters with his own eyes.

That there was a dualism in the government of Germany in 1914, as between the civilian and the military sections, could not be un-known to British diplomatists either there or in London. But in general they failed to attach anything like sufficient importance to it. Grey recognized its significance in retrospect (*Twenty-Five Years*, ii. 26), but his actions hardly suggest that he did at the time. Certainly neither the British cabinet nor its diplomatic advisers were on the look-out for a war in August 1914; though to not a few private observers the signs seemed unmistakable. The probable explanation is a natural one; men following an occupation like diplomacy fix their gaze on their opposite numbers. To the foreign office in London the foreign office in Berlin seemed to hold the keys of Germany's war and peace; though in 1914 it really did not. The mistake has its counterpart among historians to-day. Not a few of them seem to think that the roles played by each nation in the 1914 war-crisis can be deduced entirely from the diplomatic papers. In the case of Germany that is certainly not so.

3. *Grey and the Liberals*

Whatever be thought on other grounds of Sir Edward Grey's foreign policy, it was a source of weakness that the bulk of the party behind him neither understood nor liked it. On the brink of the European war most liberals were, in effect, pro-German and anti-French; and had not the Germans violated Belgium, it seems probable that the foreign secretary would have failed to carry with him either the cabinet or the party, when the critical question was posed of supporting France or leaving her to her fate.

How had this come about? What was the mind of these liberals? The more intelligent of them, e.g. C. P. Scott, the famous editor of the *Manchester Guardian*, were really isolationists; they wished Great Britain to revert to an attitude of impartiality between the Powers. It may not have been a practicable ideal; but, if it had been, its recommendations to them were obvious. They thought it would leave the country free and untrammelled to assert in all foreign disputes the pure liberal doctrines of free trade, the open door, international justice, and the rights of nationalities. But as the entanglements deprecated happened to be entanglements with France and Russia, the argument, even as developed in these highest-minded quarters, tended to run a good deal in anti-French and anti-Russian channels. The less intelligent rank and file of the party, when they thought about foreign affairs at all, commonly did so in terms of quite crude traditional prejudice against the French people and the Russian empire. They never forgot that the abandonment of isolation was the policy of a conservative government, and by instinct felt aggrieved with Grey for not automatically reversing it. The feeling was fortified among radicals by memories of earlier distrust towards Grey, Asquith, and Haldane as liberal imperialists. Lord Loreburn, the lord chancellor till 1912, who did a great deal to egg on liberal editors to attack the foreign policy of his colleagues, habitually characterized the latter as 'a Cabinet of Liberal Leaguers'. Lastly among the extremely few liberal M.P.s who paid any continuous attention to foreign affairs, a high proportion were Englishmen of that generous type which falls in love with some (usually small and afflicted) foreign nationality— Persians, it might be, or Bulgars, or Greeks, or Moors, or Poles, or

Finns, or even exiled revolutionary Russians. It is rarely possible for a foreign secretary, taking the wider view which his task necessitates, to go all the way with such enthusiasts; and Grey, through his Entente with Russia, had often to appear especially disappointing.

How did Grey deal with this hostility? Generally speaking, by leaving it alone until something like a serious revolt threatened, and then coming to the house of commons and delivering a speech, which by its tact and moderation and the obvious loftiness and nobility of the man behind it swept the assembly off its feet and silenced criticism for the time being. But these speeches rarely instructed their hearers in the realities of the situation; nor was it often possible that they should. A foreign secretary, who made a habit of stating in public the real considerations which motived his action, would be like a man exposing naked lights in a fiery mine. Grey was very adroit in avoiding such perils, as a single instance may show. In the spring of 1913 he threw the weight of Great Britain on the side of the view that Scutari, which the Montenegrins besieged and eventually reduced, must go not to them but to the Albanians. Now his real motive for doing this was to save the peace of Europe. Russia having stolen a march on Austria-Hungary through the success of the Balkan League, Austria-Hungary had retorted by insisting on the creation of an independent Albania, to keep the Slav kingdoms off the Adriatic. For such an Albania Scutari was conceived as essential, and had Grey not supported the Austrian demand against Russia, there might probably have been war. It was a boldly pacific step; it proved the turning-point in the London Conference; and it disproved, if any fact could, the German legend of British 'encirclement'. But Grey did not say those things to the house of commons. He said (what was the case) that Scutari was a genuinely Albanian town, and told the house, to the heart-felt satisfaction of the liberal benches, that in this matter he was on the side of the rights of nationality. Thus he scored a great parliamentary success without saying anything that was dangerous or anything that was not in itself true. But at the same time his party was left uninstructed as to the real mainsprings of the policy pursued.

How ought Grey to have made this defect good? By realizing—as neither he nor Asquith ever did realize—that parliament was not everything, and that to keep democracy in step with their policy it was essential to educate it through the press. Both these men exerted a consummate mastery over the house of commons, and both perpetually made the mistake of thinking that a debating victory, which carried the house, carried the country also. There was only one liberal journalist—the editor of a paper with an influential but very small circulation—whom either of them ever ordinarily deigned to see; and in Grey's case no provision whatever was made for keeping what should have been the friendly press informed. At each international crisis it was the easiest thing in the world for any highly placed London journalist to discover just what view the German or the French government wanted to put forward; indeed these views would constantly be pressed on him from all sorts of unexpected quarters. But to get reliable knowledge of what the British government thought, or wanted to be thought, was far more difficult. As a rule it was eventually obtained, if at all, by leakage from cabinet ministers; but as those who recognized the importance of journalism nearly all belonged to the left in the cabinet, it was apt to come with a strong anti-Grey bias.

If it be said that, despite this failure to keep reasonable touch in regard to foreign policy either with their party in the country or with M.P.s or even with the majority of their cabinet, Grey and Asquith nevertheless brought an all but unanimous nation and Empire into the war, the answer is that they owed their success almost entirely to the supervening issue of Belgian neutrality. But for that they would never have attained it.

4. *British Policy and Belgian Neutrality*

Gladstone's views on this topic, as expressed in 1870 (Hansard, III. cciii. 1787, 1788), may be summarized as follows: (*a*) there is no absolute obligation on a guarantor to act 'irrespectively altogether of the particular position in which it may find itself at the time when the occasion for acting on the guarantee arises' ('The great authorities upon foreign policy', he went on, 'to whom I have been accustomed to listen, such as Lord Aberdeen and Lord Palmerston, never to my knowledge took that rigid and, if I may venture to say so, that impracticable view of the guarantee'); (*b*) the existence of the guarantee is nevertheless 'an important fact and a weighty element in the case'; (*c*) a further consideration, 'the force of which we must all feel most deeply', is 'the common interests against the unmeasured aggrandisement of any Power whatever'; (*d*) Belgium has set Europe a fine example of good and stable government associated with wide liberty and 'looking at a country such as that, is there any man who hears me who does not feel, that if, in order to satisfy a greedy appetite for aggrandisement, coming whence it may, Belgium were absorbed, the day that witnessed that absorption would hear the knell of public right and public law in Europe?' (*e*) the Gladstonian appeal to the concept of justice: 'We have an interest in the independence of Belgium which is wider than that which we may have in the literal operation of the guarantee. It is found in the answer to the question whether, under all the circumstances of the case, this country, endowed as it is with influence and power, would quietly stand by and witness the perpetration of the direst crime that ever stained the pages of history, and thus become participators in the sin.'

Nine days before Gladstone spoke thus, the policy of supporting Belgian neutrality had been urged in the House of Commons by Disraeli. What he, however, emphasized was the historic British interest. Of the original treaty he observed that 'the most distinguished members of the Liberal party negotiated and advised their Sovereign to ratify it amid the sympathetic applause of all enlightened Englishmen'. They had been 'influenced in the course they took by the traditions of English policy. They negotiated the treaty for the general advantage of Europe, but with a clear appreciation of the importance of its provisions to England. It had always been held by the Government of this country that it was for the interest of England that the countries on the European coast extending from Dunkirk and Ostend to the islands of the North Sea should be possessed by free and flourishing communities, practising the arts of peace, enjoying the rights of liberty, and following those pursuits of commerce which tend to the civilization of man, and should not be in the possession of a great military Power, one of the principles of whose existence necessarily must be to aim at a preponderating influence in Europe' (Hansard, III. cciii. 1289).

Having, as they had, these utterances before them, it is remarkable that the majority of the 1914 cabinet were so slow to take the view which most of them eventually took regarding the importance of the Belgian issue. Gladstone's arguments (c) and (d) had each more and not less application in 1914 than in 1870; and Disraeli's perennial principle had only increased its validity since the advent of long-range artillery, 30-knot warships, aeroplanes, and submarines. The fact seems to be that the members of the cabinet were too busy wrangling about the Ententes to spare much time to think about Belgium. (Such, at least, is Lord Morley's account: *Memorandum on Resignation*, 3.) It was not till 3 August—when, following the German ultimatum of the previous day, the king of the Belgians addressed a personal appeal to King George—that opinion both in the cabinet and in the country swung right round on this issue. The main motive in the revulsion, perhaps, was not any clearer perception of Gladstone's and Disraeli's arguments, but the stripping of a veil off the character of Germany. For years past the liberals (latterly much fortified by the attractive personality of Lichnowsky) had been making it an article of party faith that militarist Germany was not so black as it was painted. Now in a flash it seemed to them self-revealed as much blacker.

BIBLIOGRAPHY

GENERAL

For the history of this period the wealth of sources and authorities is a greater embarrassment than their occasional deficiency. No one has attempted an exhaustive catalogue, though for the years down to 1901 there is a bibliography (1907) in the 12th volume (by Sidney Low and Ll. C. Sanders) of *The Political History of England*. Classified lists, covering the whole period and several decades on each side of it, will be found at the end of Sir J. A. R. Marriott's two volumes, *England since Waterloo, 1815–1900* (1913) and *Modern England (1885–1932): a History of My Own Times* (1934). The fullest English guidance to books is afforded by the *Catalogue* and *Subject Indexes* of the British Museum. The latter are printed for periods covering publications in the years 1881–1930 inclusive, and may be consulted at other important libraries; the index for the years since 1930, which is in process of compilation, can be seen at the Museum itself. The 3rd edition (1910–31) of W. A. Sonnenschein's *Best Books*, is also useful; especially the later volumes, whose publication was deferred till after the European War. The one-volume American publication *A Guide to Historical Literature*, by W. H. Allison, S. B. Fay, A. H. Shearer, and H. R. Shipman (New York, 1931) is convenient and compact.

Much bibliographical information can be obtained from the various general encyclopaedias, which will naturally be often otherwise required for reference purposes. At least five of them may be consulted with advantage in one case or another—the *Encyclopaedia Britannica* and *Chambers's Encyclopaedia* in English, those of Brockhaus and Meyer in German, and the large Larousse in French. For the historical student earlier editions of these, reflecting more immediately the times in which they were compiled, are often more useful than the current editions of to-day. In this way the 11th edition (1910) of the *Encyclopaedia Britannica* is worth going back to for the latter half of the period, while for the earlier half, the 14th edition of Brockhaus (1894–5) will often be found the best book of reference, even on British subject-matters.

Among general sources, the most important are British official publications, including the *Public General Acts*, the *London Gazette*, the *Official Reports* of debates in parliament (usually referred to as *Hansard*), and the *Parliamentary Papers* (often referred to as 'blue-books' or 'white-papers', according to the colour of their exterior). The Stationery Office issues temporary indexes with the *Parliamentary Papers* as they come out, and every year (earlier for periods of years) a permanent index is issued consolidating these. As no library which files the *Papers* will fail to have the indexes, it suffices to know the name of the item and the year of publication, in order to ascertain the number of the volume in which any particular item will be found. Some official publications of special importance will be mentioned in different sections below. The category covers a great variety of documents—official returns; accounts and estimates; correspondence; the text of treaties; the findings of parliamentary committees, departmental committees, and royal commissions, and the evidence given before them; and other items. Their value as evidence varies with their nature and subject. Where a parliamentary paper states an official fact officially, it is a primary authority for that fact; e.g., where a Census Report records that a certain population was enumerated in a certain area on a certain date. But many official papers deal with many facts only at second-hand; and where what are presented are calculations or inferences or theoretical matter of any kind, the officials responsible only differ from other experts in virtue of occupying an exceptional vantage-ground for collecting and checking data. It should, however, be said that the statistical work of the British government departments—especially that of the board of trade from the eighties onwards—was on a very high level. It was not only able, but well above party 'tendency'; which is more than can be said of official figures in some of the neighbouring foreign countries during the same period. Lastly, one must remember that, even where a blue-book's contention may be found wrong, the mere circumstance that it was advanced is an historic and sometimes an important fact. The same may be said of the evidence recorded before commissions or committees.

The other most important category of general sources comprises the files of newspapers and periodicals, presenting an all-round picture of their age more copious than can be obtained of any earlier one. For public speeches made outside parliament their reports supply our sole record, and in the case of great journals were during this period made with the utmost care.

Files of *The Times*, with its invaluable though sometimes inadequate *Index*, normally suffice in the first instance; but speeches or events localized at a distance from London and in the sphere of some great provincial paper will often be found more fully recorded in the latter. Papers of the popular type introduced by Lord Northcliffe can too seldom be relied on for their distinctive evidence regarding facts, but are of value as mirroring social history and illustrating currents of opinion. Ideas among the governing classes were best reflected in the monthly reviews— the *Fortnightly* and *Contemporary* throughout the period, the *Nineteenth Century* from 1877, the *National Review* from 1883; after 1890 a good many shorter-lived magazines attracted from time to time much of the best writing and thought. The two old quarterlies still ran, but were relatively in the background. Visual pictures of how people dressed and looked are supplied by the illustrated journals; and after the advent of the process-block (in the early nineties) these were based increasingly on photographs instead of drawings.

A third category is that of almanacs and periodical reference books. The most generally useful of these—*Whitaker's Almanack*, *The Statesman's Year Book*, and *Who's Who*—have no official status, but high standards of reliability; though even in the last-named, where the biographies were furnished by the persons biographized, serious mis-statements may occur if those persons so desired. *Who's Who* has published two memorial volumes, *Who Was Who*, *1897–1916* and *1916–1928*, which are of service for this period. Other useful annuals in the same class are the *Directory of Directors* (from 1879), the *Municipal Year Book* (from 1897), and the *Year Books* issued in the Edwardian period and after by the *Daily Mail* and the *Daily News*. On a rather different footing are those annuals, which, covering the personnel of a particular profession or association, have for it a more or less official character. Such are the *Law List* (for judges, barristers, and solicitors), *Crockford's Clerical Directory* (for the Anglican clergy), the *Medical Register* (statutory and official for medical practitioners), the *Calendars* of the various universities, &c. *Dod's Parliamentary Companion* should perhaps be included under this type rather than the other.

Two secondary authorities of wide general value for this period are the *Annual Register* and the *Dictionary of National Biography*. The former might almost be classed with the newspapers; for, in effect, it is a comprehensive annual journal on a level of quality corresponding to *The Times*, and its judgements, emphases, or omissions, may often, like those of a newspaper, be in themselves of historical interest. Similarly, though in less degree, a quality of contemporaneity may often be noted in the *Dictionary*, where it deals with persons deceased since 1880.

POLITICAL HISTORY

GENERAL AND DOMESTIC. The leading English text-books, each of which covers part of the period, are the three volumes first mentioned above. Designed on a much larger scale and admitting far more detail are the two concluding volumes of Élie Halévy's *Histoire du peuple anglais*. These treat the last nineteen years (the volumes to cover 1870–95 being not yet published); viz. *Épilogue I. 1895–1905* (1926) and *Épilogue II. 1905–14* (1932). Among earlier books are Herbert Paul's *History of Modern England* (5 vols., 1904–6; epigrammatic and sometimes luminous, but marred by Liberal partisanship), which reaches 1870 in the middle of vol. iii and goes down to 1895; Justin McCarthy's *History of Our Own Times* (popular in its day, but not of much permanent value), the last of whose 5 vols. (1899) goes down to 1897; J. Franck Bright's *History of England*, whose last volume (1904) covers the period 1880 to 1901 on a scale quite different from that of its school-book predecessors and, though nominally attached to them, is, in effect, a distinct and meritorious essay in contemporary political history; and vol. xii (1910) of the *Cambridge Modern History*, which ends substantially with the year 1905, though glancing for some purposes a little beyond it. Prof. G. M. Trevelyan's *British History in the Nineteenth Century, 1782–1901* (1922) gives much less than 30 per cent. of its attention to the years after 1870, yet at not a few points suggests valuable lines of thought; and others may be gathered from the relevant pages in Dr. J. A. Williamson's *Evolution of England* (1931).

The principal sources, other than those described in the general section, are biographies, autobiographies, collections of letters, and collections of speeches. The number bearing on this period is very large indeed, and only some of the most important will be mentioned here.

For our first two sub-periods an exceptionally rich source is *Queen Victoria's Letters* (which include large extracts from her Journal); those relevant here are the last 5 vols., all edited by G. E. Buckle (1926, 1928, 1930, 1931, and 1932). Sidney Lee's

Queen Victoria (revised edition, 1904) also contains a good deal of first-hand material. Lytton Strachey's *Queen Victoria* (1921), and E. F. Benson's *Queen Victoria* (1935) are well-known secondary authorities, the former apt to be opinionated, the latter able to draw at some points on family records and experiences. Frank Hardie's *The Political Influence of Queen Victoria, 1861–1901* (1935) seems to be the first attempt made to estimate that side of the queen separately. In the case of King Edward VII, no mass of documents corresponding to the Queen's *Letters* has yet seen the light, if indeed it exists; but a large literature has been written round him, some of it embodying original knowledge. The leading source of material is Sir Sidney Lee's *Life* (2 vols., 1925 and 1927); others are Edward Legge's *King Edward in his True Colours* (1912), Viscount Esher's *The Influence of King Edward* (1915), Lord Redesdale's *King Edward VII* (1915), and Sir Lionel Cust's *King Edward and his Court* (1930). Notable secondary authorities are H. E. Wortham's *The Delightful Profession* (1931), and E. F. Benson's *King Edward VII* (1933). The relations between the king and his mother have been specially studied in Hector Bolitho's *Victoria the Widow and Her Son* (1934).

For Disraeli, vols. v and vi of his official *Life* (both by G. E. Buckle, 1920) throw very broad lights on our first decade. Supplementing them are *The Selected Speeches of Lord Beaconsfield*, ed. by T. E. Kebbel (1882, 2 vols.), and *The Letters of Disraeli to Lady Bradford and Lady Chesterfield*, ed. by Lord Zetland (1929, 2 vols.). For Gladstone, besides the official *Life* by Lord Morley (3 vols., 1903), there is a collected edition of *Gladstone's Speeches*, ed. by A. Tilney Bassett with a valuable descriptive index and bibliography (1916). The enormous mass of the Gladstone Papers, of which some use has been made in the present work, are now housed in the British Museum and in process of being arranged; among several recent books specially based on them the most important for this period is P. Guedalla's *The Queen and Mr. Gladstone* (2 vols., 1933). For Gladstone's last premiership a valuable source is *The Private Diaries of Sir Algernon West*, ed. by H. G. Hutchinson (1922), West having served his chief at that stage as a political factotum. Other books which supply special Gladstoniana are Viscount (H. J.) Gladstone's *After Thirty Years* (1928); the *Reminiscences* of Lord Kilbracken (1931); Lord Rendel's *Personal Papers* (1931); the second volume of the eighth Duke of Argyll's *Autobiography and Correspondence*, ed. by his widow

(1906); G. W. E. Russell's *Malcolm MacColl, Memoir and Correspondence* (1914); and F. W. Hirst's *Gladstone as Financier and Economist* (1931), which contains an interesting chapter of recollections by Lord (H. N.) Gladstone. For Lord Salisbury, the main source is the *Life* by his daughter, Lady Gwendolen Cecil, of which four volumes (1921, 1931, and 1932) have appeared; the fifth is yet to come. The most important sidelights are those in Lord Balfour's *Chapters in Autobiography* (1930). The great *Life of Joseph Chamberlain*, by J. L. Garvin, of which three volumes (1932-3-4) have appeared (with a fourth to come), is as rich in political information as any source of the kind for this period. It may be supplemented by the collected edition of *Mr. Chamberlain's Speeches* (by C. W. Boyd, 2 vols., 1914). Three official biographies—of Lord Rosebery by Lord Crewe (2 vols., 1931), of Sir William Harcourt by A. G. Gardiner (2 vols., 1923), and of Campbell-Bannerman by J. A. Spender (2 vols., 1923)—show the main currents of Liberal politics in the nineties; the last takes us far into the Edwardian epoch. Of Balfour no corresponding account has yet appeared; but that of Asquith by J. A. Spender and Cyril Asquith (2 vols., 1932) is the leading biographical document for the eight years before the War. Asquith himself wrote a good deal in his old age—*The Genesis of the War* (1923), *Fifty Years of Parliament* (1926), *Memories and Reflections* (posthumous, 1928); beside which may be recalled the *Autobiography of Margot Asquith* (1920). Of Mr. Lloyd George's pre-war career there is no satisfactory record, but his best speeches down to the end of the Budget struggle may be read in a collected volume (*Better Times*, 1910).

Other books in this class include the following lives (an asterisk marks the more important): *The Fourth Earl of Carnarvon*, by Sir A. H. Hardinge, 3 vols., 1925; *Lord Sherbrooke* (Robert Lowe), by A. Patchett Martin, 1893; *Gathorne Hardy*, by A. E. Gathorne Hardy, 2 vols., 1910; *H. C. E. Childers*, by E. S. E. Childers, 2 vols., 1901; *Lord Playfair* (Lyon Playfair), by Sir T. Wemyss Reid, 1899; *James Stansfeld*, by J. L. and B. Hammond, 1932; *Sir George Otto Trevelyan*, by G. M. Trevelyan, 1932; *Thomas George, Earl of Northbrook*, by Bernard Mallet, 1908; *The Second Earl Granville*, by Lord Fitzmaurice, 2 vols., 1905; *Memorials of Roundell Palmer, Earl of Selborne*, 4 vols., 1896-8; *Lord Randolph Churchill*, by Winston S. Churchill, 1906; *W. H. Smith*, by Sir Herbert Maxwell, 1893; *Viscount Goschen*, by A. R. D. Elliot, 2 vols., 1911;

Sir C. W. Dilke, by Stephen Gwynn and Gertrude M. Tuckwell, 1917; *Lord Wolverhampton* (Sir H. H. Fowler), by Edith H. Fowler, 1912; *Sir Michael Hicks Beach, Earl St. Aldwyn*, by Lady Victoria Hicks Beach, 2 vols., 1932; *The Milner Papers*, ed. by Cecil Headlam, 2 vols., 1931–3; *The Eighth Duke of Devonshire*, by Bernard Holland, 2 vols., 1913; *Parliamentary Reminiscences and Reflections*, by Lord George Hamilton, 2 vols., 1916–22; *Lord James of Hereford*, by Lord Askwith, 1930; *George Wyndham*, by J. W. Mackail and Guy Wyndham, 1925; *Journals and Letters of Viscount Esher*, ed. by M. V. Brett, 2 vols., 1934; *Lord Lansdowne*, by Lord Newton, 1929; *Recollections*, by Lord Morley, 1917; *Autobiography*, by Lord Haldane, 1929; *C. P. Scott*, by J. L. Hammond, 1934; *Lord Courtney*, by G. P. Gooch, 1920; *Letters to Isabel* (autobiographical), by Lord Craigmyle, 1931; *Memoirs*, by Sir Almeric Fitzroy, 1925.

The early courses of labour politics must be traced largely from sources of their own. Among the few attempts to record them historically are A. W. Humphrey's *History of Labour Representation*, 1912; E. R. Pease's *History of the Fabian Society*, 1916; the second volume (1920) of Max Beer's *History of British Socialism*; the third volume of G. D. H. Cole's *Short History of the Labour Movement*; and Lord Elton's *England, Arise!* (1929).

Important sources are the reports of the public conferences held annually by the Trade Union Congress (from 1870), the I.L.P. (from 1893), and the Labour party (from 1900); these reflect constantly the active influence of the moment. The records of the Social Democratic Federation are only of national significance in the eighties. The early Socialist newspapers, whose files are of most value, are the *Commonweal*, *Justice*, the *Labour Leader*, and the *Clarion*. The most interesting source of pamphlets was the Fabian Society, whose monthly bulletin, *Fabian News*, is also useful for reference. Among biographical and autobiographical sources are the following (others are listed later in the Economic section): W. Stewart's *J. Keir Hardie*, 1921; Tom Mann's *Memoirs*, 1923; A. P. Grubb's *John Burns*, 1908; Henry Broadhurst's *Story of His Life*, 1901; Will Thorne's *My Life's Battles*, 1925; George Haw's *Will Crooks*, 1907; G. Lansbury's *My Life*, 1928; W. S. Sanders's *Early Socialist Days*, 1927; the second volume of J. W. Mackail's *William Morris*, 1899; J. Bruce Glasier's *William Morris and the Early Days of the Socialist Movement*, 1921; H. M. Hyndman's (vivid but often inaccurate)

Record of an Adventurous Life, 1911, and *Further Reminiscences*, 1912; R. Blatchford's *My Eighty Years*, 1931; Mrs. Mary A. Hamilton's *Mary Macarthur*, 1925, and *Sidney and Beatrice Webb*, 1933; and Mrs. Sidney Webb's *My Apprenticeship*, 1926.

On the women's suffrage movement the best general authorities are Dame M. G. Fawcett's *The Women's Victory and After*, 1920, and Miss Sylvia Pankhurst's *The Suffragette Movement*, 1931; but the subject has a considerable literature.

FOREIGN RELATIONS. Among the *Parliamentary Papers* may be found (*a*) the texts of treaties, (*b*) the *British and Foreign State Papers*, forming a collection of the diplomatic reports and correspondence, that have been laid before parliament. The latter, however, though covering much ground, seldom reveal the springs of diplomatic action. For the fact that official dispatches might be printed led during the nineteenth century to a practice of duplicating correspondence between the foreign secretary in Downing Street and the various ambassadors abroad; the dispatches being kept colourless, while the real business was transacted through private letters. This is what adds peculiar importance to biographies like Lady Gwendolen Cecil's of her father or Lord Fitzmaurice's of Lord Granville.

But for the period between 1898 and 1914 the great series of *British Documents on the Origins of the War*, edited (from 1927 onwards—one volume is still to come) by Dr. G. P. Gooch and Prof. H. W. V. Temperley, give a vastly fuller picture of British official policy. Not only dispatches are printed, but also the confidential minutes written on them, together with letters and intimate papers of various kinds. This publication was preceded by, and to a considerable extent modelled on, the even greater one made in Germany, entitled *Die Grosse Politik der europäischen Kabinette*; which appeared in 1922–6, covering the whole period 1871–1914 in 40 nominal and 54 actual volumes. A selection of some of the more interesting documents in *Die Grosse Politik* has been translated into English by E. T. S. Dugdale in 4 vols. (1928–31) entitled *German Diplomatic Documents*. Similar disclosures of diplomatic documents, but for a much shorter period, have since been made at Vienna, entitled *Oesterreich-Ungarns Aussenpolitik 1908–1914* (9 vols., 1930); for the earlier period, starting from the first Austro-German alliance, the chief authority is A. F. Přibram's, *Die politischen Geheimverträge Oesterreich-Ungarns* (1920), of which the English version (2 vols., 1920) is entitled *The Secret Treaties of Austria-Hungary, 1879–1914*. For France there is an official series of *Documents diplomatiques français 1871–1914* issued by a 'commission de publication' (from 1929). Parallel to all these, but not quite analogous (because presented with an air of propaganda) is the Bolshevik publication of Russian documents, *Un livre noir: Diplomatie d'avant-guerre d'après les documents des archives russes* (Paris, 2 vols., 1922 and 1923). Lastly it may be noted that during the European War most of the leading governments published sets of dispatches covering the events that immediately preceded their becoming belligerents. The original British set, which was the first, is often referred to simply as the White Paper of 1914. The best collection of all the sets is that of J. B. Scott (New York, 2 vols., 1916). A smaller but useful collection in 1 vol. was published by H.M. Stationery Office in 1915—*Collected Diplomatic Documents relating to the Outbreak of the European War*.

Of the English secondary authorities surveying the mass of material, the best in many respects is J. A. Spender's brilliant *Fifty Years of Europe* (1933). G. P. Gooch's *History of Modern Europe, 1878–1919* (1923) has also high merits, but suffers from having been written and published before most of the documents just mentioned had seen the light. The same is true of the treatment of the period in vol. iii (1923) of the *Cambridge History of British Foreign Policy*; though the defect is naturally felt more in the later chapters contributed by Dr. Gooch himself than in the admirable chapters on the years 1874–99 written by W. H. Dawson. Dr. Gooch's *Recent Revelations of European Diplomacy* (4th edn., 1930) and his *Studies in Modern History* (including essays on Holstein and on Bismarck) form, therefore, an important supplement to his work. Asquith's (i.e. the late Lord Oxford's) *Genesis of the War* (1923) and Haldane's *Before the War* (1920) are in part secondary authorities, in part autobiographical. Of many American historical works on the same subject the best known is Prof. S. B. Fay's *The Origins of the World War* (2 vols., 1929). From the Continent comes Prof. A. F. Přibram's *England and the International Policy of the European Great Powers 1871–1914*, which within its moderate compass is singularly just and discerning.

In this field, as in that of domestic politics, much material must be sought in biographies, autobiographies, and letters. Besides those of Queen Victoria, King Edward, Disraeli, Gladstone, Granville, Dilke, Salisbury, Chamberlain, Lansdowne, and Asquith already enumerated, which combine foreign with domestic interest, there are others concerned mainly or solely with the foreign side. Records of statesmen include Viscount (Sir Edward) Grey's indispensable *Twenty-Five Years, 1892–1916* (2 vols., 1925); Earl Loreburn's *How The War Came* (1919); and Lord Morley's *Memorandum on Resignation* (1928). Essential lights are thrown upon certain incidents by vol. i. (1933) of the *War Memoirs of Lloyd George*. Among records of diplomatists the most valuable is the *Life of Lord Carnock* (1930) by Harold G. Nicolson, especially for the decade ended by the War. In studying earlier decades reference should be made to *Lord Lyons* (1913) by Lord Newton (for the earlier Anglo-French relations); *Sir William White* (1902) by H. Sutherland Edwards (for Balkan events between 1875 and 1891); and *Lord Pauncefote* (1929) by R. B. Mowat (for the course of Anglo-American relations in the years before and after Mr. Cleveland's Message). Lord Zetland's *Lord Cromer* (1932) might be added for the story of Anglo-French relations under Gladstone's second ministry and the negotiation of the Anglo-French Agreement during 1903–4. The *Diplomatic Reminiscences* of Lord Augustus Loftus (4 vols., 1892–4), and the *Further Recollections of a Diplomatist* (1903) and *Final Recollections* (1905) of Sir Horace Rumbold (covering 1873–85 and 1885–1900 respectively), are autobiographical works more often, perhaps, of value for 'atmosphere' than for contributions to our knowledge of events. To these records of British diplomatists three should be added of Americans: W. R. Thayer's *John Hay* (2 vols., 1915); Burton J. Hendrick's *Walter H. Page* (2 vols., 1922–5); and *The Intimate Papers of Colonel House* (4 vols., 1926–8).

Some special topics can be studied in monographs of exceptional quality. A case in point is Dr. R. W. Seton-Watson's *Disraeli, Gladstone, and the Eastern Question* (1935); which examines the events, that preceded and culminated in the Congress of Berlin, by the light not merely of British but of Russian secret documents, and brings together a greater mass of evidence than can be found in any previous writing on the subject. Another is the monograph on British policy regarding arbitration, which now forms ch. 2 of the late Sir James Headlam-Morley's *Studies in Diplomatic History* (1930). Another is the exhaustive examination of the Anglo-German naval rivalry in E. L. Woodward's *Great Britain and the German Navy* (1935). On a limited scale, but of value still is a famous monograph on the Bagdad Railway negotiations in the *Quarterly Review* for October 1917. Some pre-War books of special authority, such as H. Wickham Steed's *The Hapsburg Monarchy* (1913), W. Miller's *The Ottoman Empire* (1913), or E. G. Browne's *The Persian Revolution* (1910), may be mentioned with these.

Foreign authorities for the period are extremely numerous. Partly because Germany was the leading continental power, and partly because the courses that she took came to determine Great Britain's, the German literature is the most important for us. Writings by public men include Prince Bismarck's *Gedanken und Erinnerungen* (2 vols., 1898; English version entitled *Bismarck the Man and the Statesman*); Prince Hohenlohe's *Denkwürdigkeiten* (2 vols., 1907; Eng. version entitled *Memoirs*); Prince Bülow's *Deutsche Politik* (1914; Eng. version entitled *Imperial Germany*); his 3 volumes of *Reden* (not translated); his 4 volumes of *Denkwürdigkeiten* (Eng. version, *Memoirs*); Count von Bethmann-Hollweg's *Betrachtungen zum Weltkriege* (2 vols., 1919 and 1921; Eng. version of vol. i only, entitled *Reflections on the World War*); William II's *Briefe an den Zaren 1894–1914*, ed. by Walter Goetz (1920; Eng. version, *Letters to the Tsar*); his *Ereignisse und Gestalten* (1922; Eng. version, *Memoirs*); Prince Lichnowsky's *My Mission to London* (1918; see above, p. 408, n. 1); G. von Jagow's *Ursachen und Ausbruch des Weltkrieges* (1919); Baron von Eckardstein's *Lebenserinnerungen und politische Denkwürdigkeiten* (3 vols., 1919; Eng. version—of selections only—*Ten Years at the Court of St. James*); Alfred von Tirpitz's *Erinnerungen* (1919; Eng. version, *My Memories*); and his *Politische Dokumente* (1927). On the side of the general staff the book of most authority is General H. J. von Kuhl's *Der deutsche Generalstab in Vorbereitung und Durchführung des Weltkrieges* (1920); there are also the younger Moltke's *Erinnerungen, Briefe, Dokumente* (1922); for Schlieffen and his Plan, see Wolfgang Foerster's *Graf Schlieffen und der Weltkrieg* (1921), and also Baron von der Lancken's *Meine dreissig Dienstjahre* (1931). Of German histories on this period the best is Erich von Brandenburg's *Von Bismarck zum Weltkriege* (1924; Eng. version, *From Bismarck to the World War*). Among others are Otto Hammann's *Der neue Kurs* (1918), *Zur Vorgeschichte des Weltkrieges* (1918), *Bilder aus der letzten Kaiserzeit* (1922), *Deutsche Weltpolitik 1890–1912* (1925); E. Fischer's *Holsteins grosses Nein* (1925); Johannes Haller's *England und Deutschland um die Jahrhundertswende* (1929) and his *Die Aera Bülow* (1922); H. Lutz's

Lord Grey und der Weltkrieg (1927; Eng. version, *Lord Grey and the World War*); K. F. Nowak's *Das dritte deutsche Kaiserreich* (2 vols., 1929–31; Eng. version of vol. i, *Kaiser and Chancellor*, of vol. ii, *Germany's Road to Ruin*); and Theodor Wolff's *Der Krieg des Pontius Pilatus* (1934; Eng. version, *The Eve of 1914*).

On the French side, A. Debidour's *Histoire diplomatique* (last 2 vols., 1916) is still worth consulting. For our earliest sub-period there are G. Hanotaux's *Histoire de la France contemporaine* (4 vols., 1903–9; Eng. version, *Contemporary France*), which runs to 1882; Paul Deschanel's *Gambetta* (1919; Eng. version 1920); and C. de Freycinet's *Souvenirs 1878–93* (1914). For the later stages there are *Les origines et les responsabilités de la grande guerre*, by E. Bourgeois and G. Pagès (1922); R. Poincaré's *Les origines de la guerre* (1921; Eng. version *The Origins of the War*); A. Tardieu's *La France et les alliances* (1908); J. Caillaux's *Agadir* (1919); and Élie Halévy's *The World Crisis of 1914–1918* (1930). A short list of important books from other countries might include: (*a*) Russian—Count S. J. Witte's *Memoirs* (Eng. version 1921), A. P. Isvolsky's *Memoirs* (Eng. version, 1921), and A. Nekludoff's *Diplomatic Reminiscences* (Eng. version, 1920); (*b*) Austrian—*Aus meiner Dienstzeit* (4 vols., 1921–5) by Baron F. Conrad von Hötzendorf (former Austro-Hungarian Chief of Staff); (*c*) Belgian—*Albert of Belgium* by E. Cammaerts (1935); (*d*) Bulgarian—*The Balkan League* (1915) by I. E. Gueshoff (one of its chief artificers); (*e*) Japanese—Viscount Hayashi's *Secret Memoirs* (ed. by A. M. Pooley, 1915).

There is also a mass of important material scattered about in leading European periodicals. To most of this, however, references will be found in one or other of the secondary authorities cited above.

LEGAL AND CONSTITUTIONAL

Three years before the period of this volume begins, Walter Bagehot published his classical *The English Constitution* (1st edn. 1867; 2nd, revised, 1872). It defines the point from which subsequent changes start. Their effect was shown near the end of the period by another standard authority, *The Government of England*, by A. Lawrence Lowell (1908); which not only passes in detailed review all the chief external features of government and administration, but devotes special attention to more intimate matters like the growth of the party system. With it may be compared Sidney Low's *Governance of England* (1904), a slighter book but in some respects very acute. Some broader characteristics of legal development between 1870 and the end of the Unionist supremacy are indicated in A. V. Dicey's *Lectures on the Relation between Law and Public Opinion in England during the Nineteenth Century* (1905).

On the legal side of the constitution, the text-books and editions used during the period will in general be better guides to what was then the law than those in use now. Of Sir W. R. Anson's well-known *Law and Custom of the Constitution* the earlier portion, *Parliament*, first appeared in 1886 and went into a 4th edition before the War; the later, *The Crown*, dates from 1892, and a third edition was issued in two parts, published in 1907 and 1908. *Parliament* has since been carefully re-edited (1922) by Sir Maurice Gwyer, *The Crown* (1935) by Prof. A. B. Keith. A text-book of more restricted scope, but very useful within its limits, is D. Chalmers and Cyril Asquith's *Outlines of Constitutional Law* (4th ed., 1930). Of May's *Law, Privileges, Proceedings, and Usage of Parliament* the best edition for our period is the 12th, edited by Sir T. L. Webster (1917). T. P. Taswell-Langmead's much-used but rather slipshod *English Constitutional History* originally appeared in 1875, when far less was known of its subject than now; and seven subsequent editions only tinkered with its revision. But the 9th (1929), edited and practically re-written by A. L. Poole, is a much more satisfactory authority. *Legislative Methods and Forms* (1901) by Sir Courtenay Ilbert (then parliamentary counsel to the treasury) contains detailed accounts of the procedures under which laws were drafted and piloted through Parliament at the end of the queen's reign.

Of the development of the central departments in Whitehall H. D. Traill's *Central Government*, published in 1881, gives an interesting brief description down to that date. In 1908 a revised edition by Sir Henry Craik carried some of the facts 17 years farther. The Reports of the Royal Commission on the Civil Service towards the end of our period (Cd. 6209 of 1912, and Cds. 6434 and 6739 of 1913) show in a much more substantial way for the different chief departments the further development then reached.

Of the central government's developing activities in the prevention and detection of crime no one has written a satisfactory history covering this period. George Dilnot's *Scotland Yard* (1926) is the best of its class. Prison administration, on the other hand, is the subject of a copious and serious literature. Three books—*English Prisons under Local Government* (1922) by Sidney and Beatrice Webb, *The Punishment and Prevention of Crime* (1885) by Sir Edmund du Cane, and *The English Prison System* (1921) by Sir Evelyn Ruggles-Brise—cover the period between them (Du Cane and Ruggles-Brise were successively chairmen of the prison commission, each for over 20 years). In addition there are the annual official reports and statistics of the commission from 1878.

On the side of local government the best systematic treatise on things as they were at the beginning of the twentieth century is *Local Government in England* by J. Redlich and F. W. Hirst (2 vols., 1903). A much briefer but very clear description is *An Outline of English Local Government* by E. Jenks (1st edn. 1894; 2nd edn. revised, 1907). The best law text-book for that period is the 13th edn. of 'Glen's *Public Health*', edited by A. Glen, A. F. Jenkins, and R. Glen (3 vols., 1906). Published annually from 1899, *Local Government Law and Legislation* contains for each year (*a*) the relevant statutes; (*b*) a digest of cases; (*c*) circulars, orders, and other official information. Other important sources for the historian are the periodicals devoted to local government; they include the *Justice of the Peace* (from 1837), the *Local Government Chronicle* (from 1872; earlier since 1855 as *Knight's Public Advertiser*), the *Local Government Journal* (from 1892; earlier since 1872 as the *Metropolitan*), the *Sanitary Record* (from 1874, but in its present form from 1880); the *Municipal Journal* (from 1899; founded as *London* in 1893); and (last but not least) the annual *Municipal Year Book* (from 1897).

ECCLESIASTICAL

The main currents of official policy in the church of England during the period are well shown in the biographies of successive archbishops of Canterbury—the *Life of Archbishop Tait* (2 vols., 1891), by Dean Randall Davidson and Canon Benham; the *Life of Archbishop Benson* (1899), by A. C. Benson; the *Memoirs of Archbishop Temple* (2 vols., 1906), edited by Archdeacon Sandford; and *Randall Davidson Archbishop of Canterbury* (2 vols., 1935), by Dr. G. K. A. Bell (bishop of Chichester). Chapters X and XI of *Church and People 1789–1889* (1933), by Dean S. C. Carpenter, contain good accounts of the bishops and clergy prominent in the seventies and eighties, and especially of the church's extended social work. *Henry Scott Holland* (1921), by Stephen Paget, and *Brooke Foss Westcott* (2 vols., 1903), by Arthur Westcott, throw light on the best High and Broad Church tendencies respectively; the sketch of *The Evangelical School in the Church of England* (1901) by H. C. G. Moule gives an idea of the Low. No full biography of Charles Gore has yet appeared, though the sketch by Gordon Crosse (1932) is good within its limits. Nor is there any adequate account of the considerable progress made in England at this time by Roman catholicism; but the much-discussed *Life of Cardinal Manning* (2 vols., 1896), by E. S. Purcell, throws into prominence some features of it.

On the Free Church side, a history of the British Methodist churches down to the end of the nineteenth century will be found in the last of the three vols. on *British Methodism* in the *History of Methodism* by J. Fletcher Hurst (1901). *The Methodist Church: Its Origin, Divisions, and Re-union* (1932) by A. W. Harrison (Wesleyan), B. Aquila Barber (Primitive Methodist), G. G. Hornby (United Methodist), and E. Tegla Davies (Welsh Methodist) contains historical sketches of all the four bodies now re-united. The largest of them, the Wesleyans, was very notably rejuvenated during this period; *Hugh Price Hughes* (1904), by Dorothea P. Hughes, and *Mark Guy Pearse* (1930), by Mrs. George Unwin and John Telford, are biographies of the two men most concerned in the process. The too brief *Reminiscences* (1928) of Dr. J. Scott Lidgett forms also a valuable document. For the Congregationalists Albert Peel's *History of the Congregational Union of England and Wales 1831–1931* is an official record of the Union published (1931) for its centenary. Nothing similar has been done for the Baptists, but their progress may be studied in the biographies of their great preachers. C. H. Spurgeon's *Autobiography* (4 vols., 1897–1900) is rambling and egotistical, but full of material. Among many other books on him is a recent biography (1933) by J. C. Carlile. Dr. John Clifford is another leading Baptist figure, round whom much has been written; the official *Life* is by Sir James Marchant (1924). That of *Alexander Maclaren* (1910), by David Williamson, commemorates the greatest Baptist preacher in the north of England. For the Society of Friends the second volume of Rufus Jones's *The Later Periods of Quakerism* (1921) goes down to 1900; and interesting statistics of the Society's membership in 1913, with some lights on its relative position at that period, will be found in J. W. Graham's *The Faith of a Quaker* (1920).

Of the Salvation Army, which was the most important religious body originating within the period, the best account, at any rate for its founder's lifetime, is in *God's Soldier: General William Booth* (2 vols., 1934) by St. John G. Ervine.

MILITARY

The changes made in army organization by Cardwell were thoroughly discussed in parliamentary debates, for which see Hansard. The useful book on them is *Lord Cardwell at the War Office* (1904) by General Sir R. Biddulph, who as a young officer had been one of his private secretaries. The next stages of advance are shown in the biography of Hugh Childers by Edmund Childers (1901); and later the fruits of 17 years' progress are described by Lord Wolseley in his extended contribution to T. H. Ward's *Reign of Queen Victoria* (1887). In 1888 came the (Hartington) Royal Commission 'on the Civil and Professional Administration of the Naval and Military Departments', whose main report is Cd. 5979 of 1890. Most of the chief campaigns earlier than the South African War are recorded either in Lord Wolseley's *Story of a Soldier's Life* (1903) and his biography by Sir Frederick B. Maurice and Sir George Arthur (1924), or in Lord Roberts's *Forty-One Years in India* (1897) and his biography by Sir G. W. Forrest (1914). Of the exceptions, the Majuba campaign is described in Sir W. F. Butler's *Life of Sir G. Pomeroy-Colley* (1899), and the reconquest of the Egyptian Sudan in the *Life of Lord Kitchener* (1920) by Sir George Arthur.

For the South African War itself the leading authority is the official *History of the War in South Africa 1899–1902*; 4 vols. of text (1906-7-8-10) and 5 of maps. Sir J. Frederick Maurice's name appears on the title-page of the first 2 vols.; the others are 'compiled under the direction of H.M. Government'. With it may be compared *The War in South Africa: Prepared by the Historical Section of the Great General Staff, Berlin*; which is an English version in 2 vols. (1904 and 1906) of *Aus dem südafrikanischen Kriege 1899 bis 1902*, describing the war mainly as seen from the Boer side. Equally important in another way are the publications of the Royal Commission on the War in South Africa. Its Report is Cd. 1789 of 1904, and vol. i of the *Evidence* is Cd. 1790. Lord Newton's *Lord Lansdowne* throws some lights on the war office side, and more can be obtained from the debates in Hansard. The latter sufficiently explain the various attempts at army reform sponsored by the Balfour government. A good deal about the Esher Commission, and also about the development of the Committee of Imperial Defence, can be learned from the *Journals and Letters of Viscount Esher* (1934), as listed above. H. Spenser Wilkinson's autobiography, *Twenty-Five Years* (1933), presents a vivid record of hopes and fears for the army during this long season of incubation.

The Haldane army policy was also fully discussed in reported speeches, and Haldane collected some of his into a small volume (*Army Reform*, 1907). *The Territorial Force* (1909) by H. T. Baker (an intimate adherent) shows how carefully that part of his policy had been thought out. Sir Ian Hamilton's *Compulsory Service* (1910) exhibits the reasons which motived Haldane and his military advisers in opposing the conscription policy of Lord Roberts. Haldane's own *Autobiography*; J. A. Spender and C. Asquith's *Life of Asquith*; Sir C. E. Callwell's *Sir Henry Wilson: Life and Diaries* (2 vols., 1927); Sir William R. Robertson's *From Private to Field-Marshal* (1921); and the *Life of Sir John French, First Earl of Ypres* (1931), by Major the Hon. G. French, illustrate the developments of the closing years, after the Expeditionary Force took firm shape and the use of it on the Continent became the subject of regular conversations with the French general staff. A recent expert re-appreciation of Lord Haldane's work will be found in Sir Frederick B. Maurice's *Fifth Annual Haldane Memorial Lecture* (1933).

Much miscellaneous information about the pre-war Regular army can be gathered from Rudyard Kipling's works, and also from such books as Sir C. E. Callwell's *Service Yarns and Memories* (1912) and *Recollections* (1923), or Sir G. Arthur's *Septuagenarian's Scrap Book* (1933). And there are striking reminiscences of life as a private soldier and N.C.O. at a very interesting transition period, 1871–8, in Robert Blatchford's *My Eighty Years* (1931).

NAVAL

The changes in the design of warships after the abandonment of 'wooden walls' may be traced by experts in the *Transactions* (since 1860) of the Institution of Naval Architects. Attempts to describe them for the public have not been numerous. In 1869 Sir Edward Reed, designer of the *Devastation* and till 1870 Chief

Constructor to the British navy, published *Our Ironclad Ships*, explaining fully the principles of warship construction down to the stage then reached. In 1888, with E. Simpson, he wrote *Modern Ships of War*. But for the work of his principal successor, Sir William White, see the *Life* (1923) by Frederic Manning. In 1903 Sir W. Laird Clowes published the last of 7 vols. of composite authorship on the history of *The Royal Navy*, and in a chapter on its civil history, 1856–1900, surveyed the technical changes between the Crimean War and the end of the century. By that time there were already being issued the two annuals, which are the chief guides for the rest of the period—*Brassey's Naval Annual* (from 1886) and F. T. Jane's *All the World's Fighting Ships* (from 1898).

One other biography is of high value as throwing light on the developments—that of *Lord Fisher of Kilverstone* (2 vols., 1929) by Admiral Sir R. H. S. Bacon.

ECONOMIC

(*a*) GENERAL. The best general economic history that touches the period is the 2nd vol. (1933) of Prof. J. H. Clapham's *Economic History of Great Britain*. Unfortunately it only accompanies us to 1886. Dr. Gilbert Slater's *Growth of Modern England* (1932—a much enlarged revision of an earlier book) has also great merits; it is not, however, solely an economic history, but is concerned rather to depict the interplay between industrial and political movements. Both the late Dr. Lilian C. A. Knowles's *The Industrial and Commercial Revolutions in Great Britain during the Nineteenth Century* (2nd edn., revised, 1922), and Dr. C. R. Fay's *Great Britain from Adam Smith to the Present Day* (1928) are books of high quality. One can also, for this period, refer to the files of the *Economist* all through, and from 1878 to those of the *Statist*.

Government sources for economic facts were before 1886 relatively meagre; after that they rapidly and progressively became copious. The turning-point was the Royal Commission on the Depression of Trade and Industry, whose *Reports* are Cds. 4621, 4715, 4797, and 4793 of that year (each of the last three with *Evidence* and *Appendices*). The board of trade's statistical activities were thenceforward greatly expanded under Sir Robert Giffen and H. (afterwards Sir H.) Llewellyn Smith; the annual *Abstract of Labour Statistics* began its invaluable career in 1889. The depression of 1892–4 and the organization of the labour department of the board of trade led to further extensions; but as from 1886 the foundations had been laid. Thus in the important report (Cd. 6889 of 1893-4) *On the Wages of the Manual Labour Classes in the United Kingdom*, the tables of wages and hours given are for 1886 and 1891. In the first *Statement Showing Production, Consumption, and Export, of Coal, and the Number of Employees in Coal Production, in the Principal Countries of the World* (No. 317 of 1894—it subsequently became annual) the retrospective starting-point is 1883. The next expansions resulted from the raising of the fiscal issue. The 'fiscal blue-books' properly so-called are three—Cd. 1761 of 1903, Cd. 2337 of 1904, and Cd. 4954 of 1909; but there are two other great blue-books, No. 294 of 1907 and No. 218 of 1914, which are of similar scope and importance, and only differ in that they were *Returns*, that had been moved for in parliament. One might add Cd. 2145 of 1904, the very interesting *Charts illustrating Statistics of Trade, Employment, and Conditions of Labour in the United Kingdom*, which were prepared for the St. Louis Exhibition; and Cd. 321 of 1903, the board of trade *Report on Wholesale and Retail Prices*, which gives prices from 1871. Then in 1910 comes the *Preliminary Report* (Cd. 5463) of the Census of Production; the subsequent reports are Cd. 5813 of 1911 and Cds. 6277 and 6320 of 1912-13. Of the many unofficial writers who since the publication of this wealth of blue-books have tried to elucidate or supplement their results, the most conspicuous is Prof. A. L. Bowley, whose works on *The Change in the Distribution of the National Income 1880-1913* (1920) and *The Division of the Product of Industry* (1919) more particularly concern us here.

For knowledge of the period before 1886 we have to depend more on private enterprise. The *Journal* of the Royal Statistical Society makes throughout an important contribution. A. Sauerbeck's *Course of Average Prices of General Commodities in England* (1908) gives computations from 1815 to 1907. Sir Robert Giffen's *Essays in Finance* (1879-86) range over the whole of our first sub-period. Giffen, who as comptroller-general of the commercial, labour, and statistical department of the board of trade afterwards took an important part in the earlier expansion of its work, had till 1876 been a financial journalist. His later writings include *The Growth of Capital* (1890) and *The Case Against Bimetallism* (1892). A convenient and reliable channel for much information covering foreign as well as British statistics is M. G. Mulhall's *Dictionary of Statistics* (4th edn., 1899). A valuable continuation of it, the *New Dictionary of Statistics* by A. D. Webb, appeared in 1911.

(*b*) POPULATION. The primary sources are the decennial census reports and the annual reports of the registrar-general. With the development of public health administration, however, the study of death-rates and, to a less extent, of birth-rates became local as well as national; and much may be learned from the annual reports of the more enterprising local medical officers of health as well as (after 1908) from those of the medical officer to the Local Government Board. Useful books are: *The Population Problem* (1922), by A. M. Carr-Saunders; *Population* (1923) by Harold Wright; and *The Declining Birth-Rate* (1916) edited by Sir James Marchant. The last gives the *Report* and *Evidence* of a non-official but very influential 'National Birth-Rate Commission', which sat during 1913–15 and heard highly important witnesses; and includes a bibliography of French, German, and some American writings. In addition there is an extensive literature on the subject termed eugenics, starting from F. Galton's *Hereditary Genius* (1869) and continued most notably by him and by Prof. Karl Pearson; see the publications of the Eugenics Education Society, and K. Pearson's periodical *Biometrika*.

(*c*) BANKING AND FINANCE. For the ways of finance in the City during this period, the best general authority is Ellis T. Powell's *The Evolution of the Money Market* (1915). The standard account of the Bank of England by A. Andreades does not come down far enough in the century to help us. But there is a more recent book which does—*The Bank of England from Within* (2 vols., 1931) by W. Marston Acres; vol. ii gives some details about Goschen's conversion scheme and about the Baring crisis. In regard to the joint-stock banks, no general history of the amalgamation movement, which so greatly reduced their numbers and increased their scale, has yet been written. There are, however, histories of individual banks; e.g. P. W. Matthew's *History of Barclay's Bank* (1926) and Neil Munro's *History of the Royal Bank of Scotland* (1928).

During the eighties and nineties bimetallism attracted serious attention in England, though it never (as in the U.S.A.) became a popular issue. The *Report* of the Royal Commission on Gold and Silver is Cd. 5512 of 1888.

(*d*) INDUSTRIAL AND TECHNICAL. This side is covered pretty

fully by Prof. Clapham down to 1886. For Gilchrist Thomas and his discovery, see R. W. Burnie's *Memoir and Letters of Sidney Gilchrist Thomas* (1891). For iron and steel generally, see Sir Isaac Lowthian Bell's essay on 'The Iron Trade and Allied Industries' in T. H. Ward's *Reign of Queen Victoria* (1887). For the period 1886–1900 Talbot Baines's *The Industrial North* (1928), a reprint of articles which originally appeared in *The Times* in the late nineties, surveys the industries of iron and steel, shipbuilding and engineering, armaments, Sheffield manufactures, West Riding cloth, Lancashire cotton, coal-mining, and chemicals. In the following decade a corresponding description of the Lancashire, Yorkshire, and West Riding industries may be found in Dr. A. Shadwell's *Industrial Efficiency* (1906); accompanied by comparative studies of corresponding industries in Germany and America. Practically contemporary is Sir Sydney J. Chapman's important monograph, *The Lancashire Cotton Industry* (1904). Railways and railway management (which altered relatively little during the period) may be studied in Sir W. M. Acworth's *The Railways of England* (5th edn. with supplementary chapters, 1900). The best general account of nautical developments down to nearly the end of the nineteenth century is in R. J. Cornwall Jones's *The British Merchant Service* (1898); see also A. C. Hardy's *Merchant Ship Types* (1924). J. T. Critchell and Joseph Raymond's *History of the Frozen Meat Trade* (1912) is the standard work on its subject; but it does not cover chilled beef, for which see G. E. Putnam's *Supplying Britain's Meat* (1923). For the early history of the bicycle and also for that of the motor-car the most reliable general authority is H. O. Duncan's encyclopaedic book, *The World on Wheels* (1926).

(*e*) AGRICULTURE. The *Reports* of the Royal Commission on 'the Depressed Condition of the Agricultural Interest' are Cd. 2778 of 1881 and Cd. 3309 of 1882. There were also published a vast mass of assistant commissioners' reports, evidence, and appendices, which will all be found indexed for the years 1881 and 1882. The (later) Royal Commission 'on Agricultural Depression' issued its first *General Report* in 1894 (Cd. 7400), its second in 1896 (Cd. 7981), and its *Final Report* in 1897 (Cd. 8540). Twenty reports of assistant commissioners appeared in the years 1894–6; the *Evidence* is Cd. 7400 of 1894 and Cds. 8021 and 8146 of 1896; and the *Appendices* are Cds. 8541 and 8300 of 1897. A most valuable report by A. Wilson Fox on the *Wages and Earnings of Agricultural Labourers* is Cd. 346 of 1900; a second report by him on the same subject is Cd. 2376 of 1905. Much subsequent information about agricultural labourers' wages was given in the annual *Abstract of Labour Statistics*. A report by Sir H. Rew on the *Decline of the Agricultural Population 1881–1906* is Cd. 3273 of 1906. The agricultural results of the census of production are given in Cd. 6277 of 1912–13. A return listed above, No. 218 of 1914, includes detailed comparisons of British, German, and American agricultural development. The German comparison was carried farther in Sir T. H. Middleton's *Recent Development of German Agriculture* (Cd. 8305 of 1916).

The best-known book which surveys farming through the period is *English Farming Past and Present* (1912; 4th edn. 1927), by Rowland E. Prothero (Lord Ernle). *Agriculture After the War* (1916), by Sir A. Daniel Hall, gives also a lucid review of the pre-war developments; the same author's *Pilgrimage of British Farming* (1912) records the actual faces of British farms as seen by an expert traversing the country not long before. Dr. W. Hasbach's *Die englischen Landarbeiter in den letzten hundert Jahren* (1894) is a careful German monograph; partly brought up to date, it was translated by Ruth Kenyon (1908) as *A History of the English Agricultural Labourer*. The small holdings policy, of which so much was heard in the 1906–10 parliament, was reported on in 1906 by a departmental committee. The best unofficial survey of English small holdings at the time was *Small Holdings* (1907) by L. Jebb.

(*f*) MUNICIPAL ENTERPRISE. The *Report* from the joint select committee of the house of lords and the house of commons on Municipal Trading (1900) was accompanied by *Evidence* and an *Appendix* containing a wide range of information. More was embodied in the annual publications of the local government board. Unofficial writings on the subject during the period were nearly all vitiated by strong prejudices for or against. Almost the only objective study is Douglas Knoop's *Principles and Methods of Municipal Trading* (1912).

(*g*) POVERTY. The rival *Reports* of the Royal Commission on the Poor Law fill Cd. 4499 of 1909, a gigantic blue-book with some 1238 folio pages, in which the main facts about pauperism in the period are fully stated and analysed. See also the *Report* of the departmental committee on Vagrancy (vol. i is Cd. 2852 of 1906). The *Report* of the select committee on Home Work is No. 246 of

1908. The most important studies of poverty undertaken by private enterprise were Charles Booth's *Poverty*, which forms the First Series (4 vols.) in his *Life and Labour of the People of London* (collected edn., 1904), and B. Seebohm Rowntree's *Poverty: A Study of Town Life* (1901); above at p. 513, n. 4, is given a select list of later books like them. Sir W. H. Beveridge's *Unemployment* (1909) is in a class apart. A book with exceptional influence on contemporary opinion was Sir L. G. Chiozza Money's *Riches and Poverty* (1905). Mrs. Bernard Bosanquet's *Social Work in London 1869–1912* (1914) is a history of the Charity Organization Society; Sir C. S. Loch's composite *Methods of Social Advance* (1904) applies the society's principles in various fields. General William Booth's *In Darkest England and the Way Out* (1890) is the most famous social manifesto of the Salvation Army.

(*h*) HOUSING. The *Report* (1885) of the Royal Commission on the Housing of the Working Classes was the starting-point for systematic study of the problem. Details of all the chief municipal housing schemes adopted in the ensuing 17 years will be found in W. Thompson's *Housing Handbook* (1903), and much classified information covering the whole topic. Local housing reports for the larger towns are legion. Two special historical volumes issued by the London County Council are *The Housing Question in London 1855–1900* (1900) and *Housing of the Working Classes 1855–1912* (1913); they cover the whole housing record of the metropolis down to two years before the War. See also C. E. Maurice's *Life of Octavia Hill* (1913). For the influence of German town-planning ideas, see T. C. Horsfall's *The Example of Germany* (1904); and for the history of the Garden City idea see Dugald Macfadyen's *Sir Ebenezer Howard and the Town Planning Movement* (1933).

(*i*) TRADE UNIONISM. The standard book is *The History of Trade Unionism* by Sidney and Beatrice Webb (original edn., 1894; revised edn., 1920); with which goes their *Industrial Democracy* (1898). For the changes in the law, see *The Legal History of Trade Unionism* (1930), by R. Y. Hedges and A. Winterbottom. Useful biographies of trade-union leaders in addition to those listed above in the Political section are *Memories of a Labour Leader* (1910), by John Wilson (of the Durham Miners); *Life of Thomas Burt* (of the Northumberland Miners), by Aaron Watson (1908); and *Labour, Life and Literature* (1913), by F. Rogers (of the Vellum Binders). For a general review of the advanced movements in trade-unionism at the close of the period, see G. D. H. Cole's *World of Labour* (1913). For Syndicalism, see the eleven numbers of Tom Mann's *Industrial Syndicalist*, beginning July 1910; Rowland Kenny's 'The Brains Behind the Labour Revolt' in the *English Review* (March 1912); and the famous pamphlet, *The Miners' Next Step*, published at Ton-y-pandy in 1912.

RELATIONS WITH IRELAND

For most of the last thirty-five years in this period the Irish question was so strongly to the fore in British politics that this section must largely be regarded as continuing the Political section above. Many books there cited are greatly concerned with it; and conversely the biographies of *C. S. Parnell*, by Barry O'Brien (1899), *John Redmond* (1932), by Denis Gwynn, and the 2nd vol. (by Ian Colvin, 1934) of the *Life of Lord Carson*, are just as necessary for English as for Irish political history.

For the agrarian revolution certain *Parliamentary Papers* are important, viz. the *Report* of the Duke of Richmond's Commission (1881); the *Report* of Lord Bessborough's Commission (1881); and later that of Lord Cowper's Commission (1887). For the story of the Land League generally there is the *Report of the Special (i.e. Parnell) Commission with the Evidence and Speeches taken verbatim before the Judges* (12 vols., 1896). For the part played by the Irish-American secret societies, see also Henri Le Caron's *Twenty-five Years in the Secret Service* (1892). Michael J. F. McCarthy's *The Irish Revolution* (1912) treats the period from 1879 to 1886 with wide knowledge, much of it first-hand, and an historic sense for the really important currents and under-currents. G. Locker Lampson's *Consideration of the State of Ireland in the Nineteenth Century* (1907) is also worth referring to. Justin McCarthy's *Reminiscences* (2 vols., 1899) supply evidence at certain points regarding Parnell's fall and the developments in the nineties. For the early twentieth-century developments, see Hansard and the biographies of Asquith, Redmond, and Carson. For the whole period 1880–1914 much interesting, though not always reliable, information may be gained from T. M. Healy's *Letters and Leaders of My Day* (2 vols., 1928).

OVERSEA POSSESSIONS

(*a*) GENERAL. Almost the whole British Empire is covered by the *Historical Geography of the Dominions beyond the Seas* designed by

Sir Charles P. Lucas and written chiefly by him or by H. E. Egerton (1888–1923: all but Canada, Newfoundland, Australia, India, and the Introduction, appeared in the nineteenth century). 'Dominions' is there used in the wider sense; it is used in the narrower sense in A. B. Keith's *Responsible Government in the Dominions*, the 1912 edition of which (3 vols.) is authoritative for the constitutional development down to the War of what is now the British Commonwealth. See also his *Selected Speeches and Documents on British Colonial Policy, 1763–1917* (2 vols., 1918). The consolidations of Canada, Australia, and South Africa, which had gone forward during the period, were treated by H. E. Egerton in *Federations and Unions within the British Empire* (1911). For the Colonial and early Imperial Conferences, see Richard Jebb's *The Imperial Conference* (2 vols., 1911), and cf. his *The Britannic Question* (1913); also W. P. Hall's *Empire to Commonwealth* (1928).

(*b*) SOUTH AFRICA. The events from Lord Carnarvon's return to the Colonial Office down to the London Convention with the Transvaal are dealt with in vols. x and xi (1919) of G. M. Theal's *History of South Africa*. For Shepstone's annexation of the Transvaal, see also H. Rider Haggard's *Cetewayo and His White Neighbours* (1882); for Frere's conduct, John Martineau's *Life and Correspondence of Sir Bartle Frere* (2 vols., 1895); for the Zulu war, the *Narrative of the Field Operations connected with the Zulu War of 1879*, published (1881) by the Intelligence Division of the War Office. For the Jameson Raid and its circumstances the Report of the Select Committee (Cd. 311 of 1897) is the principal source, but the biographies of Harcourt and Chamberlain throw much additional light. Of Rhodes there are many biographies: an official one by Sir L. Michell (1910), and others by Basil Williams (1921), J. G. Macdonald (1927), Sarah G. Millin (1933), and J. G. Lockhart (1933). For further events up to the South African War, see the list of authorities given above at p. 248, n. 1. For authorities on the war see the Military section above; and for the settlement of 1906–7 see J. A. Spender's *Life of Sir Henry Campbell-Bannerman* (1923).

(*c*) TROPICAL AFRICA. For the British acquisitions generally, see J. Scott Keltie's *The Partition of Africa* (2nd edn., 1895) and Sir H. H. Johnston's *History and Description of the British Empire in Africa* (1910). For Stanley's decisive explorations, see his *How I Found Livingstone* (1872), *Through the Dark Continent* (1878), *In Darkest Africa* (1890), and *Autobiography* (1909). For British policy in East Africa, see Sir F. (afterwards Lord) Lugard's *The Rise of Our East African Empire* (2 vols., 1893); Sir Gerald Portal's *The British Mission to Uganda* (1894); and Sir H. H. Johnston's *The Uganda Protectorate* (2 vols., 1902). For West Africa, see Sir W. N. M. Geary's *Nigeria under British Rule* (1927); Lady Gerald Wellesley's *Sir George Goldie* (1934); and Lord Lugard's *The Dual Mandate in British Tropical Africa* (1922).

(d) EGYPT, though not at this time a 'possession', became a very important part of the British Imperial system. See Lord Cromer's *Modern Egypt* (1908), Lord Milner's *England in Egypt* (1892), and Lord Kitchener's biography as above. For the Gordon episode, see B. M. Allen's *Gordon and the Sudan* (1931) and the biographies of Gladstone, Wolseley, and the Duke of Devonshire; for the Mahdist story as a whole, Sir F. Wingate's *Mahdism and the Egyptian Sudan* (1891).

(e) INDIA. For the frontier policies of the seventies and eighties, see Lady Betty Balfour's *History of Lord Lytton's Indian Administration* (1899); Martineau's *Frere* (as above); Lucien Wolf's *Marquess of Ripon* (2 vols., 1921); and the biographies of Disraeli, Salisbury, and Gladstone. For later events, see Sir A. Lyall's *Lord Dufferin* (2 vols., 1905), Lord R. Churchill's biography, and the the *Life of Lord Curzon* by the Marquess of Zetland (3 vols., 1928). For the evolution of the Morley-Minto reforms, see *India, Minto, and Morley: 1905–10* (1934), by Mary Countess of Minto.

(f) AUSTRALIA. C. E. Lyne's *Life of Sir Henry Parkes* (1897) describes the movement which led to the National Australasian Convention of 1891. For the achievement of Australian federation see J. Finney's *History of the Australian Colonies* (1901) and W. H. Moore's *The Constitution of the Commonwealth of Australia* (1902).

LITERATURE, THOUGHT, AND SCIENCE

The chief writers and thinkers dying between 1870 and 1900 (or those who at the end of that period appeared such) will be found catalogued and discussed in vol. 4 (by Edmund Gosse, 1903) of R. Garnett and E. Gosse's large *English Literature Illustrated*—a useful index to the taste of its time. Later surveys of more recent authors must naturally be regarded as more provisional; perhaps the best is that by Louis Cazamian forming the extension of the last part of Émile Legouis and Louis Cazamian's

History of English Literature (1933 edn.). F. A. Swinnerton's *The Georgian Literary Scene* (1935) describes with insight some features of the last pre-war period. Biographical works worth consulting include H. G. Wells's *Autobiography* (2 vols., 1934), Archibald Henderson's *Bernard Shaw, Playboy and Prophet* (1932), S. M. Ellis's *George Meredith* (1919), Sir Graham Balfour's *Robert Louis Stevenson* (2 vols., 1901); Florence E. Hardy's *Thomas Hardy* (2 vols., 1933); Ford Madox Ford's *Joseph Conrad* (1924); and the same author's critical study of *Henry James* (1913).

The development of the Press during the period has not yet been adequately recorded. R. A. Scott-James's *The Influence of the Press* (1913) and G. Binney Dibblee's *The Newspaper* (1913) give the best general accounts. Many books have been written about Lord Northcliffe; the best is Hamilton Fyfe's biography (1930); others, by Sir Max Pemberton, Sir J. A. Hammerton, and Tom Clarke, each add something to the rest. J. L. Hammond's biography of *C. P. Scott* (1934) portrays the editor most successful in maintaining the best qualities of the older journalism against the tendencies for which Northcliffe stood.

The progress of science during the period can be accurately traced by two sets of records, the *Proceedings* of the Royal Society and the *Annual Reports* of the British Association—the first designed for the scientists themselves, the second for the larger educated public. Corresponding to these were two standard periodicals—*Nature* (from 1870) and the *Popular Science Monthly* (from 1872). Among the few attempts made to survey the progress of science as a whole at this time, and to describe its impacts on the mind of the generation, perhaps the best is in Sir W. C. D. Dampier-Whetham's *History of Science* (2nd edn. revised, 1930). That in Gerald Heard's *These Hurrying Years* (1934) is by comparison rather superficial. A. N. Whitehead's *Science in the Modern World* (1926) and Lord Haldane's *Philosophy of Humanism* (1922) each throw certain lights on the subject.

THE ARTS AND MUSIC

(*a*) ARCHITECTURE. Quite the best sources of information are the files of the contemporary periodicals concerned with it: notably, for this period, the *Architectural Review* (from 1896), the *Architect* (since 1869), and the *Builder* (since 1843) besides others later. There are informative lectures and discussions in the *Journal of Proceedings* of the Royal Institute of British Architects.

A special number of the *Studio* entitled *Modern British Domestic Architecture* (1901), and special issues of the *Architectural Review* entitled *Recent English Domestic Architecture* (1908–10), all largely illustrated, show the tendencies to smaller houses and simpler, more vernacular styles, which set in from the late nineties. Hermann Muthesius's *Das englische Haus* (3 vols., 1904) is the best illustrated book on English domestic architecture down to its own date. The architecture of public buildings is illustrated in Sir Banister Fletcher's *History of Architecture* (7th edn., 1924) and A. D. F. Hamlin's *History of Architecture* (revised 1922); but in these historical and cosmopolitan works not much space can be given to a short period of a single country. For churches see *Recent English Ecclesiastical Architecture* (1912) by Sir Charles Nicholson and C. Spooner.

(*b*) PAINTING AND SCULPTURE. There were no equally good periodicals for these arts, until the introduction of process-blocks made it possible to reproduce pictures and sculptures from photographs. But after the starting of the *Studio* in 1893 we have a good running record for the rest of the period. For earlier dates we have A. Grave's *Dictionary of Artists who have exhibited works in the principal London exhibitions from 1760 to 1893* (1895). The *Annual Register* habitually included a short critical record of the exhibitions of the Royal Academy and a few others. We can also refer to biographies, among which may be cited the 'official' *Lives* of *James McNeill Whistler* (1908) by Joseph and E. R. Pennell; *Sir J. E. Millais* (1899) by J. G. Millais; *George Frederick Watts* (3 vols., 1912) by Mary S. Watts (his widow); and the exquisite *Memorials of Edward Burne-Jones* (1904) by 'G.B.-J.' (his widow). With the last may be associated J. W. Mackail's *Life of William Morris* (1899); which is more particularly important for the early history of the Arts and Crafts movement. Sir Wyke Bayliss's *Five Great Painters of the Victorian Era* (1902) is interesting as showing how these men appeared to contemporary critics (the five are Leighton, Millais, Burne-Jones, Watts, and Holman Hunt). M. H. Spielmann's *Millais and his Works* (1898) has the same sort of interest; it contains a revealing chapter of 'Thoughts on the art of to-day' by Millais himself.

(*c*) MUSIC. Vol. vii (1934) of the *Oxford History of Music* contains a long and valuable chapter by H. C. Colles on English musical history from 1850 to 1900. English music, both before and after that date, is likewise fully handled under different headings in the 3rd edn. (5 vols., 1927–8) of Sir G. Grove's *Dictionary of Music and Musicians*. The following biographical or critical works may also be mentioned: *Life of William Sterndale Bennett* (1907), by J. R. S. Bennett; *Hubert Parry* (1926), by C. L. Graves; *Charles Villiers Stanford* (1935), by H. Plunket Greene; *The Music of Parry and Stanford* (1934), by J. A. Fuller-Maitland; *Elgar: His Life and Works* (1933), by B. Maine; *Cecil Sharp* (1933), by A. H. Fox Strangways and Maud Karpeles. Sir A. C. Mackenzie's autobiography, *A Musician's Narrative* (1927), gives a lively picture of what working conditions in the musical world during this period were like.

SOCIAL LIFE AND EDUCATION

Future historians of the manners of this period may rely not a little on the novelists. They are good guides, except that they tend to draw on their memories and describe states of society somewhat earlier than the generation in which their readers are living: this is noticeably true of George Eliot, Meredith, Hardy, and Galsworthy, less so of Bennett and Wells, and not at all of Mrs. Humphry Ward. But the best sources are actual letters, diaries, and other biographical matter. The number published which emanate from 1870–1914 is already large. Three may be named, which illustrate the life of different sections of the governing class: *Mary Gladstone: Her Diaries and Letters*, ed. Lucy Masterman (1930); the *Autobiography of Margot Asquith* (1920); and Mrs. Sidney Webb's *My Apprenticeship* (1926). *Memories and Notes* (1927) by Anthony Hope (Sir A. H. Hawkins) exhibits the change in London from the period of the barouche and the hansom to that of the motor-car. George Sturt's *The Wheelwright's Shop* (1923) describes the passing of an old industry from a craft to a commercial basis, and from dependence on local to dependence on non-local custom.

Another source will be the newspapers. R. H. Gretton's *Modern History of the English People 1880–1922* (originally in 3 vols., 1912, 1914, and 1929) seems largely based on them, and is an interesting attempt to exhibit from year to year how the world of events and people appeared to newspaper readers. Not the least informative feature in old newspaper files are the advertisements. Illustrated periodicals are the main authorities for costume.

Education down to the Balfour Act is well described in two books: Sir Graham Balfour's *The Educational Systems of Great Britain and Ireland* (2nd edn., 1903) and J. W. Adamson's *English Education 1789–1902* (1930). No authoritative general account covers all the developments since; but much may be learned from a great variety of board of education reports. The best recent account of the growth of technical education is A. Abbott's *Education for Industry and Commerce in England* (1933); for some of its earlier phases, see the biography of *Quintin Hogg* (1904) by E. M. Hogg. Of the expansion of the public schools in the latter half of the nineteenth century to meet the vast increase in the number of people desiring to send their sons to them, much may be learned from Sir G. R. Parkin's *Life of Edward Thring*; where the origins of the Headmasters' Conference are shown. The origins and passing of the Balfour Act are well shown in B. M. Allen's *Sir Robert Morant* (1934); which also describes the nine subsequent years of rapid educational expansion, while Morant remained head of the board.

LIST OF CABINETS 1870–1914

1. GLADSTONE'S FIRST CABINET

(formed December 1868)

First lord of the treasury: W. E. Gladstone.
Lord chancellor: Lord Hatherley (Sir W. Page Wood).
Lord president: Earl de Grey (cr. Marquess of Ripon **1871**).
Lord privy seal: Earl of Kimberley.
Chancellor of the exchequer: Robert Lowe.
Home secretary: H. A. Bruce.
Foreign secretary: Earl of Clarendon.
Colonial secretary: Earl Granville.
Secretary for war: E. Cardwell.
Secretary for India: Duke of Argyll.
First lord of the admiralty: H. C. E. Childers.
President of the board of trade: John Bright.
Chief secretary for Ireland: Chichester Fortescue.
Postmaster-general: Marquess of Hartington.
President of the poor law board: G. J. Goschen.

Changes

July 1870: W. E. Forster, vice-president (education), entered the cabinet; Lord Granville became foreign secretary (following Lord Clarendon's death); Lord Kimberley became colonial secretary; and Lord Halifax (Sir C. Wood) lord privy seal. *December 1870*: Chichester Fortescue succeeded John Bright (resigned) as president of the board of trade; Lord Hartington became chief secretary for Ireland (the new postmaster-general, W. Monsell, was not in the cabinet). *March 1871*: G. J. Goschen succeeded H. C. E. Childers (resigned) as first lord of the admiralty; James Stansfeld became president of the poor law board. *August 1872*: H. C. E. Childers rejoined the cabinet as chancellor of the duchy of Lancaster. *October 1872*: Lord Selborne (Sir Roundell Palmer) succeeded Lord Hatherley (resigned) as lord chancellor. *August 1873*: H. A. Bruce (cr. Lord Aberdare) succeeded Lord Ripon (resigned) as lord president of the council; Robert Lowe succeeded Bruce as home secretary; W. E. Gladstone succeeded Lowe as chancellor of the exchequer (combining the office with the premiership). *September 1873*: John Bright rejoined the cabinet as chancellor of the duchy of Lancaster, in place of Childers (resigned).

2. DISRAELI'S SECOND CABINET

(formed February 1874)

First lord of the treasury: Benjamin Disraeli.
Lord chancellor: Lord Cairns (cr. Earl 1878).
Lord president: Duke of Richmond.
Lord privy seal: Earl of Malmesbury.
Chancellor of the exchequer: Sir Stafford Northcote.

Home secretary: R. A. Cross.
Foreign secretary: Earl of Derby.
Colonial secretary: Earl of Carnarvon.
Secretary for war: G. Gathorne Hardy.
Secretary for India: Marquess of Salisbury.
First lord of the admiralty: G. Ward Hunt.
Postmaster-general: Lord John Manners.

Changes

August 1876: B. Disraeli succeeded Lord Malmesbury (resigned) as lord privy seal (combining the office with the premiership), and went to the lords as Earl of Beaconsfield. *February 1877*: Sir Michael Hicks Beach, chief secretary for Ireland, entered the cabinet. *August 1877*: W. H. Smith succeeded Ward Hunt (deceased) as first lord of the admiralty. *February 1878*: Sir M. Hicks Beach succeeded Lord Carnarvon (resigned) as colonial secretary (James Lowther succeeded Hicks Beach as Irish secretary, but without a seat in the cabinet). The Duke of Northumberland took the post of lord privy seal. *April 1878*: Lord Salisbury succeeded Lord Derby (resigned) as foreign secretary. Gathorne Hardy (cr. Viscount Cranbrook) succeeded Lord Salisbury as secretary for India, being himself succeeded as secretary for war by F. A. Stanley. Viscount Sandon, on succeeding C. E. Adderley as president of the board of trade, was brought into the cabinet.

3. GLADSTONE'S SECOND CABINET

(formed April 1880)

First lord of the treasury:
Chancellor of the exchequer: } W. E. Gladstone.
Lord chancellor: Lord Selborne (cr. Earl 1881).
Lord president: Earl Spencer.
Lord privy seal: Duke of Argyll.
Home secretary: Sir William Vernon Harcourt.
Foreign secretary: Earl Granville.
Colonial secretary: Earl of Kimberley.
Secretary for war: H. C. E. Childers.
Secretary for India: Marquess of Hartington.
First lord of the admiralty: Earl of Northbrook.
President of the board of trade: Joseph Chamberlain.
President of the local government board: J. G. Dodson.
Chief secretary for Ireland: W. E. Forster.
Chancellor of the duchy of Lancaster: John Bright.

Changes

May 1881: Lord Carlingford (Chichester Fortescue) succeeded the Duke of Argyll (resigned) as lord privy seal. *April 1882*: Lord Spencer, while retaining his seat in the cabinet, became Irish viceroy. Forster resigned the Irish secretaryship, which went to Lord Frederick Cavendish and after Cavendish's murder to G. O. Trevelyan—neither having a seat in the cabinet. *July 1882*: Bright resigned the chancellorship of the duchy of Lancaster, and Lord Kimberley combined it with his office of colonial secretary. *December 1882*: Gladstone resigned the chancellorship of the exchequer to Childers; Lord Hartington succeeded Childers at the war office; Lord Kimberley succeeded Lord Hartington at the India office; he himself was succeeded as colonial secretary by Lord Derby and as chancellor of the duchy of Lancaster by J. G. Dodson; Dodson was succeeded at the local government board by Sir Charles Dilke. *March 1883*: Lord Carlingford succeeded Lord Spencer as lord president, combining the office with that of lord privy seal. *October 1884*: G. O. Trevelyan succeeded Dodson (resigned) as chancellor of the duchy of Lancaster, being himself succeeded in the Irish secretaryship by H. Campbell-Bannerman (without a seat in the cabinet). *February 1885*: C. J. Shaw-Lefevre, postmaster-general, was brought into the cabinet. *March 1885*: The Earl of Rosebery was brought into the cabinet, taking over from Lord Carlingford the office of lord privy seal.

4. LORD SALISBURY'S FIRST CABINET

(*formed June 1885*)

Premier and foreign secretary: Marquess of Salisbury.
First lord of the treasury: Earl of Iddesleigh (Sir Stafford Northcote).
Lord chancellor: Lord Halsbury (Sir Hardinge Giffard).
Lord president: Viscount Cranbrook.
Lord privy seal: Earl of Harrowby.
Chancellor of the exchequer: Sir Michael **Hicks Beach.**
Home secretary: Sir R. A. Cross.
Colonial secretary: Sir F. A. Stanley.
Secretary for war: W. H. Smith.
Secretary for India: Lord Randolph Churchill.
First lord of the admiralty: Lord George Hamilton.
President of the board of trade: Duke of Richmond.
Irish viceroy: Earl of Carnarvon.
Postmaster-general: Lord John Manners.
Vice-president (education): Hon. E. Stanhope.
Lord chancellor of Ireland: Lord Ashbourne.

Changes

August 1885: the Duke of Richmond was appointed secretary for Scotland, and E. Stanhope succeeded him at the board of trade. *January 1886*: W. H. Smith, while retaining his seat in the cabinet, became chief secretary for Ireland, succeeding Sir W. Hart Dyke, who had been outside the cabinet.

5. GLADSTONE'S THIRD CABINET

(*formed February 1886*)

First lord of the treasury: }
Lord privy seal: } W. E. Gladstone.
Lord chancellor: Lord (Sir Farrer) Herschell.
Lord president: Earl Spencer.

Chancellor of the exchequer: Sir William Vernon Harcourt.
Home secretary: H. C. E. Childers.
Foreign secretary: Earl of Rosebery.
Colonial secretary: Earl Granville.
Secretary for war: H. Campbell-Bannerman.
Secretary for India: Earl of Kimberley.
Secretary for Scotland: G. O. Trevelyan.
Chief secretary for Ireland: John Morley.
First lord of the admiralty: Marquess of Ripon.
President of the board of trade: A. J. Mundella.
President of the local government board: J. Chamberlain.

Changes

April 1886: Chamberlain resigned, and was succeeded by J. Stansfeld; Trevelyan resigned, and was succeeded by the Earl of Dalhousie (but without a seat in the cabinet).

6. LORD SALISBURY'S SECOND CABINET
(*formed August 1886*)

First lord of the treasury: Marquess of Salisbury.
Lord chancellor: Lord Halsbury.
Lord president: Viscount Cranbrook.
Chancellor of the exchequer: Lord Randolph Churchill.
Home secretary: Henry Matthews.
Foreign secretary: Earl of Iddesleigh.
Colonial secretary: Hon. Edward Stanhope.
Secretary for war: W. H. Smith.
Secretary for India: Viscount (Sir R. A.) Cross.
Chief secretary for Ireland: Sir Michael Hicks Beach.
First lord of the admiralty: Lord George Hamilton.
President of the board of trade: Lord (Sir F. A.) Stanley.
Chancellor of the duchy of Lancaster: Lord John Manners.
Lord chancellor of Ireland: Lord Ashbourne.

Changes

November 1886: A. J. Balfour, secretary for Scotland, was brought into the cabinet. *January 1887*: G. J. Goschen succeeded Lord Randolph Churchill (resigned) as chancellor of the exchequer. Lord Salisbury succeeded Lord Iddesleigh as foreign secretary. W. H. Smith succeeded Lord Salisbury as first lord of the treasury. Stanhope succeeded Smith as secretary for war. Lord Knutsford (Sir Henry Holland) succeeded Stanhope as secretary for the colonies. *March 1887*: A. J. Balfour succeeded Sir M. Hicks Beach as Irish secretary (Hicks Beach resigned, but remained in the cabinet). The Marquess of Lothian succeeded Balfour as secretary for Scotland. *May 1887*: Earl Cadogan, lord privy seal, and C. T. Ritchie, president of the local government board, entered the cabinet. *February 1888*: Sir M. Hicks Beach succeeded Lord Stanley (appointed governor of

Canada) as president of the board of trade. *October 1891*: A. J. Balfour succeeded W. H. Smith deceased as first lord of the treasury, relinquishing the Irish secretaryship to W. L. Jackson.

7. GLADSTONE'S FOURTH CABINET

(formed August 1892)

First lord of the treasury: ⎫
Lord privy seal: ⎬ W. E. Gladstone.
Lord chancellor: Lord Herschell.
Lord president: ⎫
Secretary for India: ⎬ Earl of Kimberley.
Chancellor of the exchequer: Sir William Vernon Harcourt.
Home secretary: H. H. Asquith.
Foreign secretary: Earl of Rosebery.
Colonial secretary: Marquess of Ripon.
Secretary for war: H. Campbell-Bannerman.
Secretary for Scotland: Sir G. O. Trevelyan.
Chief secretary for Ireland: John Morley.
First lord of the admiralty: Earl Spencer.
President of the board of trade: A. J. Mundella.
President of the local government board: H. H. Fowler.
Chancellor of the duchy of Lancaster: James Bryce.
Vice-president (education): A. H. D. Acland.
First commissioner of works: G. J. Shaw-Lefevre.
Postmaster-general: Arnold Morley.

8. LORD ROSEBERY'S CABINET

(formed March 1894)

First lord of the treasury: ⎫
Lord President: ⎬ Earl of Rosebery.
Lord chancellor: Lord Herschell.
Lord privy seal: ⎫
Chancellor of the duchy of Lancaster: ⎬ Lord Tweedmouth.
Chancellor of the exchequer: Sir William Vernon Harcourt.
Home secretary: H. H. Asquith.
Foreign secretary: Earl of Kimberley.
Colonial secretary: Marquess of Ripon.
Secretary for war: H. Campbell-Bannerman.
Secretary for India: H. H. Fowler.
Secretary for Scotland: Sir G. O. Trevelyan.
Chief secretary for Ireland: John Morley.
First lord of the admiralty: Earl Spencer.
President of the board of trade: James Bryce.
President of the local government board: G. J. Shaw-Lefevre.
Vice-president (education): A. H. D. Acland.
Postmaster-general: Arnold Morley.

9. LORD SALISBURY'S THIRD CABINET
(*formed June 1895*)

Premier and foreign secretary: Marquess of Salisbury.
First lord of the treasury: A. J. Balfour.
Lord chancellor: Earl of Halsbury.
Lord president: Duke of Devonshire.
Lord privy seal: Viscount Cross.
Chancellor of the exchequer: Sir M. Hicks Beach.
Home secretary: Sir Matthew White Ridley.
Colonial secretary: Joseph Chamberlain.
Secretary for war: Marquess of Lansdowne.
Secretary for India: Lord George Hamilton.
Secretary for Scotland: Lord Balfour of Burleigh.
Irish viceroy: Earl Cadogan.
First lord of the admiralty: G. J. Goschen.
Chancellor of the duchy of Lancaster: Lord James of Hereford.
President of the board of trade: C. T. Ritchie.
President of the local government board: H. Chaplin.
President of the board of agriculture: Walter Long.
Lord chancellor of Ireland: Lord Ashbourne.
Commissioner for works: A. Akers-Douglas.

Changes

October 1900: Lord Salisbury relinquished the foreign office, and became lord privy seal, Lord Cross retiring from the cabinet. Lord Lansdowne succeeded him as foreign secretary, being himself succeeded at the war office by the Hon. St. John Brodrick. Goschen retired from the cabinet, and was succeeded as first lord of the admiralty by the (second) Earl of Selborne. Sir M. W. Ridley retired from the cabinet, and was succeeded as home secretary by C. T. Ritchie. Ritchie's place as president of the board of trade was filled by G. W. Balfour (till then since 1895 chief secretary for Ireland without a seat in the cabinet). Chaplin retired from the cabinet, and his place there as president of the local government board was filled by Walter Long, whose place as president of the board of agriculture went to R. W. Hanbury. The cabinet was enlarged by taking in the postmaster-general, the Marquess of Londonderry succeeding the Duke of Norfolk in that office. As Lord Cadogan, the Irish viceroy, remained in the cabinet, the new chief secretary for Ireland, George Wyndham, was outside.

10. BALFOUR'S CABINET
(*formed July 1902*)

First lord of the treasury: A. J. Balfour.
Lord chancellor: Earl of Halsbury.
Lord president: Duke of Devonshire.
Lord privy seal:
President of the board of education: } Marquess of Londonderry.

Chancellor of the exchequer: C. T. Ritchie.
Home secretary: A. Akers-Douglas.
Foreign secretary: Marquess of Lansdowne.
Colonial secretary: Joseph Chamberlain.
Secretary for war: Hon. St. John Brodrick.
Secretary for India: Lord George Hamilton.
Secretary for Scotland: Lord Balfour of Burleigh.
Chief secretary for Ireland: George Wyndham.
First lord of the admiralty: Earl of Selborne.
Chancellor of the duchy of Lancaster: Lord James of Hereford.
President of the board of trade: G. W. Balfour.
President of the local government board: Walter Long.
President of the board of agriculture: R. W. Hanbury.
Lord chancellor of Ireland: Lord Ashbourne.
First commissioner of works: Lord Windsor (cr. Earl of Plymouth, 1905).
Postmaster-general: Austen Chamberlain.

Changes

August 1902: Lord James of Hereford retired from the cabinet, and was succeeded as chancellor of the duchy of Lancaster by Sir William Walrond (cr. Lord Waleran 1905). *May 1903*: the Earl of Onslow succeeded R. W. Hanbury (deceased) as president of the board of agriculture. *September 1903*: Chamberlain resigned and was replaced as colonial secretary by the Hon. Alfred Lyttelton. Ritchie resigned, and was replaced as chancellor of the exchequer by Austen Chamberlain. Lord George Hamilton resigned, and was replaced as secretary for India by St. John Brodrick, whose post as secretary for war went to H. O. Arnold-Forster. Lord Balfour of Burleigh resigned, and was replaced as secretary for Scotland by Graham Murray. The duke of Devonshire resigned, and was replaced as lord president of the council by Lord Londonderry, who retained the presidency of the board of education, but was followed as lord privy seal by the (lately succeeded) Marquess of Salisbury. *March 1905*: Lord Selborne left the cabinet to become governor-general of South Africa, and his place as first lord of the admiralty was taken by Earl Cawdor. George Wyndham resigned, and his place as chief secretary for Ireland was taken by Walter Long. Long was succeeded at the local government board by G. W. Balfour, who himself was succeeded at the board of trade by Lord Salisbury. Lord Onslow resigned, and was succeeded as president of the board of agriculture by the Hon. Ailwyn Fellowes (cr. Lord Ailwyn, 1921).

11. CAMPBELL-BANNERMAN'S CABINET

(formed December 1905)

First lord of the treasury: Sir Henry Campbell-Bannerman.
Lord chancellor: Lord Loreburn (Sir R. T. Reid).
Lord president: Earl of Crewe.
Lord privy seal: Marquess of Ripon.
Chancellor of the exchequer: H. H. Asquith.

Home secretary: Herbert J. Gladstone.
Foreign secretary: Sir Edward Grey.
Colonial secretary: Earl of Elgin.
Secretary for war: R. B. Haldane.
Secretary for India: John Morley.
Secretary for Scotland: John Sinclair.
Chief secretary for Ireland: James Bryce.
First lord of the admiralty: Lord Tweedmouth.
Chancellor of the duchy of Lancaster: Sir Henry H. Fowler.
President of the board of trade: D. Lloyd George.
President of the local government board: John Burns.
President of the board of agriculture: Earl Carrington.
President of the board of education: Augustine Birrell.
Postmaster-general: Sydney Buxton.

Changes

January 1907: Bryce being appointed ambassador at Washington Birrell succeeded him as chief secretary for Ireland, and R. McKenna succeeded Birrell as president of the board of education. *March 1907*: L. V. Harcourt, first commissioner of works, was brought into the cabinet.

12. ASQUITH'S FIRST CABINET
(*formed April 1908*)

First lord of the treasury: H. H. Asquith.
Lord chancellor: Lord (cr. Earl 1911) Loreburn.
Lord president: Lord Tweedmouth.
Lord privy seal: Marquess of Ripon.
Chancellor of the exchequer: D. Lloyd George.
Home secretary: Herbert J. Gladstone.
Foreign secretary: Sir Edward Grey.
Colonial secretary: Earl of Crewe.
Secretary for war: R. B. (cr. Viscount 1911) Haldane.
Secretary for India: Viscount (John) Morley.
Secretary for Scotland: John Sinclair (cr. Lord Pentland 1909).
Chief secretary for Ireland: Augustine Birrell.
First lord of the admiralty: R. McKenna.
Chancellor of the duchy of Lancaster: Sir H. H. Fowler (Viscount Wolver-
   hampton.)
President of the board of trade: Winston S. Churchill.
President of the local government board: John Burns.
President of the board of agriculture: Earl Carrington.
President of the board of Education: Walter Runciman.
Postmaster-general: Sydney Buxton.
First commissioner of works: Lewis Vernon Harcourt.

Changes
(down to August 1914)

September 1908: Lord Tweedmouth was succeeded as president of the council by Sir Henry Fowler, who was created Viscount Wolverhampton.

Fowler was succeeded as chancellor of the duchy of Lancaster by Lord Edmund Fitzmaurice, who was created Lord Fitzmaurice. *October 1908*: Lord Ripon was succeeded as lord privy seal by Lord Crewe, who combined the post with that of colonial secretary. *June 1909*: Lord Fitzmaurice was succeeded as chancellor of the duchy of Lancaster by Herbert Samuel. *February 1910*: Herbert Gladstone (appointed governor-general of South Africa) was succeeded as home secretary by Winston Churchill, who was himself succeeded as president of the board of trade by Sydney Buxton. Herbert Samuel succeeded Buxton as postmaster-general, and was himself succeeded as chancellor of the duchy of Lancaster by J. A. Pease. *June 1910*: Lord Wolverhampton was succeeded as lord president of the council by Earl Beauchamp. *November 1910*: Lord Morley became lord president of the council, being succeeded as secretary for India by Lord Crewe. Lewis Harcourt succeeded Crewe as colonial secretary, and Earl Beauchamp succeeded Harcourt as first commissioner of works. *October 1911*: Winston Churchill replaced R. McKenna as first lord of the admiralty, and R. McKenna replaced Winston Churchill as home secretary. Lord Carrington became lord privy seal, being succeeded as president of the board of agriculture by Walter Runciman. Runciman was succeeded as president of the board of education by J. A. Pease, and Pease as chancellor of the duchy of Lancaster by C. E. Hobhouse. *February 1912*: Lord Carrington retired (as Marquess of Lincolnshire), his post as lord privy seal reverting to Lord (now Marquess of) Crewe. Lord Pentland (appointed governor of Madras) was succeeded as secretary for Scotland by T. McKinnon Wood. *June 1912*: Lord Loreburn retired, and Lord (R. B.) Haldane succeeded him as lord chancellor. Col. J. E. B. Seely (cr. Lord Mottistone 1934) succeeded Haldane as secretary for war. Sir Rufus Isaacs, attorney-general since October 1910, came now into the cabinet, being the first law-officer to do so. *February 1914*: Buxton (appointed governor-general of South Africa) was succeeded as president of the board of trade by John Burns, who was himself succeeded as president of the local government board by Herbert Samuel. Samuel was succeeded as postmaster-general by C. E. Hobhouse, who himself was succeeded as chancellor of the duchy of Lancaster by C. F. G. Masterman. *March 1914*: Seely resigned, and was succeeded as secretary for war by Asquith, who combined the office with that of prime minister. *August 1914*: Lord Morley resigned, and was succeeded as lord president by Earl Beauchamp. John Burns resigned, and was succeeded as president of the board of trade by Runciman, who himself was succeeded as president of the board of agriculture by Lord Lucas. Asquith relinquished the post of secretary for war, to which Earl Kitchener was appointed.

INDEX

S S

MAPS

1. THE BALKANS

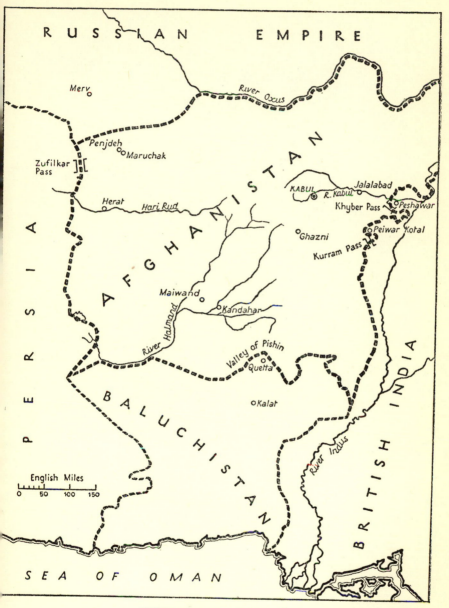

RUSSIAN EMPIRE

Merv

River Oxus

Penjdeh

Maruchak

Zufilkar
Pass

A F G H A N I S T A N

KABUL

Jalalabad

Herat

Hari Rud

R. Kabul

Khyber Pass

Peshawar

Ghazni

Peiwar Kotal

Kurram Pass

P E R S I A

Maiwand

Kandahar

River Halmand

Valley of Pishin

Quetta

Kalat

B A L U C H I S T A N

B R I T I S H   I N D I A

River Indus

English Miles

0   50   100   150

SEA   OF   OMAN

2. AFGHANISTAN ABOUT 1880

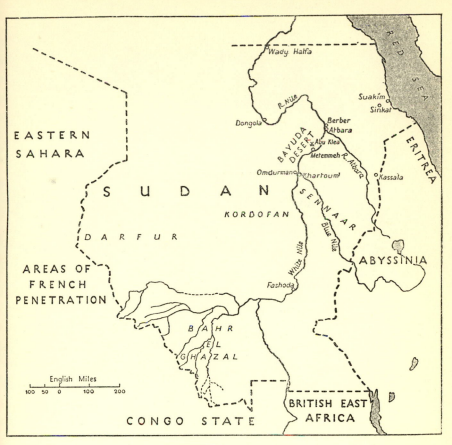

3. EASTERN SUDAN
Boundaries at the close of the 19th century

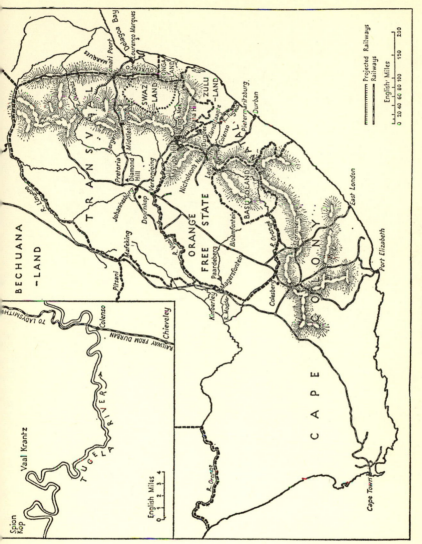

4. SOUTH AFRICA, 1899–1902

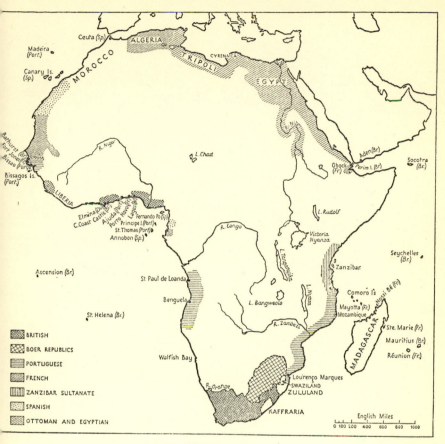

Madeira
(Port.)

Ceuta (Sp.)

Canary Is.
(Sp.)

MOROCCO

ALGERIA

TRIPOLI

CYRENAICA

EGYPT

R. Niger

L. Chad

R. Nile

Aden (Br.)

Bathurst (Br.)
Port James
Bissao (Port.)

Bissagos Is.
(Port.)

LIBERIA

Elmina (Du.)
C.Coast Castle (Br.)
Ajuda (Po.)
Porto Novo (Fr.)
Principe I. (Port.)
St. Thomas (Port.)
Annobon (Sp.)

Fernando Po (Sp.)

Obock
(Fr.)

Perim I. (Br.)

Socotra
(Br.)

R. Congo

L. Rudolf

Victoria
Nyanza

Seychelles
(Br.)

Ascension (Br.)

St. Paul de Loanda

Benguela

St. Helena (Br.)

L. Tanganyika

L. Nyasa

L. Bangweolo

R. Zambezi

Zanzibar

Comoro Is.
Mayotta (Fr.)
Mozambique

Nossi Bé (Fr.)

Ste. Marie (Fr.)

Mauritius (Br.)

MADAGASCAR

Réunion (Fr.)

Walfish Bay

R. Orange

Lourenço Marques
SWAZILAND
ZULULAND

KAFFRARIA

BRITISH

BOER REPUBLICS

PORTUGUESE

FRENCH

ZANZIBAR SULTANATE

SPANISH

OTTOMAN AND EGYPTIAN

English Miles

0 100 200   400   600   800   1000

5. AFRICA, 1871

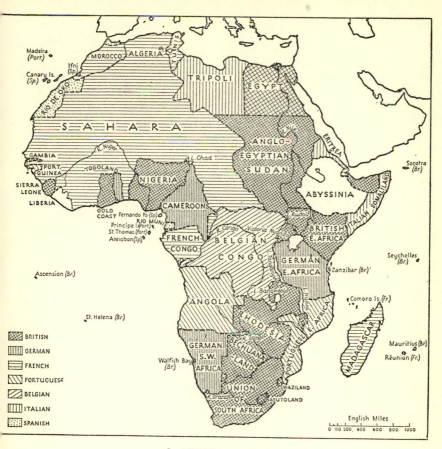

Madeira
(Port.)

Canary Is.
(Sp.)

MOROCCO ALGERIA
Ifni
(Sp.)

RIO DE ORO

TRIPOLI

EGYPT

Socotra
(Br.)

S A H A R A

R. Niger

L. Chad

ANGLO-
EGYPTIAN
SUDAN

ERITREA

GAMBIA
PORT.
GUINEA

TOGOLAND

NIGERIA

ABYSSINIA

SIERRA
LEONE

LIBERIA

GOLD
COAST   Fernando Po (Sp.)
        RIO MUNI
Principe I. (Port.)
St. Thomas (Port.)
Annobon (Sp.)

CAMEROONS

FRENCH
CONGO

BELGIAN

CONGO

R. Congo   Victoria Nya

Rudolf

BRITISH
E. AFRICA

ITALIAN SOMALILAND

Ascension (Br.)

GERMAN
E. AFRICA

Zanzibar (Br.)

Seychelles
(Br.)

St. Helena (Br.)

ANGOLA

L. Bangweolo

RHODESIA

PORTUGUESE E. AFRICA

Comoro Is. (Fr.)

Walfish Bay
(Br.)

GERMAN
S.W.
AFRICA

BECHUANALAND

UNION
OF
SOUTH AFRICA

R. Orange

SWAZILAND

BASUTOLAND

MADAGASCAR

Mauritius (Br.)

Réunion (Fr.)

English Miles

0 100 200 400   600   800 1000

	BRITISH
	GERMAN
	FRENCH
	PORTUGUESE
	BELGIAN
	ITALIAN
	SPANISH

6. AFRICA, 1914

County Boroughs (61) scheduled to the Local
Government Act 1888 are shown thus ●
County Boroughs (20) granted that status
between 1889 and 1914 shown thus ○
The county borough of Hanley disappeared
in 1910, being incorporated in the (then created)
county borough of Stoke-on-Trent.

Newcastle Tynemouth
South Shields
Gateshead Sunderland
Carlisle
West Hartlepool
Middlesbrough
Barrow
York
Blackpool Preston Burnley Bradford Hull
Blackburn Leeds
Nelson Wigan Bury Halifax
Southport Oldham Dewsbury
Bootle St Helens Huddersfield Grimsby
Wallasey Salford Barnsley
Birkenhead Warrington Manchester Rotherham
Stockport Sheffield
Chester Lincoln
Hanley
Stoke on Trent Derby Nottingham
Burton on Trent
Yarmouth
Wolverhampton Walsall Leicester Norwich
Dudley West Bromwich
Smethwick Birmingham
Coventry
Worcester Northampton
Ipswich
Merthyr
Tydfil Gloucester
Swansea Oxford West Ham Southend
Newport Reading Croydon
Cardiff Bristol Canterbury
Bath
Southampton Brighton Hastings
Eastbourne
Exeter Bournemouth Portsmouth
Devonport Plymouth

0 10 20 30 40 50 miles

7. COUNTY BOROUGHS, 1888–1914